TWO PATHS TO PROSPERITY

Two Paths to Prosperity

CULTURE AND INSTITUTIONS
IN EUROPE AND CHINA, 1000–2000

AVNER GREIF

JOEL MOKYR

GUIDO TABELLINI

PRINCETON UNIVERSITY PRESS

PRINCETON & OXFORD

Published by Princeton University Press
41 William Street, Princeton, New Jersey 08540
99 Banbury Road, Oxford OX2 6JX

press.princeton.edu

GPSR Authorized Representative: Easy Access System Europe - Mustamäe tee 50,
10621 Tallinn, Estonia, gpsr.requests@easproject.com

All Rights Reserved

Library of Congress Control Number: 2025931301

ISBN 9780691265940
ISBN (e-book) 9780691267715

British Library Cataloging-in-Publication Data is available

Editorial: Joe Jackson, Emma Wagh
Production Editorial: Elizabeth Byrd
Production: Erin Suydam
Publicity: James Schneider (US), Kathryn Stevens (UK)
Copyeditor: Susan McClung, 1st Choice Publishing Services

Jacket art: (left) Illustration of guildhalls on the Grand-Place / Grote Markt, Brussels,
Belgium. Anastasiaromb / iStock; (right) Illustration of the Imperial Ancestral
Temple, Beijing, China. MightyRabbittCrew / iStock.

Printed in the United States of America

10 9 8 7 6 5 4 3 2 1

CONTENTS

TABLE 0.1. Chinese Imperial Dynasties

Unified or Fragmented	Name of dynasty	Years ruled	Territories covered
Unified	Shang	1600 BC–1046 BC	Northeastern China
Unified	(Western) Zhou	1046 BC–771 BC	Eastern China
Fragmented	"Spring and Autumn"	770 BC–481 BC	Most of China
Fragmented	"Warring States"	481 BC–221 BC	Most of China
Unified	Qin	221 BC–207 BC	Most of China
Unified	(Western) Han	202 BC–9 AD	Most of China
Unified	Xin	9 AD–25 AD	Most of China
Unified	(Eastern) Han	25 AD–220 AD	Most of China
Fragmented	"Three Kingdoms"	220 AD–280 AD	Most of China
Weakly unified	Jin	280 AD–420 AD	Southern China
Fragmented	"Sixteen Kingdoms"	386 AD–581 AD	Northern China
Fragmented	Southern Dynasties	420 AD–589 AD	Southern China
Unified	Sui	589 AD–619 AD	Most of China
Unified	Tang	619 AD–907 AD	Most of China
Fragmented	"Five dynasties"	907 AD–960 AD	Northern China
Fragmented	"Ten Kingdoms"	907 AD–979 AD	Southern China
Partially unified	(Northern) Song	960 AD–1127AD	Central and Southern China
Divided in two	Southern Song	1127 AD–1279 AD	Southern China
Unified	Yuan (Mongol)	1279 AD–1368 AD	All of China
Unified	Ming	1368 AD–1644 AD	All of China
Unified	Qing (Manchu)	1644 AD–1912 AD	All of China

ACKNOWLEDGMENTS

THIS BOOK grew out of a long, fruitful interaction between the three of us that started in 2003 within the Institutions, Organizations, and Growth research program supported by the Canadian Institute for Advanced Research (CIFAR) and more recently by the University of Chicago. We are grateful to Elhanan Helpman, who directed the CIFAR program and encouraged us to put our ideas and thoughts into this book. We are also grateful to the participants in meetings organized by CIFAR and the University of Chicago for their feedback and stimulus, as well as to CIFAR and the University of Chicago for their general support.

We presented preliminary versions and parts of this book in several workshops and conferences. We are grateful to Tel Aviv University and especially to Dean Itai Sened and his staff for organizing a special one-day conference around an earlier version of the book. The comments and ideas of the participants contributed substantially to its development. We are also grateful to participants in workshops, lectures, and conferences at the Association for the Study of Religion, Economics and Culture; Bocconi University; Corvinus University in Budapest; Delhi School of Economics; the Center of Research in Economics and Statistics (CREST) in Paris; Harvard University; Hebrew University in Jerusalem; King's College in London; the London School of Economics; the University of Oxford; the National University of Singapore; the University of Utrecht; and the University of Warwick.

At various stages during this project, we received valuable input from colleagues who had read parts of our book. We are particularly grateful to Guido Alfani, David de la Croix, Matthias Doepke, Nicola Gennaioli, Laurenz Guenther, Ron Harris, Joseph Henrich, P. J. Hill, James Kai-sing Kung, Debin Ma, Melissa Macauley, Luigi Pistaferri, Gerard Roland, Jonathan Schulz, Carol Shiue, Tuan Hwee Sng, Matthew Somers, Joachim Voth, Peer Vries, Gavin Wright, Melanie Meng Xue, and two anonymous referees, along with our editor, Joe Jackson, for their very helpful comments. We thank Ruixue Jia, Michel

Serafinelli, and Eric Weese for sharing some data that we use in this book. We are extremely grateful to George Zhijian Qiao (Amherst) and Professor Hongzhong Yan (chair of the Economic History Department at Shanghai University of Finance and Economics) for valuable discussions and for the dataset on Chinese genealogies.

We are also supremely grateful to the many graduate students who have provided outstanding research assistance through the years, and in particular to Pietro Buri, Joy Chen, Tommaso Crosta, Davis Kedrosky, Roy Mill, Xueyan Li, Franco Malpassi, Yongwei Nian, Myera Rashid, Emiliano Rinaldi, Nicole Saito, Chris Sims, Elena Stella, Yannay Spitzer, Philip Thai, and Luca Zanotti.

Some parts of this book grew out of other papers that we had published previously or that appeared in preliminary forms in other published papers. The entire book, particularly chapters 3, 4, 5, and 6, build on Greif and Tabellini (2010, 2017). A preliminary version of chapter 7 was presented by Guido Tabellini as the Phillips lecture at the London School of Economics and published as Mokyr and Tabellini, "Social Organizations and Political Institutions: Why China and Europe Diverged," *Economica*, December 2023. Some parts of chapter 9 overlap with Kelly, Mokyr, and Ó Gráda (2014, 2023).

Joel Mokyr thanks the Northwestern University Center for Economic History, the Charles Koch Foundation, and the John Menard Foundation for continuous support. Guido Tabellini thanks Bocconi University for continuous financial support throughout this period. Avner Greif thanks Stanford University for its continuous support for this project.

Finally, our deepest gratitude of all is to our spouses, Esther (Estee), Margalit, and Giovanna, who stood by us patiently during the many years of writing this book.

1

Introduction

1. The Question

Toward the end of the first millennium, China was ahead of Europe in many dimensions. China's population had grown from about 50 or 60 million in the early 700s AD to about 100 million toward the turn of the millennium. During the Northern Song period (960–1127 AD), population growth is estimated to have averaged around a rate of 0.87 percent per year (Broadberry, Guan, and Li 2018). The capital city of the Northern Song Empire, Kaifeng, had reached 1 million inhabitants, including its nine suburbs (Fairbank and Goldman 2006, p. 88). Western Europe, by contrast, was much less densely populated, particularly in the north. Although precise estimates are not available, there is little doubt that European population growth (excluding immigration) was much slower than in China. The rough estimates available suggest that the European population in 1000 AD was about the same as in 200 AD, having declined for the first centuries of this period and then made a slow recovery. Certainly no European settlements came close to the size of the largest Chinese urban centers of this time (Mitterauer 2010, pp. 20–25).

The demographic differences between China and Europe mirrored gaps in their agricultural productivity. Song China employed advanced agricultural techniques, including the use of new rice varieties, extensive irrigation systems, terrace farming, crop rotation, and fertilizers. Its canals and waterways supported an extensive trade network. Northern China was not only the world's most populous trading area, it also produced large amounts of iron, much of it for military use.[1]

---

1. In 1078, northern China produced more than 114,000 tons of pig iron per year—double the amount produced by England at the beginning of the eighteenth century (Fairbank and Goldman 2006, p. 88).

In Western Europe, the early Middle Ages did see some improvement, especially in the introduction of wheeled plows and the slow adoption of the three-field rotation method (White 1962, pp. 39–78; Duby 1974, pp. 186–197). All the same, European agriculture was primitive by comparison, characterized by localized economies centered around self-sufficient manors, with only thin trickles of trade with more remote regions. Any excess production would primarily serve local markets or the local feudal lords (Mitterauer 2010, p. 24).

China's advantage over Europe in technological and scientific achievement was not limited to agriculture. The compass, gunpowder, and the printing press—that Francis Bacon famously coined as the major inventions of the millennium—all originated in China. During the Song period, scientific fields in China grew significantly as well: Chinese astronomers made significant contributions, and Chinese medicine became more refined. This progress was catalyzed by knowledge transmission becoming more systematic thanks to the establishment of state-sponsored academies to prepare people for entry into the state bureaucracy. As a result, Chinese nautical technology led the world: there is evidence that as early as the Southern Song dynasty (1127–1279), Chinese ships navigated to India and to East Africa. Foreign trade was a major source of revenue, and the government issued paper money—an epochal innovation—that circulated widely throughout the country (Fairbank and Goldman 2006, p. 88). Although medieval Europe showed evidence that it was open to absorbing technological and intellectual advances from China and the Islamic world, it was clearly far behind in its capacity to innovate until the later Middle Ages.

The proximate cause of these gaps between East and West is easy to identify. China had a strong and effective unitary state, while Europe was virtually stateless. As stressed by Scheidel (2019), China was able to preserve its state infrastructure despite frequent and intense internal wars. The state had maintained its coercive capacity and was able to subordinate and force cooperation from Chinese elites. This was reflected in the country's remarkable state capacity, which was also used to provide public goods such as defense, major infrastructure, some elements of social order, and a commonly accepted fiat money. During the Song Dynasty, central tax revenue is estimated to have approached one-tenth of the country's total output, and it could support an army of about 1 million soldiers (Scheidel 2019, p. 253). Meanwhile, in Europe, the collapse of the Roman Empire caused such prolonged devastation that by the turn of the first millennium AD, state infrastructure had almost completely disappeared (cf. Strayer 1970). Political and military power was fragmented among multiple local actors that were in frequent conflict with each other, and cooperation could not be enforced beyond the local level (Scheidel 2019, chapter 7).

Nine centuries later, however, China and Europe's relative positions had completely reversed. Europe occupied a position of global economic, political, and intellectual dominance, while China had fallen behind in most dimensions. Around 1850, gross domestic product (GDP) per capita in China was about one-fifth of that in Great Britain, one-fourth of the Netherlands', and less than half of Italy's (Broadberry et al. 2018). The Industrial Revolution, made possible by European innovation in science and technology, had transformed the Continent's economies, while China remained stagnant, having seemingly lost its innovative capacity. Several European nation-states had developed sophisticated and inclusive political institutions and boasted significant state capacity, with tax revenues around 10 percent of national GDP in the second half of the nineteenth century (Tanzi and Schuknecht 2000, Table III.1). By contrast, Chinese state capacity had declined, with tax revenues falling below 2 percent of GDP (Zhang 2022, p. 4), and political institutions remaining autocratic.

What explains this dramatic reversal of fortune and the social and political bifurcation between these two parts of the world? One recurrent explanation stresses the contrast between a politically fragmented Europe and the early formation of a unitary central state in China. Because Europe was so politically fragmented, its rulers were quite weak. When nation-states finally began to emerge in the late Middle Ages, European rulers had to bargain with a plurality of local elites to earn their cooperation, leading to the formation of more inclusive political institutions. In China, despite frequent internal struggles, centralized and autocratic state infrastructure never disappeared (although it weakened over time). The asymmetry of power between the central authority and weak local elites was much more pronounced in China, allowing autocratic political institutions to persist over time (Stasavage 2020; Jia, Roland, and Yang 2020).

In turn, it is commonly argued, European political fragmentation facilitated economic development in ways that were not viable in the unified, albeit more despotic China. In Europe, for example, innovators found it easier to escape censorship and the persecution of so-called heretics because sovereign states competed for intellectual and economic supremacy and were often in conflict with each other (Mokyr 2016). Scientists and innovators, when at risk of persecution, could flee to neighboring countries for refuge. In a similar vein, frequent wars forced emerging European states to invest in tax capacity (Gennaioli and Voth 2015) and in military technology (Hoffman, 2015), both of which accelerated the process of urbanization, as walled and well-defended cities offered much-needed protection to its residents (Rosenthal and Wong 2011). The relatively inclusive European political institutions, borne out of political compromise, also protected business interests because economic power-holders enjoyed some degree of political representation (Acemoglu and Robinson 2012). None of this could have happened in China, where an autocratic central state controlled education and the flow of knowledge, was not threatened by comparable external rivals, and had no interest in protecting property rights from political abuse. Thus, the great economic and institutional reversal is viewed as a by-product of the same forces that explain why China was ahead of Europe in the past: namely, the initial contrast between prolonged internal and external political fragmentation in Europe, as well as the early formation of a unitary central state in China.

Although these arguments contain many elements of truth, the importance of the distinction between prolonged fragmentation in Europe and early unification in China should not be exaggerated when it comes to explaining the Great Divergence. After all, China too was subject to severe external threats and invasions of nomad tribes from the steppe, and it was frequently ravaged by insurrections, civil wars, and violence. Moreover, although conflicts had some beneficial side effects for development, particularly in the accumulation of state capacity and city fortification, they were also disastrous for human welfare. Wars brought lasting destruction and poverty. Histories of prolonged conflict between neighboring sovereign states and political fragmentation are not unique to Europe, and yet in other parts of the world, these patterns did not bring about comparable positive effects on economic and institutional development in other parts of the world.[2]

In this book, we take a different perspective on the issue of the Great Divergence and its relationship to the institutional bifurcation between China and Europe. Our approach does not deny the relevance of the contrast between political fragmentation in Europe and unification in China to this reversal of fortune. Rather, we highlight other crucial elements that distinguished Europe from China beginning around 1000 AD, which were inherited from their distinct historical trajectories and emphasized the importance of

---

2. Dincecco, Fenske, and Onorato (2019) show that precolonial warfare is positively correlated with indicators of state capacity and local economic development within India. Yet, overall, India did not reach the levels of economic development of Western Europe despite comparable and long-lasting political fragmentation. We return to a comparison between Europe and India in chapter 11.

nonstate social organizations and cultural traditions. These additional initial differences enhanced and accentuated the consequences of the contrast between European fragmentation and Chinese unification. Our perspective not only contributes to explanations of the Great Divergence between Europe and China, it also illuminates more generally how the evolution of institutions and the process of economic development are shaped by culture and the internal organization of society.

Some caveats are in order before we proceed. Given the breadth of the questions that we investigate, we lump together large and heterogeneous geographic areas and time periods, at times neglecting important differences among them. Above all, there is ambiguity as to the exact geographical definition of "Europe."[3] Throughout this book, we use "Europe" to refer to that part of the Continent west of the "Hajnal line" between Saint Petersburg and Trieste, although much of what we will say about "Europe" may not apply to some regions in the Mediterranean (Hajnal 1965). Furthermore, our analysis covers the entire second millennium, but two periods are of special interest: the Middle Ages and the Industrial Revolution. Yet the Industrial Revolution cannot be properly understood without taking a closer look at intellectual and technological developments in the two centuries before 1750. One may also ask: Why start the comparison between China and Europe at the turn of the millennium and not earlier? In fact, we seek to explain the many divergences between these two parts of the world in terms of "initial" differences, which were already in place at the turn of the millennium and had developed over several previous centuries. The turn of the millennium is an appropriate place to begin because it was the point when the foundations of the emerging European states were being laid down and the differences between China and Europe were becoming increasingly pronounced. Finally, our focus also implies that we must inevitably neglect temporary reversals in the tendencies that we describe, along with important differences within Europe and within

3. On September 29, 2023, *The Economist* reflected on the ambiguities of the concept of "Europe." It noted that "English-speakers may call Europe 'the continent,' but that is because their language evolved on an island off its coast. In fact it is simply a convoluted promontory of Eurasia. This sets geographers a puzzle: where does Europe end? The eastern border especially is fuzzy.... The idea of Europe started with the ancient Greeks, who contrasted it with despotic, barbarian Asia.... The Enlightenment sense of who belonged in Europe rested on Europeans' alleged rationality and cosmopolitanism." As we will see throughout this book, Europeans shared some other features, which may have been decisive in defining the role of the "Eurasian promontory in world history."

China, as well as between different time periods. That said, despite such heterogeneity, the two civilizations exhibited significant common denominators, making a generalized analysis meaningful.

It is also important to clarify at the outset one important aspect of our conceptual framework. Following recent literature discussed below (e.g., Tabellini 2008a; Enke 2019 and 2023; Henrich 2020; Schulz, 2022), we rely on the important distinction between universalistic and communitarian value systems (or, equivalently, between generalized and limited systems of morality). This distinction refers to how the intensity of moral sentiments changes in relation to the social distance between individuals. In a utilitarian and consequentialist approach, it also refers to how altruism is affected by social distance. A universalistic value system is one where altruism and moral sentiments are not very sensitive to social distance: moral beliefs are applied with similar strength in interactions with friends and strangers. By contrast, in a communitarian value system, altruism and moral sentiments are much stronger toward socially close people than toward strangers. As emphasized by Enke (2023), this distinction is about the *slope* of the relationship between altruism and social distance (how much moral sentiments change as social distance changes), but not about the average strength of altruism and moral sentiments. In the pithy words of Enke (2024, p. 136), "A communitarian is a great friend to have, while a universalist in a great stranger to encounter."

When using this conceptual framework to discuss the divergent histories of China and Europe, our intention is not to imply that the Western Christian tradition, which we argue is more universalistic, is in any sense morally superior to the Confucian traditions, which we argue is more communitarian. Throughout the course of history, Europeans pillaged and enslaved much of the rest of the world and committed heinous crimes, no less (although perhaps more effectively) than other civilizations. Nevertheless, we argue that the differences between these two traditions were significant and contributed to the dramatic bifurcation in social arrangements, economic development, and political institutions between China and Europe.

2. Social Organizations and the Enforcement of Cooperation

Our starting point is the premise that sustaining cooperation outside the narrow nuclear household is a major challenge for any society. A single household is simply too small to supply a host of essential goods and services that have public-good and club-good dimensions, such as risk sharing, religious worship, protection against theft and external threats, market and transportation infrastructures, settlement of disputes, education, and water management. In modern societies, cooperative behavior that supports the provision of these basic public and club goods is largely (but not exclusively) facilitated by state agents, thanks to the rule of law and the government's enforcement powers. However, in the distant past, the state was much weaker, if not totally absent, in many parts of the world. Even a relatively effective state like Song China did not have the resources to adequately provide all the kinds of public goods described and to enforce cooperation at the local level. Yet cooperation was particularly essential. Limitations in transportation and communication made social and economic interactions over long distances very difficult. Without adequate enforcement of local cooperation, social life would have been all but impossible.

Our analysis builds on a basic observation with respect to Europe's and China's methods of addressing this problem. Gradually over time, but increasingly so after the start of the second millennium, Europe's and China's methods of sustaining local cooperation diverged. Although both civilizations used nonstate social organizations, the nature of these organizations differed. In China, cooperation was increasingly sustained by kin-based social networks, the clan being the prototypical organization. In Europe, a different kind of social organization gradually emerged among *unrelated* individuals. Following Greif (2006b), we refer to these organizations as "corporations." Examples of such corporations can be traced all the way to the Middle Ages and thereafter: fraternities, guilds, monastic and religious orders, universities and academic associations, self-governing cities, and the modern business corporation. We will describe these social organizations in detail in Chapters 5 and 6.

Chinese kin-based organizations and European corporations performed seemingly similar functions essential to the effective organization of social life: they shared risk, provided individual protection, facilitated market transactions, provided financing, organized education, provided religious services, settled disputes, and assisted the state in collecting taxes and providing military resources. Yet they differed in one key respect: *with whom* one cooperated. Chinese clans and lineages were associations of individuals who claimed to descend from a common patrilineal ancestor. European corporations were associations of individuals unrelated by kin, who got together for a specific purpose.

Of course, there was considerable heterogeneity in the nature, scope, and form of these social organizations, both within China and Europe and over time. Nevertheless, Chinese and European methods of sustaining local cooperation were clearly distinct and became increasingly so during the later Middle Ages and the Early Modern era (these historical terms refer to periods of European history, although we will use them to refer to the coinciding periods in China as well). In short, Chinese clans were held together by common kin, while European corporations were held together by a specific common interest.

This basic distinction between corporations and kin-based organizations, in turn, implied other differences in function and day-to-day operations. Chinese clans and lineages were multipurpose organizations: the same kin-based network provided a variety of local public goods and club goods: ancestral ceremonies and worship, risk sharing and protection, financing, dispute settlement, and so on. Many (but not all) European corporations were instead formed for a primary specific purpose—sometimes religious, other times economic or political—or to provide education.

This distinction, in turn, had a second implication for membership. Chinese kin-based organizations created a firm partition of society along the lines of mutually exclusive and ascriptive dynastic groups, which often competed with each other. For all intents and purposes, there were no exit options for members. In medieval Europe, in contrast, individuals often belonged to several overlapping organizations: their guild, their fraternity, their parish, their city, and others. European society was formed by dense overlapping networks and associations, which fostered a cultural practice of cooperation and conflict resolution among unrelated individuals in a variety of domains (cf. Reynolds 1997). As discussed later in this chapter, this feature of European society made it easier to scale up cooperation from the local level to the national level through inclusive political institutions. The formation of European corporations would have vast unintended consequences. The same was true for the persistent commitment to kinship in China.

A third and related significance of the difference between Chinese kin-based organizations and European corporations concerns their methods for enforcing cooperation and the governance of social organizations. Cooperation is easier to enforce between members of the same dynasty than among unrelated individuals because of reciprocal altruistic ties. Moreover, the threat of exclusion is much more fearsome in a society formed by kin-based, multipurpose associations than in a society of overlapping, single-purpose associations: once excluded from a Chinese kin-based network, an individual had practically nowhere else to go to seek protection. For both reasons, Chinese clans could rely mostly on informal methods of enforcing cooperation, whereas external and formal enforcement procedures had to be used in several European corporations. Furthermore, Chinese clans were typically hierarchical organizations based on seniority, where elder members supposedly acted in the interest of the entire clan, without much need for consultation and accountability. European corporations instead being associations of unrelated individuals carefully regulated collective decisions through consensual practices. Corporations too were hierarchical organizations, but their rules often spelled out membership rights, paid attention to agency problems, and imposed checks and balances on leaders' authority.

How and why did these distinct social arrangements to sustain local cooperation emerge and diffuse across the two civilizations? And how did they affect the subsequent evolution of political institutions and economic development? These questions are the main focus of our analysis. The remainder of the chapter summarizes how we answer them.

3. Cultural Origins of Social Organizations

For social organizations to withstand the test of time, they have to be self-sustaining and complementary with other features of society. In particular, they have to be consistent with the surrounding cultural context. Using the conceptual framework of social network analysis, social interactions exhibit a strong degree of homophily: simply put, individuals prefer to interact with people who are similar to them (Jackson 2008, pp. 100–101; Fu et al. 2012). But similar in what way? In China, the kind of similarity that mattered most for social organization was primarily sharing a common ancestor, although in the late days of the empire, more inclusive attitudes emerged and some liberties were taken with respect to the constraint of shared ancestry. In Europe, the kind of similarity that mattered most for social organization was based on other criteria, such as location (living in the same town), occupation (belonging to the same guild), religious devotion (members of the same monastery), or more generally, sharing a common set of values and interests. These distinct preferences for social interaction were clearly consequential for future development. So the question of why kin-based organizations emerged in China and corporate organizations spread out in Europe can be posed as follows: Why did the Chinese prefer to interact mostly within kin groups, while Europeans were willing to interact with strangers? One answer suggested by Greif and Tabellini (2010, 2017) is that when the need to cooperate in the provision of local public goods started to become more acute, and increasingly so after the turn of the first millennium, these two parts of the world had different value systems (see also Henrich 2020 and Enke 2019). In what follows, we trace the general trajectories of these distinct value systems and their relevance for the development of both civilizations' respective cooperative institutions.

Starting roughly at the start of the millennium, a major cultural transformation occurred in China. During the Song Dynasty, neo-Confucianism became the dominant social and intellectual culture in China. As many scholars of Chinese history have pointed out, neo-Confucianism—especially as formulated by the preeminent Southern-Song philosopher Zhu Xi (1130–1200) and his followers—was to become "the living faith of China's elite down to the twentieth century" (Fairbank and Goldman, 2006, p. 98; see also Bol, 2008). A series of doctrines governing both personal and public life, neo-Confucianism emphasized kin-based values as the basis of social order. Interpersonal relations, including cooperation, were to be governed by filial loyalty, strict gender hierarchy, and respect among relatives. An archetype of the communitarian value system, neo-Confucianism made it easier to sustain cooperation among kin, who were tied together by clannish norms: strong bounds of reciprocal loyalty, strict gender hierarchy, and respect among relatives.

Western Europe was very different. Although tribal and kin-based values were also widespread after the fall of the Roman Empire, particularly because of the Germanic invasions, they were gradually and deliberately undermined by the Catholic Church. Beginning in the early Middle Ages, the Latin (Catholic) Church actively discouraged a variety of practices that had traditionally strengthened and consolidated kin networks, such as adoption, polygamy, concubinage, consanguineous marriage, and nonconsensual marriage. Violating these bans carried the threat of harsh punishment, including social sanction and religious excommunication. As documented by Schulz (2022) and others, these Church policies influenced the European family structure: the extended family gradually became less important and was replaced by the smaller nuclear family. Marriage in Europe also increasingly became neolocal: a young couple intending to establish a new household would typically live separately from both parents, which made kin-based cooperation less effective. This is not to say that the extended family was eliminated from social life. It certainly continued to play an important role in many cooperative arrangements across the Continent. However, it is undeniable that over time, the nuclear family replaced the extended family as the basic building block of society. This transformation in turn gave rise to other social arrangements to sustain cooperation.

In addition to weakening extended kinship ties, Christian culture, as elucidated by the Church, also strongly rejected the values associated with patrilineal descent groups and strengthened the commitment toward bilateral descent (i.e., from both parents), which was already part of the post-Roman Germanic traditions. But large kinship groups are unfeasible if ancestry is determined by symmetric maternal and paternal criteria because the number of ancestors to keep track of quickly becomes too large (cf. Roland 2020b). Last but not least, over the years, the Church reinforced universalistic values. It stressed that all human beings are equal in front of God, individuals are responsible for their own choices, and loyalty to the community of believers takes priority over kin loyalty.[4]

The Church policies that weakened European kinship are credited with creating what is called the European Marriage Pattern (EMP): neolocal nuclear family units with bilateral lineages (Hajnal 1965; Todd 1987; Mitterauer 2010). The EMP was highly distinct from prevalent family patterns in China and other parts of the world. That said, the Church's policies were not the only factor responsible for the evolution of Europe's social organizations away from kin-based loyalty. The centrality of the individual was already a feature of Greek philosophy, and the legal formalisms that sustained European corporations also benefited from the rediscovery of Roman law. Moreover, European agriculture—depending as it did on livestock—created economic opportunities for women that may not have existed elsewhere, and thus contributed to unique social developments such as relatively late marriage and neolocality, a topic to be discussed in Chapter 2.

Nevertheless, Church policies exerted significant influence over large kinship groups during a crucial period when religion was particularly important in people's lives, political power was highly fragmented, and social arrangements were necessary to sustain local cooperation. Therefore, it is largely thanks to the Church that the seeds of universalism and individualism were sowed in Europe around the turn of the first millennium. In such an environment, cooperation among individuals who were bound by interests rather than ancestry became easier to sustain.

4. In line with this, Bergeron (2019) shows that exposure to former Christian missions in Democratic Republic of the Congo is correlated with more universalistic values and preferences in lab-in-the field experiments.

From this historical overview, it is now apparent that the social organizations of the kin network and corporation were complementary to the respective value systems in place in China and Europe at the beginning of the time period that we are studying. But causality went both ways. The different social organizations that began to emerge in China and Europe to sustain cooperation exerted strong feedback effects on their prevailing cultures, which in turn strengthened their relevance in society. As shown by Tabellini (2008b), an environment in which most interactions occur within a kin-based social network reinforces kin-based and communitarian values. In such a world, people deal with relatives whom they can trust and minimize contacts with strangers. This kind of society inevitably produces a larger gap in trust for kin than for nonkin. Conversely, frequent interactions among socially distant people reinforce generalized trust and universalistic values.[5] The diffusion of communitarian or universalistic values, in turn, further consolidates social organizations that are complementary with the prevailing culture. Thus, the complementarity between values and organizations can amplify initial differences among civilizations, leading to progressive social and cultural bifurcation.

This is highly relevant to the divergent trajectories taken by China and Europe. At the turn of the first millennium AD, their civilizations were sufficiently different in terms of prevailing values and methods of organization; although the extent of these differences is debated, they were significant enough to be documented in historical records. Over time, these differences became more pronounced and widespread as the societies evolved along different paths. As we discuss next, interactions with state institutions and different patterns of economic development reinforced these complementarities and the resulting bifurcations.

Our argument draws on interdisciplinary research carried out by social scientists. Recent scholarship has increasingly stressed the importance of cultural differences and family structures in explaining the Great Divergence. Many ideas in this book are consistent with important work by Henrich (2020), Schulz et al. (2019), Schulz (2022), and Enke (2019). These authors explore the contrast between Europe and China, emphasizing the uniqueness of

---

5. Tabellini (2008b) models the distinction between communitarian and universalistic values with reference to how rapidly moral obligations decay with social distance. Following Platteau (2000) and Banfield (1958), he refers to these value systems as limited versus generalized morality. Enke (2019) uses the terminology of communitarian and universalistic values, and we use these terms throughout this book.

European economic development and cultural evolution relative to the rest of the world and stating the importance of the Catholic Church in reshaping social organization in Europe Their work explores the psychological and cultural foundations that differentiate Europeans from other populations. Schulz's work also stresses the important cultural role played by the Church in European history and the link between communitarian value systems and strong historical kinship ties. Our approach builds on this literature, but we focus on the differences between Europe and China as opposed to other parts of the world. Furthermore, we specifically elucidate the historical mechanisms and the evolution of social organizations that contributed to the economic and institutional divergence between China and Europe. Our main emphasis is on how this divergence derived from the positive feedback effects between cultural, organizational, and institutional factors. We refer more precisely to these contributions in context in the following chapters.[6]

4. Social Organizations and Institutional Bifurcation

When the state was absent or incapable of supplying public goods and social services at the local level, social organizations often acted as its substitute, doing so in its stead. This substitution was often spontaneous and implicit, but in some instances, the state explicitly recognized the arrangement and used social organizations as agents of a decentralized administration. This was the case in both Europe and China. With recognition from the state, self-governing European cities administered justice, enforced tax collection, organized the provision of military resources, and built infrastructure. Similarly, Chinese clans settled disputes, provided poor relief, assisted state magistrates in enforcing tax collection, and took responsibility for fielding soldiers. In these roles,

6. Our approach is also related to the interesting work of Gorodnichenko and Roland (2017); Roland (2020b); and Eruchimovitch, Michaeli, and Sarid (2024). Their distinction between individualistic and collectivistic societies is conceptually and empirically not quite the same as our distinction between communitarian and universalistic values, however. Communitarian cultures entail a strong attachment to a local community, and in this sense, they are also more collectivist. As stressed by Enke (2023), however, the distinction between universalistic and communitarian value systems is about how fast altruism changes with social distance, whereas the distinction between individualistic and collectivistic cultures could also be interpreted as referring to the overall amount of altruism. Moreover, while these authors mostly emphasize statistical correlations between cultural features and economic and political outcomes, we build our arguments from historical analysis and put social organizations at center stage.

the formal state authorities and respective social organizations often enjoyed a symbiotic relationship: the two entities influenced each other. But the details of how this happened differed in Europe versus China because of the different features of clans and corporations, and this contributed to setting these two worlds increasingly far from each other. In particular, the corporation would amplify the effects of political fragmentation in Europe, and the clan would amplify the effects of an early unitary state in China.

The evolution of legal systems, discussed at length in Chapter 8, is a striking example. In China, where the state was stronger from the beginning, the legal system was designed top-down with two main goals: to maintain peace and stability and to govern the relations between the public administration and its subjects. Civil law played only a secondary role because commercial disputes were primarily resolved by clans through arbitration and compromise. State magistrates got involved only if clans failed to reach settlement. In Europe, by contrast, where the state was initially much weaker, the legal system had a bottom-up origin, and corporations influenced its evolution both on the demand and the supply side. The prevalence of impersonal exchange and contractual arrangements among unrelated individuals created a demand for external enforcement and well-functioning legal institutions, which provided the basis for the evolution of commercial and civil law. Legal principles first appeared in private contractual agreements within and between corporations. Over time, they evolved as best practices in communities of merchants, accompanying the Commercial Revolution of the twelfth and thirteenth centuries, and eventually were codified into law. This process was also influenced by corporations from the supply side because the codification and generalization of best practices were carried out by jurists and legal scholars who had served as administrators of corporations or received specific training by corporations.

The evolution of the legal system in Europe and its priority on civil law, in turn, had several important implications. First, the legal system defined and clarified the nature of corporations as separate legal entities and holders of specific rights. This made corporations more powerful and resilient and facilitated their acquisition of important political rights and prerogatives. Second, the emergence of legal institutions very early in European history coincided with the beginning of the formation of states. Their coevolution thus influenced how political institutions developed. The administration of justice and law enforcement was among the first functions performed by European sovereigns, and other institutions emerged subsequently to deal with specific domestic affairs (Strayer, 1970). This sequence in the emergence of state functions gave prominence to the principle of the rule of law, which encompassed two notions: the legislative and executive sovereign authority would be limited by a preexisting body of law, and the courts would uphold the principle (if not the practice) of equality before the law. The early emergence of judicial state functions in Europe also explains the growing influence acquired by national parliaments. As discussed by Boucoyannis (2021), early parliamentary assemblies performed several judicial functions of public importance, such as resolving disputes between nobles and other elites, overseeing instances of corruption among judges and other administrators, and addressing petitions.

The corporation also influenced the evolution of European political institutions in a more direct way: they provided a concrete example of how to regulate collective decisions through *consensual practices*. The diffusion of corporate arrangements throughout European civil society made consensual practices and ventures the norm. Citizens' notions of fairness and legitimacy were derived from their firsthand experiences with guilds, city charters, religious organizations, and other corporations. More concretely, best practices from corporations became built into the foundations of political institutions via jurists and scholars who were well acquainted with the regulation of collective decisions within corporations. As such, they were able to create a body of theory that justified consensual practices. Overarchingly, several important principles of corporate governance were adapted from corporations and transplanted into political bodies. Two prominent examples come via the principle of representation: namely, the notion that a delegate can bind the group that it represents to its decision, and the sufficiency of the majority in collective decision-making as opposed to unanimity. These principles, like several others, first emerged in corporations and were subsequently adapted to political institutions.

Ecclesiastic organizations played a special role in this process. The Church itself can be seen as a corporate body, being a self-governing group of unrelated people. Scholars of canon law thought carefully about how to regulate collective decisions inside religious organizations, drawing on their personal experience with the administration of other corporations. Often, the sequence first involved the adaptation of a norm of private law into the Church's administrative structure, and then its return to the secular domain as a constitutional norm (Tierney 1982).

Matters were very different in China since kinship organizations relied on informal and more hierarchical principles of governance, often based on seniority. The neo-Confucian doctrines of ancestor worship and kin loyalty strengthened the legitimacy of the emperor—who promoted himself as the patriarch of an enlarged family—and his dynasty, as they were chosen by heaven. This was contrary to the notion of equality before the law that developed in Europe.

In addition, the Chinese state had a long tradition of relying on a powerful and effective central bureaucracy to fulfill its aims. However, its members were not recruited based on their social status or previous administrative experience in civil society, as was the case in Europe. Instead, they were selected through a demanding civil service exam that required lengthy preparation and extensive training in Confucian doctrine. This meritocratic process had several advantages from the perspective of regime stability. It created a cohesive social group of talented administrators who shared a basic ethic and a very similar education, all with a large stake in preserving the regime. Simultaneously, these administrators were—at least formally—separated from their clans of origin, preventing the rise of powerful elites or external social groups that could have created a countervailing power and challenge imperial authority.

Arguably, the diffusion of corporations in European society by itself cannot wholly explain why the political institutions that emerged in Europe were more inclusive than those in China. Certainly, the institutional divergence also reflected the greater initial political fragmentation in Europe, and the much weaker bargaining power of European sovereigns vis à vis other elites. Nevertheless, the internal organization of society amplified the effects of this contrast between a fragmented Europe and a unified China by providing concrete examples of how governance could be arranged and shaping expectations of fairness and legitimacy.

Two sets of corporations had a particularly strong impact on the evolution of European political institutions: the Church and self-governing towns. As previously discussed, the Church played a critical role in eroding extended kinship values and provided a successful example of how corporate governance principles could be adapted from the private to the public sphere.[7] In

---

7. In some ways, the Church can be seen as a corporation operating on a continental scale, as it was clearly independent of kinship networks while also being capable of self-governance. Yet unlike other European corporations, members of the Church quickly lost their exit options and were outlawed from membership in rival religious organizations. What is decisive is that nothing like the Church emerged in China, and insofar that the Church was a countervailing power to the medieval state, its importance to the bifurcation was substantial.

addition, after the Investiture Conflict between Pope Gregory VII and the Holy Roman Emperor in the late eleventh century over who had the right to appoint bishops, the Church deliberately enhanced European political fragmentation by strategically undermining the centralization of political powers between and within emerging nation-states (Møller and Doucette 2022; Grzymala-Busse 2023). One reason the Church could retain its independence from secular political powers so effectively was that it had organized itself as a corporate structure. It is interesting to note that by way of contrast in China, Buddhist monasteries, which had not formed a congregation but were isolated and self-relying entities, did not survive as a political power once the Tang emperors became hostile.

Self-governing cities, too, exerted a key influence over the evolution of European political institutions, enhancing the effects of political fragmentation. Like Chinese clans, autonomous cities in Europe—known as "communes"—enforced tax collection and contributed to other aspects of decentralized administration. Unlike Chinese clans, however, communes enjoyed exclusive control over their territories. This feature enhanced their bargaining power against sovereigns, who did not yet have adequate resources to collect tax revenues on their own. When their financial needs were particularly acute, as in war episodes, sovereigns had to concede political rights to self-governing cities in exchange for the additional tax resources. Often, these political rights took the form of representation in national parliaments. A key step in the evolution of European parliaments is the inclusion of representatives of corporate groups in councils previously exclusive to the nobility. As shown by Cox, Dincecco, and Onorato (2024), this step occurred only in Europe, but it was much more likely to happen if two conditions were satisfied: first, the presence of self-governing cities; and second, the occurrence of a war. In other words, conflicts were necessary to facilitate the emergence of inclusive political institutions, but sufficient only in the presence of strong corporate organizations like self-governing cities. China too had large urban centers, but they had little autonomy and did not play an important role in decentralized state administration. Clans, which were important for local administration, were not powerful enough to extract political concessions. One reason is that their dynastic origin limited their scale and did not allow them to have exclusive control over their territory, except perhaps in scarcely populated areas.

The fact that corporate and territorial interests enjoyed political representation in Europe but not China helps to explain the divergent paths in

European and Chinese tax capacity. In Europe, corporate groups responsible for tax collection eventually gained political rights, which gave them influence over how revenues would be spent. This made it easier for them to raise revenues during times of need. In China, clans who enforced tax collection had no political representation, nor could they influence the state bureaucracy over what state revenues would be spent on. Consequently, agency problems and resultant corruption were much more severe in China than Europe, and in the long run, this state of affairs was deleterious to state capacity in China. That said, there was a countervailing measure to corruption in China; governing elites held a paternalistic attitude toward the masses. Confucian values drove them to engage in acts of charity, especially during times of emergency. Over time, of course, much charity was carried out within the clans, but several examples of government welfare in China (see the government program of granaries discussed in Chapter 8) reflect a state attuned to the needs of the people.

5. Social Organizations and the Great Divergence

The different social arrangements in China and Europe also shaped economic development in several ways. The most important reason why Europe surged ahead of China in the eighteenth and nineteenth centuries is that the Industrial Revolution occurred in Europe, not in China. Of course, this was not due to chance, and social organizations are part of the explanation of why it happened, as we will argue at length in Chapter 9.

The Industrial Revolution was driven by a host of scientific and technological innovations. European corporations were at the heart of the creation and accumulation of knowledge, following centuries-old norms and traditions. Monasteries, universities, and later scientific societies—all corporate organizations—played a crucial role in creating the conditions that made the Industrial Revolution possible. European states themselves were not a direct part of this creative process; however, the European political environment, as it had evolved since the fall of the Roman Empire, facilitated scientific and industrial innovation in three main ways. First, as already noted, the polycentric nature of political power and competition among fragmented states allowed innovators to escape censorship and suppression. Second, the Catholic Church, despite its ambiguous and often inconsistent relationship with useful knowledge, on balance created conditions that proved conducive to technological progress (even if that was not its intention). Indeed, much of medieval Europe's progress in science and technology was carried out by devout clergy, providing the basis for future innovation. Third, as we have recently outlined, the state had conceded some manner of political representation to business interests, which limited state interference with wealth accumulation and the functioning of markets.

In China, by contrast, knowledge accumulation and education were largely controlled by the state administration. Clans played an important role in the provision of education, but the purpose of schooling was ultimately to prepare students to pass the civil service exam, not to contribute to the advancement of science. Hence, its content was entirely determined by the state, and mandarins and other government officials largely controlled the market of ideas and the course of intellectual innovation. Moreover, the Chinese bureaucracy increasingly privileged the study of traditional Confucian doctrine, bent primarily on social peace and preserving regime stability, over subjects more relevant to the natural sciences. This conservative intellectual environment became particularly detrimental in later centuries, when innovation in Europe was increasingly driven by highly trained experts and people in the upper tail of the human capital distribution, such as chemists, engineers, mechanics, artisans, and natural philosophers (Lin, 1995). Hence, China was at a disadvantage: it had a huge supply of bright and industrious youngsters, but their learning was channeled into studies that had few or no spillovers into production technology and useful knowledge.

In addition to their role in knowledge accumulation and scientific discoveries, European corporations contributed to economic progress in two additional ways. First, they facilitated the creation of thick and well-functioning financial markets and the diffusion of long-distance trade. Arm's-length financing of major trade and business ventures, such as the East India Companies, were used in Europe at least a century before similar instruments appeared in China (Harris 2020). These impersonal economic arrangements reflected a long tradition of economic and social interactions among unrelated individuals and a legal system that supported such interactions. The Chinese social environment, where social and economic networks were predominantly comprised of related individuals, faced more difficulties in transition from a local to an impersonal, global economy. This constraint on whom to deal with and trust became a liability when transportation and communication costs decreased, making transactions among strangers and with remote markets much more important.

The second way that the corporation facilitated European industrialization was via its model for the organization of production. In a capitalist firm, investment decisions are made by capital owners who are also the residual claimants of the returns from investment, while labor earns a fixed wage. This organization of production creates strong incentives to invest in labor-saving innovations because the returns accrue to those who control the investment decisions. Moreover, the separation of ownership from control implies that business corporations could be easily scaled up in an environment of well-functioning financial markets. European economies could reap the benefits of this mode of production during the Industrial Revolution because their economies were already organized along these lines in agriculture. The early statistician Gregory King estimated in 1688 that two-thirds of the rural population owned little or no land (Overton, 1996, p. 178), and the 1851 census reported that 73 percent of the population living in the countryside consisted of wage earners. Long before the rise of the modern business corporation in the nineteenth century, European firms already had adopted the corporate form as defined previously. In China, by contrast, household production was more common because land ownership was much less concentrated and labor-sharing arrangements were relatively more prevalent. Wage labor employed in agriculture is estimated to have been less than 10 percent of the rural population during a comparable period. In this environment, clans were responsible for the survival of their members, and thus they drew no benefit from replacing labor with machines. Consequently, labor-saving innovations (such as mechanization) were less attractive unless production could be scaled up quickly in proportion to the productivity enhancements. Moreover, control rights over investments typically rested with senior (i.e., older) clan members, who were less inclined to innovate.

6. General Lessons

A large body of literature has argued that culture directly influences economic outcomes, as well as the functioning of existing institutions, by shaping the beliefs and values of individuals (e.g., Greif, 1994; Guiso, Sapienza, and Zingales 2016; Tabellini 2008a; Roland 2020a). Culture is viewed as an important mechanism of historical persistence because, although endogenous, it is slow moving, so current cultural traits often reflect features of a more distant social and political environment. Our analysis of the Great Reversal points to another mechanism of cultural persistence and influence: the embedding of specific cultural traits into social organizations. Culture (whether Catholic religion or Confucian doctrine)—and in particular the difference between communitarian and universalistic values—influences with whom people cooperate, which social networks are formed, and how this local collaboration is sustained. Once these networks crystallize in organizational form, they exert unintended and lasting influences on future economic and political outcomes. In other words, the effects of culture are not only direct; they are also mediated by social organizations that are complementary with specific cultural traits. Once in place, these social organizations are hard to dismantle, and they contribute to spread and maintain the cultural foundations on which they are built. As we shall see in Chapter 10, the clan structure in China proved to be a tenacious institution, surviving despite the efforts of the communist regime to eradicate it.

The histories of China and Europe exemplify how culture influences the evolution of political institutions through social organizations, and reciprocally, how state and local organizations reinforced prevailing cultural traits. Here, too, the interactions between culture and institutions are not only direct, but also mediated by social organizations. Historically, social organizations such as clans and corporations fulfilled important administrative functions and had significant control over day-to-day life. They could thus be exploited by the state as instruments of local administration. This interaction was a source of reciprocal influence. On the one hand, social organizations were strengthened by acting as agents of the state. On the other hand, the evolution of state institutions also reflected the nature of underlying social arrangements.

Little of this relationship was in place at the start of the second millennium AD. However, the seeds of this divergence were nonetheless planted around that time. The histories of China and Europe during the second millennium illustrate how initial differences in prevailing cultural traits, or specific historical circumstances that led to cultural innovations (e.g., a new norm introduced by a religious authority), can set into motion a set of cascading, long-lasting transformations in cultural, social, and institutional environments.

Although this book focuses on the historical divergence between Europe and China, the analysis of social organizations can also shed light on other historical episodes, as well as other problems of institutional and economic development. The fundamental challenge of state formation is how to scale up cooperation from the local to the national level. Most societies have found ways to sustain cooperation locally, be it within small communities such as tribes, villages, clans, or other groups. But scaling up cooperation among strangers poses new challenges and requires different social arrangements. Our historical analysis of China versus Europe, along with the work of Henrich (2020), Schulz et al. (2019), and Schulz (2022), suggest that these challenges are more easily overcome by societies that hold universalistic values and have developed social organizations to sustain cooperation among strangers, as was the case in Europe with the rise of the corporation as the dominant organization. In China, starting with the reunification of the country under the powerful if short-lived Qin Dynasty (221–207 BC), cooperation was scaled up and conflicts were resolved thanks to the early emergence of a strong autocratic regime, which relied on the enforcement powers of a centralized bureaucracy. In Europe, peaceful resolution of internal political conflicts and the emergence of inclusive institutions were facilitated by social practices that encouraged cooperation among strangers. However, the European path of economic and institutional development took many centuries. Is it possible for this process to be accelerated? And how can cooperation be scaled up in social environments where communitarian rather than universalistic values are prevalent? What if social organizations encouraging cooperation among strangers have not yet emerged? Addressing these difficult questions is of fundamental importance for future research on economic and political development.

7. Outline of This Book

The rest of the book is organized as follows.

In Chapter 2, we review the debate on the Great Divergence in economic history. We describe the reversal of economic fortunes between China and Europe in detail, as well as the many dimensions of their divergence between the eleventh and nineteenth centuries, critically discussing some explanations that have been put forward in the literature. The chapter emphasizes two initial differences between China and Europe that arguably played an important role in their subsequent divergence: the contrast between internal and external political fragmentation in Europe and early unification under a strong central state in China; and their different family structures.

In Chapter 3, we lay out our conceptual and analytical framework, explaining the two mechanisms that we argue are central to the observed social and cultural bifurcation. First, the prevalence of communitarian as opposed to universalistic culture leads to different organizational forms to sustain local cooperation. Second, the diffusion of one or the other organizational forms (between kin versus between strangers) contributes to the diffusion of cultural traits that are complementary with the prevailing social organizations. The central conclusion of this chapter is that initially, small differences in cultural traits or in organizational forms can set into motion a lasting process of cultural and social bifurcation. We discuss how this conceptual framework applies to China and Europe, and then we summarize the main logical implications of the analysis, which are more thoroughly investigated throughout the remainder of the book.

In Chapter 4, we describe the main cultural differences between China and Europe at the start of the first millennium AD, emphasizing the revival of Confucianism in China after c.1000 in comparison with the norms supported by the Catholic Church at about the same time. We also discuss how these different doctrines influenced family structures and the resulting strength of kinship ties in these two parts of the world. We point out that the influence of the Church went beyond family ties and norms of good behavior. The Church also provided a concrete and influential example of how to design corporate structures in a complex and large organization of unrelated individuals.

Chapters 5 extensively documents the prevalence of kin-based organizations in China versus corporate arrangements in Europe. We describe in detail the key features of these social organizations, as well as when and where they emerged. We identify significant differences and similarities between kinship organizations and corporations and discuss how they evolved through time and space.

Chapter 6 discusses in detail the most important corporations that spread throughout Europe during the Middle Ages, including fraternities, monasteries, guilds, universities, and self-governing cities. We contrast these organizations with their Chinese counterparts during the same period. Although the concept of a "corporation" is often associated with the modern business firm, which emerged in Europe in the early seventeenth century, Medieval corporate structures did not primarily serve an economic purpose (except for guilds). Instead, they fulfilled other social functions, including important political responsibilities that required some form of cooperation. Business corporations also emerged in China, although much later than in Europe. But importantly, unlike in Europe, Chinese corporations never acquired much of a role in the political and public sphere.

Chapter 7 discusses the institutional divergence. We first summarize the key features of Chinese state institutions, discussing why they remained stable over several centuries despite dynastic changes and internal wars, and emphasize their complementarities with prevailing kin-based organizations. We discuss the emergence and evolution of state institutions in Europe during the

Middle Ages, explaining how they developed under the influence of the corporate structures that permeated European society. We also stress the special role that the Catholic Church and self-governing cities played in the evolution of European political institutions. The main theme of this chapter is that distinctive organizations of society in China and Europe amplified the effects of their initial differences in political unification as opposed to fragmentation.

Chapter 8 discusses other aspects of the institutional bifurcation between China and Europe that resulted from the interaction of the state with prevailing social organizations. In China, the state exploited the enforcement power of clans in its decentralized administration. European states did the same with self-governing cities. These relationships strengthened social organizations while also shaping state development. In this chapter, we focus on the evolution of the respective legal systems in East and West and their various state capacities.

Chapter 9 turns to economic divergence, discussing why the Industrial Revolution occurred first in Europe and not in China. We argue that geography alone is not an adequate explanation. Instead, this chapter emphasizes the role of corporations and universalistic values in shaping the scientific and technological innovations that led to the Industrial Revolution, and explains why similar innovations did not happen in China.

In Chapter 10, we turn to modern China. The main question that we pose is how to explain the country's exceptional economic convergence with the West after the death of Mao Zedong in the mid-1970s. We emphasize two aspects of historical continuity that facilitated economic convergence. First, although the Maoist cultural revolution deliberately sought to erase clans and Confucian traditions, kin-based social networks reemerged in China after Mao's death. These social networks absolved important economic functions in an environment characterized by weak property rights and a lack of familiarity with global markets. For instance, the Chinese diaspora abroad, who had retained links with their native country, acted as an intermediary between China and the rest of the world. The second aspect of historical continuity rests in the political sphere. Although sustained by a different political ideology, the post-Mao system of government bears many similarities with the imperial regime. In particular, starting with Deng Xiaoping, local administrators enjoyed considerable leeway and discretion in initiating policy changes and reforms while still being subjected to control from the central government via meritocratic performance criteria. With a new emphasis on economic growth rather than stability and revenue maximization, this system of decentralized administration created strong incentives for local officials to promote economic development. The chapter concludes with a discussion of whether Chinese growth can continue under the centralization of power imposed under Xi Jinping beginning in 2012.

Finally, Chapter 11 concludes, drawing brief comparisons between India and the Islamic Middle East, and reiterates general lessons that can be drawn from our historical analysis.

2

The Great Divergence

1. Introduction

The term "Great Divergence," coined memorably by Pomeranz (2000), conveys the notion of two competing forces—here, economies—where one surges forward and the other one falls behind. This phrase aptly describes what happened in Europe and China between 1000 and c.1500 AD. If we take a step back and look at the entire millennium rather than just 500 years, however, a better term for what happened to the two economies might instead be "Great Reversal." Europe did not just overtake China; China stagnated, despite having enjoyed a far more advanced state in c.1000, while Europe surged ahead. In view of the clear economic and technological superiority that had been attained by Western economies by 1850, "Great Reversal" seems more apposite.

Yet the terminology of divergence and reversal obscures the fact that the two societies differed in dimensions beyond just their economic performance. As such, their trajectories may be more aptly described as a "Great Bifurcation." By "bifurcation," we mean that Europe and China embarked on paths that were very different in many dimensions besides economic performance. The economic gap that opened between the two societies in the nineteenth century could be seen as the unintended result of a number of earlier bifurcations, in which the two worlds embarked on different trajectories. Besides economic performance, there were numerous other ways in which the two worlds diverged: in their political institutions, in the economic and political importance of their urban centers, in their family structures, in their arrangements to sustain cooperation and provide local public goods, in their educational systems and what kind of knowledge was accumulated by their residents, and in their cultural and value systems.

One of the main messages in our book is that these numerous bifurcations were complementary to one another, and through their interaction, they reinforced the overarching divergence of China's and Europe's development. For instance, China and Europe diverged economically partly because they accumulated different types of knowledge. This in turn reflected their different educational systems and the role of their government institutions. Their political institutions diverged because of initial differences in state fragmentation, but also because their evolutions reflected different social arrangements to sustain cooperation at the local level. Different local arrangements emerged from divergent family structures, which in turn reflected initial differences in value systems and religion beliefs.

This chapter describes the many divergences between Europe and China, discussing how they interacted with one another and why the divergences occurred. We start by reviewing the debate on the Great Divergence, pointing out that the term does not sufficiently emphasize the importance of earlier historical periods, where China sprang forward and Europe declined. Next, we describe the many other dimensions in which Europe and China diverged, briefly reviewing how the existing literature has accounted for these phenomena. We then ask whether geography by itself can explain some of these differences, as some scholars have argued. We close the chapter with a discussion of three initial differences between Europe and China that, in our view, may have caused subsequent bifurcation. First, China enjoyed political unification early (for at least a substantial number of periods), while Europe remained politically polycentric and fragmented. Second, by c.1000 AD, China had a large and highly functional state administration that managed much of the affairs of society, whereas in Europe, central government—wherever it existed—was both weak and poor. Third, initial differences between European and Chinese family structures and inheritance rules led the two civilizations onto increasingly different trajectories. The implications of these three initial differences are a recurrent theme that will be revisited in subsequent chapters of this book.

2. The Puzzle of the Great Reversal

Since the publication of Pomeranz's seminal work in 2000, a large flow of articles and books have emerged, attempting to explain the phenomenon of the Great Divergence.[1] Much of this history remains in dispute, including the question of

---

1. See in particular Rosenthal and Wong (2011); Goldstone (2009); Vries (2013); and Brandt, Ma, and Rawski (2014). More recent contributions focusing on different aspects of the comparison include Scheidel (2019) and Stasavage (2020).

timing: When exactly did the economic gap between the two civilizations emerge? The question seems particularly acute with respect to the past few decades: recent economic successes in China seem to contradict many of the old chestnuts about Chinese culture or attitudes being somehow inconsistent with capitalism or economic progress. These arguments, such as the one made by Landes (1998), trace to an older intellectual tradition that tends to rely on the idea of a profound and immutable cultural gap between China and the West and has fallen out of favor among scholars.

Pomeranz's book provided a useful antidote to some of the more extreme arguments of such cultural gaps by pointing out a number of "surprising resemblances" between China and the West (Pomeranz 2000, p. 29). Yet we argue below that the intellectual pendulum has swung too far in the direction of emphasizing similarities and therefore has blurred the deep differences between China and Europe in many areas of economic, social, and political life. A number of key differences proved instrumental in bringing about the huge gap in income per capita and living standards experienced after the Industrial Revolution. As we discuss in chapter 10, despite the rapid growth and economic transformations experienced in China since 1980, the income per capita gap with the West remains in place.[2] As the experience of recent decades has shown, there are more avenues to industrialization and economic prosperity than the one traveled by the West. All the same, the fact that the Industrial Revolution occurred in the West and not elsewhere has had a momentous impact on world history. It is not triumphalist to point out that China's impressive economic growth since 1980 has been concentrated in industries and techniques based primarily on useful knowledge originally developed in Europe; neither is it so to acknowledge that China's policies are driven by a powerful desire to level the playing field and emulate Western success. Whether China will fully catch up with the West in its living standards is impossible to say. Ian Morris's (2010) suggestion that in the long run, the advantage of the West may well prove ephemeral may or may not be correct—many of the scholars in the so-called California school seem to think that it is. In any event, Chinese history was forever changed by the impact of Western technology. China's worldview, which formerly regarded

2. According to the *CIA World Factbook*, China's income per capita in purchasing power parity (PPP) in 2017 was on the order of Costa Rica's and 41 percent of the European Union's (EU's).

Western culture with an air of condescension and suspicion, transformed into one that saw it as something to imitate in many ways.[3]

As already noted, the term "divergence" understates the dramatic dynamic of global history in the long run. What took place between China and Europe was more than a divergence; it was a reversal. By all indications, China under the Song Dynasty (960–1279) was in the midst of a Golden Age, and by any and every measure, the nation was far ahead of Europe, which during this period was only slowly recovering from dramatic economic and political backwardness. Around 1250, Chinese technology was far more advanced than that of Europe in many ways. It developed techniques and innovations that Europe adopted only centuries later, many of which are often identified with progress, including "Bacon's Big Three"—the "modern" techniques that Bacon in his Great Instauration thought had transformed the world: printing, gunpowder, and the compass. Moreover, the list of Chinese advances is much longer that Bacon's Big Three; it includes cotton manufactures, ceramics, advanced ship design, hydraulic technology, paper, and iron casting, as well as more mundane yet useful items such as toilet paper, umbrellas, and toothbrushes with bristles.

Yet at some point after the fall of the Song in 1279, China fell into a slow process of technological decline, at least compared to what happened in Europe. While Joseph Needham and his collaborators have compiled an extensive list of the many scientific discoveries and technological advances that originated in China, a tabulation of the breakthroughs reveals that very few of these were made after 1200, and none after 1500 (Winchester 2008, pp. 267–77). Two recent contributions make valiant efforts to measure the true significance of the decline of science and technology in China. Huang et al. (2024) developed a database called the Chinese Historical Inventions Database, which documents 10,350 inventions. They conclude that the rate of Chinese inventions embarked on a downward trend as early as the sixth century—many centuries before the Ming Dynasty, which is frequently thought to be the start of this decline. Furthermore, Chinese inventiveness had completely stalled following the thirteenth century (Huang et al. 2024, p. 17). A different

---

3. It is striking how Huawei's new campus in Dongguan is constructed entirely along European cultural themes, replete with an imitation of a castle from Luxembourg, a palace that imitates Versailles's buildings, and a tower inspired by the Czech Republic (Hu 2019). For a fascinating case study of the impact of Western culture on twentieth-century China, see Cai and Melvin (2016).

approach is taken by Chen and Duan (2024), who looked at the subjects of books published in China. They showed a break in the publication of science, technology, engineering, and mathematics (STEM) content at around the rise of the Ming Dynasty in 1368. Either way, these contributions point toward the same fact: China was declining as a major source of innovation and scientific progress at about the same time that Europe began its path toward economic and technological dominance.

The precise timing of the Great Reversal remains a matter of controversy. The eleventh century marks the beginning of the emergent gap in social organizations between East and West. It also coincides with the nascent revival of markets and the reawakening of intellectual activity in Christian Europe. Yet the fifteenth century stands out as significant, too, with the flourishing of the *Rinascimento* (Italian Renaissance), the impact of the printing press, the effects of the great voyages, and the emergence of a secular intellectual community—all of which contrasted with the growing "closing" of China during the late Ming and Qing eras. All the same, technological developments had little impact on living standards and income in Europe for many decades.

Pomeranz and other scholars in the California school such as Goldstone (2009) insist that on the eve of the Industrial Revolution, there were only negligible differences in living standards between China and the West. Pomeranz (2000) has amassed a fair amount of evidence supporting this claim. However, new evidence, both quantitative and qualitative, rebuts his hypothesis. Wage data compiled by scholars in the years following the publication of Pomeranz's influential book indicate that Chinese wages were already substantially lower than in the most advanced parts of Europe in the seventeenth century and probably earlier as well. The silver wages of unskilled labor in China were far lower than they were in the richer parts of Europe, and while the gap is considerably smaller for real wages (and is sensitive to the exact price index used), it is nonetheless preserved (Van Zanden 2009, pp. 269–91; Allen et al. 2011). The picture for real gross domestic product (GDP) per capita paints an even more dramatic picture. The recent numbers computed by Broadberry, Guan, and Li (2018) and displayed in figure 2.1 are startling.

In the middle of the Song Dynasty, China's GDP (measured in international 1990 dollars, the standard—though controversial—measure of national income) was significantly higher than that of Britain. By 1500, they were roughly equal. By the time of the first Opium War—when China's inability to compete with the West was becoming brutally obvious—the GDP per capita estimates reveal a ratio of 5:1 in Britain's favor (Broadberry et al. 2018, p. 5). These estimates

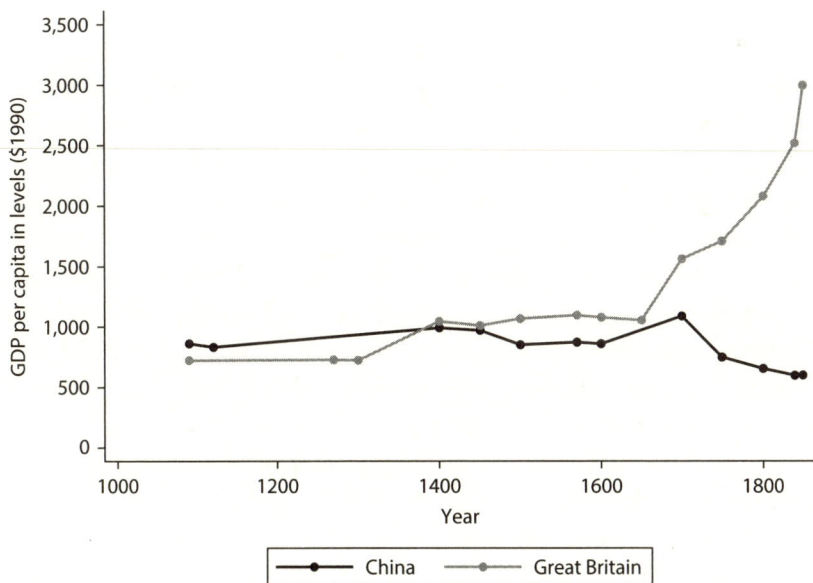

FIGURE 2.1. GDP per capita in China and Britain. *Source:* Broadberry et al. (2018).

are fragile, of course, and they have inevitably been criticized (e.g., Solar 2021). Changes in the assumptions underlying these estimates push the start of the income divergence to considerably earlier in time. One often-overlooked factor is the effect of the great voyages on living standards. Europeans encountered a number of new goods or goods in the Old World that had been prohibitively expensive before 1500: tobacco, coffee, tea, sugar, potatoes, and maize all enriched European living standards in one way or another (Hersh and Voth 2022).[4] That said, the European voyages also exposed Chinese consumers to New World crops, especially sweet potatoes and peanuts. It remains true that much if not all of the income gap emerged during the Industrial Revolution. Yet it is important to emphasize that the roots of that reversal go back many centuries prior to when its effects were first observed.[5]

4. Hersh and Voth (2022) imply that the contribution of new colonial goods such as coffee and cane sugar to economic well-being in the eighteenth century matched that of total factor productivity growth in 1700–1800.

5. Solar's revised figures (table 2.1) imply that by 1100, Britain and China had comparable levels of income, but that by 1400, Italy's income already exceeded that of China's by a ratio of 2.5:1 and Britain exceeded China by a ratio of 1.75:1. By 1700, the Britain-China gap had changed little since 1400. By 1800, it had mushroomed to 3.6:1.

To be sure, Britain was the fastest-growing country in Europe, and comparing standards of living in two economies that consumed very different baskets of goods across a period spanning close to a millennium is difficult, to say the least. However, other evidence points decisively in the same direction. By 1850, GDP per capita in the Netherlands was four times larger than that of China, and in Italy and Spain, it was about twice as large (Broadberry et al. 2018, tables 6 and 7). Perhaps nothing is more emblematic of China's decline relative to the West than its humiliation during the disastrous Opium Wars, its need for Western military assistance in stamping out the Taiping Rebellion, and its ignominious defeats in subsequent conflicts with both the West and Japan. The causes of these setbacks went beyond the inability of the Chinese state to defend itself and maintain internal order. Qing China after 1644 became increasingly conservative and inward-looking, and economic and technological progress was simply not prioritized by its rulers and intellectual elites. The West kept advancing, and the resulting gap left China weak and vulnerable.

This is not to say that China was a failure—the Chinese state and its bureaucracy during the Ming and Qing dynasties for centuries had striven for stability and peace above all, and at least until the early decades of the nineteenth century, they were significantly successful in its achievement. The neo-Confucian ideology that emerged triumphant in the Chinese Empire after the fall of the Song believed above all in the virtuousness of social and political stability and continuity and became increasingly hostile to disruptive progress. The Western concept of progress as it emerged in the two centuries before the Industrial Revolution was alien to the paradigms of China's rulers and intellectual elites, and nothing like an Industrial Enlightenment, with its emphasis on improvement and progress, the cultural taproot of the Industrial Revolution, can be discerned in China (Mokyr 2009, 2016; Friedel 2007; Slack 2015; Vogelsang 2020). Nothing like a belief in progress emerged in neo-Confucian China. Peter Bol (2008, p. 101) notes that for neo-Confucians, antiquity was the ideal period, and there was no promise of salvation in the future.[6]

Modern Chinese scholarship has maintained that viewing this absence as a failure stems from the implicit assumption that economic growth is somehow indisputably more desirable than stability, and it has criticized such assessment as inherently applying Western values to a different culture. There is

6. Bol (2008, p. 101) quotes Yan Fu, a late nineteenth-century translator of European social thought, as remarking that the "way China is today is eighty to ninety percent attributable to the Song Period."

merit in this argument, but it misses one point: the objective of preserving the status quo turned out to be a bad strategy for China in large part because different strategies emerged in the West (and later also in Japan), which eventually upset the peaceful equilibrium that characterized the long eighteenth century of Qing rule.

3. One Divergence or Many?

The emphasis on income per capita and living standards as the main outcome variable in discussions of the Great Divergence comes naturally to economists. However, it may leave out many other historical divergences of comparable interest. Economic historians interested in political economy, demography, social order, household structures, technological change, or gender issues can point to many other chasms between China and Europe, all of which may be of interest independent of their impact on living standards. These divergences predated the Industrial Revolution and the subsequent gap in economic performance by many centuries.

States and Institutions

Walter Scheidel (2019, pp. 227–32) defines the "first great divergence" as the critical events that occurred in Eurasia around the sixth century AD. This first divergence, Scheidel argues, put Europe and China onto distinct political trajectories. Until then, however, the Roman and Chinese polities had been on comparable paths, characterized by centralized and coherent bureaucratic empires. Ultimately, although both civilizations were subject to major shocks (such as invasions), the Chinese Empire eventually was able to recover and remained intact, whereas Europe splintered into smaller political units that never quite congealed back into a single entity. Scheidel lays out a long line of arguments concurrent with this theme, tracing many unique European developments leading up to political polycentrism in the middle of the first millennium (e.g., Jones 1981; Bernholz, Streit, and Vaubel 1998; Karayalçin 2008).

This initial political divergence would have important consequences for future development: whereas European state institutions eventually evolved toward some forms of constitutional participatory democracy, comparable forms of government never appeared in China. In chapter 7, we discuss at length the causes of this institutional divergence, pointing out how the early consolidation and centralization of state powers facilitated the stability of imperial autocracy in China, while the fragmentation of political powers, together with the form of its social organizations, had a profound impact on the evolution of European political institutions.

State Capacity

One of the most widely discussed differences between China and Europe remains their historical divergences in state capacity. As dramatic as the divergence in the size and fragmentation of political units was, it is not obvious a priori what polycentrism implied for state capacity and the ability of authorities to raise revenues and provide public goods. After all, the Roman Empire had possessed considerable administrative competence and impressive fiscal capabilities for centuries. Yet the Merovingian and Carolingian entities of Western Europe had nothing of the sort, and it was not until the late Middle Ages and the Early Modern era that European nation-states began to develop the administrative tools needed to raise substantial revenues. European growth contrasted sharply with the steady fiscal decline of the Chinese imperial government. This reversal in state capacity is no less dramatic than the reversal in economic performance.

Under the Ming and Qing dynasties, the Chinese bureaucracy became increasingly ineffective and corrupt, and it proved unable to provide China with the public goods that it needed—including a strong modern army and flood protection (Ma 2013; Sng 2014). The traditional depiction of Ming-Qing China as a prototototalitarian state in which Asian despots ruled without constraints, as described by Montesquieu and later Wittfogel, has not held up well (Mote 1961). Although the state had a centralized bureaucracy, whether it exercised real power on the ground depended on the cooperation of local gentry.[7] The system became increasingly unwieldy during this time, and it eventually collapsed when it came under increasing external pressure after 1840.

The Great Reversal in state capacity is illustrated in this discussion by the best estimates available, reproduced in figure 2.2 and the following tables. The differences in tax revenues raised by nations in terms of GDP demonstrate the decline of Chinese state capacity relative to the European counterparts.

Table 2.1 reports an indicator of per-capita tax revenues collected by the Chinese central government at different points in time, starting from the Song Dynasty to the Qing Dynasty and spanning a period of roughly 700 years.

---

7. A more detailed description of the Chinese gentry is provided in chapter 7.

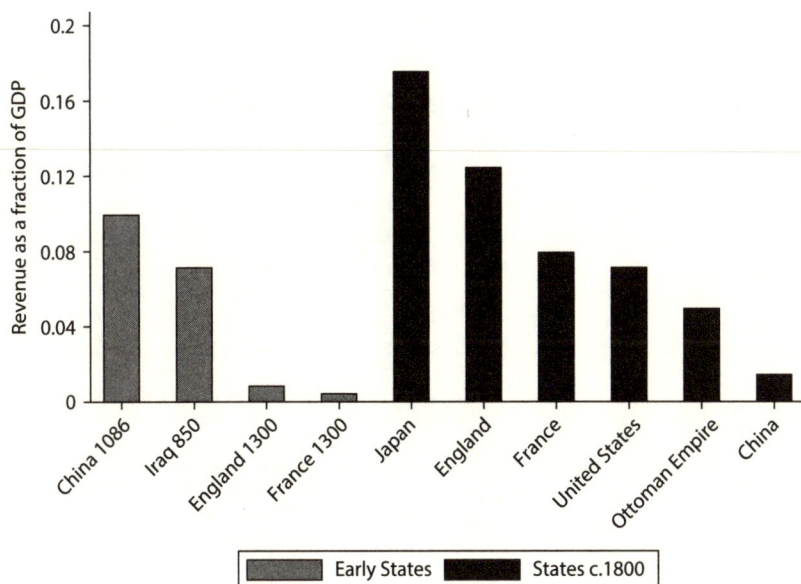

FIGURE 2.2. The Great Reversal in state capacity. *Source:* Stasavage (2020) and Brandt et al. (2014).

TABLE 2.1. Tax Revenues in China, 1085–1776 (in *shi* of rice)

Dynasty	Per-capita land tax	Per-capita indirect taxes	Per-capita tax burden
Song (1085)	0.26	0.54	0.8
Ming (1407)	0.54–0.75	0.02–0.03	0.56–0.79
Ming (1577)	0.21	0.03	0.24
Qing (1685)	0.18	0.04	0.22
Qing (1776)	0.09	0.03	0.12

Source: Brandt et al. (2014).
Note: 1 *shi* of milled rice weighed approximately 175–195 pounds.

Note that around 1776, per-capita tax revenue in China had diminished to less than one-fifth of what had been collected around the year 1085.

Tables 2.2 and 2.3 compare per-capita tax revenue in China and other European states between the seventeenth and nineteenth centuries. Per-capita tax revenue in Britain and the Dutch Republic at that time was several orders of magnitude higher than in China. Even France and Spain, which historically

TABLE 2.2. Qing Central Government Annual Revenue in International Comparison

International comparison of per-capita tax revenue (grams of silver)

Date	China	France	Spain	England	Dutch Republic
1650–1699	7.0	46.0	35.8	45.1	
1700–1749	7.2	46.6	41.6	93.5	161.1
1750–1799	4.2	66.4	63.1	158.4	170.7
1800–1849	3.4			303.8	
1850–1899	7.0			344.1	

Per-capita revenue expressed in days' wages for unskilled urban workers

Date	China	France	Spain	England	Dutch Republic
1650–1699		8.0	7.7	4.2	13.6
1700–1749	2.26	6.7	4.6	8.9	24.1
1750–1799	1.32	11.4	10.0	12.6	22.8
1800–1849	1.23			17.2	
1850–1899	1.99			19.4	

Source: Brandt et al. (2014).

TABLE 2.3. Per-Capita Tax Revenue (Grams of Silver)

Date	France	Spain	Britain	Dutch Republic
1650–1659	56	57	31	114
1700–1709	43	29	92	211
1750–1759	49	46	109	189
1780–1789	78	59	172	228
1820–1829	131	47	300	144
1850–1859	180	117	250	170

Source: Vries (2015).
Note: "Britain" includes Scotland from 1707 onward, and Ireland from 1801 onward.

had less fiscal capacity than Britain, collected more than ten times the per-capita taxes of China toward the end of the eighteenth century.

That said, state capacity is not measured solely through *fiscal* capacity; that is, the amount of revenue that the government is able to extract and how much can be spent on defense and public goods; it also depends on the nature of taxation and its predictability. As Ma (2013, p. 493) points out, it was perhaps the "informal, unregulated and often arbitrary nature of these extractions that may help explain the apparent contradiction of the very low rate of tax extraction measured by the receipts of the Board of Finance and the rapacious image of the Qing regime." It also highlights the apparent paradox that the Qing Dynasty declined and eventually collapsed because taxes were too low rather than too high—in contrast with the Ming Dynasty, which was overthrown in a peasant rebellion against exorbitant taxation. The underlying factor was the inability of the Chinese to design an effective fiscal apparatus.

As both Ma (2013) and Sng (2014) note, the decline in state capacity in Imperial China may have been a function of size. They hypothesize that diseconomies of scale had set in at the administrative level. Zhang (2017, p. 22) summarizes the history of Chinese state capacity in the past millennium, as characterized by the gradual erosion of the central government's control over local communities, when both population growth and geographical expansion exceeded the growth of state capacity. Four layers of administration lay between the imperial government and the masses of peasants: central government, provinces, prefectures, and counties. Collecting taxes from the masses suffered leakages at each level, and fiscal authorities had to take care to choose taxation rates to minimize the probability of rebellion. In addition to local corruption, Qing rulers were reluctant to raise agricultural taxes due to fears over peasant uprisings (Zhang 2020) and growing ideological resistance to a powerful, high-tax state (Zhang 2022). Despite government offices such as the Censorate, which were specifically intended to reduce leakage and pilfering, reducing corruption in the Imperial bureaucracy and theft of tax revenues proved daunting.

Urbanization

An additional bifurcation important to discuss in the Great Divergence literature is urbanization.[8] European urbanization was very low in c.1000 AD, but it advanced steadily in subsequent centuries. As such, it has become common for economic historians to use estimates for urban density as proxies for economic performance and development (De Long and Shleifer, 1993). The widely cited data compiled by Maddison (2007, p. 43) depict a dramatic reversal (see table 2.4).

This comparison has faced valid criticism. The lower Yangzi region is the most densely populated and richest part of China and is therefore most comparable

8. For an important exception, see Rosenthal and Wong (2011).

TABLE 2.4. The Great Urban Reversal

	Europe	China	Europe	China
		>10k		>40k
Date				
1000	0	3.1		
1500	5.6	3.8	1.9	
1600	7.6	4	3.5	1.7
1700	9.2		5.2	1.9
1800	10	3.8	5.6	1.7

Sources: Columns 1, 3, and 4: Woods (2003, p. 219, table 2); column 2: Maddison (2007, p. 43).

Note: The table reports the percent of the population living in cities. In columns 1 and 2, cities are restricted to those with more than 10,000 inhabitants. In columns 3 and 4, more than 40,000 inhabitants.

to the highly urbanized and rich regions of the Low Countries. There, patterns of urban settlement developed a distinctive set of clusters of market towns concentrated along the dense regional network of waterways. As a result, the economic geography of the Yangzi region had relatively ambiguous boundaries between urban and rural districts compared to Europe, where cities were walled and clearly delineated. This makes exact comparisons between China and Europe rather tricky (Brandt, Ma, and Rawski, 2014, p. 55), leading some scholars such as Li Bozhong to argue that Chinese urbanization is understated.

However, more recent work has confirmed the urbanization divergence. Table 2.5 clearly indicates that during the Song and Yuan dynasties, China was far more urbanized than Europe. In subsequent centuries, however, Chinese urbanization more or less stagnated. We thus observe in concurrence with other scholars that "[Chinese] developments are almost diametrically opposed to those of Europe, which in the same period underwent a long-term rise of urbanization and the emergence of very large cities" (Xu, van Leeuwen, and van Zanden 2018, p. 24). As we will discuss in chapter 6, this also reflects different patterns of migration: in Europe, migration flowed from the economic periphery toward its core; in China, migration flowed in the opposite direction.

Notwithstanding the difficulties of producing accurate figures from this time, there remains a consensus among most scholars that between 1000 and 1890, China's urban population as a percentage of its total population was more or less constant, whereas in Europe, it dramatically increased. Still, the exact reasons for this divergence have not reached a similar consensus, although there was surely more than one factor at play. We return to this point in chapter 6.

TABLE 2.5. Urbanization Rates in China and in the Lower Yangtze Delta

Year	China	Lower Yangtze Delta
1109	11	
1205	12	25
1291	12	18
1391	10	19
1630	12	23
1644	11	20
1776	7	19
1851	7	20
1893	7	17

Source: Xu et al. (2015), Table 11.

The divergence in urbanization is significant in its own right, but for our purposes it serves as a proverbial canary in the coal mine; that is, it reflects the different trajectories and further bifurcations to come. While China did not deurbanize (as Europe had in the early Middle Ages), its development was nothing like Europe's rapid post-1000 AD urbanization. There were great cities in the Middle East, China, and India, but none rivaled Europe's autonomous, prosperous, proud, and often rebellious urban centers. Not all European cities were created equal, but the ones that achieved some measure of autonomy and the status of the commune developed high levels of creativity (Serafinelli and Tabellini 2022). European cities competed among themselves for resources, trade routes, and top-notch artists and artisans, which in turn led to the kinds of institutional changes that were necessary to carry out long-distance trade.[9] For example, urban institutions promoting local autonomy and protecting economic and political freedoms encouraged the production and attraction of creative talent.[10] Urban centers were the location of universities, scientific societies, libraries, printing houses, and other centers of intellectual activity.

9. See especially Bosker, Buringh, and Van Zanden (2013). An example is provided by Gelderblom (2013), who focuses on three of the commercially most successful cities in Europe, Bruges, Antwerp, and Amsterdam, and shows how their political status and government eventually led to wealth, as well as to more open and inclusive societies.

10. These effects are quantitatively large. Becoming a commune was associated with an increase in the births of famous people of about 40 percent relative to the average during a century, while the attraction of famous immigrants almost doubles in size upon becoming a commune (Serafinelli and Tabellini 2022).

As we discuss more in chapter 7, cities contributed significantly to the evolution of European state institutions.

Family Structure

Another divergence between China and Europe lies in the realm of demographics. In ancient China, the dominant family structure was the communal or joint family (*yihu*), an extended household comprised of several generations defined by shared patrilineal descent, which lived in close proximity and shared resources (Lang 1946; McDermott 2013, pp. 112–16). As we will discuss in chapters 4 and 5, after the first millennium, dynastic ties became increasingly dominant as a mechanism for cooperation in China. The joint family remained the basic unit for many decisions, but interfamily cooperation was organized through the clan, a dynastic group that traced its origins to a common patrilineal ancestor. The clan was a social organization, a cooperative entity composed of households; it was different from the *yihu*, which was much more like an extended household.

Europe, by contrast, moved in the opposite direction. The role played by joint and stem families in providing local public goods and services declined, and kin-based ties lost their central role in organizing cooperation, while the nuclear family (which included only married parents and their young children) became the prototypical household structure (Goody 1983; Mitterauer 2010; Henrich 2019). At some point in the Middle Ages, Western and Central Europe developed a series of social patterns dubbed the "European Marriage Pattern (EMP)" by John Hajnal (mentioned in chapter 1). The EMP encapsulates the phenomenon whereby European women increasingly delayed marriage until about four to eight years after menarche (between the ages of twenty to twenty-four). This pattern essentially meant that women were not having children during a considerable part of their most fertile years, hence curbing European birth rates. Furthermore, a significant percentage of European women remained unmarried altogether. In a Malthusian framework, such a permanent decline in fertility would count as a preventive check on population and imply rising living standards rose beyond "subsistence" (e.g., Voigtländer and Voth 2006). The EMP also had far-reaching implications with respect to the social status of women (Voigtländer and Voth 2013), creating what is now known as "girl power" (De Moor and Van Zanden, 2010).[11] Moreover, the EMP helped to

11. De Moor and Van Zanden (2010) argued that the EMP contributed to European growth (as compared to China) by empowering women and facilitating the emergence of labor markets

facilitate the eventual transition to a new demographic equilibrium defined by lower birth and death rates—an earlier (and much weaker) version of the equilibrium that currently prevails in rich societies today. Conversely, in China—or so the argument goes—there were fewer preventive checks on population growth. Early marriage, polygamy, and low female celibacy rates implied high birth and death rates. The only Malthusian checks on population growth in a high-fertility society like this tended to be socially costly: infanticide, famines, banditry, and wars.

The view that the direct *demographic* impact of the EMP set Europe apart from China becomes clearer when examining the seventeenth century, as Hajnal had originally conjectured. Subsequent studies confirmed that late Imperial China and postmedieval Europe differed in all realms of the EMP by this time: the age of marriage, premarriage work patterns, and postmarital settlement (e.g., Herlihy 1985; Telford 1992; Razi 1993; Zhao 1997). In line with our previous discussion, a scholarly consensus emerged, neatly captured by De Moor and Van Zanden (2010, p. 1): the EMP "played a fundamental role in Western Europe economic development." The demographic shifts that it encompassed enabled the Europeans to escape—or at least to mitigate—the persistent cycles of poverty implied by the Malthusian trap, as lower birth rates led to a higher growth of per-capita income than would have been possible otherwise. Although the mean household sizes in China and Europe did not differ by much, the consensus was that China had no preventive checks on population and therefore experienced very high costs of population growth.[12]

More recently, scholars have mounted criticisms of this view. In particular, academics like Wang Feng, James Lee, and Cameron Campbell have argued that China developed a different preventive check on population that was not sufficiently considered in past work: within-marriage infanticide, as observed by Jesuit missionaries in the late sixteenth century.[13] While tragic, this practice did lead to lower fertility rates. This revisionist claim, however, gave rise to a

---

(see also Moring and Hall 2017). The mechanism through which this seems to have happened was the growth in livestock raising after the sharp decline in population due to the Black Death in the mid-fourteenth century. Women had a comparative advantage in rearing animals, and the structural changes in the economy both pushed up the age of first marriage and the contribution of women to household income.

12. Regarding household size, see, for example, Lang (1946) and Herlihy (1985).

13. For example, see Lavely et al. (1990), Lavely and Wong (1992, 1998), Lee, Campbell, and Feng (2002), and Lee (1999).

strong dissent by the proponents of the consensus.[14] Similarly, recent studies have cast doubt on the idea that the *demographic* impact of the EMP contributed much—if anything—to European growth.[15] In short, the direct impact of the EMP on long-term living standards remains in dispute. All the same, European demographic behavior was still exceptional by global standards, and it proved very different from that of China. In chapter 4, we discuss how the EMP contributed to the distinct path of European development indirectly through its effects on social organizations.

Culture

Another striking divergence between Europe and China was cultural: while Europe proved to be a group of outward-looking societies eager to explore and exploit foreigners, China was characterized by a much more complacent and inward-looking worldview, both in terms of trade relations and information flows from external nations. Europeans were open to learning from foreigners—both other Europeans and non-Europeans—even before the technological advances in shipping and navigation of the fifteenth century allowed them to sail to the New World and Asia. They not only repeatedly organized armed expeditions to the Middle East (which is what the Crusades really were), but even before Marco Polo, travelers such as Giovanni da Pian del Carpine and William of Rubruck made it to the court of Genghis Khan in Mongolia in 1245–1247 and 1253–1255, respectively. They recorded detailed and relatively fair accounts of their travels, even if their books were less well known than Polo's. Europeans did not deny the superior knowledge of other societies, even if they regarded them with hostility. For example, from the Islamic world, Europeans adopted the use of windmills and paper, as well as a great deal of knowledge and thought from fields like medicine and philosophy.[16]

14. In particular, Arthur Wolf, a historical demographer of China, argued that although the revisionists make "important claims," he "think[s] these are mistaken" (Wolf 2001, p. 134). He particularly challenged the three main data sources that the revisionists used as unrepresentative (e.g., wealthy Chinese and Manchu nobility) or unreliable (e.g., underreports of birth).

15. Notably, see Goody (1996a, 1996b) and Dennison and Ogilvie (2014), which point to the absence of direct quantitative evidence that either the EMP or the related pattern of work influenced growth.

16. The great Muslim philosopher Ibn Rushd (1126–1198) was far more influential in the Christian world than in his own Muslim one, and Muslim physicians wrote the textbooks taught in medical schools in medieval Europe.

By contrast, it is striking how little interest Asians—be they Confucian Chinese, Hindu Indians, and even Muslim Middle Easterners—showed in Europe. Before the modern age, it seemed that inward-looking perspectives were the default in most societies, with the Europeans constituting one re- markable exception. Although Chinese sailors had the know-how and techni- cal ability to explore foreign shores—as demonstrated by the celebrated ex- peditions of Zheng He—the Imperial government discouraged further such voyages after Zheng's death in 1433. Half a century later, China had implicitly ceded the management and control of globalization to Europeans.

Armed with a combination of downright greed, religious zeal, and curiosity, and supplied with firearms, Europeans set upon the task. More important than spoils like spices, silk, porcelain, and silver, Europeans benefited from global- ization by exposure to foreign ideas and techniques. From cotton textiles, chi- naware, ship design, antimalarial drugs, tea, potatoes, and smallpox inocula- tion, Europeans learned, transplanted, and improved on a variety of foreign crops and techniques from the civilizations with which they made contact.

To be sure, the rest of the world was equally exposed to European knowl- edge and goods. Sometimes this exposure took the form of missionary activi- ties, such as that of the Jesuits, who exposed China to advanced clocks and instruments that proved useful to the Chinese literati (Elman 2005). In other instances, ecological arbitrage was driven by European sailors and merchants, who brought to Asia new crops such as sweet potatoes and peanuts, leading to considerable improvement in living standards (Bray 1984, p. 458; Jia 2014). But these expansions in ideas and items were almost invariably the result of European initiatives. Moreover, China experienced more difficulty with ac- knowledging the usefulness of European innovations and adopting them. The Jesuits' presence in China depended on the goodwill of the emperor and his court, who tightly controlled their actions, remained suspicious of their reli- gious objectives, and eventually turned against them.

It has been argued that the unintended consequences of the sudden rise in European global trade and the Atlantic ports that it created were momentous. Acemoglu, Johnson, and Robinson (2005), in a famous paper, maintained that it led to and amplified institutional progress. However, some institutional di- vergences had clearly preceded the great voyages by many centuries. The emer- gence of the EMP, the evolution of corporations, and the rise of formal civil law (see chapter 8) are all prominent examples. The great voyages to Asia and the New World amplified and accelerated the institutional divergence between East and West, but they were not the original cause.

The European voyages had profound consequences for Europe's subsequent history (as well as for the rest of the world, of course). As previously noted, the voyages exposed Europeans to new crops and production techniques and introduced domesticated animals and crops from Europe to the American continent (in the "Columbian Exchange"; see Crosby 1972). Moreover, they made many Europeans question the wisdom of classical canons of geography such as those of Strabo and Pliny, who had been unaware of these lands and implied that traveling such distances would be impossible. Once such doubts were planted in their minds, much of the faithful adherence to the canonical science of Aristotle, Ptolemy, and Galen slowly melted away.

By contrast, aggressive exploration beyond its borders (except for expansion westward that occurred in the eighteenth century) proved absent from China, especially alongside the increased weakness of the Chinese central government. In Early Modern Europe, states developed a set of policies now known as "mercantilist." They involved active state support for long-distance trade (including colonial trade), and the encouragement of European colonial control and settlement in overseas areas. While Chinese trade and long-distance migration were substantial (especially to Southeast Asia and newly settled regions in the Chinese West), there was little armed trade and state-sponsored colonialism. In Peer Vries's succinct summary, there was no Chinese version of mercantilism (2001, p. 439). It is far from clear whether the absence of such policies by itself was a detriment to China's long-term policies. Arguably, nineteenth-century Europe could take off only after Europeans shed the worst forms of rent-seeking and protectionist policies of mercantilist ancien régime rulers. Whatever the reason for it, the absence of mercantilism in China is another telling divergence between East and West. Mercantilism should therefore be understood in the context of an interstate competition in Europe, leading to the gradual increase in state capacity to regulate, control, and tax. In China, the absence of mercantilism points toward the limited capacity of the state to wield these same tools with comparable stability and efficiency, thus indicating the unique position that the Ming-Qing Empire would find itself in amid a rapidly changing global order.

Human Capital and the Great Intellectual Divergence

The intellectual divergence between China and Europe has often been referred to as the "Needham Question," highlighting the growing gap between the two civilizations' scientific and technological capabilities. This gap helped drive

Europe toward the Industrial Revolution, while China's science and technology—though still ahead of Europe at the end of the Song Dynasty— eventually stagnated and fell behind.

During the Tang and Song dynasties, China produced a stream of inventions indicating unparalleled technological creativity. By all standard measures, China was a nation brimming with high-quality human capital. We do not know what literacy rates were at that time, but literacy rates in Qing China in the nineteenth century ranged from 30 to 45 percent of the male population and an estimated 2 to 10 percent of the female population. This meant that in most households, there was likely to be at least one literate person per family (Rawski 1979; Woodside and Elman 1994). China's cultural emphasis on education was an ancient tradition. In the eleventh century, education was very much part of Chinese daily life, and not just among the elites. One authoritative scholar has noted that "even in the poorest and most remote rural places there gradually appeared lower-level country schoolteachers in the smaller villages. . . . The norms of the higher levels of culture, transmitted through the various kinds of local education, broadly penetrated the level of the ordinary people" (Mote 1999, pp. 159–60). Yet despite the widespread diffusion and appreciation of education, China began a slow decline after the Song Dynasty, eventually falling behind Europe. This is reflected in the number and distribution of printed books across the two civilizations. According to Buringh and Van Zanden (2009), the number and variety of books published in Europe in the seventeenth century was forty times larger than in China (per capita). Even accounting for duplication of titles and translations in Europe, much of the gap remains, highlighting a much more diverse and competitive market for ideas in Europe. Measures of technological and scientific activity, such as scientifically oriented books and pamphlets, even if they are admittedly rough proxies, uniformly substantiate a declining trend after the rise of the Ming Dynasty in 1368 (Huang et al. 2024; Duan 2024).

It has been argued that fixed cultural characteristics account for this divergence (Landes 1998). Among historians, these suggestions have developed a (deservedly) bad reputation because they cannot account for the long periods of time when Chinese science and technology flourished.[17] If fixed culture is

---

17. Needham himself (1969, p. 119) thought that there was a "spontaneous homeostasis" about Chinese life, which he attributed to Chinese agriculture, but such a quality is hard to discern either during the Chinese Golden Age during the Song or in modern China. He also suggested at one point that perhaps the difference between China and the West was the existence of a personalized deity in Judeo-Christian religion, which implied a supreme law-giver

to blame, then why was China initially ahead of Europe, only to fall behind later? Historians of Chinese science following Needham have proposed other explanations. Among the many suggested factors are a few that are particularly worth noting. Nathan Sivin (1982 [2005]) puts forth the notion that China's scientific knowledge was never as unified and methodologically rigorous as the West's. Furthermore, China lacked an effective competitive intellectual market, in which novel ideas about science were tested and discussed. In Sivin's widely quoted words, China had "sciences but no Science" (Sivin 1982 [2005], p. 4). Derk Bodde (1991) has suggested that the Chinese language itself was an impediment to progress, claiming that its ambiguities proved an obstacle to the precise transmission of knowledge that is necessary for science. Furthermore, he argues that the gap between written and spoken language made formal knowledge almost completely inaccessible to people who worked with their hands, even if they were literate. Moreover, despite the early invention of book printing and moveable font in China, the ideographic script did not lend itself to the printing of a large number of diverse books.

As we show in chapters 6 and 9, a more promising explanation of the technological and scientific divergence between China and Europe has to do with incentives, as well as the environment in which science and technology developed. Technological progress in the modern age was typically a top-down process driven by a fairly small number of members of the educated elite, such as scientists, mathematicians, inventors, entrepreneurs, engineers, highly skilled artisans, progressive farmers, and estate managers. This group of innovators is often captured by those whom we refer to as "upper-tail human capital." The attitudes of these educated elites and the incentives that they faced were a decisive factor in the long-term economic dynamics of the Great Divergence. The incentives that they faced were not just monetary; they also included incentives related to social status, prestige, and economic security. As is well understood, it is often the case that knowledge cannot be easily appropriated and monetized by its creators. This creates a thorny economic problem of underproduction in innovation since those able to produce it have limited incentives to do so when the gains are not guaranteed to them. Hence, designing institutions that incentivize intellectual and technological innovation had large social payoffs for society.

---

whose laws were eternal and could be discovered and explained by humans. This belief created a willingness to accept natural laws that he thought was foundational to modern science, which he thought was lacking in China (1969, pp. 311–28).

Moreover, what mattered is not only *how much* new knowledge is generated in the market for ideas, but also *what kinds* of knowledge are produced. Here too, we observe a dramatic divergence between China and Europe. The types of knowledge accumulated in these two parts of the world were quite different. In Imperial China, education was driven almost exclusively by the goal of preparing for one thing: the highly competitive Civil Service Examination, the *keju* system. The exams served as the gateway to economic and social success. Hence, Chinese parents invested in the human capital of their sons, and both the state and large kinship networks allocated resources to the creation and upkeep of schools. Chinese schools and their curricula were largely controlled by the Imperial bureaucracy even in the Song period, and in later years, this control may have become stronger. By the late Ming period, authorities used private academies as a form of social control and a means to ensure stability. The Mandarin bureaucracy laid down the rules: the academies were "to serve the needs of the administration" and become part of the establishment, utterly opposed to anything that would disturb the order of society (Meskill 1982, p. 151).

The fact that Chinese households focused so much on the Imperial examinations introduced a fateful bias in the formation of human capital in China. Studying for these examinations meant a huge investment in education, but over time, most of the curriculum came to be based on rote learning and an exegesis of the neo-Confucian classics. Practical studies, such as science and mathematics, were increasingly excised from the curriculum. If economic progress had been an objective of the state, the Imperial examination system represented a misallocation of the resources allotted to human capital formation (Elman 2000, 2013). To be sure, the *keju* system augmented the overall stock of human capital. However, much as was true for other backward-looking societies whose human capital was dedicated to the exegesis of ancient texts, this had at best a minor effect on economic progress (Huang 2023, p. 239). By the time the Jesuits arrived in China, they could not help but notice this bias in Chinese education.

Recent quantitative research has confirmed this impression. Duan (2024) has utilized bibliometric evidence to document a consistent decline in the percentage of books published in China related to STEM fields, while the percentage of books classified as statecraft increased. The driving motive, as his evidence shows, was the overwhelming influence of the *keju* Imperial Service (Civil Service) Examination. The clan's drive to use education as a tool of placement of one of their members in the bureaucracy was exemplified by the Confucian dictum: "Learn, excel, and then serve in government" (Duan

2024, p. 6). The exact time when this decline takes place is hard to determine, but it appears that 1350 was a watershed, marking a point where the probability that a book was classified as STEM was significantly lower than earlier times. Moreover, the number of original books (as opposed to derivative and exegetical titles) declined as well. Insofar as the themes of books reflect the overall ideas of a nation, this can be taken as support of the argument that from the Ming Dynasty onward, China's priorities turned away from educational fields conducive to technological progress.

There was no analog to the Chinese Civil Service Examination in Early Modern Europe, especially after the Catholic Church definitively lost the remnants of its monopolistic influence as a result of the Protestant Reformation. Even before the Reformation, the Church's ability to enforce orthodox beliefs significantly diminished during the Renaissance. As we discuss in chapter 9, European intellectual life was governed by an institution decidedly different from that of the Chinese meritocracy: namely, the Republic of Letters, a competitive market for ideas increasingly infected by skepticism toward the classical canon inherited from the Greco-Roman world. Sacred cows were slaughtered mercilessly: from the notion of a geocentric universe to the idea of divine authorship of the Bible and the writings of the bogus classical author Hermes Trismegistus. Skepticism was paired with the growing belief in the progressiveness of knowledge. Intellectuals in Europe realized that contradicting and refuting Aristotle, Pliny, and Galen was justifiable, precisely because of the inescapable asymmetry of knowledge. That is, it was apparent that the scholars of the Early Modern age knew what the classical writers did in 200 AD, but obviously not the reverse.

Moreover, new tools and instruments such as microscopes and telescopes never available to the Greeks had diffused across the Continent, and the great voyages during the Age of Exploration provided everyday Europeans with information that classical civilizations could not have dreamed of.[18] New ideas were proposed and debated in an increasingly lively market for ideas, from

18. An interesting argument has been proposed by Jin (2016), who relies on cognitive science to observe a unique "great transcendence" in European scientific thought that took place nowhere else. The driving force was that the cognitive system of European intellectuals was disrupted by unexpected discoveries and instruments that allowed people to observe hitherto unsuspected natural phenomena. These disruptions happened to become available in a cluster lasting approximately a century and forced Europeans to reconstruct what they thought they knew about the universe.

which the Republic of Letters sprang into existence. The Republic's signifi-cance will be discussed at length in chapter 9, but for now it suffices to say that by 1700, the intellectual community and the market for ideas in Europe was quite different from China's. This would have far-reaching consequences for the region's long-term economic development.

Skills and Competences

Artisanal skills were the other component of useful knowledge necessary for the technological transformations that drove economic progress.. Artisans provided the workmanship and materials that turned new ideas into economic reality. The economic history of the development of artisanal skills (the domi-nant form of human capital before the nineteenth century) is truly fascinating for both economists and historians. It has been the subject of considerable research (e.g., Roberts, Schaffer, and Dear 2007; Smith and Schmidt 2007b). Artisanal skills and competence were the main form of human capital that contributed to economic performance until the eighteenth century, when for-mal science first started to inform production in a few industries. Unlike the natural philosophers and astronomers of the Republic of Letters, even highly skilled artisans were rarely well educated (in the modern sense of having ac-quired intellectual knowledge and capabilities beyond the three Rs), did not know Latin, and often possessed only rudimentary numeracy. Their skills were largely intuitive and tacit and were transmitted over time from father to son or through apprenticeships (Harris 1992a, p. 33). Written materials were much less important at this time. Even though both China and Europe produced numerous large encyclopedic volumes describing techniques and equipment in a variety of fields, it is far from obvious whether such books were much used in the training of artisans.

As late as 1500, it was still hard to argue that European artisanal skills were in any way superior to those in the Middle East or Asia. Furthermore, it is clear that the products of Asian artisans were in great demand from Europeans. By contrast, it is striking how few European products appealed to Asian consum-ers. Yet by 1600, there are signs of a reversal. Europe was pulling ahead in basic mechanical technology: screws, cranes, levers, hoists, and pulleys, as well as optical instruments, hydraulic technology, and precision mechanisms such as mechanical clocks, watches, firearms, and high-end toys. Asians may still have been ahead in iron-making, high-end textiles, and ceramics and certainly could hold their own in shipbuilding. By the eighteenth century, however, those gaps too had been closed. The great industrialists of the Industrial Revolution made it their goal to outdo Asians in producing pottery and fine cotton, and they succeeded beyond their expectations. Another great reversal of positions had taken place.

The Enlightenment and the Great Divergences

Among the many cultural and intellectual differences between Europe and China, the one that was critical to subsequent economic development but has been mostly overlooked was the Enlightenment. As already noted, much of late seventeenth- and eighteenth-century Europe experienced an Industrial Enlightenment, which should be seen as the cultural background of the Industrial Revolution (Mokyr 2005, 2012, 2024b). One element in that movement was the emphasis on the importance of the interaction and cooperation between *savants* and *fabricants,* or between the spheres of propositional knowledge (science and related forms of knowledge) and prescriptive knowledge (technology).

The distinction between propositional knowledge and prescriptive knowledge, or between the world of people who knew things and that of people who made things, is as much an epistemic one as a social one. In many cases, "local knowledge" (technical expertise associated with a particular town or region) was created by "mindful hands" or "handy minds," and the distinction between technology and science becomes blurry (Roberts and Schafer 2007). In recent years, many scholars have correctly pointed out that a great deal of useful knowledge was accumulated by what we might call "practitioners": people like surveyors, painters, architects, physicians, clockmakers, botanical collectors, and even pyrotechnicians. Indeed, a special and pivotal role was played by these practical arithmeticians, who applied mathematical tools to a growing array of concrete problems in the production of goods and services (Kelly and Ó Gráda 2022). We shall return to the contributions of these applied mathematicians in chapter 9.[19]

The root of Western technological progress, then, was not just in its growing science or its technological innovations, but also in the growing interactions among them, which created a synergistic effect that ended up eventually

---

19. Some historians have indeed argued that the concept of "mindful hand" erases any distinction between such ex post categories as "science" and "technology" altogether (e.g., Roberts and Schaffer 2007).

changing the dynamics of the economy (Mokyr 2009). Information flowed from various spheres of propositional knowledge to applications and led to sustained improvements once enough was known about the underlying physical or chemical processes, which could take decades or even centuries. Yet in areas as distant from one another as oceanic navigation, cotton bleaching, coal prospecting, hydraulics, and gas lighting, eighteenth-century scientific discoveries and advances in applied mathematics led to improved practices. At the same time, the artisanal elite—clockmakers, engineers, millwrights, ironmasters, and coal viewers—played a major role not just by coming up with many inventions themselves, but also by supplying the ingenious mechanics who were indispensable in constructing, installing, maintaining, and operating the designs dreamed up by inventors (Kelly, Mokyr, and Ó Gráda 2023). Some of the great inventors of the Industrial Revolution were artisans themselves— above all, textbook names such as Abraham Darby, Thomas Newcomen, Benjamin Huntsman, and James Watt himself.

Nothing of the sort can be found in China. China had a substantial class of educated literati (who had trained for the Civil Service Examination), but there is no evidence that they had much interaction with industry, even those with an interest in natural phenomena. China also had a highly skilled population of well-trained and competent artisans, who produced the silk clothes, jades, fine metalwork, and ceramics desired so much by Europeans that they were willing to haul them around Africa to markets in the West. Yet much like the sophisticated crafts practiced in South Asia and the Middle East, little progress comparable to Europe's advances can be discerned after 1500 or so. The idea that techniques could be improved by a deeper understanding of natural regularities and an uncovering of scientific phenomena seemingly failed to gain wide acceptance in China. Sivin (1995, chapter VII) observed that in China, science and crafts moved along nonintersecting trajectories, and tacit, artisanal knowledge was privately transmitted. This stood in contrast to intellectual knowledge, where books were at the center of the learning process.[20] Moreover, as argued next, technological progress in China was much more of a political process than it was in Europe.

---

20. Needham (1969, p. 142) emphasized the distance between the world of scholars and that of artisans and noted that Chinese intellectuals continued for a long time to "harp on the primitive theories of the five elements and the two principles of yang and yin," which in his judgment clearly had little to contribute to technological progress.

4. The Causes of Divergence: Geography and Location

What accounts for all the divergences between China and the West? It seems almost inevitable that geography had some kind of effect on the reversal; to use Ian Morris's (2010, p. 427) pithy term, it was "maps, not chaps" that gave the West its advantage. But what precisely about location and physical environment was so advantageous to the West? Some scholars have pointed to Europe's favorable physical features, such as a moderate climate and long coastlines, but some of these arguments have been severely criticized.[21]

Pomeranz (2000) proposed two geographical hypotheses. He argued that the absence of coal in China, or at least its location in inconvenient areas, made industrialization less feasible there compared to Britain. This widely repeated argument loses sight of the fact that the role of the sheer abundance of coal in the British Industrial Revolution, while important, was far from decisive. As has been pointed out many times, there were substitutes for coal as a source of heat and motive power, and many areas could industrialize by using low-energy-intense industries. Moreover, coal had been known to exist in Britain since the time of the Roman invasions, yet remained underexploited until the Early Modern period. What was required, above all, was the knowledge to find, extract, transport, and utilize it—and that knowledge was not limited to coal; had there been no coal, other sources of energy would have driven the factories, if perhaps at a higher cost. Moreover, China also possessed extensive coal fields and used them intensively throughout the past three decades. In fact, China's economic expansion during the Han and Song dynasties relied quite heavily on its coal abundance. As Jan De Vries (2011, p. 15) memorably summarized in his critique of Pomeranz's *The Great Divergence*: "The exploitation or failure to exploit coal does not answer questions, it raises them."

The other geographical argument made by Pomeranz (2000) is that Europe, unlike China, had access to colonial lands and resources termed "ghost acreage" by Jones (1981, pp. 70–85). These resources did not directly include slavery as such (since few slaves were deployed in Europe), but they did consist of the colonial goods that slaves produced in the New World: sugar, tobacco, and eventually raw cotton. That said, the magnitude of the impact of products associated with slavery on the Great Divergence through the expansion of

---

21. The argument about coastline was made by Diamond (1997, p. 414), among others; for an effective demolition of the case, see Turchin (2007, pp. 199–200). Hoffman (2015) showed that China is actually more mountainous than Europe.

consumption goods is questionable: tobacco consumption's effect on well-being may have been positive (although it made a significant and negative contribution to respiratory ailments). Sugar supplied people with some raw carbohydrates, but as De Vries points out, its dietary value is likely overstated because it was expensive. De Vries (2011, p. 15) concludes sensibly that "to the extent that poorly nourished 18th-century workers added sugar to their diet—and in Britain they certainly did—it worsened the dietary problems of the time rather than relieved them." Cotton, of course, was a different story. Because it could not be grown in Europe, it needed to be imported from colonies; therefore, colonial supply made the rapid expansion of the textile industry during the Industrial Revolution possible. In China, on the other hand, cotton was indigenous—which should have provided them with a prima facie advantage.[22] Most of the colonial goods imported into Europe before the nineteenth century were high-value/weight goods such as spices, furs, and silk. These were desirable goods, and they increased economic welfare, but true globalization, and thus full exploitation of the ghost acreage in North America and elsewhere had to wait until long-distance trade in bulky goods such as food and raw materials (apart from cotton) became feasible with the revolution in shipping in the second half of the nineteenth century. In short, ghost acreage may have been a factor in the economic performance of the West, but as a *primum movens,* it seems unconvincing.

However, the historical phenomenon of ghost acreage is still significant, if more as a symptom than as a driving cause. It was a signal that different cultural beliefs and attitudes and higher capabilities rather than a major advantage in resources drove commercial expansion and economic growth. As noted previously, after 1500, Europeans engaged aggressively in exploring and exploiting the rest of the world. Moreover, the abovementioned Columbian Exchange (really a combination of global technological arbitrage and an exchange of ideas, techniques, and crops) was almost entirely brought about by European travelers and sailors (Nunn and Qian 2010). This kind of openness to new ideas and intellectual aggressiveness can hardly be found in China.[23]

22. Moreover, China imported large amounts of raw cotton from India. Pomeranz's figures indicate that as late as 1830, when the British cotton industry was approaching maturity, it imported about a quarter of a billion pounds of cotton, compared to a Chinese production of 1.85 billion pounds in 1870 (but which probably was not much different from earlier decades).

23. An example of a European invention introduced into China, which failed to make the impact on science that it made in Europe is the telescope (Huff 2011, pp. 110–14). There are a

While the trade winds might have made it more difficult for Chinese ships to sail to the New World, the highly seaworthy ships built during the early Ming Dynasty made the rest of Asia and much of Africa readily accessible to China. And yet nothing of the sort took place. Few tourists or traveling scholars from China visited Europe before the middle of the nineteenth century, nor did those who went write home to communicate the useful ideas they found, unlike myriads of Europeans who visited and explored China. Europeans in the age of voyages acted aggressively to spread knowledge and carry out a kind of information arbitrage.

While coal and colonial expansion may not have been causal factors, geography may still have mattered. Location and geography may have led to Europe's fragmented state system, which, as already noted, had momentous consequences. Furthermore, it is possible, as has often been pointed out, that the achievements during the Song Dynasty were undone by a combination of external factors, such as war, climate change, famine, and disease (Morris 2010, p. 392). It should be kept in mind, however, that the horsemen of the apocalypse visited Europe as well. To be sure, apart from the brief though devastating invasion of Eastern Europe by Batu's forces in 1241–42, Europe was spared from the Mongol Conquests that proved so fatal in the Middle East and South Asia. But what the invading Mongols did not do to Europe, Europeans did to one another—and in spades. All the same, with the exception of some especially destructive conflicts such as the Thirty Years' War and the wars fought against Louis XIV, these conflicts seem to have had little persistent cost, and whatever damage they did to the population, capital, or trade was somehow quickly repaired.

On the contrary, constant warfare in Europe is sometimes viewed as having favored long-term political and economic development because it encouraged state capacity and urbanization (Dincecco and Onorato 2018). The argument that organized violence in Europe helped the evolution of state capacity is almost a cliché, although the full economic implications of said development are far from clear. Preparing for war, as much as war itself, perfected the military apparatuses of Europe and provided states with superior weapons that allowed them to eventually subjugate and exploit much of the rest of the world

---

few records of Chinese travelers making it to Europe, such as Shen Fuzong (known in the west as "Michael"), a Chinese mandarin who was brought back to Europe by a Flemish Jesuit priest and eventually became a Jesuit himself. Very few of them left travel accounts or tried to use their visit to transmit useful knowledge back to China. The flow of European ideas to China before 1800 was almost entirely carried out by Europeans, most of them Jesuit missionaries.

(Headrick 2010; Hoffman 2015). Moreover, constant warfare encouraged urbanization in Europe, as walled cities were better protected against marauding bands of mercenaries than the open countryside. Hence, wars are seen as having been unintentionally salutary, given that cities were the main loci of progress in trade and industry, as well as loci of intellectual activity (Rosenthal and Wong 2011; Dincecco and Onorato 2018). We critically discuss these arguments in chapter 8.

The same argument applies to the Black Death: while devastating in the very short run, some European historians have made a powerful case that in the longer run, it had important positive spillover effects on technology and culture (Herlihy 1997, pp. 48–51). The plague also played a big role in bringing about the Hajnal EMP and improving the economic position of women (Voigtländer and Voth 2013; De Moor and Van Zanden 2010), but it did nothing of the sort in China (which was less affected by the plague than Europe).

5. Interactions and Complementarities

A more promising explanation of why China and Europe diverged in so many dimensions, leading to different trajectories of economic development and institutional evolution, has to do with complementarities among different features of their societies. Logically, what we mean by that is that rather than focus on one factor or a few factors, what drove the divergence was the synergistic interaction among them, creating forces stronger than the sum of the individual components. For example, the initial allocation of power facilitated the evolution of political institutions in specific directions. This in turn had implications for the accumulation of knowledge, feeding back into institutional evolution. Family structures and value systems shaped social interactions, leading to the emergence of specific organizational forms. The interaction between state actors and social organizations mutually reinforced these differences between China and Europe and had feedback effects on economic arrangements, industrialization, and cultural evolution. In this way, initial differences between China and Europe were amplified over time, leading to radically divergent trajectories in many other dimensions.

These interactions and complementarities are discussed at length throughout this book. Before closing this chapter, however, we introduce two initial differences between China and Europe that deserve particular attention, whose influence will be discussed in several of the following chapters: first, the question of political fragmentation versus unification and how this difference influenced scientific and technological innovation; second, differences in family structures and family values and how this influenced which social organizations emerged to facilitate cooperation.

Fragmentation and Empire

A central strand in the argument about the growing gap between the West and China revolves around the theme of China being a unified single state since the Mongol Conquest of 1279, as opposed to Europe remaining politically fragmented. The causes and consequences of this difference have been widely discussed in the literature. As mentioned, there is a case to be made that geography may account for this difference. Recent scholarship, relying on sophisticated simulations, has made a powerful case that the difference can be attributed to a host of geographical differences (e.g., Fernández-Villaverde et al. 2023). For more details, see chapter 7.

It has been argued that this is how geography mattered: Europe was fragmented naturally by mountain ranges, rivers, and internal seas, whereas China appears at first blush to be a large, coherent continental mass (Diamond 1997). But a closer look at China shows that its geographical coherence is more apparent than real (Hoffman 2015, pp. 107–14). Much like Europe, China's landscape is riven by mountains. Furthermore, although China has no internal seas such as the Baltic and North seas or the Mediterranean Sea in Europe, these bodies of water were actually more unifying than dividing, as water transport was cheaper than movement over land. Some parts of China are connected to the rest through narrow mountain passes such as the Hangu Pass, which separates the upper Yellow River and Wei valleys, where the ancient capital Xi'an is located, from the fertile North China Plain in Shaanxi Province. River communications in China are limited because the rivers flow from west to east, which forced the Chinese to build the Grand Canal, spanning over 1,000 miles. However, as Turchin (2012) put it, it was not the canal that made Chinese unification possible, but rather the reverse: political unification (under the Sui Dynasty between 581 and 618) made the Grand Canal's construction possible. In Europe, rivers flow in all directions and were often used by armies. Moreover, the North European Plain is flat, meaning that militias faced little difficulty moving across it; hence Paris fell to Russian armies and Moscow to French armies. Furthermore, political fragmentation had not always been the rule in Europe. The Roman Empire successfully united large parts of the Continent into a single empire for five centuries, and China at various stages before the Yuan reunification in 1279 was split into a number of political entities. In short, the power of geographical factors in bringing about and maintaining this political divergence therefore seems underwhelming. As we will discuss in chapter 7, geography may still have mattered in some respects, although not in the somewhat simplistic way proposed by Diamond.

Whatever the reasons, the implications of European polycentrism have been explored in great detail by the literature. Enlightenment scholars in the eighteenth century had already observed its importance. As shown by Mokyr (2016), the argument goes back to Enlightenment thinkers such as David Hume and Immanuel Kant.[24] To paraphrase Morris's quip, it is here that "maps may have affected chaps" most directly. Insofar that the physical environment mattered, it may have operated mostly through how it affected "chaps" and the institutions and social organizations that they created.

As noted previously, geography may have been a factor in this divergence. All the same, other factors besides geography were at play in the political fragmentation of Europe. Hoffman (2015, pp. 107–34) and Møller and Doucette (2022, chapter 5), argue that beyond geography, the Catholic Church played an important role in the splintering of Europe. For many centuries, the medieval Church was immensely powerful and sought to ensure that no single secular ruler could become strong enough to threaten its influence. Once the papacy itself split in the fourteenth century and Western Christendom became fragmented, the Church's power weakened; however, by that time, some of the nation-states and powerful dynasties had already become faits accomplis. It might be added that a fair amount of contingency was also at play in European

24. One famous contemporary observer expressed this eloquently: Edward Gibbon (1789, vol. 3, p. 636) wrote that "Europe is now divided into twelve powerful, though unequal, kingdoms, three respectable commonwealths, and a variety of smaller, though independent, states. . . . In peace, the progress of knowledge and industry is accelerated by the emulation of so many active rivals; in war, the European forces are exercised by temperate and undecisive contests." The latter effect, sadly, was soon to be refuted by the deadly effective armies of Napoleon, but the "progress of knowledge" remains at the heart of the story. Hume ([1742] 1985, pp. 119–20) wrote, "Nothing is more favorable to the rise of politeness and learning than a number of neighboring and independent states, connected together by commerce and policy. The emulation, which naturally arises among those . . . is an obvious source of improvement. . . . The divisions into small states are favorable to learning, by stopping the progress of authority as well as that of power . . . where a number of neighboring states have a great intercourse of arts and commerce, their mutual jealousy keeps them from receiving too lightly the law from each other, in matters of taste and of reasoning, and makes them examine every work of art with the greatest care and accuracy." See also Kant ([1784] (2010), pp. 30–31).

fragmentation, as attempts to unify Europe under a single ruler failed militarily (but might have succeeded under slightly different circumstances). Inheritance rules also played a role at a key historical juncture. The Germanic tradition of partible inheritance led Charlemagne to divide the territories that he had conquered among his three legitimate sons: Charles, Pippin, and Louis. After that, Europe was never successfully reunified. At the same time, China's unified political structure did come under stress repeatedly but survived since the late thirteenth century.

Whatever its causes, the fragmented polities created a competitive environment in Europe. As we will discuss in chapters 7 and 9, when contrasted with the unified empire in China, this is one of the important reasons why radical institutional and technological innovations were eventually possible in Europe, but not in China. In a centralized state, progress depended on the bureaucracy's attitude toward innovation. For much of China's history, the bureaucracy initiated, diffused, and encouraged new techniques. But when Chinese rulers became more conservative, this innovative momentum slowed and eventually ceased altogether. As fate would have it, these centuries constituted the very period when Europe's taste for innovation became stronger.

European technological innovation was facilitated by its political characteristics. In a pluralistic system, it was easier to challenge the status quo and to escape persecution if one could find protection from a neighboring state. Given that this option was common knowledge, the incentives of reactionary authorities to persecute troublesome innovators weakened. The role of interstate competition as a source of European progress has been reformulated by economic historians, economists, and political scientists (North 1981; Jones 1981; Bernholz, Streit, and Vaubel 1998; Karayalçin 1998; Baechler 2004; Scheidel 2019). The consensus is that exit options constrained rulers and prevented them from overtaxing and mistreating their most productive citizens too much, although this was an equilibrium that did not always hold on the ground.[25] No ambitious ruler wanted to fall too far behind in the competition for influence and power in the European international arena. Hence, rulers tried to lure away their neighbors' most talented and famous citizens, and hence the upper tail of the intellectual community enjoyed a high rate of mobility. Recognizing this, many rulers increasingly turned a blind eye to the beliefs and behaviors of their often

---

25. Louis XIV's foolish decision to revoke the Edict of Nantes in 1685 led to the departure of many thousands of Huguenots, many of whom were clearly part of the upper tail of the human capital distribution, and in the eighteenth century, the French government quietly allowed many of them to come back.

eccentric dissenters and most brilliant citizens. Moreover, being exposed to a plurality of economic, social, and political arrangements, Europeans also found it easier to learn from the successes and failures of others and to acquire new ideas. While politically fragmented, Europe displayed a high degree of intellectual integration, with ideas and knowledge moving easily across the Continent: first through the Catholic Church and its clerics, and after 1500 increasingly within the Republic of Letters (Mokyr 2016).

The competitive character of European society went deeper than just inter-state rivalries. Many nonstate entities, especially corporations, were almost equally competitive with one another, as states were. This was especially true for cities, which were often effectively self-ruling even if they were formally part of the same state (e.g., Ghent and Bruges in Flanders and Amsterdam in the Dutch provinces). In many cases, urban authorities attempted to poach skilled artisans from one another. Although cities often cooperated in some dimensions, typically out of necessity (such as the Hanseatic League and the Dutch United Provinces), the competitive nature of what may be called the "Cities System" was preserved.

Another example of European polycentrism was the evolution of competition between religions after the monopoly of the Catholic Church was broken in the sixteenth century. In England, dissenting churches and the established Anglican church competed fiercely with one another. One unintended consequence of this competition was the improvement of education. The English dissenting academies were widely praised for the quality of their education. The same was true for Jesuit schools, whose original purpose was to persuade youngsters of the merits of the true faith.[26] That said, religious competition, like all other forms of competition, was a double-edged sword, leading to violent clashes such as the French Wars of Religion (1562–1598) and other conflicts. Still, it led to substantial improvements in factors important for economic development.

As a result of interstate competition, the persecution of heterodox and "heretical" intellectuals gradually faded in the age of Enlightenment and eventually rarely amounted to more than lip service and symbolic book burnings. As no single ruler was ever able to unite Europe, radical ideas and propositions that might have seemed unacceptable to many could flourish and compete in

---

26. Many of the leading intellectuals of the French Enlightenment had trained at Jesuit schools: Denis Diderot, Voltaire, Gianluigi Buffon, Nicolas de Condorcet, Jean-Charles de Borda, Charles Bossut, Jean Baptiste Joseph Delambre, Bernard Le Bovier de Fontenelle, Pierre Méchain, Denis Papin, and Maximilien Robespierre come to mind.

the market for ideas. The Copernican model of the universe, Paracelsus's iatrochemical system of medicine, Galileo's mechanics, and Baruch Spinoza's pantheism could be disseminated and discussed by intellectuals all over Europe. If reactionary authorities decided to suppress a particular idea or avenue of research or thought that they regarded as heretical or subversive, the work just moved elsewhere.[27] Censorship was more or less ineffective, as books could be printed abroad if the local censors treated it harshly (Mokyr 2016, pp. 175–78). Since the censors knew this too, the actual control that authorities had on intellectual life and the market for ideas through censorship weakened during the Enlightenment and became little more than window-dressing, even if it never quite disappeared. Given the fragmentation and competitive nature of the European system, the best strategic response for rulers in Europe was to tolerate brilliant dissenters in their realms, even if they were a considerable annoyance at times.

The history of China demonstrates what could have been, as well as what was. As Huang (2023, p. 245) notes correctly, there was a time when China had its "European moment"—namely, the era of weak or absent unity prior to the reunification of the country by the Sui Dynasty (220–581 AD). It was a period of ardent political and ideological competition, chaos, and violence, but also one of vibrant intellectual and technological creativity. The reunification of China under the short-lived Sui Dynasty and the establishment of a nationwide bureaucracy, increasingly driven by *keju*, may well have been key to the eventual stagnation of China. Huang, somewhat wistfully, adds, "Imagine what would have happened in China if the spirit of free exploration had survived and thrived" (2023, p. 249).[28]

The absence of this kind of pluralism in China may have been one of the decisive drivers of the indisputable intellectual stagnation that set in during

27. For example, the Catholic Inquisition south of the Alps felt that infinitesimal mathematics was an inappropriate area of study and contradictory to its view of the universe, and the Jesuit order actively banned it. As a result, the cutting edge of mathematical research shifted from Italy to Switzerland, France, and Germany, where no such aversion existed (Alexander 2014).

28. It is inconvenient for this approach that the Song period was as creative as the 220–581 interregnum, and Huang needs to fall back on demand-driven arguments to explain this fact away. The more obvious explanation is that, despite China being mostly unified, the Song had a central government that encouraged and fostered progress. A monopoly on power and the market for ideas is not inconsistent with technological and scientific progress, so long as the government itself is progressive and encourages innovation that enhances prosperity.

the Ming Dynasty and continued into the Qing years. David Hume sensed this already in the middle of the eighteenth century. In China, he argued, the authority of one teacher was propagated easily from one corner of the empire to another: "None had the courage to resist the torrent of popular opinion, and posterity was not bold enough to dispute what had been universally received by their ancestors" (Hume [1742] 1985, p.122). In fact, there was more dissent in China than authors such as Qian (1985)—who with many others subscribed to the Hume view—suspected. Both in the late Ming and early Qing eras, there were heterodox writers who challenged the neo-Confucian orthodoxy. One of the most prominent was philosopher Li Zhi (1527–1602), who seems to have felt that one did not have to be a Confucian scholar to be a philosopher—a truly iconoclastic position for the time (Jiang 2001, p. 13). Yet the influence of Li and others was limited and fleeting. China did not produce a Descartes, a Spinoza, or an Isaac Newton, who could form entirely new paradigms that attracted a large following among the learned. Li's main concern was reconciling the undeniable private needs and desires of human beings with the obvious constraints of public morality (Huang 1981, p. 198). In any event, his heterodox views were extremely costly to him: following the publication of his heretical (and significantly titled) book *A Book to Burn*, he was arrested by the emperor's guard, jailed, and committed suicide in prison (Huang 1981, pp. 189–221).[29]

Another key difference between China and Europe was that in the latter, scholarly reputations more or less disregarded political and religious boundaries. Hence, internationally reputable scholars such as Comenius, Descartes, Locke, and Grotius could find a hospitable environment abroad when needed. In China, there were creative minds who thought outside the box, but they failed in the Chinese market for ideas because it was not sufficiently competitive. Moreover, under the insecure and conservative Qing emperors, the Chinese state directly slowed society's intellectual progress by forcefully suppressing heresy and subversive writings and increasingly creating a conformist culture (Xue and Koyama 2020; McDermott 2022, p. 617). Again, the divergence

---

29. Other heterodox writers in China fared no better. Zhu Shunshui (1600–1682) was one of the few Chinese intellectuals who can be compared with European intellectuals in his itinerancy and who actually left China in an attempt to escape persecution and ended up in Japan. His belief was that the extension of knowledge applied not only to knowledge of the Confucian classics, but also to "all that is useful in life" (Ching 1979, p. 217). This sounds remarkably Baconian, but Zhu's work remained unknown in China until his rediscovery in the late nineteenth century.

between China and the West was a matter of degree, and instances of the suppression of radical dissenters also took place in Europe. However, by 1650, the suppression of so-called heretical ideas had become increasingly ineffective in Europe, and by the end of the seventeenth century, resistance to new ideas in science and technology had weakened beyond repair. In the "War between the Moderns and the Ancients," the Moderns had won a resounding victory.

Although it is widely agreed that technological progress is always and everywhere at least partially a political phenomenon, the degree to which politics played a decisive role differed among different economies. One of the most striking differences between West and East that featured in the Great Divergence is that in Europe, the practice of advancing useful knowledge (both propositional and prescriptive knowledge) and its transmission from generation to generation was largely left to the private sector, and hence was driven by competition. Individuals may have been part of corporate bodies such as universities, monasteries, or learned societies and academies, but these were private-order organizations. To be sure, many great physicians, philosophers, and astronomers enjoyed some form of patronage from royalty, nobility, and wealthy citizens, but they were rarely formal parts of the administration, and they were rarely strong-armed by their patrons into supporting a particular doctrine. The rich and powerful individuals employing them at their courts, such as Emperor Rudolph II of the Habsburg Empire, did so on their own account. Scientific societies and academies of intellectuals were not entirely independent of the state, and they usually were sponsored (or at least tolerated) by authorities, but in their daily operations, they enjoyed a high degree of autonomy, as one would expect from corporations. Furthermore, their work was rarely controlled by secular authorities or their patrons.

The emergence of the state as the central form of political organization and its subsequently formed capacity to levy taxes and provide public goods was one of the most striking features of European history. All the same, the *direct* influence of any European government on the frontiers of useful knowledge— that is, the progress of science and technology—was usually second order. In a few cases, to be sure, governments and people in power sponsored applied research (often for military purposes). More often, their support amounted to providing patronage to leading intellectuals and otherwise not getting in the way. Natural philosophers, engineers, inventors, and scholars rarely belonged to the ruling classes (i.e., the aristocracy and higher clergy). With some exceptions, talented and creative people not born into the right families could not occupy positions of political power, and thus they channeled their energies elsewhere. As the social prestige of successful scholars rose in the sixteenth and seventeenth centuries and more lucrative and desirable patronage positions became available, careers in natural philosophy, mathematics, and medicine became increasingly attractive.

Not so in China: the Imperial government was historically an active and dominant player in the market for ideas. Many of the great Song-era inventions, so far as their origins can be established at all, were made by bureaucrats. The state administration was the agency that encouraged technological progress in agriculture and the adoption of better equipment and hydraulic projects (Mokyr 1990, pp. 233–36; for a recent restatement, see Huang 2023, pp. 220–25).[30] China had an official "bureau of astronomy," established in the third century BC by the Qin dynasty, which functioned for many centuries. Government officials promoted the adoption of faster-ripening and more drought-resistant strains of rice, especially the Champa varieties introduced from Southeast Asia in the eleventh century, which revolutionized much of Chinese agriculture during the Song Dynasty.[31]

The massive treaties on agricultural technology published during the Yuan and Ming dynasties were written by government officials such as Wang Zhen (act. 1290–1333) and Xu Guangqi (1562–1633). The government managed the great iron foundries, mines, and shipyards and played an active role in the diffusion of cotton growing.[32] For centuries, this strategy worked well, and China's technological advances during the Han and Song dynasties succeeded largely thanks to the initiatives of the Imperial administration. Moreover, in China, the Imperial government was far more active in printing and publishing books

30. Data covering Chinese history in the very long run show that somewhere between 60 and 66 percent of prominent Chinese individuals supposedly in technology were government employees, and they were incentivized by promotion within Imperial government service, as well as by financial incentives (Huang 2023, p. 220).

31. Champa rice was a drought-resistant variety that permitted double-cropping under the right circumstances and made growing rice on higher and sloping lands possible. According to the Buddhist monk Shu Wenying, when the Song emperor Zhengzhong (998–1022) learned that Champa rice was drought-resistant, he sent special envoys to bring samples back to China and then helped diffuse its cultivation.

32. When an invention was made by a person of an "unofficial position," this was seen as worth mentioning. Bi Sheng, who was the first to use moveable type in China, was one such inventor, and the source on this, the great Chinese polymath Shen Kuo, thought it necessary to mention this. Further improvements in the technology were made by officials such as Wang Zhen, who described his invention in his enormous work on agriculture, *Nong Shu* (1313).

than European governments were. As Brokaw (2005, pp. 17–19) points out, "Government offices at all administrative levels often made what were clearly commercial decisions to publish certain popular texts for public sale and profit." The Imperial government also participated in the commerce in books and tightly controlled its content through what has become known as the Chinese Literary Inquisition (Wénzì yù). The market for ideas in China was thus far more monopolistic than in Europe. Yet for a long time, it worked well.

The problem with such monopolies was not that they completely blocked progress, but that progress was vulnerable to the whims of rulers. At some point during Ming China, the drive to discovery and progress slowed, and under the Qing, the government lost both its interest in and its capacity for initiating further progress. For instance, political decisions ended the construction of the sophisticated seaworthy ships used by Zheng He in the fifteenth century and the sophisticated clocks built for the Song emperor by Su Song.[33] China's brief exploration of more remote regions using large fleets of highly advanced large ships was commenced by the Yongle emperor in 1405 and terminated by his successors, the Hongxi and Xuande emperors. The conservative forces, which prioritized stability and security over progress and openness, triumphed, and stagnation set in. China's tragedy was that this kind of retrenchment took place at around the same time that the West was surging ahead.

It is hard to know when exactly technological and intellectual stagnation set in: it was the result of struggles within the Chinese government, and progressive forces kept trying to keep some openness alive.[34] Under the Ming, the

---

33. The famed clock was, in Landes's (1983, p. 17) phrase, "a magnificent dead end." It is worth reciting his explanation for the astonishing disappearance of what appears to have been a technological triumph: "There was no marketplace of ideas, no diffusion or exchange of knowledge, no continuing and growing pool of skills or information—hence a very uneven transmission of knowledge from one generation to the next" (Landes 1983, p. 33). The statement is not altogether accurate, as there was some further progress in clock-making during the Yuan Dynasty, but by the time of the arrival of the first Jesuits in China in the seventeenth century there is no evidence that the Chinese artisans had much knowledge of clockworks. Clocks were particularly important because clock-makers and watchmakers were artisans skilled in high-precision manufacturing—the very sort of artisans who played a central role in transforming the great technological advances into an economic reality in the British Industrial Revolution.

34. Huang (2023, p. 236) dated the beginning of stagnation to the Sui Dynasty, which he regards as "the turning point in the historical arc of China," and he argued that it was "the first wave of technological stagnation." Yet clearly there was a revival of technological creativity during the Song, ending with the subsequent dynasties. For more details on the timing of the decline of Chinese science and technology, see the rest of this chapter and chapter 9.

Chinese Imperial court still had a modicum of cautious curiosity about Western knowledge, and hence the Jesuit presence was tolerated in Beijing. The Jesuits brought to China their knowledge of astronomy, reformed the calendar, and brought certain instruments such as firefighting pumps, eyeglasses, and telescopes to China. The influence of Catholic missionaries on Chinese culture faded in the eighteenth century (in part due to internal squabbles between competing rival orders) but it never disappeared, and indeed, it affected the practice of Chinese science by the local literati.[35] The Kangxi Emperor (r. 1661–1722) was intrigued by the Western science that the Jesuits taught him; and a Jesuit painter, Giuseppe Castiglione, painted Chinese emperors and helped design Imperial mansions (Rowe 2009, p. 139). Still, their influence remained dependent on the goodwill of the emperor, and over time, the Qing rulers, especially the Yongzhen Emperor (r. 1722–1735), became increasingly suspicious of Western influence. In 1792, the first Earl Macartney, who visited China with an exhibit of Western devices, was politely told that if these inventions had been useful in China, the Chinese would have thought of them themselves.[36]

One telling consequence of the divergence in scientific and technological progress between China and the West is that until the twentieth century, China had nothing that resembled intellectual property rights. It had no patent system or copyright. It never developed any formal, centrally enforced protection of intangible assets. Indeed, as Alford (1995, p. 17) points out, the only cases in which the Chinese state made an effort to provide protection for intellectual property before the twentieth century were "directed overwhelmingly toward sustaining imperial power." In a world in which the scientific and technological envelopes were normally pushed by officials rather than entrepreneurs, there was little need for an incentive structure that encouraged private innovation of any kind. Indeed, as the empire turned more conservative, the mandarinate became less and less involved in any kind of intellectual

---

35. Elman (2002) has argued, for example, that under Imperial patronage influenced by Jesuit teachings, mathematical studies were upgraded from an insignificant skill to an all-important domain of knowledge that complemented classical studies. In terms of rhetoric, this sea change was justified by an appeal to the "Chinese origins of Western learning" (p. 225).

36. This incident may to some extent overstate the cultural differences between China and the West, as by that time, the aging Qianlong had become unusually conservative, and further, Macartney did not bring with him the most advanced inventions. That said, there is no evidence that the Chinese authorities had any interest in Western science and technology, and the culture shocks of the nineteenth century elicited much less of a dramatic response than they did in Japan, which found itself similarly falling behind (Cranmer-Byng and Levere 1981).

innovation, technological or otherwise (Mokyr 1990, pp. 233–38; see also Root 2020, pp. 164–74).[37]

In short, unlike in the West, what we would call "research and development (R&D)" was *choses du roi*—an official activity in China. That said, the absence of a patent system and a tradition of respecting intellectual property rights in and of itself is not a satisfactory explanation of why technological change in China slowed and why it was not able to take full advantage of techniques that it did deploy (e.g., military technology). It is better to think of this absence as a symptom of deeper historical factors. The lack of a tradition of intellectual property rights, however, is perhaps a good historical background to help us understand the current contempt that China has for Western intellectual property rights, which underlies much of the trade disputes between China and the West.

Family Structures and the Scope of Cooperation

While the contrast between a unified China and a fragmented Europe has been extensively discussed in the literature, there is a second key contrast whose profound implications are often neglected. It is the divergence in family structures that has been described in this chapter. As discussed in greater detail in chapter 4, this divergence originated in large part from policies implemented by the Latin Catholic Church during the early Middle Ages, although the Germanic bilineal kinship tradition also played a role. These policies eventually undermined the extended family as the main building block of society in Europe. Schulz et al. (2019) and Schulz (2022) point to the Merovingian Era as the period when the assault of the Church on cousin-marriage and incest brought about the decline of a social organization system based on extended families.

The question of why the Church engaged in these policies that turned out to have such momentous unintended consequences has multiple answers. One is that it weakened clannish and tribal power simply because these competed with the control over daily life that the Church had over its members. By the early medieval times, one area of control was the family; the Church became obsessed with the issue of incest and monogamy and was increasingly committed to what eventually became known as the EMP (Schulz et al. 2019; Schulz 2022). Tribal

37. Zhao (2015, p. 363), in his analysis of the decline of technological creativity in what he calls the Confucian-Legalist state, points out that "no matter whether the inventors were gentry or hands-on artisans, the nature of the Confucian-Legalist state determined that neither inventions nor scientific discoveries would yield wealth, prestige, or authority."

and clannish marriage customs were regarded as pagan traditions that Christianity had to eradicate. Another argument, espoused by Goody (1983), who was one of the first to point to Church policies as a driver of the move toward nuclear families, was that the Church could acquire the property of unmarried individuals or heirless nuclear families—something that would have been impossible in a clan-based society.[38] Moreover, after the fourth Lateral Council in 1215, the prohibition of cousin-marriage promulgated by the Church could be set aside on a case-by-case basis by purchasing dispensations, which was another source of revenue for the Church.

The transition to a world of nuclear families was a slow and drawn-out process, of course, and it is hard to know with any certainty where and when a society became dominated by the nuclear family.[39] Schulz (2022) maintains that cousin-marriage became difficult, if not impossible, for ordinary peasants as well. The parish system, created by Carolingian rulers, mandated prenuptial investigations and incentivized relatives and neighbors to denounce incestuous marriages by promising that the property of consanguineous marriages would be distributed to relatives. That said, demographic evidence supporting this view is lacking until much later.

That said, it seems logical that, as extended kinship ties and commitments gradually weakened, something else had to step in, and that is where corporations emerged as the answer to the question "What supported and enforced social cooperation?"

Thus, the divergence in family structures between Europe and China emerged at some point after the first millennium AD. In China, social cooperation was increasingly achieved through the extended family and kin-based social networks. In medieval Europe, by contrast, once the nuclear family became the fundamental building block of society, cooperation had to be organized outside the family. Households cannot exist in isolation; they need to cooperate with others to attain many of their essential needs, ranging

38. Goody (1983, p. 44) asserted that if the authorities prohibited close marriage and adoption, discourage remarriage and divorce, and delegitimize concubinage, 40 percent of all marriages would be left without an immediate male heir.

39. In the view of Schulz et al. (2019), "The Church's marriage policies and prohibitions, which we will call the Marriage and Family Program (MFP), meant that by 1500 AD, and likely centuries earlier in some regions, Europe had lost its strong kin-based institutions, and was instead dominated by relatively weak, independent and isolated nuclear or stem families." Yet clearly, in many areas, this was accomplished much earlier; for instance, see MacFarlane (1978), who sees in England an individualist society consisting of nuclear families as early as the thirteenth century.

from defense to insurance (see Seabright 2010 for an excellent exposition). When states were relatively weak or unable to exercise effective authority on the local level, extensive kinship relations such as clans or tribes made such cooperation possible. The corporation, which was independent of shared ancestry, became attractive as an alternative solution in Europe once the extended family and kin ties weakened. During roughly the same period, China was moving in the opposite direction: extended family ties (clans) became more pervasive in China as Imperial power slowly waned after the fall of the Song Dynasty.

The interplay between the rise of corporations and the gradual disappearance of extended kinship in Europe is one of the deeper sources of bifurcation between the two worlds. After corporations such as fraternities, monasteries, guilds, and urban communes arose, they may well have further strengthened individualism and the central role of the nuclear family. This in turn accelerated the decline of extended kinship in Europe even more, thus creating a positive feedback mechanism. Public goods produced by local governments and corporations made it easier for people to dissociate themselves from their extended kin and become more individualistic in their culture and behavior.

As discussed throughout this book, this bifurcation of social organizations was a major factor in the unique European pattern of economic and political development. It had far-reaching implications for the subsequent evolution of legal and informal institutions. Differences in social organization eventually drove the very different ways in which cooperation was achieved, how the economies worked, how markets operated, and how contracts were enforced. Moreover, as emphasized by Henrich (2020) and Schulz et al. (2018), the differences between a society of extended kinship and one of nuclear families have far-reaching psychological and behavioral effects. This bifurcation affected the accumulation and diffusion of useful knowledge, and hence long-term economic development. It also determined the different evolution of political power and the way that states emerged.

In chapter 3, we present a conceptual framework that can explain how family values and structures influence the emergence of different kinds of social organizations. The rest of the book then uses this conceptual framework to explain the historical origins and implications of these different social arrangements, as well as their role in explaining the Great Divergence.

3

Morality and Social Organizations

1. Introduction

The main idea guiding this book is that China and Europe diverged in so many dimensions because the structure of their societies and their social organizations had very different cultural and social foundations. These structures emerged and spread when the state was basically absent (as in Europe) or not as far-reaching as modern states (as in China). Both China and Europe had to sustain local cooperation and provide local public goods in areas and domains that were outside the reach of the state. Cooperation was achieved within and through social organizations that largely emerged spontaneously. But these co-operative arrangements were very different in these two parts of the world.

In premodern China, the clan based on shared male ancestry became the paramount social organization. In premodern Europe, as we have seen, coop-eration was achieved through a variety of organizational arrangements that Greif (2006a, 2006b) has called "corporations." Both the clan and the corpora-tion were organizations whose perpetuation did not depend on the participa-tion of one particular individual. They fulfilled comparable roles in supporting interhousehold and intergenerational cooperation, and they had some features in common. They also evolved in similar directions over time, reflecting how the needs and demands of their members changed with economic development and through interactions with the state. A more detailed comparison between a society dominated by clans and one that was characterized by corporations is provided in chapters 5 and 6. The rest of the book discusses at length these features of Chinese and European social organizations, their historical origin, and their implications for subsequent institutional evolution and economic and technological development. In this chapter, we outline our conceptual frame-work in a more abstract setting, studying the interaction between local culture and prevailing social arrangements. We view social organizations as social networks that facilitate interaction and cooperation among their members, and we address two fundamental questions. First, what led to the emergence of kin-based networks in China and corporate structures in Europe? Second, what effects did these different social networks have on the subsequent cultural evolution of society? Since the goal of the chapter is to provide a sharp conceptual framework that delivers specific predictions, some oversimplifications of a much more complex and variegated reality are unavoidable.

The chapter develops two distinct arguments. Starting with the first question, which social networks are formed depends on the prevailing value system because morality has key implications for how cooperation is enforced. A society with strong ties among kin and patrilineal traditions facilitates the formation of kin-based networks. Such organizations can rely on enforcement methods that take advantage of its members' strong reciprocal moral obligations and repeated interactions, as well as of the very high costs of exit in a society in which membership of organizations is ascriptive (i.e., determined by birth). A universalistic value system with bilineal kinship, instead, does not favor kin-based networks over other criteria, while it facilitates interactions among strangers through generalized trust and trustworthiness. Members of a common-interest organization have weaker and more impersonal moral obligations compared to kin-based organizations, however. As a result, common-interest organizations have to rely on more explicit, and possibly more costly enforcement procedures, and they are more constrained by members' possible dissent and options for exit compared to a kin-based network. This argument leads us to conclude that differences in social networks between China and Europe have cultural roots, even if other factors also played a role in their emergence. Different organizations emerged because these two parts of the world had different value systems and different cultural contexts. Strong kinship loyalty, patrilineal traditions, and kin-based morality made the clan more attractive in China, while in Europe, a universalistic value system and the diffusion of nuclear families gave a comparative advantage to the corporation.[1]

Then we turn to the second question: How do prevailing social networks in turn influence cultural traits and social norms? Here, we rely on the insights

1. We will use throughout this discussion the term "universalistic values" for a moral code that is based on the application of norms of good conduct in a society of abstract individuals entitled to specific rights, and who thus in theory treat nonkin as well as relatives (a generalized morality), as opposed to a communitarian society, in which people strongly differentiate between kinspeople and strangers (limited morality). See Tabellini (2008a; 2010).

of a large body of literature on cultural evolution (for a survey, see Bisin and Verdier 2022). The cultural traits that spread through society are those that are relatively more fit in that particular social and economic environment, much as is the case in biological systems that are subject to natural selection, where fitness is defined as adaptive to the existing environment. Because of complementarities in the diffusion of social networks and economies of scale in their size, a culture of kin loyalty is relatively more fit compared to universalistic values in an environment in which collective goods are mainly provided by tight kinship networks. The opposite is true if, instead, society is mainly organized through corporate structures that are open to all. Widespread clan-based interactions foster loyalty to the kin, while more diffuse interactions within common-interest organizations spread universalistic values and generalized trust. Thus, culture and organizations coevolve in a positive feedback dynamic. In addition, as discussed in later chapters and not formalized here, existing social organizations are strengthened by interactions with the state.

Combining the answers to these two questions, we formulate our main argument. The spontaneous and bottom-up aggregation of individuals in social organizations, in two environments with different initial cultural conditions, led to an institutional and cultural bifurcation between China and Europe. As we will discuss at length in chapter 4, at the turn of the millennium, when the demand for collective goods provided by social organizations was particularly strong, China and Europe had developed different value systems: kinship loyalty in China, universalistic values in Europe. These initial cultural differences, which reflected the specific content of prevailing religions or philosophical systems, facilitated the emergence of different organizational structures. A powerful mechanism of positive feedback further reinforced the initial cultural differences, which in turn contributed to the wider diffusion of these social organizations, leading the two continents to different paths of cultural, social, institutional, and economic development.[2]

The outline of this chapter is as follows. In section 2, we contrast the two social organizations, clan versus corporation, and discuss how their emergence depends on the prevailing culture. In section 3, we discuss how the prevailing network structure of society influences cultural evolution and may lead to cultural and institutional bifurcation. Section 4 summarizes the main

2. A similar model (clearly inspired by Greif and Tabellini 2017) is presented by Eruchimovitch, Michaeli, and Sarid (2024), with a greater emphasis on the distinction between collectivism and individualism but a very similar structure.

implications of the analysis, and an appendix provides a simple, formal model that captures our key theoretical arguments. This model is a simplified version of the more general setting analyzed in Greif and Tabellini (2017).

2. The Emergence of Social Organizations

Historical and Social Context

As we discuss at length in chapter 4, clans and corporations emerged and flourished as the dominant forms of social organization between the eleventh and fifteenth centuries, the former in China, the latter in the West. Clans existed before the Song period in China (960–1279 AD), but their diffusion among nonaristocratic dynasties increased substantially during the Song. In Europe, corporate structures can be discerned earlier, but they were not widespread before the turn of the millennium.

The period of the "High Middle Ages" (between AD 1000 and 1300) saw intense migration to and settlement in new lands in both continents as a result of population growth. People cleared lands and prepared them for cultivation, created new villages, and built transport infrastructures. These were spontaneous, decentralized processes, without coordination from the center. New settlers, as well as residents of presettled areas, needed a variety of local public goods such as defense, infrastructure, and insurance. In Europe, states and authorities were weak by and large, law and order were spotty at best, and local public goods—insofar that they were provided at all—were supplied mostly by local lords. In contrast, the imperial administration in China during the Song Dynasty had considerable state capacity and played an active role in agriculture, manufacturing, flood control, and other areas of life. Its authorities were "model rulers," and the state was one of the most "humane, cultured and intellectual societies of Chinese history and perhaps in all of human history" (Kuhn 2009, p. 9). But after the Song Dynasty fell, state capacity began a downward trend, increasing the need for some way to supply public goods that the state was progressively unable to provide. Despite these difference between Europe and China, both societies needed similar local public goods such as protection from external threats, risk sharing, adjudication of private disputes, irrigation, drainage, and land clearing, as well as some method for coordinating the pursuit of specific goals (e.g., diffusion of knowledge or of religious practices). Local communities had to find effective arrangements to sustain the cooperation and collective action required to address these challenges. Without the provision of local public goods, an economy could not function. How did these societies go about solving this problem, and why were different arrangements chosen in China and Europe?

A large body of literature drawing on social psychology and economics suggests that the answer to this question varies with the prevailing cultural background. Several experimental and empirical studies have shown that patterns of cooperation are strongly influenced by cultural traditions. These studies contrast individuals who grew up in environments with strong kinship ties and where patrilineal dynastic traditions were important and pervasive against individuals who grew up in environments in which family ties were less important and traditions emphasized individual responsibility and achievements (see, for instance, Henrich 2020; Enke 2019; Schulz 2020; Haidt 2013). This literature suggests that individuals with strong and extended family ties identify with their kin, exhibit strong loyalty to other members of their extended family, and respect the authority of senior members of their network. However, they are less respectful and less trusting of unrelated individuals, and they are less willing to cooperate with strangers than are individuals with weak and narrow family ties. In the words of Tabellini (2008a), strong kinship ties are associated with communitarian or limited morality, in the sense that altruism decreases rapidly with social distance. Notions of good and bad behavior and value systems are mainly applicable to members of one's kinship network, not to strangers. Different value systems also correlate with psychological traits of individuals: stronger kinship ties are associated with greater conformism, with more importance attached to the opinions of others and more contextual thinking. On the other hand, weak family ties and individualistic traditions are associated with generalized morality and universalistic value systems, more widely diffused trust, and universalistic patterns of cooperation and good behavior toward unrelated people. There is considerable historical and experimental evidence, much of it summarized in Gorodnichenko and Roland (2017) and Henrich (2020), to suggest that such societies tend to be more successful in creating a civil society in which strangers frequently interact.

These findings suggest that the evolution of social organizations and the formation of social networks reflect historically prevailing cultural traits. Cooperation is also sustained by intrinsic motivations and what Enke (2019) calls "moral emotions," not just by extrinsic and material incentives. Hence, organizations that match with prevailing social norms and value systems have lower enforcement costs. In a society of kin-based values and social norms based on tradition and ancestor veneration, kin-based organizations had a comparative advantage, and cooperation and interactions took place primarily among kin. Cooperation among unrelated but like-minded individuals, instead, is easier to sustain in a world of individualistic and universalistic cultures. The Republic of Letters (discussed in chapter 2) was one instance of such cooperation, but so are many other corporate organizations (discussed at length in chapter 6).

The emphasis on traditions of course raises the question of where such cultural differences come from in the first place. This issue is one of the central and most difficult topics in social science, and we will take a rather minimalist approach here. In part, we argue in this chapter that the social structures discussed previously coevolved with their cultural foundations, each reinforcing the other. Kin-based social organizations induce interactions mostly among kin. As shown by Tabellini (2008b), this in turn strengthens communitarian value systems because holders of these traits tend to be more successful in such social environments. Conversely, looser and more open social networks, where interactions tend to be among unrelated individuals, facilitate cultural evolution toward universalistic value systems. Such two-way positive feedback and complementarities, from culture to social organizations and vice versa, imply that neither is purely causal, but instead the two coevolve and reinforce one another. Economists have increasingly emphasized this line of thinking (e.g., Tabellini 2008a; Bisin and Verdier 2017; Alesina and Giuliano 2015), which is also supported by several recent empirical studies surveyed in Enke (2023). In these models, the emphasis shifts from the often-fruitless search from *causality* to the joint evolution of culture on the one hand and institutions and organization on the other.[3] One of the implications of such positive feedback models is that initial cultural and social differences can be amplified over time and eventually create great divergence. A similar account is provided by Roland (2024), who develops a database of institutions and shows how initial differences going back to antiquity end up producing a world characterized by a bimodal distribution of values and social/political organizations. He stresses, much as we do, that these two clusters were driven by complementarities that reinforced and amplified existing differences.

---

3. As Bisin and Verdier (2017, p. 3) put it, "In these environments the origin, and hence the causation, question loses most of its interest: culture and institutions are jointly and endogenously determined and they jointly affect economic growth and prosperity, indeed all sorts of economic activity. The focus is moved from the cause (both culture and/or institution can have causal effects) to the process as determined by the interaction."

One of these initial differences between China and the post-Roman West was the role of Christianity and the Catholic Church, not just as a source of beliefs and rituals but also as a concrete organization. We will see in chapter 4 how the Church played a pivotal role in setting into motion this coevolutionary process.

Two Kinds of Social Organizations

To make this argument more precise, we shall think of social organizations as social networks or clubs that individuals unilaterally choose to join. The emergence of social organizations corresponds to an equilibrium allocation of individuals across social networks, where individuals optimally self-select into different types of networks or clubs according to their individual features and cultural traits, taking as given the equilibrium allocation (and hence the equilibrium size of each network). The appendix to this chapter provides a formal model of the equilibrium allocation of individuals across organizations. Here, we sketch the main argument.[4]

Suppose that individuals draw utility from their private consumption and from using a given amount of a collective good. The collective good is excludable and can be enjoyed only if the individual belongs to an organization and contributes to its costs. There are two types of organizations to choose from: an individual can obtain the local public good either by collaborating with his or her kin (a *clan*), or by joining an association of unrelated individuals who cooperate in the provision of the collective good (a *corporation*). These organizations have similar objectives but differ in how cooperation is enforced. Within a clan, cooperation is sustained by repeated interactions with other individuals over several domains. Noncooperative or opportunistic behavior in one domain is punished by the clan through ostracism and exclusion from future interactions in other domains. Moreover, cooperation among kin is also sustained by bonds of kin solidarity, internalized social norms of loyalty, affinity to common ancestors, and a strong sense of belonging. A corporate organization instead is an association of previously unrelated individuals brought together by common interest as opposed to common descent. Their

4. *Club goods* are goods that are excludable but nonrivalrous. The economics of clubs (or club goods) was originally laid out in a classic article by James Buchanan (1965). See also, for example, Berglas (1976) and Berglas and Pines (1981). Jackson (2008) is the classic reference on the theory of social networks; see also Goyal (2022).

cooperation is usually confined to the purpose for which the organization was created. Repeated interaction remains important in a corporation as well, but to a lesser extent than in the clan. The latter is a more comprehensive social network that governs cooperation and individual behavior in a much wider range of areas. Hence, in a corporation, enforcement of cooperative behavior requires more formal and explicit procedures than in a clan.

These different features entail a trade-off in the individual's choice between the two organizations. The trade-off concerns effectiveness versus cost in the provision of the collective good: the corporation is more effective, but the costs could be lower in the clan. The corporation is likely to be more effective in fulfilling the needs of its members compared to the clan because its activities, by design, are directed toward fulfilling those specific needs for public good provision. Furthermore, because its members can always exit and join another corporation, the organization is incentivized to provide these goods. On the other hand, having more formal and explicit enforcement methods and decision-making procedures raises enforcement costs and agency problems for a corporation relative to the clan.

The formal model in the appendix makes two assumptions about the nature of this trade-off between the two organizations. First, it is affected by the size of each organization. Because of the economies of scale inherent in producing local public goods, the average per-capita cost of providing them is decreasing in the organization's size. Hence, ceteris paribus, a larger organization is more attractive (at least over a certain size range before a point at which diseconomies of scale may kick in). This implies that there is a strategic complementarity in individual decisions of which organization to join. If many individuals interact through their clan, this makes the clan more attractive; conversely, if cooperation mainly occurs through a corporation, more individuals are attracted to the corporation.

Second, as discussed previously, the evaluation of this trade-off also depends on the cultural traits of each individual. For simplicity, suppose that individuals can be of two broad types: communitarian or universalist. Communitarian individuals strongly identify with their kin, to whom they are tied by strong moral obligations, and are relatively reluctant to cooperate with unrelated individuals. Universalists instead subscribe to values of generalized morality and generalized trust and are more open to interacting with strangers, while they have weaker loyalty to their kin compared to communitarian types. Thus, a communitarian culture fits more naturally with the organizational structure of a clan, whereas a universalistic individual is equally at ease in both organizations (or may prefer a corporation because it is less hierarchical and provides an easier exit option).

To capture these differences, the model in the appendix assumes that individuals draw a psychological benefit from joining and contributing to the organization with which they identify and to which they feel they belong. The size of this benefit depends on how the individual culture fits with the features of the organization. Communitarian types only identify with their kin and draw a psychological benefit if they cooperate with them, but not if they cooperate with unrelated individuals. Universalist types, instead, can identify with any organization, regardless of the composition of its members, and draw a benefit from behaving cooperatively and according to the rules of the organization with which they identify, regardless of the organizational type. The psychological benefit received by universalists when cooperating within the organization that they joined, however, is smaller than the benefit enjoyed by the communitarian types who cooperate with their kin. The logic here is that for universalists, belonging to a corporation is primarily transactional, weighing benefits and costs, whereas communitarian types see their extended family as an *identity,* satisfying their need to belong, as well as a source of benefits from cooperation. In other words, kin loyalty is stronger than impersonal moral ties.[5] Hence, for a given size of each organization, the communitarian types are more likely to be attracted to the clan compared to the universalists, while the latter are more likely to be attracted to the corporation.

Greif and Tabellini (2017) study a richer model, where besides choosing which social network to join, individuals also choose a level of effort exerted (or whether to cheat in their contribution to the collective action or tax) within that organization. The difference among individual types can then be interpreted as the internalized psychological cost of cheating the other members of the organization. Communitarian types bear a high cost from cheating their kin, and none from cheating strangers. Universalists bear a smaller cost from cheating, but it is the same cost regardless of the organization that they joined. This richer model yields essentially the same implications as that given in the appendix.

---

5. This is not to deny that a sense of belonging and identity can be associated with corporations, as we observe for instance in sports—yet the high rate of churn indicates that such sentiments are relatively weak compared to family ties in communitarian societies.

Equilibrium Size of Organizations

The complementarities resulting from economies of scale imply that there could be multiple equilibria: if everyone chooses to join the clan, then the clan becomes more attractive for everyone because its costs are lower, and the same applies if everyone joins the corporation. To avoid corner solutions and indeterminacy, we assume that economies of scale are not so strong (relative to the other elements of the trade-off described here) as to drive everyone to the same organization. This assumption, which is formulated more precisely in the appendix, implies that the communitarian types prefer the clan to the corporation even if clan size is minimal, and the universalists prefer the corporation to the clan even if clan size is maximal. With only two types, this assumption implies *full sorting*: in equilibrium, all communitarian types join the clan and all universalists join the corporation. Thus, the relative size of the two organizations coincides with the fraction of each type in the population. A population with more communitarian types has larger clans and smaller corporations, and vice versa if the fraction of universalists is larger. In other words, the mechanism described here and formalized in the appendix implies that the prevailing social organization reflects the prevailing culture.

A couple of remarks about this result are in order. First, the property of full sorting is a simplification due to the presence of only two types of individuals. Suppose instead that individuals also differ in the value that they attach to the collective good. Because the corporation is more effective in providing the public good, those who care more about the public good are more attracted to the corporation regardless of whether they are universalists or communitarians, compared to those who attach less value to the public good. Under this assumption, a shock that raises the value of the public good will lead to a rise in the number of people choosing the corporation if it is more efficient at providing the relevant good. This extension (or other equivalent forms of heterogeneity among individuals) implies that the equilibrium need not exhibit full sorting: depending on how this additional form of heterogeneity is distributed across the population, in equilibrium, communitarian types may be found in both the clan and in the corporation, and/or universalist types may be found in both the corporation and in the clan. Nevertheless, in general, the equilibrium size of each organization still reflects the fraction of communitarian versus universalist types. A larger fraction of communitarian types in the population is still associated with a larger clan size in equilibrium, and vice versa, a larger fraction of universalists implies that in equilibrium, the size of the corporation is also larger—see also Greif and Tabellini (2017) for this extension.

Second, so far we have only considered how individuals self-select in either their clan or a corporation. In the historical circumstances of interest, these alternatives were not necessarily mutually exclusive. Individuals could join a specific corporation while still cooperating with their kinship network in parallel. Moreover, whereas individuals could normally belong only to a single clan, they could join several corporations, each one fulfilling the need for a different local public good. Our analysis abstracts from these possibilities because we have assumed that individuals care only about a single public good and everyone belongs to a single dynasty. If instead there were a need for several public goods, then some of them could be provided by different organizations. Similarly, communitarian individuals belonging to different dynasties would belong to different clans. The basic trade-offs described here would still apply, but other considerations would gain relevance. In particular, the *number* of organizations of a specific type would also matter, besides their relative size. As we discuss in chapter 6, some corporations extended their reach by interacting with other similar organizations through specific agreements and conventions (e.g., the Hanseatic League of European cities). These interactions were another important source of complementarities, besides economies of scale within each organization. This fact strengthens the argument that once an organizational type becomes more diffused across society, it continues to proliferate because it becomes more attractive.

Furthermore, clans competed with other clans and corporations often competed with similar corporations. Such competition was often beneficial, but it differed across organizational types because corporations, unlike clans, could compete with one another to attract members. Moreover, since clans partitioned society in ascriptive and nonoverlapping associations, competition among clans often led to interclan violence and was less benign than competition among corporations. As we discuss in the following chapters, in Europe the same individual often belonged to several overlapping corporations such as fraternities, guilds, and other associations. In this environment, cooperation among unrelated individuals was widespread and competition was less likely to degenerate in conflict. For example, the competition among various universities for faculty and students and among guilds for members was a major element in the improvement of the functioning of these organizations (Henrich 2020, pp. 350–59). Intergroup competition, Henrich maintains, created a society that was more individualistic, nonconformist, creative, and capable of dealing with strangers—provided that it followed clear-cut rules. The same principle holds for religion: following the Reformation in Europe, major religious organizations competed for the souls of Christians, and while for more than a century, this competition consisted of savage and violent armed struggle, over time, it became more benign and did a lot to improve education, as illustrated by Jesuit schools and dissenter academies.[6]

Summary

Why did clans begin to spread throughout China and corporations in Europe around the beginning of the second millennium? These social organizations performed similar functions: they sustained cooperation in the provision of local public goods such as protection, risk-sharing, land clearing and irrigation, religious and cultural services, dispute resolution, trade infrastructures, dissemination of knowledge and traditions, and other actions. In the absence of strong central authority, these local public goods could be provided only through local and spontaneous arrangements among individuals. The more successful social arrangements employed prevailing value systems and cultural traits to facilitate cooperation. As we discuss in chapter 4, China had a tradition of strong kinship ties and loyalty, and this gave an advantage to kin-based organizations. Thanks to the influence of the Church, European value systems grew more universalistic and rule-based, while tight kinship ties were eroded. The decline of extensive kinship groups in the West facilitated cooperation among unrelated individuals within more formal, rule-based organizations. Economies of scale within organizations and complementarities in the interactions among similar organizations then transformed these initial comparative advantages into an ever-greater prevalence of corporations in Europe. In China, society evolved in the opposite direction, with clans growing more and more prevalent, also in reaction to a gradual decline in state capacity after the Song, and with a correspondingly greater demand of public good provision supplied by nonstate organizations.

6. Historians of the Reformation have concluded that the tighter definition of dogma and belief known as "confessionalization," which took place in the century after the Peace of Augsburg of 1555, led to a more dynamic society in which religious and secular authorities cooperated to strengthen state control (Schilling 2008, pp. 18–21). Economists have argued that religious competition led to more efficient local government and a reallocation of resources toward more secular and productive uses (Cantoni, Dittmar, and Yuchtman 2018; Dittmar and Meisenzahl 2020).

3. Dynamics

So far, we have emphasized how initial cultural traits influence the emergence of social organizations. But although culture is persistent, it is not fixed once and for all. As emphasized by a large body of literature on evolutionary dynamics and cultural transmission, the social and economic environment exerts a strong influence over how culture evolves over time (cf. Bisin and Verdier 2022). We now analyze how the prevalence and diffusion of specific social organizations in turn influence cultural evolution. Again, here we provide a general and intuitive discussion, while the appendix illustrates these arguments with a formal model.

Evolutionary Dynamics

How are cultural traits and moral beliefs acquired, and how do they change over time? There is no single, universally valid answer. New generations inherit the value systems and traditions deliberately or inadvertently transmitted by their parents. Adopting their parents' cultural values is the default option for each individual, and yet over a lifetime, people can abandon these inherited traits and adopt different ones.[7] This may happen for a variety of reasons. Successful role models trigger imitations. Interactions among peers induce changes in attitudes and beliefs. Salient events such as the Black Death or a devastating war may change the way that people see their environments.

All these different mechanisms share some basic features. They concern a large population of individuals who interact repeatedly over time and who make choices whose relative payoffs depend on the actions of other possibly unknown individuals. When an individual chooses whether to imitate the social behavior of others or what education and social norms to transmit to their children, their future welfare (or that of the children), depends on how effectively the acquired traits will guide future social interactions with other similar or dissimilar individuals. The choices behind mechanisms of cultural transmission and social learning thus entail complex judgments, where the future consequences of alternative decisions are hard to assess.

Evolutionary game theory has proposed a simple mechanism that captures the central aspects of these complex situations. Average cultural traits in the

---

7. A detailed examination of such biases that drive how and why people may choose beliefs and values that differ from their parents is provided in Mokyr (2016, chapter 5).

population are assumed to evolve over time in the direction of the traits that have proved more successful in previous periods (or, in more sophisticated formulations, that are expected to be more successful in the future). More precisely, cultural traits evolve according to what is called a "revision protocol"; namely, a function describing how the probability that an individual acquires a specific trait depends on the fitness of that trait relative to others in the current (or expected future) environment. Aggregating across a large number of agents, the revision protocol implies that average cultural traits in society evolve in the direction implied by their *relative fitness*. A specific trait is more fit if individuals carrying that trait are better off on average. The analogy with biological evolution is obvious. In the specific instance of cultural transmission, this assumption captures the plausible idea that if a cultural trait is more successful, it is more likely to be imitated by others, parents are more likely to devote effort to transmitting that trait to new generations, or it is more likely to be selected by other mechanisms of social learning.[8]

The Relative Fitness of Clans versus Corporations

Let us now apply this idea to the setting described in the previous section. There are two types of individuals in the population: the communitarian, who is loyal to their kin, and the universalist, who is individualistic and behaves according to norms of impersonal and generalized morality. As described previously, these two types sort themselves into different social organizations. Communitarians join a clan, while universalists join a corporation. Which type is better off?

The answer depends on which organization is more efficient overall. As argued in the previous section, this in turn depends on their relative size and prevalence in society, all other things being equal. Because of economies of scale and the resulting complementarities in the interactions of different organizations, a clan delivers higher utility to its members if it is larger or more

---

8. This mechanism can be given alternative microfoundations in more detailed specific models. See Bisin and Verdier (2001), Tabellini (2008b), and Besley and Persson (2019) for specific examples, and Sandholm (2010) for a more general discussion of evolutionary game theory. Besides vertical transmission from parents to offspring, horizontal transmissions among peers can also play a role. In a world in which most people are communitarian, that by itself would make most people want to conform. Similarly, individuals are driven toward universalism if most people are universalists.

effective at providing local public goods, and the same is true for a corporation. Thus, in general, either organization can be more efficient, depending on its size and/or diffusion across society.

The appendix compares the relative fitness of the two organizations as a function of their size. It shows that, if economies of scale are sufficiently sensitive to the size of the organization, then there is a threshold relative size that makes the two organizations equally fit for their members. At this threshold size, the communitarian types in the clan have the same welfare as the universalist types in the corporation—that is, the two types have the same relative fitness in equilibrium. If clan size exceeds this threshold, the communitarians are better off in equilibrium, and vice versa: if clan size is below this threshold, the universalists have greater relative fitness.

Equilibrium Dynamics

Recall that in equilibrium, clan size is given by the relative fraction of communitarian types in the population. Thus, at any given moment in time, the relative fitness of the two organizations depends on the distribution of types in society. If the population consists of a large fraction of communitarian types (i.e., above the indifference threshold), then the percentage of society committed to clans is large and the one organized by corporations is small (in size and/or numbers of members). This makes the communitarian types better off than the universalists. By the revision protocol described earlier, the communitarian population expands in the next period, while the universalist population shrinks. This makes the communitarian type even more fit compared to the universalist because clan size grows further. Thus, in future periods communitarian types diffuse even more, further increasing their relative fitness. The dynamic process eventually comes to a stop when communitarian types have taken over the whole population and the clan has become the dominant organizational form. The opposite evolution takes place, toward universalist diffusion and dominance of the corporation, if the initial fraction of communitarian types in the population is small (i.e., below the indifference threshold).

Thus, the interaction between the sorting of types across organizations and the revision protocol for cultural evolution generates a phenomenon of self-reinforcing cultural and institutional bifurcation. Even small differences in initial cultural traits of otherwise identical societies can lead to lasting divergences in social organizations, value systems, and institutions. China started around the turn of the millennium with a stronger and more diffuse communitarian culture and evolved along a mutually reinforcing path of developing more intense and pervasive kinship networks and organizations. This in turn contributed to increasing the diffusion of kin-based norms and traditions even further. By contrast, Europe started with universalistic and individualistic values and took the other path of mutually reinforcing open and rules-based organizations and universalistic value systems.

That said, the theoretical result that the dynamic evolution of the system converges to an extreme steady-state with a corner solution in which only one type of organization and only one cultural type prevail is a simplification that need not hold in more general settings. In particular, in the richer model of Greif and Tabellini (2017), there is another dimension of heterogeneity in individual preferences besides the distinction between communitarian and universalist types. In this more general setting, the steady-states are less extreme and cultural bifurcation leads to alternative steady-states where one or the other organizational form and culture prevail, but the minority culture and organizations never disappear.

In such a setting, communitarian organizations could survive in a universalist world like Europe, and conversely, some nonkin-based organizations can be found in Imperial China. Similarly, a more mixed result could be obtained if the economies of scale within the organization apply only over some range of size and membership. Once an organization becomes too large (or too widespread), diseconomies of scale or (benefits from variety) may become relevant. Furthermore, if there are people who are contrarians, then negative frequency dependence would not lead to complete domination. Similarly, minoritarian cultures could survive in equilibrium if parental effort to socialize their offspring depends on the features of the social environment (Bisin and Verdier 2023).

Of course, other exogenous factors (not just relative fitness) could play a role in cultural transmission. As noted, a traumatic or salient event may make enough people change their beliefs such that a new equilibrium becomes possible. In some cases, a highly influential cultural entrepreneur, such as the prophet Muhammad or the philosopher and economist Karl Marx, may act as the coordinating or focusing agent for a new set of values or beliefs (Mokyr 2016, chapter 6). Religious organizations were as important as religious beliefs. As we will see in chapter 4, the growth of universalist types in Europe also reflected the efforts of the medieval Church to actively discourage large, kinship-based social organizations.

Summary

At the heart of the cultural and social bifurcation described in the previous pages lie the following key concepts. First, cooperation within any organization is sustained not just by material and extrinsic incentives, but also by *intrinsic motivations* determined by the values and identities of its members. Such values and beliefs sustain voluntary compliance. They can take the form of ancestor worship in clans or loyalty to organizations in corporations (e.g., the pride of being a citizen of a city). Hence, well-functioning organizations require a good match between organizational features and the cultural and psychological traits of its members. The second concept is that of a *complementarity* that makes an organization more efficient if it is larger (because of economies of scale) or more widespread in society. This complementarity attracts individuals to the larger and more diffuse organizations and increases the relative fitness of the cultural traits that are matched with the prevalent organizational form. The third concept is a mechanism of endogenous *cultural transmission* guided by relative fitness: over time, cultural traits evolve in the direction of those values that are relatively more fit given the prevailing organizational structure in society, creating a positive feedback dynamic. These three concepts jointly explain how and why different initial value systems led to the emergence of different types of social organizations in China and Europe, sending them on divergent paths of cultural, social and institutional development.

4. Discussion

The theory summarized in this chapter highlights the importance of some key differences in the initial cultural conditions of China and Europe in the years around 1000 AD and predicts specific trajectories for their subsequent social and economic development. These predictions raise several questions that will guide the historical analysis of the following chapters. In this concluding section, we outline the road ahead.

Value Systems.

Our starting point is the premise that China and Europe had different value systems at the turn of the first millennium, when the need for developing new social organizations was particularly acute. We document these differences and discuss their historical origin in chapter 4, where we argue that differences in value systems between China and Europe originate partially from religion. Christianity was dominant throughout Europe at the time, and the Western Church engaged in a successful new policy of dismantling extended family networks and weakening kinship ties. In addition, the Germanic tradition of bilineal descent made it more difficult to preserve large lineage organizations. As a result, the dominant value system in the West was increasingly founded on universalistic moral principles and individual responsibility. In China, by contrast, Confucianism became dominant during the late Tang and Song dynasties (and subsequent ones) and prioritized moral obligations toward kin, respect for elders, and patrilineal ancestor worship. We discuss the origins of these initial differences in chapter 4.

Social Organizations

The next step in our argument is to establish that the features of the social organizations that emerged in China and Europe were very different and matched their respective cultures. Chapters 5 and 6 document that kinship-based and corporate structures started to proliferate among the commoners in China and Europe, respectively, in the first few centuries of the second millennium, mostly through a spontaneous bottom-up process and with little or no coordination from the central authorities. Rapid transformations, including intense waves of migration, created new demand for local public goods in both continents. But the social networks that sustained cooperation were very different in these two parts of the world. Chinese kinship organizations relied on implicit enforcement methods; they were hierarchical and multipurpose organizations, restricted to members of the same lineage. European corporate structures instead—at least in theory—were open to all, relied on explicit, legal enforcement rules, had formal and more inclusive decision-making procedures, and were often created for a single purpose. Unlike clans, they were not ascriptive, members had exit options, and they did not partition society among mutually exclusive groups. Overall, they constituted a more competitive system.

Complementarities and Institutional Bifurcation

Complementarities in the diffusion of social organizations and their coevolution with cultural traits were central to the historical dynamic that we seek to explain here. The theory predicts that the initial cultural and social differences between China and Europe became more pronounced over time. This bifurcation occurred in multiple dimensions, and the following chapters attempt to explain this in a coherent framework. As the organizational structure evolved and became more complex, initial differences between the two worlds became more pervasive and extended to new domains. Corporate structures extended their reach through agreements with other organizations, creating a network of arrangements among similar institutions that permeated society. European monasteries, for instance, were parts of larger orders that coordinated their activities.

Moreover, in both China and Europe, the state relied on existing social organizations for law enforcement, conflict resolution, tax collection, and the provision of local public goods. This interaction with the state strengthened and legitimized existing organizational forms and was reflected in the evolution of legal systems and state administration. It also had long-term effects on the gradual emergence of state capacity, which evolved in opposite directions in China and the West. We discuss these bidirectional influences between social organizations and state institutions (legal systems, state administration, and state capacity) in chapter 8.

Bifurcation of Political Institutions

Social organizations also exerted a profound influence on political institutions. In Europe, state institutions were built on top of existing corporate arrangements and inherited several key features of smaller-scale organizations: in particular, forms of representative democracy and attention to checks and balances. In China, by contrast, the hierarchical form of clans, their being nonscalable institutions that had no territorial control, and the weaker prominence of legal systems in Chinese civil society all contributed to the stability of an autocratic regime not bound by the rule of law. We discuss this bifurcation of political institutions in detail in chapter 7.

Economic Divergence and Catch Up

What were the economic implications of all these bifurcations? Our central argument is that they have clear implications for long-term economic development and thus need to be placed at the center of the literature on the Great Divergence. Enke (2019) and others have argued that tight kinship ties do not constitute a major disadvantage in economic development within agricultural and simple commercial societies, although they may be an obstacle once technological progress accelerates. As noted in chapter 2, the lion's share of the economic divergence between Europe and China took place only after the Industrial Revolution. The Industrial Revolution, however, was not unrelated to the organization of society. Productivity shocks produced by the generation and dissemination of useful knowledge are far more likely to occur in a society based on weak kin ties that encourage nonconformism, thinking outside the box, and individualism, yet within a moral framework that induces cooperation with like-minded persons. Moreover, economic development goes hand in hand with greater specialization, and this in turn increases the potential benefits of transacting and interacting with strangers. As Henrich (2020, p. 39) has argued, in societies with loose kinship ties, it is more likely that reverence for ancient wisdom will be eroded and disrespect for the received canon will create a culture of intellectual contestability. In chapter 9, we discuss how the intellectual and social environments created by corporations in Europe were essential to the occurrence of a major wave of radical innovations.

Appendix

The Clan and the Corporation

The Model

Consider a population of size 1. The material utility of each individual is given by

$$u = c + \delta g,$$

where c denotes private consumption, g is the consumption of a good that can be only collectively provided (e.g., protection of private property, dispute resolution, or contract enforcement); and $\delta > 1$ is the marginal utility of the collective good. Good g is excludable, and, in the absence of the state, it can be provided only by a social organization. Thus, to enjoy the benefit of g, each individual has to join an organization and pay the cost charged by the organization. Since we do not model the decisions of organizations, we take the quantity of public good g to be fixed (e.g., a bridge), although its quality is allowed to vary across organizations.

There are two types of social organization, indexed by $z = 0, 1$: the clan $(z = 0)$ and the corporation $(z = 1)$. The individual has to decide which organization to join. There are two differences between these organizations:

- Each organization has an enforcement or functioning cost charged to each member, denoted by e_z, that is a decreasing function of the size of the organization. Thus, there are economies of scale in providing the collective good. It is plausible to think that, for the same size, the corporation is more expensive than the clan $(e_1 > e_0)$ because the clan can exploit ongoing relationships among its members, whereas the corporation's enforcement procedure are more formal, but it turns out that we don't need an explicit assumption to this effect. Alternatively, if the quantity of the public good were variable, economies of scale could also be exploited by providing more public good for the same individual cost; see Greif and Tabellini (2017) for such a formulation.
- The collective goods provided by a corporation are more effectively tailored to the needs of its constituents compared to a clan. The reason is that the corporation is designed for the purpose of delivering that particular collective good, whereas the clan is a multipurpose organization defined by dynastic relations among individuals. Thus, the clan structure need not be suited to all kinds of collective goods. Specifically, we assume that $g = 1$ if it is provided by the corporation, and $g = a < 1$ if it is provided by the clan.

Each individual has an endowment of 1. Thus, if the individual joins the clan, the material utility is $u = 1 - e_0 + \delta a$, while if it joins the corporation, it is $u = 1 - e_1 + \delta$. These material utilities are increasing in the size of each organization since enforcement cost e_z is decreasing in size (more on this next).

Individuals also enjoy a psychological benefit p by joining the organization with which they identify. These psychological benefits can be thought of as a reduction in the cost of complying with the enforcement rules imposed by the organization. There are two types of individuals, who differ in their identities or values:

- The communitarian type, who is loyal to the clan. Communitarian individuals can identify only with their clan. They draw a benefit $p = \lambda > 0$ by contributing to the activities of the clan but get no psychological benefit from contributing to the corporation.

- A universalist type, who can identify with any organization but draws a smaller psychological benefit $p = \gamma < \lambda$ from contributing to the organization (regardless of whether it is the clan or the corporation).

Equilibrium Allocation of Types to Organizations

Let us denote the utility derived from each type of individual when joining either organization as W_z^p, where $p = \lambda, \gamma$ denotes the individual type, and $z = 0, 1$ denotes the organizational type. Given our notation, the overall utility of a communitarian type if it joins the clan $(z = 0)$ or the corporation $(z = 1)$ can be written, respectively, as

$$W_0^\lambda = 1 - e_0 + \delta\alpha + \lambda, \qquad \text{or} \qquad W_1^\lambda = 1 - e_1 + \delta \qquad (3.1)$$

Likewise, the overall utility of a universalist type if it joins the clan or the corporation can be written, respectively, as

$$W_0^\gamma = 1 - e_0 + \delta\alpha + \gamma, \qquad \text{or} \qquad W_1^\gamma = 1 - e_1 + \delta + \gamma \qquad (3.2)$$

Thus, the communitarian types are always more willing to join the clan than the corporation compared to the universalists. The reason is that they identify only with their clan and draw a larger benefit from identification than the universalists do $(\lambda > \gamma)$.

This can be seen by considering the utility difference in the two organizations for each type. Consider the communitarian types. They prefer to join the clan rather than the corporation if

$$W_0^\lambda - W_1^\lambda = e_1 - e_0 + \lambda > \delta(1 - \alpha), \qquad (3.3)$$

and vice versa, they prefer the corporation if the inequality is reversed. Similarly, the universalist type prefers the clan to the corporation if

$$W_0^\gamma - W_1^\gamma = e_1 - e_0 > \delta(1 - \alpha) \qquad (3.4)$$

and vice versa if the inequality is reversed. Clearly equation (3.4) is a more demanding condition than equation (3.3) since $\lambda > 0$

To describe how individuals choose to allocate across organizations, we need some assumptions on the properties of the enforcement technologies. Denote as $x \in [0, 1]$ the relative size of the clan (to be determined in equilibrium). Since population is normalized to 1, the relative size of the corporation is $1-x$. It is natural to assume that the difference in enforcement costs between the corporation and the clan is a strictly decreasing function of the clan size:

$$e_1 - e_0 = F(x),$$

where $F(.)$ is a continuous and strictly *increasing* function. Intuitively, as clan size grows, the size of the corporation shrinks. Economies of scale then imply that the enforcement cost of the corporation relative to that of the clan ($e_1 - e_0$) rises. To easily pin down the equilibrium, we need the following additional assumption:

$$F(0) + \lambda > \delta(1 - a) > F(1). \tag{3.5}$$

By equation (3.3), the first inequality implies that communitarians prefer to join the clan rather than the corporation even if clan size is minimal. By equation (3.4), the second inequality says that universalists prefer to join the corporation even if clan size is maximal. Thus:

Proposition 3.1 *Under equation (3.5), the equilibrium exhibits full sorting: in equilibrium, all the universalists join the corporation and all the communitarians join the clan.*

Hence, we immediately obtain that in equilibrium, the size of the clan coincides with the fraction of the communitarian types in the population, also denoted as x.

Note that equation (3.5) requires $\lambda > F(1) - F(0)$. Stated in words, the enforcement technologies must be not too sensitive to relative size (i.e., economies of scale cannot be too strong), and the psychological benefit λ associated with clan identification must be sufficiently large.

Relative Fitness of the Two Types

Before turning to the dynamic evolution of types in the population, it is useful to ask which type is better off in equilibrium (i.e., which type is more fit to the socioeconomic environment) and how this depends on the fraction x of communitarian types in the population.

Let $\Delta(x)$ denote the difference between the equilibrium utilities of communitarian and universalist types, given the state x of society; that is, $\Delta(x)$ is the relative fitness of communitarian rather than universalist types.

Proposition 3.1 implies that in equilibrium, there is full sorting, with the communitarian types in the clan and the universalists in the corporation. Hence by equations (3.1) and (3.2):

$$\Delta(x) = W_0^\lambda - W_1^\gamma = F(x) + \lambda - \gamma - \delta(1-\alpha). \tag{3.5}$$

This expression can be either positive or negative, depending on the difference in enforcement costs $F(x)$ between the two organizations, the psychological benefits of joining either organization, and the relative efficiency of the two organizations in providing the required collective goods. In what follows, we assume

$$F(1) > \delta(1-a) - (\lambda-\gamma) > F(0). \tag{3.6}$$

This condition says that enforcement costs are sufficiently sensitive to size (i.e., economies of scale in the organizations are sufficiently important) relative to the remaining parameters.

Condition (3.6), together with equation (3.5), implies

$$\Delta(1) > 0 > \Delta(0). \tag{3.7}$$

Namely, if the equilibrium size of the clan is maximal, then in equilibrium, the communitarian types are better off than the universalists because they can fully reap the benefits of the economies of scale in their preferred organization. Conversely, if the equilibrium clan size is minimal, then in equilibrium, the universalists are better off for the same reason. By continuity and monotonicity of $F(.)$, the inequalities in equation (3.7) imply the following:

Proposition 3.2 *There is a value $\bar{x} \in (0,1)$ such that $\Delta(\bar{x}) = 0$. If $x > \bar{x}$, then $\Delta(x) > 0$, and if $x < \bar{x}$, then $\Delta(x) < 0$.*

Stated in words, the relative fitness of the two types depends on the fraction of communitarian types in the population. If the communitarians are sufficiently large, then in equilibrium, they are better off than the universalists because their preferred organization (the clan) can reap the benefits of the economies of scale. Conversely, if the fraction of communitarian types is small, then the universalists are better off because the corporation can be scaled up to an efficient size.

Finally, note that conditions (3.5) and (3.6) can be combined into a single condition; namely,

$$\delta(1-a) > F(1) > \delta(1-a) - (\lambda-\gamma) > F(0) > \delta(1-a)-\lambda \qquad (3.8)$$

The inequalities at the extremes are needed to ensure full sorting (proposition 3.1). The inner inequalities are needed to ensure that both organizational forms are feasible in equilibrium; namely, there is a value $\bar{x} \in (0,1)$ such that $\Delta(\bar{x})=0$ (proposition 3.2).

Dynamics

We now discuss how the fraction of types evolves over time depending on the organizational structure of society. We assume a very general form for the evolution of preferences, based on models of evolutionary dynamics. Specifically, let t subscripts denote periods. We assume that the fraction of communitarian types in the population evolves over time according to

$$x_{t+1} = x_t + q(x_t)(1 - q(x_t))Q(\Delta(x_t)), \qquad (3.9)$$

where $q(x_t) \in [0,1]$ is an arbitrary increasing function with $q(1)=1$ and $q(0)=0$, $Q(.)$ is an arbitrary continuous and strictly increasing function with $Q(0)=0$, and $\Delta(x_t)$ is the difference in equilibrium utility between communitarian and universalist types, given the state x_t of society, as defined in equation (3.5). Equation (3.9) is a general form of replicator dynamics widely used in evolutionary theory; see Sandholm (2010). It can be given explicit microfoundations, as in Tabellini (2008b) or Besley and Persson (2019). Equation (3.9) says that the fraction of communitarian types in the population increases over time if these individual types are more fit in the given environment than the other types (if $\Delta(x_t) > 0$), and they decrease if instead relative fitness favors the universalists.

It is easy to prove the following:

Proposition 3.3 *Suppose that equation (3.8) holds. Then there are three steady-states:* $x_s = 0$, $x_s = 1$, *and* $x_s = \bar{x}$. *The steady-state xs = 0 is stable, and it is reached if the initial condition xo satisfies* $x_0 < \bar{x}$ *The steady-state* $x_s = 1$ *is stable, and it is reached if the initial condition* x_0 *satisfies* $x_0 > \bar{x}$. *The third state,* $x_s = \bar{x}$, *is unstable.*

Thus, if initially there are enough communitarian types $\left(x_0 > \overline{x}\right)$, the clan size is large and clans are efficient organizational forms. This makes communitarian preferences relatively more fit, and eventually communitarian culture prevails throughout the society. If instead communitarian types are initially few, then corporations can better exploit economies of scale, and universalists are relatively more fit, which induces the diffusion of these types in society.

Note that the simple form of equation (3.8) implies that the stable steady-states are always at the extremes: either the entire population is communitarian and joins the clan $\left(x_s = 1\right)$ or it is universalistic and joins the corporation $\left(x_s = 0\right)$. This feature of the steady-state is not a general result. Alternative microfoundations to equation (3.8) generally allow multiple but interior steady-states, and hence for the survival of minoritarian cultural traits and organizational forms. This is true, for instance, in the richer model of Greif and Tabellini (2017), which combines both vertical and horizontal cultural transmissions (i.e., the cultural traits of new generations reflect both the culture of their parents and that of the social environment in which they grew up). Similarly, Bisin and Verdier (2001) show that steady-states are always interior (and hence they allow a plurality of cultural traits) if vertical and horizontal cultural transmissions are substitutes; namely, parents have a stronger incentive to transmit their own traits to their offspring if these traits are minoritarian in the population. Hence, the general result of proposition 3.3 is that there is hysteresis (different steady-states are reached from different initial conditions), not that these steady-states are always at the boundary of the distribution of types in the population. Bisin and Verdier (2023) provide a more general discussion of this point.

4

The Social and Cultural
Origins of the Great Bifurcation

1. Introduction

In previous chapters, we have argued that China and Europe evolved along different trajectories because they started from different initial cultural conditions: strong kinship ties in China versus universalistic values and individualism in Europe. Although many of these cultural differences date back to antiquity, the social bifurcation between Europe and China accelerated around the turn of the millennium. In this chapter, we discuss how these cultural backgrounds were intimately related to the different family structures that prevailed in these two parts of the world toward the end of the first millennium, and in particular to the decline of the extended family in Europe and its strengthening in China.

Our arguments are consistent with a growing body of literature written by historians and social scientists that emphasizes how kinship relations and marriage customs determine a host of psychological and behavioral outcomes (Todd 1987; Mitterauer 2010; Enke 2019; Henrich 2020; Schulz 2022). In particular, Henrich (2020) and Schulz et al. (2019) show that on average, Westerners have a more universalistic value system than other modern societies. They are more individualistic, independent, analytically minded, and impersonally prosocial (e.g., trusting of strangers and less inclined to cheat nonkin), while exhibiting less conformity, blind obedience, in-group loyalty, and inclinations toward nepotism than non-Westerners. The explanation that these scholars put forward for these cultural differences is similar to ours: it is based on the relative importance of extended kinship and kin-based social organizations. Schulz et al. (2019, p. 1) point out that in a society in which cooperation is mostly among kinsfolk, "people's psychological processes adapt to the collectivistic demands and the dense social networks in which they are enmeshed." In this way, these cultures create incentives for the emergence of conformity, loyalty to kin, and deference to elders. Ancestor worship, too, is more common in kinship-based societies.

As pointed out by Henrich (2020), European family relations are peculiar: throughout time and space, strong family ties and extended families were the norm world-wide rather than the exception. This was not true in Western Europe, however, where extended family ties instead became much weaker a long time ago, leading to the emergence of a particular marriage and family pattern centered around the nuclear family. What led to the decline of extended kinship relations in the West? We are not the first to pose this question. In his *General Economic History,* Weber (1927, p. 46) suggested that one of the factors that led to the disappearance of clans was the rise of political bureaucracies; he felt that "the Royal power feared the clan and encouraged the development of a bureaucracy," whereas in China, Weber thought that the rulers had failed to break the clans. Yet the reverse may have been closer to the truth.

An influential view proposed earlier (pp. 66–67) is that the Catholic Church was at the core of the turnaround in European family structures. Family traditions in Germanic Europe differed from those in China, even before the influence of the Church began to be felt: whereas China traced descent strictly based off of patrilineal ties, Germanic tribes allowed for maternal influence in the formation of extended families. This discouraged the formation of large lineage structures (Roland 2020a). Nevertheless, as emphasized by Goody (1983), and more recently by Schulz et al. (2019), Henrich (2020), and Schulz (2022), the Church's influence was the main factor that erased clans and extended families as the basic building-block of Western social organizations. By undermining extensive kinship networks, the Church unintentionally created a society that differed from the rest of the world. As Henrich (2020, p. 113) puts it, the "accidental genius" of the medieval Church was that it gradually dismantled kin-based institutions, and thus slowly but inexorably dissolved the tribal nature of Europe, replacing it with organizations of unrelated people. Such "loose kinship" organizations, as Enke (2019) calls them, lay at the heart of the game-changing evolution of European institutions that produced a different way of enforcing cooperation. This in turn affected social interactions in all domains, from economics, to politics, to science and innovation. It was a truly momentous example of history-changing unintended consequences.

But the Church's influence went beyond the severing of extensive family ties. The Church itself can be seen as a corporation, or at least it had many of the features of corporations. Its internal organization (which in turn was inspired by contemporaneous monastic orders) influenced the evolution and design of secular associations. The Church exerted a strong influence on other European organizations, both directly, by providing an example of how corporate structures could be designed, and indirectly, by favoring the emergence of other corporations such as self-governing cities, which could provide countervailing power to the emperor. In a precise sense, the Catholic Church was really the "mother of all European corporations." As we further discuss in chapters 7 and 8, in this way the Church also influenced the evolution of European political institutions and legal systems.

In the next section, we briefly review the evolution of family structures in Europe and China. We then discuss the role of the Church in bringing about the transformation of family ties in Europe, as well as its role as a concrete example of corporate arrangements. Next, we turn to China, discussing the origins of its cultural background of strong kinship ties. We close the chapter with a discussion of the importance of ancestor worship in Chinese culture and its implications for social organizations.

2. The European Nuclear Family and the Chinese Joint Family

For most of human history, extended kinship groups such as clans and tribes have been central to the social organization of cooperation. How human cooperation might be sustained beyond immediate kin remains one of the main questions in social science and "the fundamental problem of human existence" (Enke 2019, p. 954). People needed to cooperate in the provision of local public goods and social services such as protection, mutual insurance, agricultural work, dispute resolution, religious services, education, and poverty relief. Of course, the nuclear family and the joint (extended, communal) family or the household (which included nonrelative permanent residents such as servants) were often the primary units of cooperation. But these entities are generally too small to provide such public goods effectively. The natural affinity among kin renders the larger kin group a natural unit to provide local public goods and social services. According to anthropologists, kin-based institutions have long been the fundamental building block for organizing social life and have proved "remarkably resilient" throughout much of the world, the West being the most notable exception (Henrich 2020, p. 159). These institutions affect most social relationships by providing constraints, obligations, and privileges that regulate within-community interactions (Schulz 2022).

In many contemporary societies, large kin groups remain central to the social organization of cooperation. For people living in modern Western societies, in which public and club goods are provided by governments or corporations, the historical importance of large kinship groups may not be obvious. But kinship groups were historically central to the social organization of cooperation in both ancient China and Europe. As previously noted, clans prevailed among aristocratic families in pre-Song China (Lang 1946, p. 15), and to some extent they could also be observed among commoners. Similarly, in pre-Roman Europe, Celtic tribes were central to the social organization of cooperation, and in post-Roman Germanic society, tribes and clans were basic building blocks of local communities. Germanic clans were different from those in China, however, especially since they accounted for bilineal descent. Needless to add, in both China and Europe, nuclear families were important, but they mainly existed within the frameworks provided by extended kin groups.

Around the start of the second millennium AD, however, the two worlds began to bifurcate. In China, the joint family remained an ideal, but the clan—a patrilineal, interfamily alliance that traced its origins to a common ancestor—became an increasingly important element in facilitating cooperation.[1] A clan's constituting families—be they joint, stem, or nuclear—remained the basic units of procreation, consumption, and production. The Chinese clan, however, increasingly became the main social unit through which interfamily cooperation was organized.[2] Meanwhile, medieval Europe evolved in the opposite direction. The Celtic and Germanic clans and tribes

1. Watson (1985 [2011], p. 35) describes how the Teng clan in southeast China was formed—namely, via the fusion of smaller units by building an ancestral hall and endowing it with land. She notes that this happened as a response to political and economic environments but fails to recognize the centrality of the club goods that the clan provided to its members.

2. The insight that the clan should be seen as a community or a social organization was driven home by the highly influential work of the anthropologist Maurice Freedman (1958, 1966), who pointed to the common ancestor as the key to membership in a social organization that has clearly defined objectives, fosters the ability to own common property, and provides services to its members. See also Faure (2007).

lost their roles as important units of social organization.[3] Corporations of unrelated individuals became central to the way that members of different families interacted.

The central feature of the peculiar European evolution is the prevalence of the nuclear family and the decline of joint and stem families. John Hajnal (1965, 1982), Peter Laslett (1977), and Jack Goody (1983), among others, have called attention to the growing prevalence of nuclear families in northwestern Europe prior to the Industrial Revolution. Specifically, Hajnal (1982) pointed out that in seventeenth-century Europe, a peculiar marriage pattern had become prevalent: men and women married relatively late (above twenty-six and twenty-three years of age, respectively), worked outside their parental households prior to marriage, and established a new household once married. Celibacy was relatively common. New households usually took the form of a nuclear family. MacFarlane (1978) documents that in England, the nuclear family already was the dominant arrangement by the thirteenth century. Using historical records in St. Germain de Prés, Herlihy (1985) estimates that in the early ninth century, average and median household size were about six persons; these patterns are deemed to be quite uniform throughout most of Europe.

The European Marriage Pattern (EMP) consisted of three basic elements: relatively late marriage, nuclear families, and neolocality. Yet, as we shall see, it involved some other rather radical changes in the institutions of marriage and procreation: increasingly strict prohibitions of consanguineous marriage, polygamy, divorce, adoption, levirate and sororate marriage, and infanticide. In addition, it supported the growing custom of requiring bridal consent before concluding and formalizing marital unions. Larry Siedentop (2014, p. 116) argued that Christianity was one of the sources of the relatively better treatment of women in Europe, who were no longer "mere chattels . . . completely subject to the authority of the paterfamilias." Although others have argued that improvement in female welfare was driven by economic factors, either way, the bond of marriage became more symmetric and priests helped augment women's bargaining power. European customs in this sphere were thus very different from the ones associated with Asia and the Middle East. In Imperial

---

3. More specifically, they lost any important role they might have had in providing local public goods. See Murray (1946), who gives an interesting critical evaluation of the common assertion regarding the importance of tribes in the German society. Similarly, see Lang (1946) for doubts regarding the prevalence of the joint family in China.

China, men and women married early and women rarely worked outside their parents' household prior to marriage. After marriage, a woman typically joined her husband's parental household. Clearly, there were variations in both regions, but these general patterns distinguished Europe from China.[4]

Did the EMP directly contribute to the Great Divergence in income per capita through its effects on demographics? We saw in chapter 2 that the answer to this question remains unsettled. The EMP's indirect effects on institutional evolution and individual behavior, however, seem more important in the long run. Joseph Henrich (2020) and Schulz et al. (2019, p. 1) have argued that the rise of the nuclear family caused important changes in the psychological makeup of the European population. Schulz et al. (2019, p. 1) summarize the position of this school as follows: "Small, nuclear households, weak family ties, and residential mobility fostered greater individualism, less conformity, and more impersonal pro-sociality." As we saw in chapter 3, these cultural traits facilitated the emergence of corporate arrangements that were unique to Europe and strongly affected its economic and political development. Schulz (2022, pp. 2594–600) further shows that the decline of extended kinship in Europe was strongly associated with participatory institutions such as urban communes (a prime example of European corporations).[5] Moreover, he shows that proxies for the weakness of kinship ties correlate positively with what he calls "civicness" in modern times—basically, unselfish acts in the public interest that are evidence of overcoming free-riding in collective action problems, such as voter turnout in elections. We extensively discuss these feedback and causal effects between cultural traits, social organizations, and political institutions in chapter 7.

Along similar lines, Hajnal (1982) conjectured that the nuclear family and public (governmental or private) poverty relief were institutional complements because with the weakening of extended families as a source of mutual insurance and relief came a demand for substitutes to provide these services. Because the nuclear family was too small to effectively insure its members,

---

4. For additional evidence regarding Europe, for example, see Laslett (1969, 1977). Wrigley et al. (1997), Razi (1993), Herlihy (1985), Gottlieb (1993), and Goody (1982). Regarding China, see, for example, Lang (1946). Watson (1982), and Huang (1985).

5. Schulz (2022) also shows that the emergence of communes is strongly correlated with two proxy variables measuring the weakness of extended families in Europe: the length of exposure to the Western Church and to the extended prohibition of marriage to members of the extended family in the eleventh century.

some form of public poverty relief and insurance was necessary to maintain social order. The connection between public insurance and the prevalence of nuclear families can be seen in the historical record. It is no coincidence that England, which had led Europe and the rest of the world in the race toward industrialization, had also created the most generous and reliable public poverty relief system in the centuries before the Industrial Revolution (Greif and Iyigun 2013; Greif, Iyigun, and Sasson 2012).[6] Through its impact on the emergence of public and impersonal poverty relief, the EMP also may have indirectly stimulated the emergence of an industrial labor force, which in turn was a precondition of a capitalist mode of production (e.g., Solar 1995; Smith 2008; Greif and Iyigun 2013). We return to the issue of poor relief in chapter 6.

3. The Catholic Church: The Mother of the European Corporations

The Church and the European Marriage Pattern

The Catholic Church was a major factor in the restructuring of the European family through the EMP. In his recent summary of the role of Christianity in Western history, German historian Heinz Schilling (2022) summarized what it meant to be a Christian in medieval Europe. Among the many important characteristics that Schilling described, the most pertinent to our argument is Christians' firm belief in the soul as the indestructible and inalienable seat of human equality, including—at least de jure—that of man and woman. Traditional societies organized around clans contradicted this belief, argues Schilling.

We know very little about the marriage customs of peasants. The information that we do have about marriage during this period comes mostly from members of the aristocracy. There was certainly resistance to the Church's policies, and enforcement could not have been perfect among peasants even when the Church was at its strongest, since many of the rules, such as the prohibition of divorce and the requirement of bridal consent, must have contradicted accepted practices. Nevertheless, given the pervasive influence of the

---

6. Dennison and Ogilvie's (2014) dismissal of the importance of the EMP does not take into account such complementarities. During the Reformation, the wealth of the Catholic monasteries was expropriated. England thus lost its main source of nongovernmental poor relief. The crown's response was to pass the Old Poor Law of 1603.

religion on people's lives, it seems plausible that the Church's policies and principles affected broader swaths of the population.

Basically, Church policies were based on three principles, none of which ironically were drawn from the Scriptures. They were that marriage was permanent and indissoluble, that valid marriage required consent by both parties, and that matrimony was permissible only between nonconsanguineous couples, even if the degree of consanguinity was often disputed (Morris 1989, pp. 329–32). In the long run, these principles played a major role in the emergence of the EMP.

The medieval Church, from the Merovingian and Carolingian times onward, strongly discouraged marriage between cousins and other relatives. The Church Synods (congresses of high Church officials) increasingly sharpened and widened the prohibition of cousin marriages; this prevented extended families from retaining their strength and serves as a good indicator of Church policy weakening tight kin-based groups.[7] The Church also actively discouraged other practices that enlarged and strengthened the family, such as concubinage, divorce, remarriage, and legal adoption. As a result, many lineages disappeared due to a lack of legitimate heirs (Schulz et al. 2019, p. 2). While adultery by the mighty and rich could not be prevented, of course, the offspring of those relations were not regarded as legitimate and not admitted as bona fide members of their kin. In this way, the Church was able to effectively implement a strategy that prevented the perpetuation of clans and other forms of extensive kinship-based organizations.

The Church also curtailed parents' abilities to retain kinship ties through arranged marriages by prohibiting unions that the bride didn't explicitly consent to. The Church demanded that the bride consent to her marriage in a public ceremony administered by a religious official.[8] This empowered women and undermined parental control over marriages, which were the key to constructing and maintaining large kin groups. The importance of women in the construction of interfamily alliances is well documented in European

7. In the Synod of Douci (874), third-cousin marriage was prohibited, whereas a century and a half later, the Synods of Diedenhofen (1003) and of Seligenstadt (1023) went as far as prohibiting marriage of cousins of the sixth degree.

8. See also Mitterauer and Sieder (1982), Ekelund et al. (1996), Schulz (2018), Schulz et al. (2019), Henrich (2019), De Moor and Van Zanden (2010), Korotayev (2003), and Greif and Tabellini (2010, 2017).

history.[9] The need for a bride's consent to her marriage to render it valid was a main factor leading to the North European peculiar marriage pattern, although the effectiveness of bridal consent was clearly endogenous to other factors that determined the bargaining power of women. Comparing the marriage practices in China and Europe reveals that they differed in their attitudes toward women, particularly regarding marriage. One main relevant distinction is that in China, a bride had no say in her own marriage and bridal consent was immaterial. A bride's guardian, usually her father, had to consent to her marriage and sign the marriage contract. The cultural implications of the prevalence of so-called girl power in Europe are significant. Research on modern data has established a strong case for a positive association between gender equality and individualism (Davis and Williamson 2019), which is consistent with the cultural changes that occurred in Europe as a result of the emergence of the EMP.

The relatively stronger status of women in European societies probably not only reflects these Church policies, but also earlier customs. In particular, Europe was unique in that ancestry accounted for both maternal and paternal descent. This custom originates in Germanic traditions, although, as noted by Goody (1983, pp. 44–46), the Christian marriage doctrine also emphatically rejected group values characteristic of unilineal descent. As pointed out by Roland (2020a), bilineal (or "bilateral") descent may have discouraged the clan as the core form of social organization. With bilineal descent, membership in a particular clan becomes ambiguous because as one traces ancestry back further and further, the number of people to keep track of grows exponentially. In a bilineal world, people were more likely to be organized by nuclear families, with less extensive ties to distant family members. By contrast, unilineal kinship systems, including the patrilineal system of equal division among male heirs in China, were more likely to be associated with strong clans. Indeed, Roland (2024) notes that societies with bilineal kinship (such as Europe) tended to be more market-oriented and less dominated by

9. In twelfth-century Genoa, for example, the outcomes of civil wars depended on interfamily alliances created through marriages (e.g., Annali 1190, vol. 2, 1164, 1170, 1189). In 1239, the *Annali* reports that "many marriages or espousals had been secretly contracted in the city of Genoa between such persons who were believed to be in disagreement and were accustomed to hatred more than love" (Epstein 1985, p. 95). Rather than rejoicing, the annalist spoke soberly about these events, reporting that they caused "wonder and fear in the greater part of the good men of the city" (vol. 4, p. 153). See the discussion of such "political marriages" in Hughes (1978, pp. 127–28).

autocratic statist systems than societies that adhered to unilineal (i.e., mostly patriarchal) kinship. This is because in unilineal systems, economic activities such as exchange and education were carried out within the clan or tribe, whereas in bilineal systems, economic activities took place in the market. This kind of difference, Roland argues, is strongly correlated with the bifurcation of societies into collectivist as opposed to individualist societies.

All the same, bilineal descent in and of itself does not uniquely predict the corporative mode of social organization. In the Middle East, for instance, bilineal descent and tribes are both common. We could also point to the ritual obligations to in-laws (i.e., the wife's parents) that prevailed in patrilineal China (Lang 1946). Watson (1985 [2011], p. 17) stresses the importance of patrilineal principles in China, and their relevance to explain ancestor worship, household organization, and other rituals, although she rightly warns that these principles did not necessarily imply the presence of a lineal descent group and many Chinese were not really part of the clan system.

To be sure, the two worlds were similar in some ways. Chinese custom and law also forbade marriage among close relatives, discouraged divorce, and frowned upon remarriage by widows. The Confucian dogma prohibited consanguineous marriage and encouraged women to make vows of chastity after widowhood (Lang 1946). Furthermore, polygamy was not prohibited in principle in China, but it was an expensive luxury, and only the wealthy could afford more than one wife. Nevertheless, no religious official administered the marriage ceremony; rather, the fathers of the groom and bride administered it (Lang 1946). In other words, marriage did not require certification by a third party such as the church or the state, as was the case in Europe. Moreover, Confucianism indirectly encouraged early marriage through its deep commitment to ancestor worship, and a main duty of the family was to worship its paternal ancestors.

Christian Doctrine and European Values

In addition to its impact on family structures, the Catholic Church disseminated the universalistic cultural beliefs that accompanied Europe's transformation into a society centered around corporations. These beliefs viewed humans as sharing fundamental qualities, such as being created in the image of God and possessing an immortal soul. The notion of sin committed against fellow humans played a significant role as well. These concepts were self-enforcing and eventually evolved into a generalized morality, in which people felt moral obligations to other humans regardless of social distance or differences.

The early Catholic Church also encouraged individualism, another key cultural element that complemented the rise of the corporation.[10] As already noted, the Church's marriage rules empowered individuals to make choices regarding whom to marry (if at all), removing this decision from the influence of greater society. Moreover, a basic tenet of the New Testament is that all humans share original sin, but redemption is personal and depends on individual choices.[11] Some biblical stories also forcefully illustrate the importance of individual decision-making: in particular, the choice to join the community of believers should take precedence over loyalty to parents and kin. The early Church arguably encouraged individualism because it sought to attract believers despite the possible objections of their pagan or Jewish family members. Centuries later, the Reformation built on and amplified Christian individualism by encouraging Christians to read the holy books on their own and interpret God's plan themselves. To be sure, individualism in the West had more influences than solely religious ones, and it clearly exhibited deep roots in the Greek and Jewish civilizations.[12] The role of the Church in enforcing and amplifying individualism, however, should not be underestimated.

Yet there is more to the claim that the value system promoted by the Catholic Church was congenial to the emergence of corporate associations. The Church also directly promoted corporatism, with itself at the center. The early Church advanced a dogma that an individual's loyalty should be to the congregation and transcend kin loyalty. This can be seen in many religious beliefs, such as the Christian congregation's priority in caring for fellow members in need and providing impersonal poverty relief.[13] In China, by contrast, poverty

---

10. The connection between Christianity and the rise of European individualism is the central argument made by Larry Siedentop (2014). In his view, the fundamental concern with the salvation of the soul of each person fostered an individualist attitude and explains the higher incidence of values associated with it, which he terms "western liberalism."

11. The New Testament promoted individualism in particular by emphasizing saving one's soul. Individualism is reflected in the need of Jesus's earlier followers to make different choices than their relatives did. For instance, the apostles Matthew and Mark (among others) tell how Jesus met two of his disciples, the brothers James and John. They were in a boat with their father, Zebedee, preparing their nets. Jesus called them, and they left their father without consulting him and followed Jesus (Matthew 4:21–22, Mark 1:19, 3:17).

12. In a wide-ranging survey, Roland (2020b) stresses the important geographical and agricultural origins of individualism.

13. "Since the time of Gregory 'the Great' (590–604), it was the custom that parish income was to be divided four ways: to the bishop, to the poor, for the upkeep of the church and for the support of the priest" (Volz 1997, p. 148).

relief was the first responsibility of the clan trust when it emerged during the Song period, as discussed later in this chapter. Moreover, clan trusts, as rich as they were, could not cover all Chinese. Many uncovered families organized themselves in secret societies that provided their members with impersonal poverty relief (Chesneaux 1973). Nevertheless, as clans expanded and their number increased, these secret societies remained marginal.

The Church as a Corporation

The Church did more than just spread values and cultural traits that were congenial to associations among unrelated individuals. The Catholic Church was also the mother of all European corporations, in that it was originally *itself* a corporation until the late Middle Ages.[14] First and foremost, the Church was a voluntary association of like-minded and (in theory at least) equal people. Prior to the Edict of Milan in 313, Christianity was still an illegal, monotheistic religion in the officially pagan Roman Empire. The early Christian congregations were local and rather isolated from each other (Ascough 1997).[15] Persecution of Christians was common, and congregations were in no position to force individuals to become members. Moreover, even the Christian doctrinal unity was in dispute, as various Christian groups held distinct beliefs about scriptural issues.[16]

The early Catholic Church confronted the challenges that it faced during this time by organizing itself in a form that we now recognize as a corporation. It was an interest-based, self-governing association of individuals not affiliated by kinship, with perpetual life. As Tierney (1982, pp. 19–20) points out, in legal

14. As discussed in chapter 5, the corporation in Europe was used during the Roman period, but the Roman corporation differed from the later, European corporations. The emperor had to authorize each new corporation, and corporations were to serve the interests of the empire. The Roman corporation was not widely used and was not a means for the social organization of cooperation.

15. In 313, Constantine I issued the Edict of Milan, which gave Christianity legal status and protection from persecution. The Edict of Thessalonica of 380 made Christianity the state church of the Roman Empire.

16. This was true during the first three centuries of Church existence, when as many as seven schisms can be counted (Kelly 1977). The struggle to define European Christianity continued and even increased in the final days of the Roman Empire (Rubenstein 1999). The struggle raged again following 1517, with the Reformation. Only during the late medieval period (1055–1515) did the Church face relatively little doctrinal competition.

terms, a corporation (*universitas*) is a group possessing a juridical personality separate from that of its members. Consistent with this definition, the Church had an infinite horizon and remained the same legal entity even when the identities of its members changed. By the thirteenth century, canonists described it as a "fictitious person."

The description of the Church as a corporate body, similar in many ways to other corporate arrangements that already permeated European society, was easily transferred to secular institutions. Fifteenth-century political thinkers pointed out that a "commonwealth" could be considered akin to a corporation, and an assembly representing the single personality of the commonwealth must be as well (Tierney 1982, p. 21). Moreover, as we discuss in chapter 7, the Church developed practices of corporate self-government, representation, and consent that influenced emerging state institutions (see also Møller and Doucette 2022, p. 13). As pointed out by Gryzmala-Busse (2022), and as we further discuss in chapters 7 and 8, the Church was the first complex European organization to develop an effective, centralized administration during the Middle Ages. Its administrative structures reflected ongoing practices in other medieval corporate organizations, and then they were emulated and adapted by the emerging European states. Moreover, the administrative challenges addressed by ecclesiastic experts gave a critical impulse to the evolution of European legal systems.

The Catholic Church developed an Episcopal (from the Greek word *episkopos*, meaning "overseer") regional structure, headed by the five equal patriarchs of Constantinople, Antioch, Alexandria, Rome, and Jerusalem. The leaders of the main congregations were bishops, whose authority was derived from their election by members of their congregations (Volz 1997, p. 146).[17] By the late eleventh century, the Church had become much more hierarchical and bishops were appointed by the Church; but even then, their approval from their people still mattered.[18] Popes had to be elected as well. During the early Middle Ages, they were chosen by the clergy and the nobility of Rome, with

17. In the twelfth century, the cathedral canons (the cathedral priests) began to play a "decisive role in the selection of new bishops" (Volz 1997, p. 145).

18. "In theory the concentration of a bishop took place following his confirmation by the archbishop . . . [nevertheless, t]he Decretum of Buchard of Worms (c.1012) stated that bishops should be 'elected by the clergy, asked for by the people, and consecrated by the metropolitan (archbishop).' It was only later in the 14th century and beyond that popes claimed the right to intervene in episcopal election, and only since the 16th century that such claims have been practiced" (Volz 1997, p. 146).

the agreement of the cardinals and the assent of the emperor. In 1059, Nicolas II sought to remove secular influence from elections via a decree that cardinals alone should elect the pope (Volz 1997, p. 148). In 1179, this decree was revised to approve an election with the consent of two-thirds of all cardinals.

Various other practices of the early Church reveal its corporate structure, including equality among all members in the eyes of God. Consider, for example, the physical setting of early places of worship. Until the ninth century, the priest conducted ceremonies from an altar in the center of the church. Over time, the rituals changed and became increasingly hierarchical, with a sharp division between priest and audience. By 1200, the church altar had moved to the end of the prayer hall, allowing the priest to conduct the ceremony with his back to the congregation, which had acquired a passive role and did not participate in the chants (Volz 1997, p. 152). This evolution is informative: in the early centuries of the Catholic Church, a Catholic priest was a leader of the congregation of which he was one member among equals.[19] By the twelfth century and beyond, this feature of the Church had slowly disappeared.

Over time, some of the corporate features of the Church underwent modification. For one, as the Church established absolute dominance over areas under papal control, the voluntary nature of participation became more theoretical than real. People were born and baptized in the Church, and before the Reformation, there was no realistic exit option for members. Dissenters were persecuted mercilessly as heretics. Similarly, the egalitarian nature of the Church was irretrievably lost: the Church developed a rigid hierarchical structure, with the pope at the top and the lowly parish priests at the bottom. Moreover, the sharp distinction between ordained priests and laypersons became a hallmark of the Catholic Church (and one of the driving motives behind the Reformation). The practices of absolution as they evolved over the Middle Ages were formalized by the 1439 decree "Pro Armenis" by Pope Eugenius IV at the Council of Florence.

Eventually, then, the corporate nature of the early Catholic Church eroded. By 1200, when the Church was at the peak of its power, the priest differed from the other members of his congregation by acting as the designated intermediator between God and the congregation as a whole. The Reformation can be seen as aiming to return the Church to its corporate roots, and English Puritans

---

19. "But you are not to be called 'Rabbi,' for you have only one Master and you are all brothers. And do not call anyone on earth 'father,' for you have one Father, and he is in heaven" (Matthew 23:8–9).

(among other Protestants) insisted on the cooperative arrangement as the ideal.[20]

Finally, as we further discuss in chapter 7, internal and external developments prompted the Church to create and support corporations inside and outside its ranks. Beyond monasteries, which were an integral part of the religious structure, the Church supported the emergence of another paradigmatic corporation in Europe: the self-governing town. Before c.1400, Italian bishops were often the guarantor of the *patta iurata* (the sworn pact), which formed the legal basis of the northern Italian autonomous cities. Møller and Doucette (2022) document in detail how the Church supported the rise of urban centers, and they claim that for a century after the eruption of the investiture struggle between the papacy and the emperor, urban self-government was limited to towns ruled by bishops (pp. 18, 58–61).[21] Guiso, Sapienza, and Zingales (2016) document that towns that were a bishop seat by the year 1000 were more likely to become a free city-state in the following centuries. To be sure, cities rebelled at times against their bishops, but the Church favored and supported communes, an emblematic example of the kind of corporations that emerged in Europe in the Middle Ages.

4. Cultural and Political Factors in the Rise of the Clan in China

At roughly the same time that much of Europe abandoned extended kinship as the main unit of social organization, China turned in the opposite direction. What were the cultural and political factors that contributed to the emergence of the clan as a central unit of society in China? We showed in chapter 3 that a cultural heritage favoring interactions with and loyalty to relatives facilitates the emergence of clans. As is well known, Confucianism, with its emphasis on kin loyalty and respect for one's elders, provided such a heritage. The *Analects*

20. Yet the ancient legacy of the voluntary nature of the early Church was still reflected in the way that the pope approached the believers as late as the thirteenth century. For instance, a statute directed by Pope Gregory IX to the University of Paris in 1231 begins by stating "Gregory, the bishop, servant of the servants of God, and to his beloved sons all the masters and students of Paris" (Tierney 1999, p. 266).

21. Moreover, there was a strong correlation between the establishment of self-governing institutions in medieval towns in the period 1000–1200 and the proximity of monasteries that spread the reforms inspired by the monastic order of Cluny (Møller and Doucette 2022, p. 18).

(sayings) of Confucius reveals this emphasis in the following conversation between Confucius and the governor of *She* (representing Legalism, or rule by law): "The Governor [of She] . . . said to Confucius, 'In our village there is a man nicknamed 'Straight Body'. When his father stole a sheep, he gave evidence against him.' Confucius answered, 'In our village those who are straight are quite different. Fathers cover up for their sons, and sons cover up for their fathers. Straightness is to be found in such behavior'" (*Analects*, XIII, 18).

Neo-Confucianism reached full cultural dominance in China only during the Song period. It was at this time that neo-Confucianism earned constant and widespread state support and became the main philosophy that dominated Chinese culture. One recent scholar of its triumph assesses that of all the major persuasions, "Confucianism was the only one that was tailor-made for the support of the state. The nature of Confucianism facilitated a symbiosis between the political actors and the ideological actors" (Zhao 2015, p. 280). The canon of neo-Confucianism (the *Four Books* and *Five Classics*) became the core curriculum for the *keju* examinations, and hence the material that every ambitious and bright Chinese lad studied. While it merged elements from other philosophies, it became dominant because its values were consonant with a world where extended kinship governed social interactions.[22]

The origins of Confucianism date back to the Warring States Period, long before the creation of the unified Qin Empire in 221 BC. With the creation of the empire, Confucianism had to contend with competing philosophies such as Legalism, Buddhism, and Daoism (Taoism). In fact, the ruler of the Qin state, who unified China and created the empire, adopted Legalism, an alternative political philosophy that emphasized obedience to the law (for more details, see chapter 8). The first emperor of united China, Qin Shi Huang (r.221–210 BC), forbade Confucianism, a harsh measure that may have been a factor in the very short duration of his dynasty. Confucianism became a recognized state philosophy only in the first century BC, during the Han Dynasty. Religious pluralism, and hence competition in China, clearly persisted, but it was different from Europe in that competing philosophies often merged with one

22. Huang (2023, pp. 50–51) argues that the dominance of Confucianism was due to a "technicality," in that it was much harder to master than the alternatives due to the large amount of the material to be mastered, and hence it served better as a selection mechanism. Such an argument ignores the possibility that alternative curricula could be enriched by other (and arguably more useful) topics such as science, mathematics, medicine, and commerce.

another to create a syncretic worldview, unlike the sharply delineated boundaries of religious identities in Europe.

Thus, in the first millennium AD, alternative philosophies and religions
competed with Confucianism and challenged its familyist philosophy. In particular, the introduction of Buddhism around the first century AD was very
successful, expanding rapidly during the period of the "Six Dynasties" (Wright
1990, pp. 220–581). Chinese translations of major Buddhist works, including
the *Diamond Sutra*, appeared around 400 AD. The popularity of Buddhism
increased in China during the Tang Dynasty (618–906 AD), when mass production of Buddhist texts took advantage of newly invented woodblock printing (Twitchett 1983). Buddhism promoted cultural values that differed from
Confucianism and emphasized the individual as part of nature, the belief in
incarnation, and spiritual rewards for impersonal altruism.[23] Buddhist monks
and nuns lived in monasteries and practiced impersonal charity. Like European
rulers, who relied on Christian monasteries to provide social safety nets, the
Tang relied on Buddhist monasteries to provide individual-level poverty relief,
although the Tang government did its part in systemic welfare through tax
exemptions and operating granaries.

As the wealth of the tax-free Buddhist monasteries increased, they became
a tempting political target. When the Tang Empire declined, the emperors
confiscated the wealth of the monasteries, particularly after 846.[24] The collapse
of Buddhists' social safety net during the later Tang contributed to the rise of
Confucianism during the Song period (Liu 1973). The consequent decline of
Buddhism just prior to the Song period helped bring about the rise of neo-
Confucianism, masterminded by the great philosopher Zhu Xi and his colleagues. "Under the influence of both Buddhism and Daoism, Confucian

---

23. Buddhist emphasis on the individual differs from Western individualism, however. As
pointed out by Weber (1958b, pp. 206–20), Buddhism has a mystic (world-fleeing) component,
where individuals adjust to the world as is, whereas the Abrahamic religions are activist and see
individual salvation as dependent on actions to change the world.

24. In the 840s, the Emperor Wuzong (r.840–846) initiated a violent campaign (known as
the "Huichang persecution") against non-Confucian religions that were regarded as foreign,
Buddhism being the most prominent of these. A strong motive behind this campaign was fiscal,
as the emperor had fought expensive wars against Uighur tribes in the west of China. By some
estimates 40,000 shrines and temples were closed, 260,000 monks and nuns ended up as laypersons, and large plots of land owned by the monasteries were confiscated and sold. Subsequent emperors tried to reverse this persecution, but Buddhist temples suffered irreversible
damage.

thinkers began to reorganize ancient Chinese thought to create the basis of a philosophical system known as the Learning of the Way" (Kuhn 2009, p. 99; see also Bol 2008). Neo-Confucianism became a dominant ideology, and its symbiosis with the clan system became decisive. As David Faure (2007, p. 39) summarizes, "In time, the Neo-Confucian tradition was so successful that it totally changed the shape of Chinese society." The significance of the triumph of neo-Confucianism for the role of the clan in Chinese society is in how it illustrates the argument that culture affected the economy through social organizations. Neo-Confucians focused "on the family as a kinship-based ritual unit that could serve as the building block of local society" (Bol 2008, p. 238).

Neo-Confucianism retained Confucius's position on the appropriate scope of morality. It emphasized the personal scope of morality, particularly one's moral obligation toward kin. In the words of Fei (1992, p. 74), "Extending out from the self are the social spheres formed by one's personal relationships. Each sphere is sustained by a specific type of social ethic." The most basic social sphere is kinship, and the corresponding values are filial piety and fraternal duty. An additional social sphere is based on friendship, and the corresponding values are loyalty (*zhong*) and sincerity (*xin*). This communitarian perspective clearly differs from the universalism that stemmed from the Western religious principles that everyone is equal before God.

Neo-Confucianism received a major boost during the Song Dynasty, in connection with recruitment into the state bureaucracy through the civil service exam. The Song administration created state schools whose curricula included the teachings of neo-Confucianism from books that the government published and required the schools to purchase (Twitchett and Fairbank 2009, pp. 585–89). The production of books by the state benefited from technological advances that reduced production costs, while private demand was strong because of the Civil Service Examination (Twitchett 1983, p. 60).

During the Song Dynasty, the influence of Confucianism thus became central to Chinese society. China's intellectual life changed as neo-Confucianism triumphed in the market for ideas, which then weakened the dissent of its competitors.[25] To survive in a world of increasing family-based values, Buddhism adopted the family orientation that is central to Confucianism (Wright 1990). Thus, by the eleventh century, all the main philosophical schools in

---

25. "A largely temple-based world of principally Buddhist textual learning, centered at one main site during the Sui and the Tang, evolved into the far more secular and dispersed network of Confucian learning based on private holding during the Song" (McDermott 2011, p. 67).

China emphasized personal morality and loyalty to a kin-based collective. The culture was primed for the emergence of clans. The historiography on this topic seems remarkably unanimous. The main components of a clan-based society, such as filial piety, ancestor worship, respect for elders, and intraclan solidarity enjoyed a general moral legitimacy and were consistent with the forms that social organization took.

The triumph of neo-Confucianism in the market for ideas was gradual but unquestionable for nearly a millennium. Not until the early twentieth century have we seen respected intellectuals begin to seriously question kinship hierarchies and ancestor worship. One reason for Confucianism's sustained success was the scholar-official system governing the mandarinate; this system meant that most serious intellectuals were also members of the administration and thus had a vested interest in its continuity. Moreover, the examination system that selected the officials was based on a curriculum that stressed Confucian family values. Lineage-based groups developed a symbiotic relationship with the Imperial bureaucracy based on a shared Confucian morality. This positive feedback between cultural elements and institutions created resilience, and hence longevity. That system could have continued to be dominant but for the encroachment of the outside world into China during the nineteenth century.

As we discuss in chapter 5, the diffusion of neo-Confucianism during the Song Dynasty coincided with the spread of clans among commoners. The Song imperial government permitted and at times encouraged the creation of clans. For the first time, it allowed commoners to compile the genealogies necessary for the clans to function. From the perspective of China's central administration, clans solved the dilemma of providing local public goods—particularly assisting the poor and refugees—while upholding the Confucian principle of keeping the government as small as possible and mitigating social problems.[26]

5. Ancestor Worship in China

The family and the larger clans and lineages were permeated by a culture of ancestor worship (Lang 1946, pp. 18–19; Baker 1979, pp. 71–106). Ancestor worship was a means to foster the coherence of the lineage and became a feature of Chinese society in antiquity (Lakos 2010). It operated at two levels. The

26. See Scogin (1978); the term "policies" in his argument means *what* is being done, while governance is about *how* it is being done.

family worshipped its close lineal forefathers, while the broader clan worshipped more remote ancestors (Lang 1946, p. 19).[27] The more pronounced forms of ancestor worship and clan lineages emerged only during the Song Dynasty. Religion in China, unlike anything in Europe, was diverse and inclusive, and in large part designed to support the emperor.

While religion was not explicitly political, it functionally served the interests of people in power. In one interpretation, religion in China was defined by the kinship structure that fulfilled the functions of religious organizations and structured churches in other civilizations. As religious scholar Mou Zhongjian put it, "Respecting Heaven and honoring ancestors (*jingtian fazu*), taking good care in seeing off the deceased, and maintaining sacrifices to distant ancestors (*shenzhong zhuiyuan*) were the basic religious concepts and emotional expressions in this religion. This religion is closely entangled with the hierarchical structure of the clan system and with patriarchal ideology, thus it is also called 'traditional patriarchal religion'" (cited in Zhuo 2012, pp. 280–81). Traditional ancestor worship provided the structure of the organization and the rituals; Confucianism provided the ethics and the metaphysics. It was, almost literally, a marriage made in heaven.

Ancestor worship became a defining characteristic of Chinese society and thus constitutes one of the most salient cultural differences between Europe and China. David Keightley (1990, pp. 44–45) notes that ancestor worship was a "strategic custom," and it legitimated and sanctified "all other aspects of life." As early as the Zhou Dynasty (after c.1045 BC), the values of ancestor worship went hand in hand with strong lineages, where families spanning several generations lived under one roof. This combination of clan loyalty and ancestor worship would have far-reaching implications. Keightley also points out that ancestor worship meant that the kind of class struggles between the "few" and the "many" over economic issues, which plagued Western capitalism, did not play an important role in China. Even more important, kinship ties and their political extensions took priority over economic interests, and hence merchants in China never attained the kind of political independence and influence that they did in Europe (Keightley 1990, p. 47). We return to these issues in chapters 7 and 9.

---

27. There is a consensus that a distinction should be made between ancestor worship by the clan as a whole and that by individual families who might or might not have belonged to a clan. Family-level worship was quite often practiced even by commoner households in the village, but the former was predominantly run by the gentry (Hsiao 1967, p. 335).

All the same, the triumph of ancestor worship in Chinese culture and society and the dominance of neo-Confucianism were far from inevitable. As already noted, Buddhism was a more individualistic religion, but along with Daoism, it eventually accepted religious life centered on the family (Mote 1999, p. 158). Overarchingly, in Europe, religion was a driving force in the organization of family life; in China, it was the reverse. Yet the latter's trajectory in cultural evolution came fully to the fore only in the Song Dynasty, with what Mote (1999, p. 159) calls "the popularization of the great clan-family tradition."

Whether or not one wants to think of this as a wholesale "Confucianization" of Chinese society, as Mote suggests, it clearly entails the diffusion of a coherent set of values in some ways akin to a religious doctrine, even if very different from the Abrahamic monotheistic religions of the West and the Middle East. There was no Confucian church, no formal religious organization of rabbis, pastors, or clerics of any kind; worship occurred within the family and thus exhibited interhousehold variation. Yet the great neo-Confucian philosophers of the Song Dynasty, especially Cheng Yi (1033–1107) and Zhu Xi himself, wrote influential books that guided the performance of family rites (Ebrey 1990, p. 212; Lakos 2010, p. 26).[28]

As Joseph McDermott (2013) showed in his study of Huizhou in the Guangdong province in southern China, religious practices for many years remained far more complex than mere ancestor worship in kinship institutions. He describes in detail village worship associations, Buddhist institutions, and even popular cults that existed side by side with kinship institutions. How did these relate to one another? He sees the relationship as "sometimes harmonious and sometimes not" (McDermott 2013, p. 53). At least in the

---

28. Von Glahn (2004, p. 152) in discussing the evolution of non-Confucian doctrine in China, points out that the most salient feature of Chinese religion in Song times was "the emergence of a unified realm of the sacred that amalgamated religious beliefs and practices of disparate origins." This amalgamation was increasingly attained by merging Daoism and Buddhism, as well as variety of cults under a Confucian umbrella. Confucian purists nominally restricted ordinary subjects to veneration of their ancestors (and a limited number of household tutelary deities). In theory, all other forms of worship were deemed "profane cults" (*yinci*) and strictly prohibited, but the Song government remained committed to a strategy of cooptation of cults and other religions. Their insight was to bring about religious harmony through regulation through official recognition, rather than outright suppression, "as the most effective means of curbing the excesses of popular devotion" (Von Glahn 2004, p. 158). In this way, ancestor worship was made consistent with a host of local and idiosyncratic cults and religious beliefs.

region that he studied, the transition to ancestor worship based on the clan (as opposed to other local associations) was slow and finished only during the Ming Dynasty.[29] The neo-Confucian clan-based social organization prevailed because it adopted many of the practices and ideas of Buddhists and village-worship social organizations, and it supplied a range of services and local public goods to kinfolk that was unavailable to other residents of the village community (McDermott 2013, p. 107). This method of outcompeting other institutions was slow and costly, requiring clans to use their joint property to help pay for the services that they provided. Yet it proved successful in the end.

The growth of lineages and the deepening of ancestor worship went hand in hand and continued apace during the Ming and Qing dynasties. On the one hand, the tradition of ancestor worship facilitated the diffusion of clans, which were associations of descendants of a common male ancestor. On the other hand, the diffusion of clans strengthened the dominance of this cultural trait. Lineages were often founded and led by senior members of the gentry, educated scholars, and often degree holders. Moreover, the twin cultural features of ancestor worship and clan loyalty led to the construction of the ancestral hall (*citang*), a kind of religious temple where people practiced the veneration of their ancestors. Ancestor worship varied from region to region. In some places, it was mostly done within the homes of people, whereas elsewhere, ancestral halls and clan temples were of greater importance.[30]

Certainly, by the early Qing, the ancient practice of ancestor worship had become entrenched within local communities. Under the early years of the Kangxi Emperor (also known as Emperor Shengzu of Qing) in the 1690s, it seemed that Christianity would start making serious inroads into China. Significantly, the emperor did not object to the idea but insisted that Christian

29. In his review of McDermott's book, Chen (2017) argues that there is a sharp distinction between village worship associations and clans, with clans eventually pushing out alternative local social organizations promoting public goods. Such a schematic description defies the complicated relationships among different forms of worship and organization at the village level, which were often overlapping and cooperated with one another (Du 2007, p. 282). Clans were clearly active on a wide scale from the Song times forward, and Chen's failure to recognize the importance of ancestor worship and the influence of neo-Confucianism and their role in creating the cooperation needed for local government underlines the one-sidedness of his argument.

30. Home-based worship in theory was restricted to five generations back. As the clan grew larger, though, there were more and more ancestors, and the need arose to agree on a founder, who became extremely important to the functioning of the clan.

converts be allowed to continue to practice ancestor worship side by side with their Christianity. The Jesuits in China did not object, but the papacy and Church leadership forbade the practice. The emperor did not take kindly to this position and expelled many Catholic missionaries who refused to accept his position from China. As Jonathan Spence (1990, p. 72) remarks, "This mutual hard line wrecked the power base of the missions in China and effectively prevented the spread of Western teaching and science. Had either side been more flexible, the new knowledge and techniques might have led to significant changes in Chinese attitudes about thought and nature."

This quote points out an important downside of ancestor worship. Because it implies an unwavering respect for earlier generations, it also incorporates a conservative bias, great respect for ancient knowledge, and a suspicion of heretical or deviant views. The veneration of ancient knowledge is not a watertight obstacle to technological or intellectual innovation, but it is understandably more difficult to innovate where such beliefs are present. As we discuss in chapter 9, there was relatively limited private innovation in China, and most consequential inventions were introduced and diffused by government officials. At least in those times when the imperial court was favorably disposed toward technological progress, these officials were less constrained by what Kuran (1988) famously called "the tenacious past." After the Song, however, the court became more conservative and the flow of intellectual and technological innovation gradually slowed to a trickle.[31]

Furthermore, with ancestor worship came the influence of older people. Greif, Iyigun, and Sasson (2013) suggested that conservatism in China was

---

31. Recent research has confirmed that intellectual ancestor worship and too much respect for classical learning can impede industrialization and economic development. Ma (2022) points out that in China, there were actually shrines to ancient intellectuals, a clear sign of the importance of this veneration to the ancient canon. Many classical masters were acknowledged as "sages" (literally, holy, wise, and virtuous men). Their texts constituted the core of the curriculum of the imperial examinations, and their writings were seen as sacrosanct by many. Ma is able to show that the presence of these shrines impeded industrialization between 1858 and 1927, precisely the era in which Western technological ideas were slowly penetrating China, supported by progressives and strongly resisted by conservatives and entrenched interests. Ma concludes, sensibly, that "the prevailing worship of classical wisdom may impede a region's transition from a traditional to an industrial economy, at least in the context of China, because it increases the entry costs of new learning that is pivotal to industrialization. Therefore, the intellectual origins of modern economic growth are based not only on what intellectuals know, but also on what they believe" (Ma 2022, p. 24).

reinforced by the decisive influence of elders in decision-making at the clan level, a point that we return to in chapter 9. In any event, a system in which an internal hierarchy is based on age and generational seniority seems to make little sense from the point of view of functionality. As Zhang (2017, p. 202) notes, there are far more effective ways to ensure that capable as opposed to experienced people are in charge. But the seniority system had one overriding advantage—namely, stability and the absence of power struggles at the clan level. Here, too, Chinese society seems to give preference to continuity and stability over efficiency and growth. That said, seniority was probably decisive only when all other things (such as managerial competence) constituted not too glaringly different criteria, and in some clans, merit was clearly a criterion for leadership (Hsiao 1967, p. 332).[32]

Most relevant to long-run economic and technological development is that ancestor worship and kinship-based religious worship were on the whole backward-looking institutions. In China, the idealization of the past was remarkably strong, exceeding that in Europe during the Middle Ages. While in principle, it is also possible to observe ancestor worship where society is organized by bilineal nuclear families, in practice, bilineal descent made the number of ancestors to be venerated much too high to be feasible. A world of gerontocrats, where the elderly hold respect and power by cultural consensus rather than proven record, is unlikely to accept intellectual challenges by radicals and young firebrands who want to overthrow ruling paradigms. Ancestor worship was a method of retaining power by the existing elite, and the scholar-officials of the Song and later dynasties found it perfectly consonant with the equilibrium that they established between religious institutions and cultural beliefs. In such an equilibrium, there was no room for radical new ideas that could not be incorporated into the neo-Confucian culture. Ancestor worship was inherently conservative and could easily slide into intellectual ancestor worship, in which the writings of the ancients were the font of all wisdom and knowledge. Only in the second half of the nineteenth century did the encroachment of European imperialism poke holes in the conservatism of Chinese education, and both missionaries and Chinese modernizers established

32. The exact division of intraclan decision-making between elders and wealthy people owning more real estate has been contested. Watson (1985 [2011]) explicitly denies that elders (*fu lao*) constituted a managing elite, and Zhang's work has been criticized by some, such as Faure (2020).

schools that taught curricula more consistent with economic progress (Kung 2022, pp. 390–99).

This was not so in Europe. By the Renaissance, Europeans had already demonstrated their willingness to disrespect the past and engage in "apostasy" and "heresy" to overthrow long-standing customs and beliefs. The skepticism of ancient knowledge far exceeded anything seen in China before the twentieth century. The core tenet of contestability was part of the foundation of European intellectual innovation. The old intellectual order in Europe crumbled around 1500, and the venerable and admired canons of the past were tested—most of them found wanting—and then abandoned. Historians have long described the "quarrel between the ancients and the moderns" in Europe, and by 1700, there was no doubt that the "moderns" had won this battle decisively. In China, ancestor worship made such a triumph far more difficult. While there were serious debates within the Confucian paradigm on what the master really meant, there was never any serious attempt to abandon Confucianism until the next master (i.e., Karl Marx) replaced him, at least temporarily.

None of this is to suggest that intellectual ancestor worship in China was absolute, or even as rigid and doctrinaire as in the more orthodox versions of Islam and Judaism. Within the Chinese class of scholars and literati in the Qing era, the Kaozheng movement created a more rigorous approach to knowledge and restored the study of mathematics, astronomy, linguistics, and other forms of science. Yet none of these advances would produce a Chinese Galileo, René Descartes, or Isaac Newton. Learning and research were undertaken in adherence to the belief that "it would lead to greater certainty about what the true words and intentions of China's ancient sages had been and hence to a better understanding of how to live in the present" (Spence 1990, p. 103). Scholars who strayed too far from the neo-Confucian orthodoxy, such as the heterodox Ming-Dynasty philosopher Li Zhi (1527–1602), were persecuted and met unfortunate ends.[33]

Ancestor worship for obvious reasons was anathema to the communist regime, and by the 1950s, many ancestral halls had been closed. During the Great Leap Forward (1958–60) and the Cultural Revolution (1966–76), the suppression of ancestor worship became more intense. Ancestor worship was not eliminated altogether, however. Some traditional rituals like burial were

33. Li Zhi's second book was appropriately entitled *A Book to Hide*. Ray Huang (1981), who discusses Li's career in detail, points out the political rigidity driven by the heavy reliance on the classic canon embedded in *the Four Books* and its suppression of creativity.

preserved in rural regions. As we discuss in chapter 10, ancestor worship re-emerged after Mao's death, although not in full due to urbanization, population mobility, and diffusion of Western culture. Ancestor worship still prevails in certain areas, like Guangdong province. Descriptive spatial distributions suggest that ancestor worship has become distinctly more popular in reform-era China, and its demographic effects can be discerned (Hu and Tian 2018).

5

The Clan and the Corporation

1. Introduction

During the European Middle Ages, China and Europe came to rely on very different social organizations to sustain the cooperation needed to provide local public goods. In premodern China, clans were the paramount social organizations, while in Europe, corporations were becoming increasingly common. Clans and corporations evolved to meet similar needs over time, reflecting how the circumstances and demands of their members changed with economic development and through interactions with the state. As the market economy developed on both continents, social organizations evolved to fulfill important economic functions supporting market activity, sustain commerce and specialization in production, and facilitate cooperation. In this respect, the evolution of social organizations was similar in China and Europe, as it accompanied the process of economic development. European corporations acquired important political roles and, as we will discuss in chapter 7, they contributed to the evolution of political institutions—something that did not occur in China. Moreover, as we shall explain later in this chapter, the modern-day limited liability joint stock business corporation emerged in Europe at the beginning of the seventeenth century, while it took much longer to appear in China (Harris 2020).

In this chapter, we describe the key features of these organizations, their similarities and differences, when and where they emerged, what they did, and how they evolved over time. The next chapters then discuss several examples of specific social organizations in greater detail, highlighting how similar functions were performed by very different social arrangements in Europe and China.

2. The Hallmarks of Clans and Corporations

Throughout the book, we refer to the Chinese clan as a social organization that includes some of or all the patrilineal households tracing their origin to a self-proclaimed common male ancestor. Thus clan members belong to a common descent group (zu) tracing its origin to a first male ancestor who lived in a given locality. The clan is a much broader and less closely knit organization than the family (jia). The latter is typically the basic economic unit, and it consists of close family members living together and sharing a common budget.

Clans differed greatly in their scope, size, activities, and internal organizations, both across time and space. Anthropologists and historians use more precise terminology to define different kinship groups, but since we are interested in comparing China and Europe, we stick to a broader and less precise definition, and we interchangeably use the terms "clan," "lineage," and "dynastic group" to refer to any kin-based organization, regardless of its scope and activity (for more extensive discussions, see Hu 1948; Freedman 1958; Ebrey and Watson 2018; and Watson 1986). By way of contrast, we refer to the European corporation as a "social organization," established by unrelated individuals to pursue common objectives and interests, regardless of kinship. This definition of "corporation" is broader than that commonly used today and corresponds to its premodern use and conceptualization of the word (Greif 2006a, 2006b).

While both clans and corporations were arrangements for interpersonal cooperation and the provision of local public goods, they exhibited several key differences. As noted in chapter 3, clan membership was ascriptive (i.e., based on kinship), while corporation membership was a matter of choice, based on common interest. Furthermore, clans were multipurpose organizations: members shared risks and provided mutual protection, organized religious ceremonies, supported education, settled disputes, and organized production and exchange. Most corporate arrangements instead had a single main specific purpose. Due to these different membership rules, individuals in China belonged to a single clan, while people in Europe could (and often did) join several corporations active in different domains. Because loyalty and altruistic ties among kin were normally much stronger than those among strangers united by interests, clans and corporations relied on different methods to enforce cooperation. Finally, both clans and corporations were self-governing organizations, but they had very different governance rules. We will provide a more detailed comparison between clans and corporations at the end of this chapter.

The conceptual distinction that membership in a clan was based on kinship, while membership in a corporation was based on common interest, was in practice more nuanced and should be qualified to some extent. First, although memberships in clans were determined by inheritance through kinship, Chinese lineage organizations were often formed for specific purposes and by voluntary association. Especially in the later years of the Qing Dynasty in the nineteenth century, kinship was still a prerequisite to membership, but not all members of an existing lineage would join (Zheng 2001, pp. 122–31). Second, in practice, kinship was not entirely predetermined; it could be manipulated through adoption or marriage, or even be outright manufactured (Ruskola 2013, chapter 3). Kinship ties could be invented for people sharing a common business interest or regional origins. Third, in some instances, the same person could belong to more than one lineage-related organization since the same lineage could have several organizations and lineages were also subdivided into branches. Similarly, while membership in a corporation was theoretically a matter of choice, in practice, long-term permanent residence in a town normally made one a town citizen (i.e., a member of the town corporation), although such a status was neither immutable nor ubiquitous (Prak 2018). Exercising a craft or occupation usually made membership in the local guild mandatory. Last but not least, social organizations and partnerships that included nonkin were also present in China. Conversely, Europe too had kin-based social organizations, and family relationships remained of primary importance in European business partnerships.[1] In short, the distinction between Europe as a world of corporations and China as a world of clans should not be overdrawn. That said, the relative diffusion of clans and corporations was vastly different in China and Europe, and the evidence leaves little doubt that the clan and the corporation were the quintessential social organizations in these two continents up to the modern period, and they differed in several key respects.

3. Clans

Family and Lineage

During the Tang and Song dynasties, the prevalent unit of organization among elites and commoners was the "communal family," an extended household that included several generations who lived in close proximity and held common

---

1. Hawk (2024, chapter 8) discusses several examples of Chinese business partnerships that also included nonkin as business partners, while chapter 9 discusses the role of family relationships in several medieval European business partnerships.

property.[2] Ebrey (1986, p. 31) provides examples of families of 700 individuals with common patrilineal descent, which around the turn of the millennium had maintained a common household for eight to ten generations. Within such extended families, there was no sharp distinction of status except those related to age, generation, and gender; property was held in common, risks and income were shared, and social life was governed by rules for management, budgeting, and courtesy, reflecting their organizational complexity. Communal families were an important building block of Chinese society during the Song Dynasty, but eventually they evolved into larger units (Ebrey 1986, p. 32). While the communal family remained in some ways the ideal, cooperation among kin became increasingly organized within clans (Lang 1946, pp. 12–21).

When large differences in status or income emerged within the communal family, or when individuals moved across localities, communal families split up or lineage groups consisting of several communal families were formed. Lineage groups were much looser, internally more heterogeneous organizations, but they were still based on common ancestry. Some lineage groups held common property while others did not, but they were all aware of their common origins and group identity, and they practiced collective rituals to honor their ancestors and observed in-group solidarity. Several distinct households belonged to the same lineage group, each household having its own assets and standard of living. When they held common property, few common estates lasted for more than two centuries, and as they became too large or too heterogeneous, they split into different branches of the same lineage (Ebrey 1986).

Economic changes under the Song Dynasty accelerated the transition from communal families to clans. During the Song Dynasty, agricultural productivity increased due to new rice varieties and new cultivation techniques. Food surplus in the rice-producing regions in central and southern China supported large-scale craft production, urbanization, and commercialization (McDermott 2022, pp. 611–17). Population growth coupled with partible (i.e., male-only) inheritance threatened to create fragmentation of family assets. These changes further undermined the communal family by increasing the moral hazard and

2. A "household" in China included the parents, their unmarried children, any relative in residence, married sons (whether in residence or not), and these sons' family members. In Europe, a household included the nuclear family and any adult child or other relative in residence.

adverse selection problems associated with communal living. The clan enabled adhering to the Confucian principles of loyalty to family and lineage without imposing equality. The Song thus extended the right to maintain genealogies for their clans (or lineages, *zu*) to commoners and to create clans' estates (Bo 2008, pp. 236–46). Clan solidarity increasingly became a central pillar on which the coherence of Chinese society came to rest. As Zelin (2022, pp. 325–26) puts it, "Patriarchal authority and generational hierarchy, key Confucian expressions of a well-ordered society, were baked into both the imperial code and social practice" as household members were linked through time to common ancestors, and thus to one another. This kind of solidarity was eroded in medieval Europe with the disappearance of extended kinship, and alternatives were created to secure social cooperation.

Moreover, the policies of the Imperial administration during the Song contributed to increase the diffusion of clans. First and foremost, the government fostered the scholarship associated with neo-Confucianism that emphasized obligation to the extended family and kin (Bol 1982, p. 155). As already noted, as late as the Tang Dynasty Buddhism was widely practiced in China. The Tang emperors even welcomed the introduction of Islam into China (Lewis 2009, pp. 161–72, 214–25). In contrast to Confucianism, these religions placed more emphasis on the individual, his moral responsibility toward the community, and the notion that humans are equal. Such worldviews were even more popular among the many non-Han rulers that controlled parts of China after the fall of the Han Dynasty in the second century AD. The Song Dynasty brought about the revival of Confucianism, also thanks to the writings of Zhu Xi (1130–1200), widely regarded as the most influential intellectual in China after Confucius himself.[3] Furthermore, the Song Dynasty no longer relied on the pre-Tang Chinese aristocracy for the management of state affairs (Hartwell 1982, p. 408). Instead, the civil service examinations allowed members of local society to ascend to the imperial bureaucracy. Once successful, these officials founded lineages to signal their elite status, while at the same time "becoming middlemen between government and local society," which also benefited their kin (Chen and Peng 2022, p. 701). Strengthening and broadening kinship relations combined with the imperial examination system constituted one way to identify and select able administrators.

---

3. Zhu Xi extended the duty to build ancestor worship shrines to the population at large, thus initiating a process in which much of the Chinese population practiced ancestor worship, the centerpiece of the clan system (Chen and Peng 2022, p. 701).

Organizational Forms

Lineage-based organizations in China were flexible, and they took very different forms as they adapted to the needs and goals of their members. In the earlier stages of family organization, their main function was to preserve a common estate (consisting mostly of land) left by previous generations for ancestor worship and avoid property fragmentation. Lineage organizations were also used to promote the social status of members and facilitate their continued cooperation. Their property mainly consisted of ancestral halls and land (including income-generating land). In his study of local society in the Ming and Qing Fujian province, Zheng (2001, p. 25) calls this type of organization an "inheritance lineage" to stress that the main link among members was a common patrilineal descent.

As the economic and social status of different families in the lineage became more heterogeneous and as the lineages themselves grew larger, organizations became more structured and hierarchical. Lineage property and responsibilities were separated for specific purposes under a unified management. Many of these lineage-based organizations provided local public goods such as risk sharing through mutual insurance, irrigation and transportation infrastructure, and education. In the late nineteenth century, intraclan risk sharing, which had been of great importance during the Song and subsequent dynasties, was often more symbolic than real. Investment in education was paramount since it contributed to the prestige and welfare of the clan.[4] Common descent was still normally a prerequisite, but in some cases, it could be relaxed via adoption, by fusion of separate sublineages, or by accepting households with the same surname who lived in the same region into the lineage group.[5] Typically, lineages were localized, and they often took over functions of local government.

In the nineteenth century, in some densely populated and commercialized areas with high social mobility, some lineage organizations took yet another form that started to resemble European corporations. If ties of consanguinity or common locality were too loose, kinship networks could be complemented by specific contractual agreements. Zheng (2001, p. 26) refers to these

4. When the member of a clan passed the Imperial Civil Service Examination, his glory and political influence were assets to the entire clan.

5. "Ties of consanguinity had only symbolic importance; adopted sons and their descendants, who were excluded from inheritance lineages, could usually be accepted in control-subordination lineages." Zheng (2001, p. 119).

organizational types as "contractual lineages" to stress that they were based on relations of common interest and hinged on contractual agreements. These artificial lineages in some ways resembled European corporations, and yet they differed in that they were not mere abstract companies formed between strangers. Although there were exceptions, most contractual lineages evolved from control-subordination and inheritance types of lineages.[6] The lineage-based business enterprise was a typical Chinese institution of the late Qing period. It distributed profits to its member households, and membership shares in common property could be transferred through inheritance, indicating that these agreements were more than just partnerships between living individuals (Harris 2020, pp. 358–62). There are examples from the nineteenth century where shares were sold within the same branch of the lineage or at most between different branches of the same broader lineage. But sales outside the broad lineage were rare. They generally concerned land, not commercial activities, and they occurred in the late Qing era.[7] It is noteworthy that the sellers of lineage property were required to give members of their lineage branch right of first refusal. Only if the other original owners were not interested could the property rights then be sold to members of other branches, or even other lineages.

The Chinese system of clans thus showed unmistakable signs that it was more flexible than some scholars have given it credit for, especially in the later decades of the Qing Dynasty. Yet the lineage remained the central unit of organization. As pointed out by Harris (2020, pp. 360–61), the connection

6. An example is provided by how independent lineages claiming to descend from the same ancestor founded a market in the Changting County: "When the market was established in 1779, the Yesheng branch was already a control- subordination lineage, while the descendants of Lichong, Xiong, Ximeng, and Yongsheng comprised four mutually independent inheritance lineages. These different lineage organizations, each oriented around an ancestor of a different generation and each with its own distinct character, were the shareholders who invested in the establishment of the market. Through this contract the five lineages, one control-subordination and the other four inheritance, together formed a contractual lineage" (Zheng 2001, p. 126).

7. The first example of a sale to a nonlineage member harks to 1881, where a member of a lineage sold his share of common property to a nonmember belonging to the same village. Even in this case, however, some of the shares in the property remained under the control of members of the original lineage, and the common property remained tied to the original kinship group. Thus, even when common interest replaced common kin as the exclusive criterion for association, the lineage continued to define the control structure of the organization. "In other words, . . . lineage–village collective ownership was simply an extension of lineage collective ownership" (Zheng 2001, p. 320).

between lineage and economic activity could take place at three levels. First, bonds of mutual loyalty generated trust and facilitated economic cooperation among related individuals, regardless of any institutionalized structure. Second, the existence of a common pool of assets created for ancestral worship and status promotion facilitated risk-sharing arrangements and the provision of local public goods. Third, common property was used for specific business ventures to distribute profits, appoint a unified management, and diversify risk. On this third level, which was observed during the eighteenth century, or later in the more prosperous parts of China, the lineage organization may indeed have shared some features with the European corporation. However, as we will describe shortly, even contractual lineages did not raise equity financing from outsiders in impersonal markets, could not be created overnight by charter, and did not deploy the concept of limited liability.

The differences between the Chinese and the European business corporation were thus to some extent a matter of degree, and it may be true that they have been exaggerated. Some contractual lineages were often set up for purely commercial purposes. Ruskola (2000, pp. 1610–11) claims that Chinese business organizations have a unique history of an ideological insistence on kinship as a fictional cover for their organizing principles—even in the case of large clan corporations, in which kinship was the most threadbare fiction.[8] Lineages also fulfilled important functions in noneconomic domains. But the primary purpose of the semicorporate contractual arrangements sustaining lineages that emerged late in the Qing Dynasty was business-related. As we discuss shortly, this is a key difference with European corporations, which in addition to business purposes were often established for specific political, religious, and cultural purposes.

Finally, there were also systematic differences in the prevalence and diffusion of lineage organizations across regions. Since the seminal work of Freedman (1958), most anthropological and historical studies have focused on southeastern areas of China such as Guangdong and the New Territories of Hong Kong, Fujian, and Taiwan. This has created a perception of the lineage that nearly exclusively reflects the southeastern ones. While lineages in northern China were similar in many respects to the southeastern ones, there were important differences. One of the most basic of these was inheritance customs.

---

8. Ruskola's (2000, p. 1610) critique of the literature that stresses the contrast between China and Europe as an "orientalist myth" and "colonial epistemology" appears to be little more than an exercise in strawmanship. Harris (2020) provides a far more level-headed analysis.

In northern China, primogeniture was prevalent, whereas in southeastern China, lineage branches established between brothers all had the same claim to the original corporate holding. In northern China, inheritance rules functioned differently: the branch of the eldest son would be superior to that of younger brothers. This would apply both to common property and to decision-making power within the family.[9]

Overall, clans were more prevalent and powerful in the southern parts of China, especially the southeast, than in the northern regions.[10] The exact causes of this difference are the subject of an interesting body of literature. Anthropologist Maurice Freedman, who has more than anyone else stressed the importance of clans in Chinese society, suggested that a major factor in regional variation was the massive immigration from the North to the South in the Song era, especially during the twelfth century (Freedman 1966, pp. 5–6). Immigrants tended to be more inclined to rely on kin and thus were a major factor in the proliferation of clans in China.[11] Faure (2007, p. 9) maintains that during the settlement of the South, membership in a clan was sufficient to claim access to plots of unclaimed land.

Immigration was driven by pull factors (new agricultural technology in rice production made the South more attractive) and push factors (more violence in the North due to conflicts with steppe people). But other factors were also at work. Talhelm has argued that the rice-growing regions of China (mostly in the southern provinces) required more cooperation due to the intricate irrigation systems needed for the rice paddies (e.g., Talhelm et al. 2014;

9. As a result, in northern China, lineage seniority was not only vertical (with elders higher ranked), but also horizontal (with higher status of older brothers), and the leader of the lineage was the eldest son. This position was hereditary, so it would always be the eldest son of the eldest son's descent line, with any descendant of younger sons being denied leadership in the lineage. This lack of flexibility in this area was sidestepped by creating other dynastic organizations within the lineage, so-called Qingming associations, which would set their own governance rules, held common property, and were often used for business purposes. The lineage itself was typically not the owner of the commonly held property, but only of the common graveyards (Cohen 1990). This also explains why lineages in the north of China generally had small-property holdings.

10. Even this observation, which seems to be widely accepted, has been contested. Faure (2007, p. 363) states ex cathedra that "in North China, it can now be said quite categorically that it is simply untrue that the lineage as a form of social organization was any less common than in South China."

11. A dissenting view of Freedman's argument is expressed by Pasternak (1969).

Talhelm and Oishi 2018).[12] These technological constraints led to the development of a more collectivist and interdependent culture in southern China, in which trust and cooperation between clan members was essential. The interaction between rice cultivation, greater uncertainty of living on the frontier, and smaller agricultural plots in the South all help to explain the proliferation of clans (Noblit 2023). There is little evidence that clans had explicit rules regulating agricultural cooperation, but clearly any such cooperation required trust and reciprocity, which clans provided. In contrast, wheat farming in the northern regions, which was less labor intensive and more reliant on individual effort, fostered a more individualistic and self-reliant culture.

What Did Clans Do?

Clans were basically trust-based, private-order institutions that cohered through kinship (e.g., Wang 2022). In the second millennium, clans became increasingly responsible for supplying local communities with the public goods that the Imperial government became incapable of supplying. The Imperial government outsourced these responsibilities to local elites that managed the clans. Initially, the activities of clans centered on strengthening group consciousness through ancestral worship, collecting resources to pay for group rites and gatherings, and holding common land for burials and ancestral halls. In the words of Ebrey (1986, pp. 55–56), "Lineages organized around large estates appear to be the functional successors of communal families, like communal families they exerted considerable control over individuals, regulated their access to material benefits, and acted as a social and political unit in the larger society." But even when they did not hold common property, lineages were important and flexible. Ebrey adds that by 1350, descent groups had become more complex and structured than they had been at the turn of the millennium: they had ancestral halls, followed collective rituals, updated their

---

12. In a symmetric argument, Ang and Fredriksson (2017) have argued that wheat farming (driven largely by exogenous environmental factors) leads to weaker family ties because there is less need for intrafamily cooperation. Oddly enough, however, the authors hang their argument on the assumption that women raised the arable crops while men tended to the livestock (p. 239), which is wholly contradicted by the evidence for Europe and other regions. It is also unclear if other cereal crops such as rye and barley show the same pattern. Yet their argument may well survive a reversal of this specialization, and the idea that agricultural practices may have been a major factor in the structure of the family and the division of labor has been an important theme in economic history (Boserup 1970; Alesina, Giuliano, and Nunn 2013).

genealogies and so on (1986, pp. 53–54).[13] This trend toward tighter organization and more extensive activities continued in the subsequent centuries. As described next, lineage groups evolved to provide a variety of local public goods to their members, such as common schools and education, risk sharing through support for widows and orphans and, when necessary, protection against bandits or pirates.

In their earlier stages (during the Song Dynasty), the main purpose of the clan was religious, and their main concern was whom and where to worship. As in most religions, worship was a group activity, and the age-old admiration that the Chinese held for their ancestors made the clan a natural congregation for joint worship (Chang 2013, pp. 39–44). Joint worship groups of descendants of such venerable ancestors had to cooperate in setting up ancestral shrines and halls, and hence it was perhaps natural for them to cooperate in other dimensions. This evolution may be seen as another characteristic of the dynamics of institutions: organizations that are established for one purpose often assume completely new and unintended functions.

As Chinese society evolved, so did clans' ranges of activities. Clans promoted the social status and welfare of their members, organized markets, carried out local public works, cooperated with state officials in acts of public administration and taxation, resolved commercial and other disputes among clan members, and acted as political lobbyists. Eventually, they created militias to defend themselves from rebels, thus undermining the state's monopoly on violence and weakening the Qing regime even further. In short, clans were adaptable organizations that found ways to pursue their collective purpose of social organization to produce for a community what individuals could not provide for themselves. Clans provided club goods, meaning that they largely limited their activities to their members. As Rankin (1990, p. 19) has noted, their cooperative activities were a "by-product of their business and kinship purposes that had a more private, albeit corporate, character." Among their most widely known activities was the establishment or support of schools,

13. In his detailed and well-documented survey of the Chinese Ye clan, Esherick (2011, p. 21) traces this clan to its founder in the fifteenth century, Ye Sheng'er, and points out that "the central organizing principle was to identify a single founding ancestor and then endow some property for the benefit of all recognized descendants of that ancestor. Land was granted to the entire lineage, and rental income from this land supported the annual rituals of ancestor worship that helped maintain family solidarity ... and ideally, generate enough income to support a lineage school to educate talented young men to pass the examinations and bring further glory to the extended kinship group."

foundling homes, and community temples. They are thus best regarded as a "corporate societal institution" representing only part of the larger local community. Moreover, many clans were not specific to a location and had members spread out over large areas. In this regard, clans were similar to the corporations that arose in the West.

Clans were social organizations meant to facilitate cooperation, but they were not egalitarian organizations any more than European corporations. Watson (1985 [2011], pp. 168–75) has emphasized the class differences between rich and poor members of the same clan, and even argued that clans and lineages played a central role in perpetuating an economic and political system in which the landlord-merchant class was dominant. Yet Watson's Marxist approach obscures the importance of clans in supplying local public goods and services.

Wang (2022) sees the clan as a private-order institution that eventually took over the functions of the state, as the Imperial administration became increasingly ineffectual in providing local public goods, including law and order, poor relief, water management, and defense. More recent scholarship has affirmed the clan as the central unit of social organization in China. Shiue and Keller (2023), using the violence of the Ming to Qing transition in the mid-seventeenth century as a plausibly exogenous treatment effect, used multigenerational lineage data about 500 couples from Tongcheng (a county of China's province of Anhui) to show that clan effects were central to the acquisition of human capital as a response to the shock. Their data show that kinship-based group effects appear to be larger than village-based group effects. Furthermore, the resources of the male clan, as well as the clan of the in-marrying wives, affect the speed of recovery from a big shock (Shiue and Keller 2023, p. 48).

This finding is consistent with important role of clans in education. Loyalty, solidarity, and preferential treatment characterized intraclan relations, and members had clear incentives to provide education to other bright children in their extended family in the hope that one of them would beat the odds and pass the challenging civil exam. If that happened, and one of their family became an official, this success would spread fame and wealth through the entire family. Hence, clans provided free education in clan schools, usually financed by the income from communal properties such as real estate. In principle, income from those properties was to be shared among all members of the clan, but in practice, the elites spent much of it on local club goods such as these schools, essentially gambling on the success of a few talented boys to succeed and become members of the mandarinate. There is also evidence that large kinship groups were active in building and maintaining hydraulic infrastructure such as irrigation and flood control (Huang 1990, pp. 39–40; Pomeranz 2022, p. 498).

Clans were based on intraclan mutual trust relations, which allowed them to become the central social organizations providing mutual insurance and credit. Charitable assets were an important part of the insurance functions of the clans. They consisted of charitable lands and charitable estates, essentially trust properties held in the name of a clan, endowed out of the charity of the clan members and inalienable assets. They produced an income to support members who found themselves needing assistance (Twitchett 1959, p. 98). These charitable estates were established by wealthy clan members or by pooling resources, and they created networks of reciprocal relations between families and kin as a basic method to deal with risk shocks (Chen and Peng 2022, p. 701). Clans also were instrumental as a substitute for financial institutions. As Zhiwu Chen et al. (2022, pp. 1382–83) point out, Confucian norms and clan rules helped create *tangs* (literally: ancestral halls) as an organization for intraclan fundraising, providing an effective method for internal financial intermediation in premodern China, but they rarely reached investors beyond the clan membership. As a result, clans were a substitute for financial institutions and slowed the development of the impersonal, formal financial institutions that supported economic activity and investment in the West. Chen et al. (2022) show empirically that in regions in which clans were strong, banking development in the twentieth century was seriously delayed.

McDermott (2022, pp. 624–27) describes in detail the lineage-based commercial organizations in which family members pooled their resources for commercial purposes. Enterprising families throughout China, he notes, came up with "creative blends of kinship and business" involving kin in what became clan-based commercial partnerships. These partnerships, often taking the shape of commenda-like partnerships, were essential to the evolution of long-distance trade in China. To be sure, family firms could be found in Europe from the earliest times until today, but corporate forms of cooperation were dominant. In China, even larger and more encompassing joint-share partnerships, intensively used in Ming and early Qing days for long-distance trade, were successful enough to support the "efflorescence of kinship-based institutions" until modern times (McDermott 2022, p. 630).

Clans, however, did more than provide local public goods and cooperation. They also became a pillar of local public administration. There was a symbiotic partnership between the state and the clan system, which jointly provided the cooperation needed for the economy to function (Wang 2022). Above all, clans became essential to tax collection. Freedman (1958, p. 74) described the governing elite of the lineage as the "fiscal intermediary between the state and landowners" and noted that in practice, landowners did not make payments directly to the government but used the local gentry as tax collectors. Moreover, as noted in chapter 4, the decline of Buddhism removed an important mechanism for poverty relief, and the burden of supporting needy individuals shifted to the extended family.

There is some reason to believe that widespread poverty became more prevalent under the Song despite of—or rather, possibly because of—rapid economic growth, migration from the North, and population pressure (e.g., Liu 2015).[14] The imperial administration, while debating the scope, details, and feasibility of some of its programs, rarely debated the pressing need to provide for the poor and therefore increasingly outsourced local relief to the clans. By playing an increasingly central role in poverty relief, clans helped the Imperial bureaucracy solve a major social problem, and one could almost say that they provided the Song with a free lunch. The ability of clans to benefit the state by providing these local public goods was clearly expressed by the prominent eighteenth-century scholar-administrator Chen Hongmou: "The reason that peace does not prevail among the people is because of differences in wealth. The poor are often not capable of supporting themselves.... Confucius once observed that it is not poverty itself which leads to the disaster [of class warfare], but rather inequality." He added that "the implementation of the lineage system is designed to stimulate the basic human impetus to share foodstuffs on the basis of seasonal need, and to foster the collective husbanding of resources to smooth over good and bad years" (cited by Rowe 1998, p. 383).

To be sure, the Song Dynasty's central bureaucracy did not cease altogether to provide local public goods (e.g., Kuhn 2009, pp. 55–56; Bol 2008, pp. 72–76; Scogin 1978; Levin 2009, pp. 596–600). Initially, it still provided many of them, including orphanages, pauper cemeteries and clinics, elderly care, hospitals, fire protection units, and irrigation/transportation projects. Yet after c.1000 AD, the clans increasingly took over those responsibilities. Detailed studies of various localities reveal an empirewide trend where clans were created to provide public and club goods (e.g., Brook 1989; Rowe 1998; Faure 2007; Bol 2003). These studies reveal that clans formed, compiled genealogies, regularized the

---

14. As Hugh Scogin (1978, p. 35) has noted; "We should not ... let economic successes blind us to the fact that a great many Chinese were rendered destitute by the economic forces of the time. On the land, where the vast bulk of the people lived, several factors worked to lower independent farmers' margin of subsistence." Land per capita declined 30 percent between 976 and 1072 (Chao 1986, p. 89). Liu (2015, table D-1) reaches different quantitative results but shows the same conclusion.

assignment of generationally specific names of lineage offspring, constructed lineage halls, wrote lineage rules, standardized liturgies for funerals and ancestral rites, and in many cases mobilized resources to accumulate endowments to finance these tasks. As Zhang (2017, pp. 198–99) summarizes the case for the benefits of the clan system, it was efficient and provided much of what local social organizations set out to do: resource and information sharing, labor pooling, economic security through social insurance, and a more orderly social life.

The support that clans provided to the government in providing local public goods was an unintended consequence of their growth. Clans emerged primarily not to support and benefit the state, but from people trusting others with whom they shared a lineage and a culture of ancestor worship. Yet the Chinese bureaucracy came to understand that this structure could be exploited to impose Imperial rule and aid in local administration. As we discuss next, over time, clans became a central pillar of local government. By the time of the Qing Dynasty, the Imperial government had withdrawn from most local government, leaving tax collection, dispute resolution, and other matters to clans and guilds that often overlapped (Zhang 2017, pp. 51–52). The Imperial government increasingly encouraged lineage networks and their activities, and while it clearly was not the case that the system emerged *as a consequence* of official policy, the harmony that emerged between the mandarinate and local clan-based social organizations became a source of stability in Chinese society that lasted close to a millennium.

In nineteenth-century China, clans were so common that Westerners considered them the hallmark of Chinese culture. A widely circulated English book in 1869 asserted flat-out that the "Chinese nation is divided into" clans, and members of "these clans are bound to assist each other in any way that may be required" (Reynolds 1869, p. 157; see also McCulloch 1851, p. 604). Although Chinese social history was far more complex than that, the observation that kin-based organizations were central to the social organization of cooperation is apt.[15] Although, to repeat, lineage organizations were not all

15. The central role of clans as social networks in mid-nineteenth-century China is illustrated by Bai, Jia, and Yang (2023). They show that personal networks were an important factor in the recruitment of the army that defeated the Taiping Rebellion in the 1850s and early 1860s. Although clans were not the only base of these networks, they suggest that clan relationships provided information and served to build trust in recruiting soldiers. The use of the surnames of elites and soldiers to proxy for clan membership differs from our definition and may overestimate the connections. All the same, they find (Bai et al. 2023, p. 25) that "elite connections had

the same and did not all perform such functions, dynastic organizations were "the most systematized form of organization in local society, playing critical roles in the fields of politics, economics, and culture, among others" (Zheng 2001, p. 22). Lineage organizations took an active part in the cultural life of their community and were responsible for hiring teachers, arranging education and apprenticeships, promoting candidates for the Civil Service Examination, as well as in religious rituals and other cultural activities.

The economic importance of clans is extensively documented. Clan trusts owned about 33 percent of the cultivated land in Guangdong Province during the interwar period (Pang 1981, p. 40), and about 44 percent of the cultivated land in the Pearl River Delta (Mok 1995, p. 77).[16] In Fujian Province during the Ming and Qing periods, common property held by lineages included not only land, but also houses, halls, capital for usury, commercial activities, canal systems, and other property and activities. During the Ming and Qing dynasties, each generation in a lineage would contribute part of its holdings to a common pool, effectively expanding lineage property continuously. By the Republican period, lineage property in several areas of Fujian was greater than that held by individual households (Zheng 2001, chapter 5).

The practice of common ownership also thrived with the commercialization of the economy. One reason was economies of scale in specialization. As lineages (or branches thereof) specialized in specific occupations or sectors, such as the silk and salt trades, they could no longer take care of administering the land themselves, and it became efficient to have a central administration of all lineage property. The second reason was risk. Many lineages wanted to diversify their economic interests and enter into commercial activities. To minimize individual risk and accumulate enough capital, they used collective property. Lineages were also considered more credible by creditors and joint venture partners (Zheng 2001, p. 316; Harris 2020, p. 359).

---

a significantly larger effect for soldiers from the same clan as the elites," indicating that clan solidarity was quite powerful.

16. The Chinese "clan trust" was first introduced during the Song Dynasty (960–1279), and it enabled clan members to jointly hold property. Trusts were endowed by wealthy clan members, and some clans, particularly in the south, were very wealthy. In the North, lineage organizations had at first little, if any, property, and their operations were financed by ongoing contributions. In multiclan villages, the local temple collected contributions and assisted members of the local clans (Huang 1985).

When Did Clans Emerge?

Chinese clans were rooted in ancestor worship and patriarchy, and they gradually morphed into social organizations providing local public goods. As such, they were a permanent although protean feature of Imperial China's social landscape. During the Northern and Southern dynasties (317–589), genealogy was used to prove membership in a "great family," to obtain privileges, and to enhance status among the elites (Ebrey 1986, p. 20). Wealthy but nonaristocratic individuals often lived in communal, multigenerational families whose members lived together and shared a common purse. Although the Chinese aristocracy declined during the period of social, economic, and political unrest from the late Tang to the early Song eras (Tackett 2006, 2008, 2014), nonaristocratic clans became more prevalent as the families that comprised them became more organized. By the Qing Dynasty, such clans were very common, particularly in South China.

When exactly did commoners' clans emerge? When exactly did the clan begin to prevail as a major form of social organization outside the Chinese elites? These seemingly simple questions are inherently difficult to answer, given the scarcity of historical sources (particularly for the pre-Ming period), given regional variations and the nature of social change.[17] The origin of the diffusion of clans among commoners is often dated to the Song period. Denis Twitchett (1959, pp. 97–98), for example, maintained that "the close-knit clan which we tend to think of as the norm [in China] is to a very large extent the product of Song times."[18] Similar conclusions were reached by subsequent scholars, who have also estimated the duration of clan dominance: "The clan as a Chinese institution in the pre-modern period is generally believed to have prevailed some 800 years, beginning with the Song dynasty" (Fei and Liu 1982, p. 393).[19] Yet other scholars have disagreed: Du (2007, p. 194), in her study of

17. For example, thousands of local gazetteers survived the Ming and the Qing periods, providing a valuable source for local history. In contrast, only thirty gazetteers survived the Song Dynasty (Wilkinson. 2018, p. 220).

18. He attributed the rise of the clan, in particular, to the Song policy authorizing commoners to establish clan trusts to care for their poor. "The joint trust properties held in the name of a clan, endowed out of the charity of clan members . . . produced an income to relieve needy clan members and to help pay those expenses—weddings, funerals, and the cost of education" (Twitchett 1959, pp. 97–98).

19. "The Sung period heralded not only the beginning of the epoch of clan institution but also the development of the art of local government and market system in traditional China.

Zezhou County in Shanxi Province, claimed that the construction of lineage-based local organizations was limited to the gentry, and not accepted by commoners.[20] Others have dated the emergence of lineages even later.[21] Clearly, the spread of clans was not uniform, and it may have reached some areas relatively late. Jianhua Chang (2013) showed that most of the early functions of the clans during the Song Dynasty were confined to the realm of religion (i.e., concerning worship and the necessary ancestral halls and shrines that required their cooperation). In later centuries, their functions were gradually expanded to providing local public goods. The communal worship at the tombs and ancestors' shrines helped create a sense of unity and identity among clan members (Chang 2013, pp. 64–66, 110).

There were, of course, precedents. Liu (1959, pp. 4–5) described the rise of clans during the era of the Six Dynasties, but a subsequent decline of their importance took place under the Tang due to wars and recruitment of public officials based on merit rather than blood. Liu argued that their revival happened during the Song Dynasty (960–1279): "The essential achievement of the Sung [Song] scholar-officials was to engraft parts of the ancient heritage of the clan institution upon a broader basis of organization. . . . Following the Song period, the ramified clan institution permeated the entire traditional Chinese society" (1959, p. 5). McDermott (2013)'s study of Huizhou complements this claim; he described the transition from communal families to trust-based lineages (clans) and noted that large communal families continued to

These new developments thus limited the functions to be performed by the clan in education and rearing the youth, providing social security for the seniors and needy members, arbitrating minor disputes, and performing certain ceremonial functions" (Fei and Liu 1982, p. 398). Liu (1959, pp. 4–5) dates the rise of clans to the Six Dynasties (220–589 AD). Liu then argues, however. that the clans' rise was largely during the Song and was mainly top down: "The essential achievement of the Sung [Song] scholar-officials was to engraft parts of the ancient heritage of the clan institution upon a broader basis of organization. . . . Following the Song period, the ramified clan institution permeated the entire traditional Chinese society" (1959, p. 5).

20. Du (2007, p. 194) uses the example of the Tian family in Yangcheng to illustrate that the common people's indifference toward lineage organizations, which can be seen as the most direct reason why the gentry's continuous efforts in lineage construction were futile.

21. David Faure (2007, p. 11), in his otherwise magisterial study of lineages in Guangzhou, states flatly that "the lineage was [a] product of China's commercial revolution from the sixteenth century on," although this is contradicted by his acknowledgment that Patricia Ebrey's study of Song dynasty lineages "have been the most influential" on his understanding on the subject. Faure regards lineages almost exclusively as a means for worshipping and rituals and has little interest in the role of clans as the providers of club and local public goods.

exist, but the clan became the preferred large kinship organization in rural South China. The Huizong emperor (r.1100–1126) established rules for worship among both officials and commoners, specifying the number of generations to be worshipped (Chang 2013, pp. 39–40). There is little evidence, however, that clans played a role in the provision of local public goods at that time beyond ancestor worship. This began to change under the Yuan, when other features of the lineage system were established under the influence of Zhu Xi's *Family Rites*.

Yet other scholars have questioned to what extent the clan structure actually penetrated to the masses at that time. Du (2007, p. 194) claimed that in Shanxi Province, the gentry's efforts to impose a clan structure on the wider population were futile until the Ming and Qing eras, especially in the northern regions of China. Still, others have dissented and reinforced the argument for an emergence during the earlier times of the Song Dynasty (for a survey, see Chen 2017).

The best we can conclude is that the diffusion of kin-based organizations among commoners accelerated during the Song Dynasty, although it may have occurred before that time. However, clans as the primary social organizations for providing local public goods became dominant only during the Ming. By that time, clans were dominant in the South, but other local organizations remained important, especially in the North. All the same, clans were also ubiquitous in the North: during the Qing, they were observed to provide the social basis for villagewide organizations (e.g., Kelliher 2019, p. 77).

While the growth of clans was thus a gradual, partially bottom-up process and hence hard to time with any precision, a few dates stand out. The Song administration enacted policies that should have helped push China's movement toward a society of extended kinship networks, such as the reforms initiated by Fan Zhongyan (989–1052). These reforms encouraged the keeping of genealogies and established clan-based trusts to hold property in perpetuity to be used to finance local public goods. In particular, trust income was to be used for rituals and to provide poverty relief to needy clan members. Moreover, in 1041, the Song administration permitted all government officials to engage in ancestor worship according to their ancient rituals. This right was extended and clarified in 1108, when the Ministry of Rituals officially permitted all officials to worship their ancestors, although the number of generations that one could worship varied depending on officials' seniority and may have been a status symbol at this stage. This was extended by the early Ming in 1384, which allowed all commoners to worship three generations back, and later, in

1536, it was further extended to five generations (Zhang 2017). In short, the rise of clans was strongly encouraged by the government and eventually became the "dominant institutional form by which village society was organized." Yet it is an overstatement to declare categorically that "lineage institutions spread only as government ideology permeated village society" (both citations in Faure 2007, p. 2).

The Yuan Dynasty further encouraged the formation of clans by focusing on taxation rather than local public goods, which further increased the need for clans' assistance in both realms. The introduction of the *lijia* fiscal system under the first Ming emperor (which will be discussed in chapter 8) was instrumental in bringing about the growing importance of the clan. Faure (2007), who emphasizes this connection, however, points out that the establishment of *lijia*-driven lineages in the Pearl River region that he studied was very uneven and gradual, and often driven by narrow interests such as tax evasion. The Ming reforms strengthened wealthy families and further motivated them to consolidate clans by weakening direct Imperial administrative control and creating a rift between the central and local administrations. This literature highlights that the Ming period was crucial to the eventual predominance of clans in Chinese society. McDermott (2013, p. 430), in his comprehensive analysis of social organizations in the South (900 to 1600), argued that the civil wars of the mid-fourteenth century (which ended with the rise of the Ming) were crucial in leading to the proliferation of clans. The Qing emperors were even more vigorous in their encouragement of ancestor worship and Confucian family values, which supported the dominant position of clans in the local management of social and economic affairs.

In a recent paper, Kung and Wu (2025) show that the 1536 reform led to a sudden increase in the construction of ancestral halls, which served as places of worship in which members of the clan congregated. Such halls were still fairly rare until the mid-Ming era, when they proliferated afterward. The completion of an ancestral hall was not the start of clan activity and its engagement in the provision of local public goods, but it might have been its culmination. It provided a convenient venue for joint ancestral worship—the glue that kept the clan together; it was also the center of civic, legal, and financial activities.

Kung and Wu (2025) then use the number of ancestral halls as a proxy for the importance of the clans. They assume that the demand for cooperation at the local level is primarily driven by the needs for hydraulic control in rice-growing regions, as suggested by Freedman (1966) and Talhelm et al. (2014). They show that the interaction between rice cultivation suitability and a post-1536 indicator is strongly correlated with the emergence of ancestral halls and surmise that hydraulic projects carried out by clans were a main driver of the need to cooperate. Kung and Wu (2025) do not argue that the ritual reform explains the origins of the clan; it would be more correct to say that it marks the culmination of a long process in which clans increasingly assumed responsibility for local public goods.[22]

One institution that supported the rise of the clan system was a set of rules known as *xiangyue* (literally, a public contract of a village). The term refers to a traditional system of social contracts or village pacts that were ordered by the administration and implemented during the Ming (1368–1644) and Qing (1644–1912) dynasties to maintain order, promote "moral behavior," and organize collective activities in rural communities. The system functioned as a local governance code to help villagers cooperate and resolve disputes peacefully. It emphasized community harmony, social responsibility, and adherence to Confucian values such as filial piety and respect for elders, The code sometimes included written documents, and the head of the village, often a respected elder or local scholar, was responsible for the implementation of these agreements. While this system already existed in Song times, it was promoted by the Ming administration, which elevated it from a local practice to a national policy; in 1370, it required all villages to form such associations that carried out much of local governance. Like many other Imperial edicts, it was not uniformly implemented; for example, in Huizhou, it was not fully implemented until the sixteenth century.[23]

These regulations were complemented by a set of rules known as *tongzong cigui* (literally, ancestral hall regulations of the unified clan) that specified that lineage heads were responsible for resolving disputes, caring for the infirm and old, and coordinating the maintenance of public order (Chang 2013). Importantly, these rules gave lineage leaders the authority to punish clan members for disobeying imperial edicts. Clans were thus supported by the Imperial administration because of the fundamental symbiosis between them and the

22. The data collected by Kung and Wu (2025) also show that ancestral halls were associated with contemporary "clannish values" or collectivist morality, such as the tendency to relate to and support relatives much more than strangers, as argued by Enke (2019) and Henrich (2020).

23. An example is the rise of the Jin clan in Hongdong, Shanxi Province, which received a boost from the local official who promoted the implementation of the *xiangxue* rules. The clan was exceptionally successful in educating its members and having them succeed in the Imperial Civil Service Examinations in the sixteenth century (Chang 2013, pp. 194–221).

government, in which the government increasingly delegated local public good provisions to clans (Chang 2013, p. 140). The *Jiaomin bangwen* (literally, instructions to the people), issued in 1398, specified that worshipping four previous generations was allowed not just for officials but also for clans of commoners (Chang 2013, p. 119). These edicts were supplemented by later Ming emperors, especially the Jiajing emperor (r.1521–1567). It may be concluded that, in part, the rise of the clans can be attributed in part to top-down policies, and they can be seen as *choses du roi*, a tool by which the state controlled its subjects. It stands to reason that clans arose primarily spontaneously, but they were supported and used by the central administration. It is a classic example of symbiosis between centralized and decentralized institutions.

To be sure, clans were never the only body that solved the problem of cooperation for the purpose of producing local public goods and club goods. Many villages, especially in the North, had organizations known as Village Worship Associations (*cunshe*), which also were instrumental in meeting those needs (Du 2007, pp. 217–20; Chen 2017). These associations turned into an "institutional space for cooperation and negotiation" in the North (Chen 2017, p. 146, see also pp. 164–67; McDermott 2013, chapter 3).

The Village Worship Associations were at times separate from lineage-based ones, but the overlap was substantial, and the two groups often merged seamlessly into one another.[24] Given the prevalence of ancestor worship in China, it seems plausible to assert that Village Worship Associations and lineage-based ancestor worship overlapped, and that over time, many worship associations morphed into clans by excluding nonclan members (Du 2007; McDermott 2013). In this regard, Chen's (2017) argument, trying to date the rise of clans to a later period and dismiss their role as the providers of public goods in earlier times (because these services were provided by Village Worship Associations), is not altogether persuasive. Certainly, by the Ming Dynasty, the dominance of kinship-based social organizations had become widespread, especially in the South. As noted previously, lineage-based social organizations were less developed in northern China, but there too they provided local public goods and club goods.

---

24. McDermott (2013, p. 183) describes how in the town of Mingzhou in Xiuning County (Zhejiang Province on the coast), members of the Wu lineage in 1447 evicted all nonkinsmen from the local Village Worship Association. After that the lineage and the association were indistinguishable. In Huizhou (Guandong Province), similarly, in the mid sixteenth century, all members of the association had to belong to the Zhu family (McDermott 2013, p. 184; see also Du 2007, p. 282).

In sum, early traces of the clan as a form of local social organizations are visible even before the Song years, but their diffusion clearly accelerated during the Song. As already remarked, North-South emigration during the Song era was remarkable: southern provinces such as Liangzhe and Fujian experienced a population increase of 30 percent in the first half of the twelfth century (Kuhn 2009, p. 74), and immigration to the South helped stimulate the diffusion of clans. Still, the system did not come to full bloom until the Ming Dynasty. In this sense, the development may indeed mirror Europe's, where the dismantlement of kinship-based organizations by the Catholic Church was slow, and individualistic societies based on nuclear families were not convincingly documented until the fourteenth century (MacFarlane 1978). That said, we are looking at a tectonic change that took multiple generations and was never quite universal in a vast and heterogeneous nation.

Data on clan genealogies confirm this chronology. The recently published printed registry of all known clan genealogies is a particularly useful source (Greif and Tabellini 2017; Wang 2008).[25] Genealogies were used during the Northern and Southern dynasties (317–589) to prove membership in a "great family" to obtain privileges and enhance their social status (Ebrey 1986, p. 20). As lineage organizations became more widespread and important, compiling and updating genealogies became common practice among descent groups from a wide array of social statuses (i.e., not just among the elites). Their purposes varied from enhancing prestige, fostering alliances among distant kin, establishing claims to common property, or even fabricating evidence of common descent. The database contains about 51,200 observations regarding 38,429 clans. It also provides information on holdings of common property.

The most obvious problem with this source as an indicator of the rise of clans is survival bias: the more recently compiled genealogies are more likely to have survived the ravages of time. This biases the use of this source against claims of earlier origins of clans (Song era or before). On the other hand, since these data rely on self-reported information, the bias could also go in the other direction: namely, toward earlier dynasties in view of the prestige associated with belonging to ancient clans. Another deficiency of the genealogy data is that they do not provide information regarding alternative organizations for facilitating cooperation.

25. See the seminal study of Liu (1959). General discussions of genealogies as a historical source can also be found in Telford (1986) and Shiue (2017).

Nevertheless, these data confirm the importance of the Song period in the diffusion of clans and the presence of clans even before the Song. Greif and Tabellini (2017) exploit the genealogy data to support this statement.[26] In the dataset, 10,852 genealogies report the dynasty during which the clan's ancestor lived, and 22,141 report the dynasty of the founder. An "ancestor" is the individual from whom the clan traced its blood line, while the "founder" is a specific descendant of the ancestor who established a branching clan. To illustrate this distinction, the founder might be the grandchild of the ancestor. In this case, the genealogy would mention the grandfather (and possibly his sons and their sons) but would subsequently delineate only the households in the founder's bloodline. Put another way: an ancestor is the trunk of the family tree, while the founder and his clan constitute a particular branch.

The distinction between ancestor and founder can thus be used to date the transition to a clan-based social organization. If the clan is created by an ancestor, we can reasonably assume that the lineage was not previously organized as a clan. If instead the clan founder is not also an ancestor, then it is likely that the new clan is a branch of a preexisting dynastic group, and the true founding date could be earlier than that indicated in the genealogy.

The left panel in table 5.1 reports the total number and percentage of ancestors from each (row) period, as well as the average by decade, thus adjusting for the duration of each dynasty. The Song Dynasty (960–1279) accounted for the largest number of ancestors reported: 36 percent of ancestors lived during this dynasty. The Tang Dynasty (618–906) came in second, with 21 percent. The period in between, the Five Dynasties (906–960), accounted for an additional 4 percent. Thus, 61 percent of the clans that updated their genealogies after 1644 traced their ancestors to the period from 618 (when the Tang Dynasty began) to 1279 (when the Song Dynasty was ended by the Mongols). The pattern is reversed in the right panel of table 5.1, which refers to clans created by founders. Here, most founders date from the post-Song period, but presumably these clans are branches of preexisting lineages whose ancestors originated in earlier centuries.

In short, the genealogy data suggest that clans started to proliferate during the Tang and Song periods. In other words, the transition to a clan-based society in China was well on its way during the Song, and possibly even earlier. Note that this is approximately the same time when Europe began to abandon its commitment to extended kin networks and increasingly organized society into

26. For earlier work along these lines, see the pioneering study of Telford (1986).

TABLE 5.1. Ancestors and Founders, by Dynasty

	Ancestors			Founders		
	Total	Share	Decade average	Total	Share	Decade average
Pre-Tang	220	2%		106		
Tang	2252	21%	78	644	3%	22
Five Dynasties	481	4%	93	289	1%	55
Song	3,857	36%	121	4,772	22%	149
Yuan	1,060	10%	119	2,663	12%	299
Ming	1,778	16%	64	8,295	37%	300
Qing	1,204	11%	45	5,372	24%	200
Total	10,852	100%		22,141	100%	

Source: Greif and Tabellini (2017). The genealogy database without repetitions. Ancient, probably mythological clans are excluded. Most (550/849) came from the Han Dynasty.

nuclear families. While this was happening, China had already started to move in the opposite direction. Thus, this was another Great Divergence. That said, the genealogy data cannot illustrate precisely how important clans were as social organizations, and clearly, their functions expanded during the Yuan and Ming dynasties. In short, there remain many unanswered questions on the extent of clan importance, although we have a general timeline of clan diffusion.

As already mentioned, the Song Dynasty was a period of rapid population growth and large-scale migration, possibly the largest in Chinese demographic history in terms of population share.[27] This migration wave forever altered the territorial distributions of the Han people. Previously, the majority of the Han Chinese resided in the North, the birthplace of Chinese civilization. By the end of the Song Dynasty, the population center gravity had shifted to the East. The North's population share during the Tang Dynasty (c.742 AD), was between 49 and 56 percent, compared to between 12 and 34 percent in the East. At the end of the Song Dynasty, however, the North's share had fallen to about 11 percent, compared to between 46 and 68 percent in the East. Although the North recovered somewhat by the Ming period, the East retained the largest share.[28]

27. Xu et al. (2015) estimate that Chinese population growth during the twelfth century was 25 percent.

28. Population data come from Perkins (2013, p. 195) and are based on provincial data. The population ranges reflect changing provincial boundaries.

Migration was triggered by political, climatic, and economic shocks that also weakened the state (e.g., Kuhn 2009, chapter 4; Lary 2012; Liu 2005). Migration probably peaked during the Song, when "military pressure from the North and climate changes in that region led to a near-panic flight migration" (Lary 2012, p. 48). Large-scale resettlement created demands for local public goods and protection, both of which the state could not provide; therefore, social organizations based on lineage were formed to meet demand (Perkins 2013, appendix H; Lary 2012).

The genealogy data confirm that the emergence of lineage coincided with these large-scale migrations, and they flourished in the seven provinces in East China around the same time as when new settlers arrived in this region. Table 5.2 presents the spatial and temporal distribution of the 13,000 clans for which we know the dynasty and regions in which the ancestors or founders lived. The top panel presents the number of observations for each region and dynasty pair, while the bottom panel provides the regional percentages. Three regions—the Northeast, Southwest, and Northwest—are combined in the "Others" column.[29] The East was the birthplace of the Chinese clans. In each dynasty, more new clans originated there than in all other regions combined; on average, almost 80 percent of all clans trace their history to the east.[30]

The genealogy data can also be used to estimate how many individuals migrated independently (i.e., abandoned a clan that already existed and subsequently formed a new branch of their clan in a different province), compared to how many individuals migrated collectively (i.e., migrated with their entire clan).[31] The Tang and Song migration waves were mostly by individuals; in later centuries, clans more often migrated in their entirety. This time pattern

29. Regions in contemporary provinces: North: Beijing, Tianjin, Hebei, Shanxi, Neimenggu. East: Shanghai, Jiangsu, Zhejiang, Anhui, Fujian, Jiangxi, Shandong. South-Central: Henan, Hubei, Hunan, Guangdong, and Guangxi.

30. The various pieces of evidence given here also cast doubt on the possibility that the data collection process was biased in favor of preserving relatively more clan information in the east. This possibility cannot simply be dismissed because only in the East were there early scholarly efforts to preserve genealogies before the Cultural Revolution, during which genealogies were systematically destroyed. However, this early preservation was due to the process of clan formation itself. The scholarly effort to save genealogies is not exogenous but is due to the longer history and stronger impact of clans in the East.

31. Migration of the entire clan can be estimated by observing how many clans updated their genealogy in a different province from that of the clan founder; see Greif and Tabellini (2017) for more detail.

TABLE 5.2. Regional Distribution of New Clans

Dynasty	East	North	South Central	Others	Total
Pre-Tang	498	16	99	19	632
Tang	917	50	159	43	1,169
Five Dynasties	318	7	32	21	378
Song	2,880	56	444	66	3,446
Yuan	1,216	50	217	34	1,517
Ming	3,116	306	610	111	4,143
Qing	1,193	61	402	59	1,715
Total	10,138	546	1,963	353	13,000

Dynasty	East	North	South Central	Others
Pre-Tang	79%	2.5%	16%	3.0%
Tang	78%	4.3%	14%	3.7%
Five Dynasties	84%	1.9%	8%	5.6%
Song	84%	1.6%	13%	1.9%
Yuan	80%	3.3%	14%	2.2%
Ming	75%	7.4%	15%	2.7%
Qing	70%	3.6%	23%	3.4%
Total	78%	4.2%	15%	2.7%

Source: Greif and Tabellini (2017). The genealogy dataset without repetitions. The provinces (UN 2005 boundaries) in the East are Shanghai, Jiangsu, Zheijang, Anhui, Fujian, Jiangxi, and Shandong.

makes sense: early on, when clans were less important, individuals could more easily abandon them to settle in a new region. But once clans became a key part of the structure of society and every individual's social environment, abandoning one's clan by moving away became more costly, as it involved the loss of the local public goods and social capital that the clan provided. Settling as an isolated individual in a new region already populated by well-organized clans was also more difficult. As a result, by the mid-eighteenth century, migration increasingly became a collective decision, and the entire clan typically moved together.

Economic Development and Clans

The lack of comprehensive historical data has led some historians to view Chinese clans as a backward form of economic organization, which emerged and survived primarily due to their role in maintaining social and political

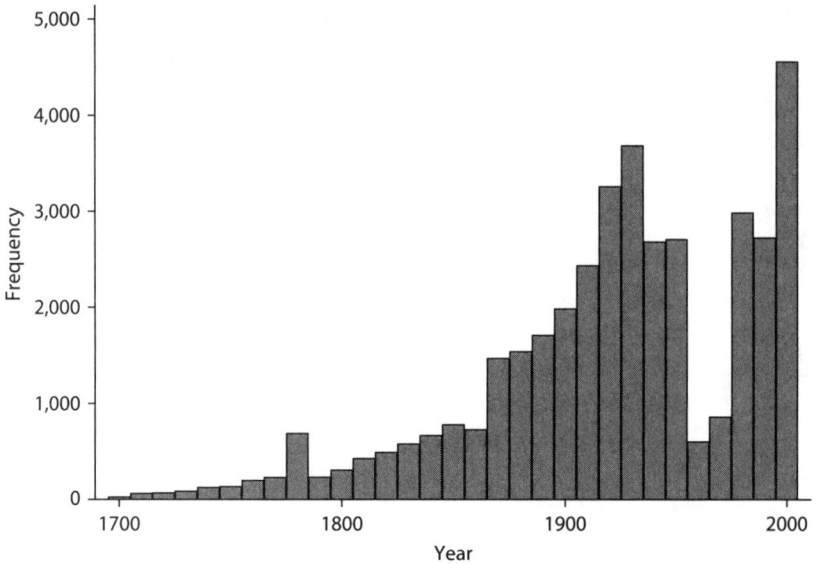

FIGURE 5.1. Year in which genealogies were updated, as reported by Wang (2020). *Source:* Wang (2020), using digitized data from Wang (2008).

order in late Imperial China (e.g., see Esherick and Rankin 1990). If this had been the case, clans should have been more common in less advanced areas of China, and they should have declined by 1912, when the republic replaced the empire. Moreover, the decline should be visible in the later stages of imperial China because authorities had begun turning on clans at this time. The opposite was actually the case: clans were more common in the more economically advanced areas of China, and their importance kept growing over time, even in periods when they were opposed by the state, as was the case in the waning years of the Qing Dynasty in the late nineteenth century.

To demonstrate this, we can rely again on genealogy data. Typically, genealogies were first created when a new lineage organization was formed, and they were updated if the lineage was viable as an organization. Thus, the act of updating a genealogy can be used as an indication that the specific lineage continued to perform important economic, social, or administrative functions.

As shown in figure 5.1, most updates (98.6 percent) were made between 1700, when the Qing Dynasty had fully consolidated its power, and 2005, the last year of data collection. About half of the observations are from the Ming, Qing, and

TABLE 5.3. Clans and Common Property in China, 1368–1949

Period	Genealogies		Adjusted: population and years		Ratio	Fraction holding common property	
	Y	R	Y	R	Y/R	Y	R
Ming	417	68	2	0.3	6.1	0.21	0.21
Qing	10,455	2,271	10.2	1.6	6.4	0.27	0.21
Republic	7,306	1,844	46.6	6	7.7	0.28	0.22
Total	18,178	4,183				0.27	0.216

Source: Greif and Tabellini (2017). The genealogy database without repetitions. Yangtze (Y): Anhui, Zhejiang, Jiangsu, Hunan, Hubei, Jiangxi (2005 provincial boundaries). Rest (R): rest of sixteen core provinces. Population data from Chao (1986) and Chen (1923).

Republican periods (1368 to 1949), suggesting that the social significance of lineage organizations continued to grow over time.

Table 5.3 presents the data for the more recent period, aggregated by area: the six economically advanced provinces of the low and middle Yangtze River (column Y), and the rest of China's sixteen core provinces (column R).[32] The number of genealogies increased over time in both the Yangtze region and the rest of China. Columns 1–2 show the raw data, while columns 3–4 are adjusted for population size. The data confirm that clans were not associated with economic backwardness. On the contrary, the adjusted number of genealogies was higher and increased faster in the economically advanced Yangtze region than in the rest of China (column 5). Moreover, in both regions, the demise of the empire was followed by a substantial increase in the number of genealogies updated.

The last two columns in table 5.3 display the per-dynasty probability that a clan held common property in each region. The percentage of clans holding common property ranged from 21 percent to 28 percent. The weighted average was 27 percent in the Yangtze region and 21.6 percent in the rest of China. These figures are consistent with the data presented by Liu (1959, p. 29), which examined the content of the book rules directly and found that 21 percent of the clans held common property. Applying the same procedure to other regional divisions of China reveals that the northern provinces had the lowest

32. Provinces in current (2005) boundaries: Yangtze: Anhui, Zhejiang, Jiangsu; Middle Yangtze: Hunan, Hubei, and Jiangxi. The rest: Fujian, Guangdong, Guangxi, Guizhou, Hebei, Henan, Shaanxi, Shandong, Shanxi, and Sichuan.

probability of common property (11 percent in the Northeast to 16 percent in the North), while the East had the highest (24.4 percent), followed closely by the South-Center (23.7 percent).

These data, and particularly the measure of property holdings, are subject to various measurement errors, and they cannot be interpreted without consideration of these issues. Yet they still suggest that clans were more common in the economically advanced Yangtze regions and more updates to genealogies were made as China was growing economically. Similarly, the data do not support the view that the perpetuation of Chinese clans depended on political support. During the Qing, a series of edicts were enacted to curb the influence of large clans, but they proved unsuccessful (Watson 2007). During the late Qing, authorities became increasingly hostile toward larger clans, which came to be seen as a threat to Imperial authority. In fact, as shown in table 5.3, the adjusted number of genealogies updated after 1912 (when the Chinese republic formed) increased over four times previous figures in both regions. Once ensconced in Chinese society, clan proved to be remarkably tenacious.

Although clans were numerous, the share of clan members in the population by period and place is unknown. We do know that some historical clans were very large, as was the case in Liaoning Province (1789–1909), on the northern coast of China, for which the data were particularly good. In Liaoning, the five largest clans (*tzu*) together comprised 75 percent of the population in 1789, and 70 percent in 1909 (Lee and Campbell 2014). At the same time, there were several hundred small clans with fewer than fifty individuals.

How Clans Evolved

As noted previously, clans accelerated their proliferation during the Song Dynasty in connection with migration toward newly settled areas in the East, where state presence was weaker. The support lineage (*yizhuang*), sometimes defined as a "charitable estate," was the most common form of clan during this period. The clan would provide several charitable goods, such as schooling, protection, rice rations, and wedding and funeral expenses, while also organizing common rituals. Several of these functions, and particularly the funding of schooling and protection, continued in later periods. Most clans had local defense corps consisting of professionals trained in military arts, which protected the properties and lives of all members (Watson 1982, pp. 600–601). The importance of schooling among the activities of clans varied over time depending on the chance of entering the civil service. The higher the likelihood of success on the Imperial examination, the more that clans would invest in education because a successful examination benefited and reflected well on all the members of the clan.

Schooling became particularly important during the early Ming Dynasty, as lineages sought to produce scholars who attained imperial degrees and achieved positions in the bureaucracy. Even when few civil servants were recruited, education remained a high priority for most lineage organizations. Until the 1920s, the chances of a peasant attaining a minimal level of literacy in rural Guangdong depended largely on his access to a lineage-sponsored school (Watson 1982, p. 601). Not surprisingly, lineage reputation was paramount, and this also led to dynastic specialization: lineages that invested less in education specialized in unorthodox occupations, such as racketeering or providing mercenaries.

Over time, especially in the nineteenth century, the role of lineages changed and clan-based organizations became more business oriented. With the growth of commerce and urbanization, clans became involved in multiple business activities. Economies of scale and the lure of trade monopolies led clans to specialize in specific sectors, like the salt, spice, or silk trade. This evolution also affected their organizational structures. Contractual lineages became more important, and by the late Qing/early Republican eras, ancestral estates were run as "hard-nosed business corporations," not as charitable trusts; they distributed profits, and their only social priority was to subsidize ritual and educational expenses (Watson 1982, p. 602; also see Ruskola 2000).

That said, and despite the continuous evolution of clans over time, they remained different from Western corporations. David Faure, in his comparison of Chinese lineages and Western-style corporations, notes the fundamental difference: the Chinese clan existed not to make profits and enrich its members but rather to provide certain services: religious ones (which are his main focus) and local public goods. He notes that "no company law ever granted them [clans] the independence and maneuverability inherent in western trading companies"—and, one could add, to all western corporations (Faure 2007, p. 6).

4. European Corporations

In Europe too, there was a compelling need to cooperate in the provision of local public goods and mutual assistance, given the absence of effective state institutions. But with the loosening of family ties largely due to the Church's influence, these needs were fulfilled by a plethora of organizations, which took different forms and held different goals. Nonetheless, these myriad organizations still shared a common feature: they were based on the voluntary association of unrelated individuals who joined forces for specific purposes.

To distinguish these European organizations from kinship-based organizations, we refer to them as "corporations," although this term should not be interpreted as a precise legal definition. Collective action and jointly owned property among nonkin were already found in the tenth century, and probably earlier, even though a formal distinction between corporate and non-corporate groups appeared later, in the twelfth century.[33] Until then, social interactions were governed by customary law since formal legal codes did not exist yet. But even without formal legal recognition, from at least the tenth century onward, a variety of groups acted in ways that later centuries would associate with formal corporations: they owned property, had their own internal rules, were represented by delegates in higher-level assemblies, claimed rights, and accepted responsibilities. They could even be punished.

European corporate groups emerged to address the same basic social needs that Chinese lineage organizations did: they provided local and club goods that were essential to the proper functioning of society: education, defense, conflict resolution, and at times infrastructural projects. As in China, these functions changed over time, together with the economic, cultural, and political evolution of society. Chinese and European social organizations differed in their membership rules, however: ascriptive and kinship-based rules dominated in China, while rules that were voluntary and mostly between nonkin dominated in Europe. This key difference in turn had other significant implications for the internal organization and the functioning of social organizations.

Who belonged to corporations? To illustrate how membership rules affected the divergence between China and Europe, consider the social organizations that held common property for the purpose of mutual insurance. During the Song Dynasty in China, such property was held customarily in clan trusts, also known as "lineage trusts." European kinship groups sometimes established trusts holding their common property, and of course in many cases family members supported each other (e.g., King 2000). Yet the main social organizations for mutual insurance and poverty relief in Europe were religious and secular corporations and municipal authorities. As we will see in detail in chapter 6, medieval guilds—both merchant guilds and craft guilds—also provided various forms of mutual

33. Even in the twelfth and thirteenth centuries, there was no necessary connection between having all the prerogative features of a corporate group and having the formal seal of a corporation (Reynolds 1997).

insurance to their members. So did the more loosely organized social organizations, known as "confraternities." Some of those organizations that originated in the Middle Ages were persistent. As late as nineteenth-century England, common property for mutual insurance was held by the corporations known as Friendly Societies,[34] voluntary associations whose members contractually pledged to pay a premium regularly in return for insurance. Kinship played little or no institutionalized role in membership selection in a world of corporations, whereas it was the only thing in a world of clans.

Other corporate organizations emerged in the Middle Ages in Europe. One of the earliest were monasteries and convents, already common in Merovingian times. Universities emerged much later and would become an unusually striking and viable form of the corporation. With the urbanization that accompanied the slow but unmistakable recovery of the Continent's economies, Europe witnessed the reemergence of self-governing cities and communes, as well as a number of independent city-states.[35] In those places, smaller corporations emerged, such as guilds, militias, and charitable organizations that managed orphanages and hospitals. Above all, as we saw in chapter 4, the Church itself can be seen as an entity that shared many of the features of a corporation. We discuss several examples of these corporations in more detail in chapter 6. In what follows, we outline some general features and patterns that were common to most corporations and highlight their similarities and differences compared to clans.

When Did Corporations Emerge?

In Europe, the legal concept of a corporation emerged in the Roman period.[36] Corporations were used by the state to facilitate negotiations and settle disputes. *Grand Collegia* conducted imperial business and sponsored public

34. In 1801, about 32 percent of English families had a member in a Friendly Society (Marshall 1833, p. 33). This is about 64 percent of the working class families that needed insurance (i.e., excluding the wealthy, who could self-insure, and the very poor, who could not afford the premiums and who qualified to be supported by the English Poor Laws if needed). Membership as a share of households increased to 39 percent by 1815 (Powell 1827) and to 50 percent by 1904 (Cordery 2003; Greif and Iyigun 2013). For other examples, see Van Leeuwen (2012), which examines the Netherlands.

35. Self-governing cities had been very prevalent in Mediterranean antiquity, but in the end, they were unable to survive the military superiority of Rome (which itself, of course, had its beginnings as a city-state).

36. Hawk (2024) documents the evolution of business organizations around the world, from antiquity until the eighteenth century, and also discusses the Roman period.

circuses and games. At a lower level, professional *collegia*, associated with specific trades or parts of a town, created social groups that supported trust between its members, protected their members' interests, and acted as lobbying groups with the authorities. As far as we know, they did not participate in the governing of their cities in the way that guilds clearly did in medieval cities. Roman *collegia* were thus legal entities, much like medieval guilds, although their precise function is still debated (Verboven 2011). In addition, voluntary associations sometimes operated informally around the household (Porterfield 2018; Kloppenborg and Wilson 1996). But the organizations that proved most important and durable in the late Roman world were Christian associations that organized religious and charitable activities. Saint Paul the Apostle's letters to the Corinthians provided the influential image of society as a human body (*corpus*), consisting of a variety of members, each with different roles but all of them indispensable and integrated with the rest, and all equal before God. Paul's letters provided guidelines for a growing network of Christian organizations that eventually consolidated into the early Catholic Church (Porterfield 2018, chapter 1).

While corporate structures thus existed in the ancient world, Roman society at large was not organized via corporations. Only during the High Middle Ages did corporations become salient social organizations in Europe. Some of the earliest evidence that we have on corporate organizations in the Carolingian period comes from Italy. At this point, Italian cities were still heavily dominated by the presence of Catholic bishops and nobility with large landholdings. In fact, it was common for these local elites to reside in the town center and live off the rent earned from their country estates. However, some documents reveal instances of corporate action and self-governance within the city by the late eighth and early ninth centuries, such as regular public meetings and consultative assemblies (Nicholas 1997).[37]

The period between 1200 and 1500 marks the pinnacle of economic and political associationism. Merchant guilds emerged to facilitate long-distance trade (Greif 2006). Joint ventures were formed to share risks and exploit economies of scale in trading arrangements. Merchants acquired responsibilities toward their financiers and had to manage complex networks of relations with suppliers, customers, and subcontractors. Accumulation of theoretical and practical legal knowledge was organized and diffused in universities. Artisanal

---

37. In an act from 808, the amphitheater of Lucca was called the "place where discussions are held" (*parlascium*; Nicholas, 1997, p. 45).

skills were maintained and transmitted by the apprenticeship system, regulated by guilds. Self-governing cities developed sophisticated administrative arrangements, invested in tax capacity, and bargained with sovereigns to gain national political representation. In short, corporations in Europe were central in many ways to the medieval economic revival.

As discussed in the next chapter, city autonomy was an integral part of this economic and social evolution. The ruling class of European cities often took the initiative to codify and refine existing commercial practices, as reflected in court decisions and documents drafted by notaries. Berman (1983, p. 355) quotes *Customs of Genoa* (1056), the *Constitutum usus* of Pisa (1161), and the *Book of Customs* of Milan (1216) as examples of this process. These legal innovations were driven by competition among cities that sought to attract merchants through favorable regulation and market integration. As pointed out by several scholars, the European market miracle reflected a unique blend of two ingredients: first, intense political competition and fragmentation between several territorial political units; and second, a remarkable degree of economic integration and cooperation. Corporations made a major contribution to both ingredients. On the one hand, they served as the instrument for exercising city autonomy, and hence creating political competition. On the other hand, they contributed to economic cooperation by sustaining market integration, enabling contract enforcement, setting uniform standards, and protecting property rights (De Moor 2008, Van Zanden 2009, Gelderblom 2013, Cavanagh 2016).

Migration

Much as in China, several European corporate organizations were created in the context of demographic upheavals, either due to large-scale migration or after pandemics such as the Black Death. In the period following the fall of the Roman Empire, migration took place via the movement of entire tribes. Various areas in Europe still bear the names of the kinship groups that founded them: for instance, Saxony is where the Saxons settled in Germany, and Sussex is where Saxons created a kingdom in Britain during the fifth century. But as individualism slowly came to prevail, migration by individuals became more common, often aided by corporations. Once settled, migrants created new corporations in the process.

Large-scale migration was driven by population growth after c.1000 AD. Forests were cleared and areas previously inhabited by Slavs (in Eastern Europe) and Muslims (in Iberia) were resettled by others in an environment of weak central authority (either political or religious). The most extensive movement of population was the migration of German, Dutch, and Flemish settlers in regions east of the Saale and Elbe rivers, known in German as *Ostsiedlung*. This period started in the mid-eleventh century and accelerated in the twelfth century, continuing until the early fourteenth century. These settlers included farmers as well as monks, artisans, and missionaries. Most important, they moved mostly individually, not as part of a larger group. The push to the East and the settlement of Eastern Europe was driven by population growth in the West, as previously noted, but there were also pull factors, such as local princes making efforts to attract and invite these settlers (Piskorski 2008).

In medieval Europe, urban and rural expansion required cooperation among nonkin who joined to advance their economic and other interests. In the countryside, feudal lords organized groups of settlers to clear new lands, granting them forms of self-government in exchange (Reynolds 1997, chapter 5). Lords also endowed monasteries with marginal land to develop and encouraged urban growth to increase demand for their estates' agricultural product and to raise their income through taxing commercial activity (Duby 1962, chapter 1).

Migration and demographic instability, above all the Black Death and the subsequent recovery of the population, were particularly pronounced during the fourteenth and fifteenth centuries. Other epidemics and harvest failures contributed to this process too, both by creating labor scarcity in some areas and by leaving many individuals as singles or in search of economic opportunity. Many young men and women who had just moved to the towns did not have the support of a family network and had to cooperate with strangers in unfamiliar environments. Not surprisingly, they sought companionship and protection in local fraternities and similar organizations. Historical records in fourteenth-century England point to a significant correlation between personal mobility and the incidence of fraternities: the most overcrowded and economically developed counties, between London and East Anglia, were also the ones that recorded the largest number of guild foundations. Concentrations of late-medieval fraternities were also found in the towns of Norfolk and Suffolk, as well as in the more densely populated areas near Cambridge. Comparable evidence from other parts of Europe, where it survives to this day, supports the impression that guild recruitment was prevalent in areas of demographic instability and among young migrants to the towns (Rosser 2015).

Thus, cooperation among unrelated individuals was the hallmark of urbanization and migration in Europe, and evidence of this fact survives from a diverse array of sources. The earliest Venetian public document enabling the study of family structure is from 1090, concerning a gift from the Byzantine emperor to a local monastery. The 127 individuals mentioned in the document have 91 different last names, exemplifying the highly diverse family backgrounds of the organization's members (Folena 1970–71). Later documents containing the lists of the people elected to the Great Council from 1261 to 1296–7 contain names of 392 individuals with 119 last names (Folena 1970–71). Similarly, in Genoa, 136 families constituted the top nonaristocratic merchants from 1375 to 1450 (Van Doosselaere 2009, appendix E).[38] Another well-documented case can be found in England, which attracted at least 64,125 immigrants from 1330 to 1550.[39] These immigrants came from all over Europe, with only 17 percent coming from the top three regions (France, Scotland, and Normandy). Social relations among migrants are known in more than 17,000 cases and reveal that less than 1 percent of migrants came with any relatives beyond their nuclear family. Servants (1,850 of them) were the largest group outside members of the nuclear family that accompanied the migrants. In fact, servants were the single largest group of immigrants; 11,732 of them arrived to serve nonkin unrelated to the people they migrated with.

The individualistic character of European migration and settlement and of Europe's social organization more generally is also evident from the broad distribution of last names within cities and villages, which were decidedly nonkinship based. To illustrate, in 1541, only 7.85 percent of the population of London had the top ten most common surnames. More generally, English surnames were relatively unconcentrated, according to the 356,834 English marriage certificates in the Vicar-General Marriage License Index (1694–1826). There are 52,872 different names in the index.[40] The same can be seen in urban areas of England in the late nineteenth century.[41] In other words, England exhibited higher diversity in background and lineage than one would expect in say,

38. It should be added, however, that over time in some Italian cities, trade became more concentrated and a fairly small number of aristocratic families came to dominate it, such as happened in Venice after the *serrata* (Puga and Trefler 2015).

39. These statistics are based on information collected by the National Archive (https://www.englandsimmigrants.com). The data are mainly based on tax records.

40. For the sources on London surnames, see http://www.ellipsis.cx/~liana/names/english/engsurlondon1541.html (Index of Names in the 1541 Subsidy Roll of London). For data on surnames of English men and women, see "Vicar General Marriage Licence Allegations Index 1694–1850," Society of Genealogists, accessed April 7, 2025, https://sogdata.org.uk/bin/aps_browse_sources.php?mode=browse_dataset&s_id=359&id=390.

41. In the distribution of last names in English towns according to the 1881 English census, the mean proportion of the population with the most common single surname was 0.079 and the mean proportion of the most common ten surnames was 0.39. These figures are calculated from the 1881 Population Census (http://www.britishsurnames.co.uk/1881census/).

China, where social organizations would have been determined by sharing the same male ancestor, and therefore the same surname. And because English marriages were between people with different surnames, this also points to far fewer within-lineage marriages, meaning that extended kin networks were not sustained via consanguineous unions.

To sum up, individuals in both China and Europe migrated and settled in regions remote from their place of birth. Yet the effects of migration differed across the civilizations because of underlying social norms and organizations. Chinese settlement was based on kinship ties, and migrants "constructed a new kin-group on the frontier for the purpose of land clearance and developing an irrigation infrastructure" (Rowe 2002, p. 534). A similar pattern of kin migration also transpired in later periods, when migrants moved to repopulate regions devastated by natural and artificial disasters. In Europe, by contrast, migration from medieval times was largely carried out at the level of individuals or nuclear families. Settlements and colonies, both on the Continent and later in the New World, were created through cooperation among unrelated individuals who more often than not voluntarily formed corporations.

The Rise of the Business Corporation

The modern business corporation occupies a special place in the history of the emergence and evolution of corporations as a broad category—see Hawk (2024) for an account of its development around the world. A modern business corporation is commonly regarded as having the following key features (Harris 2020, chapter 9; Dari-Mattiacci et al. 2017): (1) a separate legal personality; (2) rules for collective decision making and for representation of the corporation by its delegates; (3) joint-stock equity financing and transferability of shares; (4) lock-in of capital (i.e., shareholders cannot take their money out of the corporation unless the corporation engaged in a share buyback); (5) limited liability (i.e., shareholders' assets are protected from corporate creditors); and entity shielding (i.e., corporate assets are protected from shareholders' creditors). Harris (2020) also adds (6) protection from expropriation by the sovereign, although this feature is a de facto political characteristic of the state rather than a legal property of the corporation.

Features (1) and (2) were a by-product of the legal revolution in the twelfth and thirteenth centuries. They were observed in religious corporations, self-governing cities, and other public corporate entities, but not in private enterprises, whose goal was profit (agriculture was typically with sole proprietorship, and manufacturing was mostly carried out by artisans in urban workshops). Public (i.e., nonprofit) corporate entities also often granted limited liability to their administrators. Equity financing with profit-sharing, elements of limited liability, entity shielding, and some transferability of shares also existed in private joint ventures and similar contractual arrangements during the Middle Ages, particularly to arrange for long-distance trade (Dari-Mattiacci et al. 2017; Harris 2020; Hawk 2024). But generally, they were features of private contracts between individuals who knew each other, not properties of corporate bodies.[42]

All the elements of the modern business corporation, and in particular capital lock-in, emerged for the first time in Europe at the beginning of the seventeenth century. This evolution was spurred by the special challenges posed by long-distance trade with Asia and the Americas. As emphasized by Harris (2020), in the sixteenth to eighteenth centuries, transoceanic trade posed novel and radical economic and organizational challenges that were comparable to those of organizing the Church and creating independent cities in earlier centuries, or digging canals and constructing railways in later centuries. It is not surprising that organizations in charge of long-distance trade were at the frontier of institutional innovation. The main innovation that emerged in 1600 and 1602 was the creation of the English and Dutch East India Companies, respectively.[43] In particular, these two corporations introduced the key novel feature of capital lock-in: investors could sell their shares in the company, but they could not withdraw their capital from the corporation. This commitment enabled both companies to undertake long-term investments on a scale that soon dwarfed that of their rivals. During the 1620s, the English and Dutch East India Companies sent almost 200 ships on the Cape Route to Asia, more than three times as many as Portugal could send. Their advantage over their rivals further amplified in later decades. By the end of the seventeenth century, they were sending almost 400 ships each

42. An exception was the grain mills in Toulouse, which in the fourteenth century had limited liability and tradable shares. But as argued by Harris (2020) and Dari-Mattiacci et al. (2017), they promoted cooperation between neighbors, not strangers, and their main motive was service to the community rather than profit.

43. The two East India Companies are widely seen as the first large-scale joint stock corporations. In fact, the Muscovy Company (founded in 1553) and the Levant Company (founded in 1581) both met the criteria of a modern business corporation, although they were by comparison small and experimental and not as successful as the East India Companies.

decade on the Cape Route, in practice enjoying a full duopoly over trade with Asia (Harris 2020, p. 324).[44]

The emergence of these new corporations gave England and the Netherlands an edge on the lucrative transatlantic trade. Moreover, they also encouraged complementary legal and financial innovations that helped shape English and Dutch economic development. To finance one of its voyages in 1617, the English East India Company managed to raise funds from nearly 1,000 private investors, which constitutes one of the first documented examples of the general public investing in a foreign-trade corporation for the sole purpose of getting an economic return. Similar large corporations emerged in later decades, like the Bank of England in 1694 and the South Sea Company in 1711, both investing heavily in national debt. In the late eighteenth and early nineteenth centuries, Parliament incorporated over 100 canal companies in England, further contributing to the growth of capital markets and paving the way for the large, diffusely owned companies that were set up in the nineteenth century (Turner 2017).[45] For a long time, most corporations were active in commerce, finance, and infrastructural activities; manufacturing firms before 1850 were still too small to adopt the corporate form.

The emergence of these large-scale corporations also had important political implications. The East India Companies became an essential tool for diplomacy, as they eventually grew to develop their own embassies, as well as naval and military facilities. Indeed, some nations used corporations to outsource their colonialist ambitions to the private sector. Moreover, corporations of this size and wealth created the temptation of expropriation by the sovereign. The risk of expropriation perhaps explains why these big

44. According to Harris (2020, p. 370), the main benefit of being large was that there were economies of scale in the use and acquisition of valuable information, not monopoly pricing. Prior to the East India Companies, other regulated corporations had already replaced the merchant guilds in the organization of long-distance trade in England. Examples are the Spanish Company (chartered in 1577) and the Eastland Company (chartered in 1579). But these associations of traders did not have the legal features that emerged with the creation of the East India Companies (Harris 2020, p. 261).

45. In England, the Joint Stock Companies Registration and Regulation Act of 1844 was an important turning point, since it allowed incorporation by registration (rather than through royal or parliamentary charter). This led to a great expansion of business corporations, with market capitalization increasing to over 20 percent of gross domestic product (GDP) by the end of the 1840s. Limited liability came later, with two acts in 1855 and 1856. This was followed by an immediate increase in the number of incorporations (by the end of 1856, over 5,000 limited liability companies had registered) and a rapid growth of the stock market in the second half of the nineteenth century (Turner 2017).

corporations emerged in their purely private form in England and the Netherlands, where political institutions provided more checks and protections against state interferences, rather than in more absolutist countries like Portugal, France, and Spain (where monarchs remained in control of the largest corporations). Most interestingly, the economic power of the corporations and their diffuse ownership in turn had feedback effects on political institutions, reinforcing the incentives of members of Parliament to protect private property (Dari-Mattiacci et al. 2017; Acemoglu et al. 2005; Jha 2015).

Despite its many efficiency advantages over alternative organizational forms, and despite migrating to the rest of Europe after several decades, the modern business corporation did not emerge in China until much later (Harris 2020). This long delay was not due to chance. Social organizations coevolved with the cultural, economic, legal, and political features of society, exploiting complementarities and reciprocal influences. For this reason, they could not easily migrate or be transplanted across societies. If those complementary features are lacking, transplanted organizations will be resisted and rejected.

Support for this claim is found by the response to the legalization of corporations in early twentieth-century China. In 1904, the Chinese imperial government legalized corporations with the explicit intention to foster industrial joint stock companies. The legal change, however, had limited impact. From 1904 to 1920, "only 1,116 'companies' of any type registered with the government ... of these only 451 were industrial enterprises, that is, enterprises of the kind that the 1904 and 1914 company laws had especially been designed to encourage" (Kirby 1995, p. 50). Personal moral beliefs, such as universalistic as opposed to communitarian values, social norms, and long-standing but very different social practices in China limited the impact of legalizing corporations.[46] Changing the law failed to change behavior because doing so did not change the society's commonly known beliefs and value systems.

In contrast, the rise of the modern business corporation in Europe was favored by a number of conditions that were absent in China: a corporate tradition of people cooperating for a common purpose, a system of universalistic values, a long practice of trusting and cooperating with nonrelatives, a formal and professional legal system that could be trusted to enforce complex financial arrangements, and a set of political institutions that protected individual

46. As one Chinese scholar explains, "The idea that members of the public would be invited to join one's business and share in its control and profit was indeed repugnant. On the other hand, the notion that one's money be put into the pocket of some strangers for them to run a business was just as unthinkable" (Kirby 1995, citing Chun Li 1974).

economic rights from government abuse and abitrariness. Chapters 7, 8, and 9 discuss these fundamental differences between Europe and China and why they led to a deep social, economic, and institutional bifurcation. Before turning to that, though, we summarize in the next section some of the main similarities and differences between the Chinese and European social organizations.

5. Clans and Corporations: Differences and Similarities

As we have stressed, clans and corporations performed similar functions, diffused at roughly the same time and in similar circumstances as society evolved, and they were adaptive organizations. In the rest of this chapter, we discuss in further detail the similarities and differences between these two organizational forms. Given the multitude of organizations that fall under the general labels of "clan" and "corporation," our discussion will unavoidably be broad and cannot do full justice to their real-world complexities and subtleties. All the same, however, the bifurcation in social organizations is a main source of the many divergences discussed in chapter 2. The basic historical fact remains that corporations were the road not taken by China, just as clans were the road not taken by Europe.

Membership Rules

As previously noted, the European corporation was a voluntary association among unrelated individuals who were organized to pursue specific goals. The Chinese clan was an organization based on kinship. In other words, clan members cooperated and shared interest because of the family into which they were born, while corporations were formed by individuals who chose to be members because they shared a common interest. That said, some clans had elements of voluntary association; not all members of an extended kinship group joined specific lineage organizations, and one could belong to more than a single lineage organization within the same broad dynastic group. Moreover, especially in the later Qing period, the definition of common kinship was becoming more elastic.[47] Still, though, kinship was flexible only to a certain degree, and one could not stray too far from the designated path of one's clan.

---

47. There are several examples of relatives (including distant relatives) voluntarily reuniting to establish a common trust. According to Ruskola (2000, p. 1636), many clan trusts that traced themselves to a distant ancestor were in fact contractual arrangements formed posthumously by their living members, sometimes not even related by blood.

Nevertheless, the ease with which unrelated individuals could form special-purpose organizations in Europe is not comparable to what happened in China. In medieval Europe, there was not one dominant corporate group, and people belonged to several overlapping corporations. In China, networking among common kin remained the dominant mode around which organizations were built. Its relevance is confirmed by the fact that even in the more business-oriented organizations of the late Qing period, sales of shares in common property outside the lineage were generally prohibited and, even when allowed, they were rare (Szonyi 2002). Moreover, participation in the lineage organization was hereditary, and typically heirs could not renounce their inheritance even if debts exceeded liabilities (Ruskola 2000).[48]

Activities

Both clans and corporations facilitated a similar set of activities, which changed over time in accordance with economic development, commerce, and the extent of labor specialization. These similarities are not surprising, given that the basic social and economic needs of their members were not too dissimilar. Nevertheless, there are two important differences in the activities of the two organizational types. First, European corporations were often more specialized: universities only provided advanced education, monasteries had the primary purpose of organizing and sustaining monastic life and worship, merchant and craft guilds primarily regulated specific branches of economic activity, militias provided local security, and so on. Chinese lineage organizations, by contrast, were often more general, catering to a broader range of activities: they provided education, while also managing religious worship and handling family enterprises. Consequently, a clan-based social structure created a partition of society between largely mutually exclusive and predefined groups, whereas corporate arrangements created open and overlapping social networks that changed over time.[49]

---

48. As noted by Ruskola (2000, p. 1655), the provision of clan penalties for sales of genealogies is evidence that there was a market for constructed genealogies, and there are instances where shares in large lineage organizations were sold to nonkin. Nevertheless, transferability of ownership in clan corporations was neither easy nor widespread, and this limited the organizations' ability to raise capital.

49. The exclusivity of Chinese dynastic groups was more blurry in reality because some social strata did not belong to any active clan, and clan boundaries could be manipulated and constructed to some extent.

Second, some European corporations had clear political and administrative purposes, which they pursued autonomously over well-defined territories. Within their own borders, they enjoyed the rights to enforce their rules. The two most obvious examples are free towns and the Catholic Church, which also enjoyed political rights and responsibilities in national government. Although these corporations were used as instruments of governance by the state, they held some degree of power and self-determination at the local level. In China, by contrast, public administration was formally controlled by the central bureaucracy. While clans often participated in local administration and had de facto enforcement powers, they never had full self-governing autonomy, nor did they have territorial jurisdiction over the proscribed communities that they served, and they certainly never had political representation or formal rights in the central government. The only way that a clan could affect the central administration was by petitioning the emperor or having one of its members enter the imperial government by successfully passing the Imperial Civil Service Examinations. As a result, clans never developed a set of articulated representation and governance principles comparable to that of the Western Catholic Church or of European self-governing cities.

Enforcement of Cooperation

Given the length of time and size of space under discussion, it is to be expected that both clans and corporations displayed a great deal of diversity in their internal structures, modus operandi, and enforcement methods. Nevertheless, some systematic differences between the two types of organizations are clearly discernible that hold across both time and space. Whereas clans were hierarchical organizations largely based on seniority and ancestor worship, corporations were also hierarchical, but they regulated collective decision making through sophisticated and often formalized rules, paid attention to the individual rights of members, and imposed checks and balances on their leaders' authority (who were not necessarily the most senior members). In China, although clans had legal authority over their members, clan rules rarely specified formal punishments for transgressions; instead, they relied on informal sanctions and rewards to incentivize appropriate behavior.

Clan rules in China had primarily a moral rather than a formal legal character: they mostly admonished members to behave in ethical ways and protect the weak and the poor (Ruskola 2000). As one clan book rule states, "A clan without rules leaves its members with no moral standard of conduct to follow"

(Liu 1959 p. 22). The frequent, repeated interactions among family members clearly facilitated the use of reputation mechanisms to encourage ethical behavior, and the threat of ostracism or even expulsion from the clan was a key deterrent against rule violations. Many of the rights and duties between family members did not even have to be written, as they simply followed Confucian philosophy and filial piety. For example, the biggest punishment for being an unfilial son was de facto expulsion from the clan (Teng 1977 p. 142). Moreover, even when formal and explicit, most internal enforcement systems were extrajudicial. Violators of clan rules and of internal agreements in principle could be reported to the authorities for punishment, but generally this happened only as a last resort, after the clan had exhausted its internal procedures for enforcement and dispute resolution. The Chinese word referring to a civil lawsuit is *xishi,* meaning "minor matter," which is informative about how imperial officials tended to view civil lawsuits (Ruskola 2000 p. 1659; Huang 2010 pp. 21–22). At the highest level of abstraction, this reflects the Confucian ideals that viewed formal law as redundant in a society in which wise men realized the unity of their interests. Social order was achieved through obeying social obligations and rituals, with everyone supervising the actions of other members of their social network (Fei 1992 p. 28).

In accordance with this attitude, civil disputes in China were mainly resolved by mediation within the clan or village. This was not entirely due to any failing of the state's legal administration. Rather, civil matters were seen as something that should rest in the hands of the family and the community, and only if their efforts failed would the imperial judicial system become involved in resolving a situation. Furthermore, it was believed that if the state ruled on all matters, then they would have to rule by law, and the law was not flexible enough to deal with the moral complexity of specific situations, as the clans were. During the Qing period, most disputes in civil matters were resolved through social mediations by clans or local communities (Huang 2010, p. 64).

In about 40 percent of the cases in a selected sample, compromise was facilitated by comments issued by the magistrate, who briefly reacted to complaints and petitions as they were received. The magistrate's preliminary opinions gave parties a sense of the implications of their potential adjudication, and this typically induced one of the parties to change its position. Importantly, the magistrate himself was generally not directly involved with mediation, which instead was conducted by the social groups. Only a small remaining fraction of cases were formally adjudicated by the magistrate, who was expected to apply the very detailed and concrete provisions of the Qing legal code. Yet since these magistrates did not have any formal legal training, this adjudication process of last resort was often quite inadequate and consequently occurred only in rare cases.

In contrast, European corporations generally relied on legal procedures and coercive measures to solve disputes, reflecting the weaker moral obligations within a group established on the basis of common interest as opposed to blood. In the merchant communities, the ultimate sanction resulting from a transgression was the loss of one's business reputation and ostracism from the network, but even without the power of enforcing penalties, disputes were resolved by courts based on codes of law or previous jurisprudence (Berman 1983). Such formalities are most transparent in the late medieval European cities, which developed legal codes to enforce cooperation and compliance. The late medieval urban communes progressed from informal norms and rules to legal codes, and from elected judges to professional ones (e.g., Clark 1987). As we discuss in chapters 7 and 8, self-governing cities adopted and enforced formal codes of law that applied to commercial transactions. Moreover, urban law developed to lay out rules and procedures for governing autonomous cities.[50] At the end of the day, both civilizations developed some kind of rule of law. However, in Europe, it was codified and formal, embodied in institutions such as juries and carried out by professionals such as judges and bailiffs, with little to no role for the extended family.

Differences in enforcement methods between clans and corporations, particularly cities, are evident in the organizations' distinct revenue sources. European cities depended on taxes and fees levied on the local population, whereas Chinese clans provided public goods financed by voluntary contributions from members and common assets. In northern China in particular, lineage organizations had less property and their operations were financed by ongoing contributions. In multiclan villages, the local temple collected donations and assisted members of local clans (Huang 1985). This is not to say that voluntary contributions were not common in Europe; fraternities and parishes relied on donations by their members to finance activities. Fraternities were often financed through a system of tithes (Reynolds 1997, p. 92). But the

---

50. Between 1143 and 1475, 190 cities in Germany alone adopted one of the twenty law codes that had been specified by the leading towns. For instance, the laws of Lübeck were used by 43 cities, those of Frankfurt in 49 cities, and those of Magdeburg were applied by over 80 new cities (Berman 1983, p. 376).

financing of guilds was based on compulsory fees, and municipal authorities established sophisticated systems of tax collection.[51]

Governance

Both clans and corporations were hierarchical, often complex organizations. But the hierarchy criteria were different in each. Seniority, measured by generational proximity to the clan ancestor as well as age, was often an important criterion within Chinese clans, in addition to wealth. The concept of filial piety, the submission of younger kin to more senior members, gave clans a natural hierarchy, along which they organized their power. Consistent with orthodox Confucianism, older members of the clan exercised authority over the younger ones, ruled by the principle of *xiao* (filial piety), which often left children at their fathers' mercy, with little recourse to the law (Ruskola 2000, p. 1626).

Hierarchical roles based on seniority were also recognized by the law. The *lijia* reform, promulgated by the Hongwu emperor in 1370, gave legal authority regarding administrative matters to village elders; and, in 1397, the Ming legal code granted lineage heads (*zuzhang*) legal authoritative status and acknowledged their role as presiding over the ancestral rites (Rowe 1998, p. 389).[52] Under the *lijia* taxation system, groups of households were liable to pay taxes and provide labor according to a decennial rotation (every group paid taxes and supplied labor every ten years).[53] The fulfillment of these obligations rested on the group's leader, typically the largest and wealthiest household in the group. After 1494, the *lijia* families also served as local militia members (Huang 1998, p.135). These group registrations remained fixed in time, despite the fact that some households grew in size and others shrank or even

---

51. In the late twelfth and early thirteenth centuries, several Italian cities introduced a system of proportional property taxes, determined by formal declaration of the value of the assets. In some cities, these declarations were then recorded *in catasti*, which enabled regular assessments by city officials (Nicholas 1997, p. 257).

52. The *zuzhang* (or *zuzheng*) system was revived during the reign of the reform-minded Yongle emperor in 1726, who ordered that each clan elect a *zhuzeng* that would be an intermediary between the state and the clan. Yet within a few decades, these local leaders usurped more local power than the Imperial administration was happy with it having. Either way, effective power on the local level had shifted decisively to the clans and their leaders by then (Zhang 2017, p. 211).

53. Deng (2004, p. 37) describes the *lijia* system as "a state-endorsed guild" for fiscal purposes, which was anything but a branch of the state bureaucracy.

vanished.[54] The fine details of how the clan was to be organized were not imposed by the central administration. Instead, administrative arrangements gave a formal imprimatur to *xiangyue* rules and contracts (as mentioned earlier) that governed how the clan was to be managed (Faure 2007, p. 74). In short, "the legal and rhetorical support for the lineage system, the state sponsorship and systematization of local religion, the creation of village schools . . . all aimed to stabilize and strengthen the local community" (Bol 2003, p. 13).[55]

An illustration on how the hierarchy worked in a clan system is provided by Taisu Zhang (2017), who examined lineage registries produced during the Ming and Qing dynasties in Zhejiang Province, near Shanghai.[56] These lineages had two organizational features. First, in the registries that he examined, none of the registries relied on wealth or landholding as a relevant criterion for higher status and authority. In fact, in some lineage registries, this was explicitly forbidden. Second, when a selection criterion for leadership was explicitly mentioned, only generational seniority and patrilineal proximity to the founding ancestor and using material wealth as a criterion were regarded as immoral. Even those who felt that wealth should matter felt that age and seniority were to remain central to the determination of status and rank (Zhang 2017).[57]

Deference to seniority also extended to local politics and was reflected in power relations. Zhang (2017, chapter 4) analyzed the composition of local elites, including village chiefs, deputies, and other local authorities in seven villages in northern China during the late nineteenth and early twentieth centuries. Zhang found that almost half of local leaders owned land whose size

54. The local administrators treated all the families of the male descendants of the original household as one unit and held them responsible for paying the taxes of the original household (Nimick 2008, pp. 38–39). Because local magistrates wanted to conceal any increase in local taxpaying capacity, they also did not report population increases, although the Ming ordered that a census every ten years. County officials "usually just wrote in the last decade's figures or switched a few numbers to give the appearance that new count had been done." The official records thus suggest a stagnant population of around 60 million to the end of the Ming Dynasty (Brook 2010, pp. 42–45, quote from p. 44).

55. One drawback was that the system was inflexible. There was no mechanism to work out mutually agreeable changes. Formal changes could come only from the central authority (e.g., Nimick 2008; Huang 1988).

56. The views expressed by Zhang (2017) are not uncontroversial, however; see, for instance, the critical review by Faure (2020).

57. The exact division of intraclan decision making between elders and wealthy people owning more real estate has been contested. Watson (1985 [2011], p. 39) explicitly denies that elders (*fu lao*) constituted a managing elite, and Zhang's work has been criticized (e.g., Faure, 2020).

was below the village's average holding, meaning that wealth did not explain their positions. Rather, they occupied influential positions due to their advanced age or because they belonged to a larger clan. Furthermore, the richest households in the village often lacked formal political authority. In more prosperous areas of the Southeast, where business-oriented, contractual clans behaved similarly to European corporations, internal clan hierarchy was more often directly determined by wealth and economic power. Nevertheless, even there, Zhang (2017, p. 151) argued that "generational hierarchies were at least the 'default state' from which wealth-based forms of lineage organization might mutate given sufficiently compelling socioeconomic circumstances."

European corporations developed a variety of governance rules and criteria, but generational seniority as well as age rarely played an outsized role in the distribution of power, and lineage was seldom an important criterion for authority when not correlated with wealth. As voluntary associations, corporations often assigned control rights to all major stakeholders and held leaders accountable to corporate members. As will be discussed in chapter 7, several key principles of modern democratic governance—including the majority principle, the principle that *quod omnes tangit, ab omnibus approbari debetat* ("what touches all should be approved by all"), and important principles of delegation of powers—first emerged in corporate organizations and were then adapted to political institutions. Corporations were not egalitarian or democratic; on the contrary, decision-making authority was often closely related to economic power and wealth. Belonging to a powerful and wealthy family within a corporation, even in Europe, was associated with influence and social status. But this power was derived from contractual arrangements that included specific provisions for how to allocate control rights and executive authority in light of the specific goals of the organization and the composition of its members.

The evolving structure of European local government is most evident in the charters and governance rules of self-governing cities. Initially, cities appointed their own courts and also had legislative prerogatives. At first, the general meeting of all citizens was the chief legislative body, but soon such mass assemblies became too large and administration was delegated to committees of "good men" or *boni viri* (Nicholas 1997, p. 159). Rural settlements, too, had forms of collective decision making, as open-field agriculture required a high level of coordination. Within small groups, it seems that decisions were taken by unanimity, while in others, decisions in rural areas too would be delegated to "good men." Within communes, executive authority was sometimes exercised by consuls, who represented different groups or economic interests in the city. Not everyone residing in the city enjoyed political rights; only formal citizens did, and although the conditions to gain citizenship differed based on time and location, to become a citizen, one usually had to have some wealth and pay taxes for some period of time. Benefits from citizenship also differed, but Prak (2018) notes the importance of the possibility of joining a guild and holding public office.

Legal Personality

Both clans and corporations exhibited a de facto legal personality (i.e., an identity separate from that of its members), which was recognized by the law and could last in perpetuity. But legal personality was a much more formal for the European corporation than for the Chinese clan. The European legal tradition had to invent the notion of legal personhood for the corporation because the original holders of legal rights and responsibilities were individuals. The definition of a corporation as a legal entity, separate from that of its members, was first applied to religious and political organizations in the twelfth and thirteenth centuries. In this tradition, the corporation is a "nexus of contract" between its individual constituents.[58]

Ironically, assigning legal personality to a collective entity rather than an individual came much more naturally in China, despite the absence of a formal concept of legal personhood. For traditional Chinese law, the legal and administrative unit of reference was the collective, and collective legal personality was the natural standard. "In the Confucian tradition . . . the collective was morally prior to the individual . . . in many ways the family was the Confucian 'natural person,' just as the individual is the 'natural person' of the modern Western legal system" (Ruskola 2000, pp. 1606, 1652–53). This philosophy meant that in China, groups were typically the bearers of rights and liabilities: penal responsibility in China was collective, and tax and military responsibilities were borne by households and transmitted across generations. It was thus natural that in China, civil law would be part of family law. For Confucians, the extended family was a single entity, and therefore the property of the

---

58. The "nexus of contracts" theory (e.g., Easterbrook and Fishel 1996) regards the corporation as a voluntary, market-oriented creation. The definition sees corporations as a collection of contracts among different parties such as managers, workers, and suppliers. Since the corporation is contractual in nature, corporate structure reflects what the participants have freely chosen. The way that the corporation operates, according to this approach, reflects the free choice of investors, directors, boards, and indeed all stakeholders involved with the corporation.

family also belonged to a single entity, even after generations. The head of the household acted as a trustee for subsequent generations. Household property was not his personal property. Family heads had authority over the members but were regarded as custodians or trustees of the household's property and had no testamentary powers (Ruskola 2000, pp. 1627–28).

Separation of Membership and Control

The separation of membership and control, too, was common to clans and corporations. European corporations often entailed a distinction between the executive authority of whoever had management responsibilities, and the control functions of corporate members, who in theory may have been the residual claimants on any rent that the corporation generated.[59] In practice, this meant that guild members, for example, were often the beneficiaries of their organizations' monopolies, but the rank and file were rarely in control over daily group-level operations. Similar arrangements could be found in Chinese clans. The ancestral trust already involved a separation between ownership and management: while the property belonged to the whole lineage, it was actively managed by only a few individuals. As clans became increasingly complex, so did their management structures. In small clans, it was common for management power over the estate to rotate annually among branches, or among brothers. In more recent times (such as in the nineteenth century), as clans grew along with their commercial interests, some clans began hiring professional managers (usually within their own members), along with assistants and auditors.

Late nineteenth- and early twentieth-century ancestral trusts, or *tang,* increasingly came to resemble European corporations in a few dimensions. They had complex organizational structures that employed full-time, professional managers, who were accountable to councils of elders in semiannual meetings (Ruskola 2000, p. 1649; Zelin 2022, pp. 328–32).[60] Clans also developed ways of dealing with agency problems: the most common example being the case

59. In some cases, the separation of ownership and control was more formal than real. For instance, many medieval monasteries controlled a great deal of real estate and accumulated large amounts of wealth. In theory, such wealth was shared by all members of the corporation, but in fact, it was controlled by the leaders of the corporations, such as the abbot of the monastery or the burgomaster of the town.

60. Lineage trusts had their origin in Song times, with the growth of the clan as the main form of social organization. The authorities encouraged the creation of entities that controlled endowments that would not be subdivided among male heirs, and its income created "a focus of solidarity for the descendants of the founders" (Zelin 2022, p. 328).

where one branch was elected to management and chose to further its own interests rather than those of the entire lineage. This often led to the imposition of rules for serving as manager, as well as duties and punishments to ensure managerial honesty. Sometimes the managers were required to provide bonds before assuming office; that is, securities to forfeiture if they were found guilty of misbehavior (Ruskola 2013, p. 83). They were also required to present financial reports at clan meetings and to keep archives of accounting records. Penalties for misbehavior were generally not spelled out, although there are examples of provisions specifying severe punishments (Ruskola 2000, p. 1651).

Yet these arrangements, which clearly began to close the gap between Western-style corporations and Chinese clans, became more prevalent and prominent only in the late nineteenth and early twentieth centuries. In many ways, the social organizations between East and West continued to differ. There is no evidence that clans resorted to an arrangement such as limited liability or a complete separation between ownership and control, as in modern business corporations, and much less of their having shares traded freely on financial markets. The legacy of the clan remained powerful: the senior male member of the senior lineage branch remained all powerful, and profit-sharing was confined to kin members (Zelin 2022, p. 330). The diffusion of corporations met resistance in Imperial China, unlike other forms of business management and finance that took root more successfully (Harris 2020). As we will see in chapter 10, clans were remarkably tenacious, and their effects can still be discerned during and after the hostility of the communist regime determined to eradicate the institution in the twentieth century.

6. Conclusion

In premodern societies, when the power of the state was not as pervasive and far-reaching as we are now used to, many social and economic interactions occurred where political authority was absent or irrelevant, especially where it came to the provision of local public goods. As such, nongovernmental social organizations such as the clan and the corporation emerged to facilitate cooperation and provide essential services that no individual could supply on his or her own. After the turn of the first millennium, these social organizations proliferated in China and Europe. They performed similar functions and evolved in similar directions, accompanying the processes of economic development and the accumulation of state capacity.

Nonetheless, the clan and the corporation, as social and cultural building blocks of their respective societies, were very different in ways that proved fundamental for future divergences. This, of course, is the central contention of this book. The clan is a dynastic organization, whereas the corporation is a voluntary association. This foundational difference had a profound influence on their trajectories of evolution, future interactions with the state, and subsequent economic and political development. In the coming chapters, we discuss the roles of the clan and the corporation in sustaining the social, economic, and political bifurcation between China and Europe during the second millennium.

6

Social Organizations
in Europe and China

1. Introduction

In this chapter, we describe in more detail the most important and best-known European medieval corporations: fraternities, monasteries, guilds, universities, and self-governing cities. We discuss how they contributed to economic development and contrast them with their counterparts in China. Our goal is to highlight the role of social organizations in the bifurcations between the two civilizations.

There are several reasons to focus on these corporations. They are the best-known, the most comprehensive, and the most important premodern European corporations. They also illustrate the deep penetration of cooperation in various areas of medieval life. Monastic orders and parishes were associated with religious activities, welfare provision, and the creation of local communities; universities were concerned with the transmission of knowledge and the accumulation of human capital; guilds were associated with impersonal charity, the training of apprentices, and the regulation of craftsmanship and trade. Encompassing these corporations and facilitating their continued development were cities, which provided legal enforcement, defense against predators, schooling, and commercial infrastructure. Cities were also a source of an early form of local patriotism and provided a sense of belonging, as well as a basis for social capital. This plethora of corporations highlights that in Europe, individuals could sort themselves according to their interests, capabilities, and resources to pursue shared goals. Moreover, an individual could belong to several corporations at the same time and over time. Finally, these four types of corporations reflect the strong influence of the Catholic Church and of the culture that it diffused.

Before discussing these examples in detail, it is worth making a somewhat ironic point. A central thesis of this book is that corporations were one of the main moving forces in the economic modernization of the West. Yet, perhaps paradoxically, by the Early Modern Age, many of these medieval corporations were either considerably weakened or disappeared altogether, and it would be hard to point to any of them in isolation as a powerful modernizing agent (except for self-governing cities).[1] For example, monasteries were eventually dissolved in all Protestant countries, and even in Catholic countries, their economic and social impact was significantly diminished after 1500 (Cantoni, Dittmar, and Yuchtman 2018). Guilds remained important for economic activity until the late eighteenth century, but in England and the Netherlands—the most developed countries—they were much weakened. Elsewhere, the French Revolution abolished surviving guilds, but by that time, they were widely regarded as a harmful relic. The function of some corporations in aiding the poor was taken over by government in England with the Elizabethan Poor Law of 1601, and it remained a state responsibility.[2] Even universities, which of course survived, had to compete with other voluntary gatherings of intellectuals. City autonomy came under the growing pressure of powerful centralized states, and many of the autonomous city-states disappeared, absorbed into larger national units. However, it is not the parts but the whole with which we are concerned. Even as specific corporations found their influence waning over time, the corporation as a concept remained central to European development, embodied above all in the modern business corporation. Indeed, the business corporation is seen by many as one of the epochal innovations made in the West that set it apart from the rest of the world (Harris 2020). Without its predecessors—which became defunct over time but influenced subsequent organizational innovations—it is difficult to argue that its evolution would have been guaranteed.

2. Fraternities and Guilds

Fraternities and guilds were among the oldest medieval corporations. Although the two terms are sometimes used interchangeably, they refer to

1. We are grateful to Peer Vries for pointing this out to us.
2. Dittmar and Meisenzahl (2019) have pointed out that the Reformation triggered a sharp increase in the role of secular municipal authorities in providing public goods in Protestant towns that passed the so-called Church Ordinances (*Kirchenordnungen*), laws ensuring that the legal jurisdiction over public goods changed and secular magistrates took control of institutions that particularly concerned the laity, including schools, poorhouses, and hospitals.

different types of organizations: fraternities (or "confraternities") were primarily religious and social, whereas "pure guilds" were primarily economic in nature and in many ways resembled modern professional associations or chambers of commerce.[3] As Jack Ross (1983, p. 7) points out, "The basis of both was an oath-bound obligation among several equals legally capable of willful contract to perform certain collectively defined duties, accompanied by the right to certain benefits defined more in relation to need than investment." Guilds applied the idea of voluntary association with nonkin to economic and political affairs, while fraternities were religious organizations concerned with common religious rituals, prayers, and burials, as well as charity and support for the sick. Of course, fraternities were also used to facilitate social gatherings. Reynolds (1997b, p. 73) stresses that many fraternities were basically drinking clubs, with some religious and charitable actions thrown in for good measure.

Fraternities

In the fourteenth century, most English urban dwellers belonged to a fraternity or a guild (Richardson 2004; Ashley 1909; Sommerville 1993). Rosser (2015) estimates that over 30,000 fraternities were active in the United Kingdom alone at some point between 1350 and 1550. medieval fraternities were voluntary associations whose members were bound by oaths and sometimes by pecuniary subscriptions. An individual could join more than one such organization. Unlike kinship, membership was not for life, and an exit option existed, though normally costly. The size of guilds and fraternities varied, ranging from very small groups to several hundred individuals, with most fraternities having between 50 and 100 members. Some fraternities, despite the name, included women.[4] Fraternities often offered a social organization to which the many unmarried men and women in medieval Europe could belong and where they could form relationships (Rosser 2015, pp. 111–14).

Many fraternities went beyond serving members' needs to provide public goods that benefited the larger community, such as administering and

---

3. Ogilvie (2019, p. 20) points out that devotional confraternities were often organized around shared occupations, whereas occupational guilds often shared religious observance "for motivating cooperation and organizing collective action."

4. Half of the members of the confraternity of San Paolo in Florence in the year 1480 were unmarried, and several confraternities in Italy and France had the specific purpose of nurturing or assisting the young. The percentage of unmarried women (including widows) in Normandy ranged between 20 percent and 50 percent of members (Rosser 2015, pp. 51, 111).

providing resources for hospitals or hospices, assisting the poor, or contributing to monuments, churches, schools, and infrastructures for their town (Rosser 2015, pp. 84–86). These charitable activities fulfilled the Christian and universalistic goals of the organization, and at the same time enhanced the reputation and prestige of its members. In several instances, fraternities took over social tasks that had previously been performed only by ecclesiastic institutions. Through the activities of fraternities, individuals participated in the public and political life of their community.

Religious rituals and moral principles were of particular importance in the formation of many corporations, and as Christianity deeply permeated medieval European societies, religion affected the collective actions of laypeople. The beliefs that underlay fraternities were thus influenced by the Church, in particular both by local priests and their superiors, as well as by members of the wider Church (monks, nuns, and the monastic orders in which monasteries and convents were organized). This was true of the Dominicans and Franciscan orders in the late thirteenth and early fourteenth centuries (Rosser 2015, p. 39). Universalistic values of piety and care for others, and not just for one's relatives—an example of generalized morality—were founding principles stressed by many fraternities and apparent in their rituals and activities. These values reflected the widespread idea that practicing charity and generalized compassion (i.e., an obligation of charity toward strangers) was the responsibility of any good Christian, not just of the clergy or monks. By joining a fraternity, individual members were expected to subscribe to a shared value system and act as "an ethical member of the community" (Rosser 2015, p. 44; see also Porterfield 2018).

This fact points to an important difference between European fraternities and Chinese clans. Moral and religious principles were also paramount in Chinese dynastic organizations, of course, but the scope of the system of ethics stressed by Chinese clans was very different: the Chinese were far less obsessed with salvation and universalistic values of love and compassion toward other human beings, and more with ancestor worship and solidarity with relatives descending from the same ancestors. Ironically, the term "fraternity" widely used in European associations denoted organizations that constituted a break with family ties. A fraternity was an artificial household: its members were supposed to behave toward one another *as if* they were brothers and sisters, even if they were totally unrelated, and even if doing so might undermine their real family relations. Saint Francis, who had rejected his father upon his conversion, was a widely known and venerated example of model behavior at the time. Similarly, there is evidence that members of the guild of the Trinity at York in 1306 had sworn to assist each other even against their direct family members.[5] Tellingly, the ideal sentiment stressed by fraternities was that of *brotherhood*, not of cousinhood—a further symptom that the value system of the extended family was no longer significant at the time.

Fraternities periodically reviewed the behavior of members, to make sure that it was consistent with the ethical principles of the organization. They could administer fines and other punishments, and members in gross violations could be expelled. Consistent with the ideal of friendship and brotherhood, however, and in contrast to Chinese lineages, the governance of most European fraternities was fairly egalitarian. Obligations were reciprocal and among equals who had voluntarily decided to join the organization. In principle, official roles rotated over time, and in most fraternities, the power structure was horizontal except where members had acquired a political role (Rosser 2015, pp. 111, 172–73).

In short, European fraternities provided individuals with networks, aid, and social capital. By joining a confraternity, young men and women gained many benefits: they obtained friendship and assistance, as well as a sense of belonging and identity; they nurtured their ethical principles during a period of life where they were most vulnerable; they gained social status and built reputations of trustworthiness; and of course, all of these in turn increased their economic opportunities and promoted their social mobility.

Guilds

Merchant and craft guilds, which overlapped with fraternities to some extent, were particularly widespread in urban centers. Although kinship and endogamy were often present, membership rarely made common ancestry a formal requirement. Often, new guild members were young men (and occasionally, a few single women) who had left their households in search of better economic opportunities.[6]

5. This is not to say that fraternities often broke up families, but rather that they acknowledged the Christian ideal that "in order to reach God, one was required to put aside the natural ties inherited at birth in favor of a deliberately willed engagement with others" (Rosser 2015, p. 59).

6. Craft guilds were on the whole male-dominated organizations and mixed-sex guilds were fairly rare. Ogilvie (2019, p. 245) presents data for guilds in France, Flanders and Germany that indicate that mixed-sex guilds constituted at most 10 percent of the total.

The rapidly growing number of guilds reflects the increasingly fine division of labor among European urban artisans.[7] Merchant and craft guilds engaged in a large variety of activities. Some were clearly social and religious, as in fraternities: they performed select religious rituals, organized meetings and festivities, and overall created considerable social capital among unrelated individuals. But the objectives of guilds were above all economic. Guilds engaged in forms of risk sharing for members struck by bad luck and provided members with loans (which sometimes were forgiven). They resolved conflicts and arbitrated disputes, regulated and supervised master-apprentice relationships, offered protection, organized periodic gatherings to strengthen friendship, and labored to consolidate a common identity among people of the same trade. Guilds provided a variety of other economic services to their members, such as monitoring product quality and guaranteeing standards, enforcing contracts, regulating trade and setting prices, and coordinating the purchase of raw materials. They helped their members in overcoming collective action problems in negotiations with city government and rulers, organizing political lobbying, and deciding collective punishment against sovereigns or other external entities.[8] Guilds were active in local government and often presented petitions or organized riots when needed against excessive impositions by the ruling feudal lord. As Prak (2018) notes, guilds did a lot more than just the kind of activities expected from professional associations: they took responsibility for fire protection, policing, tax collection, and jury duty, among other services. Guilds had financial autonomy, elections, and membership meetings and were "miniature versions of the urban community" (Prak 2018, p. 107). It has even been argued that guilds were "a mainstay of the urban community," although clearly that varied considerable from town to town as well as over time (Prak 2018, p. 108). Ogilvie (2011) points out that the combination of social, political, and economic functions made merchant guilds more effective. Members who did not play by the rules would lose out not only on a host of economic benefits, but also the highly valuable social capital embedded in guild networks. The bundling social capital and religious

---

7. A "book of trades" (*livre des métiers*) was compiled for Paris in 1260, listing no fewer than 101 different trades. At the same time many occupations, such as copyists and dancers, were never part of a guild. See Epstein (2009, pp. 117–18).

8. A large body of literature discusses the activities of merchant guilds and craft guilds. In particular, see Greif (2006), Gelderblom and Grafe (2010), and Ogilvie (2011, 2019). For discussions of apprenticeship, see Epstein (2013) and Mokyr (2019).

worship with economic coordination turned out to be key to the success and survival of both merchant and craft guilds.

Merchant guilds continued to be dominant in most cities and were particularly important in the regulation of local markets. Many medieval English towns show close relationships between the local merchant guild and the municipal government, giving rise to a confluence of interests that came at the expense of the rest of the community (Ogilvie 2011). In England, this included the creation and enforcement of rules regarding products and prices, markets, tolls, and wages. On the Continent, guilds were less invasive in local affairs but more involved in long-distance trade, often acting as the primary institution governing the city's foreign affairs. English and Dutch merchant guilds lost their dominant position in the sixteenth and seventeenth centuries, but on the Continent, their power lasted until late in the eighteenth century (Ogilvie 2011, p. 33).

Craft and merchant guilds, like religious fraternities, affected nonmembers as well. At times, they acted as surrogate forms of local government until towns were formally incorporated and recognized as self-governing. At this point, the same individuals who held administrative offices in guilds ended up acquiring similar responsibilities in their municipality government. Thanks to their example, guilds and fraternities led the evolution of urban government, playing an important role in steering urban policy and strengthening a common identity for the larger community, as will be discussed at length in chapter 7. As always, however, not all these activities were economically beneficial for everyone else. There are also examples of merchant guilds created to corrupt public officials or engaged in malicious activities that benefited their members while reducing economic prosperity for everyone else (Ogilvie 2011; Rosser 2015).

Whether guilds were overall socially beneficial remains a matter of controversy, but their widespread proliferation indicates that they served their members well. Among other things, guilds supported members' widows and orphans, provided social insurance, fostered social capital, and strengthened group identity by organizing social events and religious processions. Economists have argued that merchant guilds were an important means to make long-distance trade possible by providing security and arbitration in disputes. There is no question that medieval Europe indeed experienced a Commercial Revolution, and merchant guilds indeed made this revolution possible. Because the state capacity necessary to suppress brigandry and opportunistic behavior was still absent, guilds stepped in to fill this void. Greif, Milgrom, and Weingast (1994) argued that merchant guilds used the threat of possible trade embargoes to compel rulers to enforce security for foreign merchants. On the

other hand, guilds clearly engaged in what we would now call "anticompeti-
tive" practices, such as limiting entry to protect the exclusionary rents of
current members. Merchant guilds regulated how their members could do
business and lobbied officials and rulers to enforce their privileged positions.

Craft guilds were similar. They regulated the production process, stipulating in detail which techniques could be used. Such supervision supposedly
ensured the quality of the product (and thus the reputation of the products made
in that town), but it also crystallized technology and thus may have slowed
innovation. Some economic historians have followed Stephan R. Epstein in
highlighting the positive contributions of craft guilds to the smooth operation
of markets, the recruitment of workers and capital, and the transmission of
artisanal and commercial knowledge (Epstein and Prak 2008; Prak and van
Zanden 2013). Others, especially Sheilagh Ogilvie (2011 2019), have rebutted
this movement with detailed critiques, arguing that guilds were rampant in
lobbying authorities for rent-seeking and helped masters collude in labor markets by regulating the employment of apprentices and journeymen. This prevented newcomers from competing with more senior workers. Furthermore,
guilds also regulated the employment of women and foreigners, who were
often the victims of monopsonistic practices.

Given guilds' pervasive importance for many centuries, it would seem unavoidable that they would have a variety of effects, some favorable, some dam-
aging. What matters above all is that guilds were a prime example of corporations and represent the fundamental features that made European social
organizations so unique. For better or for worse, guilds made markets work
and sustained the cooperation and knowledge that drove local economies,
forming an inseparable part of European commercial and artisanal sectors.

Guilds emerged in China too, where they performed seemingly similar economic functions. By the nineteenth century, guilds became increasingly important in providing Chinese communities with local public goods and services:
regulating markets, maintaining quality standards of artisanal goods, and sometimes collecting taxes. They also sponsored local relief, organized education and
festivals, and handled other matters of general community significance. Clan
managers, particularly in single-lineage villages and areas of strong corporate
lineages like Southeast China, also assumed public functions. Rankin (1990)
suggests that the term *gong* (public) might be used to describe their activities.
Nevertheless, they differed from European guilds in several key respects.

First and foremost, Chinese guilds emerged much later than their European
counterparts. To be sure, a few merchant guilds emerged during the late Ming

period, starting as associations of traveling merchants taking over the functions of licensed brokers. However, they become common only from the eighteenth century onward. Craft guilds emerged even later, sometime during the nineteenth century (Moll-Murata 2008; Peng Zeyi 1995; Kwang-Ching Liu 1988). By the mid- and late nineteenth century, they had attained considerable political power (e.g., Brown 1979).

Second, as mentioned in previous chapters, the tradition stressing that apprenticeships take place between family members remained intact (Macgowan 1888–1889; Van Zanden and Prak 2013). In some sense, guilds were subsumed by lineages in managing the transmission of intergenerational skills and knowledge. In twentieth-century southern China, "not only were the elders of the town the heads of the clan but the entire industry was organized and monopolized by the clan" (Burgess 1928, p. 71). Even in modern China, some skills are often kept within the family and experienced artisans intentionally inhibit the acquisition of knowledge by new workers who are not dynastically related (Zhu, Chen, and Dai 2016; see also Gowlland 2012). The practice of within-family training was especially prevalent in high-skilled crafts such as medicine (Islam 2016).

Third, before the nineteenth century, membership in Chinese guilds was often based on common geographic origin (which correlated with kinship). This criterion also reflected an urban context where it was common for people sharing the same native place to specialize in the same trade. According to Golas (1977, p. 563), "The requirement in many guilds that members be native of a single area other than in the city where the guild was located provides one of the most striking contrasts between European and Chinese guilds." Over time, this requirement was weakened or abandoned, often through the confederation of guilds from different areas, but there are several examples of Chinese guilds that maintained common origin until recently.[9] The apprenticeship system also often preserved geographic exclusion and remained based on extended family connection to a great extent (for detailed evidence, see De la Croix, Doepke and Mokyr 2018, pp. 12–13).

---

9. Golas (1977, p. 564), provides the example of the Leather Box Guild in Beijing, founded in 1689, that during ,World War II still consisted of people originating from Shantung. Rowe (1984, table 14) lists the membership criteria of over 100 guilds founded in Hankow between 1644 and 1920. Most of the guilds founded until the end of the eighteenth century required common origin as a membership criterion. For guilds founded from the second half of the nineteenth century onward, instead, common trade had become the most important criterion.

Fourth, Chinese guilds were primarily economic associations, and they did not have the much broader social, religious, and altruistic goals of European corporations, whether they were guilds or fraternities. In China, these goals were pursued first and foremost by lineage organizations.

Finally, unlike in Europe, Chinese guilds did not play a formal role in city governance—although they did informally shape local enforcement and exerted considerable influence over local administration, as discussed by Rowe (1984) in his study of the city of Hankow during the nineteenth century.

3. Religious Associations: Monasteries and Parishes

European Monasteries and Monastic Orders

Once Christianity became the recognized religion of the Roman Empire in the second half of the fifth century, the Church faced a dilemma. How could it set out to capture the hearts and minds of pagans, both within the empire and outside it, without making doctrinal and ritual compromises? Doing so risked alienating the Church's most zealous followers, who resented any concessions with respect to their faith (Davis 1961). Monastic orders helped resolve this dilemma by providing the most committed Christians with a place where they could live as devoted believers.

The evolution of Christian monasteries in the West reflects its increasingly corporate nature. Whereas in Eastern Europe, Christian monasteries began as communities of isolated hermits, in the West, they took on a more explicit corporate structure: they were formed, governed, and administered by individuals who had elected to join and were committed to cooperative behavior.[10] European monasteries became organizations of monks and nuns living together, who worked with one another and with the surrounding population. They located themselves in settled areas and followed a strict code of conduct. Monasteries were self-governing and were always outside the structure of the

---

10. The Church promoted monastic orders mainly because it was spiritually weakened once it gained political recognition, power, and wealth. Monasteries enabled the Church to cultivate and benefit from the most pious Christian adherents (i.e., the monks), while the Church itself sought to appeal to the less devout believers. The monks' zeal implied that the Church was never able to fully absorb monasteries into its structure. Effectively, the Catholic clergy was split into a secular clergy (priests) and a regular one (monks). Thus, the way that the Church could take advantage of the monasteries was to "accept their fruits" of religious zeal and purity by filling its own hierarchy with monks (Davis 1961, p. 81).

secular Church, which was increasingly based on the local parish and church, and the hierarchical Episcopate (deacons, bishops, and others). Western monastic orders were formally answerable to the pope and normally collaborated with him, but in practice, they operated independently. They assisted the papacy in spreading the faith inside and outside Europe and usually supported it in its struggles against the state, national churches, and heretics. The monasteries constantly provided the papacy with the reformers and strong leaders required to preserve collective vitality (Davis 1961). In fact, a considerable number of influential popes, such as Gregory VII, Victor III, and Urban II, came from monasteries.

Christian monasteries emerged as early as the fourth century in the eastern segment of Christianity, particularly Egypt (Davis 1961). These monasteries had little or no structure that we would recognize as corporate. In Merovingian times, many Western monasteries were still in part family affairs and run more like clans than corporations. Subsequently, however, as kin-based institutions diminished in importance, monasteries became increasingly corporative (Henrich 2020). One of the first organized and structured forms of monastic association was the Benedictine Order, founded in 529 by Saint Benedict in Monte Cassino. The rules that governed Benedictine monastic life lasted for over 1,000 years and were used as a founding model by later monasteries. These monasteries—as all subsequent ones—emerged and took shape through a bottom-up process, not at the initiative of the Church.

Although Benedictine monasteries were numerous, they had no organic connection with each other. This changed in the tenth century, when several monasteries joined in congregations under a common governance. This movement was initiated by the monastery of Cluny in southern France (established by William I of Aquitaine in 910). To avoid corruption and abuse, several monasteries delegated the choice of their abbot to the abbot of Cluny, who had displayed exceptional strictness in enforcing the Benedictine rule in his monastery. This led to a federation of monasteries ("a congregation") that in the twelfth century included 2,000 monasteries in France alone. These resultant characteristics were distinctive of corporate structures: voluntary association, shared identity, and representative decision-making. The Order of Cluny is the first example, besides the Church itself, of a large medieval corporation consisting of a network of smaller and subordinated corporate groups, located in different areas. Several subsequent monastic orders also were similarly organized as a corporation of corporations but adapted to the particular needs of their time and place. Examples include the Cistercians (1098), the Order of the Camaldolese (founded c.1012), and the Order of Chartreuse (1084) (Davis 1961, pp. 58–59).

Monasteries became quite numerous in Western Europe, particularly in France but also in Italy, Spain, Germany, and Belgium (Van Zanden 2009). Figure 6.1 presents the estimated number of monasteries throughout Western Europe by century (existing stock at the time and new foundations). A marked acceleration took place during the period between the ninth and thirteenth centuries, when challenges and crises within the Church drew more zealous believers to embrace monastic life, the embrace of the monasteries. One driver of the expansion of monasteries was a set of papal reforms that prohibited lay ownership of monastic assets, such as buildings and access to tithes. In many ways, these reforms embellished monastic corporations with legal privileges such as "charters of immunity," which excluded royal officers from their estates and freed the groups from services that were normally due from their tenures. In the eleventh century, the monasteries that had left some record of their size all reported doubling their ranks or growing even more (Morris 1989, pp. 57–63).

Some monastic orders such as the Cistercians, accumulated considerable wealth through gifts, skillful administration, and efficient estate management. They contributed a great deal to the economic revival of their surrounding localities (Colish 1997). By around 1300, the Cistercian Order had constructed roughly 600 monasteries from Ireland to Poland. The so-called Mendicant Orders (Franciscan, Dominicans, and others) shared ideals of humility and external charity, prohibited individual possessions, and engaged in a large range of activities without being restricted to any specific locality. These orders became so large that they had a great influence over the Church and society at large (including over fraternities and guilds) in the later Middle Ages. Some cities had to be divided into districts, which were then specifically assigned to one order or another (Davis 1961).

At the time of the Crusades, some monastic orders even pursued military objectives. The Knights Hospitallers of Saint John started as a monastic order in charge of a hospice for Christian pilgrims in Jerusalem, but later they added an oath of resistance to infidels to defend the Holy Sepulcher. This order, and other similar military corporations such as the Order of the Knights Templar and the Teutonic Order, had more complex constitutions than the first monastic congregations (Barber 1995). They could sustain large-scale cooperation, which enabled them to gain substantial political power. The Knights Hospitaller eventually ruled the islands of Rhodes and Malta, while the Teutonic Order spearheaded the Crusades to subjugate and Christianize Eastern Europe. By the

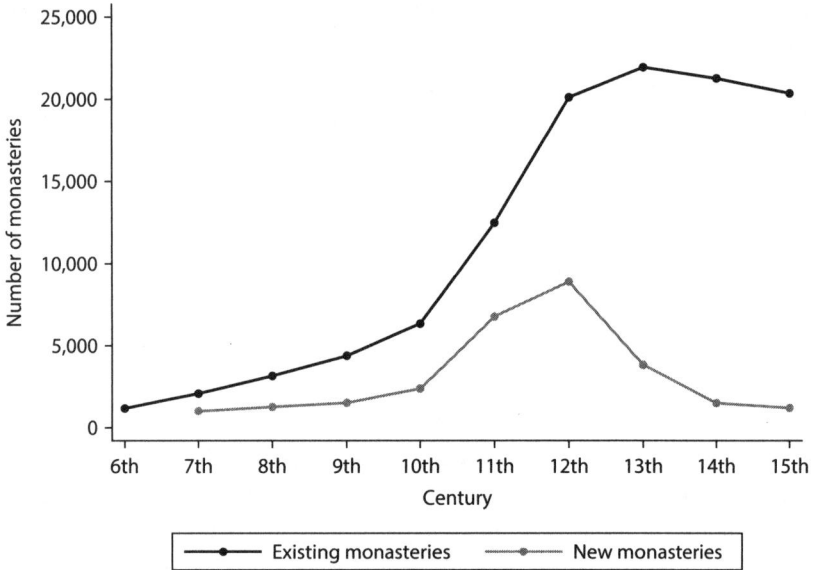

FIGURE 6.1. Monasteries in Western Europe. *Source:* Buringh and van Zanden (2006, table 5).

sixteenth century, some monasteries had become so wealthy that they tempted secular rulers to engage in expropriation, which led to their downfall.

The ideals of monastic life changed considerably over time and across orders reflecting the flexibility and effectiveness inherent in the cooperative organizational form. For example, the early Benedictines viewed monastic life as being dedicated to contemplation and prayer. Over time, however, they increasingly extolled the virtues of labor and production and committed to a *laborare est orare* (to work is to pray) ideology (White 1978, p. 183; Siedentop 2014, p. 95). Subsequent monastic orders committed to have an impact on society. Hence, many of them provided poverty relief, organized agricultural work, and invested in the preservation and accumulation of knowledge well before the growth of universities. Recent research has shown that monasteries had substantial positive externalities on the growth in the areas in which they were located. For example, Cistercian monasteries had a significant impact on economic development and population growth and seem to have increased people's willingness to work hard, ironically spreading what is known as the "Protestant work ethic" (Andersen et al. 2017). Even earlier, the Domesday Book of 1086 shows that estates under Benedictine monastic ownership were more progressive and productive than those owned by secular landlords or nonmonastic religious organizations

(Rossignoli and Trombetta 2024). In short, monasteries were at the cutting edge of agricultural technology and management, just as White argued.

Monasteries and monastic orders had several other positive externalities on local economic development. First, they increased literacy rates among men and women, as well as the number of books in circulation. Medieval science, especially astronomy, geometry, and physics, was largely advanced by members of the regular clergy, some of whom made important contributions to philosophy and science: one thinks of Roger Bacon, William of Ockham, and John of Sacrobosco (although there is no reason to believe that scientific activity contributed much to economic development in this age).

Second, monasteries contributed to a more precise definition of property rights by documenting their land holdings in charters and written documents. Because they were organized in corporate form, monasteries and monastic orders were able to acquire titles to land and real estate that they could hold in perpetuity, separate from the Church (Cavanagh 2016). This clarification and the precise definition of property rights provided an example that was followed by others. Increased literacy and more clearly defined property rights in turn contributed to the evolution of legal institutions of the twelfth and thirteenth centuries.

Third, monasteries facilitated economic development because they contributed to pacification and a reduction of violence (Van Zanden 2009, pp. 44–45). Markets for agricultural products developed in close proximity to monasteries, which often found themselves with excess food supplies that others wanted to buy. In the early Middle Ages, monasteries therefore contributed to the development of nearby cities that took advantage of these surpluses, particularly in France and Germany; Nicholas (1997, p. 32) provides several examples. The Cistercians monasteries did this by generating and disseminating a culture of diligence and stimulating higher productivity. They did in Catholic Europe what Max Weber argued happened in Protestant Europe—namely, by teaching and promoting the belief that labor ennobles and pleases God, monks used their human capital to achieve several technological breakthroughs. The Middle Ages were not nearly as technically stagnant as popular conceptions of "the Dark Ages" would have it, but any discussion of the origins of technological progress in Europe must acknowledge religious influence from monasteries.[11]

---

11. In a classic summary, Lynn White (1968, p. 65) famously stated that "for the first time the practical and the theoretical were embodied in the same individual ... the monk was the first intellectual to get dirt under his fingernails." Medieval treatise on technology and engineering were written mostly by monks, most famously *De Diversis Artibus* by the Benedictine monk

Finally, as argued recently by Siedentop (2014), monasticism proved to be a great model for subsequent corporations. Monastic orders consisted of self-governing social organizations founded on consent and "under a rule that recognized the moral equality of brothers" (p. 188).

Chinese Monasteries

Monasteries were not a uniquely European phenomenon. As we have already noted, Buddhist and Taoist monasteries existed in China long before the first European monastic order was formed in the fifth century. Comparing monasteries in the two regions, however, reveals a critical difference: in Europe, but not in China, monasteries were corporations. European monasteries were self-governing, horizontal associations established by their members to advance a common interest. In China, monasteries increasingly became neither self-governing nor intended to advance the common interests of their members. Prior to the fifth century, Buddhist monasteries were similar to European ones. They were mainly established by wandering monks (and nuns) and their lay supporters to pursue spiritual life. During the Tang Dynasty, Buddhist monasteries prospered. Eventually, however, they collided with the imperial bureaucracy and became victims of the fiscal needs of the state. The decline of Buddhist monasteries accelerated with the triumph of neo-Confucianism, and they lost most of their political power. As Brook (1993, pp. 29–34) notes in his definitive study, Buddhists were prohibited from taking the imperial *keju* exam and lost their influence on the imperial government. Neo-Confucian scholarship was the road to being part of the elite, and "[scholars] came to regard the career of a monk as a second class undertaking" (p. 31). Unlike in Europe, by the Ming Dynasty, Buddhism and its monasteries were alienated from secular power and from intellectual and technological activities (see also Gernet 1995).

A few words about Chinese Buddhism, more broadly, are in order at this point. Buddhism was introduced to China during the first century BC. In the few centuries thereafter, Chinese scholars undertook the translation of Indian Buddhist manuscripts. Afterward, the faith prospered for the next 350 years or so, gaining many lay followers, especially due to the political disorder that

---

Theophilus in 1122. White (1978) has placed monasteries at the center of technological progress in medieval Europe and suggested that monks may have been the only people who tried to bridge formal knowledge and its technological applications. For centuries, he felt, monks were at the cutting edge of new techniques in the West.

followed the collapse of the Han Dynasty. Buddhism offered spiritual comfort during this period of instability. Buddhism peaked in the mid-ninth century, as reflected by the increase in Buddhist monks over time: there were around 38,000 Buddhist monks during the late fifth century, but about 360,000 in AD 845. As noted in chapter 4, in that same year, the Tang emperor turned against Buddhist monasteries and dissolved many of them. Growth seems to have resumed under the Song Dynasty as the number of Buddhist clergy reached 458,000 in the early eleventh century; however, they declined to 213,148 in 1291 (Gernet 1995, p. 6).

Buddhism and Christianity have much in common, despite profound theological differences. Both faiths emphasize individual salvation and commit to the belief of punishment and reward in the afterlife. Both also encouraged the organization of lay believers in communities (manifested in temples in China and churches in Europe).[12] Yet while Buddhism and Christianity both led to the creation of monasteries, these institutions differed notably. After the fifth century, the abbots of the large Chinese monasteries were nominated by the Imperial court. The court also ordinated monks and nuns, and during the Tang, it went as far to administer an exam to those who sought to be ordained (Gernet 1995, p. 44). Once officially recognized, clergy and monasteries enjoyed valuable tax exemptions and legal privileges (Gernet 1955; Twitchett 1957). These privileges encouraged forgeries of ordinations and gave rise to an active secondary market in which these forgeries were traded (Gernet 1955, p. 11; Brook 1993, p. 32). Tax privileges were essential to the perpetuation of the monasteries as monks were religiously prohibited from working—another striking difference between Buddhist monks and those of the West.

Such tax exemptions increased the cost of Buddhism to the state, however, undermining the political resilience of Buddhist monasteries because they eroded the state's tax base. The expansion of Buddhist monasteries made it tempting—particularly in times of need—to dissolve them, confiscate their wealth, and subject their inhabitants (monks, servants, and slaves) to taxation. This is exactly what happened during the reign of the Wuzong emperor (814–846). Later, the state itself entered the market for Buddhist ordinations

12. The similarity between Buddhism and Christianity was sufficient to induce the first European missionaries in China to adopt a Buddhist persona. "Michele Ruggieri was the first [Jesuit missionary in China] to dress like a Buddhist monk . . . from 1582 to 1588, and he never questioned the adequacy of his Buddhist persona. From 1584 onward, he lived in a church called the Temple of the Holy Flower (Shenghua Si), a name actually identifying the church as a Buddhist temple (si)" (Amsler 2018, pp. 36–37).

(*tu-tieh*) and sold them to those who could afford and wanted to buy them. The Song emperors sold thousands of ordinations, issuing as many as 10,000 in 1084 (Gernet 1995, pp. 61–62).

Another important difference with Europe is that Buddhist monasteries remained isolated from each other and never formed monastic orders or an equivalent grouping.[13] This isolation contributed to their political weakness. Moreover, monasteries were physically isolated, as most tended to be located in remote regions like the mountains rather than in presettled areas. Socially, monasteries promoted a lifestyle alien to most Chinese. As Wright (1990, p. 69) noted, there was a "conflict between Chinese [Confucian] social morality and the ethics of Buddhism." In particular, Buddhism required monks and nuns not only to retain celibacy and to refrain from eating meat, but it also prohibited them from physically cultivating land or touching any "impure" object.[14]

Buddhism did not offer the Chinese peasantry an alternative means for the provision of local public goods. It thus failed to reverse the impact of neo-Confucianism on the organization of society. As noted previously, the Song Dynasty encouraged the influence of Confucianist thought by allowing commoners to compile genealogies and establish clan trusts, and through the requirements of the Civil Service Examination. The early Ming emperors weakened Buddhism further by restricting the number of monasteries and who could become a monk or nun. In the late Ming Dynasty, monasteries became subservient to the whims and interests of the gentry. In particular, the elite used the monasteries as resorts and meeting places in the context of an increasing rift between the gentry and the court (Brook 1993, p. 114). These trends were interrupted by the Qing emperors, who supported Buddhist monasteries as part of their strategy to expand their control over the Mongolians, who were Buddhists (Naquin and Rawski 1987, p. 18). Despite the hostility of all ruling dynasties until the Qing, Buddhist monasteries persisted for a long time. Nevertheless, Chinese Buddhism did not have the same impact on the social organization of cooperation that the Church—and the Christian monasteries—had in Europe.[15]

13. Decay of learning in monasteries began by the sixth century because Dhyāna Buddhism emphasizes looking into oneself (Johnston 1913, pp. 85–86). Gifts made many of the monasteries into large landowners (Walsh 2010, pp. 83–85).

14. Monasteries thus had to survive by relying on donations, rental income, or the labor of slaves and bondsmen (Mather 1981). Regarding lay Buddhism during this period, see, for example, Teiser (2020, pp. 155–59).

15. Chinese Buddhism, nevertheless, remained part of Chinese culture. See, for example, Fang (2015). About 18 percent of contemporary Chinese are Buddhists. https://assets .pewresearch.org/wp-content/uploads/sites/11/2012/12/globalReligion-tables.pdf

Parishes

Whereas monastic orders were associations of individuals devoted to prayers, work, and an ascetic monastic lifestyle, European parishes were religious associations of laypeople. By the thirteenth century, the parish was among the most important religious organizations for most average citizens, particularly in the countryside, where they allowed people to form strong bonds with local priests.

Parishes were not corporations. Formally, they were subunits of the Catholic Church; as such, they were neither autonomous nor voluntary, and there was no free exit for members. Yet their expansion was a bottom-up process that reflected increased demand for religious services from the citizenry beyond that which would be expected from organizations comprising the clergy hierarchy. According to Reynolds (1997b, pp. 79–80), community involvement in the parish was inversely related to clerical attention to the local church. Many parishes were built by laypeople—either by local lords or the entire community—and later given to the Church or to a monastic order. Parishes served as an important source for social capital because they provided places for ordinary people to meet and interact on a regular basis, especially in the countryside, where the vast majority of people lived.

Although the primary activities of a parish were religious, in some cases they also became involved in secular and administrative activities and provided local public goods. Some of the responsibilities of the parish had a secular and administrative nature, and secular officers were in charge. Officials were accountable in annual meetings of parishioners for how they spent the money that had been raised for the local church (Dyer 1994, p. 413). For instance, parishes in the Low Countries organized common work on drainage works and other infrastructures (Reynolds 1997b, p. 90). Churchyards also commonly served as marketplaces, and church buildings could be used as warehouses or points of assembly and collective decision making. Most rural villages did not have a formal administration, and collective decisions regarding common property, such as walls, roads, and wells, were made within the confines of the parish. The parish did not usurp local powers; rather, it gave structure to a local community that was previously absent in many rural areas of medieval Europe. In urban centers, sometimes parishes were associated with specific social groups, such as a particular trade or group of immigrants.

Regardless of who originally built them, for most practical purposes, parish churches were often regarded as common property of the local community and exhibited some important forms of self-government—even if they were formally under the control of the local bishop. Parishioners generally had to bear maintenance costs and other expenses, and in several places in the twelfth and thirteenth centuries, they elected their own priests, sometimes in opposition to higher ecclesiastic authorities. Parishes were also involved in forming guilds and fraternities and held property jointly with these other corporate organizations; in such cases, laypeople could also be in charge of administering church property. In all these instances, formal arrangements like statutes or charters did not usually create new corporate bodies but recognized communities and practices that already existed (Reynolds 1997b, p. 98).

4. Universities and Institutions for Higher Education

Europe

European universities emerged spontaneously as key corporate organizations for providing higher education. Of the many corporate organizations of the Middle Ages, the university has proved the most viable and persistent, and the shape attained by universities around 1500 determined their current structure. In the words of one of the first historians of the topic, universities "are the rock whence we hewn . . . the historic continuity is unbroken" (Haskins 1923, p. 2). Higher education had existed in classical antiquity, and in medieval times, it could be found in many parts of the world.[16] Much of the material taught at medieval European universities was derived from Greek and Islamic learning, but the organizational form—which became cemented as a classical corporation—was unique to Europe.

The first European universities emerged in the second half of the twelfth century in Paris, Oxford, Montpellier, Salerno, and Bologna. As Grant (1996) points out, universities were an urban phenomenon, but urbanization alone was not sufficient for their emergence. Most universities were fairly small: even the best-known schools, like the universities of Paris and Oxford, admitted around 500 students a year, most of whom dropped out without attaining a bachelor's degree. Yet even a few years of university study in an arts faculty and the acquisition of literacy skills in Latin and basic numeracy skills prepared one for a useful career in a royal or ducal bureaucracy. Figure 6.2, which uses

---

16. Among the precursors of the medieval university were the Platonic Academy, founded in 387 BC; Aristotle's Peripatetic School, established c.335; and the Imperial University of Constantinople or *Pandidacterium*, founded in 425 AD by Theodosius II. Even earlier institutions of higher learning can be found in India, where the University of Takshashila is dated to the sixth century BC and Nalanda University a century later. See, for instance, Peters (2019).

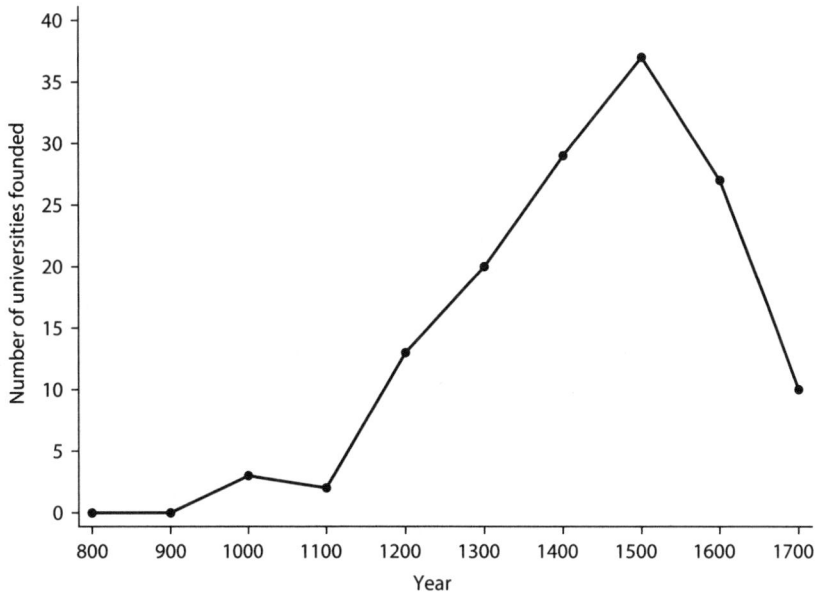

FIGURE 6.2. New universities founded in Europe. *Source:* De la Croix et al. (2023).
Note: De La Croix et al (2023) consider universities in Latin Europe, meaning Europe minus the Muslim world and the Byzantine world. The data also include important learning institutions that were not formal universities, such as the Herborn Academy (Academia Nassauensis), which was a Calvinist institution of higher learning in Herborn, Germany, from 1584 to 1817. The century refers to when universities were active which sometimes occurred before their official creation (e.g., the University of Amsterdam, which was officially established in 1877, but its roots go back to the Athenaeum Illustre, founded in 1632).

data from De la Croix et al. (2023), illustrates the number of new universities founded throughout Europe in each century between AD 800 and AD 1700. There is a continuous growth of new universities, starting in the twelfth century and peaking in the sixteenth century.

Universitas was a general term used by medieval jurists for any corporation. When accompanied by terms such as *scholarium*, or *magistrorum*, the phrase referred to a community of students or masters who had organized to pursue or provide higher education. The organizational features of medieval universities also reflected the high geographic mobility of both faculty and students. Foreigners did not automatically acquire any legal status in a city, and to attract talented individuals, cities granted faculty and students a special clerical status associated with considerable rights, including the right to be judged by an ecclesiastical court.

Like guilds and fraternities, universities were self-governing: they set their own rules for membership and advancement, had their own statutes, and could contain subcorporations, such as associations of foreign students or colleges that provided housing and other facilities. There were no superior entities that would supervise medieval universities or provide binding norms and guidelines. While the governance details of universities differed from place to place, they were normally independent from direct control by the city. In Bologna and Padua, governance was controlled by students' associations; teachers were hired by the student body, which in turn was divided by field of study, such as law or medicine, or by the students' geographic origin. Yet in other universities, governance was mixed, with students being in control of some offices but with masters integrated in the university. For instance, in the late fourteenth century, Prague's faculty of law had a student rector but its own dedicated faculty (Verger 2003, p. 39).

A main reason why universities strived to remain independent was their desire for self-determination of academic standards and freedom from external interference. Their independence was sometimes won peacefully; at other times, it was obtained only after litigation and conflict (Colish 1997, p. 267). While universities were granted privileges by rulers and the Church, they zealously defended their autonomy and "faced the world with an autonomous front" (Hannam 2011, p. 67).

As discussed in chapter 2 and in the next subsection, autonomy and decentralization were two major differences between European and Chinese educational institutions. In China, the main goal of schools and academies was to prepare students for the Imperial Civil Service Examinations, and the curriculum content was determined by the Imperial bureaucracy. Independent institutions with scholarly missions such as universities and learned societies were rare in China, and those that existed often proved ephemeral. The Donglin Academy in Wuxi in the Yangtze Delta, an independent private "discussion forum" founded in 1111 by intellectuals, languished and eventually disappeared, a common fate shared by similar organizations (Huang 2023, pp. 94–95). Although other countries developed institutions similar to the European university—like Nalanda University in India—many of them proved unsustainable.

The self-governing and autonomous organization of European universities enabled them to modify and update curricula in light of intellectual developments and of external needs. Indeed, as shown by Cantoni and Yuchtman

(2014), the legal training provided by European universities contributed to the evolution of administrative and legal institutions, exerting a positive effect on local commercial development in the late Middle Ages. Cantoni and Yuchtman (2014) show that the establishment of universities favored the emergence and formal certification of markets in Germany. Commerce and credit required contract enforcement, and as markets became more sophisticated, more professionals were needed. Universities provided the legal training of administrators, lawyers, and notaries that reduced transaction costs and made markets work properly.

Universities also were useful to actors in medieval society besides traders. The Church and the papacy found universities valuable because they provided an intellectual foundation to a cohesive and unambiguous doctrine that they could use against heterodox thinkers. Religious authorities also thought that universities would strengthen the central powers of the papacy against the claims of regional feudal interests or the emperor. Finally, universities supplied trained and learned personnel to the papal bureaucracy. Consequently, on the whole, there was a symbiotic relationship between the papacy and the universities, and the papacy helped free the universities from local control (Nardi 1992).[17] Emperors too needed a legally trained bureaucracy that strengthened their fiscal and political powers, although they were more interested in the provisions of Roman law (Rüegg 1992, pp. 15–16). Above all, however, universities have persisted as a unique institution because, as Haskins (1923, p. 24) wrote a century ago, "no substitute for the university has been found in its main business: the training of scholars and the maintenance of a tradition of learning and investigation." They thus both epitomized and perpetuated the unique trajectory onto which the idea of a corporation led Europe.

Despite their important role in training and in disseminating knowledge, it should be acknowledged that the role of university professors in intellectual innovation in Europe was perhaps less striking than would be expected. The "arts" courses were mostly about logic and philosophy, and science rarely went

---

17. The idea that a graduate of any university was ipso facto qualified to teach at any other university within the papal Christendom, known as the *licentia ubique docendi,* is described by Rüegg (1992, p. 17) as having "far-reaching historical significance." It helped create a transnational intellectual community in which both students and professors were comparatively mobile and thus helped disseminate knowledge and ideas. In his view, the combination of the shared quest for knowledge with the high degree of autonomy that universities retained was provided in a formal institutional setting.

beyond the "natural books" of Aristotle. Studies often consisted of rote learning: a "close drill on a few well-thumbed books," as Haskins put it (1923, p. 33). Medicine also concentrated on the classical works of Galen (129–216 AD) and his Muslim interpreters, Avicenna and Rhazes. Legal studies were different, and we will return to their importance in chapter 8. In medieval universities, law was one of the few areas in which learning went far further than the teachings of ancient authorities. By one calculation, in the crucial period 1450–1650, 87 percent of all scientists mentioned in *The Dictionary of Scientific Biography* were trained in universities, but less than half (45 percent) ended up teaching at them (Gascoigne 2000). Many of the truly influential intellectual leaders of European thought and science—among them Francis Bacon, Baruch Spinoza, René Descartes, John Locke, Gottfried Wilhelm Leibniz, and Antoine Lavoisier—never held academic positions, while still others, such as Isaac Newton, Galileo, and Adam Smith, left them for nonacademic patronage jobs when they had the opportunity to do so. Academics, precisely because they embodied a great deal of human capital, tended mostly to be intellectually conservative and often resisted disruptive innovation. While it was true to some extent, as Gascoigne (2000, p. 657) has noted, that in a world in which "inherited positions loomed so large, universities provided a haven for another set of values in which learning was valued for its own sake and intellectual distinction received recognition," most universities did not play a leading role in driving pathbreaking research.

That said, the significance of universities to the future development of Europe is not just in the increase in supply of human capital that turned out to have economic value. Universities fostered the competitive market for ideas, which was key to the creation and dissemination of knowledge (De la Croix et al. 2023, pp. 5–6). The institutional structure of higher education that emerged in the late Middle Ages and Early Modern Europe created a decentralized and competitive *system* of independent corporations, each dedicated to the transmission and generation of knowledge. Rather than being managed in a top-down fashion, universities were independently run from the bottom up. They competed for the best students, for resources and reputation, and above all for the best professors. Almost all the most important medieval intellectuals were educated in European universities, and some of them, such as Roger Bacon, Duns Scotus, and Albertus Magnus, taught at European universities, and almost all of them were educated there in one form or another. Universities were central to the growth of formal juridical theory. They translated and taught works of philosophy and science, often part of the Greek cultural legacy by way of Arabic writers. In some ways, the university system was interconnected, not only because faculty and students moved among them. The degrees that they conferred were recognized everywhere, creating a transnational standard of assessing education, and they shared most of the pedagogical methods, especially lectures and ensuing disputations (Verger 1992, p. 44). Yet there was a great deal of diversity across universities. This variety, coupled with interorganizational competition, lent them their dynamism and viability.

China

As discussed in chapter 2, China also invested extensively in advanced education, and did so arguably more than Europe. But, far more than in Europe, Chinese education was centralized and guided by the Imperial government. The contents of education were determined by the goal of sitting for the civil service academies and serving in the central bureaucracy, and as a consequence, Chinese institutions evolved along a very different trajectory. Positions in the civil service were very attractive and a source of privileges and social status for the individual and his relatives, and the Imperial bureaucracy was the main mechanism of social mobility in China. As a result, large investments in preparing the most promising youngsters for the exams were made by their families. Throughout Chinese history, clans were always deeply involved in assisting candidates through educational awards and travel subsidies, as well as by setting up their own schools. A successful candidate would be an advantage and an honor to the entire extended family. But the goal of privately provided education was always to prepare students for entry into public administration. The Chinese Civil Service Examination thus had profound effects on human capital accumulation, social mobility, and cultural integration. Elman (2013, p. 49), in his authoritative work on the examination system, notes that the civil examination imparted a degree of intellectual uniformity that "only a classical education could provide." This goal could never be achieved in full, however, as there was some local variation in the way that the texts were interpreted and read.

Most scholars agree that academies in China originated during the Tang Dynasty, but there is still significant debate regarding the specific time period (Xiao 2018, p. 19). It is uncontested, however, that academies were a by-product of the expansion of the Civil Service Examination system. During the reign of Empress Wu Zetian (AD 690–705), the government greatly expanded the Civil Service Examinations to weaken the power of eminent families. By the end of the Five Dynasties and Ten Kingdoms periods (AD 907–979), the public had accepted that the Civil Service Examination was the sole method for selecting talented individuals as government officials. Many descendants of the eminent families also had no choice but to take the examinations to enter officialdom (Xiao 2018, pp. 23–24). For a long time, the government directly controlled academies, but during a period of state weakness from the bloody An Lushan Rebellion (755–763), state-run schools declined. In their place, communities established private academies.

Private academies were quite prevalent during the early Song years, many of them formed by clans or lineages for the purpose of teaching Confucian values to maintain family harmony, along with, of course, preparing for the civil service examinations (Xiao 2018, pp. 37–45). As the central government recovered during the reign of Emperor Renzong of Song (AD 1022–AD 1063), the government conducted several large-scale educational reforms and reestablished state-run schools. As a result, some private academies were converted to government schools, and although some private institutions survived, they no longer enjoyed the prominence that they had in the early Song period (Xiao 2018, p. 167).

The Chinese educational system gradually became committed to neo-Confucianism during the Song period, a process catalyzed by a host of philosophers determined to revive and resurrect Confucianism, notably the Cheng brothers and Zhu Xi. The neo-Confucian school of thought grew under the Yuan Dynasty, whose rulers supported its revival. This movement culminated in the famous edict made by Emperor Renzong of Yuan (r.1311–1320)— not to be confused with his earlier namesake—which established the Cheng-Zhu school of neo-Confucianism as the standard for the Civil Service Examination. This further elevated the philosophy's status to the level of official doctrine. The academies were wholly committed to neo-Confucianism, and as government schools declined due to financial difficulties during the mid-Ming period, private academies proliferated. However, they gradually lost their independence from the government in exchange for state support. This trend continued into the Yuan and early Ming years. In the later periods of the Ming and Qing dynasties, government control became even more exacting (Xiao 2018).

Under the Song Dynasty, education increasingly fell into the purview of the state, which used neo-Confucian (or "way learning") to consolidate the legitimacy of the dynasty and of the ruling elite (Elman 2013, p. 50). By the eleventh century, provincial and local officials established publicly supported schools and the Imperial Academy became larger and more effective, with an enrollment of 3,800 students during its peak. From the early Ming period onward, "the examination and the school system became inseparable" (Ho 1964, p.171). The Yuan and Ming dynasties established village schools in every county in China (Du 2007, p. 87). Over time, however, these dynastic schools became way stations for the examinations and did not do much teaching in subjects beyond those covered by the exams. By the end of the nineteenth century, there were as many as 1,810 state schools, but much of the actual teaching took place in private domains of clans and temples.[18]

The meritocratic civil service system was very competitive. The success rate in the Civil Service Examinations was very low: only 1.5 percent passed the lowest grade, *shengyuan*. Of those who did, only 6 percent passed the next stage, *juren,* and of those individuals, only 17.7 percent made it to *jinshi.* The probability that one reached the top was thus approximately 1:6,300. The students were not limited to the most privileged families. Top families did not enjoy a large disproportionate advantage despite their affluence, although in practice, wealth and family background still mattered a lot. According to Ho (1964), during the entire Ming and Qing periods, distinguished families on average accounted for only 5.7 percent of total candidates to the *jinshi* exam, which was the third and highest level. Several anecdotes also testify that even diligent members of distinguished families repeatedly failed to pass the higher-level exam.

Even if one did not pass the *jinshi* exam, the human capital investment in a *juren* or *shengyuan* degree was not wasted. The impact of the system went much beyond the few candidates that passed the exam. Many of those who were not selected into the top of the central bureaucracy found a role in local government and became members of the local gentry, which played a crucial role in the day-to-day administration of the realm.

The Civil Service Examination and the associated educational system were thus important instruments of social mobility.[19] Ho (1964, p. 257) concluded that there were no legal or social barriers preventing the movement of

18. See Elman (2013, p. 6). Elman adds that dynastic schools never tried to achieve mass education and were a pure training ground for the *keju* examinations.

19. "The fact that in spite of their incomparable advantages members of distinguished families failed to dominate chin-shih [*jinshi*] examinations, in sharp contrast to the prolonged monopoly of political power by a few hundred aristocratic families in XVIII century England, goes far to testify to the general effectiveness of the competitive examination as a factor in the social-leveling process and to the inability of wealthy and top-status families in the long run to maintain their position" (Ho, 1964, p. 147).

individuals and their families from one status to another, and that high-status individuals had no way of perpetuating the status of inept descendants. A similar mechanism of social mobility was all but absent in Europe, where the offspring of the nobility, however lacking in merit, remained part of the social and economic elite. Until the creation of compulsory national education after the Industrial Revolution, the only comparable institutions in Europe to promote social mobility were the Church, where some commoners climbed to the highest ranks, and commerce, which allowed wealthy merchants to purchase noble titles and join the elite.

More recent scholarship has been more skeptical of the actual social mobility provided by the Chinese *keju* system in later centuries. Commoners and merchants indeed had the capability to train their most talented sons for the *shengyuan* (local) examinations; thus, at least slowly, over generations, one could crawl up the social hierarchy. Nevertheless, people designated as "commoners" were a large proportion of the successful candidates, and we should not mistake them for "working class." By the nineteenth century, the resources required to give youngsters a chance to succeed in the exams were so demanding that wealth became almost required for such preparation. As such, the sons of wealthy salt merchants had a disproportionate rate of success during the Qing (Brandt, Ma, and Rawski 2014, p. 77). As Elman (2013, p. 4) noted, peasants, small-time traders, and artisans made up 90 percent of the population, but they were not a noteworthy portion of the two to three million who regularly failed local biennial tests.

Elman describes the subtle but effective ways that elites excluded candidates from lower classes from their ranks. During the Ming and Qing dynasties, officials introduced new requirements that curtailed mobility further. One was that all candidates were required to compose "8-legged essays," a complex and sophisticated form of writing that was utterly baffling for "primer-literate" candidates from merchant, artisan, and peasant families (Elman 2013, p. 51). To attain full mastery of the classical material, a candidate had to master close to 10,000 characters. The enormous requirements made on these students for all practical purposes excluded sons of most families of the commoners (Elman 2013).

Still, the impact of the civil service system went far beyond the few candidates that passed it. Even the large numbers of candidates who failed were still imbued with neo-Confucian learning, and many of them ended up working for local administration, thus infusing them with the values and concepts that they had been taught while preparing for the examination. The system established the ideal of the scholar-statesman as the pivotal focus of power in China. The imperial examination, whether by intention or not, thus became the tool that sustained neo-Confucianism's monopoly in China's market for ideas. Huang (2023, p. 239) described the "thwarting of political and ideological competition" as the more pernicious effect of the *keju* system. In his view, the Imperial examination system was the main cause of China's relatively high literacy rates, but all together, it bred conformism and obedience rather than inspiring independent thought and originality (Huang 2023, p. 107).

Scholars have devoted considerable attention to the merits and consequences of the Imperial examination system. Critics have argued that over time, the *jinshi* curriculum became more and more removed from specific administrative needs, creating a large gap between the material studied and the practical knowledge needed for effective administration. This manifested, for example, in the safeguarding of certain information from examination materials. Most egregious was the study of maps, an essential input necessary for understanding the geography of their vast empire, which was restricted by the Qing administration (Elman 2000, p. 485). Similarly, the studies of mathematical harmonics and astronomy were prohibited for examination candidates (Elman 2005, p. 168). As Elman (2013, pp. 71, 81) stresses, the Ming and Qing dynasties took a decisive "turn to ancient studies" (*guxue*) while increasingly eschewing diversity in curriculum. The Jesuit missionary Matteo Ricci (1953, p. 32) famously described Chinese learning around 1600: "Scarcely anyone devotes himself to the study of mathematics and medicine [which] are held in low esteem, because they are not fostered by honors as is the study of philosophy." During the Qing Dynasty, the practical content of the human capital produced by studying for the examinations deteriorated even further.[20]

Thus, despite the seemingly salutary effects of a meritocracy and the advantages of government-funded education, the Civil Service Examination and scholar-statesman ideal had a fatal adverse consequence: it led the most

20. The questions became so predictable that mass-produced answer books were available to train students to succeed. By the nineteenth century, the examinations were graded primarily based on calligraphy, not content or even style (Hucker 1975, p. 321). Average students prepared answers using the officially recognized "regular" script, but the more advanced and ambitious ones also mastered "cursive" (*caoshu*), "running" (*xingshu*), and even ancient "seal" (*zhuanshu*) forms of writing. Seal and cursive script were intelligible to only the most erudite, creating linguistic barriers to mobility and crystallizing the status quo (Elman 2013, p. 51).

talented individuals to acquire a type of human capital that had little value for the advance of practical mathematics, applied science, and engineering. Because the prospects of upward mobility were so significant and the social status of the mandarins was high, the most gifted individuals were irresistibly attracted to the civil service (or pushed toward it by their families). Preparation for the exam was very demanding, but it concerned learning and memorizing the classics, writing the dreaded "8-legged essays" and poems, and reading literature, history and philosophy.[21] Over time, the areas of useful knowledge that would have been most useful to lead to technological progress were more and more neglected, and the examination's requirements of familiarity with the ancient classics were reinforced.[22]

Just as Europe was accelerating its rate of augmentation of useful knowledge in the sixteenth and seventeenth centuries, China's government shifted into reverse. Much like Europe in the seventeenth century, China experienced a "war of the ancients against the moderns." But the outcome was quite different; seventeenth- and eighteenth-century Kaozheng scholars critiqued their Song-era canon for distorting and adulterating ancient knowledge and demanded evidence for the propositions made by Zhu Xi and other scholars in the neo-Confucian school. By "evidence," however, they did not mean the same thing as Bacon and Galileo did: they looked back at ancient wisdom as the source of all truthful knowledge. Observation and experimentation were of little interest to them. The standard text for students in the Chinese Imperial medical service in 1743 was a compilation of a set of notes on a medical work written by Zhang Ji (150–219 AD) (Elman 2006, p. 57).

It is not far-fetched to see a parallel between Chinese intellectual life in the eighteenth century and the early Renaissance in Europe, when ancient classics were rediscovered and dusted off. There was a fundamental difference, however. Whereas Europeans subsequently proved willing to test and criticize

21. A Western observer in late Qing China described the education system as follows: "Pupils do not study, in school, books on mathematics, geography, and the natural sciences, but the writings of Confucius and Mencius. These they are required to commit to memory, and recite with their backs toward the book. . . . They first learn the sounds of the characters, so as to recite them *memoriter*. After years of study they acquire an insight into their meaning and use. They commence to write when they begin going to school, tracing the characters given them as patterns on paper by means of hair pencil and China ink. It requires an immense amount of practice to write the language correctly and rapidly" (cited by Elman 2000, p. 265).

22. Until 1786, students were required to specialize in one of the five Confucian classics (*wujing*); after that year, all five were required (Elman 2000, p. 286).

their classical heritage, Chinese intellectuals did not. In the European quarrel between the ancients and the moderns, the latter won hands down (LeCoq 2001). In China, because the market for ideas was controlled by a backward-looking and increasingly reactionary administration, the moderns did not have much of a chance; in the end, modernization came to China only because it was forced on it by the West's imperialist threats.

The Chinese were not the only culture in which education was focused on the study of the past. In Early Modern Europe, rote learning, such as the memorization of the catechism, was at the foundation of religious education. But within their fragmented and uncoordinated intellectual world, it was possible for dissent, skepticism, and pluralism to emerge and flourish. The reason is that there was no monopoly in the market for ideas, as it existed in China. The advantages of a meritocracy, in which ability and intellectual talent are rewarded rather than ancestry, may appear self-evident. But the Achilles heel of a meritocracy is that someone has to decide what "merit" really is and how to measure it. If merit is determined by knowledge of an ancient canon and past wisdom and traditions, technological and scientific progress is unlikely. In the end, that was the cost of the Chinese *keju* examination system.

5. Cities

The historical differences between Chinese and European social arrangements manifest quite clearly in how cities were organized and evolved over time. This is both because European corporations were more widespread in towns than in rural areas and because self-governing cities were the prime example of corporations. As we saw in chapter 2, there were marked differences in the historical rates of urbanization between Europe and China. In 1843, only 5.1 percent of the Chinese population lived in cities with more than 2,000 people, whereas in Europe in 1800, 13 percent lived in cities with more than 5,000 people. European cities were more often walled and more concentrated. To be sure, in China, the economic geography was different, with no sharp boundaries between urban and rural districts or farming and nonagricultural activity, which complicates the comparison of standard measures of urbanization.

At the same time, European cities reshaped political and military realities, punching above their demographic weight in their contribution to arts, science, and technology. The system of urban corporations that emerged in medieval and Early Modern Europe was novel. There had been substantial urban centers in large parts of Europe during the Roman Empire, and inevitably these towns were largely self-ruling, as they were remote from the capital. Yet, the managers and local elites controlling the cities were appointed by Rome even if they remained unpaid. This grand bargain between the central Roman government and local elites involved assisting with tax collection, in exchange for which the urban oligarchs were given a more or less free hand in local affairs. Yet this relationship between the central state and independent townships was very different for the highly competitive system of autonomous cities that emerged in medieval Europe (Terpstra 2025, chapter 4).[23]

Europe's city-states and self-governing communes provided the most dynamic parts of society, not just for trade but equally for technology, finance, science, education, arts, and music. The towns' dynamism derived from their competitiveness and polycentrism. European cities were centers of learning, experiments in political organization, commercial innovation, financial development, and demographic safety valves (as they had very high mortality rates, and thus served as a Malthusian check on population growth). We now examine the function and character of cities in both societies in greater detail.

Urbanization in China and Europe

Cities in imperial China lacked the kind of autonomy enjoyed in European towns; a recent survey (Lincoln 2021) notes that only in modern China did the idea of a municipality replete with councils and mayors emerge on the political landscape. Mote (1977, p. 114) summarizes the status of Chinese cities in late imperial China, noting that the typical Chinese city had no "citizens" in the Western sense of the word and possessed no corporate identity, nor a government distinct from that of the surrounding countryside. By way of contrast, European cities insisted on carefully separating themselves from the area around it. Mote (1999, p. 762) has also noted that Chinese cities were often walled, but only by permission of the central government. Rather than being symbols of autonomy as they were in Europe, they reflected the imperial authority running the city.

True, different cities in China experienced quite divergent degrees of imperial control. Zurndorfer (2022, p. 557) notes that in capitals, county seats, and walled cities, imperial functionaries controlled and managed most of the

---

23. If anything, the European competitive urban system resembled that of ancient Greece, in both its decentralization and the high degree of competition among its constituent units (Ober 2015, pp. 293–95; Terpstra 2020). The Greek urban system was fragile, however, and could not withstand the repeated onslaught of more powerful states, such as Macedonia and Rome.

infrastructure, whereas in market towns, members of the local gentry took on these duties. Other cities were not autonomous but possessed a "certain amount of practical communal self-management" (Zurndorfer 2022, p. 543). Yet the phenomenon of the urban commune, which negotiated with the ruler on taxes and enjoyed a large amount of political agency, was absent in China.

Many Chinese cities originated as administrative and military centers. The largest city was typically the state capital, which was the seat of the emperor and of the central administration; the state capital moved around according to the whims of the current dynasty. Imperial capitals were typically an order of magnitude larger than European state capitals. Kaifeng, the capital of the Northern Song, probably housed about 1 million inhabitants in 1100. A century later, the capital of the Southern Song had moved to Hangzhou, which is estimated to have had about 1.1 million inhabitants. The largest European cities in those centuries were Cordoba (80,000 inhabitants in 1100) and Paris (110,000 inhabitants in 1200) (Xu et al. 2018, p. 348).

The massive difference in the size of the largest cities reflects two facts. First, there was much higher economic development in China at the time, as a result of greater commercialization and industrialization; and second, China also had a higher degree of concentration of political power than Europe. As argued in chapter 2, the gap in the size of the largest cities between China and Europe declined over the centuries, as state capacity increased in Europe while it declined in China: by the nineteenth century, the primary urban centers of Europe had overtaken those of China.

Besides the state capital, provincial capitals formed the second level of administrative hierarchy in China. The prefecture was the third level of urban concentration and administration, and then came county administrations. Different dynasties moved provincial capitals around, so they were not too far from the national capital (whose location, as mentioned before, changed with each new regime). Bai and Jia (2020) show that the location of the province capital reflected a trade-off between being close to the state capital and occupying a central location within the province (to control the other prefectures in the province).

These political considerations implied that the provincial capital was not always the largest and economically more prosperous city in the province. This was in contrast to Europe, where the state capital was typically one of the largest cities in the state. This difference between China and Europe in the relative size of capital cities (relative to other cities in the same administrative area) is depicted in figure 6.3. Using the data by Bairoch et al. (1988) and Schonholzer and Weese (2019), we have ranked European cities belonging to the same

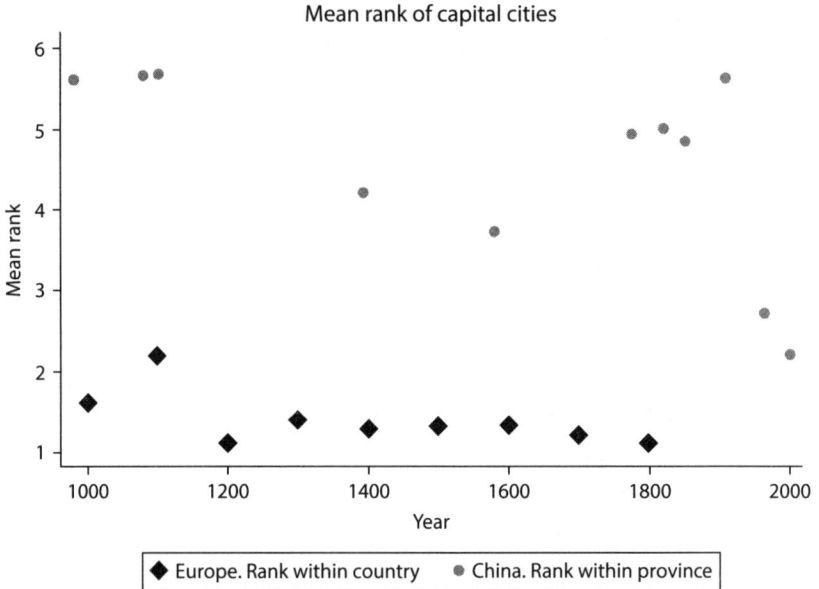

FIGURE 6.3. Rank of capital cities in Europe and China. For each European country and century, we rank the cities by their population, assigning rank = 1 to the biggest city, 2 to the second biggest, and so on. We consider two cities as belonging to the same country in a specific century if they were part of the same state for at least ninety years of that century. In case of ties between two cities, if only one of them is a capital, we rank it higher, otherwise, we split ties at random. For each Chinese province and year, we rank the prefectures by their population density. Finally, for both Europe and China, the graph depicts the means of the ranks of capital cities (state capitals for Europe, province capitals for China). *Source:* For Europe, we used data by Bairoch et al. (1988) and Schonholzer and Weese (2019). For China, we used data by Bai and Jia (2020).

historical state by their population size. Similarly, using the data of Bai and Jia (2020), we have ranked Chinese prefectures belonging to the same province by their population density—a province consists of several prefectures, and one of them was chosen as the seat of the provincial capital. Figure 6.3 plots the average rank of European state capitals (diamonds) and of Chinese provincial capitals (circles) in different centuries. A lower rank means a larger relative size. These data demonstrate that European state capitals tended to have a larger relative size (lower rank) compared to Chinese provincial capitals.

Bai and Jia (2020) also study the effects of gaining or losing the status of province capital, exploiting exogenous variation induced by dynastic changes. They estimate very large effects on population size, indicating that these urban centers were political and administrative hubs, but economic forces alone did not have large persistent effects on urbanization. Losing (gaining) the status of provincial capital was associated with a lower (higher) population density of about 50 percent. Upon losing its status of provincial capital, the city returned to a similar level of economic development as other noncapital cities within seventy-five years. The effect seems due to two mechanisms: changes in public employment and changes in transportation networks. As a city became a provincial capital, its transportation network significantly improved, increasing its market access, while the opposite happened over time if the capital was moved elsewhere. This points to the crucial role of the central state and its bureaucracy in determining patterns of economic activity in China.

In Europe too, cities that became state capitals accelerated their growth (Bosker et al. 2013; Serafinelli and Tabellini 2022), but their market access and commercial integration were less dependent on political decisions made by the central government. On the contrary, Cox (2017) shows that city growth was favored by national political fragmentation, and a key determinant of city growth was geographic proximity to other rapidly growing cities. This is consistent with the idea that the main driver of city growth in Europe was commerce rather than public administration. Such a positive correlation between the growth of neighboring cities during the period 1200–1800 is a peculiar and uniquely European phenomenon, absent in South Asia and East Asia. Cox (2017) estimates that even during China's second commercial revolution that began in the mid-sixteenth century, intercity growth correlations in China were less than half of Western Europe.

The development of markets offers useful insights on the pattern of growth of European cities during the early medieval period. Carolingian rulers used the creation and regulation of markets to centralize trade in specific locations to extract tolls and other levies. These trading centers later grew to become some of the most important merchant towns in Europe. The larger Italian cities were often located along trade routes for agricultural exchange, and merchants developed strong links with bishops and other city rulers. The same was true north of the Alps, where most early medieval cities that became important commercial centers were located on navigable rivers. Cities built canal and transport infrastructures, often in competition with other cities, to attract trade and merchants (Nicholas 1997).[24] Trade was the catalyst of

---

24. Nicholas (1997, p. 108) quotes several examples, such as Nuremberg and the cities of Brabant, Milan, Coventry, and Bristol, which prospered thanks to canals and other transport infrastructures, some of which were built at the initiatives of the cities.

change for cities in early medieval Europe and was linked to political developments, but it was followed by the growth of manufacturing: the Flemish towns, as well as many cities in Italy, thrived on the growing woolen industry, as well as glass, shipbuilding, armory, paper, and other products, further stimulating commerce on a continental scale. The cities that were able to develop a deep connection between the ruling class and the merchants prospered the most. One can think of Genoa and Pisa as examples, but there were also cities in Flanders—Bruges, Lille, Ypres, and Douai. By way of contrast, English cities were in decline under Norman rule, as merchants were taxed and local markets removed to make space for castles.

In China too, market towns became important urban centers. But the growth of market towns was not as rapid as in Europe. As pointed out by Xu et al. (2018), the decline in urbanization during the Qing Dynasty reflects a general process of migration from the core economic areas of China toward the periphery. Population growth and environmental deterioration pushed people out of the traditional lowland areas into more remote places, where new crops brought from the New World, such as maize and sweet potatoes, created opportunities and incentives to cultivate new areas. Sichuan Province is a good example of one such destination during this period. In Europe at the same time, migration took on the opposite pattern—namely, people flowed from the periphery toward the core. In the seventeenth and eighteenth centuries, a large extent of international resettlement occurred: the Netherlands attracted immigrants from Germany and Scandinavia, and England attracted Irish immigrants. As a result, the share of the North Sea region in the total population of Western Europe grew from 11 percent in the sixteenth century to over 20 percent in the nineteenth century (Xu et al. 2018, p. 357). Evidently, concentration of economic activity around urban centers in China did not have the same benefits as in Europe.

Another important difference in the patterns of urbanization between China and Europe concerns port cities. In Europe, the share of urban population living close to the sea rose from about 22 percent in 1500 to 32 percent in 1700. In China, it declined, particularly in the Yangtze Delta, where the share of the population in coastal cities dropped from 12 percent in 1205 to 2 percent in 1776 (Xu et al. 2018, p. 353). Port cities became especially important in Europe after 1500 with the growth of the Atlantic trade (to the Americas, as well as to Asia and Africa). These cities grew faster than their inland counterparts, and they did so thanks to their institutions: largely autonomous and open urban polities grew faster and eventually became key to the development of their economies (Acemoglu, Johnson, and Robinson 2005). As discussed in chapter 5, these opposite trends also reflected the different organizational arrangements supporting maritime trade in China and Europe, and in particular the rise of European business corporations that could exploit the large economies of scale in transoceanic trade.

Self-Governing Cities

One of the most striking phenomena in European urban history is the emergence and persistence of independent cities (or city-states). Early in the eleventh century, external threats to Europe declined due to the defeat of the Magyars, the weakening of the Muslim states, and the formation of stable Christian polities in Scandinavia that ended the Viking raids. Roughly around that time, a set of new players entered the political scene: self-governing cities (communes) that acquired administrative capacity and political autonomy when states were weak.

The city-state was an institution that emerged in antiquity and was able to survive for many centuries, playing a disproportionate role in the growth of European commerce and industry. Its remarkable resilience over time was due above all to its role as a trading center (Rosenberg and Birdzell 1986). John Hicks (1969), in his remarkable little book on economic history, was one of the first economists to draw our attention to the city-state; he defined its core as "a body of specialized traders engaged in external trade" (p. 42). Whether we think of the Phoenician and Greek towns before Rome, the medieval Hanseatic towns, or the Dutch Republic in its Golden Age, European cities all depended on Smithian growth supported by institutions defending property rights. Hamburg, Lübeck, Cologne, Genoa, and Venice stand out as examples of city-states that stood the test of time, even if few of them have survived as independent polities into the modern age.[25]

As cities grew in importance after 1000 AD, their role in the generation and dissemination of innovations became crucial.[26] Modern scholars have stressed

25. It is debatable whether two of the most commercially successful European towns, Amsterdam and Antwerp, should be regarded as city-states; they both were formally part of larger political units (the county of Holland and the duchy of Brabant, respectively), but basically local affairs were run by their municipal authorities (Gelderblom 2013, p. 201).

26. Ester Boserup (1981, p. 77) has no doubts when she concludes (in the context of classical antiquity) that "urbanization was accompanied by rapid progress in the technology of

the ability of cities to develop the kind of institutions that made the functioning of markets possible (Greif 2006b; Gelderblom 2013). These institutions were no happy accident. They were created and enjoyed an advantage in accessing credit markets precisely because their self-governance and relatively compact size increased their ability to tax inhabitants, which then produced efficient fiscal capacity. This capability thus made them more trustworthy and a relatively good risk (Stasavage 2011).[27]

Indeed, city-states were often fiscally responsible because of the people who wielded power. Urban communes were constitutional oligarchies that represented the interests of merchants, artisans, bankers, and landowners. Representatives of the city ruling class initially acted as the link between the town and its feudal overlord and gradually gained autonomy from external influence and became accountable to the city bourgeoisie. These communes organized independently, collected taxes from their citizens, regulated commerce, administered justice, enforced law and order, and often had their own militias boasting a surprising degree of military capability. In addition, they invested in infrastructure, commissioned works of art as symbols of citywide pride (including a bell tower with a clock), established and maintained orphanages and hospitals, and even maintained their own historical archives.

Communal institutions began to develop in some European cities during the tenth and eleventh centuries. They first emerged in southern Europe, after which they spread to northern France, northern Italy, Flanders, Germany, Spain, and beyond in the following centuries, adapting to each situation differently (Jones 1997; Van Zanden 2009). Bosker et al. (2013) have systematically coded the emergence and disappearance of communal institutions in a sample of 677 European cities.[28] The sample consists of all European cities that

---

construction, transport, and agriculture . . . the need to organize the urban economies . . . led to some of the most important inventions in the history of humanity." Paul Bairoch (1991), writing about a more modern period, asks rhetorically whether the city has not had a considerable hand in stimulating invention and ensuring its diffusion (p. 160) and then states categorically that "there are few attributes of urban life that do not favor the diffusion of innovation" (p. 169; see also Bairoch 1988).

27. Recent research (e.g., Angelucci et al. 2020) has also suggested that self-governing cities (in contrast with cities controlled by local aristocrats) were crucial in the evolution of more inclusive and representative institutions in England.

28. Bosker et al. (2013) rely on several criteria for their classification. First, they check if historical sources mention the presence of communal institutions such as consuls or town councils. The date is then attributed to the whole century subsequent to the first evidence of such

ever reached a population size of at least 10,000 inhabitants in at least one century between 800 and 1800. Figure 6.4(a) illustrates the fraction of cities that Bosker et al. (2013) classify as communes in each century, while figure 6.4(b) illustrates the flow into the status of commune using the same data (the source for these figures is Serafinelli and Tabellini 2022). By the thirteenth century, almost 60 percent of European cities in this sample had gained the status of commune, with most transitions to commune occurring during the twelfth century.

In England between 1042 and 1307, 268 cities were incorporated by charter. This number rose to almost 500 not long after (see figure 6.5).[29] Similarly, most European cities west of the Baltic Sea in the north and of the Adriatic Sea in the south achieved formal incorporation (Pirenne 1969, pp. 168–212; Cantoni and Yuchtman 2014). In 1422, Germany had at least 75 cities recognized by the emperor as "free," and by 1521 this number had increased to 84; at the same time, the Hanseatic League included about 190 self-governing German cities (Dollinger 1970, p. 116). In Flanders, authorities issued a twelfth-century urban law that recognized cities' right to self-governance (Nicholas 1992, pp. 119–23). Even in the more absolutist Castile in around 1500, about 20 percent of the population lived in its 30 self-governing cities and 60 percent lived in villages that were self-governing, although subject to a lord (Nader 1990, p. 3).

What drove the emergence of free towns, and why did this phenomenon happen only in Western Europe? First, political circumstances were favorable to gaining autonomy. As we will discuss in chapter 7, between the twelfth and fourteenth centuries, Europe was particularly fragmented, and central powers were weak. The Carolingian Empire had long disintegrated, the Papal

---

institutions. As a fallback option, they use the building date of a town hall, and if this information is also missing, they use information on the first time that city rights were granted (as mentioned in historical encyclopedias), dating the commune from the first century after such rights were first granted. The criterion for exit from commune status is symmetrical; namely, they code if local participatory institutions stopped functioning because the town council was taken over by a powerful local family (as in hereditary *Signoria*), or it was dissolved by a central authority or external power (again dating it from the first whole century after the occurrence). In the absence of a specific indication of a stop to the town council or of the inclusion of the city into a hereditary Signoria, it is assumed that local participatory institutions kept functioning until 1800, in line with local historical sources.

29. See Ballard (1913); Ballard and Tait (1923); Beresford and Finberg (1973). In Germany, 2,256 incorporated cities had been created by the seventeenth century and were included in the Deutsches Städtebuch (Cantoni and Yuchtman, 2014, p. 832).

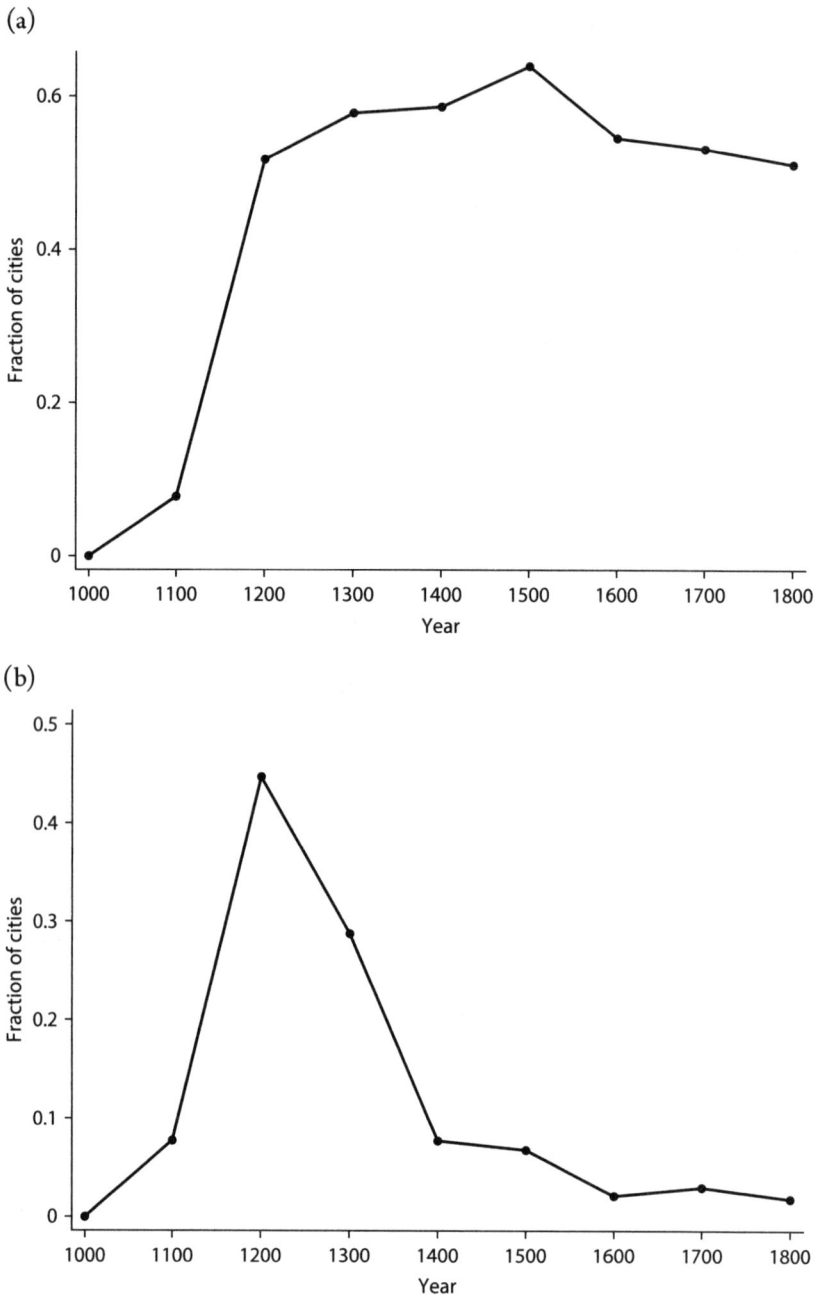

FIGURE 6.4. (a) Fraction of European cities that were communes. (b) Fraction of European cities that became communes. *Source:* Serafinelli and Tabellini (2022), using data from Bosker et al. (2013).

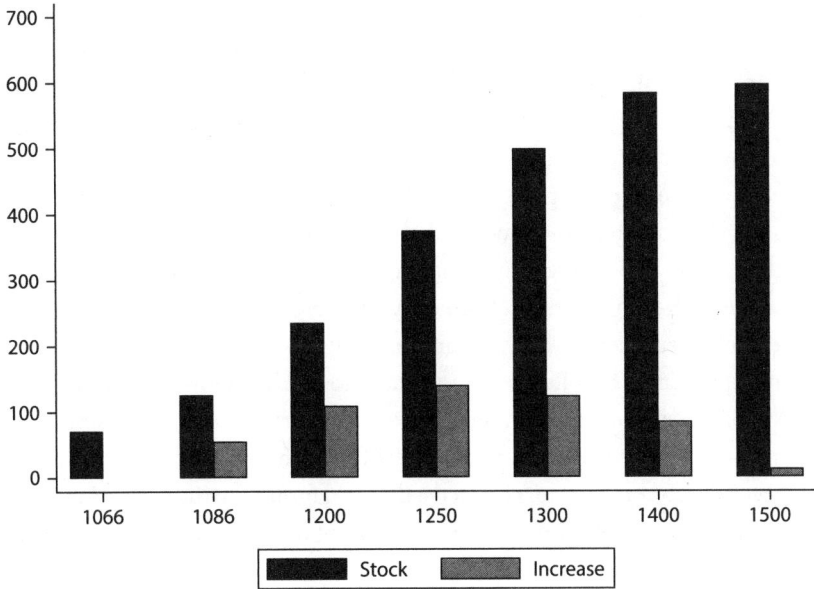

FIGURE 6.5. Incorporation of English cities. *Source:* Beresford and Finberg (1973).

Revolution created a deep conflict between the Church and imperial authority, national consolidation had not yet occurred. In this vacuum of central
power, and cities could claim forms of autonomy that were subsequently recognized by the sovereign in return for taxes or loyalty (Jones 2003). The degree of city autonomy varied across Europe and over centuries, often depending on the strength of control that a prince enjoyed over his territory. In the
Kingdom of Naples and Sicily, royal control was strong enough that communes were rare or nonexistent. By contrast, the cities of Northern and Central Italy took advantage of the conflict between the empire and the pope to
gain autonomy from both powers, with long-term effects on their political and
cultural development (Guiso, Sapienza, and Zingales 2016).[30]

Similarly, in Germany, the landed aristocracy was fully occupied "in resisting or supporting the Emperor, extending boundaries and colonizing new
lands in the north and east," which then gave German towns an opportunity
to develop their own city institutions and free themselves from central

30. The authors show that in cities that attained a high degree of autonomy in the Middle
Ages, new cultural norms were established that resulted in a higher level of civic capital today,
meaning that in these cities, collective action and voluntary cooperation were easier to achieve.

authority (Clarke 1926, p. 44). In the Low Countries, there was continuous tension between the local counts and dukes and their ever-rebellious urban subjects in Ghent, Bruges, Courtrai, and later, Amsterdam and Leiden.[31] In the Netherlands perhaps more than anywhere else, guilds and urban elites stood up to external powers and clung stubbornly to an ideology of self-determination based on consent by the governed. There, urban elites organized local politics through civic organizations and guided their cities using petitions, elections, meetings, and, when necessary, armed resistance (Prak 2018, p. 203). England was somewhere along the spectrum of autonomy and central power: the territory administered by the king was large enough that he had to delegate administrative tasks and tax collection to the major towns. Yet, unlike in Italy and the Low Countries, the king retained sufficient military capacity to prevent self-administered cities from gaining full independence (Angelucci et al. 2021).

Second, economic factors created a demand for new institutions. After the end of the first millennium, Europe underwent rapid economic transformations. The rise of commerce contributed to urbanization (Lopez 1971, pp. 86–89), and progress in agricultural technologies and increases in agricultural productivity led to the growth of a class of artisans in urban centers. City growth often occurred along trade routes or around marketplaces (Angelucci et al. 2021), and a new class of merchants emerged. As described by Pirenne (1925 [2014]), Parker (2004), and Clarke (1926), communal institutions typically evolved from within the city and were guided by the aspiration of the urban middle classes to gain freedom and independence from external influence (primarily in opposition to the Church or an external lord). Finally, the High Middle Ages were a period of intense migration and movement of people within Europe. In some cases, autonomy and freedom were granted to new urban centers by the sovereign to encourage settlement in previously uninhabited areas (Bartlett 1994).

Third, cultural factors also played a role in determining how political opportunities were exploited and new institutions were designed. Communes

---

31. Repeated wars between their local ruler, the Flemish count, and his French allies could end badly for the cities, as happened for example in 1328, following an unsuccessful rebellion led by Nicolas Zannekin, when many of their privileges were suspended or revoked. The fifteenth century was even more troublesome if possible, with the Flemish towns rebelling time and again against their suzerain rulers, and in 1488, the hapless husband of Mary of Burgundy, Maximilian of Habsburg, was taken captive by the citizens of Ghent and forced to make far-reaching concessions, on which he promptly reneged after release.

were held together by a common urban and legal consciousness and distinctive legal institutions. This is well expressed by Prak (2018, p. 41), who points out that formal citizenship in towns created both legal and political communities as well as "imagined" communities. Such communities rested on a belief in a shared identity, loyalty to the city, and local patriotism and solidarity, in addition to shared economic interests. As we will discuss in chapter 7, the cultural foundations of communes were also reflected in their citizens' active participation in city governance, as well as their commitment to mutual aid and protection. Communal institutions entailed forms of representative democracy with limited suffrage, separation of powers among the legislative, judicial, and executive branches; protection of civil rights; and commitment to economic and political freedom. These institutions created an inclusive social order that reinforced civic capital and emphasized the importance of the common good over particularistic interests. Historians have referred to this ideology as "civic republicanism," meaning that citizens demanded to participate in the exercise of local power through collective forms of representation such as guilds, civic militias, and charity organizations (Prak 2018, p. 43). Brucker (2015, p. 30) summarized the politics of European communes as follows: "Central to the Commune's function was the premise that its corporate components, representing the interests of particular groups, would reconcile their differences within its ambit and under its guidance. Once defined, the common good (*il ben comune*) was expected to take precedence over the interests of any specific group or constituency." Often the agreements between members of the elite to assist one another and city charters were confirmed by religious oaths to underline the city's communitarian character and the importance of religious principles in holding together the community.

The corporate character of communes was evident from the very beginning. Communes generally were founded by a communal oath—namely, a "sworn association of inhabitants" (known as a *patta iurata*, or "sworn covenant") that entailed solidarity against outsiders (Nicholas 1997, pp. 148–49; Pirenne 1925 [2014], p. 201). Such covenants were often mediated by local bishops (Guiso, Sapienza, and Zingales 2016). Communes assured protection and upheld basic economic and civil rights, established forms of self-governance, and built their own tax capacities. One of their most typical corporate properties was the city wall, a good example of a local public good provided by urban corporations. Strong urban growth all over the Continent in the twelfth and thirteenth centuries led to the construction and expansion of city walls. Except in England, walls were municipally owned, with construction often funded by the citizens. This was done not only to provide for their security, but also to raise funds for other activities.

Genoa is an interesting example. In the late eleventh century, some important Genoese families signed a contract to create seven districts known as *compagnia* to pursue their common interests. The *compagnia* was essentially a neighborhood association based on a sworn pact, with the bishop and the local nobility joining in. Each district was its own corporation and handled its judicial and administrative aspects. It was expected that all able-bodied men of appropriate age would be part of the company depending on the district that they were born in. The seven corporations of Genoa played important roles within the city, including the maintenance of a militia, a judicial system, and handling of public finances, and they should be regarded as the first stage in the evolution of Genoa's commune (Epstein 1996, p. 33).[32]

Within the cities, smaller corporate bodies were important to the growth of cooperation and successful collective action. Charity organizations such as *beguinages* (homes for single women), hospitals and orphanages, local militias, friendly societies, and above all guilds were instrumental in these developments. As noted by Nicholas (1997, p. 220), "the corporate structure of the Medieval city was extremely complex," and the guilds involved in the city governance often came into conflict with one another. Despite this complexity, however, the organizational features of European communes were quite similar to one another. This homogeneity was due not only to their common cultural foundations, but also to deliberate imitation and the diffusion of urban legal arrangements. This was particularly true of the charters of cities in northern Europe, which formed the blueprint for later-established communes.[33]

Self-governing city-states modeled after the commune prototypes of cities like Venice and Hamburg were an almost exclusive European phenomenon. There was a sharp divergence between European cities and towns in the Islamic towns or in East Asia. Urban centers in the Middle East or North Africa never attained autonomy from rulers (Bosker et al. 2013). Japanese cities were

---

32. Somewhat earlier, dispersed Venetian households had organized themselves as a republic to mobilize military force to assist Byzantium in blocking a Norman invasion from Sicily. The reward, lucrative commercial privileges, greatly contributed to Venice's economic success (Greif 1998; González de Lara 2008; Nicholas 1997).

33. For instance, the laws of Lübeck were adopted in forty-three cities, those of Frankfurt in forty-nine cities, and the laws of Magdeburg (on the river Elbe) spread to over eighty new cities and became the predominant legal system in Central and Eastern Europe (Berman 1983, p. 376).

administered by a centrally appointed governor (with the exception of Osaka, which was self-governing on the eve of the Tokugawa shogunate).

Chinese cities, too, never enjoyed formal autonomy except during the early period of Spring and Autumn (eighth to fifth centuries BC). Lewis (2000) wondered why the early Chinese city-states of the Spring and Autumn period left such a meager mark in the history of China. His answer was that these cities in part had to coexist and compete with the Zhou bureaucracy. In addition, Lewis noted that although the city-states came to rule their surrounding countryside, they were too small to sustain themselves and diffuse ideologically; therefore, they were "squeezed between the lingering prestige of the old monarchy and the rising power of the emerging macro-states" (Lewis 2000, p. 372). We would add to these arguments the more fundamental point that China never developed the social and legal foundations of a corporation as a self-ruling cooperative body of unrelated people coresiding in a compact region.

Throughout most of history, Chinese cities remained governed by the central administrations of the counties in which they were located. As noted by Weber (1966), to avoid the risk of political fragmentation, the Imperial administration refrained from giving Chinese cities exclusive power over their territories (urban wards were the major administrative unit below the county); cities did not have their own military force. By the time of the Song Dynasty, most local public goods in cities were controlled and financed by the central administration, and the city administration was in the hands of state officials who were responsible for administering the region (Eberhard 1956). As state capacity declined in Ming and Qing years, nongovernmental associations informally took over many of these public services, and by the late nineteenth century, many or most urban services were provided informally by guilds and native-place associations and financed from dues or from the property of these associations (Skinner 1977, pp. 548–51).

During the nineteenth century, the major urban centers of China eventually gained a fair amount of de facto, informal autonomy. In these cities, the leadership structures coordinating urban services typically grew either from merchant associations or from gentry institutions (Skinner 1977, p. 549). In the former case, confederations of guilds and of native-place associations gradually extended benefits to everyone that had previously been restricted to members. One example is the market town of Hankow, where major guilds informally gained powers to enact and enforce commercial legislation and maintain infrastructures. In Hankow, even public services like firefighting and the police came under guild and then city control (Rowe 1984). Similar arrangements emerged in several other cities described by Skinner (1977, pp. 549–50). Shanghai County instead provides an example of gentry involvement in the provision of local public goods: local elites initially gained administrative experience as they cooperated closely with the magistrate to maintain waterways and other public infrastructures. Over time, they also developed local consultative institutions that accommodated certain forms of representation to guide major decisions and allocate tasks, striking a balance of power between state officials and local leaders (Elvin 1977).

The emergence of a self-governing capacity in Chinese cities has two distinctive features that set it apart from Europe, however. First, it happened much later than in Europe (Rowe's description of the city of Hankow refers to the nineteenth century, and many of the examples discussed by Skinner also refer to this period). Second, it reflected a large gap between de facto and de jure political authority. In the words of Crissman (1967, p. 200), urban Chinese had to "govern themselves without having . . . governmental institutions." This gap between de facto and de jure political authority was critical because it prevented the emergence of a tradition of well-defined participatory polities and a system of formal urban law that, as will be discussed in chapter 7, instead played an important role in the evolution of European political institutions.

The Social Structure of Cities

European and Chinese cities differed greatly not only in their administrative structures, but also in their social fabric. Being a citizen, or "burgher," as part of the urban community was an important aspect of urban identity in Europe, and there was a clear social distinction between the city and the countryside, embedded in the boundaries set by the city walls. Not every resident was a citizen. Citizenship was usually inherited or bought, and it always required taking a sworn oath to the city. In most examples of the communal oath, members were required to swear to provide mutual assistance, which included defense of the city's limits. To be a citizen, one had to contribute to the corporate estate of the city. Contributions were not just monetary, they could also include physical activities such as labor and military service in the urban militias. Often (particularly in England and Germany) citizenship was interconnected with taxation, and gaining full residence or citizenship rights usually required some financial or labor contributions, such as having minimum wealth or paying taxes for several years (Prak 2018).[34] Until the twelfth century, citizenship in England was based on owning a house. Citizens always enjoyed a special corporate protection (also when traveling), as well as liabilities, and city courts often punished noncitizens more severely than citizens.

In medieval Europe, unlike China, those with financial means could migrate between cities with relative ease, although cities also attracted migrants who escaped political or religious persecution and accepted them as citizens. Sometimes cities liberated migrants from their serf status.[35] That said, the popular notion that one could free themselves from serfdom by living in a city for a year and a day ("city air liberates") is mostly a myth. Nicholas (1997, pp. 156–57) points out that the custom was far from universal and it varied across the Continent: Marseilles, for example, required five years of residence, and some Italian towns as many as thirty.

At least in the early stages of medieval urbanization, cities had serfs living in them, and much of the population was migratory and seasonal. Nevertheless, on the whole, European cities were migrant-friendly, and large inflows of new residents, both permanent and temporary, did not prevent the formation of strong common urban identities. It should be added that such a migrant-friendly policy was a demographic necessity as towns overall had very high mortality rates and needed to replenish their population with migrants from the countryside. Urban authorities also made efforts to attract the best journeymen and artisans from other towns to improve the skills of their craftsmen (Belfanti 2004).

In China, instead, emigration from rural clans to a city (by merchants, scholars, artisans, and others) was usually temporary. Family members, including members of the person's nuclear family were often left behind, and migrants returned to their birthplace when the business that brought them to the city ended. The permanent residents in cities were typically a minority. Immigrants accounted for at least 75 percent of the population of Shanghai at the end of the nineteenth century (Goodman 1995). Rowe (1984) describes

34. In most German cities, the tax register and citizen list were identical. The charter of Provins (a commune southeast of Paris), written in 1230, defined the commune's territory as Provins and several settlements of the environs, called the *vilois*. All persons in this area who paid tax to the local count were considered members of the commune (Nicholas 1997, pp. 202–3).

35. The practice of "liberating" serfs started in Spain with the goal of repopulating cities with Christians during the Reconquista; it then spread to France and Flanders, and eventually to the North-German Hanseatic towns.

the demography of nineteenth-century Hankow, and while he does not provide precise estimates, he mentions different sources and examples, such as a neighborhood with no native residents at all, an 1813 *Baojia* enrollment where natives made up 50 percent of the resident population (but the statistic excluded temporary residents), and an estimate of the male-female ratio of 64 percent in 1912 (visitors and migrants were predominantly male).[36] As late as the seventeenth century, typically "the majority of a city's population consisted of so-called sojourners, people who had come from elsewhere and were considered (and thought of themselves as) only temporary residents. . . . Suspicions were always rife that sojourners could not be trusted" (Friedmann 2007, p. 274). City sojourners were of two types: traveling merchants, who stopped in the city for only brief periods and made up a considerable percentage of the city's population at any given moment in time, and "resident merchants"; that is, nonnatives who lived in the city for longer periods but eventually returned to their native homes. Rowe (1984) estimates that resident merchants in nineteenth-century Hankow could have reached hundreds of thousands, out of a total urban population of close to one million people.

The place of origin of city sojourners in China typically determined: (1) their occupation and economic specialization, (2) the social organization they belonged to, (3) their social background and cultural identity. Sojourning was seldom an individual matter. People who left to try their luck in the city normally did so as "representatives" of his or her family, lineage, and native place and were "'selected' to go" (Skinner 1977, p. 539). Chinese migrants who had moved to cities retained "their allegiance to the ancestral hall for many generations, the bonds of kinship being much closer than those of common residence" (Hu 1948, p. 10). Migrants often wanted to be buried in their native villages, and an important role of native-place associations was to help send the body of a deceased person to their village of origin. According to Goodman (1995, p. 46), "The idea of the native place remained a potent organizing principle as late as the 1930s" in the urban organization of Shanghai. Urban immigration in China was perceived as temporary, and hence the rise of an urban identity and a sense of belonging to a common urban community was largely absent. Immigrants originating from different regions lived in separate neighborhoods and were separated by language, social traditions, religious practices, and economic specializations.

36. In a *Baojia* enrollment, the population was assigned to groups of mutually responsible households arranged hierarchically under headmen to achieve some form of social control over a highly mobile and transient population (Rowe 1984, p. 297).

The division of urban residents by native place was also critical for social control and how social organizations evolved in the city. In Shanghai, for example, city authorities held native-place associations responsible for the actions of their members (Goodman 1995). In this sense, encouraging associations to manage migrants based on preexisting group ties was useful to the state apparatus. The pervasiveness of native-place associations also hampered the emergence of city-level institutions that served and represented the entire urban community. One exception is nineteenth-century Hankow, where the leaders of different guilds cooperated to pursue the common interest of the town, with the blessing and support of state officials (Rowe 1984, p. 338).

Broadly, however, the norm was segmentation by group identity, which unsurprisingly generated mistrust and conflict, both among different immigrant groups and among urban natives and immigrants. This pattern also existed beyond the urban center; even in Chinese villages, newcomers tended to face suspicion and hostility (Hu 1948, pp. 91–94; Ebrey and Watson 1986 pp. 1–15).[37] Paired with the host of Chinese custom and laws that favored local clan members in the allocation of economic and political privileges (e.g., the norm that awarded local clan members first right of refusal in the land market), these forces culminated in inhibiting permanent migration, thus preventing shared group identity from developing.

6. Concluding Remarks: A Practice of Cooperation

The need for cooperation is one of the most basic requirements of a well-functioning economy. Neither China nor Europe was exempt from this condition, especially prior to the rise of the modern state. Although both civilizations developed functional solutions to this problem, their methods varied. In Europe, voluntary associations of unrelated individuals were the norm, especially during the Middle Ages. Fraternities, guilds, monastic orders, parishes, universities, and self-governing cities allowed individuals to pursue general or specific goals across the social, cultural, and economic domains. Corporate bodies also emerged in the countryside (Reynolds 1997a; Brenner 1987).

---

37. To illustrate, consider the genealogy of the Chu clan from Kiangsi. In describing the social relations in their new location, the genealogy notes that "our village is the only one inhabited by the *tsu* [clan] of Chu. It adjoins that of the tsu of Yu, but there is no community of interests or of administration between us, nor is there any ill-feeling however" (Hu 1948, appendix 10, p. 112).

Medieval farming required cooperation and coordination in open-field agriculture, as well as management of common and waste fields. Whether or not we want to regard these organizations as "corporations," they clearly demonstrated the ability of Europeans to organize themselves spontaneously into collective bodies with some kind of quasi-public function.

All these examples point to widely diffused practices of universalistic cooperation. Depending on the requirement and the community, people would be able to group themselves and collaborate on a specific project or in a range of activities, if it were in their common interest to do so. A large variety of corporate organizations emerged in Europe. People belonged to different corporate groups at the same time, including possibly their villages or towns, their parishes, their craft or trade guilds, and their militias. "Many people must have thought of themselves (if they thought consciously about the subject at all) as belonging to overlapping groups within their immediate locality and also to layers of collective activity beyond it" (Reynolds 1997b, p. 138).

The existence and features of specific corporate groups varied across time and space, reflecting the structure of society, its economic and cultural developments, and the specific collective needs. It is no coincidence that corporate structures in cities differed from those on the countryside, and corporations in maritime areas could be quite different from those in alpine communities. Nevertheless, the large varieties of European corporate groups that emerged during the Middle Ages shared two common features. First, corporate organizations were not established and controlled by sovereign or ecclesiastic elites. Rather, they emerged through a bottom-up process during a period of political fragmentation (Van Zanden 2008; De Moor 2008). Second, although medieval society was very unequal and hierarchical, the internal organization of most corporate groups was inclusive and nondiscriminatory. These organizations made collective decisions either by general consensus or through collective counsels and representative committees. This habit of community involvement and organized cooperation had a profound influence on popular attitudes toward collective activities in general.[38] As we shall see in chapter 7, the organizational practices of European corporations were then

---

38. In the words of Reynolds (1997b, p. 339), describing the early fourteenth century: "In most of western Europe lay people (. . .) believed that government depended on consultation and consent, and that its object was to achieve a harmonious consensus in accordance with the custom and the law of the whole community."

adapted and transplanted in political institutions when state consolidation started to take form.

Cooperation was equally widespread in China. But it was mostly organized within the nonoverlapping boundaries of kinship ties, and along hierarchical criteria based on seniority. As a result, society was more clearly divided in a partition of nonoverlapping groups. Chinese clans also were more ambiguously defined relative to European corporations: they had no formal legal definition, and membership was defined by common ancestry, which in practice could be rather flexible. Clans remained defined by extended kinship, and by a much deeper loyalty to clansmen, a respect for elders, and a deep commitment to the defining values of neo-Confucian ideology.

Chinese clans, like European corporations, had a complex relationship with state authorities. But in China, the power of the central government was gradually declining, making clans increasingly important in maintaining the proper functioning of society. In contrast, European state institutions were strengthening and taking on more responsibility for local order and cooperation. As we will discuss in the next two chapters, these starkly different social arrangements left a deep imprint on the divergent evolution of legal and political institutions in these two parts of the world.

7

Political Divergence

1. Introduction

To reiterate the overarching theme of this book, the "Great Divergence" or "bifurcation" between Europe and China discussed in chapters 2 and 6 is not solely economic, but also political. Throughout most of its history, China was governed by a sequence of absolutist political regimes, that ruled over most of its territory and relied on a centralized and professional bureaucracy to enforce tax collection, recruit and maintain an army, and help ensure law and order. To this day, China has never had even a semidemocratic or participatory form of central government.

Europe differed in several respects. As we have seen, the collapse of the Roman Empire fragmented the Continent both politically and geographically. After this point, it was never again ruled by a single, centralized authority. Despite the occurrence of absolutist regimes in some parts of Europe and during some centuries, European rulers were generally forced to bargain with representatives of local political groups, often in collective assemblies, and were gradually more and more constrained by the rule of law. Eventually, and at different speeds and varying degrees of success, and not without quite a few setbacks, European political institutions evolved toward liberal democracy.

How can we explain these divergent trajectories of institutional development? And how are they linked to the differences in culture and social organizations discussed in previous chapters? This chapter addresses these questions. Much as was the case for economic divergence, there is no single answer. A plurality of factors, including historical accidents and path dependence, certainly played an important role. But two aspects deserve special emphasis.

First, political power in Europe remained highly fragmented for a long time. This fragmentation went much beyond the geographical polycentrism discussed in earlier chapters. The total and prolonged collapse of the Western Roman Empire and the invasions and settlements of different tribes of barbarians destroyed the Roman state infrastructures without replacing them with viable alternative state institutions. For several centuries, power remained highly splintered across localities and within society, and it proved impossible to reestablish a sustainable central authority. When European rulers eventually started to rebuild state and tax capacity, they faced two main challenges: how to come to terms with other powerful groups in society, and how to overcome the threats coming from neighboring states. By contrast, China achieved unification and concentration of state powers early, before countervailing forces could emerge. Centralization of powers persisted even during periods of internal wars and after external invasions. Therefore, unlike in Europe, Chinese rulers were focused less on domestic and foreign competitors; rather, their main challenges were how to solve agency problems in the vertical hierarchy of the central bureaucracy, how to overcome informational asymmetries in controlling an extended territory, and how to prevent and resist internal rebellions by peasants. Although the last point is similar to Europe's struggle with internal instability, opposition to central authority in China was less organized and weaker than in Europe. Two recent books, Scheidel (2019) and Stasavage (2020), have also emphasized the relevance of this initial difference between China and Europe in explaining their divergent paths of institutional development.

But historical circumstances are only part of the story behind this political divergence. A critical role was also played by a second factor: the different organizations of society in China and Europe, at a time when state institutions were still underdeveloped or totally absent. In Europe, state institutions were built on top of other social organizations; and in China, where state institutions emerged very early on, they were deeply influenced by the dynastic organization of society. These differences in the organization of society between China and Europe were key in determining their divergent evolutions of state power and political institutions.[1]

The distinctive features of China and Europe's methods of organizing society mattered for the way that state institutions developed in numerous ways. As we have seen, Chinese clans were geographically based but had to share

---

1. In a recent survey, Grafe and Prak (2020) propose a tri-partite division of the role of institutions in long-term economic change. The microeconomic level pertains to families and households; the mesoeconomic level to firms and other local organizations; and the macroeconomic level to states and other political and encompassing organizations.

control over their territories with other similar organizations. Clans were also ascriptive and closed, and they could not easily be scaled up: people were born in a clan, and there were limits to how much lineages could be extended (although there was some fluidity in membership). These features made clans politically weaker relative to comparable European groups (free towns, guilds, the Catholic Church, and other corporate bodies), which could more easily be scaled up, and relative to feudal lords who had a tighter and more complete control over their territory. By contrast, some European corporations (free towns and the Church) were strong enough to hamper the centralization of power in the hands of European rulers during the Middle Ages. By the sixteenth and seventeenth centuries, when European states had become stronger, many of the parameters of participatory government had already been set.

Chinese clans and European corporations influenced political institutions also by shaping the evolution of legal systems and by providing concrete examples of collective governance. As already noted, Chinese clans were highly hierarchical organizations held together by traditions, informal arrangements, and social norms. They furthered a collectivistic culture that emphasized seniority as an unquestioned source of authority. These cultural traits complemented and facilitated the consolidation of an absolutist state, where the emperor was seen as the head of all Chinese people who derived legitimacy from a "Mandate from Heaven" (*tian ming*). In contrast, European corporate groups were based on formal agreements between actively consenting parties sharing common goals. Despite living in a hierarchical society, Europeans were accustomed to consensual practices in their daily life. Moreover, to the extent that hierarchies were needed within a corporate organization, a lot of thought went in how to protect the rights of individual members and how to regulate decision-making procedures. The organization of the Church is an important example of this, but it is not the only one. These corporate practices first emerged and were codified in civil law and then were adapted to constitutional law and to the governance of political entities. In other words, European political institutions evolved from principles inherited from corporate structures and an individualistic culture, such as the principle of representation, the right of consent, and the belief that collective decisions should follow due process.

A few recent books have contrasted the evolution of political institutions in China and Europe. Although several arguments in these books are similar to ours, there are also some relevant differences. Our main ideas and conclusions are very much in line with the approach of Joseph Henrich (2020) and Jonathan Schulz (2022). As discussed in chapter 4, and as argued by these authors, we agree that Europe evolved along its unique and distinctive path of economic and political development also thanks to a key historical juncture: the adoption by the Western Church of an active policy against extended kin networks. This contributed to the diffusion of individualistic cultural traits and universal (as opposed to communitarian) morality, as well as to the emergence of social organizations based on voluntary associations rather than dynastic ties. Relative to our approach, however, these scholars place more emphasis on how individual psychology and beliefs were influenced by historical developments, while we give more emphasis to social and economic relations. We also place greater weight on the historical circumstances that led to external and internal political fragmentation in Europe, following the insights of Scheidel (2019).

Two recent books, Møller and Doucette (2022, pp. 82–116) and Grzymała-Busse (2023), as well as Grzymała-Busse (2024), have also stressed the role of the Catholic Church in sustaining European political fragmentation and in the evolution of the ideas of representation and consent. As they see it, these ideas, which became the cornerstones of Western notions of democracy, first emerged within the Catholic Church in the twelfth and thirteenth centuries, and from the Church, they diffused to secular authorities. They argue that using the development of formal canon law and the resuscitation of Roman law (to be discussed later in this chapter), these political principles emerged first to resolve intra-Church disputes—those resulting from "attempts within the reform papacy of the twelfth century to find ways of handling the challenges of the administrative centralization and expansion sparked by the eleventh-century declaration of independence from secular rulers" (Møller and Doucette 2022, p. 86). Yet the Church itself, whether it was the origin of these ideas or not, became increasingly hierarchical after the reforms, and proto-democratic ideas such as consensual governance were clearly not part of its DNA. In our view, the Church was particularly important in facilitating the emergence of corporate arrangements as the prototypical social organization throughout Western Europe. As argued in previous chapters, this resulted in Europeans abandoning tribal and kin-based networks inherited from Germanic societies. The corporate organizational forms that emerged in Europe were unique and, being so familiar and widespread in civil society, they provided a model for the subsequent evolution of political institutions; they also shaped notions of political rights and sources of legitimacy.

Acemoglu and Robinson (2019) attribute the uniqueness of the European path of political development to a balance between two forces. On the one hand, they argue, Europe was able to avoid the path of failed and anarchic states because it inherited some remnants of the Roman tradition of central state institutions. On the other hand, it was also able to avoid excessive centralization based on despotic state institutions, thanks to the Germanic tradition of participatory assemblies. We instead attribute the European uniqueness to other historical forces. Rome was important not only for what remained of its central institutions, legal traditions, and intellectual legacy, but also for how it fell (Terpstra, 2025). As argued by Scheidel (2019), the collapse of Rome left a void that remained unfilled for half a millennium. The resultant political fragmentation constrained subsequent rulers and forced them to accept political compromises, contributing to keep Europe away from political absolutism. Moreover, while we acknowledge that some aspects of the Germanic tradition facilitated the embodiment of consensual practices in political institutions, particularly in northern Europe, we instead attribute the European uniqueness to the decline of tribal traditions in the early Middle Ages and their replacement by corporations as the main mechanism enabling local cooperation. The governance practices that emerged in corporations were then transplanted and adapted to the newly emerging state institutions.

Stasavage (2020) stresses the difference in the timing of the emergence of an effective state bureaucracy relative to the evolution of political institutions. China was able to build an effective central bureaucracy early, under an absolutist autocracy. This order of events mattered. The persistence of a bureaucratic apparatus enabled the authoritarian regimes that came to power to subjugate society even when the economy became more developed.[2] Instead, in Europe, political rights were conceded before a strong state bureaucracy was built, and this limited consolidation of power by the sovereign. While we broadly agree with both Scheidel (2019) and Stasavage (2020) that political fragmentation was a fundamental difference between China and Europe after the fall of the Western Roman Empire, we feel that the importance of Chinese bureaucracy in shaping the course of events must be supplemented by other factors. The Chinese empire was spread out over a very large territory. State control in China during the first millennium AD was limited and imperfect. We instead attribute greater importance to the different social organizations that emerged in China and Europe in those early centuries, when the state presence in local affairs was weak, no matter how developed its bureaucracy.

---

2. Francis Fukuyama (2011, p. 134) pointed out that during the early Han Dynasty (202 BC–9 AD), "the Chinese government of the Former Han Dynasty fulfilled virtually all of [the] criteria of modern bureaucracy."

In the rest of this chapter, we develop these arguments in greater detail. Section 2 focuses on China, describing the main institutional features of Imperial China and explaining how they came about. Section 3 turns to Europe. We refrain from a complete description of European political institutions because they varied too much across time and space. Instead, we focus on the period between the eleventh and fifteenth centuries, when several distinctive pillars of European states first emerged. Here too, we seek to explain the path of institutional development and its link with other social organizations. In particular, we pay attention to the emergence of corporations and free towns, and to the influence of the Western Church on state development. Section 4 summarizes the main ideas in this chapter.

2. China's Political Institutions

The key features of Chinese political institutions emerged early, during the brief Qin Empire (221–207 BC) and then more extensively during the Han Dynasty (206 BC–220 AD). Before the Qin Dynasty, China did not have a stable and unitary system of government. Under the Zhou Dynasty—which ruled nominally from the eleventh century BC until 221 BC, but which effectively lost power in the eighth century BC—China was mostly a feudal state. When the Zhou fell out of power, feudalism began to disintegrate. In its place emerged the Spring and Autumn period (traditionally dated between 771 BC and 476 BC), during which China was highly fragmented and with many small city-states. This was followed by the period of Warring States (475 BC–221 BC), characterized by fierce competition among the seven regional states. Conflicts resulted in fiscal and technological innovations, such as the taxation of agriculture, mass conscription of farmers, and the diffusion of cast iron.

This was also a period in which pluralism and competition stimulated intellectual and artistic creativity, in a manner perhaps familiar to historians of medieval and Early Modern Europe: urban population expanded, commercial activity increased, and the use of money spread within walled cities (Lewis 2007, pp. 75–86). Traditional Chinese history sees the era as one in which "a hundred schools of thought" (*zhuzi baijia*) flourished, among them Confucianism, Mohism, and Legalism. It was truly a competitive marketplace for ideas, reminiscent in some ways of Europe in the sixteenth and seventeenth centuries. As one scholar described it, "This was an age of bold intellectual departures and remarkable ideological pluralism, unhindered by either political or religious orthodoxies. Thinkers competed freely for the rulers' patronage, moving from one court to another in search of better employment" (Pines 2012, p. 16; also see Gernet 1982). Had it persisted, Chinese intellectual, cultural, and political history would have been quite different.

However, it was not to be. The early Zhou Empire, which effectively lost power around 771 BC, had already laid the foundations of a centralized bureaucracy. As Stasavage (2020, p. 149) notes, its officials served at the pleasure of the king and were subject to a system of promotion. These bureaucracies were maintained locally by the city-states that prevailed during the Spring and Autumn centuries and were developed further in the Warring States era. When the Kingdom of Qin unified China between 230 BC and 221 BC, it faced a choice: Reestablish autonomous princedoms in the East, as had been the case in the past under the Zhou? Or instead, develop its own system of administrative control? To preserve unity and stability, the "First Sovereign Emperor" Ying Zheng chose the latter, extending the pre-Imperial system of local government to all conquered territories. He divided the realm into thirty-six military commanderies (later, prefectures) and several counties. To prevent the concentration of local power, each commandery was run by a triumvirate of officials directly appointed by and accountable to the new emperor (Finer 1997, vol. 1, p. 472). This administrative framework was one of the most durable legacies of the Qin Dynasty.

Unity was also achieved through other means besides a central bureaucracy. As Pines (2012, pp. 21–22) observes, the "Qin sought to establish stability and uniform orderly rule through a variety of practical and symbolic means," imposing a unified system of measures, weights, coinage, orthography, laws, and a calendar, thereby establishing a standard repertoire for subsequent dynasties. The Qin Dynasty itself was short-lived, but its administration set the precedent for those that followed, in its reliance on court appointees who constituted the nonhereditary and meritocratic bureaucracy. The Han Dynasty continued this tradition.

The pursuit of unification and stability remained a central objective of the Chinese state across regimes. Under the Qing, fears of uprisings constrained the Imperial government's fiscal capacity, preventing rulers from raising the taxes necessary for basic functions (Zhang 2022). Stability included the absence of famines, and the Chinese state made a deliberate effort to smooth consumption by investing heavily in granaries intended to stabilize prices.[3]

---

3. Some scholars have seen these measures as part of an improvement of living standards under the reasonable assumption that economic security should be regarded as part of the quality of life (Chen and Peng 2022, pp. 697–700).

Perhaps as a result of this quest for stability, many of the essential characteristics of Chinese political institutions established under the Qin and Han remained remarkably sturdy in subsequent centuries despite internal wars, external invasions, and dynastic changes.

The remainder of this section describes Chinese political institutions and discusses how the organization of government was complementary with other features of Chinese culture and society.[4] We return to the discussion of why Chinese political institutions were so stable in the next section. The similarities between the Imperial institutions and those of modern China are discussed further in chapter 10.

The Emperor

Central authority in the Chinese government rested with the emperor, who was a symbol of unity and whose role was hereditary. The emperor's authority was unquestioned. The Chinese state was regarded as a "family state" of sorts, something like an enlarged family headed by the emperor, who commanded respect and obedience as the ultimate patriarch.

The absolute ruler had a number of duties toward his people: he had to care about their welfare, treat them fairly, and protect them from external threats. If he failed to do so, rebellion and disobedience could justifiably ensue. These obligations reflected a Mandate from Heaven. This notion gave the emperor legitimacy, but it imposed real constraints on Imperial despotism through the threat of rebellion. The idea of the Mandate from Heaven dates to the Zhou Dynasty, which overthrew the previous Shang Dynasty in 1046 BC. In later centuries, thinkers like Xunzi (c.310 BC—c.238 BC) developed this idea further into a right (and even a duty) of the people to overthrow a supposedly bad emperor (Pines 2008). The idea of heaven's mandate remained one of the fixed elements of Chinese Imperial history, and arguably traces of it can be found in China until today.

Even so, the notion of the Mandate from Heaven entailed no accountability of the emperor to his subordinates and did not require that he engage in negotiation with representatives of powerful groups in society (Finer 1997, chapter 5; Stasavage 2016). Consent was not a prerequisite for the exercise of state power, and the Mandate from Heaven entailed no power sharing but rather

4. Finer (1997) and Ch'ien (1982) provide more complete descriptions disaggregated by dynasty.

was unitary in nature. Only one emperor had this mandate, although it could be taken away from him. Once a revolt happened, however, whoever won the battle for power could claim it completely, and with no dissidents, over the entire territory (Wang and Nahm 2019). The contrast with England's Glorious Revolution, where the new ruler, King William of Orange, had to make far-reaching concessions of his power to succeed his predecessor King James II (who had escaped in France), is striking.

The effective powers of the emperor varied over time and across dynasties, reflecting the emperor's personality and strength, among other traits. During the Tang Dynasty, which came to power in 618 AD, Imperial decrees required endorsement from top bureaucrats, who thus had some veto rights. As Mote (1999, p. 361) pointed out, Chinese emperors had no independent sources of income, and all funds disbursed to them were "subject to bureaucratic procedures." However, in practice, strong emperors were often able to effectively circumvent these requirements. Much of the consolidation of Imperial power and the powerful civil service occurred during the Song Dynasty, relying on legitimacy and an "atmosphere of responsibility and reliability" (Kuhn 2009, p. 176). During the later dynasties, and in particular during the Ming and Qing, the powers of the emperor became more absolute (more on this later in this chapter).

Imperial succession was from father to son, and the Imperial throne was the only hereditary position in Chinese government. Succession was not unproblematic. The very large Imperial harems implied that lack of male heirs was usually not a problem, unlike in Europe. But the large number of potential heirs was a source of uncertainty. Emperor Tai-Tsung of Tang (r.626–649 AD) acknowledged this fact: "I have already appointed my eldest son Crown Prince, but the fact that his brothers and the sons of my concubines number almost forty is a constant source of worry to me" (quoted by Wright and Twitchett 1973, p. 249). Usually, the emperor designated an empress, but he could change his mind later and demote her.

Moreover, occasionally the emperor died when his designated heir was too young to take the throne, or when there were no heirs. This is how the Han Dynasty ended in the third century, when a power vacuum created by a problematic succession coincided with an internal rebellion. Unlike in the Roman Empire, however, these situations were rarely resolved by war or outright conflict, but rather by intrigue within the inner court, and often in the harem as well. This reflects another important difference between Chinese and Western civilizations: whereas Roman emperors were often warriors and political issues became military conflicts, statesmen in China were typically civilians who subordinated military generals, particularly from the Song Dynasty onward. Moreover, the ideal Chinese emperor had a ritualistic role and was detached from daily administration (Finer 1997, vol. 1, p. 484).[5] Again, these characteristics can be discerned much earlier, but they were stabilized and finalized under the Song.

The Central Government

Just as important as the Imperial regime was its bureaucracy, which made Imperial rule possible (Stasavage 2020). The structure of the bureaucracy changed over time, and its reach was constrained by administrative and communications technology. Throughout time, however, the bureaucracy played a central role in Chinese governance.[6]

The emperor was the head of state, but administrative power rested with the chancellor who headed the government. Early on, the chancellor was the chief manager of the Imperial household and also took care of palace affairs. Over time, the Office of the Chancellor evolved, imbuing him with greater powers, to the point that he became the real head of the central government. As noted by Ch'ien (1982), before unification under the Qin Empire, China was divided into many principalities and kingdoms, each ruled by a noble family. "With unification of all of China under one Imperial House, what were formerly merely clan matters became national affairs. The ruling house with all its officials became a national government. The Chancellor, formerly a household manager, became the chief administrator of such a vast national state that it is called an empire" (Ch'ien 1982, p. 11).

During the Song Dynasty, power was shared among three major departments: the central secretariat, which was close to the emperor and the decision-making process; the department of state affairs, the closest to what in modern times would be a government running finances, war, and justice; and the chancellery, which fulfilled advisory functions. Yet the emperor remained "the one man at the center, in charge of and responsible for everything" (Kuhn 2009, p. 39). Over time, effective power increasingly shifted

---

5. Unlike European rulers, Chinese emperors lived secluded lives, rarely made public appearances, and had little direct contact with their subjects.

6. At the zenith of the Han Dynasty, around 5 BC, the Chinese bureaucracy counted more than 130,000 officials, or 1 in 440 people in the population, an astonishingly high number (cited by Stasavage 2019, p. 140).

toward the emperor at the expenses of the chancellor. Eventually, the chancellery was abolished by Zhu Yuanzhang, the Hongwu emperor, founder of the Ming Dynasty, and the three departments no longer existed during the Ming and Qing dynasties.[7]

The details of how members of the bureaucracy were selected, promoted, and appointed, as well as their ultimate powers, varied over time. During the Tang Dynasty, top appointments followed a specific procedure, and the central administration had veto power over Imperial decrees. Thus, the bureaucracy provided effective checks and balances on the emperor's authority, particularly when the emperor was weak (Zhao 2015, p. 292). In later dynasties, however, the internal checks and balances exercised by the central bureaucracy were weakened, and emperors found ways of bypassing the central administration through eunuchs or other loyal palace officials. This was particularly true under the Ming (1368–1644), and even more so during the Qing Dynasty (1644–1911), which originated from the Manchu tribe in the north. The cruel Hongwu emperor accused his chancellor, Hu Weiyong, of treason and executed him and thousands of members of his family and related officials. Hu was the last chancellor in China. From then on, the emperors were their own central secretariats, responsible for coordinating the work of the ministers. The grand secretariats that subsequently replaced the central secretariat had only an advisory capacity, with no policymaking authority (Brook 2010, pp. 91–94; Huang 1988, p. 106).[8] The Qing Dynasty, which felt insecure because of their nonHan origins, further strengthened the autocratic powers of the emperor and of the inner palace. The emperor relied on the support of his own Manchu tribesmen and their military, known as "bannermen," placing them above the Chinese literati in the hierarchy of the central bureaucracy. For this reason, Ch'ien (1982, p. 126), speaks of a regime of "tribal despotism" under the Qing.

Nevertheless, modern scholarship has recognized that in many ways, the Ming emperors were subject to constraints and were not quite as powerful as

7. The flip side of this concentration was that precisely because the mandate was from heaven, if some natural disaster took place, this was seen as a sign of dissatisfaction from heaven and undermined the legitimacy of the emperor.

8. The Hongwu emperor also regularly intimidated and humiliated high-ranking officials by punishing them in public. By the early fifteenth century, officials were too scared to take the initiative in determining policy. "After a series of bloody purges that lasted from 1376 to 1396, the bureaucracy was virtually reduced to a huge clerical pool, subservient to the sovereign but not empowered to make important decisions" (Huang 1988, p. 106). That changed after the death of the Hongwu emperor in 1398, however, and the third Ming emperor, Yongle (r.1402–1424), refrained from making policy decisions regarding how to implement his orders.

earlier scholars had believed.[9] Legitimacy depended on moral behavior by the standards of Confucianism. As Brook (2010, p. 87) points out, the Ming emperors were limited by the letter of the law promulgated by the founder of the dynasty, the Hongwu emperor. Significantly, however, Brook adds that the emperor did not consider himself bound by his own codes, and the regulations that he put in place lacked the sense of reciprocity between ruler and people that Confucius had recommended, and which ironically was being put in place in Europe. Moreover, even during the more absolutist periods, the complexity of administering such a large state from the center made the regular bureaucracy indispensable. "The emperor could have his officials flogged or tortured or executed; he could act on private advice rather than theirs; but he could not rule without them. It was from them that the memorials and reports emanated in the first instance, it was they who regulated his ritual appearances, it was through them that he administered" (Finer 1997, vol. 2, p. 829). The informal checks and balances imposed by the powerful Chinese bureaucracy were very different from those faced by European rulers, however—not only because these checks and balances were not formal, much less constitutional, but also because Imperial China lacked anything like a countervailing power, such as a powerful Church, a strong aristocracy, a politically active military class, or a well-organized urban bourgeoisie. We return to this point next.

The Civil Service Exam

The transformation of the chancellor from a private official of a feudal noble house into the formal head of a professional and centralized administration was a key step in the evolution of Chinese political institutions. This evolution was gradual. Its foundations were first laid during the Warring States Period (or even before that), and later consolidated during the Han Dynasty. As the administration grew larger and more complex, bureaucrats were increasingly selected based on merit and education, through a central examination that

9. In a famous article, Mote (1961, p. 32) argued against the thesis of absolute despotism and pointed out that even the ferocious and dictatorial Hongwu emperor, founder of the Ming Dynasty, (also known as Ming Taizu) was limited "because he would have felt them obviously inappropriate to legitimate Confucian government and knew that the world would feel the same way." In any event, the draconian laws passed by the Hongwu emperor were too autocratic to be sustained by his successors (Brook 2010, p. 88). The idea that autocracy was baked into the Chinese polity by the *keju* examinations and there were no effective constraints on Imperial power in China, as proposed by Huang (2023), therefore may have to be modified.

appraised the candidates' ability as intellectuals and men of letters.[10] Eventually, this centralized meritocracy evolved into a striking institutional innovation: the Imperial Civil Service Examination, or *keju* system. First codified during the Tang Dynasty in the seventh century AD, it remained in force until the last years of Imperial rule.[11]

During the Han Dynasty (206 BC–220 AD), officials (particularly those at the local level) were recruited through a system of recommendations. Provincial, local, and central officials were all required to recommend men of merit or junior bureaucrats for appointment or promotion. Merit criteria concerned integrity, character, ability, literary attainment, and administrative expertise. An Imperial academy was also created in the nation's capital. Candidates' performance on the final examination would determine their official rank. Over time, however, the system deteriorated; increasingly, recommendations reflected the influence of clans and nepotism rather than true ability (Ho 1964, chapter 1).

The collapse of the Han Empire was followed by a long period of internal fragmentation and conflict known as the Period of Six Dynasties (220 AD–589 AD). Unification was achieved again under the House of Sui (589 AD) and maintained under the Tang Dynasty (618–907). These new regimes aimed to establish objective merit criteria for the bureaucracy and instituted a competitive exam system for recruitment. The resulting solution was both an extension and a rationalization of earlier practices of written and oral exams under the Han, but it went further, formalizing testing as an explicit requirement for promotion. The *keju* examination system evolved through time, placing more emphasis on scholarship as a basis for merit, and it came fully into being during the rule of the Song emperor, Taizong (r.976–997).[12] Initially, the *keju* consisted of two important academic degrees: the *mingching* and the *jinshi*. The former required more mechanical memorization of the classics and was

10. China's tradition of merit-based rule as a principle to be preferred over heredity goes back, and evidence of it can be traced, to the period of Warring States (475 BC–221 BC) prior to the Qin Dynasty.

11. By the time of the Tang Dynasty, professionalization and expertise had become hallmarks of administration at both the central and provincial levels. All the men who controlled the Salt and Iron Commission, which administered revenues from the salt tax, had risen to their position through competence and experience (Lewis 2009, p. 42).

12. Taizong was the younger brother of Emperor Taizu, the founder of the dynasty. Taizong awarded more degrees in a year than his brother did during his entire reign. Ability rather than hereditary ascription became the criterion for advancement in government, and the emperor declared his interest in recruiting men of proven ability for his administration.

less selective. Eventually, the *mingching* was abandoned and selection for the highest office was based only on the more demanding *jinshi* examination, which lasted until 1904.[13] There were also two lower-level examinations: the *shengyuan* and the *juren*.

In principle, a meritocratic system of selection is to be preferred over that practiced in Europe, where the accident of birth determined the distribution of political power and social status. Elman (2000, p. 14) summarized the rise of the examination system in the Tang and Song years as the transformation of the *Shih* (the class of gentry-literati) "from men of good birth to men of culture." Ability rather than hereditary ascription became the criterion for advancement in government. At least in theory, it provided an opportunity for lower-class people to rise to the top of Chinese society and create an administration of the best and the brightest.

As discussed in chapter 6, the Civil Service Examination was an important institutional innovation that lasted through time and strongly affected the incentives and attitudes of the Chinese elites. Selection into the civil service was based on objective and nonhereditary criteria, and many families devoted substantial effort and resources to acquire the human capital necessary for promising lads to succeed. Overall, the human capital accumulated to prepare for the exam was a good approximation to the Confucian ideal of liberal education. It equipped candidates with good judgment and common sense, and the system produced many successful officials (Ho 1964). As we will discuss in chapter 9, however, the Civil Service Examination also had massive unintended consequences—it induced the accumulation of a kind of human capital that actually hindered innovation and economic development.

The Civil Service Examination was also an important tool of cultural integration. It led to the emergence of a social class of erudite civil servants and scholars, trained in a self-referential Confucian culture. The emergence of such a social class did not happen by chance, but it was a deliberate goal of the early rulers, who wanted to consolidate central authority and reduce the power and legitimacy of decentralized military leaders. In the words of Ho (1964, p. 169), "To curb and eliminate the influence of the remaining regional military

13. The exam for the *mingching* consisted of three parts: (1) completion by memory of some given passages from the classics, (2) an oral interpretation of some passage from the classics, and (3) an essay on current affairs or administration. The *jinshi* required less memorization from the classics, entailed more essays on administrative matters, and replaced the oral interpretation of the classic with an essay and creative writings such as poems and rhymed prose (cf. Ho 1964, p. 13).

governors, the early Song state greatly enhanced the prestige and power of civil officials and made the examination system an increasingly important channel of sociopolitical mobility." This new social class of scholars and civil servants in some ways resembled the religious elites and prelates in the West, and sometimes it also had similar political and cultural effects in constraining central authority (Finer 1997, vol. 1, p. 479, vol. 2, p. 817).[14]

Overall, China's large, professional bureaucracy, imbued with a common culture of Confucian values, was a fundamental feature of its governance. However, while it served the purposes of the state, it also constituted a source of vulnerability: when population's demands outpaced government resources, the bureaucratic apparatus was susceptible to corruption and inefficacy, as in the later years of the Qing Dynasty, when the sale of offices to wealthy candidates undermined the strengths of the meritocratic exams (Lawrence Zhang 2022).

Moreover, as already pointed out in chapters 2 and 6, the Chinese mandarinate established a monopoly in the market for ideas, which had detrimental consequences for China's ability to innovate. Some scholars see the *keju* as the cause of the disappearance of serious competition in the market for ideas and trace the beginning of China's decline as a technological leader to the Sui Dynasty, which was the first to try examinations as a way of recruiting bureaucrats. "The closing of the Chinese mind occurred as *keju* scaled" (Huang 2023, p. 239). Increasingly, under the Ming and Qing dynasties, the Imperial examination system became a tool of stability and stagnation rather than innovation.[15]

14. In a recent paper, Chen et al. (2023) argued that the Civil Service Examination in effect erased the checks and balances that were imposed by the aristocracy on the emperor because the bureaucracy had no independent power base and all public officials all had similar backgrounds and were therefore substitutable. The result shifted power to the emperor, who could easily purge (and even execute) disobedient or uncooperative officials. The absence of any kind of checks and balances, short of violent rebellion, characterizes Chinese government throughout the Imperial period, and the authors claim that this "provides an institutional explanation of the great divergence" (p. 6).

15. In line with this view, Luo and Yu (2024) point to the initial difference in state power as a source of the Great Divergence. They note the economic importance of the state bureaucracy in Qu and Han times, and they stress state production in some sectors and active regulation and intervention in others (see also Von Glahn 2016, pp. 98–108). The powerful state bureaucracy early in China, they submit, was the critical difference that accounts for the Great Divergence. Their model is based on the assumption that in the long run, private production is more susceptible to technological progress than state production, and eventually, a society with weak government will develop faster.

Territorial Administration

Given the vast area covered by the Chinese state, enforcing law and order and tax collection throughout the empire was always a major challenge. On the one hand, the central administration needed to avoid the concentration of countervailing powers in specific geographic areas. On the other hand, coercing powers were needed for law enforcement and tax collection. Unlike Rome, which gave its provinces considerable autonomy, the Chinese state sought to impose uniformity and never allowed self-government from the Qin Dynasty on. At the same time, however, central control was limited by the size of the empire. Even the powerful Ming minister Zhang Juzheng, who ruled China between 1572 and 1582, was constrained by the technical weaknesses of an enormous empire where centralization could go only so far (Huang 1981, p. 64).

The compromise was to establish a two-track system. The central bureaucracy was organized from the top down, but it had very little control below the county level—the lowest tier of local government (Ch'ü 1962). Local affairs instead were run by informal social networks and local clans as a bottom-up system. Educated members of local clans were de facto in charge of actual enforcement and the provision of most local public goods. This made sense, as clans were the strongest sources of local authority and could legitimately exert power and control over their members. Central officials lacked this sort of influence, as captured by the popular saying, "Heaven is high and the emperor is far away." Bureaucrats seconded in the county from the central government mainly exercised supervisory tasks, collected information, and arbitrated conflicts among clans. The presence of a central bureaucracy strengthened the hand of the emperor relative to local elites and powerful clans. But the de facto powers of the center were limited because it needed to rely on local clans to get things done. Thus, this two-track system limited the absolutist powers of the central government (Fei 1992, p. 143).

As argued by Pines (2012), much of China's administrative history can be likened to a political pendulum, swinging between tighter and looser centralization. The pole of tighter centralization appealed to administrative logic: it allowed better control over local strongmen to prevent both potentially subversive political activities and corruption in the localities. At the same time, decentralization had several advantages. The delegation of power to local potentates could cut expenses and diminish the resources used by the central bureaucracy. Moreover, as Pines notes, local autonomy could allow greater flexibility in the ruling of remote territories inhabited by ethnic minorities, where Chinese administrative practices were at odds with local conditions and customs. All the same, the long-term trend was toward more centralization, in which efficiency and agility were sacrificed for the sake of stability above all.

There were three layers of local government: province, prefecture, and county. Only the lowest level, the county, dealt directly with the people; the higher levels were mainly involved with administering county officials. The higher-level units changed considerably over time, but the counties did not, and despite the large increases in population and the territorial expansion, the number of counties did not increase substantially: it is estimated that there were 1,100–1,400 counties during the Han (Ch'ien 1982, p. 11), and 1,360 counties in 1724 (one county for every 150 000 inhabitants approximately). Between 1700 and 1800, the population more than doubled, but the number of counties, and hence the number of magistrates in charge of governing them, barely increased (Sng 2014).

The central administration appointed a magistrate to head each county government. Under the so-called rule of avoidance, dating to the Sui Dynasty (581–618), county magistrates were prohibited from serving in their county of birth in order to deny them a local power base through nepotism. This rule was later reinforced by a prohibition on magistrates serving more than three or four years in the same county. Furthermore, the local military was directly accountable to the Imperial Court rather than the local government.

The county magistrate's court, the *yamen*, served as the center of local administration. Each *yamen* employed a staff of clerks and runners, but much of the day-to-day management of tax collection and peacekeeping was left to the local moral codes (*li*). Strikingly, this mode of governance was quite egalitarian in that both the rich and poor held positions of official responsibility. The only formal social distinction was between officials (*guan*) and commoners (*min*). The Chinese system was not democratic and differed from the kinds of local government that we are familiar with in the West; that said, in many ways, it still worked quite smoothly and was "ruled by an egalitarian spirit" (Mote 1999, p. 714).

In practice, although the magistrates were part of a large and coherent central bureaucracy, they had to rely on local personnel (who were typically part of powerful clans in the area) for the actual enforcement and administration. The magistrates were foreign to the region. Since they rotated areas frequently, their knowledge of local conditions was scant and they depended on local gentry (*jinshen*) for information and advice. Thus, local elites and their clans were effectively in charge of tax enforcement, administration, and the provision of local public goods.[16] The central administrators mainly focused on supervision and arbitration (Finer 1997, vol. 2, p. 768, vol. 3, pp. 1152–53). Of course, clans did not provide their services for free, and in return they enjoyed significant benefits, such as tax privileges. Peasants who were not protected by powerful clans bore the brunt of taxation (Sng 2014; Ma and Rubin 2015). At the same time, the government imposed indirect taxes on market transactions, the most profitable being the tax on salt.

Who exactly were the local elites (the so-called local gentry)? The term "gentry" is misleading. In England, it is associated with land ownership and wealth. In China, the *jinshen* are instead defined by education and social prestige. This social class consists of former and current local officials, leaders of influential clans, and literati who had either passed (or at least studied for) the lowest of the three Imperial examinations or had the means to purchase their degrees. The Chinese gentry were local clerks, teachers, physicians, accountants, and similar professionals who shared a commitment to a Confucian worldview (Zhao 2015, p. 336).[17] The rise of the gentry as a crucial actor in local society was clearly supported by the Imperial examination system. As Chen (2017, p. 158) noted, the examination system incentivized local elite families to accept the national Confucian culture, as it reinforced their status in local society. The gentry usually were the channel through which local Imperial officials transmitted orders that came from the capital. This dependency was the source of their power in running local affairs and providing local public goods (Ch'ü 1962, pp. 180–85). The gentry's power in local matters may have originated with the *shuai* system in place in the fourteenth century, in which local commoners were grouped into units of 100 families, each one led by literati and indoctrinated with Confucian texts to attain collective morality. These organizations fused normative rural communities with coercive state

16. By the eighteenth century, clans had accumulated considerable political power thanks to their indispensability in providing local public goods and local administration. Indeed, it has been argued that the power of some clans eventually became a matter of some concern to the Imperial government, fearing that kinship organizations of such magnitude were a possible threat to central authority, and the Qianlong emperor thought that large clans were more likely to cause trouble than small ones (Watson 1985 [2011], p. 27).

17. That said, there is no unanimity among historians about the *precise* definition of the gentry. Chinese scholars, such as Ch'ü T'ung-tsu (Qu 1962, p. 172; also see Chang 1955, pp. 6–8, and Hsiao 1967), have distinguished between the official gentry and the scholar gentry and pointed out that, as local leaders, they were responsible for the welfare of their community and represented it in front of formal Imperial authorities.

control and increasingly became instruments for tax collection and local administration, with mixed results (Wakeman 1975, pp. 4–6). By the time of the Ming Dynasty, in some interpretations, the gentry were accepted as the moral and intellectual leaders of their communities. Most important, they functioned as reliable local assistants to the magistrates (Heijdra 1998, p. 557).

Some scholars have argued that commoners often held anti-elite feelings and characterized the gentry as narrow-minded and selfish people who jealously defended their privileges and tax exemptions, and who were too few to effectively support the local administration (Heijdra 1998, pp. 558–62).[18] On the other hand, Wakeman (1975) defined the relationship of the gentry and the Imperial government as a "dynamic oscillation." He stressed that their provision of local public goods such as charity, education, and hydraulic engineering was indeed driven by their private interests and those of their lineage trusts. All the same, this self-motivated behavior had benefits for society. This ambiguous relationship created "the unity of Chinese society, not by eliminating the contradictions but by balancing them in such a way as to favor overall order" (Wakeman 1975, p. 4).

The power of the local gentry and the role of clans as the elemental building block of society were closely intertwined (Chen 2017, pp. 174–78). The gentry depended jointly on their local power base and on their political status, which was determined by having participated in the examination system. Having relatives with gentry status provided protection for local interests, and pooling resources at the clan level to invest in the human capital of gifted youngsters destined for the Imperial examination meant that the spoils of office—if the investment paid off—would be shared with other members of the clan. As McDermott (2013, pp. 260–61) has noted, large and successful clans depended on success on the examination.

The nature of local government in China had far-reaching implications. Unlike Europe, there was no local resident aristocrat (i.e., a ruling class that was almost defined by their access to wealth)—at first it was primarily landed wealth, and then commercial and financial as well. One consequence of the dependence of local government on clans was that day-to-day administration was often controlled by senior clan members (i.e., older people). In addition, senior clans (i.e., with longer genealogies) often yielded more local influence,

---

18. As Wakeman (1975) points out, members of the gentry might well have been incorruptible magistrates away from their county of birth, but once they retired to their home residence, they would use their superior social status to seek rents and protect the interests of their clan.

although they were not necessarily richer. Zhang (2017, pp. 22, 136–51) points out that in some sense, the Chinese social hierarchy was much more egalitarian than that of Europe, where ancestry typically implied wealth, and wealth implied power. In China, status was much more associated with age and seniority, so one automatically gained status over time. In other words, compared to Europe, the clannish organization of Chinese society greatly reduced the local political power of large landowners. As a result, the legal apparatus in China was far more protective of smallholders and tenant farmers, and the heavy concentration of land, as experienced in England as well as in Eastern Europe, was absent in China.[19] Of course, no society has ever succeeded in eliminating the correlation between political power and wealth, but in China, the causal chain was primarily from power to wealth through the increasing corruption of the Imperial administration. Only in the last two centuries of the empire did wealth buy power as well, through the increasing habit of selling offices, and the causal arrow was pointing in both directions.

Taxation

The Chinese tax system evolved over time, but the main source of government revenue was a land tax, besides other tolls and revenues from government monopolies. At the beginning of the Tang, taxation was not monetized and land was taxed according to the so-called Triple Tax System. This system, inherited from earlier times, presumed that all land belonged to the emperor, who allocated it to all males in proportion to their productive capacity, and taxes in kind (or in labor hours) were due on the allotted land. Great care went into assessing the quality of land soil and land productivity for the purpose of taxation.

In 780, under the Tang Dynasty, the system was changed to a Two-Tax or Double Tax System, or *Liangshuifa* (so-called because taxes were due in two installments, in the summer and in the autumn). Besides a much smaller poll tax on individuals, land was taxed regardless of who owned it. It was a progressive tax on all land under cultivation and an implicit recognition of the property rights in real estate. The Tang's system was put in place by Chancellor Yang Yan, who served under Emperor Dezhong in 780. The Double Tax System was intended to extend the tax base to merchants and other businessmen.

19. These rights are especially important in the mortgage markets, where borrowers (mortgagors) maintained a legal option to property even in the case of default, whereas in England, mortgagees could foreclose and take full ownership of land when the mortgage matured (Zhang 2017).

Farmers were taxed twice a year, but they still had to provide *corvée* (labor services) as well. The tax reform contributed enormously to the revenues of the Tang state, and because the payments were in cash, they stimulated monetization and commercialization. Yet its burdens were partially responsible for the growing unpopularity of the Tang Dynasty and its eventual downfall (Lihua Chen 2022). Over time, the Tang system evolved and became complex and cumbersome; for example, it eventually included payments in kind and labor services. All the same, the basis for assessment remained wealth and land holdings, and the system lasted for six centuries until the Ming reforms.

The land tax was also significant in that it established de facto individual property rights over land. Under the Song Dynasty, the government did away with explicit policies on land allocation. This enhanced efficiency and commercialization because individuals were free to buy and sell land and to move around. However, the new policy created new informational problems in tax collection because property holdings had to be assessed. To circumvent these informational requirements and the associated agency problems, the government established fixed revenue targets for each province and used a quota system to divide revenues among the different levels of government. The central government then left it to local authorities in each county to enforce tax collection, as described previously. The system became similar to a tax farming arrangement, where local tax collectors were de facto the residual claimants of tax revenue. This meant that, in concrete terms, the government delegated responsibility for tax collection to the clans.

Many of the key features of this fiscal system survived until the early twentieth century, although the Imperial administration made repeated attempts to reform it. In 1381, the first Ming emperor, Hongwu, simplified the system by specifying a fixed tax rate per unit of land, regardless of its productivity and cultivation intensity, and then allocating a tax quota to each province. The new system reinforced the owners' incentives for land cultivation, but it gave rise to huge disparities of effective tax burdens across regions and types of land. The village registers of land holdings, known as Yellow Books, were often out of date and rarely updated.[20] Moreover, to cope with the huge discrepancies among different areas, charges and surcharges were levied, yielding an impossibly complex system. No wonder that next to the official Yellow Books, many local officers kept a separate set of "white" books that were more realistic. The biggest reform of the Ming fiscal system was passed by Grand Secretary Zhang Juzheng in 1581. Known as the

20. The Yellow Books were the population registration records that were the basis of the *lijia* system, as the new Ming taxation administration was called (Huang 1974, p. 32).

Single Whip Reforms, they introduced a nationwide land and tax survey, as well as a complete reassessment of land values in terms of silver rather than rice. This change recognized that China was an economy of monetary exchange, much different from the agrarian ideals held by Hongwu. As Zhang (2022, pp. 141–43) pointed out, these reforms increased the country's fiscal intake, reduced corruption, and rationalized the entire tax system.[21] For these reasons, Secretary Zhang is credited with making the Chinese fiscal system work at peak efficiency, which allowed the country to survive many years of drought until the collapse of the reforms in the 1640s. Thus, Zhang's system is seen as the greatest tax reform since 780. Yet it was not to last. By the 1630s, the Ming Dynasty fell into serious financial difficulties and met increasing resistance to its tax policies.

Despite their innate conservatism, the Qing emperors realized the need for reform.[22] The reform-minded and autocratic Yongzheng emperor (r.1722–1735) recognized that one of the main reasons why revenue "leaked" on its way through local government into the emperor's coffers was that local and regional officials tended to help themselves to the money. One reason was that they could not survive on their very low official pay. This led to a system of gratuities and surcharges, such as the "meltage fees" (huohao) and similar customary fees that have been dubbed "a fundamental weakness in later Imperial government" (Mote 1999, p. 909). Under the Qing, the salary of local officials came for the most part from customary fees. These fees, collected locally, were neither legal nor illegal; they were unofficial, but tolerated and expected. Unsurprisingly, this system of customary fees became a source of great corruption and abuse (Finer 1997, vol. 3, p. 1150). The Yongzheng reforms put forth under the Qing addressed this problem by explicitly forbidding the practice. In addition, they gave officials "bonuses to encourage incorruptibility," which may be seen as an appeal to the fictional image of the scholar-official as incorruptible.[23] Yet in the end, even the rational and energetic rule of Emperor Yongzheng did

21. An earlier version of it had already been introduced early in the sixteenth century on a more limited scale, and in 1582, it was made a national policy. The national granaries were revived, and the government appeared to be on a sounder fiscal system.

22. The Kangxi emperor merged the head tax and the land tax, but growing resistance to land surveying meant that by the end of his reign in 1722, the Imperial government was weakened by revenues having declined precipitously, leading to large deficits, especially in view of growing demands on the state bureaucracy as the population was growing rapidly (Zhang 2022, pp. 202–13).

23. Yongzheng also unified the dual system of taxes on land and labor, in the process freeing landless laborers from taxation. Once the reform was completed, his successor Qianlong emperor in 1772 abolished the onerous need to be registered locally as taxpaying headmen (ding) who owed labor services.

not endure. After his death in 1735, his system faced strong opposition and was eventually replaced by its predecessor.[24] The idealized norms of incorruptibility and efficiency quickly evaporated (Mote 1999, p. 910).[25]

Despite the good intentions of some officials, the system of funding local government in China turned out to be impervious to streamlining, and local clans were able to sabotage the reforms' attempts to reduce their power. The reforms enacted did not change the basic fact that fiscal revenues consisted of three flows: the formal taxes reported, the additional and often informal taxes and exactions levied without authorization, and the actual amounts that local officials extracted from the peasants in the form of various payments, fines, and bribes. It is not easy to measure how corrupt the system was, but clearly the actual amounts extracted from the peasants were far larger than the official data suggest. By the end of the eighteenth century, as Zelin (1984) summarizes it in her definitive study of the eighteenth-century tax reform, "rational fiscal administration was dead, and informal networks of funding once again became the hallmark of the Chinese bureaucracy" (p. 301).

Large-scale corruption was the inescapable norm of late Imperial China— so much so that even foreign visitors commented on its pervasiveness. The missionary Père Jean-Joseph-Marie Amiot (1718–193) remarked on the Qing bureaucracy, "It is rare among the Chinese to find anyone in an official post who does not enrich himself, and the people regard as a species of rare bird any Mandarin who is disinterested up to a certain point" (cited by Park 1997, p. 968). Much of this was inevitable, simply because it was the only way to conduct the business of government. Magistrates depended on what Zelin (1984, p. 25) euphemistically called "informal networks of funding." Consequently, tax revenues were moved around in leaky buckets, and much of the revenue was stolen, wasted, or used on tax-collection costs. The administrative

24. Taisu Zhang (2022) wistfully reflects on the counterfactual that Yongzheng would not have died after only thirteen years at the helm, and he feels that it is impossible to know what Qing history would have looked like had he lived as long as his father and his son did. "With Yongzheng at the helm, there is at least the possibility that the Qing tax regime would have obtained true institutional rationality" (p. 219).

25. The best-known reform by the Yongzheng administration was the reinstitution of meltage fees to cover local expenses, which was originally a fee added to regular tax payments to compensate for the loss of silver when taxes were melted into large ingots for transporting to the central government, but eventually it came to mean any kind of surcharge for which no other name existed. The emperor clearly realized that to mitigate the problem of corruption, he had to rationalize the local fiscal base (Zelin 1984, pp. 88, 113).

budget in the revenue-sharing system that was legally available to local governmental divisions was very small. Therefore, without pilfering from the funds owed to the central government, it would have been impossible for magistrates to cover their administrative costs and do their jobs. The large size and growing population of Qing China made the principal-agent problem increasingly acute and opened the door for a sharp increase in fiscal corruption, the extortion of ordinary taxpayers by venal officials (Sng 2014, p. 111). Such fiscal corruption reduced the effective supply of public goods and reduced trust in government. In the long run, this was very costly to Imperial China and left a legacy of corruption in local governments that persisted in modern China. Huang (2023, pp. 95–96) sees capitalism in Imperial and modern China as "vertical" or crony capitalism, in which business leaders and government were in cahoots and state officials took advantage of their privileged positions to enrich themselves by exploiting state power to trade and steal state-owned assets.

Despite the reforms, the agency problems associated with assessments of land property and tax enforcement remained intact, and de facto tax collection remained a responsibility of local officials. To reduce tax leakage and corruption by local officials, the central administration set up a highly complex monitoring system. The Qin Dynasty established a special branch of the central bureaucracy, the Office of the Censorate, as early as 221 BC–207 BC. The censorate would remain part of the administration even after the end of the empire.[26] The censorate sent observers to various localities to report malfeasance and allowed private individuals to lodge complaints with the central administration. It was a tool of the emperor, who could extend or curtail it as he wished. Although the laws against corruption were harsh and rigid, the censorate did not necessarily enforce them to the utmost capacity. Park (1997, p. 975) characterized it with some understatement: "Their actual enforcement was heavily influenced by the relaxed social norms concerning corruption." Over the millennia of its lifespan, the government reformed and reorganized the censorate repeatedly; however, the agency problems plaguing the Imperial administration remained huge.[27]

In the final analysis, the inability of the Chinese state to secure efficient sources of revenue was a large part of the reason why Imperial rule collapsed.

---

26. Nothing like the censorate existed in the West. The Western term "censorate" was chosen to translate the Chinese term, in a rather inaccurate analogy with the ancient Roman institution.

27. The Yongzheng emperor moved some of the powers of the censorate to other branches of his administration in an attempt to streamline the Imperial bureaucracy, but in the process, he may have weakened the Chinese government (Mote 1999, p. 896).

Zelin (1984, p. 308) summarizes the Chinese empire's fiscal history as follows: "It was not a lack of vision or a lack of will that determined the collapse of the centralized Chinese state. It was a lack of means." The failure of the Yongzheng fiscal reforms ushered in an era of highly corrupt local administration, low official morale, and above all, ineffective Imperial control of the Chinese countryside (Zelin 1984). Clearly, the resistance of local gentry, who still effectively exercised much power over day-to-day governance, only made the issue worse.

Risk Sharing

Unlike some European states, China did not have a public poverty relief program, and risk sharing and poverty alleviation were typically left to the clans. One notable exception is with respect to preventing famines. The Imperial bureaucracy set up a system of granaries to help protect society against harvest failures and other disruptions.[28]

Granaries were one of the most important forms of local public goods provided by the Chinese state. The political commitment to grain storage was part of a larger responsibility of "nourishing the people" (yang min). From classical ideals to late Imperial practices, the storage of grain satisfied both basic political ideals and the urgent practical need to avoid famine and the political turmoil that it engendered (Wong 1991). In the eighteenth century, state expenditures on granaries constituted roughly 5 percent of all nonmilitary spending. Much as they intended, the Qing administration may have done little to grow the rural economy, but they did succeed in stabilizing it (Pomeranz 2022, pp. 509–10). Rowe (2001) argued that in Qing China, nourishing the people may well have been the single most important government policy objective, perhaps more to ensure political stability than to achieve some conscious maximization of economic welfare. When famines did occur, the emperor was held personally responsible.

Imperial policies went beyond granaries: Wang Anshi, the great statesman and reform-minded chancellor of the Shenzong emperor of the Song Dynasty (served 1067–1085), introduced a system of loans that would tide peasants over after harvest failures. At other times, private community granaries supplemented government action, extending loans to peasants rather than

28. The Guanzi document mentioned earlier insisted in the seventh century BC that "when the granaries are full, people will know propriety and moderation, when their clothing and food is adequate, they will know the distinction between honor and shame" (Rickett 1985, p. 52).

subsidizing food prices. As state capacity declined during the later Ming Dynasty, the ability and willingness of the Imperial bureaucracy to maintain granaries weakened, due to both the need to feed its armies and the lack of funds. Under the Qing, however, granaries were revived, and for many years, the government committed considerable resources to it. Will et al. (1991) argued that under the Qing, the Chinese granary system managed to alleviate famine, as well as control more routine local fluctuations in food supplies and prices.

Despite some concerns, the system worked quite well through most of the eighteenth century and even beyond. For our purposes, it also serves to demonstrate the complexity of the Chinese state's development in the Qing era.[29] In contrast with the view that the Imperial bureaucracy was thoroughly ineffectual and corrupt, this research shows that the Chinese administration under the Qing was still, in the words of one scholar, a "bureaucratically centralized, though regionally diversified system, that facilitated the demographic, territorial, and economic expansion of the mid-Qing" (Macauley 1995, p. 182). Nevertheless, as the centralized administration became weaker and more poorly funded, daily management of local affairs was increasingly carried out by the local gentry. As Liu and Yan (2020) point out, by the eighteenth century, the resources of the central government were insufficient to maintain the granaries, and they depended on the local elites to pay for and run them.[30] In those provinces where support from the Imperial government was inadequate, local elites—that is, leaders of powerful clans—filled the vacuum. Clearly, these elites played an indispensable role in supplementing the government in the presence of weak fiscal capacity.

The Military

In Europe, warlords and generals wielded dominant political influence both during the Roman periods and in the Middle Ages. In Imperial China, instead, the military exercised political influence only during times of internal wars or dynastic successions. This reflected a deliberate policy of keeping the army

29. One source of weakness was that granaries were financed in part from local sources and in part subsidized by the Imperial government. This led to inefficiencies, as the central government's support created a moral hazard and crowded out local spending (Shiue 2004).

30. Moreover, as perhaps might be expected, they favored outlying provinces in the resources allocated for their granaries. The idea was above all to avoid social unrest triggered by high food prices, and granaries were used as a price-stabilization device. Obviously, the central government worried more about unrest in more remote provinces (Liu and Yan 2020).

subordinated to central authority and avoiding military concentrations at internal locations. Under the Song, generals were given only temporary command and were rotated so troops did not become too attached to their leaders. Whenever possible, the army was kept close to the northern frontier, where the threat of external invasions was highest. This policy was not free of problems, as it made suppressing banditry and internal rebellion more difficult. When these events happened, and internal military conflict erupted, the survival of the dynasty was most at risk. As rebellions became more frequent, military buildup in the interior provinces was unavoidable, and sometimes the emperor fell into fatal confrontation with its own generals (Finer 1997, vol. 2, p. 804).

Under the Yuan Dynasty, China experienced rising militarization, perhaps because of the Mongol influence, or because the military offered an avenue of social mobility; in any event, the Ming Dynasty was established by a brilliant military leader who had access to high-quality human resources (Mote 1999, p. 557). Yet subsequently the Chinese military slowly declined and became increasingly less effective. In 1644, the Ming soldiers fell to Manchu invaders, who overthrew the dynasty. Their Qing successors in turn showed astonishing weakness during the White Lotus Rebellion, which Rowe (2009) has rightly called a multifaceted disaster from which the Qing never fully recovered. Other rebellions followed, not to mention external defeats such as the humiliating losses in the Opium Wars and the Sino-Japanese War of 1894.[31]

3. The Stability of Chinese Autocracy

The Chinese political system was remarkably stable, in three ways. First, it was institutionally stable. Dynastic changes were often accompanied by dramatic and prolonged social and demographic disruptions.[32] Yet despite these periods of instability and other shocks, the general autocratic features of Chinese

---

31. The so-called Green Standard Army, which consisted of Han Chinese who had joined the Manchu invasion after 1644, became a kind of constabulary in the eighteenth century, but as inflation eroded their pay, many of them had to moonlight, further eroding their effectiveness. The officers were often chosen through patronage and nepotism, and discipline was poor.

32. Shuji Cao's new data on the size of the Chinese population illustrate the demographic effects of the chaos and violence that accompanied the dynastic transitions. China's population was 70 million in 755 under the Tang; by the rise of the Song in 980, it had declined precipitously, to 35 million, but rose again during the prosperous years of the Song dynasty. The Mongol invasion and the establishment of the Yuan Dynasty in 1271 reduced the population from 124 million in 1210 to 75 million in 1290. The transition to the Ming Dynasty in 1368 reduced the population from 90 million in 1341 to 75 million in 1391 (Cao 2022).

TABLE 7.1. Duration of Chinese Dynasties and Emperor Reigns

Dynasty	Duration of dynasty (years)	Average term of emperor (years)
Qin (221 BC–207 BC)	14	7
Western Han (202 BC–9 AD)	211	24
Sui (589–619)	30	17
Tang (619–907)	289	19
Song (960–1279)	319	28
Yuan (1279–1368))	89	28
Ming (1368–1644))	276	22
Qing (1644–1912))	267	36

Source: Huang (2023, p. 163).

political institutions remained in place for almost 2,000 years and were resurrected by each new dynasty even after long periods of internal war. This confirms that the main features of this autocratic system of governance were not accidental but were strongly complementary with other features of society in premodern China. Second, as shown in table 7.1, the main Imperial dynasties were often long lived, frequently lasting more than two centuries, despite frequent rebellions and a slow trend toward economic stagnation. Third, emperors lasted in office for a long time, often for more than two decades, and increasingly so in the more recent dynasties (cf. table 7.1). This length of office stands in sharp contrast with the precariousness of Roman emperors, who lasted only 5.6 years on average due to assassinations, coups, and several unnatural causes of death, to the point that being an emperor has been dubbed as "the most dangerous occupation in Roman history" (Huang 2023, p. 156).[33]

After the violent and chaotic centuries of the Warring States Period, the ideology of the Chinese empire was heavily biased toward stability, which was seen as inextricably connected with unity.[34] This basic idea had been emphasized by Mencius (371 BC–289 BC). In this view, then, stability was not fully

33. Zhao (2015, p. 293) points out that even though the Roman Empire was in many dimensions more sophisticated and advanced than the contemporaneous Chinese empire under the Han, Roman civilization collapsed while the Chinese one endured. He sees the source of Chinese resilience in the synthesis of Legalism and Confucianism, which he regards as a remarkably stable arrangement.

34. The Yongzheng emperor proclaimed that "Unity of the Central Lands [China proper] began with Qin; unity beyond the border passes began with [the Mongol] Yuan [1271–1368], and peaked under our dynasty. Never before were Chinese and foreigners one family and the country so expansive as under our dynasty!" (cited by Pines 2012, p. 36).

achieved until the Mongol Conquest, which established the Yuan Dynasty in 1271 and reunited the country. But even before the Mongol Conquest, Mencius's view was a dominant ideology, and maintaining stability through unity was a source of legitimacy for Chinese rulers, even if not all dynasties were able to achieve it (especially the Song). When necessary, the government formed new administrative bodies at the royal court to reinforce this goal such as the Grand Council, a kind of informal kitchen cabinet that concentrated more and more power under the Qing emperors (Rowe 2009, pp. 40–41). Political fragmentation, when it occurred, was unstable and therefore inevitably required efforts toward centralization (Pines 2012, pp. 30–32).

That said, the dominant ideology described here—that peace and stability require unity and fragmentation leads only to chaos and strife—is a poor description of Chinese history. In terms of casualties, the biggest tragedies in Chinese history took place when the country was unified: the Taiping Rebellion of the nineteenth century and the Great Leap Forward in the twentieth. On the other hand, periods of great success also coincided with fragmentation: for example, Song China after the Chanyuan Treaty of 1005 (which effectively divided China between the Song and the Liao dynasties) experienced unparalleled progress and prosperity. In Europe too, fragmentation did not inevitably equal war, and not all wars were equally destructive; on the contrary, international competition often led to pluralism and progress. But regardless of whether it was correct, the belief that unity was a precondition for stability and peace remained dominant in Chinese political thought and supported efforts toward unification.

Given the long life of Chinese autocratic institutions, scholars have discussed at length the concepts of political resilience and stability. Root (2020) deploys social network analysis to explain the Great Divergence. Networks, in his view, can be "stable" or "resilient," and the difference between the two is critical to his account. In Root's terminology, stability means that the individual *components* of the network can "revert to functionality despite disruptions" (Root 2020, p. 80). Resilience, on the other hand, refers to how the system *as a whole* adapts to stresses. In his view, Europe was resilient but not stable, whereas China was stable but not resilient.[35]

---

35. In Europe, Root argues, even when a dynasty or a state was taken over by another, its main features remained largely intact. In China, on the other hand, its unchanging "hub-and-spoke" structure, with the Imperial Court at the center, made it vulnerable to attacks on the central node. Transitions that involved the hub were costly and highly disruptive, none more so than the rise of the Manchu-led Qing Dynasty in the seventeenth century. Equally interesting is the weakening of

The problem with using network structure as the main explanatory variable of the differential development of China and Europe is that it takes networks as exogenous, whereas in reality they evolved over time. Moreover, Root's analysis fails to explain why, despite costly transitions between dynasties, each successor always resurrected the Chinese mandarinate as the backbone of the governance apparatus. Also, the network approach cannot convincingly explain reversals in the Great Divergence: namely, why technological and scientific progress, which had thrived during the Tang and Song dynasties, declined later under similar institutions. In addition, this approach fails entirely to consider the importance of social organization and cooperation on the local level.

In this section, we treat stability and resilience as more or less equivalent concepts and discuss why Chinese autocratic institutions persisted with the same fundamental features for such a long time. The stability of Chinese institutions does not imply that they were efficient in any definable sense; functionalist explanations of institutions are especially hazardous. Dysfunctional institutions have been known to survive over centuries, in many instances leading to failed nations and poor economic outcomes. Often, institutions emerge to solve a particular problem but then develop inertia and resilience, outliving their usefulness. In other cases, societies get locked into bad equilibria because of the inability to commit credibly to compensate the losers who stand to miss out on disrupting the status quo (cf. Acemoglu 2003). What can happen then is that support for the status quo, no matter how bad, becomes internalized, and the institutional structure becomes self-reinforcing despite its high cost to economic performance.[36] In what follows, we single out the main elements that were responsible for this stability.

Culture

A recurrent explanation of the stability of Chinese autocracy is culture, particularly the official Confucian doctrine supported by the state. Unlike in ancient Greece and Rome, Chinese culture emphasized the primacy of the

the Tang Dynasty after the An Lushan rebellion (755–763), after which the Tang Dynasty was fatally weakened, eventually collapsing in 907. The traumatic experiences of a total collapse of the network's center and the subsequent chaos created a deep-seated fear of change and chaos and "could have been behind administrative policy to avoid potentially disruptive innovations" (Root 2020, p. 105).

36. Zhang (2017, p. 23) argues that such was the case with Confucian-based norms of kinship-based hierarchy.

collective and of the family over the individual.[37] As discussed in chapter 4, ancestor worship and respect for paternal authority were paramount in Chinese culture. Paternalism and patriarchy have specific implications for political relations since they accustom individuals to hierarchy, inequality of status, and unquestioned authority. The family was seen as a network of duties, not rights, and the state as an enlarged family. The close logical analogy between the extended family and the state also manifested itself in collective punishment, whereby entire families were made to answer for the crimes of a single actor, especially if these crimes were political.

These features of Chinese culture emanate from the idea that morality is based on personal relationships, of which kinship is the most important. In the words of Fei (1992, p. 74), "The Chinese pattern of social organization embraces no ethical concepts that transcend specific types of human relationships, as is the case in the West. Filial piety, fraternal duty, loyalty, and sincerity—these are all ethical principles found in private personal relationships." In line with this notion, Chinese society was ruled by social norms enforced through social networks. Social order was achieved primarily through obedience to social obligations, and control was a shared responsibility. Finer (1997, vol. 1, p. 455) describes the tenets of ancient Chinese culture as follows: "Collective and mutual responsibility, not individualism; authoritarianism, paternalism, and absolutism, not self-determination; inequality and hierarchy, not equality before the law; subjects, not citizens, duties not rights." In Western societies, by contrast, morality was guided by universalistic religious principles. Because the Church is the universal organization of all human beings and transcends any personal relationship, everyone is equal before God. Hence, individuals have inalienable rights that must be respected by any political organization, as stated at the very beginning of the American Declaration of Independence (Fei 1992).

There is no doubt that these long-established traits of Confucian culture increased the legitimacy of the emperor and were congenial to the Chinese autocratic system of government. This remains true in modern China, where survey data indicate that the strength of Confucian values is positively correlated with

37. Protection of individual rights was a founding pillar of political thought in ancient Greece. This is how Aristotle (2008, p. 280) summarizes the principles of democracy: "The basis of a democratic state is liberty. . . . One principle of liberty is for all to rule and be ruled in turn, and indeed democratic justice is the application of numerical not proportionate equality. . . . Another is that a man should live as he likes."

support for autocracy (Pan and Xu 2018). Moreover, the key principles of Confucian doctrines predate the emergence of Imperial political institutions. This value system centered on the family, and the cult of ancestors was systematized by Confucius (551 BC–479 BC) and by other sages well before the first emperor of unified China under the Qin Dynasty (221 BC–206 BC).

Over time, Confucian attitudes toward the emperor evolved and faced some pushback, although in the end, absolutism would coopt this philosophy to strengthen its rule. Initially, for example, the exact meaning of the Mandate from Heaven was open to interpretation. During the Han Dynasty, the Theory of Cosmic Resonance implied that bad government meant that the state was no longer in sync with nature. Hence, high officials could use natural disasters as the impetus to demand policy changes, and in extreme cases, undermine the legitimacy of the dynasty itself (Bol 2008). Later, during the Song, the philosophical foundations of autocracy faced more challenges. Bol (2008) argued that the true characteristic of the Song regime was not Imperial autocracy, but rather the rule of a government of scholar-officials. The reforms introduced by the New Policies of Wang Anshi in the 1070s were part of his more skeptical view of autocracy. However, Anshi's reforms faced opposition, and in the absence of an adequate infrastructure, their implementation was unlikely (Zhao 2015, p. 340). In the end, this more moderate approach was contested, and in the longer run, absolutist rulers exploited neo-Confucianism to increase their legitimacy.

The extent to which neo-Confucian doctrine supported Imperial despotism remains the subject of some debate. Some scholars, such as Wood (1995), disputed this interpretation and argued that neo-Confucianism was much more than an instrument of absolutism. In Wood's view, the power of the ruler was not absolute but constrained by Confucian morality as interpreted by scholars.[38] The great founder of neo-Confucian ideology, Zhu Xi, whose influence on Chinese culture is widely regarded as second only to Confucius, felt that the emperor could only rule well through learning; therefore, he was in some senses subordinate to his intellectual bureaucrats (Bol 2008). One of the most influential books of the neo-Confucian school, the commentary written on the *Spring and Autumn Annals* by Hu Anguo (1074–1138), was adopted as a

---

38. In Wood's words, "The full significance of the neo-Confucian advocacy of obedience to the ruler in Northern Sung China (960–1127) emerges only after we place it in the context of a simultaneous advocacy of obedience to absolute moral values that transcended the interests of any particular ruler and to which the ruler himself could be held accountable." (1995, p. 8).

formal requirement for the *keju* curriculum in 1313.[39] Wood argued that the philosophers wanted a world in which the emperor deserved obedience so long as he himself obeyed a set of natural laws.

It is conceivable that this system of values could have evolved in other directions, had political institutions and power relations in society been different.[40] Culture is not immutable and can be molded by the initiative of leading elites. Yet as a practical matter, whatever the original intentions of the neo-Confucian philosophers were, the empire became more rather than less despotic after the fall of the Song. The Mongol Conquest of 1279 and the subsequent Ming overthrow of the Yuan Dynasty brought to power emperors who exhibited increasingly autocratic tendencies: of them, none were more despotic than Emperor Hongwu, the founder of the Ming Dynasty. As Elman (2000) has argued, the early Ming emperors harnessed neo-Confucianism to support more autocratic power. The fourth son and successor of Hongwu, the Yongle emperor (also known as Emperor Chengzu of Ming, personal name Zhu Di, who ruled 1402–1424), was wholly committed to the intellectual heritage of Zhu Xi and his school. The political coherence of Imperial rule under the Ming relied on "intimate ties and selective reproduction" of neo-Confucian learning (Elman 2000, p. 70) In the end, Hongwu established once and for all the supremacy of the emperor over the bureaucracy and made it abundantly clear that he would have final say over how neo-Confucian ideas and arguments would be implemented.

The State Bureaucracy and the Civil Service Examination

The influence of culture is never unidirectional. Culture interacts with and is molded by other features of society, particularly government institutions and social organizations. In China, the organization and selection of state bureaucrats played a key role in consolidating and disseminating Confucian culture throughout society and amplified its influence in support of autocracy.

39. The *Annals of Spring and Autumn* or *Chunqiu* was composed in the fifth century BC and attributed to Confucius himself by Mencius. Wood (1995, p 55) describes it as follows: "From the early Han to the late Ch'ing [Qing], a period of more than two thousand years, it has been the single most important reservoir of ideas about politics in all classical literature."

40. Wang Anshi was challenged by his political and ideological nemesis, the historian Sima Guang, a staunch defender of strong Imperial authority. The balance of power between the two camps shifted repeatedly during and after the rule of Emperor Shenzhong (1048–1085). Acemoglu and Robinson (2021) discuss the malleability of Chinese political culture.

The key principles of Confucianism are strongly complementary with a highly educated professional bureaucracy of scholar-administrators. Confucianism posits that all things—including human beings—are unequal: people differ greatly in intelligence, ability, and moral character. A hierarchical social order thus fits perfectly with Confucian ideology (Ho 1964). Said hierarchy is then replicated in government as such. One of the key tenets of the Confucian doctrine is that education rather than coercion is instrumental to bring out humanity and benevolence in individuals. In contrast with Europe, in China the fundamental political ideology of rulers was that good government is government by good men, not of laws (Finer, vol. 1). And good men were scholars who know the classics and have invested in their education, and who gained responsibility in government "because of their ability as intellectuals and men of letters and their effectiveness in handling people. . . . Consequently, one can say that traditional Chinese government was uniquely devoted to 'rule by the cultivated'" (Ch'ien 1982, p. 17).

The Chinese principles of the "rule of good men" and "rule of the cultivated" were thus quite different from the European ideas of the rule of law and from the concept of government by representatives of different interest groups in society. The belief in the merits of technocracy was a product of many centuries of political development. It was a classic case of culture, social organizations, and institutions reinforcing and strengthening one another: the belief in the supremacy of a government by the educated, supported by the Imperial examination system (*keju*), produced a literate civil service that ran the country at the level of counties, prefectures, ministers, councilors, and other entities. It was a system that was as self-enforcing as it was stable.

The establishment of a strong bureaucracy to administer such a large empire presented a difficult challenge for the emperor, however: whom to appoint to that position. As discussed thus far, the emperor exploited the traditional strength of kinship ties in Chinese culture by promoting himself as the patriarch of an enlarged family and presenting his dynasty as chosen by heaven. This established the Imperial dynasty as being above all the others. However, the emperor could not staff a bureaucracy solely from those of his own dynasty, and he needed to coopt in government individuals from other dynastic groups. The challenge was to give these administrators authority and legitimacy, but without creating a rank order among the remaining dynasties. Doing so would have created powerful elites that could threaten the Imperial dynasty. As discussed next, the Civil Service Examination had precisely this effect. It created a new order among unrelated individuals belonging to any clan, without ranking their clans of origin. This new order was a source of legitimacy, and in fact it had manifest social implications: by law, officials were required to wear special clothing indicating their rank within the state bureaucracy. The emperor, of course, was the only one whose role or rank was not determined by the examination.

Preparation for the Civil Service Examination and the creation of a new social group of top bureaucrats, trained in the classics and sharing a common set of values and competences, had other benefits. On the one hand, it loosened the link between each administrator and the clan of origin. Rather than binding their identities to their lineages, officials identified more as part of a group of top scholars, connected by their successes and a common culture. Yet each individual official was not indispensable—he could be replaced by others with similar training, competences, and values. This increased the bargaining power of the emperor relative to his bureaucrats.

The meritocratic and competitive features of the Civil Service Examination were also an advantage from the ruler's perspective. As discussed in chapter 6, the *keju* was open to commoners, not just to members of powerful clans, although it is unclear how much it really promoted social mobility. But to the extent that it did, it played further into the hands of the emperor because it selected individuals who did not have a vested interest in protecting countervailing powerful groups.[41] And to the extent that it was really meritocratic, it sucked human talent into the public administration, depriving other groups in society of the best and brightest. Although only a small fraction eventually passed the exam, millions of individuals prepared for it.[42] Since there was no limit to the number of times that one could take the exam, it was often the case that individuals took years to prepare for it. This too was an advantage for the emperor because the *keju* tied up a large pool of the population's talent into queuing for the state bureaucracy rather than leaving them free to pursue other political goals. As mentioned previously, many of those who had passed (or studied for) the lowest level of the exam were coopted informally in the local administration. Of course, this system imposed a heavy toll on China's ability to innovate, as we will discuss at length in chapter 9.

41. According to Huang and Yang (2022), the highest level of the *keju* exam during the Ming, which opened the door to the most powerful positions in the Imperial palace, was actually biased *against* candidates of wealthier families with insider status.

42. During the Ming, between two to three million people regularly took the exam (Huang 2023, p. 104).

As pointed out by Huang (2023), the *keju* system also weakened political opposition to the emperor in subtler ways. Competing for the exam was a very individualistic and zero-sum game. Candidates were assessed for their individual merits and competed against each other. This discouraged horizontal cooperation between the most resourceful and talented citizens, who were also potential political leaders, reducing the risk that they would oppose the autocratic regime via coordinated collective action.

Last but not least, the neo-Confucian indoctrination of young students preparing for the exam constituted a form of social control over their thinking and values, infusing them with a commitment to loyalty, docility, and respect for Imperial authority. In this way, the *keju* system became a self-perpetuating mechanism that ensured the stability and survival of China's political system.[43] The single-minded focus on success on the examinations meant that students internalized and canonized the texts of the curriculum. Heretical and heterodox critical thinking, such as that which occurred in Europe in the sixteenth and seventeenth centuries—eventually leading to the Enlightenment and its era of creative dissent—were discouraged and even prohibited in such a system. The transformation of political thought and institutions in China had to wait until it was severely disrupted by invading forces. China produced many extraordinarily creative scholars, many of them amazing polymaths such as Su Song (1020–1101), Shen Kuo (1031–1095), and Guo Shoujing (1231–1316). But it produced no successful heterodox intellectuals such as Paracelsus, Baruch Spinoza, and Denis Diderot. Radical dissenters were not tolerated.

Power Relations and Social Organizations

One additional feature that distinguished Imperial China from Europe is how power was distributed in society. On the one hand, the emperor enjoyed a much stronger concentration of powers relative to the elites and other power holders in society, compared to European rulers. On the other hand, there was also less inequality and asymmetry of power between local Chinese elites and the common people compared to in Europe. As documented by Zhang (2017) and discussed in chapter 5, local political powers in China were associated with seniority both within and between clans. Wealth, ancestry, and landholding also mattered, but less so than in medieval Europe. Jia et al. (2020) argue that

43. According to Huang (2023), it is no coincidence that the Imperial regime collapsed during the Qing Dynasty, which was responsible for diluting and weakening the *keju* system.

this distribution of power created a more stable political environment than in Europe because the emperor was less likely to face threats from internal challengers, and also less likely to lose the support of the common people whenever he was challenged. In fact, coups and intra-elite conflict were much less frequent in China than in other parts of the world. According to Huang (2023, p. 176), about 38 percent of power transitions between 220 BC and AD 1911 were triggered by interelite conflicts, but such events became much rarer from the Song Dynasty onward. By comparison, Svolik (2012) finds that coups were responsible for more than two-thirds of nonconstitutional transition of powers in modern autocracies.

What explains this strong concentration of power in the hands of the emperor and the weakness of the elites both relative to the emperor and to the rest of society? A first explanation has to do with the fact that in China, feudalism disappeared very early, and by most definitions of the term, never came back.[44] In Europe, after the fall of the Western Roman Empire, landed elites remained a key countervailing power to central authority for several centuries. In the Early Middle Ages, kings were forced to grant control over lands and peasants to powerful warlords in exchange for their military support and political loyalty. Something similar happened in China during the early part of the Zhou Dynasty around the first millennium BC. However, after the country's first political unification under the Qin in 220 BC, stable feudal structures dissolved and did not reemerge in China despite prolonged periods of internal conflict. After the sixth century, all the political and legal characteristics that we would identify as being part of feudalism were absent in China: the Chinese aristocracy was not identified as a formal juridical category, its members did not hold hereditary titles of nobility, and typically aristocrats were not military leaders (Johnson 1977; Tackett 2014). Subsequently, in Tang China, a small number of important clans were highly influential in the royal court, but these great families usually did not retain their dominant positions in their places of origin (i.e., at a local level as well as a national level). Over time, local elites gained more power as the central government weakened during the Ming and Qing dynasties, but it would be a stretch to think of these arrangements as feudal in any sense.

One reason that feudalism did not continue in China as it did in Europe is due to China's early state formation and unification. The first Chinese state

---

44. Feudal structures were central to the Zhou Dynasty, and during the Warring States Period, feudal lords (*zhuangzhu*) held substantial power and governed their territories more or less independently, which might be regarded as "feudal" by some definitions.

institutions were formed when countervailing powers were weak and disorganized. For a long time, central authority was much more powerful and effective in China than in Europe. As already mentioned, the centralization of military assets, and in particular the creation of a strong cavalry, were important during the early Han Dynasty to prevent the emergence of local power blocs and to stop the evolution of feudal relations (Scheidel 2019). But cultural and social factors also prevented the emergence of strong, landed elites in the subsequent Tang China. The great clans rarely held large, landed properties over multiple generations. The absence of strong primogeniture meant more or less equal division of property among male heirs, and the practice of concubinage further diluted hereditary transitions. Moreover, in principle, the land belonged to the emperor who, during the first half of the Tang Dynasty, actively sought to redistribute it to maximize tax revenue. As a result, land was not seen as a particularly safe form of preserving wealth over the long run (Tackett 2014; Fairbank and Goldman 2006).

As discussed previously, the peculiar organization of government created by the Han and reinforced by subsequent dynasties also played an important role in preventing the rise of countervailing powers (see also Stasavage 2020). During the Han Dynasty, top bureaucrats retained strong links to their clans. However, the Tang Dynasty's reforms reduced the influence of the great families over top officials. By the eighth century, the primacy of kinship over administrative appointments underwent a reversal. High family status was linked to having a clan member who held an important position in the central bureaucracy, and it was lost if no family member retained such roles. In Tang China, the great families were still able to influence top appointments. But in the violent and chaotic transition between the Tang and the Song dynasties (a period known as the "Five Dynasties," between 907 and 960), the great Chinese aristocratic families were entirely wiped out (Mote 1999; Von Glahn 2022).[45] As a result, the nature of the Chinese ruling class was transformed, and in Song China, government passed into the hands of a professional

45. The transition from the Tang to the Song Dynasty had enormous consequences, above all the shift of the demographic and economic center of gravity from north to south, the final destruction of the little that was left of a hereditary aristocracy as a source of political power, and a sharp increase in commercialization and the expansion of nonagricultural goods and services (Cao 2022; Von Glahn 2022). While such economic developments are seen in a favorable light by modern economists, the transitions were clearly traumatic and reinforced the demand for stability and order both by the Imperial bureaucracy and the population at large.

bureaucracy, selected and promoted based on objective performance criteria and its scholarly capacities (Johnson 1977; Tackett 2014; Fairbank and Goldman 2006; Huang 2023).[46] Administrators came from several kin groups. They did not have a military background, nor did they owe their appointments to links with commerce and finance (Ch'ien 1982, p. 17). Hence, civil servants did not represent specific power groups in society, as defined by location or economic interests. "Government and administration were . . . a self-contained universe: no forces and few controls existed outside it, or at least no constitutional ones, only revolts or mass rebellions" (Finer 1997, vol. 2, p. 760).

That said, although bureaucrats on their own may not have been a threat to the emperor, the central bureaucracy was a countervailing power, sometimes in conflict with the emperor. But the bureaucracy did not represent other vested interests, and it did not have a geographic base. Hence, it was a force against political fragmentation rather in support of it. As Spence (1990, pp. 8–9) summarized, "The Chinese state was more effectively centralized than those elsewhere in the world; its religions were more effectively controlled; and the growth of powerful, independent cities was prevented by a watchful government that would not tolerate rival centers of authority."

Along with early state formation and the organization of the state bureaucracy, there are other reasons that explain the stability and absolutist nature of the Chinese autocracy. One that is especially important has to do with how society was organized. Reliance on clans as the prototypical social organization also contributed to dilute countervailing powers in society in more than one way. First, clans could not easily be scaled up because their size was determined by dynastic ties. Although clan membership could be fabricated to some extent, and the exact dynastic boundaries of lineages were porous, clan membership was much more limited than that of the more powerful and flexible European corporations. Clans had a large political influence at the local level, but they could seldom reach national relevance, and they often shared control of their territory with other clans. China had no independent cities, no organized religious associations, and no independent universities or large scholarly associations, and even business interests were organized only at the local level. As discussed later in this chapter and in previous chapters, Europe was very different in this regard. Self-governing cities, the Church, monastic

---

46. According to Johnson (1977, p. 3), over 50 percent of high office positions in Tang China were held by members of the great clans (as defined in the Tang lists), but during the first century of the Northern Song Dynasty, this proportion fell to 2.5 percent.

orders, and business corporations like the East India companies were countervailing and organized centers of power that could not be neglected and with which European rulers were forced to bargain and come to terms.

Social organizations based on kinship further discouraged effective opposition to Imperial absolutism in other ways. As discussed in previous chapters, clans partitioned society into nonoverlapping and closed groups, which often competed for local resources. Individuals had strong norms of cooperation and reciprocity toward members of their in-group, but these sentiments were not naturally extended to outgroup members. This contrasts with the overlapping social networks that were typical in Europe, where one individual could belong to several overlapping associations, such as a parish, a fraternity, a guild, a city, the Church, and its parishes. As discussed next, this more open and inclusive form of associationism facilitated the scaling-up of organized cooperation when it was needed to resist external enemies or an absolutist ruler.

In addition, the internal organization of clans contributed to enhance the legitimacy of Chinese absolutism. Citizens were used to hierarchical organizations ruled by seniority in their everyday lives. As previously discussed, China was a society ruled through rituals and social norms more than by law. Social order was achieved by obedience to social obligations that stemmed from personal relationships and one's place in the social network. In the words of Hamilton and Zheng in their introduction to Fei (1992), "The means of control [was] located in the institutionalized networks of relationships—in the patriarchal control of the family, in the elders' control of villages, and in the notables' control of other kinds of associational networks" (Hamilton and Zheng, p. 29). This organization of society facilitated the acceptance of an absolutist regime, with the emperor on top. By contrast, corporate organizations in Europe were based on more formal horizontal agreements among equals, which also spelled out individual rights and obligations, and how collective decisions were made. Of course, Europe too was a very unequal and hierarchical society. But as will be discussed in chapter 8, the adaptation of corporate practices to the public sphere facilitated the emergence of more inclusive state institutions, where authority was based on the law, not just on one's place in society, and where, at least in theory, individuals were equal before the law.

Chinese society was accustomed to vertical (as opposed to horizontal) relationships also in the economic sphere. As we will discuss in chapter 10, this cultural legacy is still reflected in economic relations in modern China. Huang (2023) draws a distinction between "horizontal" versus "vertical" capitalism. The former relies on collaboration between business interests as equal partners, through financial arrangements, partnerships, contractual obligations, and other corporate practices that were widespread in Europe. Chinese capitalism, instead, was and remains closer to a vertical model of crony capitalism, in which the state plays a much more prominent role, through a combination of intrusive regulation, state ownership, and alliances with private business interests, and where successful business ventures often require the support or the approval of the state. Not surprisingly, economic interests are much more subservient and aligned with state authority under vertical capitalism, and this also shows up in a more limited willingness and ability to introduce disruptive innovation.

There is an interesting debate about whether Imperial China had anything that we might recognize as a "civil society." If its existence is even debated, it could be taken as a signal that there was a problem in China. Rankin (1990), for instance, claims that a strong civil society failed to develop in China until late in the nineteenth century. Huang (2023, p. 88) sees Chinese "society" as "embryonic, weak, and struggling," dominated by the state. Other scholars like Wakeman (1993) and Rowe (1993) have agonized over this question. Interestingly, Xue (2021) argues that autocratic rule and political repressions reduced social capital. She exploits local variation in political repressions associated with literary inquisitions in China between 1661 and 1788, which led prominent individuals in the local community to withdraw from public life. In her findings, exposure to repressions was associated with a 38 percent drop in the number of local charities before 1900, compared to nonexposed prefectures. These effects are long-lasting and result in less trust and reduced political participation in modern China in areas exposed to the literary inquisition compared to those that were not.

Geography

A final source of the stability and resilience of the Chinese system of government is geography. As already noted, China was a large and unified state for most of its history. After the fall of the Western Roman Empire, Europe always remained politically fragmented in many autonomous and sometimes very small political entities. China, on the other hand, was either unified or split across two or three large states for four-fifths of the time between 500 and 1000 AD, and by the eleventh century, it was already a large and centralized empire. After having been reunited by the Mongol Conquest in 1279, it remained so for almost all the subsequent time. As argued by Scheidel (2019) and shown in a more rigorous model, Fernández-Villaverde et al. (2023), geography played an important role in explaining this key difference between China and Europe.[47] These scholars argue that China's navigable rivers and large plains made it more interconnected than Europe, which was instead split into several smaller core areas separated by natural boundaries. This greater interconnectivity is reflected in lower genetic variation in northern China and less linguistic heterogeneity compared to Europe, particularly in the written language used by elites (Scheidel 2019).[48] No doubt, linguistic uniformity reflects political unification, but geography too played a role. This is suggested by the fact that linguistic boundaries in China often coincide with seemingly small geographic barriers (Scheidel 2019). These geographic features and its cultural implications may have facilitated political unification in China compared to Europe.

Scheidel (2019), Turchin (2007, p. 200), and Ko, Koyama, and Sng (2018) also point out that throughout much of Chinese history, external military threats were mostly unidirectional, coming from nomads in the north. The rich agrarian populations of China's east and south, which initially lived as distinct ethnic groups, both faced similar threats from horse-riding nomads of the Eurasian Steppe. A common enemy, therefore, incentivized cooperation between the rich agrarian populations who combined forces to resist Mongol and Turkic invasion. It is no coincidence, as Scheidel (2019, pp. 281–82) points out, that the unifying elements of the Chinese empire emanated almost exclusively from the northern frontier. Over the course of 3,600 years, eleven of twelve unification events originated from the north. Similarly, most unifying dynasties were founded by individuals from the northwest, who would have been most threatened by steppe nomads. Ko, Koyama, and Sng (2018) provide evidence that the frequency of nomadic attacks in China was indeed temporally associated with

47. In a formal model that captures the effects of geographical barriers, Fernandez-Villaverde et al. (2023) demonstrate the validity of the geographical dispersion argument. Their technique is to divide the Eurasian continent into hexagonal cells that start as independent units, and then to simulate how they unify as a function of conquest or secession. The incentives for such unifying or fragmenting actions and their chances of success are determined by geographical variables such as closeness to water, ruggedness, and agricultural productivity. They then simulate the history of this world and show that in high probability, China becomes more and more unified over time, while Europe remains fragmented. The simulation technique allows them to isolate the power of geography in bringing about the observed outcomes on the Eurasian continent.

48. Scheidel (2019) points to another important ecological feature that facilitated state unification in China: the abundant supply of horses thanks to proximity to the steppe. This factor affected military technology. All dynasties retained large, powerful cavalry. The presence of a large military cavalry under the control of the central power, which could move quickly and be rapidly deployed in areas distant from the center, was an important factor that prevented the emergence of rival power blocs and facilitated the concentration of military force (Scheidel 2019, pp. 279–80).

more unification and political centralization. Moreover, the unidirectional nature of external threats made it possible to avoid military and hence political fragmentation in China because troops defending the realm were held close to the northern frontier. By the same logic, Dincecco and Wang (2018) argue that unidirectional external threats reinforced China's autocratic tendencies because they weakened countervailing local powers and created incentives to reinforce the center. By contrast, European states faced external threats from several directions, and this facilitated the formation of strong military blocs in different geographic areas, which in turn induced political fragmentation.

4. Political Institutions in Europe

Compared to China, political institutions in Western Europe exhibited much less stability over time and uniformity across space. These institutions were built on very different founding principles and evolved in a very different direction. In this section, we discuss the emergence of some unique features of European political institutions and elucidate their links to other prevailing social organizations. Many scholars have analyzed the political history of Europe (see, e.g., Finer 1997; Levi 1988; Maddicott 2004; Hirst 2010; Stasavage 2020). Rather than provide a detailed account of European political history, we emphasize key aspects in which Western Europe differed from China. We mainly focus on the eleventh to fifteenth centuries because this is the period during which the foundations of modern European states were laid.

Three main differences stand out between political institutions in Western Europe relative to China. First, state consolidation and centralization of administrative and political power came much later in Europe, and when it did happen, it never achieved continentwide centralization; to this day, Europe remains politically fragmented into many nation-states. Until the collapse of the Roman Empire, China and Europe had moved on roughly comparable trajectories of centralization and being high-capacity states. But with the decline of Rome, their trajectories diverged, as the end of the Han Dynasty in China in the early third century was not followed by a process of state dismantling and collapse comparable to what took place in Europe.[49]

---

49. Walter Scheidel (2019) has noted that until about 500 AD, China and Europe followed more or less parallel paths (despite some major differences), and he sees the Great Divergence above all as the fragmentation of the Roman Empire, in contrast with the mostly unified polity in China. A similar point is made by Stasavage (2020), who emphasizes the role of a strong central administration in explaining the stability and resilience of the Chinese system of government.

Second, the formation of state capacity in Europe went hand in hand with the sharing of power between the king and representatives of other social groups. When kings wanted to raise taxes (often to fight external wars), they had to bargain with other corporate groups, and this evolved in institutionalized forms of power sharing and political representation. None of this happened in China, where property rights on land were much weaker and elites were much more dependent on the goodwill of the emperor.

Third, from the very beginning, in Europe, legal principles were of paramount importance in defining state authority and political legitimacy. As emphasized by Strayer (1973) and as we will discuss in chapter 8, early European states were built on judicial and financial institutions even before they developed permanent military organizations. Permanent institutions responsible for internal affairs and the administration of justice emerged before those responsible for external affairs. This preeminence of legal principles is also reflected in the relevance of the rule of law as a constraint on the absolutist powers of the state—something absent from the political history of China.

We now consider each of these points in greater detail, discussing why they emerged in Europe and not in China and their relevance to Europe's political development. We also discuss two social organizations that played an important role in the evolution of European political institutions: free towns and the Church.

External and Internal Political Fragmentation

As noted previously, following the collapse of the Roman Empire, Europe never again experienced political unification. Why did Europe remain politically fragmented? Besides the geographical differences between Europe and China discussed in the previous section, Scheidel (2019) convincingly argues that the answer has to do with how the Western Roman Empire collapsed during the fifth century. The collapse of Rome was accompanied by a complete disruption of state power; this contrasts with the occasions where China splintered into smaller, yet still functional states. The fall of the Western Roman Empire was a protracted process of destruction and onslaught from all directions, which lasted several centuries and was accompanied by dramatic economic, demographic, and institutional decline.

The process started with a gradual erosion of state powers in the periphery of the empire. The collection of revenue and military mobilization in distant areas became more difficult, which gradually challenged the integrity of the empire. Nonstate actors (such as Germanic tribes) that had formed at the frontier were attracted by the rich resources of the center and became increasingly aggressive, resulting in a progressive loss of territory by Rome. By the end of the fifth century, the former Western Roman Empire splintered into five successor states controlled by Germanic tribes, as well as several smaller polities (Scheidel 2019, p. 95).

During the sixth century, when important elements of Roman institutions and organizations were still in place, no German tribe was strong enough to impose its leadership and to resist ongoing invasions from all directions. At this time, the Eastern Roman Empire attempted to regain control over its other half, but it failed despite some early victories because it was too weak and had to fight its own enemies. The destruction of wars and invasions in this era was compounded by waves of pandemic bubonic plague.[50]

By the seventh century, when the dust on the great migrations began to settle, the task of rebuilding an empire with a unified state capacity had become much harder because most elements of the Roman organizations had disappeared. Central fiscal capacity and a centrally managed military force had been eroded by the protracted invasions and by the Germanic tradition of independent warlords. Germanic rulers lacked the financial resources to raise their own armies and had to rely on the cooperation of their followers. Warlords were compensated by the ruler through land assignments, and they were directly responsible for raising troops. As a result, kings had only indirect control over their territory and lacked the tools for internal coercion. The sharp decline in commerce and output reduced surplus in excess of subsistence to a fraction of what it had been at the apex of the Roman Empire. As a result, the taxable amount of income was very low. To compound problems, changes in military technology eventually shifted the waging of warfare to the cavalry. As heavily armored knights were more expensive, the cost per warrior increased. Given the lack of fiscal capacity, European armies were small and unable to control large territories. Visigothic Spain and Anglo-Saxon England could not

---

50. The precise dimensions of the impact of pandemics on the disintegration of Europe's polities are in dispute, however. A considerable body of literature has argued that a wave of epidemics known collectively as the Justinian Plague, which hit the Mediterranean and Europe between 541 and 750 AD had devastating demographic effects and may have resulted in the deaths of between a quarter and half of the population of the Mediterranean, thus playing a key role in the fall and subsequent political disintegration of the Roman Empire. Recent research has cast doubt on this finding and shown that this pandemic was smaller by orders of magnitude than the Black Death (Mordechai et al. 2019), but this view has in turn been criticized (for a brief survey, see Harper 2021, p. 546).

field armies in excess of 5,000 men, and in the ninth century, "entire kingdoms could change hands in engagements of barely more than 10,000 men" (Scheidel 2019, p. 239). Most raids involved only hundreds, rather than thousands, of warriors.[51]

In China, by contrast, the central state was able to retain its taxing power and maintained a centralized army and cavalry, even during periods of internal conflict. As emphasized by Scheidel (2019), after the end of the Han Dynasty in 220 AD, Chinese fiscal structures were preserved and the taxation of agriculture never disappeared, despite substantial drops in tax revenue compared to the peak of the Han Empire. This enabled the state to raise and control a centrally managed and highly effective cavalry, and to mobilize civilian labor through *corvée* taxes. Intermittent collapses of the state's powers, which occasionally occurred, did not substantially alter this situation. When political fragmentation took place—such as during the fourth and early fifth centuries—incoming political rulers retained substantial portions of the bureaucracy, and hence still wielded sufficient coercive powers and tax capacity. This allowed them to check local power blocs and force other elites to cooperate.

Other forces promoted unification in China and fragmentation in Europe. In China, the nationwide Civil Service Examination system, the *keju*, became a cornerstone of the Imperial administration. Preparing for the exam was an important tool of cultural integration for the elites, who all studied the same material in the same language. In Europe, as discussed next, the Western Catholic Church encouraged political fragmentation. The papacy followed a conscious policy to divide and conquer, and it consistently sought to prevent any European ruler—and, above all, the Holy Roman Emperor—from amassing too much power and challenging the Church's role as the single pan-European political entity (see Hoffman 2015, pp. 132–34; and Møller and Doucette 2022).

Because of these different historical circumstances, by the end of the first millennium, Europe and China were in starkly different situations. In China, the young Song Dynasty had just started to rule a large and powerful empire that consisted of about 20 million households, a capital city of 750,000 inhabitants, and an army estimated to exceed a million soldiers, and had a tax revenue approaching a tenth of total output and four or five times that collected by the

---

51. By contrast, about 1,000 years earlier, Rome had fielded about 40 000 troops to subdue Gaul and Britain. Most estimates of the overall size of the Imperial army are between 300,000 and 500,000 (e.g., MacMullan 1980). Under Septimius Severus, MacMullan's best estimate is around 350,000 (p. 454).

Roman Empire at its peak (Scheidel 2019, pp. 167–68). Continental Europe, instead, was dominated by local strongmen who thought of themselves as aristocrats, while centralized state structures had almost entirely disappeared. In the often-cited words of Strayer (1973, p. 15), "By the year 1000 it would have been difficult to find anything like a state on the continent in Europe."[52]

The disappearance of a strong and unified state structure in Europe for such a prolonged period had two implications of key historical importance. First, the power vacuum led to external political polycentrism. Using the *Centennial Historical Atlas* by Reed (2016), Schonholzer and Weese (2019) estimate that the number of European states that had de facto power over at least one city in the Bairoch et al. (1988) data set of cities varied from about twenty in the twelfth century to almost fifty in the fourteenth century.[53] Moreover, as Scheidel (2019) points out, unlike at the beginning of the Roman expansion, when Rome was well ahead of its neighbors, no single political entity enjoyed a head start in medieval Europe. Hence, when the process of state consolidation eventually started in the fifteenth century, no single state emerged as a dominant and stable political entity, and external political fragmentation did not go away.

Given Europe's military and political weakness and its profound internal divisions for several centuries after the collapse of the Western Roman Empire, a natural question arises: Why wasn't Europe taken over by other emerging or preexisting empires? Scheidel (2019) argues that there was no neighboring power that could have succeeded. The Byzantine Empire had a window of opportunity early, during the mid-sixth and early seventh centuries, when Roman traditions and organizational structures were still in place. However, it failed, possibly because the Justinian Plague had weakened the empire at a critical juncture. The large empire built by Charlemagne was quickly dissolved after his death in 814 because he remained faithful to the Frankish custom of dividing his reign among his three heirs. The Arab Conquests in the eighth and ninth centuries occurred too quickly to build a powerful contender, and the Muslim political entities were not able to overcome their tribal divisions. Their military was

52. This statement needs to be qualified by the survival of the Byzantine Empire, which by that time was weakened, but not destroyed, by the rise of Islamic states. Moreover, the Abbasid Khalifate during its peak (in the ninth century) was the most substantial political entity in the Middle East, although its foothold in Europe was minimal. The other organizational unit that was both functional and centralized was the Western (Latin) Church, controlled from Rome.

53. Bairoch et al. (2018) include in their data set all European cities that ever reached 5,000 inhabitants by or before the year 1850.

organized along tribal lines, and local revenue went to the tribes that conquered a region, but it did not flow to the center, which thus remained weak. The Mongol invasion of Eastern Europe in the early 1240s had limited long-run effects because it was hindered by their internal divisions, and by a European geography that was less favorable to their military technology based on the cavalry. Moreover, expansion to the east was probably a higher priority for the Mongols.

The prolonged absence of central state structures in Europe during the early Middle Ages had a second key implication: it also led to deep internal political fragmentation within political units. Nonstate social organizations emerged to fill the vacuum created by the absence of state structures. These organizations raised revenue and provided local public goods, but they also used their coercive powers to gain privileges and more generally to consolidate economic and political power vis à vis the nascent European states.

The details of how this happened varied by place. In France and Germany, rural lords acquired direct control over their territories and had autonomous military resources. Personal loyalty, often supported by formal oaths and guaranteed by the Church, was the rather brittle mortar that held together this structure of exchanges between vassals and their lords. In Italy and Lorraine, communes and independent towns took over several administrative functions that the state could not fulfill. The Church, monasteries, universities, and other corporate bodies also filled some roles of the state and gained political power and influence. When the process of state consolidation and the building of state capacity accelerated, central powers had to cope with the corporate interests that had permeated society. As a result, they were forced to bargain with them and coopt them in key decisions. The political institutions that came into being as a result differed greatly from those of China. We now turn to a more thorough discussion of how this happened.[54]

The Right of Consent

Throughout Chinese history, the form and intensity of taxation were decided unilaterally by the central government. Tax collection was rife with agency problems and informational asymmetries, and the threat of peasant revolts limited what central authority could do. Yet fiscal decisions were made by the

---

54. It should be added that in that sense, Europe also diverged from the Islamic world, where the Abbassid Khalifate was far less stable than the Chinese administrative state. For a more detailed comparison of Europe and the Islamic world, see Bosker et al. (2013).

emperor and his central bureaucracy, with no institutionalized bargaining between the center and representatives of other organized interests. This was not the case in medieval Europe. European kings were expected to live from their own resources obtained from their private domains from the services that they provided in the administration of justice or from other special arrangements. If extra sources of revenues were required, for instance to fight a war, the king had to ask for and obtain the consent of those who were taxed (Levi 1988).

The origin of this European peculiarity lies in several distinctive features of European feudal arrangements and in the corporate (rather than dynastic) form of the social organizations that became pervasive when feudalism dissolved (Møller and Skaaning 2013). One such feature is what is known as the "vertical partition of sovereignty." Under the European feudal regime, sovereignty was formally divided between lords (suzerains) and vassals in a vertical hierarchy of delegations. Rulers could not claim direct control over large parts of the territory. The vassal received a land grant from his lord, and in return, using the resources obtained from the land, he was expected to provide military services. But control over the territory was completely delegated to the vassal, who was responsible for taxation, regulation, and the maintenance of order over his territory (Finer 1977, p. 864). Powerful vassals controlling large areas could create their own vassals through subinfeudation. This led to a hierarchy of delegations and personal loyalties. The vassal had a personal obligation of loyalty to the lord, but the lord could give orders only to the vassal, not to his subordinates. The resulting fragmentation of authority created a balance of power between the ruler and the landed aristocracy.

Importantly, this hierarchy of delegations was territorially based. As emphasized by Mitterauer (2010), the territorial basis of social organizations is a key distinction between the European manorial system and Chinese dynastic organizations. This is true even with respect to the lowest social rungs. In European peasant societies, the primary social orientation was to one's "house," not to one's relatives. The house was a community largely free of kinship ties beyond the nuclear family, defined by coresidence and hence by soil, and ultimately delimited by the farming system associated with the lord's manor (Mitterauer 2010, pp. 57, 67).

Above that, medieval knights and higher nobility were practically always associated with a territory and often named after it. The manner of distributing and exercising power was thus very different between the European and Chinese systems. Chinese dynastic organizations, unlike European lords, did not have full control over their territory. The clan was a hierarchical organization defined by dynastic ties, not by residence. Lineage was spatially diffused, and local power was often shared with other kin groups (Fukuyama 2011). Moreover, in China, the central administration relied on a large bureaucracy, such that control over the territory was formally a direct prerogative of the emperor (although as we have seen, his de facto enforcement ability was severely constrained by informational and agency problems).

In the early stages of feudal Europe, central rulers lacked the capacity to exercise some local control and to know enough about local conditions. With the collapse of the Roman Empire, security was the most important public good required for survival. Wars were small, but they cost resources. After Rome's collapse, income declined with the sharp fall of commercialization and urbanization. Hence, the local population had to be squeezed hard to extract the surplus needed to fund the military. Information about local conditions was lacking, and thus it was outsourced to people in closer proximity to the sources of taxes (Stasavage 2020). Only locally residing lords had the knowledge and control over the territory to raise sufficient resources. Horses, weapons, and supporting infantry were raised mostly in loco by noblemen, who thus functioned as independent subcontractors for the realm.

This system depended a great deal on contractual reciprocity. The ties of mutual dependence between lord and vassal didn't only descend from asymmetric relationship of status, power, and information. They also had a contractual nature with binding reciprocity. The fief (from the Latin word *feudum*, originally from an old Frankish word for "livestock") was a reciprocal, two-way obligation. The vassal had a duty to provide military services to his lord—that is, raise an army at his own expense for his lord's discretion—and also to advise him ("to give counsel and aid"). But at the same time, the lord was also obliged to protect the vassal and leave him undisturbed ("immune") in the possession and governance of the fief ("to protect and preserve") (Poggi 1978, p. 22; Mitterauer 2010, p. 101). These commitments were made credible by a set of holy oaths of "fealty" (derived from the Latin *fidelitas*), which meant that they had an implicit guarantee by divine powers to punish disloyalty. Over time, however, many of the military services were commuted into cash payments, which the kings used to hire mercenaries.

As emphasized by Hintze (1975), this reciprocity reflected the nature of social relations at the time. European feudal structures emerged from the Germanic tradition of voluntary subordination of a free man to a military chief. "The Latin-Teutonic contract was based on the principle of equality of rights and the reciprocity of both parties." Hence the power of the leader was exercised "in the name of and with the consent of the people, whether expressly given or tacitly assumed" (Hintze 1975, pp. 332, 311).[55] In his description of government in an early feudal society, *de ordine palatii* (882), Archbishop Hincmar of Reims (also a jurist, theologian, and politician in post-Charlemagne France) described how the ruler was constrained by the consent of his most important subjects (Acemoglu and Robinson 2019).[56] If the lord failed to fulfill his obligations, he lost his privileges, which gave his vassals the right to abandon him and revolt. This is precisely how the Saxon Mirror (*Sachsenspiegel*)—the most important record of customary law of the Holy Roman Empire, written in the early thirteenth century—summarized the right of resistance. As noted by Bloch (1962, p. 172), "A man may resist his king and judge when he acts contrary to law and may even help to make war on him. . . . Thereby, he does not violate the duty of fealty." This principle was first recorded in the ninth century.[57]

A few centuries later, in the thirteenth and fourteenth centuries, the right of resistance became enshrined in the formal charters of right with which several European kings granted privileges to the nobility. For instance, England's Magna Carta (1215) specified actions by the Crown that would trigger sanctions by the barons. The Aragonese Privilege of the Union (1287) and the statute of Dauphiné (1341) enumerate similar principles (Bloch 1962; Møller and Skaaning 2013). Imperial decrees known as Golden Bulls also codified the

55. Acemoglu and Robinson (2019) argued that the tradition of formal Legalism implicit in Roman law also played a role. In Acemoglu and Robinson's formulation, early medieval Europe created a unique cocktail of two very different traditions, the bottom-up customs of Germanic tribes and the top-down legal traditions of Rome, and what emerged "was something greater than sum of the parts" (2019, p. 161). Later in this chapter, we discuss the important role of legal institutions and how they evolved. But we argue that this legal evolution (or better, revolution) cannot be understood without the effect of third uniquely European institution, the medieval church, both its secular clergy (the entire ecclesiastical hierarchy and canonical legal thinking) and the regular clergy (monasteries), and of other corporate organizations. Roman legal principles were rediscovered and transformed by the Church and by the emergence of new corporate organizations, but they were not at all preserved by Germanic people during the Early Middle Ages. See also Berman (1983).

56. His description pertains to an earlier state, as it was based on a book (now lost) by St. Adelard (751–827), a cousin and close advisor of Charlemagne.

57. The oath of Strasbourg (843), formulated by Charles the Bald and Louis the German to fight their brother emperor Lothar I, stipulated that, if one of the kings violated the mutual oath, his soldiers were bound not to assist their king. A similar principle also appeared in the pact between Charles the Bald and his vassals (856).

principle of consent.[58] The notions of contractual reciprocity and the right of resistance are distinctive features of European feudalism, not seen in analogous structures from other parts of the world. In one such example, feudalism, which persisted for a long time in Japan, did not produce similar political developments. The social origins of Japanese feudalism were very different from that of Europe. In Japan, feudalism was based on power differentials between two fundamentally unequal parties—a patron and a client—which did not exhibit norms of reciprocity or rights of refusal. This was in line with the dynastic tradition that saw the lord as having paternal authority over his vassals. The Japanese vassal relation originated as a "client relation within the larger unit of the clan, which often took in strangers as younger sons or brothers in the earlies stages even through the symbolic act of blood-brotherhood" (Hintze 1975, p. 333). This resulted in a much stronger dependency of the vassal on his lord, compared to the European tradition. Contractual reciprocity was a European peculiarity.

This historical and contractual difference in feudal relations between West and East implies different sources of legitimacy of the ruler. In the Germanic tradition, a military chief's legitimacy stemmed from his personal qualities as a leader, and his subordinates were bound to him by loyalty more than by the fear of repression. In the Chinese tradition instead, the emperor was linked to a heavenly entity. If he failed to behave wisely or if some catastrophe took place, his subjects took this as a sign that the emperor had lost the goodwill of heaven and could and occasionally did rebel. But the Chinese emperor had no reciprocal obligation toward his subordinates. Unlike the European right of resistance, rebellion was not conceived as originating from the violation of an explicit or implicit agreement between the emperor and his citizens.

Corporate Immunities and the Rise of Parliaments

The landed aristocracy in Europe fulfilled administrative functions for the ruler, and in exchange was exempted from some aspects of the ruler's authority. It was not the only group to enjoy such exemptions. The Church also enjoyed certain

58. The Hungarian Golden Bull (1222) ends with these words: "We also ordain that if We or any of Our Successors shall at any time contravene the terms of this statute, the bishops and the higher and lower nobles of Our realm, one and all, both present and future, shall by virtue thereof have the uncontrolled right in perpetuity of resistance both by word and deed without thereby incurring any charge of treason" (cited by Berman 1983, p. 293). In Germany, the Golden Bull (1356) recognized the prince-electors' rights to select an emperor and specified how the electors were to be sanctioned and by whom if they failed to elect an emperor within thirty days.

immunities (i.e. privileges that relieved one from a burden otherwise due) over its extensive holdings of land. Eventually, the ruler extended important forms of self-government to free towns (communes). Next, we describe in more detail the emergence of communes and the Church's role in the evolution of European political institutions. Here, we note that the extension of immunities to corporate bodies—not just to powerful and special individuals—constitutes a significant departure from the Germanic tradition. Under that tradition, rulers granted privileges to special individuals in recognition of their personal loyalty or services. As corporate organizations gained economic importance, however, immunities were also granted to corporations. Immunities often involved mortgaging future revenues. The king, often strapped for resources needed for current military engagements, sold immunities and privileges to raise revenue.[59]

The system of immunities was a precursor of modern civil and political rights. Individuals could claim well-defined rights exclusively by virtue of their membership in specific groups (the most famous example was that members of an urban community could be released from their serfdom status). Moreover, except for feudal lords, the corporate groups that enjoyed political privileges groups were defined by common economic and political interests, not by dynastic or ethnic ties. In China, the absence of corporations implied that privileges could not be assigned to them. The most powerful Chinese clans probably enjoyed preferential treatment in the recruitment of the state bureaucracy and exerted greater influence. But nothing like the formal recognition of legal rights and immunities to representatives of powerful clans ever emerged in Imperial China.

During the thirteenth and fourteenth centuries, the system of immunities in several European kingdoms evolved into the practice of convening assemblies of representatives of corporate interests. These assemblies or diets became ubiquitous, one of many telling divergences between Europe and the rest of the world. Representative bodies went by many common names depending on time and place, but they fulfilled similar functions: one thinks of parliaments in the British Isles, *états généraux* in France, country diets (*Landtage*) in the Germanic lands, the *Staten Generaal* in the Low Countries, the *Sejm* in Poland, and *Cortès* on the Iberian Peninsula. By the end of the fifteenth

59. Common fiscal immunities included exemptions from national and local taxation, fines and assessments, and various types of charges and tolls. Entities and lords also received royal grants of immunity from military service, various personal services, and from the burden of attending communal courts (Burrell 2011, p. 15).

century, at least twenty-five national and provisional assemblies operated across the main principalities of Europe (e.g., Meyers 1975; Herb 2003; for a recent analysis, see Stasavage 2020).

This practice reflected two earlier traditions. The first is the example of old church councils, or synods. The second is the older Germanic tradition of local community gathering. These two traditions were merged during the Frankish kingdoms in the eighth century, when King Pippin started to regularly convene Church synods in conjunction with conferences held with his military elites. Royal advisory councils, which discussed both religious and secular matters, also started to be convened at about the same time in England and in Spain under the Visigoth Kingdom (Mitterauer 2010; Maddicott 2004). These councils reflected the duty (and right) of vassals to give advice to their lord, as discussed previously. They also provided some sense of unity in a highly decentralized and fragmented structure. According to Mitterauer (2010, p. 143), "The imperial diets and territorial diets provided a sort of organizing bond for the various scattered bearers of lordship autonomous in their own little sphere."

Eventually, the kings institutionalized the meetings of representative bodies into royal councils, where the Church and the nobility met to advise the king on important issues. The role and composition of these councils varied greatly across Europe, although they only or mainly existed in Western Europe. According to Hintze (1975), this reflects the tradition of the Western Church. An important prerogative of these councils was to confirm, and in some cases elect, new kings. Typically, the former was the case, and councils confirmed the heir to the throne. Yet there were cases in which a real election took place, such as in Poland, the medieval *wiec* (assembly of nobles) at times exercised real discretion. The *veche* in East Slavic kingdoms such as Novgorod was a comparable council of nobles who held some selection powers.

Early on, the individuals attending these councils participated only on a personal basis (i.e., by virtue of their individual status, rights, and duties to advise the prince). But during the twelfth and thirteenth centuries, this began to change, and participants started to formally represent territorial interests or corporate bodies. An early example is the Imperial Diet at Roncaglia in 1158, where Lombard cities sent their delegates to speak on their behalf over important issues. Other examples include the council convened in Leon by the new King Alfonso IX of Castile in 1188, as well as similar assemblies in Aragon and Catalonia in the thirteenth century, where even village communities appeared together with royal towns, and where city representatives had been elected by their local communities. The extent to which this happened varied across Europe. In

Flanders, the large towns were the only exponents of the estates system in the twelfth and thirteenth centuries, while in Hungary and Poland, only a few royal cities enjoyed representation in royal diets. The frequency with which these assemblies met also varied across nations. England was unusual in the regularity of its meetings, which convened more than once every two years during the fourteenth century (Mitterauer 2010; van Zanden et al. 2012; Maddicott 2004).

The growing political importance of corporate delegates in the system of estates was a fundamental step toward developing modern parliaments. This process accelerated in the thirteenth and fourteenth centuries in part due to changes in military technology, as well as growth in commerce and of urban centers. As armored cavalry was supplemented or replaced by mercenary troops; the cost of war rose and had to be spread over wider swaths of society. By that time, urban and commercial centers had expanded, and it became natural to include representatives of these sectors in these gatherings, to obtain their consent to raise additional revenue for military expenses (Hintze 1975; Hadenius 2001; Finer 1997). In exchange for increased taxes, delegates often demanded a strengthening of their immunities, which in turn then led to the clarification and consolidation of their corporate rights. In the words of Hintze (1975, p. 346), "The rulers found themselves thoroughly dependent on the good will of those strata of the population capable of military and financial contributions. The good will naturally had to be rewarded . . . also by giving concessions and liberties of a political nature like those enshrined in the privileges of the Estates. . . . The active elements of the population who helped to build the state also gained a share in its government."[60]

Van Zanden et al. (2012) note that the initiative to convene assemblies that included representatives of towns and other corporate bodies was usually taken by the king. In this sense, the establishment of parliaments as a new political institution was a "revolution from above." This is at first blush puzzling. Why would rulers give up power and allow associations that could coordinate actions against them?[61] Outside Europe, powerful rulers carefully

60. It is no coincidence that English cities that had gained authority to collect taxes were also more likely to be represented in Parliament later and be asked for their consent when the king needed to raises taxes, usually for foreign wars (Angelucci et al. 2021).

61. As Aristotle already noted, it was costly for rulers to allow citizens' associations. Tyrants "don't allow [even] associations for social and cultural activities or anything of that kind; these are the breeding grounds of independence and self-confidence, two things which tyrants must guard against" (Aristotle 1932, 5.11).

avoided this step.[62] The answer to this question is that the initiative of convening assemblies was generally taken by the sovereign when he was weak, or in moments of transition, such as after a controversial succession or in times of war. In such situations, the king needed to consolidate loyalty or to raise additional revenue, which led to power sharing with representatives of corporate groups. Interestingly, if the king was absent or too weak to even convene representatives to the bargaining table, as in the case of northern Italy and the Netherlands, no national assemblies would be convened and Parliaments emerged later in time.[63]

The emergence of representative assemblies went hand in hand with the demise of feudalism. Under feudal arrangements, control over the land was given to the nobility in exchange for military services. As military technology evolved and mercenary troops gained importance, the barons' military obligations were commuted into the payment of customary fees to the Crown, and the barons increasingly considered the land as their own property. But typically, the revenues from customary fees were insufficient to cover the costs of wars or other shocks. As a result, the ruler needed to seek additional resources from whoever was able to provide them. In return, he needed to make concessions, often by granting political rights, immunities, or agreeing to constraints on his powers. For instance, one of the first deals made between the cities and King Alfonso IX of Castile entailed the promise by the king that he would give up his privilege to debase the currency (van Zanden et al. 2012). Another prominent example is the Great Council, convened in England in February 1225. The assembly included "archbishops, bishops, abbots, priors, earls, barons, knights, free tenants and everyone in our kingdom" and formally granted the king the right to appropriate a general tax on movable goods to fund the war against France. In exchange, the king confirmed and reissued the Magna Carta and the Charter of the Forest.

62. In Japan, the Tokugawa Shogunate forbade the formation of horizontal alliances and organizations (Ikegami 2005, p. 11), while a European writing in 1789 reported that the African Kingdom of Dahomey (Benin) outlawed any association because he feared that they "might be injurious to the king's unlimited power" (cited by Law 1986, p. 249). In czarist Russia, the Duma was established only in the last years of the Romanoff Empire (under serious pressure), and had little power.

63. Thus, the Estates General of the Low Countries were first convened in 1464 at the initiative of Philip ("the Good") of Burgundy. After some ups and downs, the powers of the diet were established in 1477 in the Great Privilege, which recognized many of the rights and immunities of the local authorities.

These episodes are typical of how bargains were struck in medieval England and other states. The sovereign obtained permission to levy a tax to pay for an imminent war. In exchange, a representative body obtained redress for some grievances, or the confirmation (or an extension) of its prerogatives (Maddicott 2004). In many cases, parliaments refused to approve new taxes unless they received various rights in exchange (e.g., Brown 1989; Stone 2001; O'Callaghan 1989). Since the king did not have its own administrative apparatus, it had to rely on preexisting corporate groups to enforce tax collection. These groups were willing to increase rulers' revenues only in return for rights that maintained their relative power.

One interesting effect of European representative assemblies is their role in facilitating cooperation between rulers and subjects (Barzel 1997; Barzel and Kiser 1997). War was a costly project, but military success was beneficial for both kings and their subjects. The requirement of parliamentary consent for taxation implied a somewhat equitable distribution of both costs and benefits. Furthermore, it implied that both parties were obliged to collaborate for a successful outcome. The presence of powerful representative bodies entailed a higher probability of engaging in defensive rather than offensive or dynastic wars. Parliaments were less likely to agree to funding nonnecessary conflicts because, ceteris paribus, commercial interests (as opposed to political or religious ones) would prefer peace over war.[64]

By the Late Middle Ages, Western Europe housed a myriad of *universitates* (i.e., corporate bodies), each with its own special privileges, rights, and responsibilities. Inside the Church, the largest corporate body, there was a split between the regular and the secular clergy, and among the former, the various orders of monks and mendicants operated with considerable distinction. Within the typical chartered town, one could find numerous merchant and craft guilds, universities, friendly societies, and other corporate organizations. This growing corporate fragmentation heralded the end of the personalized relationship of dependency that had been characteristic of feudalism. It did not, however, replace it with a symmetrical relation between equals. "Instead,

---

64. This idea goes back to Montesquieu's famous notion of *doux commerce*, the belief that peace would be a natural effect of trade (Hirschman 1977, pp. 56–63). This belief was perhaps naive. During the age of mercantilism, trade interests could at times drive economic motives for war. That said, overall the more decentralized administrative power was in the hands of urban civilians (as opposed to the bellicose medieval nobles), the more military efforts would be directed to win a defensive rather than an offensive war.

it created dualism: a two-way relationship between corporation and the Crown, between the 'Community of the realm' on the one side and the 'government' on the other" (Finer 1997, p. 1028). As the Church's political clout began to diminish due to schisms and corruption in the fourteenth century, temporal authorities were confronted with a new countervailing power (namely, the corporations that they themselves had supported). The rise of parliaments was a way to integrate the new corporate bodies into the highly fragmented power structure of the feudal state. Such assemblies were unique to Western Europe and did not emerge in China, nor in the Middle East. The Asian empires did not have corporate social organizations with which they had to negotiate. They did not seek the cooperation of their subjects, only their mandatory contributions (Van Zanden et al. 2012).

As emphasized by Hadenius (2001), the attachment of political rights to corporate rather than dynastic groups facilitated political cooperation and inclusiveness. Because corporations were based on common socioeconomic interests, they found it easier to cooperate with other corporations with similar goals than do dynastic groups. Moreover, because they were not based on kinship, corporations were open groups with porous boundaries, and this too tended to reinforce cooperation and interactions between unrelated individuals. Thus, intergroup cooperation was easier compared to a kin-based social structure. This cooperation between corporate groups was essential in a political context because it increased their bargaining power vis à vis the sovereign. European corporations were more effective at countervailing powers against sovereign rulers compared to dynastic groups, both because they could be scaled up more easily (since they were not ascriptive), and they could more easily join forces and become political allies. The weakness of particularist groups such as clans is that they depend critically on a sense of identity, of "us vs. them". Such a culture mindset can inhibit interactions with other groups, producing "a latent suspicion and enmity, periodically erupting into open hostilities, between different segments of the population" (Hadenius 2001, p. 165).

In other words, corporations acquired political rights, which facilitated the emergence of a new and more cooperative social order. These autonomous and diverse social groups created political diversity and a balance of power. The groups were held together primarily by class, location, and occupational identity, which made coordination easier. Different groups within civil society had obtained immunities and guarantees of autonomy from the state in the form of formal declarations and letters of their rights and privileges. These groups acquired enough standing to participate in political decision making and form political alliances, and their interaction with the state was done under conditions that encouraged the peaceful negotiated resolution of conflict in most cases. In this way, the coordination capacity of society was strengthened at the national level. Social groups acquired the ability to act as a counterweight to the central power, and at times to enter partnerships with it (Hadenius 2001).

Overall, the evolution of representative institutions in Europe facilitated peaceful conflict resolution and power sharing, as well as national integration. Furthermore, the allocation of immunities to corporate groups strengthened group identity, further reinforcing their pervasiveness. While conflicts were unavoidable, corporate groups rarely became involved in long-term blood feuds and vendettas with other groups as clans did. In addition, their cohesion and relationship with others did not depend as much on concepts such as "honor" and a reputation for toughness. Intuitively, if a society is segmented in nonoverlapping groups, like clans, interpersonal conflict between individuals belonging to different groups is likely to escalate in conflicts among groups, through norms of loyalty and allegiance to other group members, as happens during fights between clans and tribes. In a world of corporations, such long-lasting feuds are less likely to erupt, and political alliances to moderate the power of absolutist rulers are more sustainable.[65]

5. The Rule of Law

Chinese emperors generally had absolute powers. During the Tang Dynasty (618–907), the central bureaucracy was able to impose checks and balances on Imperial authority, but later the emperor found ways to bypass them. At that point, his powers were significantly constrained only by the limited state capacity, the informal codes known as *li*, and the threat of rebellion. While some have argued that such constraints might be seen as some form of the rule of law (Mei 1932), it was a very different concept from the principle, prominent in early state formation in Europe, that rulers are subject to and constrained by laws.

The rule of law means different things to different scholars—see the widely cited treatise by Tamanaha (2004). A useful formulation comes from Hayek

---

65. Moscona et al. (2020) provide a different kind of evidence, consistent with the idea that strong and highly segmented kinship networks induce greater fragmentation of society and discourage broader political cooperation. Using data on 145 ethnic groups in sub-Saharan Africa, they show that ethnic groups organized along segmentary lineages are more prone to conflict.

(1973): the rule of law states that both legislative and executive sovereignties are limited by a preexisting body of law (Fukuyama 2011). As stressed by Hayek (1973, p. 72), the law is older than legislation. Existing legal rules also constrained how new legislation was written, and the sovereign could not ignore them. Individual rulers are bound by the law, and their acts of government, as well as any new legislation, cannot violate existing rules. Thus, the rule of law imposed binding constraints on the absolutist powers of the state. This idea aligns with what Mokyr (2008, p. 87) called a "meta-institution": a rule about how to make rules. The legitimacy that this implies, in turn, facilitates rule enforcement.

The concept of rule of law had already gained recognition in antiquity (from Aristotle and Cicero, among others), but it rarely became formally codified when outlining the relationship between ruler and subject.[66] It was in that capacity that the principle became increasingly influential in medieval Europe. As stressed by Hayek, "law," in the sense of enforced rules of conduct, is coeval with society; only the observance of common rules makes the peaceful existence of individuals in society possible (hence, formal legislation, from Hammurabi to the Pentateuch to Roman law, was found to be necessary long before anything like a "modern state" had emerged). By the seventeenth century, the principle of the rule of law had become axiomatic, and kings like James I of England readily recognized it, although it remained contested by many rulers.[67]

Although the principle was abandoned in some countries at certain points in time, it proved remarkably persistent overall, and it always existed in at least some sovereign European polities. Of course, the rule of law is now recognized as one of the cornerstones of modern democratic states. That said, the role of the rule of law and the basic differences in legal development between Europe and the rest of the world have been underappreciated, even by those who stressed the importance of institutions (see Fernandez-Villaverde 2016, p. 27).

66. For instance, Cicero in *The Republic* condemned the king who does not abide by the law as a despot who "is the foulest and most repellant creature imaginable" and complained that "everyone of standing had realized that the republic's rule of law and order had given place to the rule of the stronger" (Tamanaha 2004, p. 11).

67. The significance of the Magna Carta in underlining the rule of law has been stressed by many scholars. Tamanaha (2004, p. 26) notes that "then and now the Magna Carta symbolized the fact that law protected citizens against the king. . . . The language confirmed that the barons were not subject to the king's justices, who were notorious for doing his bidding, and confirmed that decisions must be based upon ordinary law, not upon the desires of the king." For a detailed defense of the role of the Magna Carta in rooting the idea of the rule of law, see Fernandez-Villaverde (2016).

The rule of law also dictates that all men are equal before the law. This concept was still alien in the Salic Law, codified by King Clovis of the Franks in the sixth century.[68] This concept originated in later medieval times, in part from Christian doctrine and canon law, in part from feudal law, and in part from the legal concepts created by cities, as Berman (1983) stressed.[69] Gratian's *Decretum* states explicitly that "all men, rich and poor, free and slave, will have to render equally an account of themselves and of their souls" (cited by Kelly 1992, p. 146). Canonists, it has been argued, maintained that any rule of law or practice affects all souls. It has also been asserted that "their concern, unknown to antiquity, was with the experience of 'all equally'" (Siedentop 2014, p. 218). The Glossators (legal scholars in the eleventh and twelfth centuries) expressed the same principle, influenced by classical Roman law rather than by Christian doctrine. The twelfth-century law professor Bulgarus (one of the famed "four doctors" of the University of Bologna) spoke of a "law of nature by which all men are equal." The *Sachsenspiegel* and the *Schwabenspiegel*, thirteenth-century compilations of German customary law, similarly acknowledged the original equality of men (Kelly 1992, p. 146).[70]

68. In these laws, the punishment depended on the identity of the victim. The laws stipulate that anyone killing a pregnant woman or a free woman after she begins to bear children be liable to pay 24,000 denarii (i.e., 600 solidi). However, the killer of a woman past middle age and no longer able to bear children would be liable to pay only 8,000 denarii (i.e., 200 solidi). Killing a Roman who was "a table companion of the king" would set one back 12,000 denarii (i.e., 300 solidi), but if the victim was not a table companion of the king, the killing would cost only 4,000 denarii (i.e., 100 solidi) (Drew 1991, pp. 104–6).

69. The concept of equality before the law already had appeared in some form in the Bible. For example, Exodus 12:49, commanding that "the same law shall apply to both the native and the foreigner who resides among you." The New Testament adds, "There is neither Jew nor Greek, slave nor free, male nor female, for you are all one in Christ Jesus" (Paul's Letter to the Galatians, 3:28). As Schwarzschild (2010, p. 161) points out, Judeo-Christian thought is "a complex tangle of egalitarian and inegalitarian tendencies. At least in some moods, Jews and Christians have perennially seen themselves as communities of believers equal before God." Given that, equality before the law is obvious. And yet, he notes, they recognized legal distinctions between Jew and Gentile, Christian and heathen, saved and damned, slave and free person, and man and woman. With regard to urban law, Lesaffer (2009, p. 233) points out that in urban areas, all citizens who had sworn the pact of loyalty to the town fell under the same jurisdiction.

70. It should be added that the principle of the equality before the law was by no means as generally accepted an axiom in medieval times as it is today. Most egregiously, the clergy was exempt from being tried before secular courts and were judged exclusively by ecclesiastical courts, which meted out far milder penalties than regular tribunals.

Economists have found the concept of equality before the law interesting precisely because it is somewhat counterintuitive: if laws are promulgated by people who have sufficient power to enforce them, why would they give others with less power some formal position of equality before the law? Acemoglu and Wolitzky (2020) have examined this question, concluding that it may be beneficial for a powerful political elite to do so under certain conditions. The basic idea is that such equality may elicit more cooperative behavior from members of the elite (who therefore become subject to the same carrots and sticks as everyone else). If such increased efforts by the elites also prompt the rest of the population to work harder, it may be in everyone's interest to have the law apply to everyone equally.[71] While Acemoglu and Wolitzky do not use the rise of equality before the law in medieval legal thought as an example, the logic of their argument extends into what happened in much of medieval Europe.

The prominence of the rule of law in European state formation reflects several factors, which we now discuss in turn (see Tamanaha 2004 for a more extensive discussion).

Legal Institutions Emerged before Other State Institutions

In many cases, legal institutions emerged before other state institutions. The first factor behind the rising importance of the rule of law in Europe is thus the historical sequence of functions that early European states performed, as well as the sequence with which different state institutions emerged. Kings and greater lords used the administration of justice to overcome the political fragmentation of their polities. Overturning the decision of a lower (baronial) court had the effect of undermining the authority of the baron and enhancing the king's authority with the baron's subordinates. The administration of justice was also a source of revenue for the king.

Building specialized institutions for dealing with domestic affairs was thus an important priority for European sovereigns. Permanent legal institutions

71. Acemoglu and Wolitzky (2020) show that certain shocks are likely to lead to the elite willingly giving up their privileged status and promulgate more equality before the law. Among those are changes in the level of violence that the elite can inflict on the rest of the population, and the economic payoffs to cooperative behavior when effort becomes more important for production or for the provision of vital public goods, such as national defense. Importantly, however, more neutral growth in productivity and prosperity may not automatically do so, which casts doubt on simplistic "modernization" theories, which regard equality before the law as a simple result of society's higher level of prosperity.

were created as early as permanent financial institutions, well before sophisticated institutions dealing with defense or foreign policy (Strayer 1970, p. 32).
Law became associated with state institutions. During the late eleventh
century, and subsequently in the twelfth and thirteenth centuries, "there
emerged for the first time strong central authorities, both ecclesiastical and
secular, whose control reached down, through delegated officials, from the
center to the localities. Partly in connection with that, there emerged a class
of professional jurists, including professional judges and practicing lawyers"
(Berman 1983, p. 85). By the end of the thirteenth century, central courts in
England and France staffed highly trained legal experts who worked for the
ruler's administration (Strayer 1970, pp. 32–33).

The emergence of legal institutions at a very early stage of state formation is
important because it left an imprint on the subsequent evolution of the state. In
the words of Strayer (1970, p. 61), "Medieval states . . . were law-states. They had
acquired their power largely by developing their judicial institutions and by protecting the property of the possessing classes. The most typical expression of
internal sovereignty was the right of final judgement in a high court." Charles
Tilly's quip that "war made the state and the states made war" (Tilly 1992) has
been cited so often that it has become a cliché. But that does not make it either
accurate or complete. It would be equally or more correct to state that the law
made the state and the state made laws. Large military capacity was built only
once states had already developed their judicial institutions. Early on, internal
political fragmentation was still too high and the cost of raising a large standing
army was unbearable. Between 1215 and 1290, European states experienced a
period of relative peace, where there were no major wars involving large states.
This gave emerging states the opportunity to focus on developing formal institutions for internal affairs (Strayer 1970, p. 81). When more expensive wars began
during the fourteenth century, legal principles had already permeated society
and state institutions. As we discuss next and in chapter 8, this would affect how
wars would later shape the evolution of political institutions.

The act of creating new formal legislation came after the reformulation of
legal concepts from antiquity within a preexisting and commonly accepted
legal order. As we will describe in chapter 8, medieval legal institutions and
jurists codified and clarified preexisting legal practices and traditions. They did
not create law—they "discovered" it (Kern 1939, p. 151). The preexistence of
judicial institutions that enforced a commonly accepted legal framework made
it easier to recognize the importance of the distinction between the existing
law and new acts of government. It also facilitated the imposition of constraints

on the absolutist powers of the ruler, and in particular, it made it possible to subordinate rulers' legislative powers to the judicial powers of the state. In Europe, "the state was based on law and existed to enforce the law. The ruler was bound morally (and often politically) by the law" (Strayer 1970, pp. 23–24). The principle that the existing body of law poses limits on the absolutist powers of the ruler was also used to bind the supremacy of the pope: the canonists asserted that the Church's consensus, expressed in the statutes of the general councils and other norms of faith, could bind even the pope (Berman 1983, p. 291). The idea of a constrained executive branch of government is central to a large body of literature that tries to quantify the quality of institutions.

The Western Church

As we have already seen in chapter 4 about the dismantling of kin ties, the Western Church also exerted a huge influence over the evolution of European legal and political institutions. Tierney (1982) argues that it was not Christianity or doctrine so much as the corporate organization of religious bodies that explains the West's unique political development. Beyond the impact of canon law on the emergence of representative institutions, which we will discuss in chapter 8, Tierney points out that the existence of the Church as a powerful and transnational institution created a fundamental countervailing force to the violent thugs and bandit leaders that carried titles like "count" and "duke."[72] At the same time, the Church was also instrumental in facilitating and supporting cooperative institutions.

The Church's influence was particularly strong with respect to legal institutions and the prominence of the rule of law. This happened in several ways. First, it occurred through the specific content of its moral and religious principles. Second, as further discussed in chapter 8, the Church created a dual structure of powers and authority between ecclesiastic and secular realms. Third, generations of scholars from all over Europe were directed toward the formal study of law, hence

---

72. In a powerful passage, Tierney (1982, p. 10) summarizes: "There was never just one structure of government, presided over by an unchallenged theocratic head, but always two structures, ecclesiastical and secular, always jealous of each other's authority, always preventing medieval society from congealing into a single monolithic theocracy. Ecclesiastical criticism diminished the aura of divine right surrounding kingship; royal power opposed the temporal claims of the papacy. Each hierarchy limited the authority of the other. It is not difficult to see that such a situation could be conducive to a growth of human freedom."

facilitating the emergence of a transnational class of legal experts and professionals. And fourth, through canon law, it set an example for secular authorities of how to organize and govern a community. We now briefly discuss each of these points.

Christianity promoted the unity of an enlarged community that transcended the kin and the tribe. All human beings were equal in front of God, no matter where they came from, where they were born, and how rich and powerful they were. Moreover, Christian doctrine insisted that rulers did not descend from God and had no "Mandate from Heaven" but rather were human beings like everyone else. These values had two important political implications. First, there was a universal community of the faithful, which could be represented by the Church as an organization with a distinctive collective and legal identity. Second, even the most powerful individuals were subject to a superior body of law, with its own absolute criteria of ethics and justice.

These two implications acquired relevance in medieval Europe thanks to the duality in the distribution of power between the Church and secular rulers. The papacy tried to make the Church the ultimate source of legitimacy for temporal rulers. When Pepin the Short, Charlemagne's father, took power in the Frankish Kingdom from the Merovingians, he sought legitimation from the papacy. Charlemagne was coronated in Rome by Pope Leo III in 800 to underline the Church as being superior to the secular rulers (although reputedly this was done to the great annoyance of Charlemagne).

As noted by Fukuyama (2011), religious principles can be effective in constraining political rulers only if religious authority is independent of political authority and it is sufficiently strong. These conditions were fulfilled after 1075, when Pope Gregory VII declared the legal supremacy of the pope over the entire Western Church and the independence of the Church from the emperor.[73] After a protracted conflict with the emperor, a compromise was found in which neither side could claim full supremacy. The Concordat of Worms in 1122 solidified the notion of separate spheres for religious and secular powers, with the division of ecclesiastic and secular authorities in competition with each other and each one limiting the authority of the other.[74]

73. Tellingly, Pope Gregory relied on a formal written legal document known as the *Donatio Constantini*, according to which Emperor Constantine willingly ceded authority to the pope and recognized him as his superior. The document first surfaced under Pepin the Short and was used extensively during the investiture struggles of the eleventh century. By the fifteenth century, it was already understood to be a fraud, an accusation famously proved by the humanist scholar Lorenzo Valla in 1440.

74. The Concordat of Worms between Pope Callixtus II and Holy Roman Emperor Henry V was one of the most important political compromises of its time, in which the investiture

This outcome had several practical consequences of great importance. First, it prevented the emergence of a monolithic theocracy, consolidating the separation of church and state. This set Western Europe apart from other societies, where it was the norm that a supreme political leader claims a direct link to God and simultaneously heads the religious apparatus.

Second, by weakening Imperial authority, the coexistence of ecclesiastical and temporal authorities reinforced both internal and external political fragmentation. The rise of communes in Europe also owes much to the new environment created by the Gregorian Revolution. Often, the Church took the side of communes seeking autonomy from bishops appointed by the emperor. The city of Cambrai in northern France is an early example.[75] Shortly after Gregory VII's declaration of Church independence, the merchants of Cambrai and a papalist priest revolted against the city's Imperial bishop, claiming autonomy as a commune. The revolt was put down, but it succeeded two years later, again under the leadership of a Gregorian priest, when a new bishop was appointed by the emperor. Cambrai remained a commune until 1106, when the emperor reestablished his authority. But after the Concordat of Worms in 1122, Cambrai was finally granted a charter of liberties.

The example of Cambrai is not unique. Other episcopal cities in northern France followed similar paths. In these episodes, and in several others in the Netherlands and northern Italy, cities defied Imperial bishops with the support of the Church (Berman 1983; Møller and Doucette 2022, chapters 3–4).

Third, each body (secular and ecclesiastic) had to develop and maintain its own legal system and organization. This clear demarcation of authority, as well as the competition with the Church, also spurred the secular powers to clarify

---

struggle between emperor and pope effectively came to an end. Experts still disagree to some extent on which side got the better part of the deal, but it created a political reality in which secular rulers eventually ended up "in possession of the field" (cited by Morrison 1969, p. 343). Basically, both sides agreed to share the power to invest Church appointments. As Morrison (1969) points out, Henry V retained the substance of his control over the German church, although he had to sacrifice the symbolic act of investing bishops-elect with ring and staff. The papacy renounced the prospect of achieving in reality "the universal and immediate headship of all churches that it claimed in theory" (1969, p. 343). As compensation, Calixtus II secured Imperial assurance of free elections to abbacies and episcopacies, and a recognition of the boundaries of the papal lands as a legal entity. Callixtus agreed to the presence of the emperor or his officials at the elections of bishops and granted the emperor the right to arbiter disputed outcomes. All in all, the Concordat was a step toward the establishment of a unique form of government, in which the law constrained both secular and ecclesiastical rulers.

75. In 925, Cambrai became part of East Francia (later the Holy Roman Empire).

their role and to consolidate their organizational and legal structures. In the words of Strayer (1970 p. 22), "The Gregorian concept of the Church almost demanded the invention of the concept of the State" and reinforced the tendency to consider the state as being responsible for the administration of justice (dispute resolution and internal protection). When the Holy Roman Emperor closely cooperated with the Church, he could exploit European religious unity to invoke supremacy over other secular rulers. The Investiture Conflict weakened the emperor since it implied that religious unity could be maintained even under a plurality of secular political organizations—including what is known as the ecclesiastical princes of Europe. This loss of authority for the emperor was compounded by a clearer demarcation of secular and religious domains. The fact that the emperor was no longer responsible for the joint guidance of the Church and for the appointment of bishops implied that secular rulers had lost some of their authority. To regain it, secular rulers became more involved in the administration of justice and protection of internal security. But this required the creation of legal and judicial capacity.

Fourth, a plurality of jurisdictions was created, secular and religious. Each jurisdiction would have to respect the rights of the other jurisdiction, as limits on its own sovereignty. This also implied that "the respective heads of each body would be bound by the law which they themselves had enacted; . . . they must rule under the law" (Berman 1983, p. 291). The rule of law, then, was a precondition for the peaceful coexistence of the secular and ecclesiastic authorities.

Thus, the institution of the Western Church played a critical role in the establishment of the rule of law. In its modern incarnation, the rule of law entails the separation of legislative, administrative, and judicial powers. Berman stresses that medieval concepts of the rule of law shared two features with its modern counterpart. First, in the medieval concept, power was divided among different bodies, providing a natural system of checks and balances based on competing polities in the same territory. Second, "law was derived from, and rooted in, a reality that transcended the existing structure of political power, first divine and natural justice and later human rights, democratic values, and other related beliefs" (Berman 1983, p. 293).

The Church played a subtle but important role in shaping the emerging European states. The pope and the synods issued new laws, which were executed by an administrative hierarchy and interpreted by a judicial hierarchy. The Church had a strong collective identity; it raised revenues and retained important secular powers, and occasionally it even raised armies. As discussed in chapter 4, in building its organizational structure, the Church borrowed secular legal ideas and exploited arrangements that were evolving in civil society. These arrangements in turn influenced the evolution of medieval state institutions in a two-way interaction between the ecclesiastic and secular spheres of government. The same individuals moved from one sphere to the other: scholars trained in canon law staffed the bureaucracy of the Church but also became advisors of kings, professors of law, and administrators. Thus, similar institutional features emerged both in ecclesiastic and secular structures (Tierney 1982, pp. 10–11).

To summarize: An important force behind the joint coevolution of political and ecclesiastic organizations was the interaction with contractual arrangements in civil society based on formal legal foundations. Both the Church and the state adapted the corporate arrangements that permeated society to a larger scale, and they transmuted provisions already existing in private law into constitutional law. We now discuss this interaction between political institutions and corporate organizations in greater detail.

The Influence of Corporate Organizations

The specific institutional features of the Church and medieval states were not the outcomes of a deliberate plan or design. They emerged from a process of trial and error that reflected the how society was becoming organized, as well as changes in the bargaining power of the main actors. The Commercial Revolution of the eleventh and twelfth centuries and the rise of a wealthy urban class made disparities between the nobility and the rest of the population harder to sustain. Changes in military technology also may have played a role in changing beliefs toward more equality. Military capabilities shifted from cavalry to pikemen and archers, strengthening the bargaining position of lower classes as opposed to horse-riding knights.

In this new environment, contractual arrangements were of paramount importance, and legal principles and procedures had a particular sanctity. Both the ecclesiastic and secular parts of society consisted of a multitude of corporate groups, such as monasteries, confraternities, universities, guilds, and communes. All these groups had to solve similar problems of collective action: defining a hierarchy, establishing a procedure for making decisions, solving principal-agent problems, overcoming free-riding and other opportunistic behaviors, holding representatives accountable, undertaking mutual obligations, and resolving conflicts of interest through negotiation or arbitrage.

Medieval jurists considering these problems on a larger political scale had firsthand experience with various corporations—guilds, universities, and religious orders—and how they were organized. "The everyday reality exercised a pervasive influence on their ways of thinking about the structures of human societies in general, including political societies" (Tierney 1982, p. 11). Thus, it was natural to transplant knowledge from corporations into political organizations.

Contemporaries were conscious of the conceptual similarities between corporate arrangements and political institutions. The new political entities that emerged between the twelfth and the fourteenth centuries (i.e., the reorganized Church, the Communes, the representative assemblies, and other secular polities) were unequivocally seen and defined as corporate bodies, not dissimilar from the corporate organizations that already existed, such as guilds or monastic orders. The underlying assumption was that a polity was not just a collection of individuals, but rather a single entity, with its own fictitious personality and legal persona, much like a corporation. Consequently, any assembly representing this single entity was also a corporate body.

The conceptualization of political entities as corporate bodies had obvious implications for how political institutions evolved. Rules of private law were transformed into specific provisions of constitutional law. Corporate charters were adapted from existing organizations to new ones.[76] The monastic order of Cluny (founded in the early tenth century) is commonly regarded as having served as a model for the Catholic Church (Berman 1983, p. 88). The order of Cluny, which controlled over 1,000 monasteries dispersed throughout Europe to the Abbey of Cluny in southern France, may have been the first truly translocal corporation besides the Church itself. The Cluniac movement staunchly supported the translocal corporation of the papacy and produced four popes itself.[77] In short, European political organizations, both secular and ecclesiastic, adopted legal and political ideas from corporations.

The adaptation of concepts from corporate organizations to constitutional provisions is reflected in several distinctive features of European political institutions. Earlier in the chapter, we discussed how representatives of

76. For instance, this is what happened when the French city of Agde became a commune, and its constitution was modeled on the chapters of the cathedral of the city that had just become a corporate body (Tierney 1982, p. 11).

77. Monasteries had existed long before, of course, but the Benedictine order founded in 529 was nonhierarchical, and each monastery was an autonomous unit.

corporate groups participated in assemblies and early parliaments. The principle of representation—namely, the idea that a representative could speak on behalf of and bind their group—came from existing corporate practice, primarily the Church. This principle is known as *plena potestas* (full powers). The novel idea is that, once the legal representative of the corporation has received full powers, he can bind the whole group with his acts, even if each single member has not consented in advance (Stasavage 2020). The principle of *plena potestas* emerged in private law; it was given a precise formulation in the canonistic doctrine, and it was then used in constitutions to define the powers of elected members in representative assemblies. Its Roman civil-law origins derive from the time of Alexander Severus (Post 1943). Before that, even in private arrangements, the agent could not bind his principal to a third party under Roman law.

By the twelfth century, *plena potestas* gained wide acceptance in legal circles in Europe and soon after was extended to diplomats (Post 1943). In the early thirteenth century, it was applied to political assemblies. The practice implied that a representative to an assembly did not have to constantly refer back to and consult with their constituencies when agreeing to a royal request (Stasavage 2019). This idea follows from the logic that a corporate body is a distinct legal entity, separate from that of the individuals that compose it. As such, the approval of the corporation does not need to coincide with the approval of all the members of the corporation. As emphasized by Finer (1997), the political application of this principle was entirely new. It was absent from the Greek and Roman republics based on direct citizenship. The idea that a political representative could bind the corporate group in whose name he was speaking emerged later, under canon law, and then it found an application to secular political institutions (see Post 1943; Tiernay 1982).[78] Nothing like the principle of representation ever emerged in Imperial China.

The right of consent is yet another fundamental principle adapted from corporate bodies to political practice. In religious corporations, canon law contained the concept that, in specific situations, executive authority cannot act without the consent of a consultative body. This notion rested on the principle that those who are directly affected by a decision have the right to participate in it. As

---

78. The first time that the concept was applied in a political context was when Pope Innocent III convened representatives with full powers of cities in the Papal States in the early thirteenth century. Other early examples of representatives with full powers are found in the general chapter of the Dominican Order, as well as in assemblies of city representatives convened in Tuscany by Frederick II in the thirteenth century (Tierney 1983).

stressed by Stasavage (2020), this idea of consent derived from a principle of Roman civil law, *quod omnes tangit*: matters that concern all should be approved by all. The canonists stressed, however, that what was required was the approval by the corporation as a whole, not by each individual member. The first formulation in a medieval text is in the *decretum* by Gratian (1140), as we will discuss in chapter 8.[79] This principle was subsequently applied to political councils, both in theory and in practice. The first application in ecclesiastic councils was by Pope Innocent III, and then later by emperors and kings. By the thirteenth century, it was widely referred to as a central principle of government.[80]

A third concept, also borrowed from canon law, was that of the *maior et sanior pars*, or "greater and sounder part," which in canonistic doctrine could express the will of a corporate group. Self-governing corporate bodies in medieval Europe needed election rules, which is where this principle came in. If the majority decision was judged unsound, members could make an appeal to a higher authority to overturn it. Within the highly hierarchical structure of the Church, where these rules originated, doing so was easy; but elsewhere, this rule was vague and unstable. As early as Saint Benedict, rule-makers discovered that every defeated minority claimed to be "*sanior*" than the majority (McLean et al. 2007, p. 43).

Majority voting, of course, was widely used in medieval Europe. The majority principle, the idea that decisions by a simple majority rather than unanimity are legitimate, was essential to corporate practices. This marked a definitive step away from the tradition of Germanic assemblies, which relied on unanimity or acclamation (a way to establish very broad consensus among all participating individuals). According to Ruffini (1976), the majority principle was first formally introduced in medieval Europe in small assemblies of guilds and other civil associations, after which it emerged in communes, and finally in larger political assemblies. Italian communes were among the first political bodies in medieval Europe to employ it formally.[81] In the early twelfth century,

79. Gratian was a twelfth-century Bolognese monk and jurist about whom little is known except his famous legal text *Decretum Gratiani* (c.1150), which earned him the accolade as the "father of canon law."

80. In 1244, the concept was cited explicitly by Holy Roman Emperor Frederick II in his letter summoning an Imperial council to meet in Verona, and it was cited by Edward I of England in his convocation of Parliament in 1295 (Post 1964).

81. Political applications of the majority principle are much older, going back to traditions in ancient Greek cities and in the Republic of Rome, where the Senate made decisions by majority vote, subject to the veto power of the plebeian tribunes.

communal councils and consuls typically used majority rule, and important decisions were often made through multiple complex voting procedures designed to prevent undue influence by powerful individuals. In Venice, for instance, the doge was elected after the late thirteenth century through a sequence of nine electoral councils.[82]

The struggle to find a voting mechanism that faithfully reflects the opinions of most people remained a topic of interest in a world of political thought, and it occupied some of the best minds of late medieval Europe, such as Ramon Llull and Nicholas of Cusa (Cusanus), as well as those of Enlightenment Europe such as Condorcet and Borda. Nevertheless, the practices that first emerged in corporations provided concrete and successful examples that were then adopted by larger political bodies. All these instances illustrate a common sequence in the evolution of institutions during the twelfth and thirteenth centuries. First, a norm of private law was absorbed by Church law; subsequently, it became a principle of constitutional law within the Church's administrative structure; and finally, it returned to the secular domain as a constitutional norm or practice (Tierney 1982; Berman 1983). This sequence also highlights that the Catholic Church and its growing reliance on legal foundations were decisive in the emergence of important modern political thought. If we are to understand the roots of the institutional Great Divergence, any account that leaves out the effects of the medieval Catholic Church would be deficient.

Modern democracies are of course built on much more sophisticated principles than their prototypes from the twelfth and thirteenth centuries. Since the late seventeenth century, it has been commonly understood that representative democracy is not sufficient to prevent political abuse by a majority, and checks and balances and separation of powers are also needed. Although these ideas became popular and influential during the Age of Enlightenment, their roots can be traced to thirteenth-century notions of mixed government and corporate politics, which in turn were derived from a specific kind of corporate organization. In particular, checks and balances were deliberately introduced in the canon law model of corporation used for some

---

82. An early example of the application of the majority principle in large political assemblies is the election of Emperor Henri VII in 1308. His brother, the archbishop Baldwin, successfully argued that the group of ecclesiastic and lay princes that elected the emperor was a corporate body, and the right of electing the emperor belonged to such a body, not to the individual princes. As such, the electoral college could decide by majority, and no single elector retained veto rights.

ecclesiastic organizations. Tierney (1982, pp. 26–27) points out that in medieval Europe, there were two broad classes of corporations: the Roman law
model and the canon law model. In the Roman law model, a corporation delegates powers to an official, who acts on behalf of the community. The powers
of the official are derived from those of the community that he represents. In
the constitutional adaptation of this principle, the emperor's power was
granted by his people. In a republican version, these powers could be revoked
by the community.

The canon law model of corporation was more complex and was mainly
used for ecclesiastic matters. Here, the executive office (typically the bishop)
had predefined powers and prerogatives. These prerogatives were not derived
from the body that elected him (typically the cathedral chapter), but they were
intrinsic to the office. Still, both the bishop and the chapter had their rights
and resources, and they governed together in a practice of mixed government
that contained some form of separation of power and authority. This second
type of corporate structure also entailed a variety of checks and balances
against the abuse of executive authority, and this was recognized at the time
in the theory and practice of ecclesiastic government.

The contractual and legal arrangements that permeated civil society were
not only relevant because they influenced the ideas of jurists and scholars.
They also had a deep impact on what citizens felt entitled to, and more broadly
on the sources of political legitimacy. As noted in this discussion, in the early
steps of state formation, besides the military, judicial, and legal institutions
were the most important manifestations of state powers. These institutions
protected private property and enforced private agreements. The legitimacy
of the state was tied to the expectation that these acts of government would
be carried out fairly and without arbitrary abuse, according to established customary rules and procedures. The political right of consent was a natural extension of this expectation.[83]

More generally, government by consent was a natural extension of the practical arrangements that permeated medieval societies. Tierney (1982, p. 40)
points out that the realities of medieval life were saturated with "consensual

---

83. When King Alfonso IX convened a parliament for the first time in 1188 in León, Spain,
he promised "to administer justice impartially and not to act arbitrarily. . . . The security of
persons and of property and the inviolability of the household also were guaranteed." He also
"acknowledged the existence of a body of law binding himself as well as his subjects" (O'Callahan
1979, quoted by van Zanden, 2012).

practices." Corporate groups chose their leaders by consent, and Church government was a structure of elective offices. Feudal contracts had a strong element of consent as well. The Enlightenment ideas of John Locke and Jean-Jacques Rousseau that connected legitimacy with consent seem almost a natural extension of these medieval concepts.[84] To be sure, medieval societies were highly hierarchical, and yet individuals were accustomed to specific rights, particularly property rights, formally defined and protected by the law. These rights and legal procedures also entailed limitations on what sovereigns could do, as well as on the meta-institutions that generated the rules by which society was organized. Existing practices could not be changed by the sovereign without due process, just as property could not be transferred without due process (Strayer 1970). Moreover, viewing the state as a corporate body entailed that it had a legal personality, distinct from that of the king or its public officials. This in turn allowed a distinction between the private domain of the king and his acts as a sovereign. It also implied that the exercise of sovereign authority could be regulated, and the agents of the Crown or of the state could even be sued by a private individual or corporation (Finer 1997, p. 1299).

In other words, individuals were not just passive subjects. For many practical purposes, they were "citizens" *avant la lettre*, entitled to specific and well-defined economic rights.[85] A legal framework had developed to sustain and enforce existing social organizations. The notion of political rights and the right of consent were natural extensions of this framework. The diffusion of consensual practices and power sharing in the realm of secular politics, as well as the principle that the ruler is also bound by the law, were natural steps (although highly significant) in the evolution of social arrangements.

China was very different in this respect. Formal legal frameworks existed but were much less important for regulating social interactions beyond criminal acts. Furthermore, the state's role as the enforcer of private contractual arrangements was much less prominent. As we discuss in chapter 8, China did

---

84. The idea of consent clearly precedes the Enlightenment and can be found in Aristotle's political writings. It has medieval roots that include the writings of the early fifteenth-century German intellectual and mathematician Nicolas of Cusa (Sabine 1960). John Milton wrote in 1649 that "the power of kings and magistrates is nothing else, but what is only derivative, transferred and committed to them in trust from the people, to the common good of them all, in whom the power yet remains fundamentally, and cannot be taken from them, without a violation of their natural birthright" (cited by Coker 1926, p. 282).

85. For a full discussion of formal and informal citizenship in medieval urban communities, see Prak (2018).

not develop a *formal* body of civil and commercial law. Commercial disputes were normally settled through arbitration and compromise within the clan if possible, and by a magistrate only if necessary. These differences in social organizations between China and Europe are reflected in the evolution of their political institutions. Because corporate structures were by and large absent, China also did not develop the concept of a legal personality. This implied that there was no formal distinction between the state and the emperor (unlike in Europe, Louis XIV's famous dictum, "l'etat c'est moi," notwithstanding).

Moreover, the absence of the concept of the state as a legal entity made it more difficult to defend individual rights against the state and to sue public officials. The notion that state authority could be subject to legal limits and formal procedures, that individuals had specific rights, and that the relation between the state and the individual was regulated by the law was alien to Chinese political thought. Imperial arbitrariness, as noted previously, was limited by Confucian moral strictures, traditional conceptions of fairness and, during some periods, also by constraints imposed by the bureaucracy. But the principle of the rule of codified formal law and the procedures for power sharing and political representation did not emerge in Imperial China.

6. Free Towns and the Evolution of Political Institutions

The rise of urban communes in the eleventh to thirteenth centuries discussed in chapter 6 played a fundamental role in the evolution of European political institutions. First, the charters of free towns contained on a small scale several of the foundational constitutional principles of modern democracies: protection of civil rights and political freedoms; elections and representative government; the separation of judicial, legislative, and executive powers; and term limits for officials. These principles exemplified how political institutions could be designed, and they shaped perceptions of legitimacy and fairness. A rich and detailed body of literature going back all the way to the work of the French historian François Guizot in the 1830s has looked at urban communes and city-states as the pioneers of representative government in Europe. From the earliest days of the revival of Roman law, legal scholars struggled with the questions of sovereign rights versus abuse of power. The solutions first applied to religious organizations found their most advanced application in the autonomous communities. Urban republicanism never amounted to a full-fledged political theory as much as a series of demands for being consulted and represented in local decision making, but it helped create the kind of political culture that influenced the evolution of sovereign constitutions. Whether they were "democratic" in the modern sense of the word remains in dispute, but what is clear is that nothing like the civic institutions that emerged in the towns of Germany, the Low Countries, and Italy can be seen in China or elsewhere in Asia and the Middle East (Bosker et al. 2013).

During the eleventh century, it became increasingly common for ordinary citizens to participate in city and local government. In small villages, participation took place in assemblies that included all citizens. In larger towns, mass participation was less feasible and a process of delegation took place. Committees of "upright men" were formed to take care of specific affairs. By the twelfth century, delegation became the norm. Most Italian cities were governed by consuls, who managed the city budget and resolved disputes between citizens and ecclesiastic authorities (the bishop or cathedral chapters). These consuls generally acted on behalf of different city sectors. In Florence, these were the parishes and the neighborhood associations. In Pisa, they represented territorial subdivisions.

Unlike the merchant guilds of northern Europe, in most Italian cities, the interests of merchants were represented in city government through dedicated consular delegations, which were often the most important consuls, although merchant guilds also existed in medieval Italian towns. In Genoa and Venice, guilds came late: in Genoa, they emerged only in the fourteenth century; and in Venice, it was said that the guilds were not needed because they all lived in one guild (cited by Ogilvie 2011, p. 52). In Pisa, Florence, and elsewhere, guilds were established much earlier. In France, communes also had councils to represent different groups of citizens. In some cases, council members represented crafts, with each occupational group having a counselor sitting on the board and participating in joint decisions. In other cases, they were based on territorial subdivisions, as in much of Italy. In northern Europe, the statutes of several municipalities reserved seats in city councils for representatives of the craft guilds, and in some instances, guilds held a majority of the seats. Whether they were guilds or neighborhood organizations, these factions were eventually incorporated into the city's administration.[86]

Wahl (2016 2018) collected detailed data on the governing institutions of about 300 cities in northern Europe (including Austria, Belgium, Germany,

---

86. Guilds and communes were often interconnected: "Sometimes merchant guilds preceded the establishment of a commune, and sometimes guilds were set up after some measure of self-government of the city was realized" (Van Zanden 2008, p. 355).

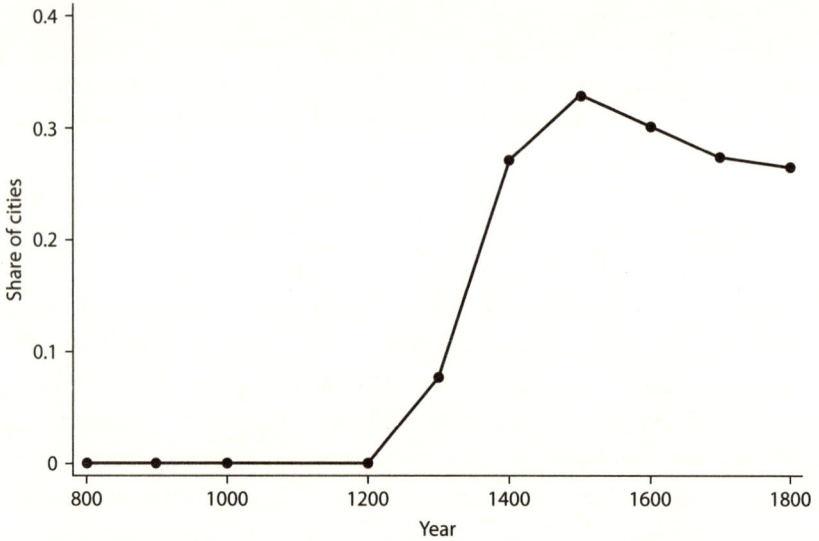

FIGURE 7.1. Fraction of cities with guild representation on city councils.
Source: Wahl (2016).
Note: The vertical axis measures the fraction of cities that reserved seats for guilds in their city council (Guild Participation Index = 1, 2), in a sample of about 300 cities in northern Europe.

the Netherlands, Poland, Switzerland, and a few cities in France). As shown in figure 7.1, guilds started being represented in city councils in the thirteenth century, and by 1400, about one-third of the cities in this sample had guild representatives on their councils.

Over time, the communal open institutions started to weaken. Many towns experienced the concentration of power in the hands of a few powerful families and turned increasingly oligarchic. This was most obvious in Venice, which underwent a *serrata* (closing), where most citizens were excluded from power between 1297 and 1327.[87] The closure spared Venice the political instability and civil strife of many other Italian autonomous cities. The naive notion of cities as autonomous, free, and democratic, as advocated by historians such as Henri Pirenne, clearly is an oversimplification. As discussed in chapter 6, originally,

87. For a highly original and striking description and economic analysis of the Venetian *serrata,* see Puga and Trefler (2014). A similar trend can be seen later elsewhere, such as the Andrea Doria reforms in Genoa in 1528, which for all practical purposes excluded the lower classes from government.

members of a commune swore to uphold the peace (*pax villae*), which created local solidarity. But in many areas, such solidarity weakened over time. This was often due to one of two cases: either a powerful, centralized state encroached upon the autonomy of the commune; or cities that retained their autonomy became dominated by a small group of powerful families or a single one (Signoria). All the same, these features of urban corporations were of decisive importance when sovereign nations began to develop more sophisticated political institutions. As Boone (2012, p. 348) states, European towns "succeeded in launching a set of social and legal constructs which in the long run did have a fundamental influence in the search for an equilibrium between private interest and the commonwealth, the *bonum commune*."

Besides being an influential example of small-scale political communities, self-governing cities shaped the evolution of European political institutions, thanks to their prerogatives within nation-states. As discussed earlier in this chapter, the attachment of political rights to corporate organizations, not just to powerful individuals, was a key step in the evolution of European representative institutions. Once cities gained substantial autonomy, they were more likely to be represented in national assemblies and parliaments. Moreover, independent cities were also more likely to support the prerogatives of Parliament to limit the authority of the sovereign and to resist his attempts to circumvent Parliament. Angelucci et al. (2021) compare English cities that were given authority by the king to raise taxes through so-called Farm Grants (and thus were given a great deal of autonomy, such as the right to appoint judges and regulate economic activity) to other similar cities that could not enjoy similar privileges because they remained under the control of local lords. They find that cities granted this independent status before 1348 were much more likely to take steps to protect and strengthen Parliament against royal authority.[88] Independent cities mostly took Parliament's side during the Civil War of 1642, and as late as the nineteenth century, their political representatives also tended to vote in favor of the Great Reform Act of 1832—an important step in the democratization of England (Angelucci et al. 2019). Not all European cities were equally successful in checking the absolutist tendencies of their sovereign, however. According to Angelucci et al. (2021), this different influence of independent cities in shaping the evolution of national institutions across

---

88. Parliament allowed such autonomous towns to coordinate their negotiations with the king and form a more or less unified front when dealing with the fiscal demands of the Crown.

Europe is one of the reasons why absolutist tendencies prevailed during the sixteenth and seventeenth centuries in France and Spain, but not in England.

As discussed in chapter 6, cultural factors and legal traditions played a fundamental role in how city institutions were designed. Urban elites were familiar with a multitude of corporate social organizations and the legal theories that they rested on, and it was natural for them to extend the principles of those contractual and legal arrangements to urban law as well. Berman (1983) argues that the rise of independent cities and their organizational features was due to a set of cultural traits and legal traditions that were unique to Western Europe. What made this phenomenon possible during the late eleventh and twelfth centuries in Western Europe and not elsewhere was a multitude of new legal concepts, institutions, and practices that permeated society through several corporate structures. Everyone belonged to a plurality of overlapping communities, each one bound by specific legal and contractual arrangements and by formalized systems of governance. "Without urban legal consciousness and a system of urban law, it is hard to imagine European cities and towns coming into existence at all" (Berman 1983, p. 362).

The idea that the emergence of European communes reflected familiarity with other corporate organizations and a universalistic, as opposed to communitarian, cultural environment is supported by quantitative evidence. Schulz (2022) has measured the extent to which different European cities were exposed to the policy of the Western Church against incest and cousin marriage. As discussed in chapter 4, these policies had an important effect on the dismantling of extended kin networks in Western Europe and on replacing kin-based cultural traits with a universalistic culture, more open to cooperation with unrelated individuals. The Church first banned cousin marriage (a proxy for the strength of extended kinship) sometime between 500 and 550 AD.[89] Schulz found that cities with greater exposure to these Church policies were more likely to become communes (according to the classification in Bosker et al. 2013) and eventually to develop democratic institutions. Moreover,

---

89. Thus, Schulz (2022) measures city exposure to this policy by the number of years that a city was within 100 kilometers of the nearest location of a bishop of the Western Church after 550. This indicator varies over time, though, because the location of bishoprics was not time invariant. Strength of enforcement is measured by being closer to a bishopric whose bishop participated in a synod that ruled over incest legislation, exploiting synodal activity over an extended period of time. The paper also exploits other sources of variation of Church policy, based on the extension of the marriage prohibition to more distant cousins or on the strength of enforcement of such prohibitions.

stricter and more extensive cousin-marriage prohibitions are positively associated with being a commune within Christian Europe.

Empirical evidence drawn from other contexts also points to a strong association between universalistic (as opposed to kin-based) culture and more democratic political arrangements. Henrich (2020) discusses extensive evidence in psychology and anthropology of how societies founded on kinship ties are less favorable to impersonal interactions, generalized trust, respect for individual rights, and participatory forms of governance in social and political organizations. Schulz (2022) studies family arrangements in preindustrial ethnicities using data from the *Ethnographic Atlas*. He shows that ethnicities that discourage or prohibit cousin marriage (and hence are characterized by nuclear families) are more likely to have local democratic traditions, meaning that their leaders are chosen by consensus rather than by hereditary rights or other nondemocratic means.[90] Although these correlations are very robust, they could be driven by omitted variables, and hence they cannot be interpreted as strictly causal. Nevertheless, they suggest that the association between culture, family organizations, and political institutions, regardless of the exact causal mechanisms, is a general phenomenon that goes well beyond the historical examples of China and Europe.

Scholars have also provided direct evidence of a dynamic complementarity between the features of lower-level organizations and those of political institutions. Giuliano and Nunn (2013) also use the *Ethnographic Atlas* to construct historical indicators of democratic arrangements at the local (i.e., village) level practiced by distant ancestors. These indicators are the same used by Schulz (2022), and they refer to the methods for choosing a local leader. After aggregating these ancient indicators of local democracy at the country level, Giuliano and Nunn (2013) show that countries with more diffuse practices of local democracy in the distant past are also more likely to be democratic and to have better institutions (as measured by respect for the rule of law and control of corruption) today. Moreover, exploiting survey data, they show that individuals currently living in countries with more village-level democracy in

90. Schulz (2022) also aggregates ethnic data on cousin marriage at the country level and measures national political institutions through the Polity IV indicator of democracy. Across countries, the prevalence of current democracy is negatively correlated with preindustrial ethnicities that allowed cousin marriage, as well as with contemporary data on the prevalence of cousin marriage. Countries that were more exposed to the Western Church ban on cousin marriage are also more likely to be democratic today.

the distant past are more supportive of democracy at the national level. This evidence too supports the idea that European political institutions evolved to incorporate checks and balances and elements of accountability and participation also because its citizens were already accustomed to lower-level organizations with similar features.

7. Concluding Remarks

The differences between the Chinese and European paths of political development came about because of a plurality of factors pushing the two societies in opposite directions. To sum up:

- The Chinese state achieved political centralization and built administrative institutions very early in its development. In Europe, instead, the protracted collapse of the Western Roman Empire and the barbarian invasions left a highly fragmented society, with different ethnic groups settling in different areas and no effective central authority within each area.
- When the development of state institutions finally resumed in late medieval Europe after many centuries, new social organizations had emerged and several groups in society held economic and political power. European rulers had to come to terms with the nobility, the Church, free towns, and other corporate bodies. In China, instead, the state evolved while the economy was still relatively underdeveloped and before the emergence of strong countervailing powers. The different order of events was important. European rulers had to share powers with other organized interests and accept that their legitimacy depended de facto on the consent of their subjects (at least the most powerful of them). Chinese emperors, instead, could exploit a strong central bureaucracy under their direct control, but they faced the challenge of controlling a vast territory through a hierarchy of scholar-bureaucrats, and faced complex agency problems when dealing with local issues.
- China and Europe developed different social organizations to sustain local cooperation. While in Song China, the clan dominated as the solution to collective action problems, in Europe, corporations increasingly fulfilled this role. This divergence mattered not only for their effect on power relations, but also for the evolution of legal institutions

and the rule of law. European corporate groups were formed by the free choice of their members and were held together by formal agreements. Principles of consent and representative decision making, paired with the granting of immunity to corporate bodies, influenced the way that legal and political institutions developed, particularly in the acceptance of rule of law. In China, clans enforced commercial agreements and cooperative arrangements through arbitration and informal social sanctions, while formal state law primarily concerned the criminal and administrative domains (as we discuss in chapter 8). Moreover, clans were ascriptive, hierarchical, and closed organizations held together by custom and social norms and a shared respect for common ancestors, and they did not have a tight control over their territory. All these features of dynastic organizations facilitated the evolution toward more unrestrained forms of government in China.

- Value systems were also very different in these two parts of the world. Value systems matter not only because they facilitate the emergence of specific social organizations, but also because they point to different sources of political legitimacy, and different notions of what are acceptable or unacceptable political actions and arrangements. Western Europe increasingly shared an individualistic culture, based on universalistic norms of good conduct and on the principle that all men are equal in front of God (Siedentop 2014). China, instead, had a collectivistic culture that emphasized loyalty to one's kin, the authority of the elders within the extended family, and the supremacy of the emperor. Since these different cultural traits were backed by different social organizations, including different religious organizations, they were resilient and not easily malleable by political authorities (Greif 1994; Gorodnichenko and Roland 2011).

The historical evolution of value systems and institutions point to a main conclusion of general validity: there was a dynamic complementarity in the evolution of social organizations and political institutions. In Europe, complex legal frameworks and judicial institutions evolved to sustain the widespread corporate arrangements. The legal foundations of civil society then influenced the evolution of political institutions. In China, dynastic social organizations and kin-based culture led to a different path of legal and institutional development. Thus, prevalent culture affected the evolution of political institutions, both directly and indirectly, through its impact on social organizations,

Of course, the dynamic complementarity between culture, social organizations, and political institutions is not like an immutable law of physics. Many other forces were at work, including the personalities of political leaders and the distribution of military and economic power in society. The trajectory of political evolution in Europe was far from monotonic. There were reversals and setbacks, such as the absolutism of the Tudors and early Stuarts in Britain, and in France, where the Estates General failed to meet between 1614 and 1789. Absolutism triumphed in several European states for prolonged periods, and it is not until the Enlightenment that it came under serious pressure (and fought back, in many cases successfully). As time passed, however, these absolutistic episodes came increasingly in conflict with prevailing culture, with prevalent social practices, and with political institutions in neighboring states. As opposition became more forceful, absolutism became more isolated, and in most places, it was eventually terminated. Yet the ongoing struggle between open, democratic, and liberal political institutions and autocracy remains a struggle to this day.

8

The State and Social Organizations

1. Introduction

In both China and Europe, state institutions interacted extensively with private social organizations. Early European sovereign states did not have extensive administrative capacities. Around the year 1000 AD, Imperial China had a much more developed central administration, but the territory that it controlled was also much more widespread. As a consequence, in both Europe and China, the state rulers utilized decentralized local adjudication and administration bodies to carry out local responsibilities. As discussed in previous chapters, Chinese clans assisted local magistrates in tax collection, resolved disputes, and invested in infrastructure. Similarly, European cities assessed and collected taxes, provided local security and several other local public goods, regulated commerce, and provided financial and military resources when needed.

These interactions would shape the development of state and social organizations. Social organizations' administrative responsibilities as delegated by the state strengthened their influence and enhanced their reputations. In return, the decentralization of some administrative roles to nonstate actors also influenced the evolution of state institutions. However, Europe and China relied on very different kinds of social organizations. As a result, the interaction between the state and social organizations led state institutions to evolve along increasingly divergent trajectories. These divergent institutional trajectories and social arrangements also influenced market interactions, causing feedback effects on the initially different value systems that prevailed in Europe and China.

This bifurcation between China and Europe is most evident in two spheres: in the evolution of fiscal capacity and of their legal systems. As discussed in chapter 2, fiscal capacity declined in China after the Song Dynasty, while it grew in Europe. One important reason for this divergence related to the political prerogatives of social organizations in both civilizations. As discussed in chapter 7, medieval European states built their fiscal capacity at the same time as they developed their political institutions. Due to bargaining with local elites over tax revenues, this led to European sovereigns often granting political rights in exchange for cooperation in raising taxes. Such political rights tended to involve corporate interests and powerful elites having some say about how the sovereign collected and used revenue. Beyond important consequences for governance principles, the notion of consent in this context became increasingly significant, as it made raising revenue in times of need easier, especially during wars.

More generally, representative institutions increased the political legitimacy of central government taxation, and this in turn enhanced tax compliance and reduced the cost of tax collection. In other words, taxpayers who have consented to the imposition of a tax are less likely to try to evade it, which makes collection more efficient. The extent to which this happened in practice, varied across Europe. England, for example, built stronger representative institutions and evolved into a much more effective and resourceful state than absolutist France. On the other hand, medieval English kings were weaker than their French counterparts vis-à-vis their constituents and were forced to make greater concessions to the nobility and to free towns on the prerogative of Parliament. Ironically, over time, this facilitated tax collection in England relative to France because there was more trust that tax revenues would not be wasted or misused (Levi 1988). Overall, tax revenue per capita grew over time throughout Europe, with a sharp acceleration after the late seventeenth century.

China developed its tax capacity much earlier than Europe. In the eleventh century, China was able to collect as much as 10 percent of national income from tax revenues.[1] But rather than increasing further, China's fiscal capacity slowly shriveled over the centuries, and by the nineteenth century, it was smaller than that of European states by an order of magnitude. While some part of this certainly reflects the difficulties of controlling a much larger territory, it was also the consequence of an increasingly inefficient state apparatus that was not able to coopt the economic interests of Chinese society to pursue priorities. As a consequence, the agency problems between the center and the periphery were much more difficult to resolve and impaired tax collection (Sng 2014).

---

1. Guo (2020, p. 64) has recently estimated total state revenue at 17 percent around 1000 AD and around 10–11 percent in the late eleventh century.

The great paradox of Chinese political history is that from the Song Dynasty onward, we see a polity in which state capacity, as conventionally defined, became weaker over time. The ability of the Imperial administration to control and tax the population was weakening as the taxing powers of the bureaucracy waned. Yet, at the same time, the emperors became more autocratic and the dynasties more durable. The political scientist Yuhua Wang (2022, p. 13) has sought to explain these seemingly contradictory trends by arguing that Chinese rulers faced a "trade-off between their survival and state strength," which he calls "the sovereign's dilemma." By weakening central elites, he asserted, rulers reduced their ability to rebel against him. But this also undermined the emperor's ability to deploy central elites and thus diminished state capacity. According to this hypothesis, Chinese emperors increasingly came to favor their regime's survival over state strength. As a result, especially under the Qing Dynasty, a process of "state involution" took place, leading to "the rapid growth of clan collective action" (Wang 2022, pp. 44). As Wang put it (2022, p. 172):

> Social organizations filled the void left by a weakened state after the Song times. Lineage institutions helped local elites overcome their collective action and coordination problems and provide public goods and services. . . . When rebels arrived, and the government army was defending only the cities, the lineages armed up. Imperial rule stayed resilient facing external and internal challenges not because the state was strong, but because social forces stepped in.

In other words, the symbiotic relationship between the Imperial bureaucracy and the clans and the gentry gradually became the mainstay of local public goods and the governance of the nation. Such a symbiosis depended, however, on appropriate cultural beliefs (i.e., between values that induced support for government and the prerogatives of local elites). In China, such support came from neo-Confucian ideology. As Faure (2007, p. 7) noted, "The growth of an ideology that posited education and scholarship as its center also promoted a body of go-betweens that brokered the relationships between government and local society." This role was played by the local gentry, educated in academies that prepared people for the Imperial examinations, focused on neo-Confucian wisdom.

Chinese lineages, much like European corporations, were not designed or created with that purpose in mind. Their growing importance in the daily management of life was an emergent property, an unintended consequence of multiple uncoordinated interactions between isolated decisions. Much like corporations in Europe, clans provided a solution to the collective action problems that were obstacles to the provision of local public goods. But unlike corporations, clans utilized a different approach to this issue. They facilitated familial solidarity through a shared ancestor, reinforced by practices of ancestor worship. The clan created the possibilities of rewarding cooperators and punishing opportunistic behavior. It owned common property through lineage trusts. Clans constituted a social system that was stable, peaceful, and effective in ensuring the kind of resilience that Chinese history displays. But this system was also stagnant. As Wang put it (2022, p. 172), the Chinese clans traded prosperity for peace and stability. Yet peace and stability turned out to be increasingly elusive with the decline of fiscal capacity in China, whereas in Europe, state capacity kept increasing in the long run, if perhaps by fits and starts.

With the divergence of state capacity, legal systems diverged as well, and the European system of law that emerged during the Middle Ages was novel and unique. Indeed, despite the heterogeneity and variability over time within Europe, the body and theoretical basis of European law remained a coherent and defining feature that set "the West" apart from other civilizations.[2] China, too, had a characteristic legal system and paved its own road to a society of law and order. The roots of the bifurcation in legal systems between the two civilizations go very far in time. To this point, Liang (1989) argued that these differences are rooted in the states' origins.[3] In Liang's opinion, the idea that

2. Berman (1983, p. 24), in his authoritative history of Western legal traditions, notes that "the legal institutions of the various nations of Europe, although they became more distinctively national and less European from the sixteenth century on, nevertheless retained their Western character. . . . There were many common bonds among the various national legal systems. All these systems share some basic modes of categorization. For example, they all strike a balance between legislation and adjudication and, in adjudication, between code law and case law. They make a sharp division between criminal law and civil law."

3. As Liang sees it, in "classical civilization," the laws of ancient Greece and Rome were born of conflicts between commoners and the elite. The two sides forged a compromise that ultimately became the essential means for defining and preserving the rights of the various segments of society. In China, on the other hand, the state and its legal structure were born of conflicts between clans and were a means by which the dominant clan imposed its will on the others using coercion. Its primary manifestation was harsh punishment. Liang (1989, p. 79) reflects the traditional view of Chinese state when he writes that "unadorned statecraft took the place of a theory of political justice. Law was seen as the will of the rulers and an instrument of suppression." Modern scholarship has significantly modified but not wholly reversed this interpretation (So and So 2022).

the emperor's subjects had rights was alien to Chinese law. Consequently, Chinese formal law concentrated on criminal matters, and nothing like what we think of as constitutional law emerged. The so-called *Canon of Laws*, allegedly written in one of the states during the Warring States Era (preceding the Qin unification of China), was "penal law and nothing more" (Liang 1989, p. 85). Recent scholarship has modified this stark picture of Chinese law. However, the overarching fact is that Chinese and European legal systems still differed dramatically and evolved in very different ways.

One of the most remarkable legal phenomena of medieval Europe was the development of a concept of a *formal* body of civil law. This principle remains one of the foundations of European society and governance. European civil law is a compilation of codified rules and scholarly analyses concerned with property, commerce, contract enforcement, and dispute resolution. It emerged after 1100, building on the foundations of Roman law inherited from antiquity. Civil law evolved through a bottom-up process as jurists and scholars worked to standardize best practices that emerged spontaneously among private arrangements, and corporations played an important role in shaping this evolution.

The contrast with China is stark. The traditional view in the legal historiography of China posited that until the late nineteenth century, formal civil law was mostly absent. This view, as noted previously, has undergone revisions. It is now recognized that civil law in China took a different form from that of Europe. In China, there were still rules and norms that allowed commerce, borrowing, and exchange and facilitated the ownership, mortgaging, and sale of property. However, these were not formally codified. The preeminence of clans in resolving intraclan disputes biased economic interactions toward intraclan transactions, which in turn reduced the incentives to invest in formal legal codes and their enforcement.

These differences between the Chinese and European legal systems thus reflect the various forms taken by social organizations in these two societies, and in particular, European corporations created demand for external and formal enforcement, while Chinese clans relied on informal procedures. Feedback went two ways, from social organizations to legal norms and vice versa. European corporations, which were formal legal entities, had a greater demand for external enforcement in the courts compared to Chinese clans. At the same time, the codification of European civil law led to formal recognition and the dissemination of legally defined corporate structures and shaped how corporations evolved. By contrast, the Chinese legal system encouraged clans to evolve in a different, less formal direction, resulting in a very different legal ecosystem.

In this chapter, we describe the interactions between state institutions and social organizations, describing the role that the latter played in supporting decentralized administrations. We also highlight how this helps to explain the divergent paths of tax capacity taken by China and Europe. We then describe in some detail the differences in the histories of their respective legal systems and take a closer look at the differences in market institutions between East and West. We close the chapter with three specific examples that illustrate our argument: criminal law enforcement, voluntary charity, and the lower echelons of local administration.

2. The Roles of Clans and Corporations in Decentralized Administrations

How Clans Evolved by Interacting with the State

As noted in chapter 5, the evolution of Chinese lineages was in part a spontaneous and unintended consequence of state policies. These policies created powerful incentives to act collectively as a dynastic group, inducing individuals related by their kin to strengthen their dynastic organization.[4] For instance, during the Song Dynasty, local security was organized in the so-called *Baojia* system, which attempted to extend Imperial authority to the subcounty level. The *Baojia* was essentially a neighborhood watch and collective responsibility network. However, the central administration had little control over its composition and, far from being a successful attempt to control local government, it remained "deeply rooted in the local clans/lineages establishments" (Deng 2004, p. 37).[5] It serves as an example of how Imperial policies helped strengthen the clans by outsourcing important aspects of local administration.

Two state policies initiated during the early years of the Ming Dynasty, land taxes and military recruitment, induced households to organize around their

---

4. Szonyi (2002, chapter 3), discusses several illuminating examples in the Fuzhou region in the southeast, during the early Ming Dynasty.

5. The *Baojia* fell into disuse under the Ming and was revived only in Qing times, when it merged with the local taxation or *lijia* system described next. Deng (2004, p. 37) describes the *lijia* system as "a state-endorsed guild" for fiscal purposes, which was anything but a branch of the state bureaucracy.

lineages and accelerated the transformation of clans into an unofficial—yet important—political force at the local level. For a variety of reasons, some households and their patrilineal descendants were registered as "military households." This entailed a requirement to fulfill military duty and other military obligations. The requirement was collective: if the current soldier designated from a family died or fell ill, the family had to send another person to replace him. It was also a hereditary requirement, which would be passed on from generation to generation regardless of living arrangements. The Ming military policy thus induced groups belonging to the same lineage to organize themselves: they updated their patrilineal genealogies and pooled resources (often land) to pay for the needs of the selected soldier and his immediate family or for other military funding responsibilities that fell to the lineage.

The Ming Dynasty also instituted a land registration policy, which had similar consequences for clan consolidation. The heads of the stronger lineages were responsible for the state. They exacted taxation according to their own systems, as opposed to the official *lijia* system. In the early years of the Qing Dynasty, further tax reforms legitimized this system (Szonyi 2002, pp. 76–77). The *lijia* system described in chapter 5 increased the wealth and power of the largest families, who had the authority to collect taxes from other groups; at the same time, it led to the almost total breakdown of the subbureaucratic Imperial governance system (Nimick 2008, pp. 36–37). By the late fifteenth century, the *lijia* system had collapsed, but the clan system continued to expand.[6] By the end of the eighteenth century, local lineages had grown even more powerful, and most attempts to curb them or harness them directly to the administration's attempts to exert local control had failed (Naquin and Rawski 1987, pp. 16–17; Zhang 2017, p. 211).

The land registration system also had important implications for the transfer of land. Without revisions to the official registration, the original owner of the property was held responsible for tax liabilities, even when the land was sold. This system therefore encouraged transfers of property within the lineage

6. The end of the *lijia* system did not bring an end to its consequences. The *lijia* system altered local society and the local administration and their relationships in a way that lasted until the end of the empire. During the fifty-odd years of the *lijia* system, the system permanently increased the power of the local clans and forced magistrates to be flexible in negotiating with them. By design, the Hundred-Chiefs were from among the richest families in the community and the *lijia* system increased their wealth and power. In the late fifteenth century, "large families, particularly in wealthier areas . . . [were able] to gain so much power that local officials had trouble dealing with them" (Nimick 2008, p. 47).

and discouraged sales to nonclan-members (Faure 2007, pp. 182, 189). The policy also induced lineages to become more involved in business activities, particularly with respect to investment and ownership. As we will discuss in this chapter, the Qing legal system was rather insensitive to the needs of business and its practices. An ancestral trust, as a landholding estate, could enforce its rights over the land in a court of law since land deeds, derived from tax registration, were recognized by the courts. The same was not true of business partnerships. Hence, if disputes were to arise on the ownership or running of a commercial enterprise, a lineage could expect the courts to ascertain and validate their right to the land (and therefore to the enterprise) through tax registration. The same could not be done for a business contract on its own (Faure 2007, p. 229). The lineage thus provided the legal claim to the land where the commercial enterprise would be located. As a result of these gradual evolutions, large lineage landholding conglomerates became common from the sixteenth century on.

As Chinese commercialization progressed and market-driven business transactions became more complex, lineage-based social organizations also worked to protect business interests in the absence of the legal system, which was often unable to protect business interests. The lineages contained systems of self-governance and loyalty that allowed business operations to be conducted and contracts to be upheld (Rowe 1998, pp. 385–86; Zelin 2022, p. 326). In many cases, lineages could utilize networks of personal connections with local officials if they had ties via the Imperial bureaucracy if some members of the lineage had been successful in passing the *keju* examinations.[7] Thus, the Civil Service Examination is another instance where state policies influenced clan evolution.

The state thus exploited these dynastic networks for public administration, tax collection, conflict resolution, and education, which in turn enhanced the clan's local political power. In short, the coevolution of clans and the Imperial administration reinforced the political architecture that formed the base of the Chinese state. Even though clans emerged through a bottom-up process, they ended up creating a deep and effective symbiosis with the Imperial bureaucracy. The combined *lijia* and *Baojia* systems rendered clans indispensable for administering the empire at the local level and marked the beginning of

---

7. For instance, in 1849, a contract for the subletting of a market stall was being debated, and an attempt to take it in front of the magistrate failed; therefore, the matter was dealt with directly by the lineage, which put in place their own system: "Reliance on magisterial authority to bar subletting must have been quite rare. Much more often, owners of the market maintained their own enforcers in the marketplace" (Faure 2007, p. 230).

China's gentry-dominated society. It should be kept in mind that despite its size, the Imperial administration had little contact with 90 percent of people in rural areas (Teng 1977, p. 122). The relationship with local elites and clan leaders provided such contacts. In short, the symbiotic relation between clans and the mandarinate was a win-win process, supported both by the central government and local notables. It delivered local public goods and was consistent with the prevailing value system.

Within the conceptual framework discussed in chapter 3, the spread of Chinese lineage organizations throughout society also reflected a dynamic of strategic complementarities: that is, the benefits of being a member of an organized clan increased, as did the prevalence of other clans. As one dynastic group gained economic and political power, other households located in close proximity would also be induced to organize in similar groups as a countervailing force.[8] Despite the system's flaws, it remained a stable equilibrium until the second half of the nineteenth century, when its astonishing resilience and longevity were eventually undone by external forces.

The Administrative Roles of European Cities

Like Chinese clans, European cities played an important role in state administration. An important reason was that self-governing cities had built considerable tax capacity thanks to their inclusive political arrangements.[9] Citizens had the right to participate in the political process of their community, but they committed to paying a fair share of taxes and being ready to defend the city. Because of their more compact size, representative assemblies of the town or some of the other corporate bodies in it could meet easier and more frequently, and participation increased.[10] As a result, independent city-states and autonomous cities that were formally part of the lands controlled by a suzerain could raise much more

8. Quoting again from Zheng (2001, p. 240): "To oppose stronger surname groups . . . a number of small lineages of different surnames might combine into a single same-surname organization. . . . The development of these kinds of same-surname lineages and multiple-surname lineages reflects the adaptability of lineage organization, and also the extent to which the entire social structure was shaped and permeated by lineage principles and organizational forms."

9. Besley and Persson (2011) discuss extensively how inclusive political institutions enable state capacity.

10. Stasavage (2011, p. 51) points out that meetings in cities could be readily convened by ringing a bell or via the town crier, whereas representative bodies that spanned larger geographical areas suffered from absenteeism.

tax revenue per capita via participatory means, compared to feudal states that relied on coercion to extract resources. Thes importance of this fact is reflected in Stasavage's (2011) finding that autonomous European cities had far better access to credit than territorial states. The existence of a representative assembly, he found, was a central factor in determining access to good credit because it meant that citizens could monitor their executives better. In such places, citizens supervised expenditures closely and representatives collected taxes effectively. Creditors therefore assigned such polities higher creditworthiness.[11]

The role of self-governing cities in state administration may seem surprising because their autonomy limited the authority of the state within their walls. But despite being at times rebellious and recalcitrant, the urban communes of Western and Central Europe were on the whole useful tools and reliable agents for the rulers. Furthermore, more often than not, rulers and communes shared common interests. Communes supported rulers financially, and in turn rulers provided public goods such as security, a system of law and wider dispute resolution, and a stable currency. Communes also supplied military resources. Their self-governance, well-organized population, and production capacity, as well as the war technology of the period, rendered cities militarily formidable.[12] Indeed, having walled and well-defended cities was an important difference between Europe and China (Rosenthal and Wong 2011) and between Europe and the Islamic world (Bosker, Buringh, and Van Zanden 2013). Recent scholarship identified this difference as one component explaining the rise of state capacity in Europe (Dincecco and Onorato 2018).

The decentralized practices of administration in Europe showed remarkable tenacity, and attempts to centralize governance and tax collection were

---

11. In the words of van Zanden and Prak (2006, pp. 115–16): "By creating the conditions for trust and cooperation, citizen arrangements radically lowered the transaction costs of the exchange between state and inhabitants. This led to an increased supply of public goods at relatively low cost to the economy."

12. The best-known demonstration of communes' military capacity is provided by the Italian cities and the famed victory at Legnano in 1176. By 1183, the emperor of the Holy Roman Empire was forced to recognize the failure of his thirty-year quest to subdue the northern Italian cities and confirmed their independence. But communes were militarily formidable elsewhere. Two thirds of the thirty-six castles that William the Conqueror built in England were situated near communes to ensure their submission and cooperation. This aim is well reflected in the fact that most of them, like the Tower of London, were built outside these cities' walls. The Flemish burghers defeated the French royal army in the Battle of the Golden Spurs in 1302. The association of northern European cities known as the Hansa was sufficiently strong militarily to defeat Denmark in the fourteenth century.

doomed for a long time.[13] It took until the eighteenth century for rulers to consolidate and standardize governance practices to the point that economies of scale could be realized. Self-governing cities provided states with administrative services and resources, including contingent military support (through an urban militia) over which the cities retained direct control.[14] This arrangement was the result of a bargain between two separate entities rather than a top-down imposition from an absolutist ruler. This finely balanced equilibrium was supported by a set of formal rules that ensured compliance with the balance of power. If the ruler overreached his prerogatives, conflict ensued.[15] It is thus not surprising that rulers tried to prevent cities from organizing

13. In England, the king attempted to centralize the assessment and collection of direct tax in the late thirteenth and early fourteenth centuries by imposing indirect taxes on movable goods. The attempt failed due to corruption and underassessment. In 1334, the revealed high cost of creating an effective centralized fiscal administration induced King Edward III to revert to a decentralized system. From 1334 to 1623, each taxpaying unit paid the same fraction that it had paid in 1334 (Brown 1989, p. 73), and the collection of the tax was left to local authorities (the counties and towns). Similarly, in fifteenth-century Florence, the authorities attempted to centralize taxation by conducting a broad census (the famous catasto). After three years, it became clear that the cost of such direct taxation was too high. Tax farming, in which the ruler literally sold administrative power to local collectors in exchange for much-needed cash, became the rule in much of Europe, nowhere more than in France (Johnson and Koyama 2014).

14. For example, after 1155, the English navy was financed, staffed, and controlled by the Cinque Ports, a confederation of cities. The chief obligation laid upon the ports, as a corporate duty, was to provide fifty-seven ships for fifteen days' service to the king annually, the costs distributed to each of the original five towns and seven more, known as "limbs." In return, the towns received a variety of privileges and tax exemptions. In France, cities contributed 64 percent of the sergeants in Philip Augustus's army in 1202, and 100 percent of the army sent by Louis IX in 1233 to restore order at Beauvais (Verbruggen 1997, p. 165). Castilian cities collected the sales tax for the Crown. while the corporation of the famous Mesta (the sheep-owners guild) was responsible for taxing wool, again in exchange for protection and many privileges. In Germany, the leagues of Swabian cities, which had had a long and difficult relationship with the emperors, established a police force in 1488 that kept the peace and suppressed rebellious local knights and helped suppress the peasant rebellion on 1525.

15. One example of such a conflict is the history of the relations between the city of Ghent and its Burgundian rulers in the fifteenth century. When Duke Philip of Burgundy (nicknamed "Philip the Good") proposed a new tax on salt and flour, the town leaders balked. War broke out, in which the Burgundians prevailed and a humiliating peace was imposed on Ghent in 1453. A generation later, Archduke (later Emperor) Maximilian of Habsburg (who was married to Philip's granddaughter Mary) was captured by the Ghent citizens (1487) and forced to make far-reaching concessions. Yet rulers could and often did play one city against another, and in the end, Ghent was defeated and its central role moved to Antwerp in the early sixteenth century.

collectively against him.[16] But in general, both rulers and those who constrained them gained from coordinating expectations regarding rights and obligations. However, after the Middle Ages, a growing tension emerged between European rulers seeking to centralize their power and corporations that wanted to maintain their autonomy. Perhaps the best-known example of such conflict is the establishment of royal intendants in France replacing local functionaries. This was made a permanent feature of royal power by Cardinal Richelieu in the first half of the seventeenth century (and unleashed a rebellion by local notables known as the Fronde).[17] Rulers increasingly came to depend, in different ways, on the growth of central bureaucracies that they controlled. The system that emerged was a fusion of centralized and local administration. For a long time, centralized government remained dependent on local agents possessing a great deal of local information and autonomy.[18]

As late as the eighteenth century, states strategically employed their local administrative power to govern and tax their residents. The Company of General Farms, created by Jean-Baptiste Colbert a century before the French Revolution, persisted as an important part of the country's fiscal system (White 2004).[19] In much of southern Europe, decentralized administrative structures were well

16. The German Golden Bull of 1356 explicitly condemned "unlawful assemblies in the cities and out of them, and associations between city and city . . . and confederations and pacts" and explicitly threatened cities that violated this with heavy fines (clause 15).

17. Another striking example is the fate of the Habsburg kings. To finance his many wars, the Spanish king Philip II mandated an increase in the sales tax (*alcabala*) the Spanish towns collected for him in 1575. The Castilian Cortes, the "standard bearer of urban elites" (Drelichman and Voth 2014, pp. 76–77), refused this demand (Nader 1990). Philip then demanded a higher tax from his non-Spanish possessions and attempted to centralize the fiscal administration in the Low Countries, where urban communes had enjoyed long-established privileges that precluded such impositions. The local Estates General that had previously collected taxes on the king's behalf now used their administrative powers to coordinate their efforts at resisting him, finance an army, and establish a Dutch republic, in which each city and province was basically self-governing and the common government's authority was limited.

18. As Johnson and Koyama (2014) point out, a major cause of information asymmetries between local officials and the ruler were the bewildering variations in local weights and measures, which made indirect taxation exceedingly difficult. One way to overcome this formidable source of information cost was to standardize weights and measures, and it is not surprising that the new governments in Europe following the French Revolution embraced the metric system, which rationalized weights and measures, nor is it surprising that the implementation of this reform ran into serious resistance and was achieved only partially, and late.

19. The power of the French *fermiers* can be gauged from the fact that when Louis XVI's minister, Jacques Necker, sought to reform its financial system, the Company was able to block the financial reform proposed by the government because it did not serve its interests. "The

entrenched and self-enforcing. They would be overthrown only by violent revolution.

Divergence in State Capacity

China's centralized bureaucracy, as discussed extensively in previous chapters, did not give the state unlimited enforcement or fiscal powers. Following the rule of the Yuan (Mongol) Dynasty (1368), even among the growing despotism of the Ming and Qing dynasties, China's administrative effectiveness declined, taking with it the ability to supply local public goods (Wang 2022). China became in some views " a small and 'doing-little' state" (Deng 2016, p. 21).

Two main factors limited the Chinese state's fiscal capacity. The first was an obvious agency problem among the several players, driven by distance and high transportation costs. The emperor was the uninformed principal who wanted to collect the land tax (Sng 2014). It delegated tax collection to state officials (the magistrate and bureaucrats in intermediate levels of government). But the magistrates had very limited knowledge of local conditions, and they could not in turn delegate actual policy enforcement to trusted subordinates. The "rules of avoidance" that rotated magistrates across localities also limited their effectiveness since they inevitably had to rely on local notables for reliable information on local conditions.[20] In addition, the sheer burdens of many different juridical, administrative, and fiscal responsibilities were extraordinarily demanding and meant that even the best officials were stretched thin. Ultimately, state officials had to rely on the gentry, who had the required locally specific information and the de facto enforcement capacity. Understandably, this system was vulnerable to abuse, and the gentry used it to evade taxes and obtain other privileges. They, along with local magistrates and other higher-level officials divided informational rents among themselves, and little revenue reached the emperor.[21] As we have seen, Chinese emperors tried at times to

---

leverage of this group prevented the Crown from pursuing radical reform" (Root 1994, p. 205). Nothing short of complete revolution could uproot them.

20. Ma (2011), Ma and Rubin (2015), Brandt, Ma, and Rawski (2014), and Sng (2014) have studied the Chinese system of land taxation as an agency problem with the features described in this text.

21. One of the factors in the low fiscal capacity under the Qing was the absence of an updated survey of landholding, which was essential to a system dependent on a land tax. Through delaying tactics and other means, the Chinese landowning class sabotaged effective taxation of their holding. In 1712, a cadastral survey was published, but assessment within each county was left to the local officials (Rowe 2009, p. 43).

reform and rationalize the system with limited success due to the difficulties of managing the bureaucracy and resistance from powerful local clans.

The second limiting factor on fiscal capacity in Imperial China was the threat of rebellion (Zhang 2022). Commoners—local county residents and peasants not belonging to the powerful clans—ended up bearing most of the tax burden. Effective tax rates reflected local political influence and differed arbitrarily across households. Commoners could fight back by rebelling, which limited how much the state and local officials could extract from them (Zhang 2020). Internal rebellions were frequent and driven by many factors, including droughts and floods when the legitimacy of the Imperial government was impaired.

Table 8.1 compares the causes of social protests in China and England during the seventeenth and eighteenth centuries. In England, protests were mostly motivated by requests for state assistance, particularly when food prices increased. Notably, there was no instance of riots being driven by taxes. By contrast, in China, the main motivation was resistance against the state. The rebels resented the states' intervention in their economic and social affairs and expected it to be unhelpful in resolving various conflicts among themselves. If one considers that actual tax revenue was much smaller in China than in England, this contrast is even more striking. The obvious inference is to support Zhang's notion that the threat of rebellion in China was an effective constraint on extraction by the state.

Zhang (2019 2022) stressed the trauma inflicted on China's elite class of scholar-officials, who felt that the collapse of the Ming was due to overtaxation of the Chinese peasants and were determined at all costs to resist such taxes to prevent another chaotic regime change driven by anti-tax peasant rebellions (p. 317). As we saw in chapter 7, this was at the core of the failure of various attempts to reform the increasingly enfeebled Chinese fiscal apparatus during the Qing. Ma and Rubin (2017) presented a similar hypothesis and argued that limited taxation was a direct consequence of China's absolutist political institutions.[22] If the state had too much power to tax, its

---

22. Ma and Rubin (2017) view limited tax capacity as a commitment technology chosen by the emperor to prevent state agents from overtaxing citizens. Because the regime had no checks and balances and its rapacity had no limits, too much tax capacity was a danger to stability. The hypothesis that the central government deliberately avoided building its tax capacity to tie the hands of its own administrative apparatus in the future might presuppose too much farsightedness and an implausible amount of patience. Moreover, this explanation does not rule out a

TABLE 8.1. Friend or Foe? Causes of Riots in China and England

	China (1740–1839)	England (1790–1810)
Resisting the state	64.70%	27.18%
	Crackdown on illegal activity (28.90%)	Military recruitment (11.23%)
	Taxation (16.10%)	Policy/official (6.09%)
	Policy/official (11.20%)	Mutinies (4.62%)
	Intervention in social conflicts (8.50%)	Others (5.25%)
Political riots	18.60%	13.22%
	Participation in decision making (15.30%)	Religion and other (6.72%)
	Sizing state function (3.30%)	Election (4.20%)
		Church and king (2.31%)
Seeking assistance	16.70%	59.60%
	Famine relief (14%)	High food price (43.65%)
	Intervention in social conflict (2.70%)	Wages & others (15.95%)

Sources: China: Hung (2011, table 23, p. 64). Based on 484 cases of known causes. England: Bohstedt (1983, table 1, p. 14; see also p. 15).

agents would overtax the citizens to the point of expropriation. Such taxes would lead citizens to rebel against the Imperial government. Hence, the threat of rebellion induced the sovereign to refrain from investing in tax capacity because state agents would abuse the tax capacity. In practice, this meant tolerating a system with extensive tax leakages, where a fraction of tax revenue was de facto retained by direct or indirect state agents.

A second possible explanation of the differences in the dynamics of state capacity between China and Europe concerns the nature of the threats that called for a military buildup. If threats are predominantly external, defense spending is a public good that benefits everyone. If instead the threat of violence is predominantly due to internal conflicts and rebellions, investments in tax capacity are more divisive, as they benefit whoever holds power only when

second predatory equilibrium, in which tax burdens were high and the high revenue supported the military power used to suppress peasant rebellions forcefully, which seems to be an equilibrium described by North, Wallis, and Weingast (2009, p. 18) as a "natural state."

these investments come to fruition.[23] Intense interstate competition forced European kingdoms to invest in fiscal capacity. Since in China violence was predominantly due to internal wars and rebellions, whereas in Europe it was mainly due to interstate wars, this line of thought could explain why European states found it easier to accumulate state capacity.[24]

However, on its own, the importance of the distinction between external versus internal wars for the incentive to build fiscal capacity is not altogether convincing. First and foremost, a distinction between civil war and external war is not always straightforward in Europe: were the Dutch revolt and the Thirty Years' War external or internal conflicts? Furthermore, even though state fragmentation was much less in China than in Europe, as noted previously, internal rebellions and external threats of invasion from the Asian steppe were a constant and very serious concern to the Chinese ruling elites. Ma (2011) estimates that recorded incidences of warfare in China were about 1.4 per year on average throughout Chinese history. Figure 8.1, reproduced from Andrade (2016), depicts the number of conflicts per year in China and Western Europe. Although there are many caveats on how warfare is defined and measured, China does not appear to be more peaceful than Europe, except during the eighteenth century (during the so-called Great Qing Peace).[25] Finally, Europe is not unique in being ravaged by interstate wars. Precolonial India was also highly fragmented among different kingdoms that were often at war against each other. Yet India did not come close to building state infrastructures similar to those in Europe.[26]

23. Besley and Persson (2011) provided evidence from a panel of modern countries that external wars are robustly associated with increases in tax capacity, but civil wars are not. A similar argument was put forward by Gennaioli and Voth (2015), who pointed out that interstate wars were an existential issue for European kingdoms, and large fiscal revenues were needed to win wars.

24. Onorato and Dincecco (2018) and Rosenthal and Wong (2011) made a similar point in the context of how the risk of interstate war strengthened urbanization in Europe, but not in China.

25. Data on Chinese wars come from the People's Liberation Army Press lists (Wang 1922), and those on European wars are from Dupuy and Dupuy (1986). But Jia et al. (2020) have coded wars that lasted at least three years, showing that these longer-lasting conflicts were more frequent in Europe than in China.

26. Dincecco, Fenske, and Onorato (2019) pointed out that within India, exposure to conflict is positively correlated with long run economic development, although the mechanism and the direction of causality remain somewhat uncertain. They compare the effects of war on state capacity in Europe and in sub-Saharan Africa.

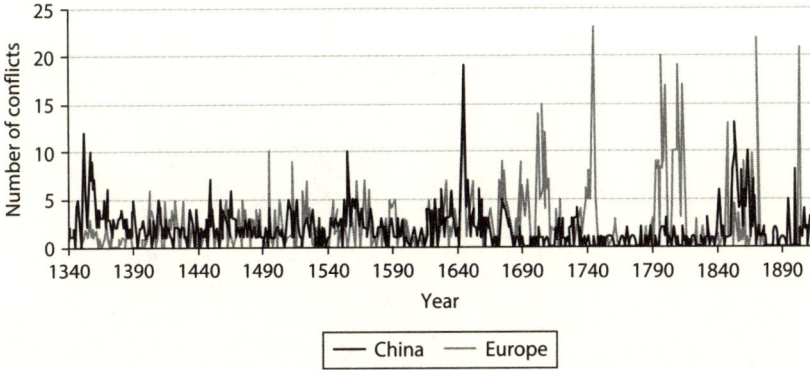

FIGURE 8.1. Warfare by year in Western Europe and China. *Source:* Andrade (2016, appendix).

In fact, all the major Chinese dynasties after the Han were terminated either by internal rebellions, by invasions from the north, or both. The consolidation of the Ming Dynasty was preceded by a warfare that lasted for almost an entire century, between around 1350 and 1450. Similarly, the Ming Dynasty was overthrown by a peasant rebellion led by a commoner named Li Zicheng. His reign lasted for a single year, as he was in turn defeated by the Manchu armies who established the Qing Dynasty, a transition followed by warfare of similar length and intensity between the 1610s and the 1680s (Andrade 2016, p. 11). The Qing in turn were fatally weakened during the nineteenth century by the White Lotus and Taiping rebellions. These interdynastic wars were not brief interruptions; they lasted for generations. Although there were relatively long periods of peace, the lack of state revenue to cover military expenses proved to be a constant and major problem throughout much of the history of Imperial China.

Furthermore, even if Chinese military strength was not often threatened by major foreign powers before the first Opium War of 1839–1842, the Qing Dynasty was very active in westward expansion of the empire's territory. The activities of the Qing in the eighteenth century, known as the "Ten Great Campaigns," led to a doubling of Chinese territory (Chinese armies also tried unsuccessfully to invade Burma and Vietnam). This expansion is illustrated in figure 8.2, which depicts Chinese territorial gains since the seventeenth century.

Furthermore, internal violence also can be a force for political centralization. Internal violence in China was often directed against local clans, and much of it originated from banditries and peasant revolts against local notables, not against the state. If the central state credibly committed itself to

FIGURE 8.2. Chinese territorial expansion since the seventeenth century. *Source:* Ebrey (2022, p. 233).

defending local gentries, however, clans requested their protection and agreed to admit and support a more effective central military. Consistent with this argument, Dincecco and Wang (2018) found evidence that during periods of more intense internal violence, affected localities also displayed a weakening of clan activity (as measured by genealogical records).[27] One might also expect that Chinese intrastate conflict could have had countervailing effects and provide incentives to higher administrative capacity—and yet such effects seem to have been largely absent.

Thus, accepting that the distinction between interstate versus internal conflict cannot fully explain differences between European and Chinese state capacity, the question remains unanswered: Why did China fail to sustain the powerful fiscal capacity that it wielded during the Song Dynasty? A more promising explanation rests on the general foundations of the system of Chinese government, particularly with the growing disconnect between a despotic central government controlled by the emperor and state bureaucracy and the clans, whose local powers increased steadily from the Song period and

27. It might be added that in Europe too, internal violence in some cases led to increased centralized power for the state. The most striking example is perhaps the French wars of religion (1562–1598), which led to the administrative reforms introduced by Henry IV in the early seventeenth century.

thereafter. The central government determined the allocation of government spending without any formal input from the clans, who were simply left in charge of tax collection. This arrangement produced poor incentives for supporting fiscal expansion. Since clans were excluded from the central administration and had no say in the spending process, they had little interest in increasing government revenue (Wang 2022). If it wanted to change and streamline this inefficient and leaky fiscal extraction system, the central government would have needed to tighten its control over local enforcement through coercion and the use of force. But this in turn would have created the danger of countervailing powers, which could one day use their coercive capabilities against the central authority.

The alternative was fiscal decentralization; one could plausibly create a federal type of state that vested more power in local government while leaving the emperor in charge of national matters like foreign policy. As Sng (2014, p. 123) pointed out, this was in fact attempted later by the Qing after the disastrous Taiping Rebellion. As Sng noted, the Qing decentralization policy split the fiscal budget in this way: the Imperial government received a fixed amount of tax revenue from the provinces, ceding the remainder to local officials. This system was equivalent to provincial governments replacing the Imperial court "as the residual claimant on the taxes collected within each province" (Sng 2014, p. 123). By decentralizing, the incentives on local authority to collect taxes more efficiently were strengthened. The problem, however, was that without stronger controls on the governors' spending, local governments would free-ride on nationwide efforts, as happened for instance during the Sino-Japanese war of 1894.[28]

Thus, ultimately, the decline of tax capacity in China can be attributed to two features of its political institutions. First, the absolutist powers of the emperor and the absence of any formal constraints on his executive powers coupled with a self-referential central bureaucracy left a huge gap of information and incentives between state institutions and the rest of society. The Imperial administration was unaccountable to external power holders, and there were no participatory political institutions through which groups representing territorial interests could express their views. This prevented the alignments of incentives between the center (the Imperial administration) and the periphery (local authorities controlled by local clans).

28. Yet the Imperial government in China was able to increase taxes and revenues, as it demanded more and more from the provinces in the closing decades of the empire, and state capacity improved dramatically (Rowe 1999, p. 261), even if it was a classic case of too little, too late.

The second key feature was the power of the local clans in actual enforcement of tax collections. The supreme irony of Chinese history was that while the regime seemed absolutist and without any kind of countervailing power, it was in fact a weak state. The Imperial administration exerted only very limited control over much of the country because it did not want to reinforce countervailing local powers that could eventually threaten Imperial authority. But this in turn limited the fiscal and administrative powers of the state, since enforcement was ultimately in the hands of nonstate agents and corruption was widespread.

In contrast, in many European political regimes, local constituencies in charge of tax collection acquired some say over the allocation of government revenue. This is because—as we have seen in earlier chapters—before 1700, most European sovereigns lacked the enforcement powers to collect taxes by themselves, outsourcing this role to tax farmers and giving them some manner of representation in assemblies. This is why European assemblies typically included individuals and corporate bodies with administrative roles. Indeed, the late medieval European estates either were assemblies of those with administrative capacity or had a standing committee with this capacity (for a summary of the evidence, see Herb 2003). The system aligned the incentives of the center and the periphery better, particularly in the face of external military threats, and made it possible to sustain investment in tax capacity.

As pointed out earlier in this chapter and in chapter 7, this trend first emerged in smaller political units such as city-states, where shorter distances between local officials and constituents ameliorated agency problems (Stasavage 2011). Later, the trend became prominent in the evolution of broader state institutions. Often a sovereign in need of cash would grant political rights to corporate bodies with administrative capacity in exchange for additional tax revenue. Consequently, a striking historical regularity emerges: in states where rulers negotiated with representative assemblies, government taxes were paradoxically higher, and their spending reflected more closely the interests of the assemblies' members. It is striking, indeed, that taxation in relatively more absolutist European states, such as Bourbon France and Habsburg Spain, was lower than in parliamentarian states such as Hanoverian England and the Dutch Republic (e.g., Hoffman and Norberg 1994, p. 299). In a recent contribution, Prak and Van Zanden (2022) describe in detail the successful cooperation that was achieved in the Dutch United Provinces, both at the level of intracity cooperation between different corporations, and at the level of intercity cooperation in the face of common threats and problems.

3. Legal Developments in Medieval Europe

Origins: Roman and Canon Law

The differences in political institutions and social arrangements between Europe and China were reflected in their legal systems. European civil law was in large part a legacy of the Roman Empire. As Lesaffer (2009, p. 19) summarizes, "Roman law was without doubt the most sophisticated and highly developed legal system from Antiquity. It was also the most influential in later history. The rediscovery and study of Roman law in the late eleventh century triggered the development of European legal science and the civil law tradition." Whereas the Greeks still lacked a class of scholars who would call themselves "jurists," such a class developed in Rome.[29] Roman law was the basis of the Justinian *Digest* (a compendium of quotes from earlier Roman jurists compiled c.530 in Byzantium). Both the *Digest* and the sixth-century legal codifications known as *Institutiones* (essentially a student textbook in civil law, also written in Byzantium) were given legal force by the Byzantine government.

Roman law fell into disuse for centuries after the collapse of the Western Roman Empire. In the centuries that followed, formal law was largely replaced by local customs and informal legal practices. Because most conflicts and civil disputes were settled within the clan or the village, there was little need for formal laws, although some early rulers found it necessary to write down these laws and rules. These efforts resulted in the Salic Law compilation, commissioned by the Merovingian king Clovis around 510 AD. From the early days, moreover, there was one additional major effort: the Catholic Church, which created a separate body of rules and practices that became known as *canon law*.

Canon law was the part of law that touched upon ecclesiastical activities and the organization of the Catholic Church, which was a complex transnational corporation It also formulated the moral codes for the rest of society. Largely separate from Roman law, canon law exerted strong influence because of the Church's pervasive role in daily life during the Middle Ages. It directly

---

29. The earliest known jurist who was engaged in codifying civil law was Quintus Mucius Scaevola (140 BC–82 BC), who composed an eighteen-volume summary of civil law (none of which has survived in its original form). He divided Roman civil law into formal categories such as the law of persons and that of obligations. A more elaborate version of his work, which has in large part been preserved, was the *Institutes* composed by an author about whom we know only his first name, Gaius. It was written c.161 AD and used and cited in the sixth century Justinian codes.

dealt with the sacraments of marriage, and hence marriage law; debt; breaches of contract; and perjury. So did many other matters that constituted sins or had some need for moral instruction (e.g., the charging of interest, regarded as "usury").

Canon law was the religious side of civil law. For centuries, it was as fragmented and heterogeneous as secular law. The first systematic codification of canon law was compiled by Gratian in a famous document known as *Decretum Gratiani*, dating from about 1140.[30] It was a treatise that organized, synthesized, and harmonized existing legal rules accumulated from diverse sources.[31]

Berman (1977, p. 921) argued that Gratian's treatise was "the first comprehensive and systematic legal treatise in the history of the West, and perhaps in the history of mankind." In it, Gratian insisted that customs—which still clearly dominated the practices of jurisdiction and conflict resolution at the time—must be made subordinate to formal legislation (whether secular or ecclesiastical). The legal revolution of canon law, formalizing and standardizing local rules and customs, was subsequently extended to the secular political and commercial domains, with the emergence of self-governing towns and the development of urban law, and to the private economic domain, with the evolution of the *lex mercatoria* or "law merchant" discussed later in this chapter.

Beyond their practical implications, the legal compilations helped to establish civil law as a coherent academic field of study, treating legal studies as a body of knowledge formally independent of religion or political ideology. Consequently, a more robust metaphysical concept of "the law" emerged in serious intellectual thought. Moreover, the theory underlying legal scholarship continued to evolve. As Pennington (1998) phrased it, thirteenth-century jurists successfully transformed legal procedures once thought to constitute "positive law" (i.e., law that was promulgated by rulers) into unassailable "natural laws" (i.e., a set of moral principles and norms inherent in nature and accessible to human reason), an idea inherited from classical philosophy. This transformation in thought removed legal procedures from the authority of the ruler and his whims, and in fact it subjected the ruler to them. What was unique and highly significant here is that, at least in theory, the idea of "the law" as a constraint on human

30. Gratian was a twelfth-century Bolognese monk and jurist about whom little is known except his legal text, which earned him the accolade as the "father of canon law."

31. Canon law was further extended, updated, and streamlined in 1234 by Saint Raymond of Penyafort into a document simply known as *Decretals*, compiled at the instructions of Pope Gregory IX.

behavior and actions therefore applied to all legal entities—thus explicitly constraining rulers and churchmen as not being above the law.[32]

The classical heritage was central to this evolution. The body of legal knowledge that we call Roman law was recovered in Italy in the late eleventh century thanks to its close connections with Byzantium and its access to the Justinian codes that contained it. The resuscitation of Roman law in the West was possibly inspired by the ecclesiastical reforms of Pope Gregory VII, together with the surfacing of copies of the *Digest* in Italy. These texts were taught by the early professors of law in Bologna, such as the legal scholar Irnerius (1050–1125). Irnerius's students, known as the Doctors of Bologna, were among the first of the so-called Glossators, who reorganized the *Digest* and established the curriculum of medieval Roman law.[33] In the following centuries, legal scholars continued to develop and expand Roman civil law.[34] At first, they simply provided exegetic glosses of the texts. Over time, however, they also became commentators who ventured far from the original texts to propose new combinations and ideas.

In short, what emerged from the great commentators of the fourteenth and fifteenth centuries was a new and coherent system of civil law, along with an intellectual body of legal theory that "the ancient Romans would have not recognized as theirs" (Lesaffer 2009, p. 260). These developments produced general legal concepts based on theoretical beliefs about the role of law in society, unlike original Roman law, which was case-specific. Legal theory created the tools toward the formalization and standardization of existing practices and provided complete definitions of concepts such as representation (agency) and corporation (joint action). One nineteenth-century scholar

32. Gratian concluded that, as a matter of natural law, "princes are bound by and shall live according to their law" (Berman 1983, p. 145). He also stressed that customs were subordinate to local law, and thus began a process in which local custom lost their sanctity and may be overridden (Berman 1983).

33. The endeavors of the Bologna School in disclosing and understanding these texts were part and parcel of its lecturing on Roman law. The literary output of the Glossators consisted primarily of *glossae* (annotations), written in the margins around the original text. Their purpose went beyond explaining and included reorganizing the somewhat inchoate texts into a coherent structure and uncovering the true meaning implied by the authoritative voice of the Justinian collection (Lesaffer 2009, p. 255).

34. Of those, the most notable was Bartolus of Sassoferrato (1313–1357), by most accounts the most influential jurist of the Medieval Age. Bartolus and his students, known as *Bartolists*, were instrumental in the growth of European civil law in the late medieval period.

claimed that the work of the Bologna School in creating civil law was "the most brilliant achievement of the intellect of medieval Europe."[35] This may have been an exaggeration, but civil law was indeed the medieval universities' most valuable gift to economic development of the time.

In the creation of a body of legal knowledge in the Middle Ages, canon law and Roman law were studied side by side. The duality between secular (Roman) and ecclesiastical (canon) laws, which inevitably emerged here, was expressed by the term *utrumque ius* ("the one and the other law"). Both claimed to be the law common to the entire Christian world (Bellomo 1995, p. 74), which inevitably led to friction between the legal scholars representing Church authorities and those loyal to secular rulers. Understandably, as secular agents grew more powerful, their courts contested many of the decisions issued by ecclesiastical courts. While the canonists naturally defended the subordination of secular rules to those of the Church, secular authorities rebutted these attempts, citing natural law.

Despite such frictions between ecclesiastical and secular jurists, the canonists and the Romanists jointly created Western civil law. Berman (1983, p. 204) suggested that we might call their joint contribution a "Romano-canonical" legal system. The two branches of civil law synergistically created a synthetic body of systematic juridical thought in Europe (sometimes known as *ius commune*) that combined the legal techniques and sophistication of Roman law with the pragmatic, solution-oriented approach of canon law (Lesaffer 2009, p. 266). The two schools shared basic theories concerning the nature and functions of law, similar methods of analysis, and procedural foundations of legal action. Roman law, as it evolved at the hands of academic jurists at Bologna University and elsewhere after its revival in the eleventh century, borrowed heavily from the methods and theoretical concepts of canon law. From this combination, something new emerged.[36]

---

35. The author was the Oxford philosopher and historian Hastings Rashdall, whose *The Universities of Europe in the Middle Ages* was published in 1895 (cited by Haskins 1923, pp. 35–36). See Cantoni and Yuchtman (2014) for an argument linking university-trained scholars directly to market development.

36. A good example of the kind of procedure that this hybrid legal system created was the *ordo iudiciarius*, the investigation of a suspected crime by an outside agency, such as a magistrate or (in England) a grand jury. The origins of this procedure (the precursor of the modern idea of due process) were due to the Church, but it soon became a generally accepted doctrine (Pennington 1998). Intellectually, the new body of knowledge had deep classical roots: European legal scholars combined ideas from Greek philosophy, such as natural law, with Roman legal thought.

The Legal Professions

Legal administration in Europe was typically carried out by specialists who had received education and training distinct from other professional schooling (e.g., religious training). These specialists developed their own scholarly literature, formal rules, informal codes of conduct, and so on. The close interaction between academic judicial *learning* and legal *practice* became a defining characteristic of Western civil law and legal procedure in the West. The study of law did not just consist of memorizing the actual laws on the books; it also included what legal scholars had said about them and how they had analyzed and interpreted them. It was regarded as a logical and coherent living body, a *corpus iuris,* and jurists worked hard to settle internal contradictions and generalized principles from cases and rules. Much like other broad bodies of law, such as Jewish *halacha,* Islamic sharia, and Chinese legal codes, Western law was adaptable and specified the meta-rules that determined how laws could be tweaked and revised.

It is important to note that for much of its early history, the learned law taught in universities, the *ius commune* (the union of the sets of canon and Roman law), was not directly relevant to the daily operation of the legal system, such as it was. Jurisprudence followed local legal customs known as *ius proprium* (Bellomo 1995, pp. 78–111), and obviously, such local customs and procedures differed enormously across Europe. All the same, we should not infer that day-to-day law as practiced on the ground and academic legal learning developed independent of each other. Several historical facts directly evidence otherwise. For one thing, had there been no need for university-trained lawyers, there would be no explanation of the demand for attending laws schools at considerable cost. Moreover, learned professorial law became an ideal and a source of advice and inspiration for jurists who wrote laws and practiced the law.

That influence can be seen over time in the day-to-day operations and procedures of courts, increasingly influenced by the legal scholarly constructs of Roman and canon law. The *ius proprium* slowly adapted to the evolving values and underlying assumptions of learned law. Some of the more egregious customs of local jurisprudence, such as trial by combat or ordeal, were eventually abandoned. Another example is the abandonment of customary oral procedures in favor of written documents and testimonies, relying on notarial deeds (Lesaffer 2009, pp. 270–72).

Medieval Europe was not the only region in the world to develop some form of civil law. But it was different from non-European legal systems in that it was run by professionals, with both judges and advocates expected to have legal training. The legal "branch" slowly became separate from the executive and legislative parts of government (not including interactions among the branches, such as courts ruling on laws passed by the legislative branch and the executive branch enforcing their verdicts). In its early stages of development, the legal branch was a bottom-up system. Rather than being promulgated and imposed by some all-powerful ruler or a Solon-like lawgiver, Europe's body of law emerged from a combination of different sources synthesized by collaborative efforts. and hence it required top-down scholarship to be systematized and standardized.

Medieval jurists integrated different bodies of laws and legal procedures to cohere together into a "common system." Whether originally Roman, canon, or Germanic customary law, the body of law that emerged was syncretic, a fusion of the three (Herzog 2018, pp. 54, 91). This combination gave it a certain flexibility, and hence it could adapt to the daily needs of commerce, credit, and contracts more than China could. It supported the dependence of the economy on orderly cooperation rather than the desire of rulers for order and obedience. Unlike Islamic sharia law or Jewish Talmudic *halacha*, Roman civil law had little religious or metaphysical content except paying lip service to certain philosophical ideas (e.g., natural law, which was little more than what we would call "common sense" today). Moreover, many of the secular jurists involved with creating European civil law were legal practitioners themselves. Their firsthand experiences helped to inform them in creating a product that retained tight connections between formal codes and actual de facto jurisprudence.

By the fourteenth century, a coherent legal system based on juridical theory was in place in Europe. Modern research has concluded that the success of commerce and finance in medieval cities "owed much to the rise of law as a rational and systematic scholarly discipline that strengthened individual values over customary duties and generated superior rules of conflict resolution" (Schäfer and Wulf 2014, p. 299).[37] The growth of legal studies in higher

37. Schäfer and Wulf (2014) conclude that it is was not the Roman law as such, but the scientific, rational, systematic, and more individualistic approach of legal scholarship in all Western Europe that led to commercial development and urban growth. The teaching of Roman and canon "learned law" was similar in all European universities, regardless of the extent to which substantive Roman law had become the law in the region around a university. They add that "the medieval economic rise of Europe owes much to the rise of law as a rational and systematic scholarly discipline that strengthened individual values over customary duties and generated superior rules of conflict resolution" (2014, p. 299).

education was conducive to commercial development in late medieval Europe (Cantoni and Yuchtman 2014).

The Legal Revolution and the Evolution of Corporate Arrangements

As discussed in chapters 5 and 6, voluntary associations such as fraternities, guilds, and parishes were not initially recognized as corporate structures. This changed during the twelfth and thirteenth centuries due to the emergent legal system. The latter's evolution gave additional impetus to the growth of corporations, as it recognized them as legal entities while also bringing about a more precise definition of property rights and corporate organizations. The Commercial Revolution and the associated proliferation of private corporate structures (with primarily economic goals) provided a major impetus to some corporations, above all merchant guilds.[38]

The legal history of medieval Europe is central to our argument that corporations were a major driver of European economic and social development. The evolution of corporations from informal associations to formal organizations that enjoyed specific legal recognition and rights features is important for several reasons. First, this evolution clarified that the corporation was a separate legal entity, distinct from its members. By implication, corporations acquired a permanent status, unlike the transient status of individual members. Guilds, universities, and other associations were meant to last for generations, and they did. Their long-term persistence can be inferred from membership rules that spelled out how to arrange succession and sometimes even allowed inheritance clauses. It can also be inferred from corporations' high survival rates, often spanning several centuries (De Moor 2008, p. 196).

Second, thanks to the legal revolution, corporations enjoyed specific rights and responsibilities. Their legal status and personhood enabled them to engage in a variety of activities: to enter long-term contracts, to sue and be sued, and to issue debt that was an exclusive liability of the corporation (not its administrators nor members—that is, an early version of limited liability). These functions and many others allowed corporations to engage in a variety of contractual arrangements, thereby enabling them to fulfill new and important economic roles. Monasteries, guilds, and universities, all in their different ways, became integral parts of economic development in medieval Europe.

---

38. The number of merchants in Western Europe is estimated to have been in the thousands in the mid-eleventh century and in the hundreds of thousands by 1200 (Berman 1983; Pounds 1973).

Third, because corporations were not responsible for the liabilities of their members and vice versa, this paved the way to establish precedent for the idea of limited liability. The fact that corporations could act as a single body represented by delegates also facilitated their acquisition of important political roles, as discussed in chapter 7.

A Transnational Legal System

The syncretic *ius commune* proved quite useful in the development of European law. It became a *standard*—a focal point, in the terminology of Schelling (1960)—in essence, a body of rules that helped normalize and coordinate laws already in force. For this reason, the recovery of the Justinian Codes was of far more importance than solely satisfying antiquarian interest; indeed, many readers were only vaguely aware of its Byzantine origins (Bellomo 1995, pp. 61–65). What the *ius commune* provided was a legal mindset, a common terminology, and an idealized juridical standard. Moreover, the body of learned law established the transnational nature of Western legal science, which was truly pan-European even if legal practices and norms differed from place to place (Berman 1983). This helped create what Herzog (2018, p. 80) called a "fragmented yet unified world."[39] The systematization of law was a kind of legal analog of the transnational Republic of Letters in the Middle Ages. In this world, legal doctrines and ideas were not only taught but also assessed and criticized. Academic legal learning unified the understanding of legal logic and arguments, but because the universities were autonomous, the market for legal ideas remained competitive and pluralistic. This combination of fragmented polities with common traditions of rules, codes of behaviors, standards of proof, and ethics, was to become one of the keys to Europe's divergence from other parts of the world. In short, European civil law was a unique historical construct, created from the contingent and subtle interaction of traditions, customs, legal scholars, and legal practitioners.

One widely discussed example of European legal developments was the emergence of the "law merchant," or *lex mercatoria*. Thanks to its customary origin and close links to de facto commercial practices, the law merchant

39. In large part, the universities created such uniformity, as students from all over the Continent traveled to the best universities to study law. Canon and Roman laws became "disciplines without national boundaries" as Berman (1983, p. 162) put it, much like the Republic of Letters was to become in the sixteenth century.

introduced several innovations that had lasting effects on the evolution of corporations. The codification of bankruptcy procedures and the development of various financial instruments are some prime examples. Merchant law also gave a precise form to new corporate structures such as the famous *commenda*, a joint venture between a traveling merchant and a sedentary financier, which helped to resolve principal-agent problems. The *commenda* was used specifically to execute long-distance trade: it dictated that each investor was liable only for the amount he invested, and profits were shared between the investor and the traveling trader who conducted business on his behalf (Berman 1983; Harris 2020).[40] Like the larger body of law of which it was just one component, the *commenda* evolved from the bottom up, becoming a system of best practices and customs enforced by merchant courts. It reconciled widely variable local customs and minimized conflict between merchants transacting at arm's length from one another.

Often, the principles embodied in the law merchant, such as reciprocity of rights and good faith, first appeared in private agreements and were defined more precisely later. Adjudication was left to courts of merchants, local officials, and jurists. Since judges had few effective enforcement powers, their main sanction for refusal to comply with court decisions was via reputation mechanisms, which could potentially result in offenders being expelled from the community of traders (Milgrom, North, and Weingast 1990).

That said, the true extent of standardization in the law merchant remains an open question. Much evidence suggests that customs and legal principles varied widely across localities. Donahue (2004) investigated whether there was a *lex mercatoria* in the medieval and Early Modern periods. His answer was, "'no,' at least not in the sense that that term is normally used" (p. 27). He contrasted the absence of any standard codification of the law merchant with the *ius maritimum* (law of the sea), which employed formal codifications. In her critique of the same idea of standardization, Kadens (2015) pointed out that the notion of a pan-European body of laws was invented in the seventeenth century and adopted by historians without much supporting

---

40. According to Harris (2020, chapter 5), the *commenda* first appeared in Islamic Arabia and then emerged in Italy after the First Crusade. It differed from the modern business corporation in that it was a short-term arrangement established for a specific trade expedition. Long-term ventures were organized in the twelfth and early thirteenth centuries in the form of partnerships called *compagnia*, but these did not have limited liability and were mainly used among family members or partners who already knew and could trust each other (Berman 1983).

evidence.[41] Unlike other bodies of law, the law merchant was much more of a construct created by historians than the body of informal and spontaneous law system of order without law, regulating trade and constraining behavior that some scholars have made it to be (e.g., Ellickson 1991). Instead, much long-distance trade was enforced by the laws and courts of each city, and foreigners had to learn the idiosyncratic rules and customs of each town in which they wanted to sell their goods.[42] The Law Merchant, insofar that it was a coherent set of rules, depended much more than is suggested by many scholars on the cooperation and enforcement of local authorities.[43] Like many self-enforcing, seemingly private-order conflict resolution arrangements, they operated in the shadow of the law.

Moreover, the intensity and nature of interactions between customary practice, judicial enforcement, and legal scholarship differed across parts of Europe. In southern Europe, the influence of learned law came much earlier than it did north of the Alps. Even northern Europe exhibited variations. France's northern part remained loyal to customary law, while the south remained mostly loyal to the *pays de droit écrit,* possibly inspired by the University of Montpellier, one of Europe's premier law schools. England was less affected by Roman law and eventually developed its own version of we now call "common law."[44] Yet it too developed a version of civil law that was vastly more sophisticated than the customary laws and the early *ius proprium* still extant at the time of the Norman Conquest.

41. Kadens also notes that "merchant courts existed, but their very existence challenges the notion of a uniform and universal law merchant. Instead, they indicate the parochialism of traders and their preference for their own local law" (2015, p. 261).

42. At the fairs of Champagne, thirteenth-century merchants took contract disputes to the local secular or ecclesiastical authorities, the same authorities before whom the merchants attested their contracts. Only from 1274 did the local fair wardens become the merchants' preferred court. Yet they hardly resembled the standardized spontaneous merchant court of law depicted by some historians. Rather than being an informal affair adjudicated by other merchants, it was a true court, with court officers, notaries, and lawyers. The wardens were appointed by the local count governing the fair, and they were not necessarily merchants (Kadens 2015).

43. As Gelderblom (2013, p. 103) points out, even when merchants invoked the *lex mercatoria,* they referred to procedural rules set up by local institutions.

44. Common law (and its English context) is not to be confused with *ius commune.* English law consisted of a sequence of writs issued by royal courts, which implied certain legal rights. Despite its royal origins, it was a bottom-up process, as the royal courts were not directly controlled by the king.

Civil law in the West thus bifurcated into two varieties: continental civil law and Anglo-Saxon common law. Common law was heavily influenced by precedent and case law, whereas the countries that adopted continental civil law depended much more on formal legislation. The distinction between the two is important and has been used to explain differences in economic development (especially capital markets) in the various parts of the world that adopted them. According to this hypothesis, common-law (mostly Anglo-Saxon) countries had more adaptable legal systems, which led to more investor protection, less rigid regulation, and possibly more effective policies. This "legal origins" hypothesis, first fully expounded in LaPorta et al. (2008), has become a source of some controversy in the economics literature.[45]

The debate on legal origins and the relative merits of English common law and continental system of civil law has obscured the similarities between the two systems. The differences between the two in preindustrial times should not be overstated, as Herzog (2018, pp. 112–15) emphasizes. Some differences, such as the relative importance of juries versus judges, appeared in the late Middle Ages, but the basic ideas of civil rights were accepted everywhere. As Berman (1983, p. 25) stresses, "There were many common bonds among the various national legal systems" in Europe. For much of European history, England and the Continent followed somewhat different paths, but they strongly influenced one another.[46]

Despite its heterogeneity, then, there were enough common denominators of the development of law in Europe to speak of a "European legal system." It was unique in the tight connection between legal scholarship and its practice, in its bottom-up origins through formalizing extant practices rather than promulgating laws from the top down, and its basic ideological assumptions of equality before the law and that no one was above the law. Despite its partially religious origins, it was secular. It was also a specialized profession in which

45. Recent criticism of "legal origins" interpretations can be found in Guerriero (2016). For an application to the United States, where some states adopted common law as opposed to states acquired in the Louisiana Purchase of 1803 that had a tradition of civil law (see Berkowitz and Clay, 2011).

46. In a way, this debate reflects in miniature one of the central paradoxes of economic historiography: in their efforts to explain British leadership in the Industrial Revolution, scholars risk losing sight of the fact that the difference between Britain and the Continent were dwarfed by the gaps between Europe and Asia or Africa, and the various regions in Europe were in close contact with one another, with information and ideas flowing quickly and efficiently between them.

both lawyers and judges were increasingly formally trained in the law. Moreover, professionalization was encouraged and utilized by the emerging nation-states, seeking administrative support from legally trained administrators as well as legitimization for increasingly encroaching into new areas of jurisdiction and control.

4. Legal Developments in the Chinese Empire

The Chinese Legal System

Having a sophisticated and monetized market-oriented economy from early on, it would seem odd that China could have done without anything resembling European civil law. Bodde and Morris (1970, p. 92) summarize the traditional assessment of the legal structure of premodern China by stating that "written law of pre-modern China was overwhelmingly penal in emphasis . . . it was limited in scope to being primarily a legal codification of the ethical norms long dominant in Chinese society." Unlike Europe, as they stressed, Chinese law was not aimed at defending the rights—including property rights—of individuals against others or against the state. Instead, above all, it was focused on deciding matters of criminal acts. The underlying assumption must have been that such rights in the commercial spheres would be protected by other (nonlegal) means. Chinese law's emphasis on criminal acts, according to this view, was motivated by the goal of preventing disruptions to social order rather than defending individual rights. This is a subtle but critical distinction.

Traditional historiography argued that the Chinese legal system was built primarily for vertical (i.e., hierarchical), not horizontal relationships (i.e., between equals). What this meant was that a person wronged by a fellow citizen could not bring formal suit against the offender. Rather, they could only lodge a complaint with an authority (the magistrate), who would then decide whether to pursue the matter. Yet few if any magistrates had legal training, and the matter was usually decided on political grounds. A Chinese proverb illustrates this notion: "Of ten reasons by which a magistrate may decide a case, nine are unknown to the public" (Bodde and Morris 1967, p. 6). Most disputes were resolved through mediation by extralegal bodies, such as the clan or a council of village elders. Because of their informality, these bodies did not leave much written record, especially compared to those produced via formal legal procedures. As such, assessing their full impact on economic life is a difficult task.

More recent research has modified the contrast between China and Europe significantly and specifically objected to the earlier idea that China had nothing like European civil law. It would be more accurate to argue that in China, civil law was not entirely absent and can be shown to have existed in the Qing codes (Perdue 2004, p. 53). The boundaries between civil and criminal law were less clear cut (Lau 2017), even though in her pathbreaking study of civil trials during the Qing Dynasty, Liang (2007, pp. 13–14) pointed out that whereas the sharp distinction between "penal" and "civil" law is a Western feature, in China, there was also a difference between criminal and noncriminal acts.[47] Similarly, Lau (2017) pointed out that even if the boundaries between civil and criminal law in China were not as sharp as in the West, the Imperial Chinese and modern Western civil laws are "roughly common in their coverage of marriage, divorce, succession, disinheritance, property matters, and so on." Huang (2016, p. 228) noted that there was a "Sinitic legal tradition" that differed from Western legal traditions in that it saw the civil and criminal justice systems as overlapping and interactive. Consistent with Bodde and Morris's view that Chinese law was predominantly about criminal matters, he argued that Chinese legal thought has held consistently that disputes among the people over "minor matters" that did not involve criminal offenses should preferably be dealt with through nonlegal means, with the state intervening only when the matter could not be resolved through arbitration or mediation. As Huang stressed, there was nothing premodern or primitive about this: it was a choice that the Han Dynasty made, and it survived for many centuries. Chinese tradition had a strong preference for settling disputes by the customs of society rather than by formal litigation. After all, Confucius himself said that "it would be better if there were no lawsuits at all" (*Analects*, 12.13). By the time of the Qing Dynasty, this had become a fiscal as well as a moral imperative: the Qing administration, chronically short of resources, avoided litigation wherever it could (Zhang 2017, p. 51).[48]

47. As Liang (2007, p. 13) points out, the Chinese term *zuiming* roughly means "named crime," indicating that crime was a separate part of the law.

48. A telling example of the divergence of the European and the Chinese legal traditions can be seen in the late nineteenth century, when British merchants appeared in Chaozhou (which was a treaty port after 1858). Obviously, disputes arose between European and local businessmen, and the clash of the two legal systems was quite apparent. As Macauley (2021) shows, Chinese magistrates would delay judicial proceedings in the hope of attaining a resolution through mediation and were disinclined to follow the rules that the Europeans were accustomed to. Europeans often found it extremely difficult to collect from Chinese debtors and felt that the Chinese should adopt European-style commercial law, something that the local Chinese objected to. She noted that "as a practical matter this meant that Chinese plaintiffs were more likely to gain satisfaction in the British consulate than British plaintiff in Chinese courts" (p. 211).

While Europe's legal evolution traversed from informal customs to formal legal rules, in China, the two coexisted and interacted and had a synergistic effect that made trade and other economic interactions easier. As evidence of this fact, Scogin (1994) pointed to the phenomenon of *guanxi*: essentially personal connections, which underlay the trust necessary to minimize transaction costs. Guanxi supported intrafamily and interfamily transactions, with the judicial system as the ultimate enforcer of last resort. A late nineteenth-century observer noted that in China, "the family or clan is . . . much in the position of an English corporation"; it can set up its by-laws but "liable to the ordinary law for exceeding its powers" (cited by Scogin 1994, p. 29). The formal systems of the state and the informal systems of clans like *guanxi* were complements in facilitating Chinese commercial activity. In some cases, clans actually set up "family regulations," which were formally contained in the genealogies. Interestingly, these were primarily concerned with the moral character of clan leaders and intrafamily solidarity in order to preserve the clan's reputation and unity, based on the concept of reciprocity (Esherick 2011, pp. 23–25).

Enforcement of criminal law in China remained a prerogative of the state administration, although law and order depended heavily on local arbitration, often mediated within the clan or by local officials. Given the extensive responsibility of the clan over its members, criminal law held the entire kin-group liable for any serious criminal or treasonous offenses of their members. This would be unthinkable in European criminal law, even in the Middle Ages. The Great Ming Code, promulgated by the Hongwu emperor in 1397, became one of the foundational documents of Chinese governance, the core of which the country retained until the fall of the empire. Its 460 articles enumerated all crimes and their respective punishments, and all magistrates were expected to follow it (and faced punishment if they did not).[49] Not surprisingly, the harshest penalties concerned rebellion and crimes against the emperor or the state (Finer 1997, vol. 2, p. 778).

Furthermore, unlike in Europe, the Chinese legal system did not evolve from the bottom up. Although legal practices were not fixed over time, they changed slowly and often reflected codes formulated in the distant past, sometimes more than they did the current needs of civil society. The legal statutes

---

49. Unlike Europe, when a deviant intellectual was accused of disloyalty by the Chinese "Literary Inquisition" (*wénzìyù*; literally, "imprisonment due to writings" or speech crime), the authorities severely punished other clan members, largely to demonstrate collective responsibility and to activate internal controls of clans on their members to fall in line.

pertaining to economic affairs in the Qing period were largely lifted from Ming codes, which in turn came from the Tang codes of 653 AD. As such, the country's legal principles "can be said to have existed for twelve centuries," subject to minor annotations and clarifications (Jing 1994, p. 82). The changes constituted modifications of the rigid rules attributed to the Confucian moral codes. Over time, as Huang and others have noted, the various legal codes incorporated more and more civil content.[50]

As the legal system in China developed, it needed to reconcile with the Confucian moral codes. Notwithstanding the supposed rigid family hierarchy of the Confucian system, children were legally permitted to sue their parents without fear of the death penalty if their accusations were true (which, of course, was a strong condition). Private property could be owned under certain conditions by individuals without being shared by parents and siblings. More generally, while perhaps Chinese legal codes did not stress property rights as explicitly as they did in the West, the formal penal laws took informal property rights as given; for instance, by stipulating penalties for theft, they implicitly acknowledged concepts like ownership and possession (Huang 2016, p. 232).

That said, in many ways, the differences between Chinese and European civil law were stark. Much as in every society, there was a significant difference in both worlds between the formal legal statutes and the practice of law on the ground, and as the grip of the Mandarin central bureaucracy on the country weakened during the Ming and Qing dynasties, that gap probably grew. The state's priorities were above all the maintenance of stability and public security, protecting its tax base, and the resolution of conflict (Jing 1994).

Law Enforcement in China

The implementation of laws and exercise of justice was left primarily to local officials of the Imperial bureaucracy (i.e., the magistrates). Yet the magistrate's responsibilities were as much administrative and fiscal as they were judicial.

---

50. Nevertheless, Huang (2019, p. 38) pointed out similarly that "codified law retained its earlier penal framework and packaged most provisions about civil matters with punishments," although in practice, the courts rarely employed legal penalties in minor civil matters. Civil provisions in traditional Chinese legal codes, he notes, appear rather thin compared to European legal tradition. All the same, he concludes that "there can be no doubt that together they formed a vast civil justice system of very broad application" Huang (2016, p. 228).

Consequently, at times, his different functions could either be combined or be in conflict (Liang 2007). In any event, the magistrates were part of a central bureaucracy in charge of justice and other public goods. By one account, however, Chinese officials had little contact with 90 percent of people in rural areas (Teng 1977, p. 122). This is hardly surprising: county government was weak, understaffed, underfunded, and rarely in a position to challenge local interests (Zhang 2017, p. 59). One may wonder how the government maintained peace and order, given feeble third-party enforcement of contracts and transactions. The answer largely rests on clan elders and the gentry, who utilized peaceful mediation of property disputes, normally following local customs.

Local adjudication in China was complex when it reached the courts. Chinese magistrates were not judges trained in the law—they were bureaucrats. The Imperial administration discouraged litigation. In Qing China, the state went so far as to prohibit assistance to a private person in drawing up a petition or pleading a case (Finer 1997). Magistrates had de facto discretion in minor criminal cases, although said discretion diminished as the severity of the crime increased (Ch'ü 1962). Civil rights were loosely defined, and social relations were defined by hierarchy within the clan. Authority was not based primarily on the law; rather, it was the result of power relations or customs. By themselves, however, these differences do not imply that property rights and contract enforcement in China were necessarily weaker than in Europe, only that the mechanisms on which they rested were quite different.

Furthermore, Chinese county magistrates had many responsibilities besides adjudication, and their resources were usually stretched thin. The county-level judicial apparatus, such as it was, was so underfunded that it was unable to deal with its civil caseload effectively (Macauley 1994). Qing county courts were operative just a few days a month, for six months a year. Magistrates were appointed on a basis of continuous rotation and served for only three or five years, which meant that they depended heavily on the information supplied to them by their local staff.[51] This responsibility gave lower-ranked officials a great deal of leverage at the local level. Moreover, as Perdue (2004) pointed out, even if the differences between the Chinese and the European systems of legal protection of property rights were overdrawn by previous scholarship, the Chinese system was slow and inefficient, and it was

51. Moreover, other local officials were required to serve at least 250 kilometers from their hometowns, which meant that they depended on local elites to help them run the local administration (see Fu 1993, p. 84).

no wonder that most disputes were resolved elsewhere. Both the authorities and citizens preferred it that way. Thus, as noted previously, the bulk of disputes were resolved by mediation, normally within the clan, based on customary rules. The importance of these rules granted clans and kinship-based communities so much power that even "totalitarian Maoism could do little to change them" (Deng 2016, pp. 86–87).

An integral part of Chinese legal practice was the role played by so-called litigation-masters (*song shi*), as described in detail by Macauley (1998). These private legal specialists, or "pettyfoggers," were akin to informal lawyers or intermediaries between plaintiffs and the magistrates' courts. Because the overworked magistrates resisted lawsuits and the Imperial civil service felt that many such cases were frivolous, the litigation masters faced vilification and at times were even threatened with exile. Yet they fulfilled a useful function, even if in contrast with Europe, they were never formally part of the legal procedure. The inadequate and underresourced formal justice system needed such experts when the informal channels were unsatisfactory, and their persistence was evidence of the adaptability of the Chinese legal system.

As emphasized in this discussion, one of the stark contrasts between Western and Chinese legal systems was the degree of informal conflict resolution in China. Wherever possible in China, conflicts between individuals were settled through mediation, and only when all else failed did it reach the magistrates. In this regard, the system was a perfect illustration of the concept of operating in "the shadow of the law"—filing formal complaints or lawsuits with the local magistrate was a *pis aller* (a last resort). To be sure, as Macauley (1994) pointed out, when Chinese peasants could not resolve their disputes over property or marriage, they often turned to the local courts (*yamen*) for a settlement. But the Chinese bureaucratic apparatus did not help. The Mandarins found litigiousness morally repugnant and worked diligently in support of maintenance of what they thought were traditional norms of harmony.

While magistrates thus indisputably dealt with civil law beyond their duties in criminal cases, there was nothing like the *ius commune* in China. The debate between historians on the precise ways to classify Chinese law demonstrates the difficulty of analyzing it with tools forged to deal with European legal traditions. The disputes illustrate how thousands of years of separate evolution created a profound difference between the two legal traditions. The distinction that emerged during the Qing Dynasty was not so much between civil and criminal cases, but between *cisong*, lawsuits over household, marriage, land,

and some minor criminal matters and *anjian*, which dealt with more severe criminal cases (Deng 2015, p. 32). Disputes on minor matters that could not be mediated or settled within the clan were often resolved by county magistrate courts, but such cases had low priority. They were not formally bound by state law and the Qing codes; instead, magistrates maximized local peace and stability at their personal discretion—although clearly, they were informed by some formal codes. The primary function of formal law was to induce litigants in minor *cisong* cases to settle rather than appeal to the discretion of the courts, which would then be forced to make final judgments. In property disputes, officials tended to decide on the basis of "common sense, circumstances and the spirit of equity, while rarely citing specific legal provisions" (Deng 2015, pp. 33–35). On the other hand, major felonies had to be dealt with using the formal legal codes, and the penalties that magistrates could face for misapplying them were severe.

Above all, in recent decades, scholarship has established that notwithstanding the very different legal modes between China and Europe, China was no less than Europe a society of contracts and arrangements to enforce them. As early as the Han Dynasty, magistrates are known to have enforced contracts; under the Song, the country witnessed "widespread innovation in contract law and practice" (Scogin 1994, p. 35). While contract enforcement worked differently than it did in Europe, it was effective. Written contracts and the very idea of contractual relations permeated Chinese society, extending even further than in Europe, to the point where people made formal contracts with dead people and supernatural beings. When they could, magistrates were in charge of making sure that market exchanges worked properly and according to the rules, even if those rules were often different and less formal (Perdue 2004, p. 56). Scogin (1994, pp. 36–37) concludes that when examined in detail, Chinese contract practices were not all that different from the West, "but their function and meaning often differed considerably from the legal implication of those elements in the West. In China contract practice encountered needs that were rare in the West: the demands of the regulatory bureaucracy, its internal policing, and complying with the requirements of ancestor cults and clan solidarity."

In sum, China and Europe were both sophisticated market economies that depended on property rights and contracts supported by trust and third-party enforcement. While the institutional foundations of their economies differed in many dimensions, it is not easy to conclude that one system clearly dominated.

Law and Culture in China

Legal development in China depended on the development of institutions, but institutions may have had little impact if the rules that set incentives and constraints were not enforced by either legitimacy or coercion. Cultural beliefs were crucial here. Confucianism purported to be a way of life that maintained harmony and cooperation without the benefit of the law (Teng 1977). In theory, social structures based on Confucian tenets were governed by a set of rules and norms known as *li*. These rules of behavior set standards of decency and morality that guaranteed social harmony in a Confucian world. In practice, of course, this was unrealistic, not least because it was realized that such moral behavior was largely confined to the elites.[52] The concept of *Junzi* (moral and learned men) was central to the Confucian notion of a good society; such superior men had a natural right, and it implied that what later became known as the "Chinese gentry" could exercise a fair amount of independence from the Imperial bureaucracy. Furthermore, while the rules of *li* specified good behavior, they stressed family loyalty above all. Mencius, one of the intellectual founding fathers of Confucianism, stated, "If each man would love his parents and show the due respect to his elders, the whole land would enjoy tranquility" (Mencius 1861, p. 178). Hence, Confucianism supported communitarian values such as loyalty to relatives rather than universalistic. Confucian doctrine retained a strong hierarchical bend, in which the norms of behavior were strictly conditional on whether one was dealing with a superior, an inferior, or an equal.

Directly opposed to Confucian thought was the doctrine known as *Legalism* or *Fajia*, which emerged in China in the fourth and third centuries BC. Legalism postulated a Hobbesian worldview: a strong ruler needed to enforce laws strictly to prevent people from misbehaving. It minimized human agency and the discretion of officials and relied on *Fa* (a universally applicable set of laws, administrative methods, and standards).[53] In the Legalist view, China

52. The *Li-chi* (book of rites) states explicitly that "the rules (li) do not go down to the common people. The penal statutes do not go up to the great officer" (*Li-chi* 1967). In other words, adherence to the codes of conduct was a way to distinguish upper class people from commoners (Holcombe 1994, p. 82). Xunzi, one of the classic philosophers, noted that "to rule the gentlemen, we must use li; but to rule the masses, we have to resort to *fa* (law)" (cited by Mei 1932, p. 864).

53. In the words of Derk Bodde (1954, p. 168), "[The Legalists'] aim was to create an all-powerful state authority, which could forcibly put an end to the prevailing disorder. . . . Law, in

was to have a rule *by* law rather than a rule *of* law. Morality was irrelevant and unattainable, and the state needed to suppress local elites who attempted to exercise autonomy. Legalism, which remained influential in Chinese political and legal doctrine, thus presented a very different approach to power than that which emerged in Europe, where slowly but certainly the idea of the rule of law began to take root.

The sharpest formulation of Legalism was created in *The Book of Lord Shang*, an ancient Chinese text dating to the third century BC, attributed to the Qin reformer Shang Yang, who served as minister to Duke Xiao of Qin from 359 BC until his death in 338 BC. Yang is generally considered to be the original proponent of the Qin state's "legalist philosophy." The Legalists insisted that laws should apply uniformly to all: the *Guanzi* (a subsequent document that summarized the Legalist position) stated, "When ruler and minister, superior and inferior, noble and humble, all obey the law, this is called great good government."[54] More than Confucianism, Legalism was rooted in beliefs in general morality.[55]

Legalists recognized that laws should be flexible and adapt to changing circumstances. This is evident from excerpts in *Han Feizi*, reputedly written by Han Fei (c.280–233 BC), a philosopher who served the Qin emperor and the chief theoretician of the Legalist school. The text argued, "For governing the people there is no permanent principle save that it is the laws (*fa*) and nothing else that determine the government. Let the laws roll with the times and there will be good government. . . . But let the times shift without any alteration in the laws and there will be disorder" (cited by Bodde and Morris 1967, p. 25).

The Qin Dynasty (221–206 BC), which reunified China, carried out many draconian measures inspired by Legalism. This harshness may well have

---

their hands, was merely one of several such controls; others advocated by them included state rewards for public informers, the use of secret police, institution of group responsibility for crime, and suppression of allegedly seditious literature."

54. The *Guanzi* is an ancient Chinese text attributed to the politician Guan Zhong (720–645 BC), who served as a minister in the state of Qi. It is widely regarded as a foundational document of the Legalist school. *Han Feizi* stated in a famous passage that "the law no more makes exceptions for men of high station than the plumb line bends to accommodate a crooked place in the wood. What the law has decreed the wise man cannot dispute nor the brave man venture to contest. When faults are to be punished, the highest minister cannot escape, when good is to be rewarded, the lowest peasant must not be passed over" (cited by Liang 1989, p. 82).

55. In an essay on the "essence of the six schools of thought," the historian and astrologer Sima Tan (d. 110 BC) noticed that *Fajia* are "strict and have little kindness" and "do not distinguish between kin and stranger, nor differentiate between noble and base: everything is determined by the standard (or law, fa)" (cited by Pines 2018).

contributed to the dynasty's short-livedness. That said, the organization of the empire under the Qin Dynasty became the foundation on which the dynasties that followed built the Imperial bureaucracy. The Han Dynasty, which ruled China for four centuries after the Qin, reestablished Confucianism as the ruling ideology but blended it with many ideas drawn from Legalist writers. Under the framework of Legalist thought, the Qin standardized Chinese currency, introduced official weights and measures, and set up a uniform system of writing, all for the purpose of creating a monolithic bureaucracy to unify the regions of China previously in conflict during the Warring States Period. This bureaucracy was to be salaried, nonhereditary, centrally appointed, and tightly controlled by the Imperial court. Many of those reforms were retained. Legalist influences also can be seen in the establishment of a government monopoly in salt and iron trade. The bureaucratic system combining Legalist and Confucian elements survived in modified form until the fall of the empire in 1912 (Teng 1977). The bureaucratic apparatus that held the Qin and Han states together goes back a lot further; its origins can be traced to the ancient Zhou Dynasty (1046 BC to 771 BC).[56]

Under Emperor Wu of the Han Dynasty (r.141 BC–87 BC), Confucianism was nominally encouraged. This did not mean, however, that Legalism's influence disappeared, especially when it came to ideas concerning efficient governance via a professional bureaucracy. Indeed, under the Han and Tang dynasties, the two ideologies developed what Teng (1977, p. 132) called "an ideological amalgam," in which they eventually agreed on a combination of both *li* and *fa* as a means of maintaining the social order. The Tang Legal Code of the mid-seventh century AD was the culmination of this synthesis. Thus, Legalism's legacy was long-lasting and, in the end, the two schools worked out a modus vivendi.[57] Many elements of the Chinese penal code reflected the ideas of Legalism, such as the rigid formulas for meting out punishment, the implicit assumption that an accused was guilty until proven innocent, and the widespread use of torture to extract confessions.

56. Some scholars have suggested that one could see a parallel between the Chinese distinction between *fa* and *li* and the Western distinction between natural law and positive law (Bodde and Morris 1970).

57. When it became obvious that the penal codes were becoming a permanent fixture, the Confucians softened their hostility to them and grudgingly accepted formal penal law as inevitable. Even then, however, they remained true to form in their insistence that in an ideal state, such arrangements would be unnecessary, and even in highly imperfect administrations, "government by law should always be kept secondary to government by moral precept and example" (Bodde and Morris 1967, p. 18).

While Confucianism and Legalism thus appear on the surface to be diametrically incompatible, Chinese bureaucracies were improbably able to synthesize them into a syncretic blend that became the foundation of Chinese Imperial power that lasted basically until the fall of the empire (Zhao 2015). In Zhao's reading, the combination of the two created a system of government that "merged political and ideological power, harnessed military power, and marginalized economic power" (2015, p. 14). Legalist methods, he argues, provided the instruments of government and Confucianism with legitimacy and moral guidance (p. 292). He adds that the alliance between moralists and realists implied that emperors eventually committed to Confucianism as a ruling ideology and subjected themselves to the control of a Confucian bureaucracy. At the same time, scholar-officials both in and out of the bureaucracy cooperated with the government and supplied meritocratically selected officials who administered the country using "an amalgam of Confucian ethics and Legalist regulations and techniques" (Zhao 2015, p. 14). Zhao's interpretation raises as many questions as it answers (Pines 2016). Among them: Why did it take more than a millennium after the Qin's brief rule for Confucian principles to become the dominant ideological guideline of the mandarinate?

One of the most important products of the Legalist-Confucian synthesis was the abovementioned Tang Legal Code, often regarded as the most important legal work in all of East Asian history. The Tang Code influenced China's modern legal system and also shaped the systems of Japan, Vietnam, and Korea (Johnson 1995, p. 217). First promulgated in AD 653, the Tang Legal Code was standardized and universally applied. It fused Confucian ideas of filial piety and obedience to family heads with the Legalist tradition of strict enforcement of formal laws. But even the penal codes reflected the commitment to family as the fundamental unit of organization in society and the commitment to hierarchical structures within the extended family. Punishment for a crime varied depending on the identities of the perpetrator and the victim, not just the nature and circumstances of the crime. The code recognized eight "privileged groups," among them members of the Imperial family, descendants of former Imperial houses, and high officials (mandarins) and their immediate family members.[58] That said, the principles of *li* implied a more demanding moral code of behavior of those who were so privileged.

58. Persons in these eight categories were exempt from the regular rules dealing with capital crimes. The emperor's court had to consent to their being brought to trial, and if they were found guilty, determine their punishments separately. Sentences would be reduced by one

Punishment for transgressions varied with the accused's seniority within the family and within society. The closer the relationship between two people involved in an offense, the heavier the punishment for the junior offender and the lighter that of the senior one (Lewis 2009). The underlying theory—and very different from Europe—was that society was not seen as consisting of individuals; it consisted of families. Within the family, the members owed complete obedience to the head of the family. Overall, the Tang legal codes, much like the subsequent legal codes, were primarily concerned with criminal law and the relationship between the citizens and the state. Its emphasis on family loyalty and authoritarianism has been regarded as a means by which the central government tried to control the masses.

The role of the clan in the legal administration of China was substantial. The clans that became increasingly prevalent during and after the Song were governed by a board of elders made of the oldest educated heads of families. The clan held judicial power to arbitrate disputes, and its decisions were typically accepted. The role of the clan in Chinese society was fundamental. The countryside, where the mass of the population lived, would have been ungovernable without it. This kind of governance was achieved by a form of collective responsibility, in which people kept an eye on their relatives because they themselves could be held accountable for the actions of other members of the clan. Thus, clans and families were effectively in charge of local law and order (Teng 1977, pp. 139–42).

The relatively low profile of Chinese formal and codified civil codes can thus be explained, at least in part, by relatively low demand. China did not need such codes as much as Europe did; it had alternative and highly functional means of dispute resolution at the basic levels of social organization and contract arbitration, which were complementary to formal courts. The court itself preferred that parties engage in arbitration and negotiation rather than providing a ruling itself. Disputes within the extended family were settled by other kin; if that failed, the court appointed subcounty overseers (*zongli*), village heads, or even *yamen* runners as arbiters (Allee 1994). Some scholars, such as Teng (1977, p. 143), have hence concluded that "on the whole, China was well governed" and that a social structure squarely founded on families and clans "did an excellent job in keeping social tranquility."

---

degree and the maximum sentence could not be more than three years of penal servitude (Johnson 1995). It is no wonder that throughout Imperial China, placing a member in a career in the civil service would be fervently desired by all families.

A world based on families and clans had a downside, however: a deep tendency toward nepotism and corruption. As discussed previously, widespread corruption and nepotism were endemic in China, and both domestic authors and eighteenth-century foreign travelers to China frequently commented on it (Park 1997). Scholars have argued, perhaps with some exaggeration, that the family needed and was backed by the state but in the end had no loyalty to it; this was because the family "throve on particularist relationships" (Baker 1979, p. 123). The underlying cultural beliefs of China were quite close to what Banfield (1958) described as "amoral familism," as was the dominant trend in southern Italy.[59] Yet familism also had its merits: by punishing not just officials accused of corruption, but also their family members, the Imperial government used the commitment to family as a means to deter and ward off the worst excesses of nepotism and corruption.

5. Market Institutions

Both Europe and China became highly commercialized in the second millennium. The comparative development of markets in China and Europe can be better understood when it is realized that their institutional foundations rested on distinct social organizations of cooperation. In contrast with China, European markets increasingly supported more impersonal exchange, particularly in financial markets. Formal credit markets and instruments such as bills of exchange and insurance policies were widely used to support trading at arm's length in Europe from medieval times. The story in China was more complex. McCulloch's *Dictionary* flatly stated in the 1840s that "credit is little known" there (1851, vol. 1, p. 628). Modern research has refuted such oversimplified notions. Credit in some forms existed, of course: for one thing, pawnshops were already known in Song times and grew rapidly during the eighteenth century (Elvin 1973, pp. 210, 249). Small-scale credit associations could be found all over China from at least the Song era, although transactions were normally confined to kin (McDermott 2022, p. 622). Mortgage markets also existed, but they took the form of *dian*, in which the lender could never quite take full possession of the land even in the case of default (Zhang 2017).

59. Lang (1946, p. 22) noted that officials who refused to employ kin met with general disapproval and "all work depended on personal relationships." However, statistical studies have shown that, at least for advancement within the civil service, nepotism may have been somewhat constrained by the Imperial policies of the Qing government (Marsh 1960).

Finally, China adopted a variation of the European *commenda*, in which an itinerant merchant and a stationary lender agreed to share the profits; this form of contract flourished especially during the Song Dynasty, when many thousands of Arab and Persian merchants lived in Chinese port cities and in all likelihood brought the idea with them. Another Chinese arrangement known as *ortoy*, more common during the Yuan Dynasty, was a contract between rulers and foreigners, but it too involved both credit and risk-pooling (Harris 2020). That said, anything resembling a joint-stock corporation such as those that emerged in Western Europe around 1600 was not used in China prior to the late nineteenth century.

What was missing in China was a more formal credit market relying on banks and sophisticated trade credit at arm's length. Similarly rare was the use of book credit in daily transactions such as peasants selling at local markets, which remained cash-based until the twentieth century (Kuroda 2013). In a recent contribution, Chen et al. (2022, pp. 1378–79) show that the clan system in China created a substantial obstacle to the development of financial markets and "the deeply entrenched Confucian clan has historically stifled and continues to depress both the demand for and the supply of external finance in China." Clans supplied much of the need for credit, which may well have reduced risk and transaction costs, but in the long run, they left the Chinese relatively "uninterested in external finance" (Chen et al. 2022, p. 1410). Even today, they note, regions that had strong clans have relatively little demand for external finance. In short, markets in both China and Europe may have been integrated, but impersonal exchange was far more prevalent in Europe, where universalistic values supported institutions that made trade between unrelated strangers possible (Greif 2005).

One example of an institution that helped markets to function in Europe was the capability of local public officials to dispense impartial justice to foreign merchants during the medieval Commercial Revolution. The Community Responsibility System (CRS) emerged the eleventh and twelfth centuries in Western Europe (Greif 2006a).[60] The system's basic mechanism was simple: If a member of one community reneged on his contractual obligation toward a member of another community, the cheated trader's community could impose a cost on citizens of the other's residence, thus motivating the cheater's community to punish the cheater and compensate for the damage. Knowing

---

60. For other similar institutions that met this need, see, for example, Gelderblom (2011, 2013), Strum (2013), and Kessler (2007).

this, traders were more likely to enter into impersonal, intercommunity exchanges, as the CRS mitigated the risk of being cheated. In short, the CRS made impersonal exchange possible not despite the partiality of the courts, but because of it; the court cared about the community's collective reputation (Greif 2006a,b).[61] One important feature of this system was that the CRS implied de facto equality before the law. Similarly, equal legal treatment of out-of-town traders was generally mandated in European cities and had a positive and significant impact on trade (Boerner and Quint 2016; Gelderblom 2013). The CRS took advantage of repeated intercommunal relations to support nonrepeated relations among their constituting members.

One would expect that, in principle, a similar institution could have been used in interclan relations in China. Such arrangements were indeed employed with respect to various aspects of interclan relations. Clan regulations generally specified that "a clan should always watch its reputation by preventing its members from harming outsiders and by refusing its offenders clan protection" (Liu 1959, p. 152). At the same time, however, the moral obligation to kin seems to have limited the credibility and effectiveness of intraclan punishments for interclan transgressions: "The punishment of a member who misbehaves against a nonclan member is usually oral censure," while "the punishment for siding with outsiders in an aggression against fellow clan members is, however, much more severe . . . the group interest is placed higher than [interclan] community solidarity" (Liu 1959, p. 152).

More generally, the communitarian values associated with clans reduced the enforcement costs of intragroup exchanges relative to intergroup transactions. Fewer interclan interactions, in turn, reduced the return from investing in legal enforcement and undermined alternative reputation-based institutions such as the CRS. Such institutions require a sufficiently high present value of expected intergroup future relations to make threats of punishment credible and costly. Under a universalistic value system, the set of relations that had to rely on legal enforcement was more or less the same in intragroup and intergroup relations.

---

61. To illustrate the historical importance of the CRS, consider a charter granted to London in the early 1130s. King Henry I announced that "all debtors to the citizens of London discharge these debts, or prove in London that they do not owe them; and if they refuse either to pay or to come and make such proof, then the citizens to whom the debts are due may take pledges within the city either from the borough or from the village or from the county in which the debtor lives" (*English Historical Documents* 1968, vol. II, pp. 1012–13; also see the discussion by Stubbs 1913). This charter is representative; evidence from other charters, treaties, and regulations reveals that the CRS was the law of the land in England.

Consistent with this analysis, intraclan commercial networks remained important to long-distance trade in China.[62] In these networks, communitarian values and institutions based on repeated interactions supported cooperation. To illustrate, "The sprawling merchant diasporas that managed 18th century interregional trade usually were built upon kinship ties. The huge shipments of rice . . . were overseen by groups of Kiangsi merchants organized internally by lineage" (Rowe 2002, pp. 531–32).[63]

As Ma (2004, pp. 267–69) pointed out, however, such differences should not be exaggerated. Over time, the Chinese social organizations evolved, and by the late Qing era, Chinese lineages had become more dynamic and flexible than was previously thought. The lineage, as distinguished from the family, could assume an almost "corporate" character. Furthermore, inclusion in lineages was less rigid than an absolute insistence on a formal common ancestry would suggest, with lineages merged and resources pooled as needed (Ruskola 2013).[64] In the later years of the empire, the clan-based system became less rigid and progressed slowly into a more flexible institutional structure.

In turn, intraclan exchange reinforced communitarian values. Chinese clans' rules from the twentieth century still stated that "one must be very

62. Very similar phenomena can be observed in the Roman Empire, where large kinship groups sent members overseas to serve as agents in important remote trading partners (Terpstra 2013).

63. The same was true for the overseas trading network, where limited morality was still the background for the importance of kin relations in overcoming transaction costs driven by lack of trust and asymmetric information. See, for instance, Landa (1995) and Pyatt and Redding (2000). Furthermore, in the late Qing years, we can observe some nonkin organizations such as the anti-Qing "brotherhood" in Chaozhou, a mixture between an anti-Qing guerilla group and a criminal gang (Macauley 2021, pp. 68–96). These organizations extended the familial logic of group solidarity, which was the normal way of securing cooperation, to "multi-surname networks as a means of coping with unpredictable challenges" (Macauley 2021, p. 75).

64. The importance of personal relations in supporting cooperation is also evident from the creation of fictional kinship groups. The clan of Li in Wenchuan provides an example of what Zheng (2001, p. 133) called a "contractual clan." Everyone who shared the clan's surname could have bought a share (when offered to finance clan-specific local public or local goods) in return for the proportional number of prayers for the souls of his ancestors. When cooperation with kin was insufficient, the boundaries of the group were extended to individuals who were closer to their kin than others, and particularly to those with close places of residence or origin. As one had to move further away from kinlike relations, more assertive means were used to create kinlike relations. These means included adopting an adult, adopting the same surname, developing a myth of common origin, and creating a clan trust and similar setups.

careful about" friendship with strangers (Liu 1959, p. 148). About 95 percent of clan rule books called for care in selecting friends, while only 8 percent called for "helping a friend in trouble" (Liu 1959, p. 148). The impact of communitarian values on market institutions is reflected in a pervasive reliance on personal relations for facilitating exchange. Investments specific to those relations compensated for the absence of generalized trust. Clans from one locality cooperated to advance their common interests in other locations. Thus, much property was owned by the lineage, and the managers had the rights and responsibilities typically required for their roles, but they were still unable to dispose of property without the consent of the lineage segments concerned.

Moreover, in the trading and late settlement frontiers in the north and Taiwan, temple-based worship associations were established as a substitute for the absence of strong clans (for more details, see chapter 5). Advanced payment and guarantees were among the other institutionalized mechanisms widely used in China to facilitate trade among nonkin.[65] While it is probable that local markets in China before 1800 were, on average, not less developed than those of Europe, the same could not be said of long-distance commerce. "Despite China's size, trade was largely local, the disputants lived in the next lane . . . and neighborly mediation was readily accepted because, after all, everyone involved in the controversy was going to have to go on living with everyone else after the present disagreement had been smoothed over" (Gellhorn 1987, p. 3). What long-distance trade there was depended on large kinship relations. The importance of family ties in trade was particularly prominent among Chinese merchants in the Chinese diaspora in southeast Asia (Landa 2016).

6. The Coevolution of Values, Organizations, and Institutions

The bifurcation of the legal systems described in this discussion illustrates the complementarities between institutions, social organizations, and cultural traits. The legal institutions of Europe and China evolved in different directions because their societies relied on different social organizations and different value systems

---

65. "A trader in grain or goods conventionally made a large advance payment—sometimes as much as eighty percent of the agreed price—when placing the order. Disputes about the quality of what had been purchased rarely arose because, by commercial custom and private agreement, the purchaser was expected to inspect carefully and to decline acceptance of anything found to be unsatisfactory" (Gellhorn 1987, p. 3).

to enforce cooperation. The bifurcation of political institutions in China and Europe, as discussed in chapter 7, provides a similar perspective. But the argument that the institutional bifurcation between China and Europe was due to social and cultural complementarities and self-reinforcing dynamics has another relevant implication—namely, that the influence should go in both directions: not just from culture and organizations to institutions, but also in reverse. The value systems and cultural beliefs should evolve to be consistent with prevailing social organizations and with legal and political institutions by internalizing the rules and customs as virtuous.

Is this coevolution of morality, institutions, and social organizations consistent with the historical evidence? This question has attracted a great deal of interest among social scientists in recent years, and the literature on the topic is large but still unsettled (e.g., Alesina and Giuliano 2015; Henrich 2020). Examining the compatibility of social organizations, institutions, and value systems is challenging because morality is difficult to observe on its own; examining it in the past is even more difficult since it leaves behind only subtle and indirect evidence.

Yet sometimes values can be inferred from indirect evidence. Next, we present three sets of indirect historical evidence that serve as illustrative examples of how the cultural differences and divergent ideas of morality between China and Europe affected the operation of institutions. The three sets pertain to the theory and practice of criminal law enforcement, the organization and practice of voluntary charity, and the social status of law enforcers.

Criminal Law Enforcement

The punishments imposed on criminal offenses reveal a great deal about the ideas about morality in a society because crime is immoral by definition, and it is a natural human instinct to impose harsher punishments on more immoral acts. It also reflects on the ruling ideas in society about retribution, deterrence, and (in modern times) rehabilitation.[66] The histories of criminal law in China

---

66. The most influential thinker about the nature of criminal law and punishment in eighteenth-century Europe was the Italian philosopher Cesare Beccaria (1748–1794). His *Dei delitti et delle pene* (1764) marks a highlight in the Italian Enlightenment and was a powerful and influential statement that punishment should be a deterrent, not performed for retribution. The impact of his work was felt all the way to Russia and North America and clearly was strongly consonant with the belief in rational action and in a utilitarian rather than an ethical approach to the question of punishment typical of enlightenment culture (e.g., Robertson 2021).

and Europe reflect distinct and changing moral bases. Early in both histories, when kinship-based organizations prevailed in China and Europe, criminal codes similarly conditioned the severity of punishment for a given offense on the identities of those involved.[67] Subsequently, however, the two civilizations' outlooks diverged. Punishments in Europe became increasingly independent of identity, at least de jure, and as outlined previously, Europe developed an ideal concept of equality before the law.[68] In China, the identity of both perpetrator and victim became more important over time in determining the punishment.

The European legal codes reflect the temporary surge in moral obligations to kin following the collapse of the Roman Empire. They also reflected the subsequent decline of these obligations as much of medieval Europe slowly transformed into a more individualistic society. Consider the earliest Germanic legal code of the Salian Franks (sixth century) mentioned earlier in this chapter. As we saw previously, the code imposed so-called blood money on a killer of another person depending on the status and identity of the victim.[69] In subsequent centuries, however, the theory and practice of criminal law drastically changed, and identity and kinship connections mattered less and less. Moreover, the resistance to antiquated procedures such as trial by combat and ordeal became prominent in "communities that had a strong sense of the individual's responsibility and his citizenship or membership" (Kelly 1992, pp. 146–48). Consequently, European criminal codes did away with status-based punishments and no longer depended on whether parties were kin. This is most evident in communal laws, which were based on the principle of equality before the law and reflected a generalized morality.[70] By the seventeenth century, the criminal law

67. These premodern distinctions included the obvious ones between slaves/freemen and male/female.

68. Some relics of the past, however, remained in force until the nineteenth century, such as the custom of executing members of the upper class by decapitation whereas lower class people were hanged. The guillotine, which reflected the egalitarian views of the French Revolution, symbolized the end of this class-based distinction.

69. A killer of a (free) Frankish man or a woman was to pay 200 solidi to the victim's relative as compensation. If the crime was committed on a public official, the penalty was higher, reaching as much as 1,800 solidi if the victim was serving in the army. The highest blood money for killing a Gallo-Roman, however, was generally half the amount imposed for killing a Frankish person (Drew 1991).

70. To illustrate this point, consider the fourteenth-century statute of the Piedmontese commune of Bugelle (Biella). The statute declares that "the consuls can and should render justice and a fair reckoning in respect to each man of Biella, each person residing in Biella, and any one who seeks justice from them" (Sella 1904, section 1.2). The same principle prevailed in England

imposed a higher penalty on the rich for the same crime, to equalize the severity of the punishment (Kelly 1992, pp. 238–39).

In contrast, under the late Imperial Chinese law, punishments remained a function of kinship relations. Generally, penalties were most severe for crimes committed against senior relatives, less severe if committed against those outside of the extended family, and least severe if committed by senior family members against their younger kin. Even in "the early twentieth century a father could kill his son without incurring much more than a reproof and a warning, while a son who killed his father, or even his only slightly older brother, faced a very harsh punishment. Only the killing of friend by friend came to court on an even keel, so to speak" (Gellhorn 1987, p. 2).

Voluntary Charity

The customs regulating private contributions to charity are another good measure of moral obligations toward nonkin, whether personal or impersonal. Charity is *personal* when the givers donate to specific individuals whom they know; it is *impersonal* otherwise. If communitarian values were more important in China relative to Europe, then we should observe more personal charity among kin. Similarly, if universalistic values were prevalent in Europe, impersonal charity to nonkin should be more likely to predominate. This, indeed, was the case. In premodern China, kin groups were the main source of charity, either through clan trusts or local temples (as was particularly common in multiclan villages).[71] Permanent, impersonal charity organizations appeared only in the early seventeenth century, and on a limited scale.[72] Although Chinese authorities encouraged impersonal charity, some moral philosophers

---

during that period. The judges in Exeter and Southampton took an oath to "render justice indifferently to rich and poor . . . [and] to do and keep justice to all persons, rich and poor, denizens and strangers" (cited by Tait 1936, p. 275).

71. The moral aspect of this practice is clear from the analysis of the view expressed by the prominent Song statesman and poet Fan Zhongyan (989–1052), one of the most prominent of China's scholar-officials and the innovator of the clan trust. Fan decreed that the lineage should aid only relatives with lineage ties clearly documented in their genealogy, which became the norm for hundreds of years that followed (Smith 1987, p. 316).

72. In surveying the evidence, Smith noted that "the first documented benevolent society appeared in . . . Honan [Henan], in 1590" (1987, p. 311) and concluded that only "during the late Ming (1368–1644) and early Qing (1580–1750) . . . [were new organizations created] to voluntary or compassionate giving to the poor and needy outside one's family" (pp. 319–21).

asserted that the diversion of assistance from kin to strangers was immoral. A popular seventeenth-century book written on morality "tells of a generous scholar who was derided by a member of his lineage for lightly giving money away to strangers" as a charity (Smith 1987, p. 316).

Clans remained the mainstay of the social safety net in assisting the indigent. This limited morality logic perplexed Western observers. John Ramsay McCulloch's widely read *Dictionary*, in its essay on China, pondered the contradiction between destitution and generosity toward the poor. In his words, "The conditions of the poor are wretched in the extreme; they are frequently destitute of food. . . . It is a curious fact, that . . . the Chinese be remarkable for assisting each other, particularly their own relations" (1851, vol. 1, p. 361). Early twentieth-century clan rules (1912–1936) reveal the persistence of the kin-based welfare system. Liu (1959) examined 151 genealogies containing 316 clan rules, some of which were from previous centuries. These are considered representative of the traditional clan rules. About half of the genealogies (75 out of 151) contain sections concerning clan relief and aid of needy members (Liu 1959, p. 217).[73] In short, the clan was the organization that organized relief and redistribution, and generous people provided relief to their kin.

In Europe, by contrast, impersonal voluntary charity was common, evidenced by the fact that by the sixteenth century, organizations providing impersonal private charity predominated.[74] Moreover, in the early seventeenth century, the English Poor Law formalized charity and made the relief of the poor—both "deserving" and "able-bodied"—mandatory until its abolition in 1834. Moreover, the English Poor Law made impersonal poverty relief a nationwide mandate, administered by local authorities. Elsewhere in Europe, it was more haphazard. Poverty relief in cities was common, but in rural areas, it could be spotty. In Germany, the Reformation shifted the responsibility for poverty relief from religious officials over to municipal authorities (Dittmar and Meisenzahl 2020). The French poverty relief system was supervised and

73. Another piece of evidence for the extent of personal charity is found in a seminal 1925 study of country life in South China. The poor "depend largely upon the aid granted them by the village leaders from the income of the public property and upon the surplus over the cost of worship when they rotatively administer ancestral property" (Kulp 1925, p. 104). Moreover, the prominent Chinese historian of common descent groups, Hsien-Chin Hu, noted that on the eve of Communist era clans were still prominent providers of welfare assistance to their members (1948, pp. 87–90).

74. To illustrate, London in 1560 had about 35 poverty relief foundations, and by 1700, there were more than 100 of them. In late sixteenth-century Bristol, 25 percent of the wills written made a donation for the "relief of the poor," while a century later, 30 percent of the wills in England made such donations (Ben-Amos 2000).

controlled by the state but was financed mainly by voluntary contributions. Its mainstay was in-door relief through "general hospitals" funded by local organizations but mandated by royal decree (Balch 1893, pp. 40–48). It too had all the hallmarks of impersonal charity.

To summarize, an examination of charity and poverty-relief organizations illustrates the difference between the religious and cultural beliefs prevailing in China and Europe. The divergent trajectories taken by the two worlds at the end of the first millennium AD created different initial conditions that accentuated future bifurcation. In China, moral obligations toward kin became stronger, whereas in Europe, a variety of factors created a cultural predisposition toward a more generalized morality, in which kinship played a relatively smaller role. These distinctions became more pronounced over time, together with the diffusion and consolidation of different social organizations, as implied by the theory. In that fashion, differences in social organization further amplified and widened the differences in culture.

Bailiffs versus Runners

The distinct cultural foundations of cooperation in China and Europe also manifested themselves in the nature and capacities of local state administration. In China, the state depended on clans and the local elites to enforce its policies, but the Imperial administration could not rely on the local social organizations to implement policies that were contrary to their interests. Moreover, strengthening and institutionalizing the administrative power of lineages increased the ability of clans to resist state authority (Rowe 1998; Hung 2009).[75] As a result, the Chinese state operated on what may be called a "dual system": authorities delegated to the clans the implementation of mutually beneficial policies (with the local gentry serving as intermediaries), but they relied on a parallel coercive administration to implement policies that the clans objected to.

Unpopular policies were carried out by a paid local staff, typically known as "yamen runners" (the *yamen* was the office of the local magistrate).[76] The

75. Chen Hongmou, the governor of Jiangxi, granted lineage headmen considerable judicial and disciplinary powers over their kin in 1742, to be exercised in conjunction with their officiating over the sacrificial rites at the ancestral temple. Chen was a great believer in lineage organization as the preferred solution to "socially deviant behavior" (Rowe 1998, p. 384).

76. The term "runner" is a very loose translation of the Chinese *chaiyi*, meaning "drafted service" (as the occupation was originally recruited) and refers to all activities carried out by officials outside the gates of the *yamen* (Reed 2000, chapter 4).

runners were so important that a late Imperial magistrate noted that they "were an official's claws and teeth, and their services could not be dispensed with for a single day or in a single task" (cited by Ch'ü 1962, p. 57). Among other tasks, the runners collected taxes and debts, acted as a police force, arrested criminals, and imposed punishments. In terms of the tasks that they performed, the runner was roughly the equivalent of the sheriff's deputy or bailiff in England or the *vogt* in German-speaking countries.

The tasks of the Chinese runners and the European bailiffs (we use this term generically) were similar in supporting local cooperation with the government. The more generalized morality that prevailed in Europe made many of the bailiffs' tasks consistent with the prevailing beliefs and attitudes. A bailiff or other court employee pursuing a delinquent debtor or collecting the poor rate from landowners was effectively the means through which cooperation was achieved by enforcing the rules and reducing free-riding. These officials were in general respected members of the community.

By contrast, in China, runners were the means to enforce the will of the state when the interests of the state and the local officials clashed with the clan's interests; they were far more controversial and regarded as social outcasts. Runners faced disdain from much of society, even by the magistrates who employed them.[77] They were local individuals—a necessary condition for the lowest-level administration to be effective at the time—who nevertheless were willing to take actions that harmed other locals, potentially even their kin. Runners were regarded as people who placed obedience to those who paid them to enforce the law above their moral obligations. In short, a runner in China had revealed himself to be "immoral" by the prevailing standards, whereas a European bailiff did not. Hence the Chinese runners were more likely to be individuals with low social rank, who could not be trusted even by the authorities whom they served. In point of fact, most of the *yamen* runners were poor, some had criminal records, and most had no property (Ch'ü 1962).

---

77. The evidence regarding the legal designation of the runners confirms that the authorities held the runners who served them in contempt. Prior to the early eighteenth century, runners were "legally classified as 'mean' people . . . a status comparable to that of a prostitute, actor or slave. Like all other 'mean' people, they were discriminated against. They were not allowed to take civil service examinations and were prevented from entering officialdom." (Ch'u 1970, p. 62). As Reed (2000, pp. 3, 169) points out, ironically one of the functions of the magistrate was to protect the people against the villainies of "yamen vermin," as the runners were known.

The adverse selection of Chinese runners, their very poor reputations, and the institutionalized and cultural discrimination against them implied that runners were likely susceptible to corruption unless deterred by the local magistrate or the Censorate. The length to which the magistrates would go in trying to prevent corruption among the runners is striking. For example, for a considerable period of time, runners managed tax collection as follows: taxpayers would place their tax money in a locked box and runners would deliver it to the magistrate, the only person with the key to open the box. Yet despite these efforts to curb corruption, runners were still often able to abuse their positions. There were too many of them to be effectively supervised by the Censorate, and the process of recruitment broke down at the lower levels, where magistrates had little control over selecting clerks and runners. The runner positions were either hereditary or purchased from previous holders (Kiser and Tong 1992). Junior officials such as runners and lower-level clerks possessed locally specific knowledge that the frequently rotating higher-level bureaucrats lacked, making these officials costlier to replace if they were dismissed.[78]

The contrast with local peacekeepers and bailiffs in Europe is striking.[79] Recent research has shown that local peacekeepers "played a significant role not just in local justice, but in the microcosm of shire politics and society" (Musson 2002, p. 3). They worked in partnership with justices of the peace in presenting jurors, witnesses at trials, and even trial jurors. They were also in charge of arresting persons prosecuted by appeal or indictment who had been served in the county court. Their independence and capacity for initiative were vital, as was their ability to maintain a balance between the king's interests and sensitive local issues (Musson 2002). Their social status was

---

78. An inquiry into tax shortfalls in the Jiangsu province in 1788 revealed that 41 percent was the result of corruption by the runners (Kiser and Tong 1992, p. 318). Reed (2000) has revised to some extent this rather dismal picture of local administration, arguing that the rules by which runners had to operate were vague and poorly spelled out. In the absence of any formal body of standards and guidelines, they had to do their jobs by improvising, imposing their own set of rules, and they remained to some extent an informal case of administrative employment "operating without benefit of externally defined structure or supervision . . . the ability to prosper relied not only on the application of rules and standards but also on personal contacts and support from family members, patrons, and colleagues" (Reed 2000, p. 159).

79. The term "bailiff" refers to two kinds of officials: the superintendent of the manor of the lord and an employee of the sheriff, working for the so-called hundreds courts, executing writs, collecting fines, assembling juries, and performing other official duties.

accordingly higher than that of their Chinese counterparts. In England, for example, only a freeman could aspire to become a bailiff.[80] The function of bailiffs overlapped with local constables, the latter being an ancient institution originally in charge of military preparedness and defense. Local constables assumed more responsibilities with the Statute of Winchester (1285), which increased their responsibilities for local law enforcement. After the Black Death, constables were even put in charge of controlling the movement of laborers, whom local landowners tried to tie to the land. Constables (like justices of the peace) were unpaid, and until the nineteenth century, they were the chief form of local law enforcement.

In sum, while morality and attitudes in the past are hard to observe directly, the features of institutions that were set up and the local public goods that were provided can often indicate what moral principles underlay the functioning of society. The striking feature of Imperial China was that in a world of communitarian values organized around clans, local law enforcement officials such as *yamen* runners would be highly unpopular. In a world of more universalistic and individualist values, such as England, this was far less the case.

7. Concluding Remarks

The legal, administrative, and economic institutions of China and Europe were consistent with their distinctive social organizations and cultural traits. In Europe, administrative responsibilities gradually shifted from territorially small units, such as local towns and villages, to the state. With the increasing standardization of local customs and language, better access to local information, and stronger state capacity, the central governments took over enforcement and officials assumed responsibility for law and order and public goods.[81] This development contrasts sharply with China, where a communitarian value

---

80. The backgrounds of bailiffs varied, but their social status was usually substantial. Some peacekeepers came from recognizable county aristocratic families, but most belonged to the minor gentry or substantial peasants. Qualifications for these positions required some legal knowledge, as well as the necessary local social status to carry out their tasks successfully (Musson 2002, p. 20).

81. In Britain, local notables continued to have important administrative functions, such as justices of the peace and Poor Law guardians. But these functions were supervised and coordinated by the state. Blanning (2007), for example, pointed out that the British state was appreciably more effective than many of the "absolutisms" of continental Europe in terms of actual implementation of legislation. He explained that by "the substantial overlap between the national lawmakers (Members of Parliament), and the local law-enforcers (Justices of the Peace)."

system preserved and enhanced the central role of clans and local gentry in local administration. The Imperial bureaucracy, pressed increasingly by the weakness of its fiscal resources, responded by relegating more and more interpersonal legal matters to clans and to local authorities. Personal relations based on kinship ties, whether real or imaginary, were considered essential for local cooperation. The increasingly diverging state and market institutions in China and Europe reinforced their different underlying social organizations and cultural traits. The delegation of legal enforcement to the clans, for example, fostered closer and more frequent interactions among clan members and impeded interactions with nonmembers.

To sum up, a millennium ago, the differences in social organization between Europe and China were not overwhelming. Positive feedback mechanisms, however, amplified distinct initial social and cultural conditions that prevailed in Europe and China around AD 1000. The resulting divergent evolution of the organization of society affected subsequent social, cultural, and institutional developments. In China, clans increasingly became the locus of cooperation among kin, motivated by communitarian values, informal institutions, and a central government that relied on them for local administration. In Europe, extended kinship networks faded away, replaced by corporations. The difference was decisive to the evolution of both institutions and culture in both worlds. The same was true for the economy. The way that markets functioned in both worlds reflected those differences and led to divergence in the way that commerce took place in both worlds.

As the basic units of cooperation, clans and corporations affected more than markets: they determined the provision of social safety nets, legal development, and at the end of the day, the organization of the state. Their dynamics differed due to the complementarities between their cultural, social, and institutional elements. These effects persist today. Persistence, however, does not mean stasis; indeed, both systems were successful in adapting to change. The European economies responded to the technologically driven increase in economies of scale by relying on the law and universalistic values to separate firm ownership from control. In China, kinship organizations were supplemented by more agile, versatile, and contingent networks that included other kin and relatives (Thøgersen 2002; Ruskola 2000).

For instance, the Turnpike Acts, which were resisted in many places, were rammed through efficiently (pp. 10–11).

The European system had a comparative advantage in supporting imper-sonal exchange, while the Chinese system had a comparative advantage in economic activities that relied on personal relations. In both cases, these sys-tems created trust and thus reduced transaction costs, but they did so in dif-ferent ways, based on their social organizations. Each system had advantages and drawbacks, and it is difficult to assess their relative efficiency, although as we will see in chapter 9, they had different implications for the dynamic devel-opment of the economy in the long run. But whatever the assessment, Europe's and China's economic, social, and political histories bear the hallmark of their distinct social organizations and cultural heritages and the growing gap between how the two worlds functioned.

9

The Industrial Revolution

1. Introduction

One answer often provided to the question of the origins of the Great Divergence, raised in chapter 2, is very succinct and precise: Europe had an Industrial Revolution in the eighteenth century, and China did not. This answer is a favorite of members of the so-called California School, who have argued that as late as 1750, the two worlds of Europe and China were very close in their technological attainments and standards of living. In this interpretation, an economic gap in income emerged only in the eighteenth century due to the development of advanced machinery and a widespread application of fossil fuels in manufacturing (e.g., Goldstone 2009). At first blush, however, the Industrial Revolution in and of itself does not serve as an explanation. Instead, it only pushes the question of the origins of the Great Divergence further out. The question of *why* Europe had an Industrial Revolution at that time and China did not remains central to the debate. Similarly, it raises the question of how far back we can trace the deeper roots of the gap. In this chapter, we propose a new interpretation of the factors before and during the Industrial Revolution that help explain why it started in Europe and not elsewhere.

Before laying out our interpretation of the Industrial Revolution, it is important to emphasize that it was a *Western European* phenomenon, not just a British one. To be sure, Britain was the leader in the sense that most of the technological advances that formed the core of the Industrial Revolution occurred first in Britain, and from there spread to the Continent and beyond. Yet the differences between Britain and the follower nations in Europe were small in comparison to the gaps with Asia, the Middle East, or Africa. A substantial number of the pivotal inventions associated with the Industrial Revolution were made on the Continent, even if their successful deployment first took place in Britain. Moreover, the natural philosophy and mathematics on which many of the pivotal inventions were based came from all over Western Europe. Furthermore, while the Industrial Revolution clearly had its start in Britain, much of Western Europe soon adopted British technology and industrialized some decades after Britain. By the late nineteenth century, a "convergence club" of industrialized and economically advanced nations had emerged in the "West." British leadership, in other words, was important but not decisive in the longer run. Nor was it a permanent feature: by 1870, Britain's technological and economic leadership had begun to decline. By 1914, it had more or less vanished, even if Great Britain was still very rich by any standard and remained a charter member of the convergence club.[1] Hence, if we are to explain the Industrial Revolution as a broader phenomenon, we have to identify factors common to Western Europe and contrast them with China.

The literature concerned with why "the West led the Rest" is enormous. As previously mentioned, the California School argued that the divergence (as measured by gaps in living standards between states) emerged only in the eighteenth century. Opponents of the California School, however, argue that the roots of the divergence go back much further than 1750, although of course, scholars have different views on what these roots are. Yet the common thread in one way or another is the Industrial Revolution of the eighteenth century, the period where the technological and economic chasm between West and East fully opened. If we can supply a persuasive explanation of it, some of the mystery of the Great Divergence would be resolved.[2]

The importance of the Industrial Revolution in Britain and its diffusion to Europe and North America is central to any discourse on the Great Divergence or, as McCloskey (2016) has memorably and accurately referred to it, the Great Enrichment. But how deep do we have to dig for its roots? The California School's approach is that the Industrial Revolution was rather sudden, unexpected, and contingent. In their view, it could have happened almost anywhere, and Europe's advantages stemmed from the fleeting accidents of

1. For a more detailed explanation of British leadership within Europe, see Mokyr (2009); Kelly, Mokyr, and Ó Gráda (2014); and Kelly, Mokyr and Ó Gráda (2023).

2. Indeed, the scholars associated with the California School (Pomeranz 2000; Perdue 2005; Goldstone 2009), arguing that the Industrial Revolution was the true watershed, therefore must insist that before 1750, the differences between Europe and the East (mostly China) were insignificant. In view of recent scholarship, such an opinion is increasingly untenable, and in fact, Pomeranz himself (2011) has modified his 2000 position somewhat.

politics and the whims of geography. This claim also implies that such dynamics were readily reversible.[3] Our approach is quite the opposite. We see the Industrial Revolution as the culmination of several long and drawn-out processes that started many centuries before James Watt and Richard Arkwright. That said, the developments were hardly obvious. An informed observer in AD 1000, watching European, Chinese, and Islamic societies, would never have bet on Europe to emerge as the technologically and economically dominant civilization eight centuries later.

What we need to understand is how and why a group of nations located west of the Elbe River in Europe, plus the parts of North America and Oceania settled by immigrants from these countries, led the world in the biggest economic revolution since the invention of agriculture. We can roughly divide the most influential explanations into two major categories: the explanations that rely on physical and geographical features and the ones that rely on social and economic factors (institutions and culture). The former can be summarized by Ian Morris's quip (cited in chapter 2) that it was "maps, not chaps" that determined why Europe forged ahead of the East. The "chaps" school instead focuses on attitudes and aptitudes as the driving factors conditioned by the unique institutions that characterized Europe (Mokyr 2021a).

Our view is most definitely in the "chaps" camp. In this chapter, we argue that the driving force that eventually led to the Industrial Revolution and the Great Enrichment was not geography, nor was it the fortuitous outcomes of battles and political contingencies, nor even factor prices. It was above all useful knowledge—that is, the kind of knowledge that potentially can be applied to some productive purposes. However, knowledge is not created in a social and political vacuum. It is the result of human interactions, in which new ideas are distributed, vetted, and assessed by others in a market for ideas. Our fundamental point is this: the commitment of Europe to corporate forms of social organization, and the consequent ability of Europeans to interact with and trust others to whom they were not related, triggered the creation of organizational structures in which useful knowledge was propagated,

3. As Perdue (2005, p. 537) writes, "The Industrial Revolution is not a deep, slow evolution out of centuries of particular conditions unique to early modern Europe. It is a late, rapid, unexpected outcome of a fortuitous combination of circumstances in the late eighteenth century. In view of what we now know about Imperial China, Japan, and India, among other places, acceptable explanations must invoke a global perspective and allow for a great deal of short-term change."

disseminated, assessed, and used productively. In this way, the rise of corporations was one of the essential ingredients that fueled Europe's eventual scientific and technological successes and led to the Industrial Revolution.

As discussed in previous chapters, recent literature has emphasized how the demise of kinship ties was a major factor in European exceptionalism (Mitterauer 2010; Schulz 2022; Henrich 2020), but to date, the spread of corporate arrangements has not been recognized as a major factor in bringing about the Industrial Revolution. To be sure, the "institutional bend" of economic history in recent decades has helped to shed light on the causes of the Industrial Revolution. These institutional approaches follow the seminal insights of Douglass North on the importance of political changes between the English Civil War and the Glorious Revolution (and the rise of Parliament as the ultimate source of political power). These changes, as North argued, were significant for establishing the rule of law, well-defined property rights, and contract enforcement. This work is complemented by scholarship on specific English institutions' roles in advancing British technological leadership: the Poor Law, the patent system, the absence of internal trade barriers, and the weakness of its guilds. There is no doubt that these institutional factors played an important role. But they too are an endogenous outcome of an underlying cause yet to be explained. Our approach emphasizes instead the key role of social organizations that permeated European society and how they helped to shape these outcomes.

We now lay out this argument in greater detail, starting with a discussion of why geography alone cannot provide an adequate explanation of the Great Divergence. We then explain why Europe was much more successful in the accumulation of useful knowledge, stressing the role of various social organizations that enabled innovation and promoted economic development. The chapter closes with a discussion of why similar innovative developments were not set in motion in China.

2. Geography

Geography is central to several explanations of the divergence in economic history, and many have alleged that various favorable characteristics provided Europe with advantages that can account for the Industrial Revolution. Two of those arguments, made by Pomeranz (2000) in his pathbreaking *Great Divergence,* have already been referred to in chapter 2: Europe's more convenient access to its "ghost acreage" in the New World, and the more favorable location of coal.

Coal

The importance of coal has been a major theme in the economic history of Britain's Industrial Revolution. The dependence of the Industrial Revolution and the subsequent economic growth on fossil fuels have always fascinated scholars and given the importance of fossil fuels in the new technologies that emerged after 1750, and the centrality of energy in economic performance in most sectors, its centrality to the Industrial Revolution seems at first glance an almost ineluctable conclusion (Kander, Malanima, and Warde 2013).[4] But, as argued in chapter 2, attributing too much causal power to the fortunate location of coal and other fossil fuels as a resource windfall does not stand up to close scrutiny. For one thing, carbonocentric explanations of the Industrial Revolution on their own run into the problem that the resource had been in the ground for millions of years. Unless we come to grips with the growth in the technology that permitted its location, extraction, transportation, and utilization, coal explains nothing.

Moreover, as John Harris (1988, p. 26) has emphasized, the switch from charcoal to coal-based fuels in the iron industry in the second half of the eighteenth century—often believed to be the first transition of its kind, and one that helped augur in the Industrial Revolution—was in fact virtually the last. Long before the eighteenth century, coal was used as a source of heat. During the Industrial Revolution, it was far more important as a fuel than as a source of motive power. Industries such as soap boiling, brewing, brickmaking, and glass blowing, to say nothing of home heating, had switched to coal centuries earlier. To be sure, steam power was an epistemic quantum leap forward by the controlled conversion of heat into work, but at least in its early stages, the Industrial Revolution did not absolutely need steam power (and for a long time, manufacturing in many coal-scarce areas continued to rely on water power). Moreover, steam power was not absolutely dependent on coal. Peat and wood could be and were used in engines, despite having lower thermal efficiency per pound.

---

4. The output of coal in 1700 was about 3 million tons per year; by 1775, this had increased to almost 9 million, 15 million by 1800, and annual output was over 60 million tons by 1850. Wrigley (2004, 2010) has pointed to the transition from organic forms of energy to coal in Britain as the pivotal factor singling out successful industrializers such as Britain and Belgium. Coal was more efficient and cheaper than wood, and it also economized on land use since it implied that woodlands could be deployed in other ways.

Furthermore, the precise location of minerals and materials was less critical than might appear because transportation costs were declining over the eighteenth century.[5] Most strikingly on this point, the cotton industry, which is often seen as the leading sector of rapid technological change and productivity growth, depended almost entirely on raw cotton shipped from North America. Raw wool, silk, flax, and high-quality iron ore were also imported into Britain. Yet the British technological lead in the mechanization of most textile industries was as clear as it was in iron and steam. When coal was abundant and cheap, it was often used in a wasteful way, as it was at the famous "ten-yard seam" in Staffordshire in the Black Country, which yielded 20,000 tons per acre (Rolt 1970, pp. 85–86). When coal was expensive, ingenuity led to more economical ways of using being designed, as was the case of the more efficient Cornish engines. Where coal may have played a central role was not so much as a source of heat energy or power, but as a focusing device for the skills and savoir faire that lay at the core of the Industrial Revolution (Kelly, Mokyr, and Ó Gráda 2023). The technical issues in collieries stimulated new techniques and engineering breakthroughs, both in the extraction and the utilization of coal. Many of the leading engineers and mechanics working on steam power and machinery in the Industrial Revolution were trained in coal mines.

Empire

A further geographical factor already discussed in chapter 2 was the importance of empire and the exploitation of non-Europeans. How important was empire to the British Industrial Revolution? Some of the necessary resources for European industrialization were indeed extracted or grown outside Europe, cotton above all. However, the control of overseas areas did not mean that they provided cheap imports of the products that Europeans wanted before the sharp fall in transportation costs in the nineteenth century. The New World also provided Europe with some desirable resources such as sugar and tobacco (grown largely by slaves), as well as furs and indigo, but it is hard to see how these products were crucial in bringing the Industrial Revolution about.

More plausible is that profits from colonies helped to fund projects of the Industrial Revolution. The slave trade and the sugar that slaves produced in

5. Recent research does conclude, however, that coal proximity is an important factor in explaining the growth of cities, even if that is quite a different matter than explaining why the Industrial Revolution occurred in Britain (Fernihough and O'Rourke 2021).

the Caribbean were immensely profitable and made many British rich. It is hard to imagine that some of these profits did not find their way in investments and other activities associated with the Industrial Revolution, helping to finance projects, especially infrastructure ones, that supported industrialization. On the margin, then, it is possible that the benefits of empire exceeded the costs, contrary to what Adam Smith believed.[6] One perhaps could add to ghost acreage the resources grown domestically in Europe, such as wheat and timber from the Baltic area. But the Baltic and the Mediterranean trades were hardly examples of naked imperialism. Rather, they should be seen as cases of standard long-distance trade, which was a common practice all over Asia as well.

However, it is telling that the age of the Industrial Revolution itself was not a very successful time for colonial expansion, with the American Revolution robbing Britain of its most important colony (but significantly, not of what these regions—now no longer part of the British Empire—contributed to its Industrial Revolution) and France of its most remunerative one (Haiti). Much of the colonial expansion of Europe occurred *after* the Industrial Revolution had run its course. Moreover, other significant colonial empires within Europe, such as Spain and Portugal, were clearly not at the forefront of the Industrial Revolution. Above all, it was not the Atlantic trade and its profits that drove the underlying ingenuity and dexterity of British inventors and engineers that made the Industrial Revolution.

Fragmentation

The other geographical difference between Europe and China, already discussed in chapters 2 and 7, was the fragmentation of Europe into small and medium-sized states. As we have seen in chapter 7, the exact causes for this difference are a combination of geographical and contingent factors. Whatever the exact roots, the benefits of a polycentric system to assuring interstate competition is just as central to any discussion of the Industrial Revolution as it is to explaining other phenomena in the centuries preceding it. Political

6. This argument, originally associated with Williams (1944) and known as the "Williams Thesis," has been resuscitated by recent research, such as Berg and Hudson (2023) and Heblich, Redding, and Voth (2023). Europeans exploited African slave labor ruthlessly, to the point at which Inikori (2002, pp. 478–81) has written with considerable exaggeration that the British Industrial Revolution was "trade-driven," and that Atlantic commerce was made possible by enslaved Africans.

fragmentation meant that eighteenth-century Britain, unlike most of the Continent, experienced a separate and quite unique institutional evolution and became a nation dominated by a powerful representative body that looked out for the interests of property, both landed and commercial.[7] Parliament by that time had accumulated most of the political power that elsewhere mostly remained in the hands of dynastic despots.[8] By being physically separated from the Continent, Britain was spared the heavy footprint of the Napoleonic armies, even while it devoted enormous resources to their defeat. These efforts were costly and may have slowed Britain's rate of industrialization due to the closure of European markets after 1806. The keen awareness of being in a fragmented and hostile world, however, was behind the British government's support for industrialists. The dominant opinion was that if Britain did not adopt a new useful new technique, its enemies would or potentially would gain an advantage over it. Hence, the British government unfailingly chose their side as early factory masters clashed with workers. The government mercilessly suppressed unions and more spontaneous labor protests, resisting what it perceived to be threats to employment and wages. An 1806 parliamentary committee headed by William Wilberforce explained this view, arguing against workers complaints about mechanization in the woolen industry: Britain was "at this day surrounded by powerful and civilized Nations, who are intent on cultivating their Manufactures and pushing their Commerce"; furthermore, Wilberforce cited such an establishment being set up in Paris as evidence of a real threat (Great Britain 1806, p. 12).[9] In short, economic and political competition forced nations to stay on their toes and make sure that they did not fall behind.

There were, of course, substantial costs associated with the political and cultural fragmentation of Europe. The most obvious one was political conflict,

7. It should be noted, however, that the Glorious Revolution of 1688, which led to the crowning of a Dutchman, William III of Orange, as the king of England, was the culmination of an earlier process of Dutch institutional and technological influence on England (Jardine 2008).

8. Blackstone (1765–1769, book 1, chapter 2, section III) noted that in Britain, Parliament was "the place where absolute despotic power, which must in all governments reside somewhere, is entrusted."

9. It is also telling that when the brilliant French refugee engineer Marc Isambard Brunel was imprisoned for debt in 1821 (he had imprudently engaged in a number of innovative but overly expensive engineering projects), he began negotiating with the Russian czar about the possibility of moving to St. Petersburg. The duke of Wellington himself, fearing the loss of such a valuable engineer, intervened with the government, which promptly paid Brunel's debt on the condition that he stay in Britain.

including wars, arms races, and protectionist policies. Such costs must be weighed against the putative benefits of war, such as government support for techniques that had military value and the technological spillovers from military hardware to civilian industries. The most famous example was the block-making machinery of the royal shipyards in Portsmouth.[10] Another was the canon-boring technique originating in John Wilkinson's metal workshop that was indispensable to Watt's steam engine.[11] A more encompassing argument made recently by Dincecco and Onorato (2018) suggests that war led to higher urbanization and the emergence of more efficient governance and fiscal capabilities in Europe. In this interpretation, frequent wars eventually made it possible for Europe to develop more effective institutions to support markets, correct market failures, and supply public goods.

Whether the benefits of state-building offset the high costs of maintaining Britain's, France's, or Prussia's militaries remains an open question. Yet it is undisputable that fears of military conflict with other nations prevented the kind of technological complacency that we observe in Qing China. China was awakened from its technological stagnation only when the military threat of

10. The dockyards in Portsmouth have been seen as one of the first and most successful instances of the ideas of mass production in manufacturing by the use of advanced machinery to produce the blocks, pulleys, and sheaves needed to hoist sails on naval vessels. By 1808, it was producing 130,000 blocks annually by a modern and sophisticated production method. The Portsmouth facility was the brainchild of three of the most remarkable mechanical minds of the Industrial Revolution: the aforementioned Brunel, the naval architect Samuel Bentham (the elder brother of Jeremy), and the brilliant machine-tool maker Henry Maudslay. There are many detailed accounts of this enterprise (Cooper 1984; Coad 2005), and it stands out as an exceptional example of British ingenuity. The production technology deployed at the yards was built on a mechanically sophisticated foundation. From the 1760s, the manufacturing of blocks was partially mechanized (using horse-driven and water-powered machinery). The Portsmouth yard was a major step forward in its full mechanization and specialized machinery. Its exact significance has been a matter of some dispute, and perhaps the techniques of mass production deployed in Portsmouth did not spread to the rest of the economy and were not adopted in Britain as fast as one might have expected. All the same, they were a direct consequence of the European "states system," especially because of the central role played by Brunel, a royalist refugee from the French Revolution who fled France in 1793 and arrived in Britain in 1799.

11. Wilkinson's work was inspired and informed by a Dutch iron and brass founder, Jan Verbruggen, who was hired as master founder at the royal brass foundry at Woolwich. Verbruggen was one of the first to apply the technique of horizontal boring for solid-cast guns, first developed by the Swiss inventor Jean Maritz in Strasbourg in the early eighteenth century, but Wilkinson's machine was a substantial improvement and produced a tolerance low enough to create cylinders for Watt's engines.

more advanced nations—the West, Japan, and Russia—became more pressing after 1850.

3. Useful Knowledge and Innovation

A more subtle consequence of fragmentation—with potentially more severe long-term consequences—is that any kind of knowledge creation involves high fixed costs (through research and experimentation). Therefore, innovative efforts are attractive only if a large constituency is interested in it. In a highly fragmented world, in which borders, cultural and language barriers, and high transportation costs separate societies, such a constituency is hard to imagine. This could be one reason why some highly fragmented regions—such as Africa or India—could not capitalize on fragmentation as Europe did. The Industrial Revolution could happen in Europe because it was able to achieve an intellectual integration despite fragmentation. This integration guaranteed a continentwide audience for ideas and innovation. It is that propensity for novelty that prepared the fertile soil from which the Industrial Revolution sprouted.

The roots of this integration in part go back to its classical heritage and the maintenance of Latin as the lingua franca of intellectuals until deep into the seventeenth century. The cultural and intellectual unity provided by the Catholic Church through the Middle Ages, despite its schisms and internal conflicts, provided further support for this coherence. The Church was closely involved with the proliferation of universities, which created a coherent transnational system of markets for intellectuals. In these markets, universities competed for the best faculty and students. In the late Renaissance, communication technology improved through the emergence of the printing press, as well as through falling transportation costs and the establishment of better and cheaper postal services. These developments allowed more efficient correspondence between intellectuals living hundreds of miles apart. Early sixteenth-century intellectuals such as Martin Luther, Erasmus, and Juan Luis Vives, were read and debated all over Europe. They themselves readily moved between the centers of intellectual activity in various countries.

The result was that Europe ended up with the best of all possible worlds—it enjoyed the advantages of a decentralized and competitive state system that provided an environment conducive to a more or less integrated transnational market for ideas. In this market, philosophers, astronomers, mathematicians, physicians, and engineers could produce innovations that catered to a much larger audience than found in their regions of residence, and yet one in which no single entity monopolized the market for ideas. The sixteenth and seventeenth centuries were an age that produced intellectual superstars whose reach and reputation were Continent-wide. The institution that regulated it was the Republic of Letters, a virtual network of intellectuals that illustrates the kind of institution that could be produced in a world of corporations and to which we will return later in this discussion.

In the age bookended between the invention of the printing press (c.1450) and the death of Isaac Newton in 1727, the West experienced an exponential growth of useful knowledge that eventually came to fuel the engine of technological progress once it got started and then culminated in the Industrial Revolution after 1750. The growth in knowledge was much more than the classical Scientific Revolution—it involved advances in knowledge in geography, botany, practical mathematics, anatomy, engineering, hydraulics, ship design, and many other areas.

The access to useful knowledge was distributed in an extremely skewed way, especially in the centuries before the Industrial Revolution. The vast bulk of the population was hardly involved in any kind of progress. Rather, the envelope was pushed by two sets of people. The first was a relatively small group of learned individuals, whom we would call today "intellectuals," known at the time as "natural philosophers" and "practical mathematicians"; alongside them were physicians, astronomers, geographers, instrument makers, and engineers. The giants of this group from Galileo and Newton are well known, typically associated with the Scientific Revolution. But they also include more practical people who were just as ingenious, such as the Dutch engineer Cornelis Drebbel (1572–1633), the inventor of the submarine; the French Huguenot Salomon De Caus (1576–1626), a hydraulic engineer and garden architect who was one of the first to realize the critical properties of steam; and the English clergyman Edmund Gunter (1581–1626), the inventor of a variety of mathematical instruments such as the eponymous chain that used triangulation to estimate the area of parcels of land.

In addition to these educated elites was a second group of people: a small sliver of the artisanal labor force, trained craftsmen with dirt under their fingernails but with creative and original minds, were active in advancing useful knowledge.[12] A well-documented example is the sixteenth-century French

12. Modern research has emphasized (correctly) that these two groups overlapped considerably (Smith and Schmidt 2007b). That said, the intersection of the two sets is still much smaller than the union, and while intellectuals such as Robert Hooke had a strong interest in what artisans did and often engaged in building their own equipment, one would hardly designate them as "artisans."

potter Bernard de Palissy (1510–1589), who readily admitted not knowing classical languages and not being part of the intellectual community. His book *Dis-
cours admirables, de la nature des eaux et fontaines* (1580) was a provocatively
written, disputatious dialogue between theory and practice in which the practitioners were always correct (Amico 1996), and he challenged prevalent theories
that discussed the details of pottery and the processing of materials (Deming
2005). In England, his counterpart was Hugh Plat (1552–1608), whose magnum
opus *The Jewell House* offered "jewels" of experimental knowledge to help people
better their lives through practical advice ranging from making toothpaste and
preserving food to keep it from spoiling to building bridges (Harkness 2007,
p. 212). There were others like them who have left a record, but many more who
did not; yet overall, they were a small proportion of the population of artisans
and the extreme upper tail of the skill distribution. All the same, the number of
such people was rising, and by the eighteenth century, the supply of clever and
creative artisans who improved others' inventions was sufficiently high that they
constituted an indispensable component of the Industrial Revolution.

Intellectual innovations by scholars and artisanal innovations by skilled and
dexterous craftsmen had one important feature in common: they were social
actions that required interactions with others and some form of social
organization. Whereas in much of the world such interactions first and foremost took place within an extended family, by the late Middle Ages, Europe
had committed to corporate forms of social organization. The connection between the proliferation of corporations in Europe and the relatively rapid
growth of useful knowledge took a variety of forms, which we discuss next.
But these interactions shared a critical feature: they were carried out in
organizations of people who shared an interest and an objective, who cooperated and divided the work among them, and yet they were largely independent
of kinship and were not controlled and managed by the authorities.

Monasteries

As we have seen in detail in chapter 5, one of the earliest corporate forms was
the monastery. It was in monasteries that medieval natural philosophy and
mathematics thrived (White 1978). Many of the best medieval philosophers,
mathematicians, and scientists were monks.[13] Among the secular clergy (as

---

13. Most notable among them William of Ockham, Roger Bacon, Albertus Magnus, John of
Sacrobosco, Theodoric of Freiberg, and Richard of Wallingford.

distinct from the regular clergy or monks), we find many more scientists of note as well.[14] Historians have pointed out that the Catholic ("Latin") Church was strongly influenced by the rational philosophy and scientific interests of the late Hellenistic and Roman period, and these orientations were taught in the Episcopal and Monastic schools (and later universities) of medieval Europe (Schilling 2022, p. 56). Even in the seventeenth century, monastic orders in Catholic Europe were still producing innovative and influential intellectuals, such as Paolo Sarpi, Tommaso Campanella, and Marin Mersenne. Equally impressive is the list of innovative intellectuals coming from one of the most remarkable of all European corporations, the Jesuit Order. Among its most celebrated members were Christopher Clavius, an applied mathematician who helped create the Gregorian calendar, and the prodigious polymath Athanasius Kircher, "the last man who knew everything" (Findlen 2004).

Through much of the Middle Ages and the Early Modern period, then, the Catholic Church and its various institutions supported and abetted the growth of useful knowledge, so long as it remained within the confines of a certain orthodoxy. Over time, however, the character of the Catholic Church changed; it became increasingly reactionary and repressed insights that did not accord with its worldview. The Counter-Reformation in Europe led to a severe decline in the rate of progress of science and technology in those areas and the gradual move of the center of gravity of intellectual innovation to regions north of the Alps (Cabello 2023).

Universities

The dominant intellectual paradigm established in the late Middle Ages by combining Christian orthodoxy with Aristotelian metaphysics by Saint Thomas Aquinas was broken in the late fifteenth century, when increasingly rebellious intellectuals began to rethink and reexamine the recently resurrected classical heritage. The prevailing wisdom was challenged first and foremost within the universities. Universities, as we have seen, were in many ways the embodiment of the idea of a "corporation," as they were

14. Among them were Robert Grosseteste (bishop of Lincoln), Gerbert of Aurillac (later Pope Sylvester II), Jean Buridan, William of Conches, John Peckham (archbishop of Canterbury), Nicolas Oresme (bishop of Lisieux), Albert of Saxony (bishop of Halberstadt), and Nicholas of Cusa (cardinal and papal legate in Germany).

well–organized, self-governing organizations of people with a common purpose but an exit option.

In Early Modern Europe, some universities produced intellectual rebels and innovators of all types: not least Martin Luther in Wittenberg; Copernicus, who attended both the universities of Bologna and Padua; and Paracelsus, who studied at the universities of Basel and Ferrara. Like all corporations, universities could choose to be innovative or conservative. Indeed, many became conservative bastions that protected entrenched knowledge from critics while devoting little to intellectual activities.[15] However, so long as there were enough that were progressive, useful knowledge could advance and new insights could spread. No market of ideas of this sort existed anywhere else.

The track record of European universities as focal points of new knowledge-creation is rather mixed. Medieval universities had close connections with monastic orders.[16] Yet that connection began to weaken during the Renaissance. The University of Paris remained one of the most eminent institutions of late medieval Europe and a precursor of things to come. For instance, during the fourteenth century, it was home to Jean Buridan, a brilliant natural philosopher who had little interest in theology and was far more interested in logic, physics, and mechanics than in the fine points of religion.[17] That said, theology remained the queen of the sciences for some time. Had this remained the case, then perhaps the Scientific Revolution and Industrial Revolution may have looked very different (or never occurred at all). Yet there were always enough European universities in which "natural philosophy" and medicine were important parts of the curriculum. It is in these universities where another source of important useful knowledge can be found.

The importance of universities to the growth of useful knowledge in Europe continued in the age of the Renaissance and the Baroque, although the location of leadership changed over time. The most prominent institution in early modern Europe was the University of Padua, which benefited from Venice's wealth and the republic's ability to shield it from papal interference. The

15. Adam Smith ([1776], 1976, vol. 2, p. 284) famously noted that at Oxford, the dons had "long ago given up all pretence of teaching."

16. The Franciscans and Dominicans had their own priories at Oxford, which provided food and board and paid tuition. One of those signed up Roger Bacon, one of the most notable and advanced natural philosophers of his time, in 1257; subsequently, he taught both at Oxford and Paris universities.

17. Buridan was one of the few distinguished intellectuals in medieval Europe who spent his career entirely in the faculty of arts, where natural philosophy was taught (Zupko 2018).

number of superstar intellectuals who studied or taught at Padua over the years is impressive: instructors included Galileo; the founder of modern anatomy, Andreas Vesalius; and the physician Girolamo Fracastoro. Padua graduates included Nicolaus Copernicus and William Harvey.[18] In later years, a few universities north of the Alps assumed positions of leadership, especially eighteenth-century Leyden, which could count on such leading scientists as Willems Gravesande, Herman Boerhaave, and Pieter van Musschenbroek. Equally impressive is the role of eighteenth-century Scottish universities in producing leading intellectuals and natural philosophers in the age of the Industrial Revolution, among them Adam Smith and many of the leading lights of the Scottish Enlightenment, as well as the physicists Joseph Black and John Robison, who personally counseled Watt. Among their graduates were the mathematician Colin Maclaurin, who entered the University of Glasgow at age eleven and by nineteen was appointed a professor of mathematics; and James Hutton, called the "father" of modern geology, who studied at the Universities of Edinburgh and Leyden (although he was a businessman, not an academic). The chemist William Irvine was an influential academic at the University of Glasgow, with a strong interest in applied and industrial chemistry.

Yet as already noted in chapter 6, when all is said and done, the contributions of university professors to the growth of useful knowledge for the Industrial Revolution was probably a second-order effect. Their main contribution was training students—research was optional. Despite their independence from the government, European universities were rarely the loci of pathbreaking intellectual innovation. Most universities, as noted, were conservative bodies that guarded tradition and the intellectual status quo.[19] The goal of the typical university scholar was "textual purity rather than scientific truth" (DeBus 1978, p. 4). Strikingly, De la Croix et al. (2023, p. 40) noted in a sophisticated quantitative analysis of the academic market that market forces in the academic world that had had a powerful effect on the early Scientific Revolution became weaker after 1650. Furthermore, many notable innovators of the

---

18. One of the areas that flourished thanks to universities was natural history, directly related to medical education. The universities of Padua and Bologna established chairs in "medicinal simples," covering botanical knowledge, and by 1545, Italian universities had botanical gardens where professors demonstrated plans to students. These universities "promoted a new kind of natural history that emphasized evidence of the senses" (Findlen 2006, p. 444).

19. Adam Smith ([1776] 1976, vol. 2, p. 294) scathingly noted that universities were "sanctuaries in which exploded systems and obsolete prejudices found shelter and protection after they had been hunted out of every other corner of the world."

time were not affiliated with universities. As has been noted, there were important exceptions, but clearly there was a need for alternative organizations that
allowed intellectual innovators to communicate and network. Europe's
centuries-old tradition of corporations provided the intellectual backdrop for
these organizations.

Academies and Scientific Societies

The culture and traditions of corporations lent themselves admirably to the
emergence of alternative organizations devoted to the progress of useful
knowledge if existing arrangements were unsatisfactory. Such organizations
included scientific academies and societies, local organizations in which intellectuals gathered, lectured, conducted public experiments, exchanged notes
and information, collaborated, and tried to impress their peers. Many of these
congregations were spontaneous local efforts, and when the sponsoring
agent—usually a wealthy local gentleman with intellectual interests—passed
away or lost interest, the organization could vanish. Others were established
from the top down. In Italy, the best known was the Accademia dei Lincei,
founded at the initiative of Duke Federico Cesi in 1603.[20] By the middle of
the seventeenth century, such organizations had become much more common
and durable. Prime examples include the Royal Society, which grew from the
bottom up out of a spontaneous congregation of Baconians at Wadham College in Oxford, formally chartered in 1660; and the French Académie Royale,
established from the top down by Jean-Baptiste Colbert in 1665) being prime
examples. By the middle of the eighteenth century, there were many dozens
of such scientific societies all over Europe.[21] These scientific academies and
philosophical societies were a prime example of what we have defined as
"corporations"—much like universities, they were voluntary, self-governing

20. Other examples of such academies were the Accademia degli Incogniti in Venice,
founded in 1630 by intellectuals inspired by the teachings of Cesare Cremonini (1550–1631). The
Accademia del Cimento, founded in 1657, was the private venture of Prince Leopold of Tuscany;
it was mostly a group of Galileo's students and followers. It consisted of little more than a handful of notable experimental scientists, such as Giovanni Alphonso Borelli and Vincenzo Viviani
meeting in Florence under the auspices of the prince.

21. McClellan (1981) has estimated that thirty-three "official" learned societies were func-
tioning in the French provinces during the eighteenth century, counting over 6,400 members.
In Germany, around 200 such societies appeared during the half-century spanning from the
Seven Years' War to the Napoleonic occupation of Germany.

organizations that served a common interest (the exchange and vetting of scholarship) and were independent of kinship relations.

Autonomous Cities

A highly prominent corporation of Europe, as we have seen previously, was the autonomous city. Some of the most successful were independent city-states, which were often best suited to supporting trade. This was true for the city-states of Italy, as well as those in the Baltic regions. Elsewhere, urban communes proliferated. But even administrative towns and capitals of larger kingdoms such as Paris, London, and Toledo were often controlled and run by local oligarchies.

As we have seen, medieval cities were first and foremost commercial, administrative, and/or religious centers, and their role in advancing useful knowledge in the centuries before the Industrial Revolution is rarely emphasized. Yet their commercial rise occurred in lockstep with technological advances. Self-governing cities (known as "communes") were locations in which the exchange of ideas and the division of labor and knowledge could be driven further than in the countryside. Economies of agglomeration made their rise a central component in the growth of useful knowledge in Europe. Creativity in all its forms tended to cluster in urban areas for the most part. Forming a polycentric competitive system, these autonomous cities made good use of institutions that supported individual creativity and freed citizens from the shackles of conservative clerics; as such, they provided the necessary environment for the advance of useful knowledge (Serafinelli and Tabellini 2022), as well as other new ideas (Wuthnow 1989, pp. 46–51).

Italian city-states in the Middle Ages owed their growth to technological progress in manufacturing as much as to the revival of international trade: the glassblowing industry of Venice was clearly the central pillar of its prosperity before it began to dominate the Eastern Mediterranean trade. Other Italian towns led in innovations in fine textiles, in metalworking, in the use of chemicals, and later in printing, clockmaking, optics, cartography, and instrument- and gun-making. One historian, after describing the skills and technical advances of the Italian Renaissance urban centers, concludes that "these alone made its opulence possible" (Hall 1967, p. 85). The case for a technologically driven city-state could also be made for the medieval Flemish towns, which adopted the new textile technologies in cloth-making and formed what is probably the first purely industrial-urban complex in the thirteenth century.

In the sixteenth century, the central role of urban centers in advancing intellectual and technical innovations grew. A powerful example comes from the contribution made by the instrument-making centers in Nuremberg and Augsburg, as well as neighboring cities during the fifteenth and sixteenth centuries (Price 1957). By the seventeenth century, the most successful system of autonomous cities was the Dutch Republic. In its heyday, the Dutch Republic was not only a huge commercial entrepôt and financial center; it was also the technological leader of the age. Although there was no Industrial Revolution (in the standard definition of the term) in Holland, during the period between 1500 and 1700, Dutch cities were technological leaders in textiles, wind-power technology, hydraulic engineering, shipbuilding, and ceramics; furthermore, they pioneered techniques in painting and advances in mathematics (Davids 2008).

Above all, autonomous cities aimed to attract and concentrate creative and innovative skills. Their role as magnets of talents was one important source of their economic and cultural success (Serafinelli and Tabellini 2022). As a self-governing commune, urban centers fostered comparatively high levels of freedom of expression and creation. While creativity included literature, visual arts, music, and philosophy, the agglomeration effect that these cities provided helped advance practical mathematics, engineering, optics, architecture, clockmaking and instrument making, and many other high-quality crafts. To repeat, cities in premodern Europe were heterogenous, and some were more free, more tolerant of new ideas, and more welcoming to creative and original thinkers than others. The system's heterogeneity was its strength. Cities that had more open institutions attracted the best minds and skills in Europe. The more able and talented of Europe's intellectual and artisanal elites were, the more mobile they were, and modern research shows that such free and self-governing cities reaped rich rewards for their open-mindedness and liberal attitudes (Serafinelli and Tabellini 2022).

Religious tolerance was one crucial element of these attitudes. What aided the emergence of tolerant attitudes was the firm belief that having a substantial community of internationally renowned artists and philosophers would enhance the city's prestige. That cities competed with each other over the best and brightest added a further dimension to the interstate competition discussed earlier: France competed with England and Sweden with Russia, but at the same time, Edinburgh competed with Glasgow and Leyden with Utrecht. All over Europe, cities competed fiercely for the best artisans, just as royal and aristocratic courts competed for the best artists, doctors, and astrologers (Belfanti 2004). In a recent contribution, Desmet et al. (2020) point out the importance of spatial competition between cities and argue that such competition made it more difficult for incumbent producers to resist new techniques that made their skills obsolete. Even when there was strong local resistance to new technology, an economywide resistance movement would require more coordination and central-government consent than could be found in most regions. Urban dwellers were remarkably mobile. Most city-dwellers in Georgian Britain, as well as in the Netherlands, were immigrants. People who embodied upper-tail human capital, whether top artisans, musicians, or physicians, moved relatively freely between towns. This mobility enhanced the growth and dissemination of best-practice useful knowledge, both the practical and abstract kinds.

The Republic of Letters

At a higher geographical level, there was another institution that regulated and lubricated the distribution of useful knowledge at a pan-European level. This was the aforementioned Republic of Letters, a virtual rather than a brick-and-mortar organization, but no less critical in facilitating the growth of useful knowledge that eventually was the central factor in the Industrial Revolution (Mokyr 2016, chapter 12). The republic's roots can be traced to the early fifteenth century, but it came into its own during the first half of the sixteenth. By 1600, it was a well-understood feature of the European intellectual community. The Republic of Letters was a transnational network of scholars that united European scholars amid Continental political and religious fragmentation. It considered itself a "commonwealth," or an institution separate from geopolitical affairs; it was even described as a "state extremely free," as one of its central figures put it (Bayle [1696–1697] 1734, Vol. II, p. 389, essay on *Catius*). One of the republic's defining features was its built-in skepticism of classical canon knowledge and the commitment of its "citizens" to the principle of contestability, that is, that all statements and hypotheses are subject to skeptical examination and critique. The Republic of Letters fulfilled three functions: incentivizing research, distributing and testing new knowledge, and shaping the features and content of the new knowledge created.

Was the Republic of Letters a corporation? In the strict sense that we have used the term here, it was not. Membership in most corporations was binary, formal, location-specific, and sharply defined, none of which was the case with the Republic of Letters. Yet it had many features associated with corporations that were inspired by familiarity with these organizations. The republic was self-governing, and thus independent of formal political structures (i.e., the states or municipalities in which its "members" resided); furthermore, it had nothing to do with kinship. It was also a transnational and transreligious network, a market of ideas consisting of scholars who shared, discussed, and evaluated knowledge and ideas. Its historical origins are clear. As noted in chapter 4, the Catholic Church in many ways can be regarded as the mother of all corporations. The Republic of Letters in some ways was fashioned after the Church in its transnationality and its universally accepted rules of behavior. Unlike the Church, of course, the Republic of Letters had no hierarchy, and its means of enforcing its rules were limited.

By engaging in the continuous review and critique of the writings of their peers, the members created an unintended mechanism that incentivized learned people to create intellectual innovations. The valuable payoffs were reputations for those whose ideas and discoveries were deemed to be correct and worthy. Such reputational benefits and accompanying prestige could earn one a position of patronage: these might be offered by universities or powerful and wealthy individuals who provided the resources to provide successful intellectuals with economic security and the leisure to do their research. Reputations were associated with patronage positions, whether at universities or princely courts, and while these sinecures rarely led to true riches, they usually included a reasonably secure income and the leisure time to pursue one's research (David 2008).

However, the pluralist and decentralized nature of the system and the mobility of the most successful intellectuals made it very difficult for individual rulers to interfere with the market for ideas and exercise control over the content of the writings of the intellectuals under their protection. Top scientists and intellectuals were sufficiently footloose that any attempt by patrons to intervene aggressively into the research that scholars wanted to carry out would be doomed. The market for ideas in Europe was highly competitive, both on the demand and the supply side. Many wealthy and powerful people competed for the most famous scholars, and the scholars themselves competed for the most desirable positions of courts and patronage. Enjoying relatively high freedom from meddling by authorities, this market led to unprecedented intellectual creativity and eventually to technological progress of enormous economic consequences.

The Republic of Letters thus established contact and the exchange of information among persons willing to engage and exchange ideas and knowledge with strangers, provided that they met certain conditions. It established relationships and exchanges of ideas among intellectuals, who knew each other only by reputation but in many cases had not met in person or met only very infrequently. In the terminology of Granovetter (1973, 1983), it was a "weak ties" network among people who may have lived far apart but shared a common interest in intellectual topics. The network worked precisely because of Europe's generalized morality, which encouraged people to transact with others, even those who were unfamiliar or from different backgrounds. As a network, it facilitated the distribution of information on new and exciting work and examined it critically to sort the wheat from the chaff, and the scholars who were credited with true and original advances gained in reputation among their peers.

Despite its virtual format, the Republic of Letters illustrates the importance of nonstate institutions, especially in the creation of useful knowledge, which was a multinational project. Although, as noted, there was no formal admission or membership, being part of it gave the intellectual elite of the time a shared identity, involving a commitment to follow a set of implicit rules that governed their activity. Its members felt that they were "citizens" of the institution and often expressed their loyalty to it. They accepted the concepts of openness, skepticism, and the absence of a class-based hierarchy.

The difference between Europe and China is striking. The Imperial administration in China, especially under the Qing, made supreme efforts to maintain and support loyalty and orthodoxy, to the point where Western scholars have used the term "literary inquisition" to describe the Imperial policies (Goodrich 1935). While the Chinese market for ideas was never a complete monopoly, it was certainly dominated by the neo-Confucian orthodoxy that supported the status quo. As we have discussed, this was driven in large part by the Imperial Civil Service Examinations, which made the neo-Confucian canon the core of all learning (Huang 2023). As Zhao (2015) argued, while China was in some ways a more tolerant and pluralistic polity than most European nations, once they decided to repress a deviant set of ideas, they did so with devastating efficiency. European rulers and religious authorities were probably even more intolerant and fanatical, but interstate coordination on these issues was rare, and consequently repression was ineffectual in the long run.

Moreover, the Republic of Letters was permeated with a sense of independent thought and a critical approach to evaluating existing knowledge. The motto of the Royal Society, *in nullius verba* (on no one's word), which summarizes the principle of contestability discussed here, existed both in theory and in practice for a century before the society adopted it in 1660.

Indeed, "citizens" of the Republic of Letters took pride in exercising skepticism. Astronomers, physicists, biologists, and physicians challenged the hitherto-sacrosanct doctrines of Aristotle, Ptolemy, Galen, and other authorities that formed the classical canon, as well as one another. The skeptical and innovative nature and culture of the Republic of Letters, then, was very much a function of the corporate structure of Europe that had evolved in the Middle Ages. Corporations, by being independent of kinship, encouraged the shedding of ancestor worship in all its forms; that included the sacrosanct canon of ancient learning. The competition (*querrelle*) between the so-called ancients and moderns did not imply that good knowledge would in all cases drive out bad knowledge. The Copernican Revolution is an example of a case in which it eventually did, but it is much harder to assert that the iatrochemical medicine proposed by the iconoclastic Swiss physician Paracelsus was much of an improvement on classical Galenian medicine and its humoral-theory based practices.

Social organization mattered for the success of the Republic of Letters. In small communities or clans, individuals share similar sources of information and learn from the same authorities, and hence they were more likely to provide one another with trustworthy but redundant information. As noted previously, in weak ties networks, by contrast, persuasion will require higher levels of proof simply because there is relatively little information about the writer to assure his credibility (Levin and Cross 2004, p. 1480). Weak ties networks provide "bridges" (i.e., single connections that have no substitutes), and new information and ideas are more efficiently diffused. It is precisely that function that the Republic of Letters provided (Mokyr 2016). In addition to easier access to the writings of others, the existence of a lingua franca (Latin) helped ease communications in the early years (although when scholars began to write increasingly in their vernaculars, translations were forthcoming).

The generalized trust that we associate with corporate forms of social organization should be seen as conditional. A natural philosopher did not trust a new idea or finding by a colleague in a different country just on their say-so. It was expected that evidence and proof would be forthcoming precisely because skepticism was universal. Gentlemanly honor by aristocrats such as Robert Boyle would go some way toward creating trust, but in the end, supporting evidence and data were expected to go with experimental or observational data, and the idea of reproducibility began to take root (Shapin and Schafer 1985). In this, the Republic of Letters anticipated the twentieth-century engineer W. Edwards Deming's famous gag that "in God we trust—everyone else has to produce data." Because it would be unfeasible for every scientist to start from scratch, however, some level of trust of earlier work was inevitable if the results were well established and accepted. At the margins of trusted bodies of knowledge, there was skepticism, and it is exactly along those lines that knowledge advanced (Shapin 1994). The community that we associate with the Republic of Letters was the embodiment of generalized trust, the outgrowth of centuries of change in social organizations in the Middle Ages.

Intrinsic Motivation and Incentives

For an economist, perhaps the central question in such institutions was one of incentives: What was driving the scholars and intellectuals who constituted the "citizens" of the Republic of Letters?[22] One of them, as noted previously, was patronage: famous and successful intellectuals were regarded as a source of pride, and wealthy and powerful courts sought to attract them with comfortable salaries, conditions that allowed them to do their research and writing, and the legitimacy that such appointments involved (Westfall 1985; Biagioli 1990). A second was peer recognition: then as now, intellectuals were obsessed by their reputations and yearned for the respect of people of those they regarded as their equals. This motivation was also shared by artists and musicians of the time, who thrived in separate realms but often played by similar rules. To return to our comparison between East and West, there was fierce competition between members of the upper tail of the human capital distribution in both Europe and China, but it took very different forms, and these forms mattered a great deal to the outcomes. In China, candidates competed in the structured *keju* examinations; in Europe, ambitious intellectuals were operating in a decentralized market for ideas, subject only to the rules of the Republic of Letters.

Beyond material incentives, many of the leading intellectuals of the time and their original research were driven by intrinsic motivations. That is to say, the work *itself* may have had high and positive utility and would have been carried out even in the absence of any material or other rewards. Subject to a minimum consumption constraint, many creative intellectuals would work, research, and write without any obvious material incentives. In practice, only a few of the major figures of the Scientific Revolution could be thought of as

22. Some of the following is adapted from Mokyr (2024a).

altogether indifferent to material motives and uninterested in patronage: most striking, of course, were the great English scientist Robert Boyle, who was born in a very wealthy family; and Antoine Lavoisier, a wealthy tax collector. Most intellectuals, as noted, depended on patronage to survive and strived to be around royal or aristocratic courts for their social status and prestige.

The one intrinsic motive that was ubiquitous to early Europe's intellectual innovation in early Europe is what we may call "curiosity." In formal terms, economists might describe this as a property where an agent's preference function directly accounts for utility reaped from new insights.[23] Huff (2011, p. 112) asserts the existence of a "curiosity deficit" that explains the difference between Europe and China and places much of his explanation for Europe's leadership on Europeans being more "curious." A similar argument was made by Huang (2023, pp. 240–41). That argument, however, raises more difficulties than it solves. Wootton (2015, p. 61n) points out that in the early Christian West, curiosity was traditionally regarded as a vice, so its transformation from vice to virtue was itself endogenous, a consequence rather than a cause.

But things are not that simple. Saint Augustine, to be sure, condemned *curiositas* and included it in his list of vices. Saint Thomas Aquinas, however, who is often held equally responsible for the condemnation of "curiosity," did make some fine distinctions between the kinds of knowledge that were virtuous to pursue and those that were not because they were the kind of knowledge that only God possessed. The aversion to new knowledge for its own sake was thus already weakening in the later Middle Ages, but it remained powerful, and traces of it can still be found in the writings of Erasmus.

That said, there is no question that Early Modern Europe experienced a gradual cultural transformation that made curiosity a virtue, especially for the elites. The Renaissance courts and academies proudly paraded their curiosity and saw the display of new knowledge as a symbol of the superiority and power of the ruling classes. This new attitude was particularly manifest in the proto-museums, known as "curiosity cabinets," which displayed exotic animal and plant specimens and antiques (Eamon 1994, pp. 223–24).

In the many centuries separating Saint Augustine and the Republic of Letters of the Early Modern period, the attitude toward curiosity evolved. Francis Bacon warned his readers in *The Great Instauration* not to fall into the error of thinking "that the inquisition of nature is in any part interdicted or forbidden"; and cited with approval Proverbs 25:2 that stated that "it is the honor of God

---

23. Some of the following discussion is adapted from Mokyr (2018).

to conceal a thing and the honor of kings to investigate them" (Bacon [1620], 1999, pp. 74–75). While Bacon still warned that the "true end of knowledge" should not be "for the pleasure of the mind," research of any kind was turned into a virtuous activity. Thomas Hobbes, famously, defined curiosity as the desire to know the causes of things, and he clearly was free of any sense of guilt about encroaching on knowledge that was somehow out of bounds. By the mid-seventeenth century, this attitude toward curiosity had become acceptable. As Daston (2005, p. 37) phrased it, "Moralists continued to thunder away against such frivolous and potentially dangerous interests . . . but the decibel level of their complaints suggests that by the late seventeenth century they were on the defensive."

Historical scholarship has indeed recognized the importance of society's acceptance and encouragement of curiosity as one salient feature of modernity (Daston and Park 1998). It remains to be seen if these attitudes truly created a "curiosity gap" between the two worlds. The environment in which intellectuals labored just differed too much.[24] Perhaps it is closer to the truth to surmise that there was no "curiosity deficit" as much as there was a curiosity bifurcation: European and Chinese intellectuals were both curious, but their energies were directed toward different interests. Yet that difference may have had far-reaching implications for economic development. Chinese curiosity and insistence on evidence focused on the real meanings of past sages' writings. Europeans increasingly believed that they could outdo them.

In short, satisfying the curiosity of intellectuals was a function of social organization as well. The changing culture of the intellectual communities of Europe should be seen in the context of Europe's social organizations as they were formed over many centuries. In a world organized by clans, there is a built-in tendency for cultural beliefs to be dominated by elders in the family. Curiosity and the desire to propose and create new things may be regarded as disrespectful in a world of elder dominance and ancestor worship. The sense that wisdom is to be found in the writings of earlier sages ("the canon") will

24. As one review has summarized, "In China, much systematic inquiry was conducted for the sake of the emperor and was supported by the state. Such support paved the way for striking successes in some cases, and the centralization of power also made it possible that discoveries could be widely disseminated and implemented. However, this institutional framework also meant that the investigators needed to be careful about the results they presented, lest they lose their means of livelihood—or even their heads. Moreover, the fact that much systematic inquiry was funded by the state probably contributed to a certain kind of consensus among Chinese thinkers" (Hutton 2003).

suppress curiosity, as new knowledge may jeopardize the incumbent wisdom, and thus the dominant position, of elders. Greif, Iyigun, and Sasson (2013) point to the dominant decision-making position of elders in China's clans and argue that their higher risk aversion (which rises with age) meant that there was less technological experimentation in clan-dominated societies. The organization of Europe into nuclear families, where elders did not have such a dominant position, also may have affected the acceptability of curiosity, as curiosity is known to decline on average with age (e.g., Sakaki, Yagi, and Murayami 2018). At baseline, humans are probably equally (inherently) curious even across different societies. However, overarching structures of political and social organization play a role in redirecting incentives away from expressing such curiosity or acting on it. Conservative societies are especially inclined to do so.

Creative people in the upper tail of the human capital and talent distributions often have unusual preferences, and recognizing this fact should condition the search for additional motives and incentives in creating new useful knowledge. The norms prevalent in the communities in which new knowledge was created may have driven some intellectuals toward innovation without any obvious material incentives. Despite the often-heard notion (proposed mostly by noneconomists) that economists believe that most economic actions are driven by self-interest and greed, many of them have thought long and hard about what happens when people are motivated by "intrinsic motives"; that is, they carry out economic actions without any obvious material incentives (e.g., Besley and Ghatak 2008). The distinction between intrinsic motivation and status incentives can be fairly tricky.[25] In the setting of a firm, such incentives make sense if they are low cost for the owner and if they stimulate effort in areas in which output is hard to measure and verify. Peer recognition, however, was desirable for its own sake as well, as no academic needs to be told. Even such a wealthy and well-regarded scholar such as Boyle insisted on getting credit from others who used his work, and he had a catalog of his writings produced to secure his intellectual property rights in his research (Hunter 2009). Intellectual innovators, even the most modest and self-effacing ones, wanted credit for their work even if they knew there would be no profit from it.

---

25. David Kreps (1997) notes that in most employment situations (and that covers the bulk of the citizens of the Republic of Letters), it is hard to detect intrinsic motivation. He notes that "what is called intrinsic motivation may be (at least in part) the worker's response to fuzzy extrinsic motivators, such as fear of discharge, censure by fellow employees, or even the desire for coworkers' esteem."

The Growth of Useful knowledge

The net result of this unique character of the European market for ideas was not just a great deal of progress in useful knowledge between c.1500 and 1750, but also major changes in the way that knowledge was gathered, analyzed, and tested. The experimental method was essentially incompatible with Aristotelian science (Dear 1995), and it was not until the sixteenth century that experimental methods became widely accepted as a legitimate way of doing science. Mathematics, seen by many as an inferior form of intellectual activity deep into the Renaissance, was eventually recognized as an indispensable way of understanding nature. While some parts of physics and astronomy had already been mathematized in the late Middle Ages, it was not until Galileo's *Il Saggiatore* (The assayer) that a clear-cut mathematical language and methodology of the natural sciences was laid out for the age of Enlightenment—one that would lead to Newton, the Marquis de Laplace, and everyone in between.

The growth of useful knowledge was related to the social organizations. Significantly, the Republic of Letters was intimately connected to urban life (Wuthnow 1989, pp. 41–45). Centuries of urban self-government meant that many urban governments set their own rules as to what intellectual activity was permitted. This implied a great deal of heterogeneity, and not all cities were equally welcoming to skeptical and heterodox intellectuals. One thinks of the Rome of Pope Clement VIII, in which Giordano Bruno was executed, and Geneva under John Calvin, which burned Miguel Servetus for heresy. In many cities, intolerant local governments put an end to radical ideas promoted in their universities or city squares. But in the polycentric environment of Europe, there were always enough towns in which innovative intellectuals could do their work, and where they could find an audacious publisher who would print their works. Venice in the first half of the seventeenth century (which included Padua) was exceptionally tolerant and open-minded, taking in unconventional intellectuals like Galileo, Paolo Sarpi (1552–1623), and Cesare Cremonini (1550–1631) (Muir 2007). It went so far as to banish the Jesuits, who fought for a more conservative and orthodox curriculum, between 1606 and 1657. Strasbourg, a cosmopolitan border town, was famous for its tolerance; as was Basel, "a city ever hospitable to refugees from oppression in their native countries" (Grafton 2009, p. 7).

It was through this polycentrism that self-governing cities advanced the growth of useful knowledge in Europe. The importance of autonomous cities has been emphasized in recent work, such as Bosker et al. (2013) and

Serafinelli and Tabellini (2022), but their contribution to the competitive market for ideas has not been fully appreciated to date.

The open and competitive nature market for ideas was largely responsible for directing the trajectory of useful knowledge in Early Modern Europe. Market competition on both the supply and demand sides encouraged the emergence of "open science," in which intellectual innovations were normally placed in the public realm through publication or correspondence. Secrecy and guarding new techniques and innovations—previously a form of protecting one's "ownership" of propositional knowledge—became a thing of the past. Eamon (1994) described how secrecy fell in disrepute between 1500 and 1700, and while there were always some scientists who tried to maintain a veil of secrecy around some discoveries, it is fair to say that the Republic of Letters produced open science as it is practiced today (David 2008). It also meant that new insights were placed in the public realm, where practitioners who might find an application for them could access them. Secrecy remained a method of establishing property rights on practical inventions, although it was incompatible with the alternative way of doing so (namely, patenting an invention).

The market for ideas in Europe, which increasingly drove progress in useful knowledge, depended in many ways on the development of corporate forms. Monasteries and guilds in medieval times, universities and scientific societies in later centuries, and autonomous cities and organizations throughout all constituted the intellectual ecosystem in which progress could take off. Their existence was not a sufficient condition, but had Europe remained loyal to extended kinship social organizations, none of this would have taken place.

4. Artisans: The Key to the Industrial Revolution?

By 1700, intellectuals had changed the landscape of useful knowledge in Europe, developing the scientific methods and culture necessary for sustained technological growth. Yet there remains legitimate doubt among economic historians on whether formal codified knowledge, including what we call "science" today, could have created an Industrial Revolution *by itself*.[26] Despite the

---

26. The debate on the extent to which the Industrial Revolution depended on scientific advances is long and unresolved. The *opus classicus* in favor of science remains Musson and Robinson (1969). For more recent contributions, see especially Jacob and Stewart (2004) and Wootton (2015). Opposing and skeptical views have been expressed by Mathias (1979), Harris (1998), McCloskey (2010), and Ó Gráda (2016), among others.

advances of the Scientific Revolution, much of what natural philosophers knew in 1750 about essential natural regularities and laws that governed what we could produce was still meager, especially when compared to what it would become a century later. Basic phenomena such as combustion and soil chemistry were still unknown and misunderstood, and even the physics of the steam engine—the paragon of technological progress of the time—was not properly understood until the middle of the nineteenth century. The natural phenomena of electricity and selective breeding—both known early on to have large economic potential—were still profoundly mysterious. Moreover, the distance between what natural philosophers knew and did and what was actually practiced on the shop floors and in the fields where Europe's production took place was still vast by 1750. Still, contemporaries shared a widespread sense that uniting the spheres of theory and practice would be salutary to the economy (Zilsel 1942). Creating such bridges between those who knew things and those who made things was one of the great projects of the Industrial Enlightenment (Mokyr 2009). But it took many decades for such bridges to yield any serious advances in technology.

The idea that artisans and natural philosophers should collaborate to the benefit of the economy was most forcefully elucidated by Francis Bacon and Robert Hooke in England (Mokyr 2016). Yet the idea had important precursors in the sixteenth century and developed thereafter.[27] By the eighteenth century, the notion had become one of the axiomatic pillars of the so-called Baconian Program that lay at the core of the Industrial Enlightenment. Artisanal progress based on intuition and serendipity could take technology only so far on its own. In the century or so between Bacon and Denis Diderot, it increasingly dawned on Europeans that material conditions could be improved if artisans and farmers could become more efficient through a better understanding of physics and biology (chemistry was to come a bit later). Without the infusion of new propositional knowledge generated by intellectuals, Enlightenment philosophers realized, artisanal knowledge would eventually be doomed to stagnation. Background understanding provided by natural

27. The argument made here was made forcefully seventy-five years ago by Edgar Zilsel (1942), but it was largely ignored by economic historians. Zilsel stressed the significance of the various social connections between the top artisans and men of letters, and the strong conviction of contemporaries that learned academies (including London's Royal Society) should catalog and study artisanal practices in their environment—a project initiated by Robert Hooke.

philosophers and mathematicians mattered. Adam Smith spoke for the intellectuals of his age when he wrote that the "speculations of the philosopher . . . may evidently descend to the meanest of people" if they led to improvements in the mechanical arts (Smith, [1762–1763] 1978, pp. 569–72). Eighteenth-century Europe witnessed the birth of the scientific consultant—trained natural philosophers and physicians who were paid advisors of manufacturers and farmers. Their contributions to productivity were surely modest with some exceptions, but they clearly indicated the cultural changes associated with the Industrial Enlightenment and the path that Europe was to take after 1750. Again, these developments were far less likely to occur in conservative extended kinship societies.

Practical Scientists

Early Modern Europe produced many ingenious people who operated in the borderlands between crafts and natural philosophy. This was not a coincidence, but rather the direct cause of encouragement from the institutional structure in which they lived—in other words, the bridges between the two spheres of science and technology that were at times built within a single mind, straddling both. On the one hand, there were philosophers and scientists who did not mind "getting their hands dirty" and involved themselves with practical issues of production and efficiency. Following in the footsteps of giants like Hooke and Christiaan Huygens, these intellectuals built their own instruments, wrote treatises on a variety of production methods, and intently observed artisans' techniques. This group of people also included what contemporaries called "practical mathematicians." In a pioneering paper, Kelly and Ó Gráda (2022) surveyed a diverse group of "mathematics teachers, textbook writers, and instrument makers catering to a market of navigators, gunners, and surveyors." Clearly, this group should also be seen as occupying both propositional and prescriptive fields of knowledge.[28] Such individuals

28. As Kelly and Ó Gráda note, "These practitioners spanned a continuous spectrum from anonymous artisans and schoolmasters to figures now usually thought of as scientists and mathematicians but whom their contemporaries saw equally as teachers, instrument makers, and engineers." Among the examples they suggest are Jost Burgi, Johannes Regiomontanus, Peter Apian, Gemma Frisius, Gerard Mercator, and, most notably, Simon Stevin and Galileo. Many of the great scientists of the era, starting with Galileo, Huygens, and Newton, could claim to being practical mathematicians.

prospered in the open and relatively free environment of communes and other corporate forms that appreciated them and their work. Thus individuals of these occupations typically thrived in urban environments.[29] Publishing books (aimed at the literate and educated) describing cutting-edge technology belongs to the same category. Some of the most celebrated authors of books describing machinery and devices (real and imaginary) of Early Modern Europe from Leonardo da Vinci down were Albrecht Dürer, Agostino Ramelli, Vittorio Zonca, Johannes Stradanus, George Agricola, and Guido Pancirolli.

Such "borderland figures" straddling natural philosophy and the "useful arts" go all the way back to the sixteenth century. For example, the radical and heterodox Calvinist philosopher Petrus Ramus (Pierre de la Ramée, 1515–1572) reported that he had visited all mechanical workshops in Paris more than once. The Dutch physicist Isaac Beeckman (1588–1637), known as the first "mechanical philosopher of the Scientific Revolution" (Jacob 1988, p. 52), worked hard to build bridges between artisanal knowledge and natural philosophy. He worked on a range of applied issues, including meteorology, the formal analysis of music and sound, and the understanding of pumps.[30] Toward the practical end of the spectrum was the aforementioned Hugh Plat, who wrote many do-it-yourself books full of recipes and prescriptions on a range of topics (Harkness 2007). As a result of efforts from figures like these, theoretical advances from mathematicians and astronomers often led to technological breakthroughs, even if there were long lags between them.[31] For example, the eighteenth-century steam engine depended on scientific breakthroughs of the previous century. It utilized the sharp distinction between steam and air, along

29. Indeed, some scholars in this tradition (e.g., Roberts and Shaffer 2007) have gone so far as to deny altogether a meaningful separation between science and technology at this time and have proposed new concepts such as the "mindful hand"—educated and informed artisans. The notion that just because there were many individuals from both spheres who straddled theory and practice, there was no meaningful difference between them seems far-fetched.

30. One biography notes that "Beeckman in a way is the missing link between artisanal knowledge and mathematical science. . . . His mechanical philosophy of nature was grounded in both the practical knowledge of a craftsman and the theoretical knowledge of a scholar" (Van Berkel 2013, p. 4).

31. An early example of such an insight is the mathematical demonstration by the sixteenth-century Dutch (more accurately Frisian) astronomer, instrument maker, and mathematician Jemme Reinerszoon, known as Gemma Frisius (1508–1555), who suggested the possibility of determining longitude at sea by comparing the time at a location with the time at a fixed point in the world. This is precisely what the ingenious watchmaker John Harrison actually did in 1740 by building a marine chronometer of sufficient accuracy.

with the realization that the mechanical potentiality of steam pressure exceeded those of air pressure; the latter discovery was made by Salomon de Caus (1576–1630).

The eighteenth-century Industrial Enlightenment is full of examples of such people in the gray area between practice and theory. In England, a good example was John T. Desguliers, one of Newton's star students and later assistants at the Royal Society, who tirelessly spread the new Newtonian gospel but also wrote in great detail about practical mechanics, engines, and coal mines.[32] In France, a prime example is the mathematician René Réaumur, who wrote volumes on a plethora of practical and industrial topics. Trained as a mathematician and for many years the dominant scholar in the French Academy of Science, he is described by Bertucci (2017, p. 52) as a "practicing mechanical philosopher with a background in mathematics." He wrote long tomes about steelmaking, entomology, papermaking, and other practical topics. One could also mention the military engineer and physicist Charles-Augustin de Coulomb, famous for his pioneering work in applied mechanics and electricity, among others.

It was in Britain, however, that such "crossover persons" were most active and successful. They reflected a culture and mentality combining a belief in progress with a pragmatic approach to technical matters that created the background for the Industrial Revolution. Many of the leading industrialists of the Industrial Revolution were actively interested in science, believing that it could help them become more productive. The best-documented cases are that of the potter Josiah Wedgwood and Watt's partner, Matthew Boulton, but the culture of the Industrial Enlightenment was pervasive among the elite of British industry and engineering.[33] Furthermore, other bridges between the

32. John T. Desaguliers was only one of many individuals who embodied the Industrial Enlightenment. He "made the theories of the new scientific advances accessible to a wide audience [and] explained how many everyday applications worked [and] enabled others to use and develop them" (Carpenter 2011, p. 200). Watt famously stated that his knowledge of steam engines was "principally derived from Desaguliers." The frame of mind of the time was well reflected in his comment on Newcomen's engine, which he attributes largely to "accident," as Newcomen and his assistant were "neither philosophers to understand the reasons or mathematicians enough to calculate the powers" of their invention (Desaguliers 1734–1744, vol. 2, p. 533).

33. Among many other less well known examples, we could cite that of George Augustus Lee. As manager of the Salford Cotton Mill in Manchester, he was the first to introduce steam heating and gas lighting in the factory and an early member of the famed Manchester Literary and Philosophical Society, and he collaborated with the noted chemist William Henry. His

spheres of propositional knowledge and prescriptive can be discerned. One of those was the fascinating phenomenon of "Public Science," exhaustively described by Larry Stewart (1992), to which we will return next.

The strong belief that progressive manufacturers, colliers, and farmers gained from learning from scientists was embodied in the growth of consultants. This group increasingly engaged with entrepreneurs in the eighteenth century. During the first half of this period, one can already discern this trend, for example, from the careers of the aforementioned Desaguliers and Scottish chemist and physician William Cullen (1710–1790). In addition, we might look to the surveyor and engineer Henry Beighton (1687–1743), who was lesser known but no less important. He wrote a pamphlet on the power of the steam engine as a function of the diameter of the cylinder just a few years after its first operation. After 1750, the number of scientific consultants multiplied and included John Whitehurst, a charter member of the Lunar Society, and the Scottish chemistry professor Joseph Black, among others.

Skilled Artisans and Learning by Doing

Although such comparisons must always be speculative, it stands to reason that in terms of the skills and the technical competence of its artisans, there is little evidence that in c.1450, European artisans had an edge over those elsewhere in the world. In the following decades, Europeans displayed a ravenous appetite for the products of skilled Asian artisans, such as Chinese ceramics and silks, Indian cotton, and Persian rugs. An indication of the rough parity in the levels of skill is that when first exposed to the products of European artisans, those of Asia had no difficulty in emulating goods such as guns and navigational instruments at similar levels of quality.

Yet in the following centuries, there is growing evidence that at least in some critical areas, the skills of European artisans continued to improve, whereas those in the rest of the world treaded water. Two centuries after Christopher Columbus, Europeans had seen and described objects too small and remote ever to be observed by the unassisted human eye, proved the shape and dynamics of the solar system beyond any reasonable doubt, and manufactured

---

friend William Strutt, a cotton master from Derby, was a skilled architect and actually was elected to the Royal Society (an unusual honor for an industrialist). The structural engineer Charles Woolley Bage, designer of the one of the largest textile mills in Britain, was also the author of a formal paper on the strength of flanged beams in construction.

astonishing automated toys, objects that measured time and distance accurately, and musical instruments of a quality that subsequent generations have difficulty matching. By 1750, moreover, European mechanics were developing the machinery and capabilities that within a century would allow them to mass-produce consumer goods, the likes of which flooded the Indian market with cheap cotton products. They also built ships and armaments that came to dominate the Indian Ocean and easily defeated the Chinese navy in the First Opium War. Of course, these tools also allowed them to carry out worldwide colonial ventures on land and sea.

Much of this progress was due to learning by doing: the increase in the output of books improved the efficiency of printing presses and paper; the growing use of guns and constant warfare did the same for firearms; and the rising production of clocks and watches responding to a growth in demand led to a steady decline in their price and improvement in their quality. The expansion of the Atlantic trade led not only to improved ship design but also to advances in many ancillary industries such as navigational instruments, sail making, and food preservation.[34] European artisans learned both from their own experience and experiments and from one another. The diffusion of this knowledge at the most fundamental level was the result of the emergence of corporate forms in guilds, autonomous cities, scientific societies, and the like.

The elite artisans in seventeenth- and eighteenth-century Europe were critical to the Industrial Revolution, just as much as the practical scientists of the time. The former group included French artisans, whom Paola Bertucci (2017) called *artistes*; in her view, they were part of the "Artisanal Enlightenment." These people, who mostly lived in Paris and catered to the French aristocracy, were clever and good with their "mindful hands," creating things of practical use that were also of aesthetic value. Her *artistes* were a small elite of skilled, creative, and well-trained workers, the crème de la crème of French artisans: watchmakers, enamelers, toymakers, instrument makers, high-end furniture makers, and other high-skill workers. They, too, dwelled in the borderland between artisans and intellectuals. The eighteenth-century French *artistes* produced a variety of innovations, including Jacques de Vaucanson's miraculous

---

34. For more on the arms industry, see Hoffman (2015); for watchmaking, see Kelly and Ó Gráda (2016). For food preservation, the best example would be the mass production of hard tack biscuits, which sailors ate on long voyages, in the mid-seventeenth century (https://militaryhistorynow.com/2014/07/11/hard-to-swallow-a-brief-history-of-hardtack-and-ships -biscuit-2/).

proto-robots and tools, the Montgolfier brothers' hot air balloons, Etienne Lenoir (1699–1778) and his son Pierre-Etienne Lenoir's (1724–after 1789) elaborate clocks, and Jean-Antoine ("Abbé") Nollet's well-crafted instruments. The French artisans catered to a more upmarket constituency than did their British colleagues.

More than most of the top echelon of mechanics elsewhere, Bertucci's subjects were literate and read Bacon and Descartes; they also wrote books and articles on their craft. They were driven by a belief that their abilities were instrumental to economic progress, an ideological cornerstone of the Industrial Enlightenment. Their association was typical of the corporate forms that we see all over Europe in the Age of Enlightenment, institutionalized by the Paris *Societé des Arts,* established in the early eighteenth century (which thrived especially in the 1730s). She wrote that "the *Societé des Arts* constituted itself as an arena where *artistes* collaborated with savants, entrepreneurs, and aristocrats toward the common goal of improving the arts" (Bertucci 2017, p. 118).

And yet, it was Britain rather than France that was the cradle of the Industrial Revolution. Britain had an advantage over France, despite the fact that both nations had an abundance of motivated talent. Namely, Britain's artisanal elite included down-to-earth, practical mechanics who catered to a wider market; their primary concern was whether a product was useful, reliable, and cheap, rather than if it was elegant.

In the English Midlands, a group of highly skilled mechanics and clockmakers emerged over the years. They were the elite of British crafts, the right-tail of the distribution of technical competence, and without them, Britain may not have had an Industrial Revolution at all. They were more interested in the grimy mechanisms of textile equipment—which eventually became the heart of the Industrial Revolution in Lancashire and Yorkshire—than they were in the refined toys and artistic enamelwork that the French elite preferred.[35] These English mechanics were by no means ordinary workers; they were well-trained professionals who understood materials, mechanics, lubrication, transmissions, friction, levers, gears, pulleys, and belts. The best example—again, one of many—was John Wilkinson (nicknamed "iron-mad"), famous for

---

35. When Thomas Newcomen, the inventor of the Newcomen steam engine, came to the Midlands c.1712 to install his steam-powered engine, he and his assistant were "at a loss about pumps, but being near Birmingham and having the assistance of so many ingenious and admirable workmen, they soon came to methods of making the pump-valves, clacks, and buckets" (Desaguliers, 1734–1744, vol. 2, p. 533).

supplying low-tolerance cylinders for the Watt engine.[36] A good description of these men and what they did can be found in Cookson (2018), on Yorkshire textile machinery makers. Trained in such skilled occupations as clockmakers, millwrights, and whitesmiths, many of these artisans worked in small workshops, often family run. They were aided by just a handful of apprentices, journeymen, and a few skilled assistants.

What made the Industrial Revolution possible were technical competence and agility. As Cookson noted repeatedly, not only were they dexterous and well trained, but their skills were sufficiently flexible to help them adapt to a changing economic and technological environment.[37] What counted was not only their ability to scale up models and to produce reliable machinery, but also to solve unexpected problems and tweak the equipment to introduce minor improvements that cumulatively made the machinery more productive, more durable, more reliable, and more user-friendly to the textile workers using it. Competent artisans, too set in their ways or overly restricted to a production protocol cast by guild regulations, would have difficulty adjusting to the accelerating changes in the demand for skills driven by the Industrial Revolution. Overcoming that kind of inertia was a critical component of progress.

Contemporaries were fully aware of the crucial role of these mechanics. In a widely quoted statement, the great engineer Marc Isambard Brunel remarked, "It was one thing to invent, another thing to make the invention work." There was also a revealing letter authored by James Watt: "What is the principal hindrance to erecting engines? It is always the smith work" (both cited in Smiles 1883, pp. 223, 224). In this respect, Britain led Europe and Europe led the world.[38]

---

36. Wilkinson himself was well educated, having attended a dissenting academy and apprenticed to a merchant. His father, Isaac Wilkinson, conforms more closely to the model of the undereducated dexterous artisan-tinkerer: apprenticed in the iron trade, possessing only a rough literacy, he was an enormously skilled iron maker whose "business sense often did not equal his technical skill" (Harris 2006).

37. Cookson (2018, pp. 106, 127) notes, "To remain successful, engineers made structural changes, redesigned working systems, and solved technical problems in both product design and manufacturing process . . . skills requited of textile engineers were reshaped by the mass adoption of machine tools, for instance new forms of expertise in setting up machines . . . the move towards a new culture, beyond artisanship, is evident . . . changing tack came with risk attached but the great danger came from not adapting."

38. The comments of observers reflected this reality. For instance, J. L. Bradbury, a Manchester calico printer, testified in 1824 that French equipment was less productive than British, leading to far lower labor productivity (Great Britain 1824, p. 546).

However, it was not the British equipment that was decisive, but the artisans who constructed, installed, and maintained them. Jean-Baptiste Say pointed out that Britain's "enormous wealth . . . is less owing to her own advances in scientific acquirements, high as she ranks in that department, as to the wonderful practical skills of her adventurers in the useful application of knowledge and the superiority of her workmen" ([1803], 1821, vol. 1, pp. 32–33).

A few of those top artisans did more than tweak the new machinery—they actually devised major inventions. The watchmaker John Harrison, the iron-monger Thomas Newcomen, the weaver Samuel Crompton, the engineer Richard Trevithick, and the machinist Richard Roberts come immediately to mind. But only a small number of the thousands of skilled artisans left many records and are known to historians; many of them have remained anonymous. Despite this, we can get a glimpse of them by digging deeper into engineering records to learn about what drove them and how they were trained (Meisenzahl and Mokyr 2012). Artisanal competence made it possible for ideas and models of the great and minor inventors to be carried into practice, scaled up, installed, maintained, operated, and debugged. Without that kind of knowledge, the clever designs of the best mechanical minds would have remained no more economically significant than the ingenious devices designed by Leonardo da Vinci, or those of his lesser-known predecessor, the brilliant Sienese engineer Mariano Jacobus Taccola (1382–1453). What held back the realization of many technical and engineering ideas in Early Modern Europe was a barrier of inadequate skill and materials—it took centuries for these to evolve to a level where they could transform artisanal inventions and improvements into large-scale production. By the middle of the eighteenth century, Britain's artisans had reached a level of competence that allowed them to break through the barrier.

5. Human Capital Formation

What explains the increased competence of Europe's top artisans? Before the emergence of engineering schools in the nineteenth century, technical skills were acquired by and large through apprenticeship. The economics of apprenticeship have been of some interest to economists (e.g., Smits and Stromback 2001; De la Croix et al. 2017), but the central role of the institution of apprenticeship in generating the practical skills that helped drive the Industrial Revolution and the Great Enrichment have been fully recognized by only a few scholars until recently (especially Humphries 2003; Wallis 2025). Did Europe, and specifically Britain, have on average a more effective system of technical training, and if so, why?

Apprenticeship

Apprenticeship was a contract between a master of a trade and a young person, typically a teenager and their parents or guardians.[39] It was a nonrepeated, long-term transaction in which two flows were exchanged. The master committed to teach apprentices a set of skills and in most cases to provide them with room and board, as well as other services. In return, the apprentices often paid a fee up front and agreed to assist in the daily routines of the workshop. In many cases, the agreement included that the apprentices would stay on after training was completed and be employed in the workshop, much like indentured servants.

The contract underlying the relationship suffered from multiple complications. Besides the standard incomplete contract problem in economics, in which the main issue is the inability to specify all contingencies ex ante, the very nature of the service to be exchanged in the case of apprentice indentures was vague by definition because apprenticeship meant the transfer of *tacit* knowledge. Even when contracts included both parties' mutual expectations, the full details could not possibly be specified ex ante, nor could they be observed with much accuracy ex post (e.g., Smits and Stromback 2001; De Munck 2007).

The contract thus provided many opportunities for both sides to cheat. These hazards were exacerbated by the nature of the relationship between master and apprentice: it was nonrepeated, one-on-one, and long term. Moreover, the apprentices were, by definition, underinformed about the material to be taught (and their parents or guardians, often the signatories on the contract, was largely absent from the scene). This would prevent them from evaluating whether the master had actually fulfilled his obligations. The incompleteness of the contract was compounded by the further informational asymmetry that the interactions between the contracting parties were unobservable to third parties.

The possibilities for opportunistic behavior were thus multiple on the side of both the master and the apprentice. The master had a strong incentive to free-ride and renege unless a penalty was likely. Instructing a youngster took both resources and time, so a master who systematically neglected, exploited, or mistreated his apprentices might gain an advantage on his competitors.

39. Some of the following is adapted from De la Croix et al. (2017) and Mokyr (2019).

Furthermore, the master may have been underincentivized by the realization that by training a highly qualified artisan, he might create a potential competitor. On the apprentice's part, the issue can be summed up by what is known as the "credible commitment problem," which occurs widely in contract theory and political economy. The issue is basically this: if the apprentice or their guardian could advance the full cost of their training at the outset, this would be obviously desirable for the master. But when the apprentice was impecunious, and credit markets unavailable for this purpose—as was the case—the best way to cover the master's costs was to have the apprentice commit to work for him at below-market wages when the training had completed, thus securing a flow of cheap, skilled labor for the master in compensation for his teaching efforts.[40] From the point of view of incentivizing the master to teach properly, this makes sense: the productivity of the apprentice as an employee depended on how skilled they were at the time that they were to provide these stipulated services to his master. The commitment problem, however, meant that the apprentices had little incentive to fulfill this promise when the time came to do so; with sufficient skills under their belts, they could simply abscond, carrying with them the human capital they had accumulated at the master's expense.[41] Moreover, competing masters had the incentive to poach trained apprentices from their colleagues before they could reap the promised services from the contract. Because the master would anticipate these risks, he would not rationally agree to such a contract. And because the apprentice could not credibly commit to making good on their promise, the entire apprenticeship system might unravel. The contract was therefore not self-enforcing.[42]

One obvious way to solve such contractual issues was by keeping the instruction within the family and have fathers teach their sons, or at least keep the contract within the clan, where local and familial morality and loyalty to kin would protect both master and pupil from the worst excesses of

40. In medieval Paris, there was a choice of contracts. An apprentice could choose either to work more at the end of the contract or to pay or larger fee up front. See Epstein (1991, p. 144).

41. The hard-to-observe effort exerted by the apprentice working for the master is at the core of the principal-agent models that analyze such contracts, as Adam Smith ([1776], 1996, pt. I, p. 137) already noted.

42. Court records analyzed by Rushton (1991), which inevitably recorded the atypical cases of opportunistic behavior, provide a long list of ways in which the master could renege on the contract, including physical abuse, failure to instruct, nonpayment of owed wages, the disappearance of the master or his death (and replacement by his widow).

opportunistic behavior. This was de facto the case in the agricultural sector, where formal apprenticeship was rare and young boys learned the skills needed from their fathers. Outside Europe, where extended kinship was a foundation of society, this was the most common rule for artisans as well.

Yet in Europe, precisely because of its commitment to nuclear families and corporations and the ability of people to deal with like-minded persons to whom they were not related, the willingness to contract with nonkin increased. By the seventeenth century, apprentices trained by relatives were a distinct minority, estimated in London to be somewhere between 7 and 28 percent.[43] Training within the extended family or clan was less common in Europe, although training by relatives remained an option, especially in high-skill occupations such as music, as the examples of Alessandro Scarlatti, Johann Sebastian Bach, and Leopold Mozart indicate.

The significance of the wider choice of masters, as demonstrated by De la Croix, Doepke, and Mokyr (2017), is important, as the diffusion of more efficient techniques was much enhanced compared to a world in which kinship relations remained dominant. But technical knowledge also circulated by means of journeymen, who often traveled elsewhere to exercise their craft. The mobility of young apprentices and journeymen not only helped to disseminate best practices, but also created a competitive environment in which creative artisans whose ideas were not appreciated at home could go elsewhere (Belfanti 2004; Berg 2007).

In medieval and Early Modern Europe, informal and formal local organizations evolved that resolved most of the threats to apprenticeship contracts, especially moral hazard and opportunistic behavior. Municipal government became involved in this effort as well. After all, there was a collective interest at stake as well, since the entire community had an interest in the preservation of certain specialized skills and the reputational rents that came with it (Reyerson 1992).

As we have argued, apprenticeship was at the heart of human capital formation. The system served Britain exceptionally well and supplied it with a class of skilled artisans. The information system that matched apprentices with masters relied on "traditional networks of friends, neighbours, co-religionists, and . . . kin" (Humphries 2010, p. 269). The apprentices themselves had quite

43. See Leunig, Minns, and Wallis (2011, p. 42), Prak (2013, p. 153), and Goody (1989, p. 239). Fragmentary evidence for the Roman period indicates the likelihood that even in antiquity, artisans commonly sent their sons to be trained with others (Hawkins 2016, pp. 198–202).

a few incentives to complete their contracts: only apprentices with a completed term received the right of settlement in a county, and in those areas and trades controlled by guilds, they were barred from practicing their trade if they did not complete their term. This stricture was repealed in 1814, but the institution of apprenticeship survived. The institution was largely self-enforcing rather than dependent on the letter of the law or the power of the guild. In the later nineteenth century, apprenticeship as an institution was weakened, and yet it was sufficiently flexible to withstand the changes and survive until deep into the twentieth century.

On the eve of the Industrial Revolution, then, apprenticeship in Britain worked on the whole more satisfactorily than elsewhere; indeed, it remained the "recognized and sole practical route into the trade" (Cookson 2018, p. 151). Its relative independence from the guilds shielded it from some of the rigidities and obsolete rules that many guilds on the Continent still imposed on artisans and the techniques they passed to the younger generation. Its flexibility and adaptiveness prepared British mechanics to be agile enough for an age of accelerated technological progress. It is not hard to see how in a civil economy such as Britain, opportunistic behavior could be discouraged and penalized, ensuring that high-end apprenticeship would thrive as an institution.

In sum, the connection between social organizations and the Industrial Revolution runs partly through the effect that a world of corporations had on the transmission and acquisition of skills. A high level of skill and the flexibility to adapt to new techniques were associated with a world of corporations and the universalistic morality that they were correlated with. On the whole, Europe's organization led to the emergence of new and better technical competence, and these abilities created an environment in which inventors could realize their ideas and then tweak and adapt them until they became sufficiently effective to meet the market tests. The net result was that the West was able to pull ahead, creating the economic gap that lay at the core of the Great Divergence. The Industrial Revolution had deep medieval roots. Of those, the craft guild merits a separate discussion.

Craft Guilds

The craft guild was the best-known corporation for regulating European artisanship. Craft guilds were instrumental in facilitating apprenticeships in medieval and early modern times. As discussed in chapter 6, craft guilds were associations of unrelated individuals who shared occupational interests; they exerted an important influence on apprenticeship contracts (Greif 2006a). The histories of apprenticeship and the craft guild are intertwined and overlapping (Epstein 1991, pp. 103–22), and yet the two concepts are separate. Guilds regulated and controlled much more than apprenticeship. Apprenticeship could and did exist without guild supervision and was the main channel of intergenerational skill transmission. While craft guilds of some kind existed all over the world, many—but not all—European guilds actively regulated and controlled apprenticeship.[44] Perhaps the most obvious way was by solving the apprentice's commitment problem. With the power and authority of the guild behind him, the master could feel that the risk of opportunistic behavior by the apprentice was reduced since an apprentice who absconded before fulfilling the terms of their contract could be denied becoming a master or even employment altogether, or otherwise punished. The guilds had the power to enforce compliance with the contract through a variety of sanctions that they could impose on wayward apprentices, including "compulsory membership, blackballing, and boycott" (Epstein 2013, p. 61). European guilds were often closely associated with regulating apprenticeship, and they played a role in making the institution work properly by overcoming the contractual difficulties outlined here. This was especially true when the effective power of local government, to say nothing of the state administration, was limited.[45] In many cases, apprentices had to pay a special fee (known as *Lichtgeld* in Germany) to the guild to start their term, and it stands to reason that this fee was in part a payment for the supervisory functions that the guild exerted on the master-apprentice relationship (Reit 2007; Schalk 2019).

More recent work has qualified how widely guilds were engaged in explicitly enforcing the terms of the contract (Wallis 2025). In a conflict between a

---

44. The canonical statement is by Epstein (2013, pp. 31–32), who states that the details of the apprenticeship contract had to be enforced through the craft guilds, which "overcame the externalities in human capital formation" by punishing both masters and apprentices who violated their contracts. As late as the eighteenth century, for French bakers, "the guild made the rules for apprenticeship and mediated relations between masters and apprentices . . . it sought to impose a common discipline and code of conduct on masters as well as apprentices to ensure good order" (Kaplan 1996, p. 199). The radical Jean Paul Marat, no friend of the ancien régime, worried in 1791 after the abolition of the guilds that apprenticeship would disappear and lead to a decline in the quality of artisanal products. By 1803, the French state had taken control of apprenticeship, which they preferred to restoring the guilds (Fitzsimmons 2010, pp. 46, 144–46).

45. As Reith (2007, p. 181) put it, "The apprenticeship contract and the guild are . . . interdependent solution to the problem of conflicting interests of the parties to the contract."

master (and thus a member of the guild) and an apprentice (who was not), it was unlikely that the apprentice would prevail if the guild were called to arbitrate (Prak and Wallis 2019). This asymmetry would explain why eventually local officials and courts became increasingly involved in contract enforcement, creating conditions in which the market for apprenticeship could operate relatively freely and effectively without guilds. In a study of conflicts between masters and apprentices and servants in northern England in the eighteenth century, it was found that in the cases that went before the courts, the apprentice was usually the plaintiff, whereas "while the companies (guilds) offered the masters sufficient scope for correcting their apprentices, the latter had to appeal to the mercy of the more public forum of the quarter sessions to obtain justice" (Rushton 1991, p. 92).

The significance of guilds to a successful apprenticeship system was in part that they were in a position to enforce the contract between master and apprentice and arbitrate disputes between them. Moreover, they supported the institution through a reputational mechanism. Guilds provided a base for social capital by providing a venue in which people met socially on a regular basis and exchanged information and gossip, thus creating networks that supported reputation mechanisms that may have been the most natural way in which most contracts became self-enforcing. Opportunistic behavior by either side would become public knowledge, and anticipating the costs of reputational damage implies that in equilibrium, players behaved cooperatively.

The craft guilds were the locus of many social and professional activities, which created the kind of phenomenon captured in Spagnolo's (1999) model: the costs of opportunistic behavior could come from a very different corner than where the benefits came from. Spagnolo pointed out that cooperation can be attained when economic agents interact at multiple levels, so penalties for opportunism can be administered in many dimensions. Hence, even when the guild did not provide explicit adjudication and contract enforcement, it was a social network for sharing information and creating reputations. Cheating or abusing one's apprentices, in other words, could be penalized not only by formal judgments against the master, but also by social ostracism.

Guilds thus provided a way in which a highly fragile system of incomplete contracts was enforced. That said, guilds were far from a perfect solution. They erected serious barriers to entry and thus reduced competitiveness, and in all likelihood efficiency and technological dynamism as well. They may have led in many cases to the exploitation of apprentices and journeymen, to the protection of shoddy work, exorbitant prices, the exclusion of women and minorities, and many other sins, as listed by Ogilvie (2019). Guilds were a second-best solution, and their effects on long-term progress are ambiguous. Ogilvie notes that the two regions in Europe that were the most technologically progressive, the Netherlands and England, were also those in which guilds were relatively weakest in Early Modern Europe.

A stylized version of the evolution of apprenticeship in much of Europe suggests that guilds were central in enforcing apprenticeship contracts early in medieval Europe, and eventually the market (backed up by reputation mechanisms and the power of third-party enforcement institutions) took over. On much of the Continent, however, guilds remained powerful until late in the eighteenth century. As they were widely regarded as corrupt and reactionary by that time, they were one of the chief targets of the reforms introduced by the French Revolution.

The guild, however, was not the only corporate form of social organization that made the transmission and growth of artisanal human capital more effective in Europe. The urban institutional environment in which nonkinship cooperative arrangements emerged at the city level was central to the development of apprenticeship, especially in the Low Countries and Britain. In the Netherlands, local organizations associated with municipal government, named *neringen*, were established to regulate and supervise certain industries independent of the guilds. They set many of the terms of the apprenticeship contract, often including its length and other details (Davids 2007, p. 71). Even more strikingly, as we will see shortly, English guilds gradually declined after 1600 and exercised little control over training procedures, while local courts often arbitrated disputes (Berlin 2008; Rushton 1991; Wallis 2025). In reality, the two systems of corporations—guilds and municipalities—overlapped, cooperated, and reinforced one another.[46]

Apprenticeships thus functioned rather well in Europe and supplied a relatively high level of skilled labor. The strongest evidence lies in the fact that despite rising demand for skilled labor, the skill premium remained at a low and constant level for many centuries. This suggests an elastic supply response, and perhaps a great divergence between West and East in skill premia that predates the Industrial Revolution (Van Zanden 2009).

---

46. For example, Bellavitis, Cella, and Colavizza (2019, p. 9) pointed out that in Venice, the guilds monitored apprenticeships but needed the Giustizia Vecchia magistracy to enforce their regulations.

6. An Associational Society

Corporate social organizations played a key role in the onset of the Industrial Revolution—not just in the accumulation of useful knowledge, as described in the previous section, but also in bringing about a social environment that promoted economic development and facilitated cooperation across several domains.[47]

A Civil Economy

Private-order institutions contributed to the development of what we might call a "civil economy," in which most economic agents play by the rules and cooperate with one another without the threat of coercion, simply because it is in their best interest to do so. Peter Clark (2000, p. 94) pointed out that "voluntary associations of all sorts became an essential part of the social and cultural language of urban life, praised or satirized in literature and art." While this was hardly a new phenomenon, it attained special momentum after 1760. Clark called eighteenth-century Britain an "associational society" and notes that in many ways, the associations, societies and clubs were a progressive force, facilitating mobility, access, and contact: "Through their impetus to collective participation and solidarity . . . they promoted the steady accumulation of what has been called social capital" (2000, p. 469). The net result was a growth in social capital and the ability to trust strangers, with the knowledge that others behaved similarly. Above all, he notes, they fostered the tolerance underlying a more open and pluralistic society.

These associations were one more form of corporations, of course, which we see as key to the unique institutional development of Europe. In short, the civil economy was a consequence of universalistic ("generalized") morality, in which "individual values supported a generalized application of norms of good conduct in a society of abstract individuals entitled to specific rights" (Tabellini 2008a, p. 257). To repeat, economic agents were willing to cooperate with and trust people to whom they were not related and create social organizations that reflected this cooperation. The economic significance of this culture was enormous.

---

47. Some of the following is adapted from Mokyr (2008) and relies on the pioneering work of Peter Clark (2000).

In what way was a civil economy conducive to the Industrial Revolution? A market economy depended on people constraining their inclination to behave opportunistically. In other words, economic agents did not necessarily "defect" (even if that might have been in their immediate interest) and expected others to do the same. Modern economics teaches that if this was to be effective, agents needed to send out costly signals that indicated to others that they were reliable and trustworthy individuals because they belonged to a class of reliable and trustworthy agents (see, e.g., Posner 2000). Such signals were what "politeness" (in its eighteenth-century sense) was all about: gentlemanly customs and norms in dress, manners, housing, transportation, and speech observed by the British upper classes.[48] The gradual adoption of these signals by the professional, commercial, and high-skill artisanal classes in the eighteenth century marks the changes in British society, especially the growth of social capital. But the civil economy was also an environment in which important infrastructural investments such as canals and turnpikes could be organized by subscriptions of local investors, eager to show their civic spirit and enhance their reputations as local gentlemen. The success of these projects depended on formal imprimaturs from Parliament, but equally on gentlemanly behavior, trust, and a set of moral codes that were the foundation of the civil economy. Its success demonstrates the power of these moral codes, which played a much-underrated role in the British Industrial Revolution.

The success of the civil economy was part and parcel of Britain's character as a "polite and commercial society," in William Blackstone's famous words. For polite (i.e., cooperative) behavior to be an equilibrium, people had to be seen and known to behave in this way and hence have a need for social capital. This insight goes back to John Locke, in his *Essay Concerning Human Understanding*.[49] At a lower level of abstraction, the importance of a good reputation

---

48. "Politeness" meant something different in the eighteenth century than it does today: it meant, in Langford's view, a middle-class society that had accepted a set of informal moral codes that regulated behavior and sanctified acquisitiveness: "It both permitted and controlled a relatively open competition for power, influence . . . and markets" (Langford 1989, p. 5). In eighteenth-century lingo, it was equated (among others) with law-abiding behavior and an unquestioning loyalty to certain moral norms of behavior, and it was intuitively sensed that commercial success depended a great deal on politeness (Langford 2002).

49. Locke ([1690] 1975, p. 353) notes that "the measure of what is every where called and esteemed Vertue and Vice is this approbation or dislike, praise or blame, which by a secret and tacit consent establishes it self in the several Societies, Tribes, and Clubs of Men in the World. . . . For though Men uniting into politick Societies, have resigned up to the publick the disposing

in the business world of eighteenth-century Britain was clearly paramount. Daniel Defoe was only one of many to realize the value of a good reputation and observed that a shopkeeper may borrow at better terms than a prince "if he has the reputation of an honest man" (1738, vol. 1, p. 361).[50] Economic historians have emphasized the importance of groups and organizations within which the building of reputation and trust created effective markets, as trust reduced transaction costs and prevented markets from unraveling (Greif 1994; Landa 1995). It also encouraged entry into partnerships, where various parties had complementary skills that created synergistic advantages, but mutual trust was needed to make such partnerships viable.[51]

In the end, the provision of local public goods by voluntary associations was at best a mixed success, and the formal enforcement of laws and contracts by state agencies increasingly supplemented and in some cases replaced voluntary associations in this regard. Clark's judgment of the impact of clubs and associations on Britain's political and economic development was decidedly mixed. Yet in the critical area of useful knowledge, the impact of social capital and voluntary associations was quite strong. Learned societies sprung up in provincial towns such as Derby, Maidstone, and Darlington, and their members explicitly emphasized the practical utility of their ideas. Many of these organizations were voluntary associations of specialists, the most famous of which was the Society of Civil Engineers, founded by John Smeaton and eventually renamed after him; and the various botanical societies culminating in the Linnaean Society, founded in 1788. The more illustrious of these societies appealed to the very top of the intellectual elite of Britain, such as the Birmingham Lunar Society and the London Chapter Coffee House. The latter's preoccupation with useful knowledge is well described by the title of the book reproducing some of their minutes, *Discussing Chemistry and Steam* (Levere and

---

of all their Force, so that they cannot employ it against any Fellow-Citizen, any farther than the Law of the Country directs."

50. Elsewhere, he compared the reputation of a tradesman to that of a maiden, easily damaged by evil tongues and almost impossible to repair and describes how such reputations were made and lost around the coffee house through slander (Defoe 1738, vol. 1, p. 197).

51. The teaming up of such people as Boulton and Watt, or Matthew Murray with John Marshall (for more examples, see Mokyr 2009, p. 349), was a common occurrence during the Industrial Revolution. These firms were instrumental in transforming the workshops of small-time artisans and the commercial capitalism of the merchant-entrepreneurs of the early eighteenth century into the plant managers and industrial capitalists of the first half of the nineteenth.

Turner 2002). The function of these social organizations was to bring together theory and practice.

To summarize, then, the Industrial Revolution in Britain (and in Western Europe overall) was driven by the fortunate confluence of many factors; but it could have been derailed by many events and factors if they had gone wrong. It was made possible by a set of institutional factors and cultural beliefs that supported the accumulation and dissemination of formal, codifiable propositional knowledge produced by intellectuals ("science") and tacit, practical prescriptive skills, passed from master to apprentice. This knowledge explosion reached a critical point in the middle of the eighteenth century, which led to the Industrial Revolution. It relied on a social structure and an institutional ecosystem that was individualistic yet cooperative, and a generalized morality in the shadow of third-party contract-enforcing institutions. Without the social organizations established in the Middle Ages, it is unlikely that these conditions could have emerged, and indeed they did nowhere else.

7. An Industrial Revolution: Why in Europe and Not China?

Britain's leadership in the Industrial Revolution should not mislead us into believing that the Industrial Revolution was "British." It was *European*, and whereas British leadership was real and can be understood, the issue of British leadership is a different issue than the "Europe versus China" question. The latter, we argue, is rooted in the more remote past of Europe, a legacy of social and political developments going back to the early Middle Ages. In the two centuries preceding the Industrial Revolution, the Scientific Revolution and the Industrial Enlightenment planted the intellectual seeds of the Industrial Revolution in the fertile soil that were many centuries in the making. Yet for the plants to sprout and flourish, Europe needed to have institutions that were conducive to innovation and investment, as well as a cadre of high-skilled workers that could produce and maintain the machinery that embodied the Industrial Revolution. Plenty of things could have gone wrong.

As we have seen, during the period that Europeans think of as the High Middle Ages, China was a technological powerhouse and arguably may have been on the verge of an Industrial Revolution of sorts. At the time, it was developing industries that appear very similar to what we see in Britain after 1760. The widespread cultivation and manufacturing of cotton, the heavy use of iron and steel, the reliance on coal as a source of heat, and the mechanical aptitude revealed by sophisticated hydraulic and astronomical devices, to say nothing of a large upper tail human capital of literate and educated officials, coupled to a commercial, monetized, and market-oriented economy—all suggest many of the preconditions for a Chinese Industrial Revolution during the Song Dynasty. There is simply no denying that the so-called Needham Question—why Song China did not transition to continuous growth driven by sustained and accelerating technological progress—remains one of the more challenging issues in economic history. Recent work, often of uneven quality, continues to struggle with this question.[52]

As discussed in chapter 2 and as emphasized by Lin (1995), China excelled early, when technological innovations originated from the experience and luck of a very large number of farmers and artisans. If innovation is almost random or based on cumulative improvement due to learning by doing or experimentation, a larger population enjoys a comparative advantage because it can rely on a much larger number of draws. Of course, for experience-based technological progress to have widespread effects on productivity, this kind of knowledge has to be disseminated and encouraged. In a large and geographically diverse society such as China, that may have been a problem. But the distribution of useful knowledge was one of the functions that the Chinese mandarinate assumed and carried out with considerable success during the Song, Yuan, and early Ming dynasties.[53]

The Scientific Revolution of the seventeenth century in Europe generated progress of a different kind, however. Technological advances were not based only on the lucky discoveries and experience by farmers and artisans actually

52. See, for instance, Lin (2008), who complemented his 1995 paper by arguing that the Civil Service Examination misallocated human capital and hence prevented the scientific revolution that he regarded as critical to sustained technological growth. See also Chen (2012, p. 49), who placed the responsibility on a putative absence of "industrial and commercial property rights" due to arbitrary and uncertain taxation.

53. One example is the massive agricultural treatises written by civil servants during the Yuan Dynasty, such as *The Essentials of Farming and Sericulture* (1273), a state-sponsored compilation. This document, the *Nongsang jiyao*, was instantly distributed throughout the whole empire with the explicit purpose of raising agricultural output, expressing the belief that human invention and struggle can overcome the restrictions of nature and make it possible that plants like cotton can be cultivated in all parts of China. It was reprinted six times before 1332 in 10,000 copies and included in the huge encyclopedia put out by the Yongle emperor in the fifteenth century. See http://www.chinaknowledge.de/Literature/Science/nongsangjiyao.html.

engaged in production (i.e., learning by doing), although there was much of those as well. Rather, the revolution was defined by an entirely new mode of invention, based on planned experimentation, disciplined and high-precision observation, and mathematical models or hypotheses. This kind of progress relied on specialized knowledge possessed by a relatively small elite group of intellectuals and artisans in medicine, mathematics, and natural philosophy. From then on, the upper tail of the human capital distribution played an ever-growing role in generating innovation. Productivity depended not only on the *average* level of human capital and competence in an economy, but especially on the characteristics of the knowledge and artisanal elites. Upper-tail human capital thus requires specialization. China had a large, highly regarded, and well-trained community of talented scholars much earlier than did Europe. But this intellectual elite was versed in a very different kind of knowledge: in the words of one scholar, the Chinese intellectual elite studied the same material and were "not permitted to impoverish their personalities in specialization."[54] Despite its large contribution to the diffusion of education and to social mobility, therefore, the civil service tradition in China on balance hindered rather than fostered the transition from random innovation to science-led discovery and growth.

Public versus Private Roles in the Accumulation of Useful Knowledge

As discussed in previous chapters, differences between the East's and West's markets for ideas, knowledge, and skills were an essential part of why the Industrial Revolution occurred where and when it did. These differences had deep historical origins. In an increasingly individualistic and decentralized society organized by nuclear families, the incentives to innovate were different than in one of extended kinship and a centralized state bureaucracy. Innovation is a social activity, and social organizations played a central role in the divergence.

From the early Middle Ages on, innovation primarily occurred in the private sector, carried out by monks and artisans. Intellectuals, engineers, and entrepreneurs wanted to appropriate some part of the social surplus created by new knowledge, and they were thus incentivized to contribute to its advancement directly. The reason why medieval and Early Modern European states did not engage in this activity is obvious: unlike China, European states were weak, and most leaders were undereducated (and often violent) thugs.

54. Etienne Balasz, as cited in Levinson (1968, vol. 1, p. 16).

Few government officials had the background to involve themselves in intellectual or technological innovation of any kind, much less in science, even if many more refined courts sponsored it in Renaissance and Baroque Europe.

As we have argued in previous chapters, in China, intellectual activity—including scientific and technological progress—were deeply rooted in the political structure and mostly carried out by Mandarin officials. China, too, had social organizations like schools and academies to facilitate innovation, and many were run by clans, not directly by the state. However, these organizations' goal was primarily to prepare youngsters for the Civil Service Examination, not to advance scientific and critical knowledge. It is therefore unsurprising that after the Song Dynasty, knowledge accumulation did not contribute much to innovation and technological progress, certainly not to the same extent as in Europe.

The significance of the difference between an economy in which innovation was carried out by a competitive and decentralized private sector and one in which this activity was directly or indirectly carried out by a government bureaucracy may have been overlooked by scholars to some extent. The point is that if there was to be an Industrial Revolution in China, it would have had to be driven by Imperial initiative and bureaucratic support, much as it was, say, in Russia in the late nineteenth century. But Chinese authorities in the Ming and Qing dynasties lost interest in advancing innovation, so the position that China occupied as a technological leader in about AD 1100 was eventually reversed.

If not the state, who would be engaged in innovation? In medieval Europe, again, corporations played a central role. Religious organizations, especially monasteries, were at the forefront of advancing knowledge. But as the power of the Church slowly declined, secular organizations took over. Universities, academies, and informal societies emerged and contributed to the advancement and diffusion of useful knowledge. In many cases, as noted earlier, craft guilds may have also played a significant role in encouraging and diffusing innovation in manufacturing (S. R. Epstein 2009 2013).

As previously discussed, innovation in Europe took a variety of forms and was not confined solely to scientific knowledge. It also took place in the workshops of artisans, inside collieries and shipyards, and throughout the productive sectors of the economy. Why could this kind of useful and practical technological progress, intimately linked to productive activities, not be sustained in China to the same degree? After all, the more advanced parts of China housed vibrant commercial sectors, integrated markets, and employed a fine division of labor with a high level of specialization (see, e.g., the description of the city of Hankow in Rowe 1992). We now turn to this question.

The Organization of Production

One reason why technological progress linked to production was slower in China was the missing connection with scientific methods and advances, which instead became so relevant in Europe in the Early Modern period, as described earlier in this chapter. But there is a second important reason, one that has to do with the organization of production. Here, too, the different social organizations in Europe and China are particularly important. In Europe, with very few exceptions, the average firm was not much larger than a household plus at most a few servants or apprentices. Hence, any firm-specific investments were associated with full control rights by owners. They did not have to worry about other kinspeople claiming their share and having a say in management, as would be the case in social organizations based on extended kinship. This led to a proliferation of merchants and artisans organized at the household level, each of them independent (even if they were organized in guilds and other corporations). The net result was the emergence of a class of small-time capitalist entrepreneurs in the West, especially in England, thus creating something of a middle class by 1700. These people could combine commercial and financial ability, marketing and organizational skills, and the technical know-how of skilled artisans and ingenious mechanics. Eighteenth-century British observers (such as Daniel Defoe and David Hume) identified them as a people of a "middling sort." Historians have included in this group such individuals as well-to-do yeomen and farmers who had managed to augment their holdings, merchants, and high-skilled artisans and some professionals (Smail 1994, p. 26).

In China, by contrast, lineage organizations dominated productive and commercial activities. Zelin (2022, pp. 326–27) summarized the critical importance of the clan for Chinese business organizations: kinship created trust based on familiarity and mutual dependence. Moreover, the clan's ability to enforce its decisions, claim authority, and control joint resources deeply influenced how Chinese businesses organized and conducted their activities. Many scholars have noted the weakness in China of what many would call "industrial capitalism." They focus perhaps more on political aspects of capitalism, noting that manufacturing and commerce never acquired much political clout in a nation run by scholar-officials and courtiers. In Zhao's (2015) interpretation,

China was locked in by an iron-clad combination of Legalism and Confucianism, both quite hostile to industrial capitalism. Whether this unique political structure can explain the Great Reversal by itself seems doubtful, but it reflected a society in which extended families and local gentry were responsible for the supply of local public goods and jealously guarded the political power that came with it, leaving no room for alternative sources of power based on commercial or industrial wealth.

Chinese kinship organizations, as described in chapter 3, relied on seniority rather than wealth or entrepreneurial success as the criterion for allocating authority (Zhang 2017). This method of allocating control rights could give rise to obvious hold-up problems since the fruits of investments and innovation would be captured by senior clan members, and these were often not the more innovative and entrepreneurial individuals in the organization (see Hart 2017, for a general discussion of how control rights are essential in any organization when contracts are incomplete). Managerial innovation was an important component of the acceleration of productivity that accompanied the Industrial Revolution in Europe, not only in manufacturing but also in agriculture and services. The persistent quest for continuous efficiency-enhancing innovations, referred to by contemporaries as "improvements," throughout the economy was an important aspect of the acceleration of growth that preceded and accompanied the Industrial Revolution in Europe (Slack 2015). But the management of Chinese lineage organizations, which, as we saw in the previous discussion, was dominated by elder individuals, to a large extent stifled the instincts to pursue efficiency-enhancing innovations and investments at the microeconomic level.

Lineage organizations differed from European corporations in another important respect: they seldom employed wage labor, and especially not from outside the extended dynasty. Even in the most commercialized parts of China, at most 15 percent of the rural population lived primarily off wages during the mid-nineteenth century. In England, 73 percent of those working in the countryside were wage-laborers in 1851; furthermore, wage labor was also common in English cities (Vries 2013, p. 340).

Differences in the organization of production have important implications for economic development. A mode of production based on the extended family where money wages are not paid discourages labor-saving investments and innovation because redundancies are much more costly. If a machine can reduce the number of workers needed, they can be dismissed and allocated to another employer. If the worker is part of a clan, dismissal is problematic. If the lineage is in any case responsible for the survival of its members, through implicit or explicit risk-sharing arrangements, replacing labor with machines does not save resources unless production is increased proportionally. But not all labor-saving innovations lead to higher production volumes; often they are introduced mainly to save on labor costs. A recent example is provided by the findings of Caprettini and Voth (2020), who showed that labor-saving technologies such as threshing machines led to widespread riots in 1830s England. Workers feared being displaced and not find alternative employment opportunities. In China, such labor-saving innovations were discouraged by the prevalence of risk-sharing arrangements inside lineages and the infrequency of wage compensation as a part of labor contracts. In addition, large-scale investments in machinery or equipment can be more difficult for dynastic firms, to the extent that they have a smaller scale or smaller retained earnings (Vries 2012).

The Absence of an Entrepreneurial Class

As discussed in chapter 6, managerial problems at the level of the firm were compounded by issues with credit markets, specifically the rules on the redemption of mortgaged land, designed to protect small landowners and discourage capitalist farming. As pointed out by Zhang (2017), the lack of land concentration in China (and the corresponding absence of a large, landless proletariat) moderated the extent of wealth inequality in China relative to Europe. At the same time, however, it reduced the financial resources available for business investment and capital accumulation.

In addition to the absence of anything that looked like an Industrial Enlightenment or any other decentralized cultural movement that was committed to "improvement" or "progress" toward sustained innovation, China was missing an entrepreneurial class that could have brought about the transition from commercial capitalism (which clearly existed) to a technologically dynamic industrial factory system (Hung 2016, pp. 23–33). Hung's argument about the failure of China's textile industry to transform itself into a capitalist structure is that successful entrepreneurial families often tended to place their sons into a state elite of mandarin officials, which they regarded as the peak of personal achievement, instead of pursuing more aggressive business strategies. As a result, Hung pointed out, China had few entrepreneurial leaders that could help its domestic textile industry turn into factories. Wealth made in commercial enterprise was used to buy one's family way out of commerce.

In all fairness, many successful British entrepreneurs during the Industrial Revolution underwent similar transitions, and their offspring opted for a quiet life of landed gentlemen and politicians—one thinks of the Arkwrights or the Peels. But in Britain, there were always new entrants willing to challenge and replace incumbents. China was different. Opening a cotton factory in nineteenth-century China required explicit permission from the Imperial government; once receiving the permission, the licensee would exert strong influence to keep out the competition.[55] As a result, when the sons of successful entrepreneurs left the market for the mandarinate, they left a vacuum in their place.

The other argument that Hung made is that the Chinese state never unequivocally sided with industrialists—that is, they did not suppress workers' resistance to mechanization (see also Desmet, Greif, and Parente 2019). Workshop owners found it difficult to scale up their businesses to factory production. Consequently, the domestic putting-out system—which diminished everywhere in Europe under the onslaught of more efficient factories during the Industrial Revolution—remained prevalent in China (Hung 2016). Family organizations and the absence of corporate forms created a firm structure that was weaker than in the West, and Chinese business enterprises fell short of what was necessary for advanced industrial capitalism. As S. G. Redding put it, China had "weak firms in strong networks" (cited by Hamilton 2006, p. 46). One might add that Europe was the exact opposite: it had stronger firms in weaker networks.

Conservative Leadership

At the national level, some part of explaining the absence of an Industrial Revolution in China can be chalked up to contingency. The rise to power of the Qing (Manchu) Dynasty in 1644 may have been particularly prohibitive of a Chinese Industrial Revolution. The Qing emperors tended to be conservative and inward-looking. perhaps because as sinified usurpers, the Manchu rulers felt insecure about their legitimacy. Law and order, together with political stability, were regarded as far more important than progress. The Qing emperors were little interested in innovation or foreign knowledge, and they stressed continuity, discipline, and conformism. In the eighteenth century, when Enlightenment Europe had more or less abandoned the effective persecution of heretics and free-thinkers, the Chinese bureaucracy cracked down hard on subversive ideas and those suspected of thinking outside the box (Xue

55. David Faure (2006, p. 30) recounts the case of the powerful general and politician Li Hongzhang, who received a license for cotton manufacturing and yet it took him many more years to open his plant, during which time he lobbied successfully to deny a similar license to competitors.

2021).[56] In a recent contribution, Bai, Jia, and Yang (2024) analyze books published in China between the mid-seventeenth century and 1940 and show that especially between 1770 and 1840, book censorship had a serious effect on the number of publications, and the crackdown had a chilling effect on authors, who practiced self-censorship out of fear. While there is a sharp recovery in publications after 1840, the authors conclude that the suppression of knowledge in China may have had significant political and economic consequences during a critical period of global change.

Such political rigidity was especially detrimental to a country that had no tradition of bottom-up innovation and also lacked noncentral state actors who might lead innovative initiatives in the absence of the Imperial government, such as autonomous cities. Once the state lost interest in progressive initiatives and by and large abandoned them, they were unlikely to emerge elsewhere in the country until forced by increasing threats from aggressive foreign powers. Until the late nineteenth century, China did not respond seriously to the potential of such threats (a massive miscalculation, as it turned out). Most important, the Chinese bureaucracy's inability to collect taxes to fund innovation was increasingly limited due to declining tax returns (Ma 2013; Sng 2014). The fiscal weakness of the Imperial government became progressively worse after 1830. Both on the supply and the demand side, then, China was no closer to an endogenously driven Industrial Revolution in 1900 than it had been in 1700. By then, it was too late.

8. Conclusion

To understand why the Industrial Revolution took place where and when it did, it is critical to understand its cultural and social background. Contrary to what some scholars such as David Landes (and, to some extent, even Joseph Needham) believed, there was nothing fixed about culture, even if it usually changed at a tectonic pace. Between 1450 and 1750, the subtle interaction between institutions and culture paired with the growth of technical competence prepared Europe for the Industrial Revolution. Slowly, the growing sense that progress was possible and desirable became dominant. More and more intellectuals felt like Joseph Priestley (a rather emblematic figure in the Industrial

---

56. Xue (2021) shows remarkably how the "literary inquisition" reduced the formation of social capital in China, which suggests that the growth of social capital in Georgian England may be related to the relative freedom of expression and tolerance there.

Enlightenment) when he wrote in his famous *New Chart of History* in 1769 that "it is even easy to show . . . that wars, revolutions of empire, and the necessary consequences of them, have been, upon the whole, extremely favourable to the progress of knowledge, virtue, and happiness" (cited by Thomas 2023, p. 18). Whether this was in part illusory or not, by the second half of the eighteenth century, this message had fully sunk in. Needless to say, just believing in the possibility of improvement would not bring it about. But without such belief, the likelihood of continuous improvement seems unlikely (Slack 2015).

There was nothing in Chinese culture that was inherently antithetical to a belief in the idea of progress, and Needham (1969), for one, argued strenuously that in Song China, the belief in progress was almost axiomatic. However, his examples are almost all from the Song or earlier dynasties. While the idea of continuous progress in human capabilities and the human condition became one of the core concepts that drove the Enlightenment, the idea certainly had disappeared in China by the late Ming and Qing. Vogelsang (2020) stressed that the concept resurfaced in China only in the last decades of the empire and the Chinese Republic. He produced a Google Books n-gram graph that confirms the impression that the discourse of "progress," virtually nonexistent before 1895, grew significantly during the following decades (Vogelsang 2020, p. 48).

Despite the absence of a well-defined idea of progress, Chinese science in the first half of the second millennium was impressive. Needham recounts how under the Mongol emperors (Yuan Dynasty, 1279–1368), science could still flourish thanks to the work of the brilliant polymath Guo Shoujing (1231–1316).[57] Yet when the Ming came to power in 1368, there were no talented Chinese engineers and scientists comparable to Guo.[58] Guo may have been the "Tycho Brahe of China," as he was called by the Jesuit astronomer Johann

57. Guo, a government official like most Chinese intellectuals, was an outstanding hydraulic engineer, instrument maker, and mathematician, and his skills were heavily used by the emperor Kublai Khan on projects including the repair of the Grand Canal, which supplied Beijing with grain, and the redesign of the Chinese calendar, a matter of supreme importance to the rulers. His astronomical instruments and clocks continued the grand traditions of the Song Dynasty, and his armillary spheres were still in existence in the early seventeenth century, when they were described by Matteo Ricci.

58. Needham himself comments that after Guo's time, no progress of any importance was made in Chinese geometry until the arrival of the Jesuits from Europe, and Guo's astronomy "suffered in the general standstill of science during the Ming" (Ronan and Needham 1981, p. 82; see also p. 45).

Schall. Schall was impressed with the astronomical instruments that Guo designed (Engelfriet 1998, p. 72), but if Guo's achievements preceded those of Brahe, China did not produce a Johannes Kepler, a Galileo, or a Newton. In 1627, the Swiss Jesuit Johannes Schreck and a Chinese colleague named Wang Zheng published a catalog of Western inventions entitled *Diagrams and Explanations of the Wonderful Machines of the Far West*. It featured descriptions of machines catalogued by Italian and French engineers such as Agostino Ramelli and Jacques Besson, which were adapted to the Chinese audience using the Chinese pictorial style. As Elman (2006, p. 25) notes, there was a sixteenth-century revival of Chinese literatis' interest in "natural phenomena" that clearly indicates that there was nothing immutable about China's falling behind the West.[59] But this attitude melted away under the Qing. The renowned scientist and mathematician Mei Wending explicitly denied any progress in science and argued in 1693 that the moderns are in no way superior to the ancients, and there is no progress in history; indeed, "the accumulation of human knowledge is merely a token of the ancients' superior merit" (Jami 2012, p. 220).[60]

With some exceptions, neo-Confucian ideology increasingly became backward-looking and nostalgic; proponents regarded antiquity as the golden age and dismissed beliefs that the world would or could ever get better. To be sure, the European Enlightenment did produce some conservative thinkers, but during the eighteenth century, most leading intellectuals increasingly committed to the concept of progress, even if they did not agree on many of the details, much less on the path to achieve it. In China, on the other hand, the concept of progress was of little interest; instead the empire's main interest was local peace and order and social stability. The rule of the Qing bureaucracy

59. Modern research (Ma 2021) confirms that Chinese intellectuals were strongly influenced by the Western science taught by the Jesuits who appeared in China in 1582, which had a substantial influence on local intellectuals. Chinese literati exposed to Jesuit scientists actively learned European sciences and produced more Chinese scientific works than those who had been exposed to Jesuit nonscientists. A shining example was Xu Guangqi (1562–1633), who joined forces with Ricci to translate Euclid's *Elements* into Chinese. All the same, as Engelfriet (1998, p. 450) points out, "the acceptance of Western learning was totally dependent on the opinions and motivations of the thin upper layer formed by the highly cultured and traditional Confucian scholars."

60. Moreover, the way that Western knowledge was made palatable to Chinese scholars such as Mei Wending was to propagate the belief that all Western science was Chinese in origin and had been lost somehow, preserved in the West, and was now being transported back to China (Martzloff 1997, pp. 30–34).

and the triumph of a conservative ideology reinforced and perpetuated the stagnation that had set in after the thirteenth century. A recent study stresses that the backward-looking nature of the *keju* examinations encouraged this conservative bias (Chen and Duan 2024; see also Duan 2024). Duan's work demonstrates on the basis of extensive bibliometric evidence that he has assembled that the books published in China are consistent with a strong bias away from STEM fields and toward politics and classical studies.

As already noted in chapter 2, the dominant culture, as reflected in the books published, was turning away from useful knowledge.[61] Moreover, the trend was moving from original and innovative work toward more derivative and exegetical writings that Duan (2024, p. 6) has called commentary-focused scholarship.[62] Moreover, Duan's econometric work links this decline directly with the *keju* examinations; in that regard, his findings complement a similar argument made by Huang (2023). Similarly, Augier, Guo, and Rowen (2016) argued that Chinese innovation prioritized the exploitation and refinement of *existing* knowledge over the discovery, exploration, and development of radically new knowledge. It would be misleading to call this in any sense a failure: China may have been much closer to the global norm, which prized continuity, stability, and tradition and dismissed beliefs in progress. It was Europe that was the outlier.

61. An interesting example of this is an encyclopedia of Chinese technology and engineering authored by Song Yingxing (1587–1666), entitled *Tiangong Kaiwu* (The Exploitation of the Works of Nature). Disillusioned with the Civil Service Examination, Song wrote the work while employed as a county teacher. It featured a large number of extremely detailed and accurate illustrations of the techniques in use. Sometimes referred to as the "Chinese Diderot," Song openly acknowledged the encyclopedia's detachment from the conventional scholarly pursuits of career advancement and remarked that "ambitious scholars would give it no thought, as it was not concerned with the advancement of officialdom" (cited by Duan 2024, p. 35). The book was eventually destroyed, and it has only survived thanks to a Japanese reprint.

62. Strikingly, the trend toward interpretative scholarship was markedly stronger for the very top *jinshi* recipients (Chen and Duan 2024, p. 23).

10

Modern China

1. Introduction

In 1978, two years after Mao's death, China was one of the poorest countries in the world; it accounted for almost 23 percent of world population, but for only 3 percent of world gross domestic product (GDP). At the end of 2020, China was the largest economy in the world at purchasing power parity (PPP) adjusted exchange rates, with a share of world GDP of 18.3 percent, roughly proportionate to its share of the world population. During this period, its real GDP grew at almost 10 percent per year on average, doubling the size of its economy every eight years and lifting more than 800 million people out of poverty.[1] No other comparably large country has managed such an amazing feat in modern times, and in such a short period. Yet its per-capita GDP in 2019 was still only 23 percent of that of the United States (figure 10.1), suggesting that China still has much room to sustain rapid growth in the future.

China's exceptional economic growth is puzzling not only for its magnitude and duration, but also because it occurred in an environment of weak economic institutions and repressed or distorted financial markets. Property rights initially were not well defined, and even later, they were neither clear nor protected from political abuse. Private property was formally recognized by the Chinese constitution only in 1999, and even then, private business property was far from legitimate and secure without political connections. Until 2007, all property was de jure owned by the state, even if most assets were managed and controlled by individuals or companies de facto, and there were

---

1. International Monetary Fund (IMF), *World Economic Outlook*, October 2021; and World Bank, *China Overview*, 2017. As noted by Martinez (2022), however, China's official GDP growth numbers may be manipulated to appear much higher than they are.

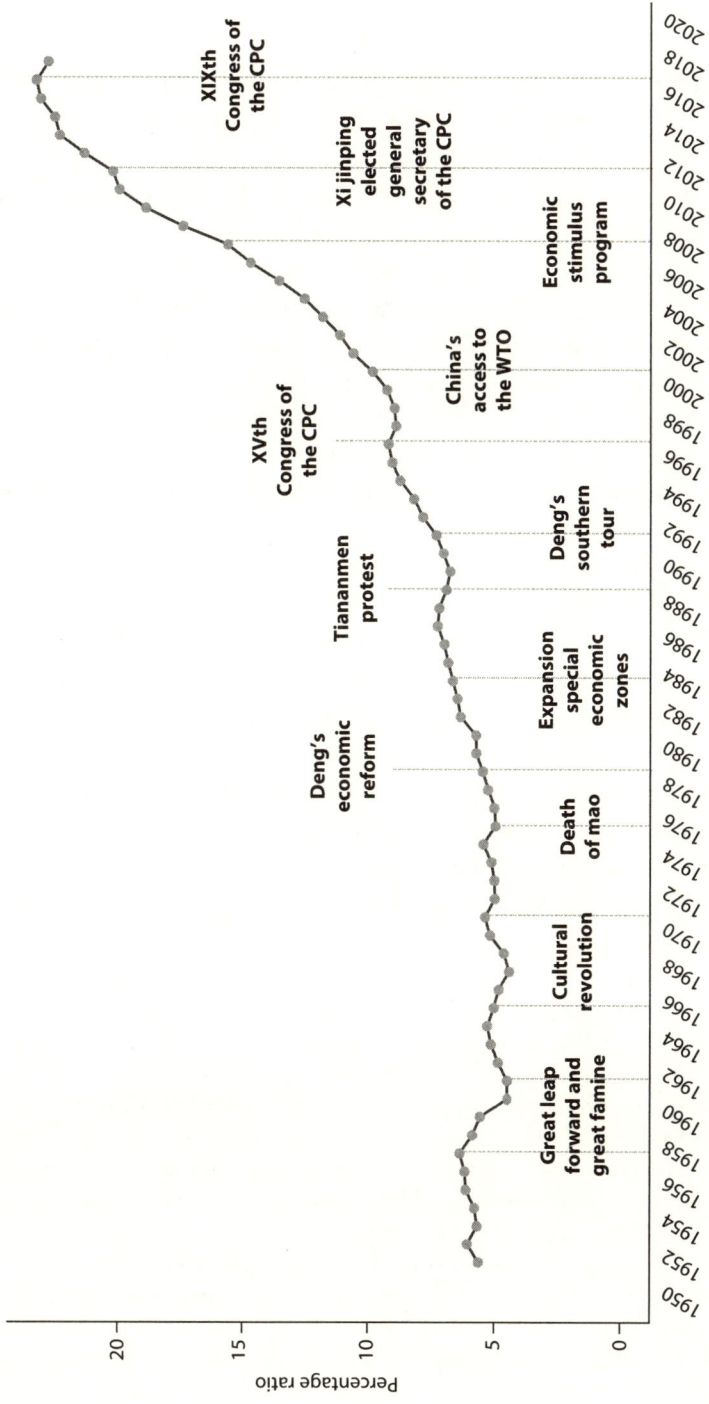

FIGURE 10.1. China versus U.S. real per-capita GDP (percentage ratio). *Source:* Penn World Table, Growth and Development Center, University of Groningen, January 23, 2023, https://www.rug.nl/ggdc/productivity/pwt/?lang=en GT.

no laws regulating private property (Zhang 2008). Often regulations were un-written and could be waived at the discretion of local officials, private firms paid higher tax rates, and entry of new private firms remained costly.[2] In the 1990s, most major contracts required government approval, without which the contract was null and void (Weidenbaum and Hughes 1996). A uniform con-tract law was formulated only in 1999, but this law remains ambiguous and lacks proper case notes (Li 2009, p. 20). To this day, there is no independent judiciary, and the legal system is subservient to the interests of the state.

In addition, throughout much of this period, financial markets were re-pressed and bank loans were mostly directed toward state-owned enterprises (SOEs). Yet despite these financial constraints, the growth of private firms and local collective enterprises (town and village enterprises) sharply reduced the weight of the state sector in the economy. In 1978, SOEs accounted for 60 percent of nonfarm employment, while by 1993, this number had fallen to 30 percent. This transformation was due almost exclusively to the growth of employment outside the state sector since privatization and restructuring of SOEs had not yet taken place. Indeed, between 1980 and 1992, the growth of output, labor productivity and total factor productivity (TFP) in SOEs was less than half that of town and village enterprises (Brandt and Rawski 2021; Huang 2012; Qian 2000b; Zilibotti 2017). Reforms enacted since the mid-1990s led to the restructuring and privatizations of many SOEs, increased competition, and improved the efficiency of the banking sector. Nevertheless, financial markets remained distorted by political interference and inefficient SOEs continue to enjoy preferential access to bank loans.[3]

Overall, China's modernization is difficult to reconcile with the view that institutions protecting property rights from political abuse, along with well-functioning financial markets, are preconditions for economic development and were responsible for Europe's economic success in the previous centuries.

2. More than 443 approval items were required to register a private firm in Beijing (Nee and Opper 2011, p. 6).

3. Cong et al. (2019) showed that the government-induced credit expansion of 2009–2010 favored SOEs and firms with lower marginal returns to capital. Bailey et al. (2011) have shown that poor financial performance and high managerial expenses increase the likelihood of obtain-ing a bank loan, and bank loan approvals predict poor subsequent borrower performance. Prob-ably this is due to corruption and to political influence aimed to preserve employment in SOEs (Chen et al 2013). Yet SOEs remain a substantial part of China's economy, creating between 23 and 28 percent of GDP in 2017 (depending on the method of calculation; see Zhang 2019). Since 2020, these firms are formally controlled by the Chinese Communist Party.

How then can this exceptional economic growth be explained, and what are its historical roots? Is China's economic miracle ultimately due to the Cultural Revolution and to Mao's break with the past, both culturally and institutionally? Or was China's modernization and transition to a market system instead smoothed by its distinctive cultural traditions and its past institutions?

This chapter addresses these questions with no pretense of providing a full explanation of China's recent economic miracle. A success of this magnitude cannot be due to a single cause. Many mutually reinforcing factors contributed to China's economic miracle. Its location allowed China to learn and benefit from the recent successes of other East Asian countries. The timing of the turnaround was propitious. China opened to the world just before the peak of an era of cooperative globalization induced by lower transportation and communication costs and new information technologies, allowing Chinese factories to be included in the global value chain. China's political leaders in the 1980s and 1990s were exceptionally competent and farsighted. A rich tradition of commercial and entrepreneurial engagement had survived Mao's regime, and it reemerged as soon as economic incentives were strengthened. Thanks to centuries of political unification, the country was ethnically and culturally homogeneous (except for the Muslim and Tibetans minorities), and education was highly valued. The preexisting misallocation of resources had created a huge gap between actual and potential output, leaving ample room for catch-up growth once the economy opened up and more efficiency-enhancing policies were pursued. A very large and cheap labor force enabled prolonged gains from sectoral and geographic reallocations.

In this chapter, we do not try to shed light on the relative importance of these factors. Instead, we relate some key aspects of China's modernization to the history discussed in the rest of this book. Our main argument is that the country's recent success is not due to a break with its past. On the contrary, two specific aspects of China's history and traditions reemerged after Mao's death: kin-based social organizations and a system of government incorporating several features of the Imperial regime. These two social and political infrastructures bear a striking resemblance to those described in previous chapters, and they allowed modern China to chart a peculiar course toward economic development.

Mao sought to destroy Confucian traditions but failed to erase kinship values. Indeed, there is evidence suggesting that, even at the height of Maoist totalitarianism with its concomitant disasters, clans remained an important component of China's economy. In a recent paper, Chen et al. (2024) showed

that clans had a significant impact on the consequences of Mao's collectivization project of 1955–1956 and were able to mitigate the disastrous policies of
the Great Leap Forward that led to the Great Famine of 1959–1961. This paper
showed that even at the height of communist rule, the persistent effects of
clans could still be observed.[4] Moreover, as we show in this discussion, ancestor worship resumed soon after the end of Mao's regime, and clan-based
organizations reemerged quickly after his death. China's economic success
cannot be attributed to a demise of its kin-based culture; on the contrary, kin-
based organizations played an important role in sustaining economic growth
in an environment of weak property rights and legal institutions. Market infrastructures emerged spontaneously through informal cooperation, sustained
by kinship ties and local social networks (what is commonly referred to as
guanxi, as discussed in chapter 8). Cooperative networks based on kin, together with local communities, substituted for well-functioning legal institutions and financial markets. Local public officials protected the business initiatives of their extended kin, and financial resources were channeled to new
enterprises through mechanisms based on reputation and personal relationships. These cooperative arrangements resemble past clan organizations in
many respects, except that in the past, they mostly supported commerce,
whereas now they are also active in industrial development. In addition, the
Chinese diaspora in Southeast Asia played a key role in supporting the export
industry by providing financial resources, managerial know-how, and international connections to relatives and friends in their regions of origin.

Historical continuity is also a feature of the current system of government.
The communist and cultural revolutions did succeed in destroying the class
of mandarins (the Imperial administrative system had already been overhauled

4. Specifically, the authors showed that the collectivization of 1955–1956 led to serious adverse consequences because Chinese peasants slaughtered their livestock rather than give the
animals up to the authorities. They also showed that in regions with a strong clan presence, these
deleterious effects were mitigated, and clan leaders were able to convince their members to
surrender their livestock to the government rather than slaughter them. On the other hand,
during the Great Famine, the clan-dominated areas suffered more. This seemingly inconsistent
finding is explained by the observation that the clan had historically been a means of government control that lubricated the mechanisms that connected the peasantry to the central authorities. Since the famine was largely caused by very large food procurements by the central
government, the prevalence of clans aggravated the situation, making the food shortages worse,
because the clan leaders may have been more effective in making the peasants surrender larger
shares of their food supply to government agents.

by the republic). Nevertheless, soon after Mao's death, the new regime built a cadre of party personnel, recruited on merit. Having a strong central bureaucracy, loyal to the top ruler and selected through meritocratic criteria, is a persistent feature of Chinese governance. Confucian training has now been formally replaced by party ideology, but China's current system remains faithful to tradition in several respects: an authoritarian and unaccountable central government, intolerance of dissenting views and heterodox ideologies, tight control over the selection and promotion of bureaucrats at all levels, and important elements of decentralization to local governments, who have considerable autonomy and are in charge of administrative enforcement but remain accountable only upward and are controlled by the center. The lack of accountability to local constituencies, the meritocratic system of selection and control of public officials, and their ideological indoctrination are important elements of institutional persistence with the Imperial administration.

The main differences with the past are that local gentries have been replaced by party cadres, corruption is more aggressively controlled, and growth is the overarching political goal. This system of government smoothed the transition to a market economy and is widely credited as one of the pillars of China's economic miracle (e.g., Xu 2011; Bai, Hsieh, and Song 2020; Qian 2017). Public officials are the residual claimants of local economic success through local tax revenue and rent extraction, and, thanks to a tournamentlike system of promotions based on economic performance, are controlled by the immediately higher level of government (Maskin et al. 2000). Although private property is not altogether safe from political predation, the default option is to respect earnings generated by successful enterprises and public officials face sharp incentives to promote local development. Moreover, many of the previous obstacles that impeded innovation have been removed: until now, Chinese scientists have benefited from open access to leading international universities, and China now invests large amounts in scientific education and research and development (R&D), about 2.4 percent of its GDP, although the data are difficult to compare with the standard Organisation for Economic Co-operation and Development (OECD) figures for R&D spending.

We now turn to a more detailed analysis of these similarities between Imperial and modern China, discussing the role of community-based networks and decentralized authoritarianism in sustaining growth in an environment of weak legal and financial institutions. We close the chapter with a discussion of what may lie ahead for China.

2. Cultural and Organizational Persistence

We first document how a kin-based culture survived and persisted despite Mao's efforts to eradicate it. Next, we discuss the important role of kinship ties and *guanxi* in sustaining economic growth in the private sector.

Persistence of Kinship Ties

Even though the state attempted to dismantle clans before and during Mao's regime, kinship-based organizations remain important and widespread in modern China. The state was explicitly hostile to clans during the moderniza-tion movement in the early twentieth century, when clans were viewed as an obstacle to economic development. Things got much worse when the com-munist regime gained power in 1949: clans were officially abolished, their properties confiscated, elders stripped of legal privileges and authority, clan legal codes were no longer recognized, and the ideology of class consciousness was promoted over kinship. Friendship ties were replaced by the universalistic morality of comradeship, under which all citizens are equally important to the state. Even family life was radically changed. For example, people in the coun-tryside all ate together in mess halls, and nurseries and kindergartens took over child-rearing (e.g., Huang 1985; Gold 1985).[5]

Despite facing persecution, there is evidence that clans and *guanxi* relations remained active and important even during Mao's regime. The hardships of the communist regime made it necessary to rely on social connections to obtain access to goods and services. Cao et al. (2022) found that counties where clan activities were more intense pre-Mao (evaluated by looking at pre-Mao pub-lished genealogies), casualties were much lower during the 1958–1961 Great Famine. The reason is that areas with stronger kinship ties were better able to cooperate in resisting Mao's disastrous grain procurement policies, which forced peasants to hand over their grain production to the state (Cao et al. 2022).

When the state stopped actively persecuting them in 1979, clans reemerged. Genealogies publication dates provide a first indicator of clans' reemergence in post-Mao China. The genealogy database discussed in chapter 5 provides some dating information for about 96 percent of the observations. As shown

---

5. A journalist returning to the West after two years in China reported the following scripts painted on the wall of an urban commune mess hall: "The machine is my husband, the factory is my family, the fruits of my labour are my children, the Party is my father and my mother" (Baker 1979, p. 186).

TABLE 10.1. Published Genealogies

Period Written	No.	%	East	North	Northeast	Northwest	Southeast	South Central
Pre-1644	596	1.21	558	6	0	4	0	28
1644–1911	18,845	38.30	13,443	275	262	128	415	4,322
1912–1949	14,306	29.07	8,927	189	97	61	479	4,553
1949–1979	2,996	6.09	2,642	9	10	24	25	286
1980–2005	10,647	21.64	6,998	101	188	142	495	2,723
No date available	1,814	3.69	1,273	24	42	21	62	392
Total	49,204	100	3,841	604	599	380	1,476	12,304

Source: Greif and Tabellini (2017).

in table 10.1, only a few genealogies were recorded under the communist regime between 1949 and 1979. Moreover, 60 percent of the genealogies written during this period were published in Taiwan, where the republic's forces had retreated. But the publication of genealogies resumed in mainland China after 1979. Out of the 46,794 post-1644 genealogies, 10,647 (22 percent) were published between 1980 and 2005, amounting to roughly 400 genealogies per year. Note that genealogies continued to be published even after the collapse of the empire in 1911. Whatever role the empire played in the diffusion of clans, by 1911, this was not necessary for their continued perpetuation.

The post-1979 reemergence of clans is particularly noteworthy because the Deng reforms were designed to restart economic development, disregarding clan organizations. Households rather than clans were given land-use rights in the former collective farms, and privately owned businesses were permitted. Yet kin-based and relations-based exclusive organizations have reemerged and resumed their traditional role in supporting cooperation.

One may wonder if published genealogies and other genealogical publications are actually valid indicators for clans, or if they just reveal curiosity about family history. The latter does not seem to be the case, however. To illustrate, a county-level survey in 2000 in Jiangxi (examined by Liu and Murphy 2006) document that seventy surnames out of ninety-nine (in 40 villages) updated their genealogies since 1981, and forty-one surnames invested in their ancestral shrines since 1991 (Lin and Murphy 2006, p. 230). A 2002 representative national survey of more than 300 villages reveals lineage activities and kinship organizations in 66 percent of the sample (Tsai 2007). Clans resumed their role as key providers of local public goods, such as securing property rights from predation by officials, organizing weddings and funerals, providing welfare, contributing to public projects, and promoting mutual aid arrangements (Tsai 2007). Interclan conflicts also resumed, and collectively owned rural firms often formally excluded nonlocals (Thøgersen 2002). About 90 percent of the 887 households that migrated to or from one of 50 villages relocated to their "ancestral village," and 60 percent relocated due to interlineage tensions (Liu and Murphy 2006, p. 623).

As one would expect, the reemergence of clans after the end of Maoism occurred in areas where they were historically strong. As shown in figure 10.2, reproduced from Zhang (2017), prefectures that updated or published genealogies before 1950 are those that also did so after 1980, indicating a remarkable persistence of clan culture.

As a second indicator of clan persistence, Greif and Tabellini (2017) studied a random sample of 4,274 individuals in seventy-six counties and 205 villages from the 2005 China General Social Survey. The survey asked rural residents whether there is a clan organization in their community. Although underreporting of clan organizations is likely, given the tradition of suppression by communist authorities, the census revealed 277 clan-based organizations. A clan organization almost always (90 percent of the time) has a genealogy, a graveyard, or both. On average, there are 1.35 clan organizations per village, and one organization for every 15.5 respondents. In 41 percent of the counties, over half the villages have at least one clan organization. As shown in figure 10.3, clan organizations currently exist in each of China's six regions. Contemporary temple-based clans are particularly common in the South-Central region, and specifically in Guangdong, the richest province, while they are not reported in the north. This geographic pattern is consistent with the history of the rise of clans associated with outmigration from the north, as described in chapter 4.[6]

The majority of clans mentioned in the survey fulfill functions such as resolving private disputes within the village, providing local public goods and economic assistance, and handling intervillage relations. For example, in River County (Jiangxi), descent groups regrouped to protect land-user rights (Liu and Murphy 2006). In addition, villagewide lineage groups are significantly correlated with the provision of public goods and with how public officials are held accountable (Tsai 2007). Using survey data on 238 Chinese villages from 1986 to 2006, Zhang and Zhao (2014) provided suggestive evidence that

6. Surname-based versus temple-based organizations differ in their assets, such as land, estates (other than an ancestral hall), and trust funds. Temple-based organizations are much more likely to have such assets.

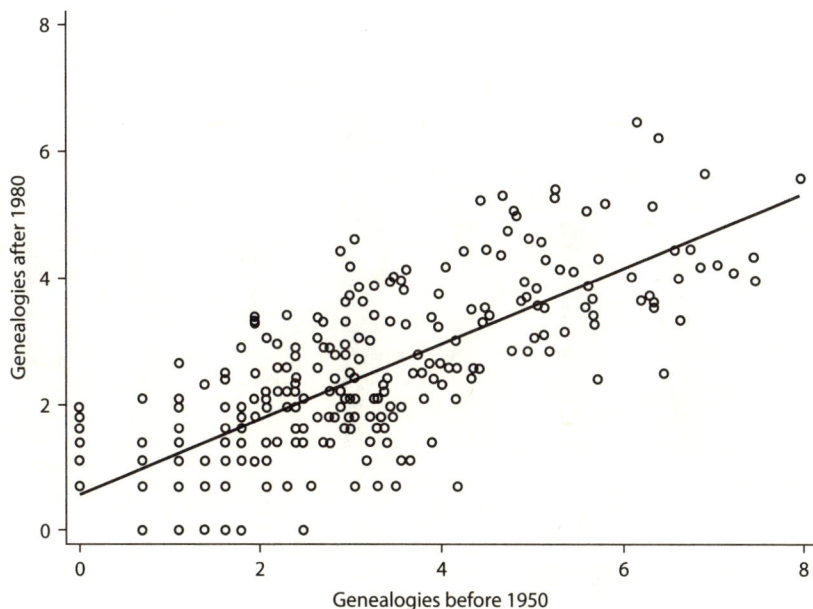

FIGURE 10.2. Persistence of clans. *Source:* Replicated from C. Zhang (2017, figure 3), using the same data as in Wang (2020, table 1.1). The number of genealogies is in logs, and the regression line is estimated across 272 prefectures. *Note*: The dots are observations of the number of genealogies in each prefecture within the time frames specified on the x-and y-axes.

kinship networks, measured by the prevalence of active lineage genealogies and ancestral halls in a village, protected villagers from land confiscation by the government. There is also a strong and significant correlation between village-level kinship and the number of private enterprises (Peng 2004). Using survey data on 220 Chinese villages from 1986 to 2005, Xu and Yao (2015) showed that village leaders from large clans increased public goods expenditures, as they were able to overcome collective action problems. Their main results are from within-village variations in leaders' clan backgrounds, and they are also robust to a regression discontinuity design that compares leaders elected with a small margin of victory, such that the election outcomes are arguably random.

Guanxi and the Growth of Private Enterprises

Several scholars have noted the importance of kin and kinlike relations in the success of Chinese market reforms (in particular, see Nee and Opper 2011). The weakness of legal and financial institutions encouraged the proliferation

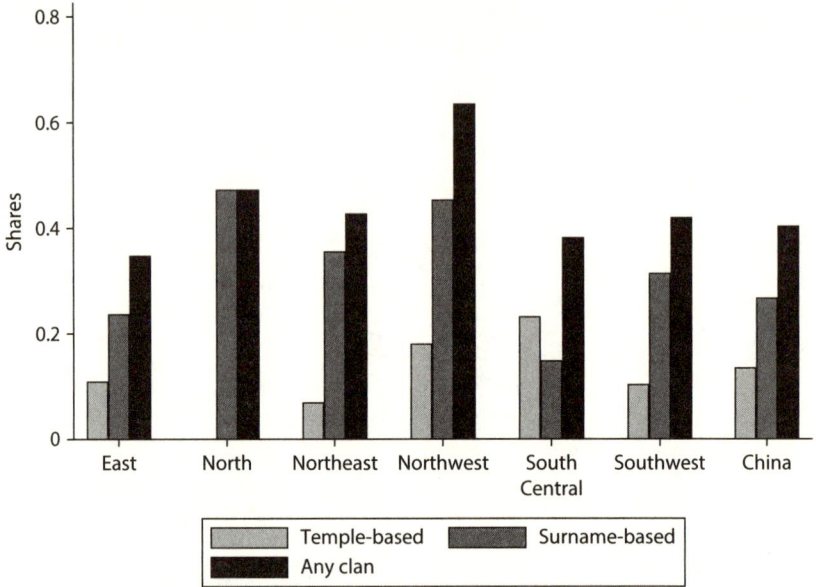

FIGURE 10.3. Probability of a village having at least one clan organization in 2006. *Source:* China General Social Survey (2005).

of social organizations meant to support private business initiatives. While these organizations were still underpinned by the communitarian values inherited from Imperial China, they often included close and trusted friends from outside the immediate family. This formed a network based on kinship and other sources of close affinity. As discussed by Hamilton (1996), Chinese private firms are typically organized around two sets of personal relationships. At the center of the network are kinship ties that define ownership and control rights of the firm. In the periphery, there is a set of regional and subethnic ties (*tongxiang guanxi*), linking people from the same region or school who often share the same surname. These relationships are exploited to support production, distribution, or financial arrangements.

The importance of family and local relationships in supporting the growth of private enterprises is extensively documented by survey data. Most job seekers find employment thanks to personal and family connections (Bian 1994), and private entrepreneurs point to networks for mutual assistance and cooperation as the most important factors to help them start their businesses (Nee and Opper 2011, chapter 3). Two mechanisms of mutual assistance stand out as particularly relevant: protection from government interference and access to capital (Xin and Pearce 1996).[7] Survey data reveal that entrepreneurs are less concerned about having access to finance or about interferences from local governments in prefectures where clans are more widespread as measured by the genealogies data (Zhang 2017).[8] Sons and daughters of party cadres are more likely to own a private business and be self-employed, and increasingly so as the government intervention in the economy becomes greater, while the opposite is true for sons and daughters of entrepreneurs (Jia et al. 2021). More generally, family ties are used to keep party cadres at bay and to impose collective sanctions if a local official doesn't protect his kin (Peng 2004), but also to extract policy favors through nepotism, such as price discounts on land sales by local governments (Diao and Zhan 2023).

Independent business owners rely on friends and family contacts, rather than legal means, to resolve disputes over financial arrangements (Potter 2002). Using the Annual Survey of Industrial Firms in 2007, Fan et al. (2021) showed that contract-intensive industries clustered in prefectures with higher clan strength (measured by the number of genealogies normalized by population), using the exogenous southward migration of Han following the Northern Song's collapse as the instrument. Further mechanism analysis shows that clans improved the contracting environment (as shown by less civil and commercial cases in a prefecture). As in the past, the typical role of lawyers and legal officials is to mediate and find a compromise after getting together privately with the parties involved, in meetings that are partly social and partly

7. This is how one respondent described his way of doing business. "There are no standardized rules on how to keep books in China, especially for private companies like ours. If they want to find fault with your income tax, they will always find something wrong. . . . In my mind, all business is connections and trust. That is all it is. No trust, no connections, no business. If you do not have connections to look after you at different levels of government, they can find excuses to suspend your business. The key connections I have are very close relationships" (Xin and Pearce 1996, p. 1653).

8. Among the private entrepreneurs surveyed by Nee and Opper (2011), short-term credit from relatives and friends is listed as the most important source of capital during the founding stage of the firm. This is how the chief executive officer of a leading information technology in Hangzou describes his sources of finance: "I do not think about banks for loans. Even to this day, I do not know how to borrow from banks. I borrow from friends. There are friends who ask to borrow from me. I lend to them" (Nee and Opper 2011, p. 100).

professional (e.g., banquets); see our discussion in chapter 8 of similar practices in Imperial China.

The role of kinship ties in the growth of private firms is also documented by hard data, not just by households and business surveys. Using data on publicly listed firms in China between 2014 and 2016, Cheng et al. (2021) document a positive relationship between clan strength (measured by the number of genealogies normalized by population) and family ownership (in 2016, for instance, 84.2 percent of listed private firms were family controlled).[9] Similarly, Xie and Yuan (2022) found that, in counties where a larger fraction of the population maintained and updated genealogies before 1949, there was a greater fraction of family firms among private unlisted firms, family firms performed better, and families were more involved in firm management in 2010.[10] Interestingly, kinship ties were only correlated with the development of private firms, while they were uncorrelated with the number and size of collective enterprises. Similarly, using more recent census data, Zhang (2017) showed that prefectures with a larger number of published and updated genealogies had a larger share of employment and assets in privately owned enterprises.

The role of community-based networks in facilitating firm growth is also confirmed by several studies on the allocation of financial flows. The growth of the most dynamic sectors of the Chinese economy and of private enterprises has mostly been funded by nonbank and nonmarket sources, such as retained earnings and loans enforced through reputation and personal connections, including trade credit and business-to-business loans (Allen et al. 2003, 2019a, 2019b, 2019c).[11]

9. Such a relationship is robust to using movers (firms located in a different place than their owners' hometowns) to disentangle the effect of clan strength from firm location effects, and also robust to using the distances to two prominent neo-Confucian academies preaching clan-related doctrines as instruments.

10. Peng (2008) measured the strength of family ties by the fraction of households in a village that belonged to the largest lineage group (or the top three lineages). In a sample of almost 400 rural villages in the early 1990s, over 20 percent of households belonged to the largest lineage, and about 40 percent belonged to the top three lineages. He found that villages with stronger family ties (i.e., larger lineages) had a larger fraction of employment in the private sector and a larger number of private firms.

11. These informal financial arrangements are not without disadvantages, however, since often they are limited in size, and there is evidence that reliance on these informal sources of finance may have hindered firm growth (Ayyagari et al. 2010). Recent years have also seen the rapid growth of Fintech arrangements, which exploit large databases on payment records to

China's recent economic development was associated with large migrations from internal rural areas toward the coast. As in the distant past, clans played a key role in assisting both migrant workers and migrant entrepreneurs. The sending county organizes migration decisions. Social networks of immigrants from the same county of origin provide mutual help and assistance, and immigrants from the same county often live together (see, e.g., Zhang and Xie 2013). The same mechanism applies to entrepreneurs who set up firms outside their county of origin. Migrant entrepreneurs from the same county of origin tend to agglomerate in the same destination counties. They typically retain strong links with their county of origin and establish networks of cooperation. Interestingly, Dai et al. (2020) showed that this phenomenon of agglomeration and mutual assistance among migrant entrepreneurs from the same county is stronger if the county of origin has a denser social network, where social interactions are more frequent.

The Bamboo Network

The growth of private enterprises was also financed by large inflows of foreign direct investment from the Chinese diaspora in Taiwan, Singapore, Hong Kong, and other locations in East Asia. These foreign investors not only provided capital, but also brought managerial know-how and international expertise and quickly became key players in supporting the growth of Chinese exports. Despite the rather complicated relationship between mainland China and Taiwan, Chinese authorities encouraged capital flow from Taiwan; since 1991, $188 billion were invested by Taiwanese businesses in China, although this has slowed in recent years as Chinese authorities ramped up their hostilities toward the island (Glaser 2021).

Throughout history, China's coastal areas always maintained mercantile ties with ethnic Chinese immigrants in the rest of Southeast Asia, and "Chinatowns" arose in several port cities outside China. Migration from Chaozhou in southeastern China started in the seventeenth century with the violent Manchu suppression of the pro-Ming elements in that region. In subsequent centuries, large numbers of Chinese migrated to Singapore, the East Indies, and Indochina (Macauley 2021). Outmigration intensified during the second half of the nineteenth century, when tens of thousands of Chinese immigrants

---

lend to small and medium-sized enterprises and to retail customers. Nevertheless, the average loan size through these channels tends to be very small (Allen et al. 2019a, Lardy 2019).

settled in European colonies in Southeast Asia and created large outposts of Chinese entrepreneurs abroad. Chinese settlements in Southeast Asia increased dramatically in the late 1940s and early 1950s, when millions of Chinese expatriates left the mainland during Mao's regime. Most refugees went to Taiwan and Hong Kong, while some dispersed through Southeast Asia. The combined total of Chinese expatriates in Southeast Asia reached about 55 million in the early 2000s (Redding and Witt 2007, p. 66). More than half of current overseas Chinese originate either from Guangdong or Fujian.[12] Another large fraction escaped from Shanghai to Hong Kong.

Many of these refugees belonged to the upper and middle classes and came from families of traders, entrepreneurs, and early industrialists. Some of them were able to escape with most of their wealth intact, while others were less farsighted or unlucky and had little besides their human capital. Many expatriates created their own enterprises abroad. Internationalization was the hallmark of these business initiatives. The Chinese diaspora of one country often traded with co-nationals located in other countries throughout Southeast Asia. Some family-owned business grew into large conglomerates, contributing to the success of their host countries.[13] Weidenbaum and Hughes (1996) provide several examples of highly successful international groups that grew out of entrepreneurial initiatives started in the 1950s and 1960s by Chinese expatriates in Southeast Asia, such as the Li Ka-shing group in Hong Kong, which now owns Hutchison Wampoa; the group founded by Ong Beng Seng in Singapore; the Formosa Plastic Group in Taiwan; and many others.

These Chinese abroad retained links to their area of origin through relatives and friends. When Deng Xiaoping created the first Special Economic Zones (SEZs) and opened China to the world in the late 1970s, several of these Chinese entrepreneurs were lured into investing in the mainland. While retaining their residence abroad, they brought to China their financial resources, managerial expertise, and international connections. China was attractive to them because of the very cheap labor and the tax advantages established in the SEZs. Thanks to their personal connections, they could navigate the unique business and political environment of mainland China. Many expatriates invested in

12. In 1945, the population of Hong Kong was just over half a million. In 1953, it had reached almost 2.5 million, and in 1961, it was 3.2 million (Redding and Witt 2007, p. 66).

13. For instance in the Philippines in 2002, ethnic Chinese accounted for about 40 percent of gross national income, and only 1 percent of the population (Redding and Witt 2007, p. 66).

their province of origin, establishing joint ventures with mainland partners.[14] Local partners were carefully selected because of their political influence, and they often included local governments and local public agencies. Relatives of local public officials were hired as employees. In other words, Chinese expatriates were able to access local *guanxi* networks, and this gave them an edge over foreign investors from Western countries. Not surprisingly, over 75 percent of foreign direct investment into China between 1979 and 1993 originated from Hong Kong and Taiwan.

According to Weidenbaum and Hughes (1996), a defining feature of overseas Chinese business is international diversification. Typically, the so-called bamboo network consists of cross-holdings of family-run and trade-oriented firms, often of small and medium sizes, that are present in more than one country and operate in different sectors. These networks tend to reduce agency and transaction costs, relative to arms'-length market transactions with suppliers or customers that are not part of the same business group. Many of these initially small overseas firms were able to grow into large conglomerates that are also present in mainland China. In 1994, the total assets of the 500 largest public companies controlled by Chinese expatriates exceeded a half-trillion dollars (not including the many enterprises privately owned by the same families). Over half of these conglomerates are based in Taiwan or Hong Kong (Weidenbaum and Hughes 1996). According to World Bank estimates, the aggregate output attributable to the 40 million Chinese expatriates in the mid-1990s was about the same size. Much of this wealth was created once China opened to the world after Mao's death. In 1976, the market capitalization of the top ten companies based in Hong Kong (one-tenth of which were Chinese-owned) was $41 billion. Ten years later, the top ten companies had an aggregate market value of $256 billion, and over half of them were Chinese-owned (Redding and Witt 2007).

The international connections of Chinese expatriates facilitated the inclusion of mainland China in the rapidly expanding global value chain. Quite literally, the Chinese diaspora acted as intermediaries between China and international markets. As shown in figure 10.4, foreign-owned firms (most of

14. Using the universe of foreign firms in China controlled by overseas Chinese, Chen et al. (2022) showed that after China opened up to the world, overseas Chinese entrepreneurs were more likely to enter prefectures with which they had higher preexisting lineage connections (measured by the fraction of population in a prefecture sharing the same surname with the entrepreneurs).

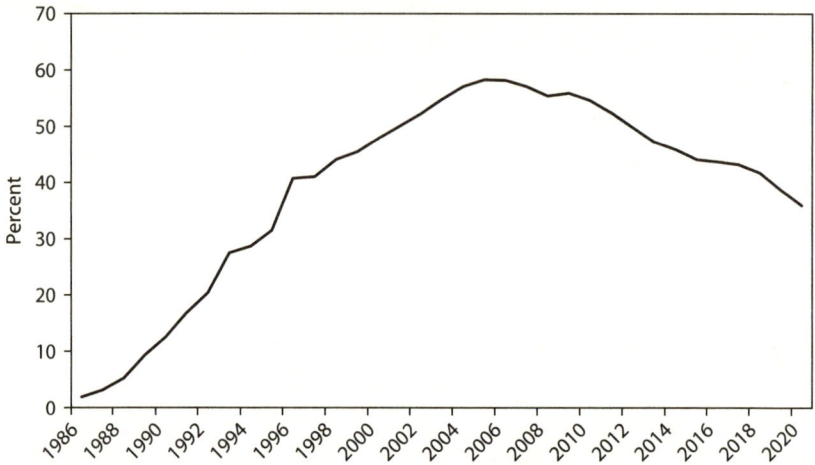

FIGURE 10.4. Share of exports originating from foreign-owned firms, 1986–2020. *Source:* General Administration of Customs, http://www.customs.gov.cn/ (accessed February 22, 2022).

which were owned by overseas Chinese immigrants) accounted for over half of Chinese exports between 2000 and 2010.

From the perspective of the Chinese political leadership, the diaspora's contributions to China's economic development were particularly welcome, not only because they created jobs and income, but also because they did so without creating domestic countervailing powers. Being based abroad, foreign investors did not fuel a powerful domestic constituency. On the contrary, they often provided riches for the sons and daughters of top Chinese political leaders—the so-called princelings.[15]

15. For instance, in the 1990s, the youngest son of Deng Xiaoping controlled a Hong Kong–based company building shopping centers across China, a son-in-law was the chairman of two Hong Kong–based real estate companies, and another son-in-law was the director of two Hong Kong–based property and insurance companies (Weidenbaum and Hughes 1996, p. 148). In the 2000s, Wen Yunsong, the son of former premier Wen Jiabao, cofounded New Horizon Capital, a Hong Kong–based private equity firm that raised capital globally and mainly invested in China. In the 2010s, Jiang Zhicheng, the grandson of former president Jiang Zemin, controlled Boyu Capital, a Hong Kong–based private equity firm that raised capital mainly from the United States and two key Asian investors, Temasek and the Li Ka Shing Foundation. Boyu made a variety of investments in China, including the online commerce giant Alibaba (Robertson 2015).

3. Institutional Persistence

Several scholars have pointed to the organization of the modern Chinese state as a key factor behind its economic success (Xu 2011; Bai et al. 2020; Qian 2017). The organization of the Chinese state combines two distinctive features. On the one hand, responsibilities for promoting economic growth are decentralized at the level of the province, the county, or even the village. This decentralization goes back to Mao's goal of creating self-reliant geographic areas. During Mao's regime, SOEs were devolved to subnational governments, together with revenue and expenditure responsibilities, and regional economies (i.e., provinces, prefectures, and counties) became quite self-contained. In 1978, the share of total revenue accruing to subnational governments exceeded 80 percent (Xu 2011, table 2). Much of this administrative decentralization was preserved after Mao's death and even extended to the township and village level. Local governments retained extensive administrative responsibilities, ranging from providing exemptions and authorizations or prohibiting the entry of new firms; transferring land; facilitating or hindering access to credit; energy and raw materials; improving local infrastructure and providing local public goods; enforcing law; and resolving business disputes. Local governments could also initiate reforms and try to attract foreign investment, and experimentation was actively encouraged by the central government (Heilmann 2008). These wide-ranging policy tools could be used as a "grabbing hand" to extract rents and infringe on private investments, or as a "helping hand" for private interests (Qian 2017, p. 37; see also Bai et al. 2020; Qian 2000a, 2017).[16]

The second distinctive feature of state institutions in modern China is that the career paths of local officials are determined by the center in systemwide competition. Unlike in a federal state, there is no local accountability to citizens. Promotions are decided de facto by the Communist Party, which exerts tight control over personnel. Deng established a network of party leadership teams that were centered around the Politburo and existed in every locality, who oversee and assess the work of the corresponding level of government

16. Not surprisingly, most town and village enterprises that emerged during the 1980s and 1990s were owned by community governments, had joint private and collective ownership, or were tied to local governments through personal relations and informal arrangements (Lardy 2014; Xu 2011). Unlike in other countries, several empirical studies have found that political connections are associated with higher firm valuations thanks to better access to credit, special deals, or other benefits (Bai et al. 2020; Calomiris et al. 2010; Allen et al. 2019a). Moreover, sons of government officials are more likely to become business owners (Jia et al. 2021).

(Vogel 2011, p. 699). In 1984, a comprehensive reform decentralized cadre management in a vertical hierarchy, whereby local party leaders control the career paths of lower-level officials in their jurisdiction: the so-called one-level-up policy (Pei 2016, chapter 2). At each level of government, the two highest-ranked positions are (1) the secretary of the local party committee (the party secretary), who oversees personnel control and other political duties; and (2) the head of the executive branch (the government head), who runs the local economy. The local party secretary is usually the de facto highest-ranking official, although he relies on the government head to implement economic policies. In theory, the former is elected by the local party congress and the latter is elected by the local People's Congress (the legislative body); in practice, though, most of them are appointed by the organizational department of the party in the immediately higher level of government.[17]

This vertical hierarchy provides sharp incentives to pursue the goals of the central administration and allows the party to impose its priorities on the entire administration (Maskin, Qian, and Xu 2001). Provincial governors are promoted or removed based on growth in their province relative to others, and they respond to this incentive by imposing similar performance criteria on their subordinates, who in turn do the same in their jurisdiction, and so on. Thus, each locality competes with other similar localities in a tournamentlike system. Between 1978 and 2005, 80 percent of provincial governors were rotated by the central government. Several papers have documented that good economic performance in one's province increases the chances of promotions to higher office, although political connections also matter. Promotion is unlikely if economic performance is weak, regardless of connections, but strong performance is more likely to lead to promotions for well-connected provincial governors (Xu 2011; Jia et al. 2015; Li and Zhou 2005; Bo 2002).

Similarities and Differences with Imperial China

This regime of decentralized authoritarianism resembles older Imperial arrangements in several respects. First, it preserves the tradition of meritocracy within the public administration. Although the Imperial exam was terminated

---

17. Below the top leadership, the party and the government also manage a number of bureaus. Bureaus under the party (e.g., the organization department and the publicity department) are in charge of party and personnel affairs, whereas bureaus under the government (e.g., the education bureau and the construction bureau) are in charge of implementing economic policies (Ang 2012).

in 1905, party members and government officials continue to be selected and trained with great care, especially in light of the discretion that they enjoy. In 1977, Deng resumed a unified exam for university admission (the *gaokao*), which remains one of the important criteria (together with school exams) for the selection of party officials and their assignment to a level in the bureaucracy (Vogel 2011).

Second, as in the past, ideological indoctrination continues to be integral to administrative training. According to Lu, Luan, and Sng (2020), only loyal supporters are admitted as party members. Every new application requires the referrals of two existing party members and the approval of a county or higher-level party apparatus. Prospective members face a probation period of up to two years, during which they are carefully scrutinized. After being accepted, they are also expected to monitor each other and to report wrongdoings. Of course, Confucian doctrine has been replaced by Communist Party principles (Koss 2018). Nevertheless, Confucian and communist ideals share several common features. Both entail a commitment to reduce inequality and inspire a paternalistic political vision. The role of the state is to harmonize society, create stability and security, mold personalities, and inspire national (as opposed to individual) goals. Under both ideologies, citizens are expected to agree with the priorities identified by political élites and to respect authority. Docility and respect for one's social superiors are basic social values (Wong 1997).

Interestingly, the system of two overlapping systems of governance at each administrative level, one within the party and the other within the executive branch, is not dissimilar from that of the past. During the Qing Dynasty, for example, overlapping governance took the form of civilian and military governors, with military personnel playing a role similar to party officials in modern China. The Qing nominated military officers—always trusted Manchu—to supervise the civilian magistrates. This supervision was subtle, as the civil and military authorities were formally distinct and separated. "De facto, however . . . the military officers were to report directly to the Emperor on the situation in the provinces." Thus, "all important business of the province was communicated to him [the garrison general], and he, in turn reported this business to the emperor" (Elliott 201, p. 152). Interestingly, despite the formal policy of separation between the military (Manchu) authorities and the civil (Chinese) authorities, the court directly instructed the civil authorities to violate the separation.

Third, decentralization of policy initiatives to local governments is also not new. By allowing policy experiments at the subnational level, modern China follows in the footsteps of late Imperial China. At least during the Qing Dynasty, policy experiments were at the discretion of local (usually provincial) administrators. Information about successful experiments were circulated, adopted, and formalized to become the new consensus (see, e.g., Rowe 1998).

Fourth, as in late Imperial China, patronage relations between local officials and their constituency is a defining feature of the current regime. Under the Qing, weakness in due legal process and a lack of formal constraints on local magistrates' power made property rights uncertain. This pushed private property owners to seek protection from and exchange favor with bureaucrats. Local officials often granted monopoly rights to powerful merchants in exchange for assistance in local tax collection (Motono 2000; Brandt et al. 2014). Today, the uncertainty surrounding private property rights and the unchecked powers of local officials induces private entrepreneurs to seek political protection and to form well-connected social networks (Brandt et al. 2014).

In Ming and Qing China, nepotism was common and patronage relations were often based on family ties. The root cause was Confucianism's emphasis on moral obligations toward relatives. An easy way to assist relatives in need was to employ them in the private or public sector. Nepotism was therefore widely practiced and morally accepted in late Imperial China. As late as the 1930s, "public opinion condemned, but not too harshly, rich families who refused to assist their poor kin. An official or businessman who refused to employ or promote a relative met with a general disapproval" (Lang 1946, p. 22). Although nepotism was seen as conducive to fulfilling moral obligations, it was costly; it implied that "men were hired not so much because their work was needed as because they needed work" (Lang 1946, p. 22). At the same time, nepotism might have been a best response in the cultural environment, given the limited loyalty of nonkin.

Nepotism has declined in modern China, but it has taken new forms. Competition intensified rendering nepotism costlier. The One Child Policy implemented between 1979 and 2015 also reduced the number of kinspeople. In an environment in which workers compete for their place in the queue to get hired or promoted, the personal morality underpinning nepotism in Imperial China took a new form. Friends, instead of relatives, assist each other to get ahead in the queue and to do well for themselves. In the state administration, this phenomenon degenerated into forms of "collective corruption" (Gong 2002, p. 87): subordinates transfer rents from the assets under their control to their direct superiors in exchange for promotions. Using data on all land sales by local governments between 2004 and 2016, Chen and Kung (2019) showed that firms linked to members of the Politburo obtained price discounts ranging from 55 percent to 60 percent of the average market price. In return, provincial party secretaries offering these discounts were over 20 percent more likely to be promoted to national positions. Similarly, Chen and Kung (2016) found that promotions of county leaders between 1999 and 2008 were correlated with revenue from land sales by the county government, particularly for officials who are well connected with their superiors, and higher land revenue reduces the correlation between GDP growth and promotions.

As discussed in chapter 8, public corruption was an important by-product of the Imperial system of governance and contributed to the decline of several Chinese dynasties. The Imperial regime frequently attempted to staunch corruption, although with varying degrees of success. Without direct accountability to citizens or an independent judiciary, corruption is endemic and widespread in modern China. That said, it is not as rampant as in other authoritarian states or former socialist countries (e.g., Russia).[18] In China, the problem increased over time, in tandem with the expanding networks of personal and economic ties between businesspeople and officials (Pei 2016).[19] As in Imperial China, corruption among public officials has become a major threat to the regime because it erodes the party's capacity to pursue its goals and undermines its authority and legitimacy.[20] This is one of the reasons why Xi Jinping started a massive antigraft campaign as soon as he was elected party general secretary in 2012. Between 2012 and 2014, over 400,000 officials had been disciplined, and more than half of them were prosecuted and convicted for corruption. In 2016, these numbers were achieved in a single year

18. In 2023, Transparency International ranked China 76 on the scale of corruption, tied with Hungary and Moldova; Russia was ranked 141, tied with Guinea and Uganda (higher ranking means less corruption). See "Corruptions Perceptions Index," https://www.transparency.org/en/cpi/2023.

19. Researchers have used different methods to find evidence of corruption. For instance, Cai et al. (2011) showed that firms' entertainment and travel costs can be used as a proxy for bribes to government officials. In their sample, these expenditures averaged about 3 percent of value added. Fang et al. (2019) used data on mortgage contracts from a large commercial bank, containing detailed information on house and buyer characteristics. Although on average, bureaucrats in government agencies earn lower income than other buyers in the sample, they are more likely to buy larger, more expensive apartments. Moreover, they often benefit from larger price discounts, which increase with the rank of the bureaucrat or if they work in an agency closer to the real estate sector. See also Quah (2013).

20. In a July 2011 speech, Hu Jintao, then the party general secretary, warned that unchecked corruption could "deal a body blow to the party and even lead to the collapse of the party and of the country" (Economy 2018, p. 29).

(Economy 2018). Of course, fighting corruption was not the only goal of the antigraft campaign, which also enabled Xi to consolidate his power and get rid of his enemies. In that sense, too, the efforts are reminiscent of the Imperial Office named the Censorate, discussed in chapter 7.

Finally, another element of continuity with the distant past concerns the relations between the state and its citizens. In Imperial China, magistrates enforced tax collection and imposed law and order with the help of locally powerful clans and the local gentry, who acted as intermediaries between the state bureaucracy and the citizens (cf. chapters 5 and 8). In modern China, the relation between the state and individual households continues to remain indirect, but party cadres (locally recruited and paid out of local revenues) have replaced the local gentry as intermediaries. In theory, local cadres do not have to be party members, but in practice, they are under the leadership of the party. Furthermore, at the village level, the villagers' committee chair position often automatically goes to the secretary or vice secretary of the village party branch (Kelliher 1997). This makes local cadres largely undergo the strict screening of the party.

The Communist Party is now a fundamental tool of social control, and as an elite group of scholar-bureaucrats, their qualifications resemble those of the Confucian mandarinate from the Imperial era. Although party officials are relatively small in number—just over half a million in 2011 (Lardy 2014)—party membership is much more widespread. In 2014, the party recognized 88 million members, corresponding to roughly one party member for every four rural households, dispersed over all social strata (Won 1997; Koss 2018, chapter 1).

This pervasiveness of the Communist Party throughout society has enhanced state capacity, enabling the implementation and monitoring of nationwide policies, even at the village level. As shown by Koss (2018), the Chinese state is much more effective in governing areas that have a higher density of party members. This is true both for economic policies (e.g., tax collection) and social policies (like the One Child Policy). Lu et al. (2020) provide further causal evidence of this relationship. Using the route taken by the Central Red Army during the Long March in the 1930s as instrument for party membership, they show that counties with more party members developed faster.

Despite these many similarities, there are also important discontinuities with the past. First, Mao's reforms have increased the reach of the state. In Imperial China, the county was the lowest level of government. In 1820, the average county was responsible for managing around 27,000 people.[21] This created difficulties for the magistrates, who were expected to supervise tax collection and enforce judgments (Qian and Sng 2021). During Mao's regime, the government organized the countryside into 26,000 communes, each of them governing about 5,000 households. Although the commune was not an orthodox territorial administrative unit but rather a large collective farm, it allowed the state to reach below the county level in an unprecedented fashion. After 1978, these communes were restructured into townships, which became a formal layer of government below the county (Qian and Sng 2021). In addition, the village level—though not a formal administrative unit of government— came under state control post-Mao via the establishment of village-level party branches (Sun et al. 2013).[22] The key administrative positions in SOEs, which contribute the most to the state's income, are also filled by appointees of the party (Qian and Sng 2021).

Second, the goals and priorities of the state are now different. Political stability remains an overarching goal, but economic development is now seen as a fundamental prerequisite for stability This priority percolates through the entire administration thanks to the promotion criteria. Unlike in Imperial China, subordinates are promoted based on their locality's economic growth rather than on success in tax collection and resource extraction.

Third, the central government's control over the bureaucracy is much improved relative to the past, also thanks to better communication and transportation technologies.[23] In Imperial China, local gentry income came from a variety of sources, such as public service, teaching and tutoring, and land rents. Although most gentry members were evaluated by county magistrates and education supervisors, this was not a very strict process, nor was it a direct determinant of their income (Hao et al. 2022).[24] In modern China, local cadres

21. The number is calculated based on Qian and Sng (2021, p. 371), who wrote that "there were less than 1,400 of counties governing a population that had reached 380 million."

22. Although village elections (to elect villagers' committees), which may attenuate the party branch's monopoly, have been introduced in the villages since the 1980s, the branch still wields ultimate authority in most cases (O'Brien and Han 2009; Sun et al. 2013).

23. For example, in Imperial China, it took about one to three months to travel from the capital to major cities such as Shenyang, Xi'an, Wuhan, Nanjing, and Guangzhou (Brandt et al. 2014, p. 65).

24. Hao et al. (2022) showed that only 0.4 percent of lower gentry (the most common form of gentry) was classified as demonstrating bad behaviors, among whom one-fifth were stripped of their degrees.

are evaluated annually by township or county governments, and their salaries, bonuses, or even promotions are directly linked to different measures, such as collecting taxes, increasing industrial output and profits, enforcing the One Child Policy, and maintaining public order (Whiting 2017, chapter 3). Using a national survey of 400 villages, Kung, Cai, and Sun (2009) bolstered this argument by showing a positive relationship between village cadres' salaries and their time spent on state tasks.

Fourth, local officials derive their legitimacy from different sources than in the past. In Imperial China, the legitimacy of local gentry among villagers rested on their ability to provide public goods such as holding ceremonies, making donations, and giving loans. Moreover, there were various ways to join the gentry, such as passing the Imperial examination or by possessing sufficient land, education, or wealth to merit recognition and buy an academic degree. By contrast, political loyalty was not emphasized (Brandt, Ma, and Rawski 2014). In modern China, instead, local cadres derive their authority from their positions in the administrative hierarchy, or ultimately, the party. This distinction makes local cadres more compliant with state directives (Ku 2003).

Finally, the meritocratic selection criteria for party cadres and government officials have also changed. Mastery of the classics and of Confucian doctrine has been replaced by modern education criteria as taught in the best universities, and scientific and technological competence is highly valued. Oddly enough, the teaching of Marxist-Leninist-Maoist ideology seems much less appreciated than science, technology, engineering, and mathematics (STEM) subjects, at least until recently, despite the ostensible commitment to communism.

4. What Next?

China's portentous economic development was mostly due to catch-up growth. China is still not a rich country, and this could leave room for further catch-up: its level of per-capita income (PPP adjusted) is only about a fourth of that of the United States. Japan and South Korea had reached this level of comparative development in the mid-1950s and the mid-1980s, respectively, and they were able to sustain spectacular growth for several decades thereafter. Nevertheless, China is now the largest economy in the world (PPP adjusted), and this reduces its potential for catch-up growth since its terms of trade are bound to become less favorable as it keeps growing. Moreover, with urban population now accounting for 60 percent of the total, the room for internal migration as a source of cheap labor is long gone. In addition, the structure of its economy suffers from severe internal imbalances, and in particular from overinvestment in real estate, financial fragility, and worsening demographics due to low fertility and population aging.[25] For geopolitical reasons, the global environment is also deteriorating, and China risks being excluded from the global value chain in important technological sectors. Last but not least, an ever more intrusive and arbitrary party oversight over economic and social life is undermining the confidence of Chinese households and businesses in the future, restraining investment and spending in consumer durables. Not surprisingly, growth is slowing to less than 5 percent per year, and several analysts predict a sharper slowdown in coming years.[26] Total factor productivity (TFP) growth, which averaged about 2 percent per year between 2000 and 2008, has slowed to about 0.5 percent per year between 2009 and 2022. To avoid the "middle-income trap" that has plagued many countries of similar levels of economic development, China must turn to innovation-based growth. Will it be able to do so? The answer remains highly uncertain.

On the positive side, China's political leaders have long been convinced that innovation is key to the country's economic success, and they are strongly committed to overcome the gaps in China's ability to innovate. Several party directives and policy resolutions have repeatedly emphasized this goal, and the state heavily invests in order to sustain scientific and technological advances. China has good universities, integrated into the international academic community. It has attracted and developed top scientists. Foreign direct investment has led to significant technology transfers from other countries. The number of Chinese patents cited abroad and approved by foreign offices has grown rapidly (Wei et al. 2016).[27] China's gross R&D expenditures as a fraction of GDP have also grown consistently since the mid-1990s. They have

25. Golley et al. (2016) estimated that the drop in the dependency ratio between 1980 and 2010 associated with the One Child Policy (that increased the labor force relative to population) could account for over one sixth of per-capita GDP growth in this period. The old age depending ratio, defined as the percentage of individuals aged 65 or older relative to working-age population, is expected to exceed 35 percent in 2045, about three times as high as it was in 2015.

26. Rogoff and Yang (2021) estimated that between 2013 and 2018, real estate–related activities accounted for 29 percent of China's GDP, and a decline in housing activity could remove a cumulative 5–10 percent of GDP for several years.

27. Since 2015, China has filed more patents than any other country. Nevertheless, it is commonly understood that these numbers are distorted by government subsidies and Chinese patents are of much lower quality than those of other advanced countries. Chinese patents have a low rate of commercialization and industrialization compared to international standards, and based on internationally comparable citation data, they seem to reach only a third of the non-Chinese quality benchmark (He 2021).

exceeded 2 percent of GDP since 2015, which is slightly above the European Union's average and a clear outlier among countries at similar levels of economic development (Wei et al. 2017). The comparison is even more favorable for China with respect to industry-related R&D spending, although with some caveats. Specifically, there is evidence that R&D investment is less beneficial to firm growth than it has been in Taiwan, a symptom that it is not always well spent, possibly because less productive SOEs spend significantly more on R&D than private firms (Storesletten and Zilibotti 2014; Koenig et al. 2022).

Market size is commonly regarded as an important driver of innovation (Acemoglu and Linn 2004). China's large internal market may provide a powerful incentive to innovate, at least in the sectors with a level playing field for all firms regardless of ownership or political connections. Moreover, having access to very large databases, Chinese researchers and firms are well positioned to experiment and use new information technologies in a variety of applications. This is already happening in the field of artificial intelligence, where China is a world leader in some specific fields, such as visual pattern recognition, also thanks to the direct support of the state. The party also is particularly interested in these technologies because artificial intelligence applied to face recognition and other social data is a powerful tool of social control (cf. Beraja et al. 2023).

Finally, not all China's past is inimical to innovation-based growth. The country has a strong meritocratic tradition, and education is deeply valued and respected throughout society. This is also reflected in its investments in human capital. In 2014, Chinese over twenty-five years of age had about 7.5 years of education on average. This is not high by international standards, but it is twice as much as in 1980 (Storesletten and Zilibotti 2014). In 2020, the gross enrollment rate in tertiary education was over 50 percent of the respective age cohorts, and since 1987, about four million young Chinese have studied abroad. Every year, China produces well over 1 million engineers (1.4 million in 2021, according to Statista.com).

Nevertheless, there are several significant obstacles to innovation-based growth. Aghion et al. (2023) showed that recent Chinese research performance owes much to the collaboration of U.S. scientists with their U.S. peers. This channel is now closing down for a variety of geopolitical reasons. Moreover, the historical and recent experience of advanced countries indicates that innovation occurs in a decentralized fashion, often in successful start-ups financed by arms-length investors. In China, however, the government has become increasingly reluctant to let the market pick the winners, and the share of investment by the state sector in overall investment has been rising again

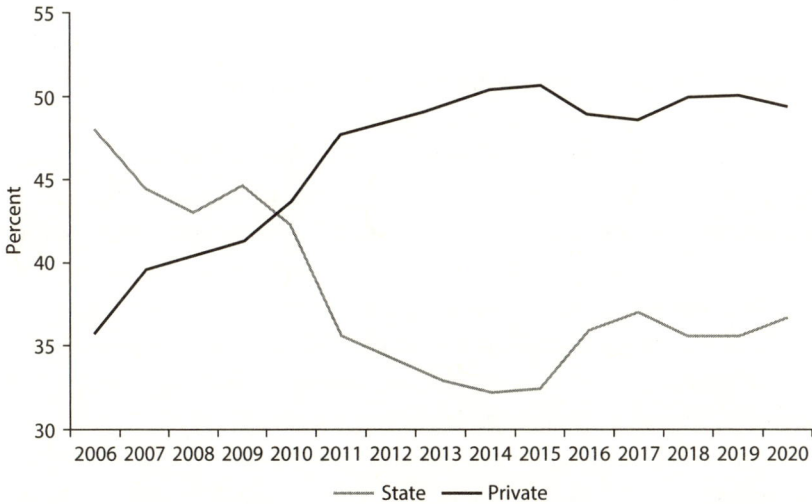

FIGURE 10.5. State and private investment, 2006–2020. *Source:* National Bureau of Statistics of China, stats.gov.cn/tjsj/ndsj/ (accessed February 22, 2022).

since 2015 (figure 10.5). Here, too, the current regime follows a time-honored tradition. When Imperial China reached its peak of technological creativity, it did so via government officials who became active inventors and agents of technological diffusion. The modern ambition to spend more on R&D and to finance innovation may be an heir of these ancient traditions and has led the state to play a large role over the allocation of resources.

The state's outsized influence on financing innovation reflects a variety of factors, not just deliberate industrial policy. It also reflects the fact that, despite several reforms, the legal and financial infrastructures that accompany decentralized innovation are still lacking in China. Several empirical studies have shown that minority investors are not well protected, particularly if firms are controlled by local governments. Earnings manipulations, transactions with related parties in potential conflicts of interest, and expropriations remain prevalent (Allen et al. 2019a). In this environment, funding to new start-ups remains small and concentrated in just a few sectors, such as internet and artificial intelligence. According to Lardy (2019), aggregate corporate funding by domestic private equity, venture capital, and angel investors in 2017 was 551 billion RMB ($81.52 billion). In comparison, total new lending by financial institutions plus bond issuance by local governments was 19.44 trillion RMB ($2.88 trillion) during the same period.

Xi Jinping enacted a series of legal reforms to streamline administrative procedures and discipline corrupt public officials. Nevertheless, these reforms also tightened the party's grip over the legal system and further inhibited judiciary independence. Judges and law enforcement personnel remain tools of the party. In the words of Xi himself, they must "vindicate the authority of the Party's policies and the state laws" (Economy 2018, p. 46). Xi's version of the rule of law means that the law is an instrument to govern the people and ensure the continued dominance of the party over Chinese society. Even for law-abiding and politically agnostic citizens, this lack of separation between political and judicial powers entails insecurity against the risk of political predation and abuse. The government crackdown on several successful entrepreneurs in the information technology sector since 2021 is a vivid illustration of this point.

Under Xi's leadership, the state also increased its political and ideological control over universities. Academic books that are published abroad or not originally written in Chinese must be approved regarding their ideological content. Western textbooks advocating Western political values are banned or restricted. Since 2016, new university hires must be assessed by interviewing to ascertain their political alignment, and universities can conduct investigations about applicants' political views. The government enacted similar campaigns to tighten its ideological grip over the Chinese Academy of Social Sciences (Economy 2018). Although these actions are unlikely to interfere with the content of research in the hard sciences, a climate of intimidation certainly does not encourage free exchange of radical new ideas, and it can aggravate the brain drain. Since 1987, only slightly more than one-half of Chinese students trained abroad returned home (Economy 2018). The increasingly authoritarian nature of China's government has diminished pluralism, which is critical for pushing out the envelope of knowledge as opposed to just catching up on best practices developed elsewhere.

To silence dissent, the party has also imposed tighter control and wider censorship of the internet, particularly over foreign sources and platforms; this is reminiscent of the "literary inquisition" in Qing China mentioned in chapters 7 and 9. Yet, obviously, innovation and creativity also require easy access to muliple sources of information. Artists, students, researchers, and creative entrepreneurs are part of an international open community, and control of the internet makes access to this community more costly and rare. For instance, censorship prevents many scientists from accessing Google Scholar (Wan 2015). Internet censorship can have even larger costs for those who are not aware of what they are missing. In an interesting field experiment, Chen and

Yang (2019) showed that Chinese university students do not demand uncensored information, probably because they are unaware of its value. However, when they are temporarily encouraged to sidestep internet censorship, they persistently keep doing it, presumably because they discover its usefulness.

In chapter 9, we described how the Industrial Revolution was largely a by-product of useful knowledge accumulated in the preceding decades. Throughout this book, we have argued that this accumulation occurred in Europe and not in China because of social organizations and political structures. Namely, corporations and political fragmentation created incentives and opportunities to innovate. China instead was ruled by a backward-looking autocracy that also deeply influenced the evolution of intellectual activity, and the organization of society hindered interactions among strangers.

Modern China has removed many of the obstacles that prevented scientific progress in the past and invests considerable resources in innovation. Nevertheless, the political regime retains tight control over how these resources are allocated, what enters the educational curricula, and what sources of information citizens can access. This makes it more likely that innovation, when it occurs, will take the form of a gradual adaptation of progress that was initiated elsewhere. Radical and disruptive breakthroughs tend to emerge in open and decentralized environments, where there is not much respect for authority and where political and economic incumbents can be challenged without fear of reprisal.

No matter how different it is from its past, modern China is certainly not such an environment. Without political liberalization, growth sustained by radical innovations seems difficult to achieve and continue. But political liberalization is certainly not in sight—on the contrary, under Xi Jinping, the regime has returned to the despotic and arbitrary personal rule of the Mao era.

11

Conclusions

This book is a study of comparative economic history. As Roland (2024) recently stressed, there is a lot of long-run stickiness in the evolution of human societies, and parameters set in antiquity may determine what kind of society we observe today. Without necessarily accepting the idea that the past is inevitably destiny, we agree that a lot of the current differences between East and West have deep historical roots, although parameters other than those set at the very beginning of civilizations in antiquity may have steered societies into different trajectories at a later time. Here, we have focused on the many divergences between Europe and China that took place after about AD 1000.

Europe was a global outlier in many ways: radically different not just from China, but also from the great civilizations of South Asia and those in the Muslim Middle East and North Africa. The outcomes of these differences are well known: by the late nineteenth century, Europeans wholly dominated South and Southeast Asia and had managed to weaken (or at least take advantage of preexisting weaknesses of) the Ottoman Empire. Can society's organization via kin-based networks as opposed to corporate organizations also help to explain the divergences between Western Europe and other parts of the world?

It is not possible here to go into the history of these civilizations in detail; however, some reflections suggest that our framework indeed sheds light on these civilizations. Economic historians, of course, have noted that the long-term history reveals "reversals of fortune" (e.g., Acemoglu, Johnson, and Robinson 2002) and proposed various explanations for them. The closest to our argument here is a line of research that focuses on the institutional and cultural foundations of markets (see Kumar and Matsusaka 2009, and other contributions surveyed by Enke 2023), and that singles out the psychological effects of nuclear families as opposed to extended kinship (Henrich 2020). In this approach, there are two kinds of markets. The first are *local markets*, based on extended-family or personal networks, which have limited reach beyond their loci. The second are *impersonal markets,* where people trade at arm's length and third parties and formal rules govern contracts. Which market arrangement emerges depends in the conceptual framework of this book on the prevailing form of social capital; the prevailing value system, whether communitarian or universalistic; and the resulting kinds of social organizations and networks.

In the early stages of economic development, most transactions naturally take place at the local level. Here, communitarian social networks perform well and economies relying on personal or kin-based social capital thrive. But as technological progress occurs, societies with communitarian social capital and local markets find it harder to transition to more formal markets and eventually will be surpassed by economies that relied initially on more impersonal market arrangements. While our account in this book has been primarily on cooperation within social organizations and less on market structures and contract enforcement, the approach in this line of research is complementary to ours. Kumar and Matsusaka (2009) applied their model not just to divergences but to *reversals* that led to the rise of the West to explain why Europe eventually overtook the sophisticated Asian civilizations that dominated in AD 1000.[1]

In this concluding chapter, we expand on this argument and briefly discuss kinship-based organizations, which were also prevalent in the Middle East and in India, albeit in quite different forms than in China, to explain other comparative trends in development between Western Europe and the rest of the world.

1. The Middle East

The Islamic world was (and is) much larger than just the Middle East and North Africa; the "core area" of Islam was quite different from South Asia, Indonesia, and West Africa. Nevertheless, the phenomenon of a reversal of

---

1. Kumar and Matsusaka (2009, p. 114) suggested that China, India, and the Middle East were inhibited from adopting market institutions by their commitment to "local social capital" in the form of family and other local networks, adding, "Kinship and tribal organizations were so entrenched that incentives to develop formal, third-party enforcement mechanisms were weak." Europe, in contrast, committed to "general social capital," making it easier to adopt market institutions there. The notion that Europe adopted a generalized morality in the Middle Ages that somehow "prepared" them for industrialization remains unexplained here, but the insight that social organizations based on communitarian values and extended kinship impeded economic and technological progress and can account for the Great Reversals of history has become something of a consensus (Enke 2019; Henrich 2020).

fortune is particularly striking in the Middle East. Islamic culture, science, and technology in the early centuries after Mohammed were by any measure much more advanced than those of the West. Yet over time, the gap closed, and eventually, the civilizations found their positions reversed. Remarkably, Europe implicitly recognized the superiority of Islamic culture during the Middle Ages and eagerly adopted their inventions and scientific tools, including windmills, paper, algebra, optics, and what passed for medicine in medieval times. The philosophy of Ibn Rushd (known as Averroes in the West) and the medical textbooks of Muslim physicians such as Al Rhazi (Rhazes) and Ibn Sina (Avicenna) became hugely influential in Europe and entered major universities' curricula.

Any notion of cultural essentialism (i.e., that there was something inherently inhibitive of economic and technological progress in Islam) is thus refuted by the early civilization's success in the arts and sciences. But at some point, their progress slowed, and Islamic intellectual life became increasingly derivative and backward looking (Chaney 2023). The ultimate culmination of this trend was the prohibition on the use of the printing press in the Ottoman Empire, but the signs were there long before. Today, Muslim nations are not contributing anything like their proportion in world population to science and technology.[2]

Despite an extensive body of literature on the little divergence between Western Europe and the Muslim Middle East (e.g., Lewis 1993; Lapidus 2002; Rubin 2017), the absence of corporations in the Islamic world, stressed by Timur Kuran (2005), has not apparently been sufficiently appreciated by scholars of the Islamic world. Kuran pointed out that Islamic law never recognized entities beyond persons, and therefore it could not award legal standing to organizations of the kind that we have defined in this book as corporations. His insight complements Ron Harris's (2020) argument that the European corporate form was not exported to non-Western civilizations. But as we have seen in chapter 8, legal development itself was determined by social organizations and the institutional environment, and clearly cannot be taken as entirely exogenous.

The importance of social organizations in providing local public goods, as we have advanced in this book, can shed light on this divergence. The early Muslim Empire housed two powerful and oppositional entities.: the tribal societies that adhered to a more traditional and orthodox interpretation of

2. Muslim countries contribute just 2.5 percent of more than 11.5 million papers published worldwide each year (Muslims constituted 23 percent of the world's population in 2010) and the 1.6 billion Muslims have produced to date four Nobel Prize winners in the sciences.

Islam, and landowners who had controlled the Middle East before the Arab conquests and remained dominant in providing local public goods (Chaney 2022).[3] The tribal type of societal organization, allied with a more conservative and literalist brand of Islam, proved to be the more powerful of the two. Muslim rulers discovered that they did not need local, landed elites for military service, as was the case in Western Europe. Instead, much of the Muslim world used military slaves (Mamluks) to populate their armies. The more professional and comparatively progressive bureaucracy lost its position, and religious scholars and tax farmers in the notorious *iqta* (tax farming) system took charge of supplying most public goods, replacing experienced administrators with a strong connection to the local population. Nothing like voluntary corporations emerged.

Chaney (2022) argued convincingly that the political and institutional changes triggered by the growing power of tribalism drove intellectual changes, not the reverse. In his analysis, Chaney (2025, pp. 1–2) has argued that the Muslim conquests eventually led to the spread and triumph of what he calls "Arabian tribal structures" and that these were "the fundamental drivers" of underdevelopment in the Middle Eastern world. During the golden age of Islam, tribal structures coexisted with a more bureaucratic regime. But in the long run, the two systems were incompatible and, at some point, tribal structures prevailed. The failure of the more bureaucratic and rationalist polity coincided with the stricter and literalist interpretations of Islam associated with the Sunni revival. Chaney argued that it was not just the tribal organizations that led to the slowing and eventually complete halting of progress. Rather, the merger of tribalist organizations with a traditionalist religious order impeded innovation.

As a result, the Muslim world "in which large kin-based social units, such as clans, lineages, and tribes have remained central until today" (Greif 2006, p. 396) remained far more anchored to collectivist structures than did their European neighbors.[4] The connection between extended kinship-based

3. Tribal forms of social organization were consonant with a more traditional interpretation of Islam because religious authority was able to create order and conformity into an otherwise fractious tribal society (Lapidus 2002, pp. 28–29; Chaney 2022, p. 9).

4. Greif (2006, pp. 254–55) also notes that consanguineous marriages and polygamy were common in the Middle East and prohibited in Europe. It may have been a tribal custom that preceded the Muslim conquest but Muslim practices encouraged it. As we have seen in chapter 4, it is widely agreed today that the prohibitions on clan-like marriage patterns of relatives were a critical element in the rise of the nuclear family in Europe as the main building block of

societies and the collectivist values we encountered above is fully illustrated in the Muslim societies of the Middle East. It remains an open question whether the Muslim world did not develop corporations because it did not need them or, if in fact they were needed, their development was only prevented by the legal and political environment of the time. The latter was argued by Timur Kuran (2011). Likely, both demand and supply factors played a role. Whatever the case, the result was the same: the Islamic world did not develop anything that resembled corporations, which made it harder to emulate the kind of growth experienced in Europe (Harris 2020).

The Arab world before Islam was organized via clans and tribes (Lapidus 2002, pp. 12–13). On top of this structure, Islam imposed the idea of an Islamic community, the *umma*, which transcended national borders. The *umma*, as Lapidus explained (2002, p. 29), redefined the meaning of the tribe: as a member, one not only defended his brothers, but also his fellow Muslims. Yet in many places, remnants of the traditional tribal and clan structures persisted, and much as in China, the central government had to rely on local elites and local tax farmers for administrative functions (Lapidus 2002, pp. 61–62).

Consistent with the argument made in chapter 7, the absence of corporations meant that the rules governing economic life were formulated by a central bureaucracy strongly influenced by clerics, without much input or participation by economic agents. Instead, Muslim clerics imposed their principles and priorities, and while there was a lively trade in the Muslim world, there was, in the words of Shlomo Goitein, "little contact between the world of the traders and that of the government" (cited by Greif 2006, p. 397). To be sure, we do not wish to argue that the governance of the Muslim world was in some sense inferior. But we do argue that unintended consequences of particular historical events led to different outcomes, and as Greif (2006, p. 398) notes, the economic system that individualism, corporations, and participatory government created in Europe gave it a dynamism and vigor that once existed in the Muslim Middle East but eventually fizzled out.

In the absence of corporate organizations, religious authorities enjoyed dominant influence in the Islamic world. As argued in chapter 7, the corporate structure of the Catholic Church made it easier for the gradual separation of church and state to take hold in Europe. This separation did not occur in the Islamic world, and the influence of religious authorities was much more

society. The consequent need for other social organizations to replace the extended kinship unit was a critical difference between the Christian West and the Muslim world.

pervasive. The phenomenon known as the "Sunni Revival," which started in the mid-eleventh century, reflected an "ideological shift away from a rationalist Islam favored by a secular bureaucracy" toward a much more conservative and traditionalist approach to religious views (Chaney 2022, p. 41). This ideological shift was caused partly by institutions (the growing power of religious-tribal leaders at the expense of secular bureaucrats) and partly driven by the growing number of non-Muslims who converted to Islam over time (e.g., Saleh 2018). Religious competition and pluralism in the Muslim world declined, and religious leaders steered intellectual activity in directions that they felt minimized the chances of skepticism and rationalism in order to preserve their political power and social prestige. The leader of this movement, an Iran-born intellectual named Al Ghazali (1058–1111), referred to by some historians as the single most influential Muslim after Muhammad, made this point the center of his thinking. The concatenation of circumstances that led to the decline of Muslim science was not preordained in any sense, but once it was in motion, the Islamic culture promulgated by conservative scholars and the increasingly conservative government reinforced one another to create a stagnant equilibrium that was overthrown only by Europe's growing hegemony in the nineteenth century.[5] Unlike in Europe, there was no political separation of religion and polity in the Islamic world (Rubin 2017).[6] Eventually, the ensuing struggles between the Church and European secular rulers led to a decline in the Church's legitimizing power, and more generally to a weakening of the Church and then to the Reformation. As a result, both before and after the Reformation, the power of the Church to impede scientific progress was ineffective in the long run, in sharp contrast with the Muslim world (Rubin 2017; Greif and Rubin 2023).

5. The contingency of the reversal of the positions of Western Europe and the Muslim world is the central message of Bisin et al. (2023), who argue that under somewhat different values of the main parameters, the two civilizations could have moved to very different equilibria than the ones they ended up in.

6. The argument about the separation between church and state in the West and its absence in the Middle East was made by Lewis (1993), among others, but it has been contested. Many scholars have stressed that in much of the Middle East, the differentiation between religious and secular spheres has been a feature of Muslim states (Blaydes 2017, p. 488). That said, there seems to be a consensus that the political power of Islamic religious elites expanded in the Middle Ages, serving as "a key intermediary between state and societal interests" (Blaydes 2017, p. 495), whereas in Europe, the Church fought the secular rulers to a standstill and eventually conceded more and more political power to it.

This argument is related to the interesting hypothesis proposed by Jared Rubin (2017); also see Bisin et al. (2024). His argument concerned Islam, but it was more related to political economy than to theological content. Specifically, he examined the ability of Muslim clerics to provide legitimacy to rulers and how this affected economic interests in governance. While the religious legitimacy of rulers was relied on in both the Christian West and the Muslim Middle East, the Church's ability to legitimize (and delegitimize) European rulers gradually weakened in the Late Middle Ages. In the Muslim world, clerics retained strong legitimizing powers; as a result, they were able to impose increasingly conservative "proscriptions" (in the terminology of Bisin et al. 2024) on the economy by threatening to withhold support for secular authorities if their interests were not heeded. This argument is consistent with ours since the power of religious authorities was supported by the tribalist nature of society.[7]

The consequences of a lack of corporate organizations in the Muslim world are also reflected in the structure of cities. One striking difference stressed by Bosker et al. (2013) (discussed in chapter 6) is the absence of self-governing cities in the Middle East and North Africa. The Middle East boasted many large urban centers, but they remained under complete control of central authorities. Furthermore, there were no formal constraints on rulers short of armed rebellion by citizens (which was often difficult as rulers could rely on high-quality professional slave-soldiers).

More generally, Makdisi (1970) stressed that whereas a Christian was a citizen of a particular city and an alien in another, a Muslim, on account of his religion, had the same political status anywhere in the Muslim world. The corporations established in the West "had no reason to develop in the Muslim East" (Makdisi 1970, p. 257). This statement sums up the differences between social organizations in the European and Islamic worlds. In its very essence, the European urban system—and especially the urban communes, which were for all intents and purposes independent entities—were competitive and pluralist. As we have seen, this placed European cities in a strong position to become the locus of both sustained intellectual innovation and politically inclusive participatory institutions.

---

7. Bisin et al. (2023) suggested that Islamic society was at first comparatively secular, but as the number of Muslims converting to Islam increased, they approached an equilibrium in which rulers increasingly depended on the Muslim clergy to legitimize their power, paying the price that reactionary clerics demanded. The model thus roughly replicates the chronology of the Muslim Middle East from a different viewpoint than the one adopted here.

A parallel development can be seen in the evolution of higher education. European universities were emblematic corporations. The Islamic madrassas were quite different. To be sure, the madrassas were effective institutions of higher learning and predate the ones in Christian Europe. Modern scholarship comparing the medieval European university with the madrassas of the Islamic world stress that a central difference was that the universities were corporate forms; that is, basically legal entities with charters that permitted self-rule and guaranteed a fair degree of independence (Makdisi 1970, 1981, pp. 224–25; Findikli 2022). Makdisi (1970, p. 258) notes that "the madrasa, unlike the university, was a building, not a community." Originally, the madrassas may have enjoyed a fair amount of independence because they often had independent sources of funding through *waqf* institutions. However, by Ottoman times, the madrassas had come under direct state control, which extended to decisions like academic and administrative appointments. Their autonomy considerably shrank, and the politico-bureaucratic logic of the state permeated, if not colonized, the madrassa system. The best that they could hope for was not to gain professional and scholarly autonomy *from* the polity, but rather to achieve a relative degree of operational autonomy *within* the polity, maintaining the notion that they had their own autonomous sphere within the empire (Findikli 2022).

The differences between the European university and the Islamic madrassa are a typical illustration of why the two civilizations diverged. The European university, as a form of organization as opposed to the content taught, owed little to Islam. Indeed, Makdisi (1981, p. 224), stressed that "Islam could have nothing to do with the university as a corporation" because the university was based on being endowed with the concept of a legal personality. Islamic law recognized the physical person alone as endowed with legal personality and did not have a concept of a corporation as a legal and autonomous entity.

One way or another, the madrassas became loci of conservative ideology and learning and a tool to undermine rationalism that was a main cause of the intellectual stasis in Islam that set in after the Sunni Revival (Chaney 2023). To be sure, European universities were often quite conservative as well, but because they were not uniformly controlled by any central power (either religious or secular), there were always some places (universities or other organizations of learning such as scientific societies) that were heterodox and provided locations where innovative and nonconformist intellectuals could go and set up circles that became breeding grounds of intellectual progress. The difference between a world in which autonomous corporations could flourish and a world in which they could not is well illustrated by this difference.

There is one more similarity between the great divergences that took place between Europe and China, and Europe and the Middle East: the reversal in fiscal capacity. Before the year 1000, both China and the Middle East wielded substantial tax collection powers. The Abbasid Khalifate was estimated to have extracted 7 percent of gross domestic product (GDP) in the mid-ninth century (Stasavage 2020, pp. 12, 312–13), whereas the nineteenth-century Ottoman Empire could extract only a small fraction of that and had the lowest per-capita state revenue in Europe (Karaman and Pamuk 2010, p. 623) and still resorted to tax farming (Özbek 2018). Much as was the case in China, the absence of any kind of consultative body that gave Muslim taxpayers a voice in both the raising and the spending of revenues reduced in the long run the ability of the central government to extract the revenues that it needed, notwithstanding their legitimization by the Muslim clergy. In Europe, as we have argued, the opposite was the case. Again, what we see is not so much a divergence as it is a reversal. The Muslim Middle East and the Chinese Empire took very different trajectories than did Europe, and as a result, so did their social organizations and culture, which had enormous consequences for future development.

2. India

The third major civilization in the Eurasian Continent was the Indian subcontinent. Its economic history was different from that of China or the Muslim Middle East, in that India's history was conditioned by European imperialism far more than that of the other two. As a result, an influential school of Indian economic history places much emphasis on British imperialism's dampening effect on economic development. The basic argument is that around 1500, when Europeans first began settling in India, their economy was not inferior to Western Europe by most metrics. The fact that the Indian subcontinent eventually fell behind was due to ruthless exploitation by Europeans (Swamy 1979; Parthasarathi 2011).

There can be little doubt that a combination of racism, arrogance, and incompetence meant that much of the British Raj had deleterious effects on the local economies of the Indian subcontinent; furthermore, the regions governed by local rulers did better in many dimensions than those ruled directly by British officials (Iyer 2010). The evidence suggests that those parts of India that remained under indigenous control (and thus were ruled only indirectly by the Raj) had far better long-term outcomes than those ruled directly by

British officials. More recent research showed that the same general trend was true for the incidence of famine (Sehgal 2023).

More balanced scholarship has warned against overstating the role of British rule in the economic and technological development of precolonial India. The complexity of the matter is reflected in the writings of the Indian scholar Dharampal, who pointed out that Europeans tended to systematically underappreciate precolonial Indian science and treated it with "ridicule and contempt." Yet he conceded, "It is possible that the various sciences and technologies were on a decline in India around 1750 and, perhaps, had been on a similar course for several centuries previously," but it was hard to know for sure because of the "general incommunicativeness of eighteenth-century Indian scholars and specialists in the various fields," which may have been due to "the usual secretiveness of such persons" (Dharampal 1971, p. 91).[8] The difference between that kind of insider science and the growth of public and open science in eighteenth-century Western Europe, which was at the very core of the Industrial Enlightenment, was symptomatic of the difference between it and South Asia. India clearly had an impressive record in science and technology, but in the absence of anything that resembled an Industrial Enlightenment, there is little evidence that its scientific achievements affected technology. It may thus be easy to fall into the trap of what Deepak Kumar (2003, p. 673) has called "a naive (perhaps revivalist) appreciation of pre-colonial science and technology."

One interesting Indian organization that could shed light on the difference between India and Europe is the curious case of Nalanda University, founded in the fifth century AD during the Gupta period (c.300–550). Established in what is now the modern state of Bihar in northeastern India, it was a Buddhist institution known as a *vihara* (basically an institution of higher education). Much like European universities, it combined religious and secular knowledge, as well as some practical fields such as mathematics, medicine, iron-casting, and astronomy. It prospered for centuries, and again much like the top European universities, it attracted foreign students from Japan, Tibet, and Korea. Its library was supposed to have had nine million manuscripts written on palm leaf.[9]

8. Dharampal (1971, p. 114) added that Indian sciences and technologies, which seem to have been very much alive about eight to ten generations ago, have been wholly eclipsed. He is careful, however, not to lay the blame on the British Raj directly, but rather on economic and fiscal decline and a general atrophy that he did not expand on further.

9. The great Indian astronomer and mathematician Aryabhata (476–550), one of the first to conceive of the concept of zero, was surmised to have been the head of Nalanda University (Sarma 2001, p. 115).

Yet the university did not thrive after the Gupta period, and c.1200, what was left of it was thoroughly destroyed by the Muslim invader Muhammad Bakhtiyar Khalji. By that time, it was already in decline and had been for a long time. Buddhism in India proved unable to compete with the Islam and Hindu religions, and a university run mostly by and for Buddhists had growing difficulty with sustaining itself. It is telling that most of what we know about Nalanda is based on the writings of two Chinese Buddhist monks who spent time there in the seventh century. The conclusion must be that Indian civilization was no less capable than Europe of creating strong educational institutions, but without the formal concept of a corporation and without the support of an organization like the Church, Nalanda University proved a false start and an example of what perhaps could have been.

How much of India's economic stagnation should be attributable to British colonialism, as opposed to indigenous conditions, in 1600? The question will continue to be debated. It may be fair to pose the naive question whether if Britain and India had really been at the same level of economic and institutional development c.1700, why was no "Western Europe Company" set up in Delhi, which would have exploited the political divisions within Europe, established an Indian "Raj" based in London, and forced Britain to accept Indian calicoes without tariffs? Furthermore, despite many just criticisms of British colonial rule, at least one economically beneficial thing that the British did was invest in infrastructure. Lord Dalhousie, governor general of India between 1848 and 1856, famously said that he introduced three "great engines of social improvements: railways, the electric telegraph, and uniform postage" (cited by Gosh 1978, p. 97).[10] The simple truth is that we have no way of knowing how the Indian subcontinent would have evolved in the absence of British rule, although the economic performance of Asian nations that were able to avoid being colonized, such as Persia (Iran) and Thailand, could provide a hint.

The leading economic historian of India in our time, Tirthankar Roy, has offered a nuanced and careful assessment: British rule had both benefits and costs. Roy (2019, p. 7) argued that "a fair assessment of the legacy of [the British Raj] should measure the *net* effect of the benefits and costs" (emphasis in original). In the end, however, such a calculation is hard to make: the people who benefited from the infusion of Western values and institutions were very different from those who suffered from them. A small commercial and

---

10. One might add the highly successful Ganges Irrigation Canal, the brainchild of a single-minded Briton, Colonel Proby Cautley.

professional class benefited from the Raj, whereas the mass of cotton spinners and weavers were impoverished by cheap British imports. Roy concluded in the end that "the legacy of colonialism is a paradox and that any story that tells us that it did more harm than good or the other way around is one-sided" (2019, p. 4).

The question of how social organizations, the main topic of this book, might have affected Indian economic development, both before and after the emergence of British rule, is highly relevant for understanding Indian economic history. Most of India's economy was agricultural and consisted of poor peasants working in low-productivity farming. Much like most preindustrial societies outside Western Europe, India was largely based on extended kinship social organizations.[11] But even in the more globalized and commercial urban sectors, most Indian businesses were family- or clan-based, managed by recruiting relatives into top positions or in the case of ethnic minorities, cooperating with members of the same caste or community (Roy 2019, pp. 70–71). Any social organization that resembled a corporation is hard to find. While there is evidence that guilds were an important part of the economy in ancient India (Thaplyal 1996), they had faded by the time the British took control of India. Guilds still existed, but they were rare and had little to no political or administrative functions (Roy 2008). Other analogs to corporations are hard to find in Indian history; cities to some extent enjoyed local self-governance, but they were hardly autonomous.

Before the Raj, Indian local government was concentrated in village communities that were largely responsible for the provision of local public goods. For example, local justice during the Mughal Empire (prior to the British Raj), only rarely involved central government; as such, villagers were unlikely to interact with Mughal law enforcement officials. Even though the Mughal imperial government was more centralized than at any other time before the British conquest, Mughal law enforcement seldom reached the village level. Most disputes were settled outside the formal Mughal courts. The Mughal legal system possessed neither the personnel nor the means of communications that would enable them to staff and operate a system of courts extensive enough to provide convenient access to villagers (Calkins 1968–1969).

11. Kumar (1974, pp. 43–46) stresses the central importance of the joint patriclocal family, often collateral extended families, which shared property, and often residences, in India's past. Needless to say, this was in many ways different from the clannish structure of China and tribal organizations elsewhere; but nuclear families were a fairly recent phenomenon.

A venerable tradition going back to the nineteenth century had it that each of these communities was, in the words of the British colonial official Sir Charles Metcalfe, who described the system in 1830, a semiautonomous "separate little state" in which village officers took care of local public goods such as public health, sanitation, education, and protection, with little contact with the outside world (cited by Chakrabarty 2017, p. 74). Metcalfe thought that "they seem to last where nothing else lasts. Dynasty after dynasty tumbles down; revolution succeeds to revolution; Hindu, Moghul . . . English, are all masters in turn, but the village communities remain the same" (cited by Mallik 1929, p. 36). More recent scholarship has questioned this generalization, arguing for a more nuanced system.[12]

At the village level, the caste and family systems were intertwined in a unique way of providing local public goods in rural India. Gune (1953), describing the state of Maharashtra in western India, explains that social organization at the village level was based on the joint family. Joint families consisted of a couple, their unmarried children, and the married sons and their families. As a functioning unit, it was quite different from the nuclear family: it was highly patriarchal, with the eldest male typically the leader of the family. The joint family owned property together, and hence no single member could dispose of or mortgage the assets. Age and gender were decisive in determining one's standing within the family. While resources were pooled, the joint family was too small to provide effective insurance and other local public goods (D'Cruz and Bharat 2001).

Castes were the other part of this dual structure: marriage took place with other members of the caste, and these groups were often responsible for local club goods such as education and poverty relief, although other matters were settled by village councils or *majlis*. Srinivas and Shah (1960, p. 1376) point to the rather peculiar structure of this system of social organization: the members of an agnatic clan (relatives connected through the father's side only) were often dispersed among several villages. The typical village had members of different castes, who were bound by ties of intermarriage with other members of the same caste in neighboring villages, and thus formed a caste-specific clan. This was especially true of some parts of north India, where members of the

12. Despite poorly developed transportation and low levels of monetization, and despite the power of the locally dominant caste that could lay down the law on many matters, the village was always a part of a wider economic, political, and religious system. The appearance of isolation, autonomy, and self-sufficiency was only an illusion (Srinivas and Shah 1960).

locally dominant caste residing in several neighboring villages were agnatically related to each other.

These networks were instrumental in maintaining commercial relations between villages and nearby towns. Yet they were relationships that relied heavily on kinship (through the male line), even if stratified by caste. Kinship was intertwined with the caste system, creating a social organization system consistent with communitarian values. There is some reason to believe that the caste system, while going back far into Indian history, was not a central feature of society during the age of the Delhi Sultanate (1206–1526) and became more prominent only after the Muslim invasions of the sixteenth century and the British Raj. In some ways, castes fulfilled functions similar to those of the Chinese clan: it was a method of contract enforcement, but it also was used as a means of rent collection and tax enforcement (Bedi 2020).[13] It has been argued that castes provided club goods, as they catered only to members and membership was purely ascriptive (Nair 2011, p. 362).

Outside of agriculture, conditions were quite similar throughout the Indian economy, particularly in the spheres of commerce and finance. One example is the Nagarathar Chettiars (also known as the Nattukottai Chettiars), a wealthy Tamil caste in South India, which became a major part of the region's commercial superstructure. Here too, caste and clan connections were essential to establish the trust needed for credit and other transactions (Rudner 1989; Nair 2011). British observers, accustomed to the formal commercial relations in Europe, failed to recognize the extent and significance of networks based on communitarian values. Indian commerce depended on a complex network of financial debts and relationships that Indian moneylenders and bankers could activate outside of Western-style banks. Credit markets operated through the connections of kinship and caste or common participation with potential investors and lenders in a variety of religious and secular institutions (Rudner 1989). The importance of extended families in India is perhaps best illustrated by the success of the wholly endogamous community of Parsis in India: a tiny group of non-Hindu (Zoroastrians) that fled Iran after the Muslim conquest. In almost every field, Parsis have punched above their weight in economic development and intellectual achievements. Tribal and clannish societies clearly were capable of successes—and yet in most cases,

13. For example, the caste "Panchayats," or panels for dispute resolution, comprised one or more respected elderly persons within the community, and they were expected to adjudicate disputes arising among caste members over both personal and commercial matters (Nair. 2011).

they found it hard to compete with organizations in the European mold. The success of the Parsis was in large part due to their ability to collaborate successfully with the British Raj (Karaka 1884, vol. 2). For more details, see Mokyr (2024a).

To sum up, while India differed radically from China in that it did not have a system of lineages and clans that formed coherent collectives, its caste system superimposed on the prevalent joint family created a system that neither needed nor encouraged organizations such as European corporations and did not experience the emergence of a culture based on universalistic values. "Amoral familism," or better perhaps "amoral caste-ism," remained prevalent and communitarian values remained the fundamental cultural foundation of society. Again, this system was not a failure, nor was it something that most Indians did not accept. But it lacked the aggressive dynamism and creativity that a world of corporations made, and in the end, this is what doomed India and created the Raj.

3. Concluding Remarks

Much of the literature on economic history has concentrated on phenomena of persistence and the perpetuation of differences among societies. Yet in the very long run, the history of economic development provides a resounding example of the opposite occurring (i.e., historical reversals). Whereas post-Carolingian Europe was an impoverished, barbaric, and backward region compared to both the Muslim Mediterranean and Song China, Europe eventually became economically and technologically dominant, creating a science and a culture that were adopted by much of the rest of the world.

Trying to understand this reversal is often denigrated by historians as Eurocentric or triumphalist, as if outlining the reversal is in some sense a celebration of the West (Blaut 2000).[14] Social science–oriented historians,

14. What this literature is arguing, almost without exception, is that by 1500, there was little difference in terms of economic development between Europe and other civilizations such as India and China, and only the extraction and exploitation by Europeans of the rest of the world, driven by a rapacious capitalist mentality, created the difference in the subsequent centuries (Frank 1998; Parthasarathi 2011). In contrast, the basic historical proposition made in this book is that the roots of the Great Reversal already existed in the Middle Ages, even if they did not lead to the emergence of a discernable gap in living standards until after the Industrial Revolution. In this interpretation, the Great Divergence can be seen as the unintended and unplanned result of very different historical forces and phenomena.

including economic historians, do not see it quite that way, and it is therefore not surprising that much of the more interesting big-picture research on the differential development of the great civilizations has come from them.

Much of the extensive scholarly literature regarding the Great Divergence, or what we think of as the Great Reversal, has focused on three themes: geography, the rise of modern science and technology, and political institutions (especially the increase in state capacity). The emphasis that we have placed on social organizations overlaps with these three themes but focuses on a separate phenomenon. The driving motive behind that emphasis is the importance of local public goods and club goods that made society work and allowed markets and day-to-day economic activity to take place. The key to the provision of these public goods was the emergence of social organizations, of arrangements that sustained cooperation between individuals, allowing them to overcome standard issues of collective action and opportunistic behavior and provide the public goods and services necessary for a proper functioning of their local economies and societies. The different ways in which Europe and China went about solving these problems had momentous (if entirely unintended and unforeseen) consequences, both in the evolution of institutions and the changes in cultural beliefs that coevolved with them. These consequences explain the rising state capacity in Europe, as well as the advances in useful knowledge that eventually led to the technological breakthroughs that created the Great Enrichment. Geography, of course, was largely exogenous, but it reinforced the consequences of social organizations.

What other general lessons can we learn from this interpretation? One is that unintended consequences of human actions can shape future developments in unforeseen ways. Inevitably, history is highly contingent. None of this denies the importance of human agency, but it does underline its limitations. Much of what we have described can be seen as an "emergent property"; that is, simple actions at the individual level resulted in totally different and far more complex outcomes at the aggregate level. In this regard, the study of history can take some inspiration from evolutionary models.[15] Decisions made at the individual level, such as when to marry, where to live, whom to

15. Emergent properties manifest themselves as the result of various system components interacting, even if it creates a feature that is not necessarily of any individual component. Thus, it is a property of a complex system or collection of system parts, but one that individual parts do not possess. It is characterized by the idea of something being "greater than the sum of its parts," such as an intellectual network.

cooperate with, and so on, culminated in a different history, where relations with nonkin and universalistic cultural values would determine economic and political outcomes centuries later. In short, local actions had global consequences.

Our argument also serves as a good antidote against what psychologists call "hindsight bias": that events that happened were inexorable outcomes of "deep" material forces such as geology, climate, resources, class structure, and technology. Few of the factors that we have invoked were inevitable. The triumph of the Catholic (Latin) Church in the West could have played out differently, by Europe eventually becoming Muslim in the eighth century or the Eastern (Orthodox) Church expanding westward. The part of Europe east of the Hajnal Line or the regions around the Mediterranean serve as an example; had the West adopted these institutions, the rise of corporations would have looked different.

Second, the resentment against the West and its historical role in creating the Great Enrichment should be modified and qualified. To be sure, the Great Enrichment did not take place without victimizing a huge number of humans, both in Europe and elsewhere. Nothing in any way exonerates European imperialists and slave traders who deployed their technological and military advantage to commit often horrendous crimes against non-Europeans. Yet in the end, the same features that allowed Europeans to pillage much of the rest of the world also led, generations later, to vastly higher living standards for many descendants of those victimized by European racism. How can we or should we weigh the economic benefits of the offspring against the suffering of their forefathers? Neither economics nor ethics have an answer to that question.

Finally, we offer one last lesson. The kind of society that the medieval corporations produced was in many ways harsh and violent, leading to persecutions, intolerance, civil and religious wars, and inhumanity toward people who were "different" (many of them, of course, being other Europeans). Nevertheless, medieval Europe also laid out the social foundations that enabled more effective and more durable cooperation among strangers. This in turn made it easier to address a fundamental challenge in any society—namely, how to scale up cooperation from the local to a higher level. But one more step was needed to soften the kind of system that emerged from the European Middle Ages, and this step was taken with the Enlightenment. After considerable time lags and many setbacks, this intellectual movement induced a liberal humanism that supported a live-and-let-live pluralism and a political system that made a deliberate effort to create a more open, equitable, and democratic society. The nations that remained largely untouched by the European Enlightenment today tend to be nations where democratic and liberal institution are absent, weak, or in decline. How that will affect their hopes of economic development remains to be seen. Either way, we should recognize that the cultural changes that we associate with the Enlightenment would not have been possible without the profound changes that preceded it, and that transformed social organizations in the centuries before.

REFERENCES

Acemoglu, Daron. 2003. "Why Not a Political Coase Theorem? Social Conflict, Commitment, and Politics." *Journal of Comparative Economics*, Vol. 31, No. 2, pp. 620–52.

Acemoglu, Daron, Simon Johnson, and James A. Robinson. 2002. "Reversal of Fortune: Geography and Institutions in the Making of the Modern World Income Distribution." *Quarterly Journal of Economics*, Vol. 117, No. 4, pp. 1231–94.

———. 2005. "The Rise of Europe: Atlantic Trade, Institutional Change, and Economic Growth." *American Economic Review*, Vol. 95, No. 3, pp. 546–79.

Acemoglu, Daron, and Joshua Linn. 2004. "Market Size in Innovation: Theory and Evidence from the Pharmaceutical Industry." *Quarterly Journal of Economics*, Vol. 119, No. 3, pp. 1049–90.

Acemoglu, Daron, and James Robinson. 2012. *Why Nations Fail*. New York: Crown.

———. 2019. *The Narrow Corridor: States, Societies, and the Fate of Liberty*. New York: Penguin.

———. 2021. "Culture, Institutions and Social Equilibria: A Framework." NBER Working Paper 8832.National Bureau of Economic Research, Cambridge, MA.

Acemoglu, Daron, and Alex Wolitzky. 2020. "A Theory of Equality before the Law." *The Economic Journal*, Vol. 131, No. 636, pp. 1429–65.

Aghion, Philippe, Céline Antonin, and Simon Bunel. 2021. *The Power of Creative Destruction— EconomicUpheaval and the Wealth of Nations*.Cambridge, MA: Belknap Press of Harvard University Press.

Aghion, Philippe, Celine Antonin, Luc Paluskiewicz, David Stromberg, Raphael Wargon, and Karolina Westin. 2023, "Does Chinese Research Hinge on US Co-authors? Evidence from the China Initiative." Discussion paper, Center of Economic Performance, LSE, Discussion Paper 1936.

Alesina, Alberto, and Paola Giuliano. 2015. "Culture and Institutions." *Journal of Economic Literature*, Vol. 53, No. 4, pp. 898–944.

Alesina, Alberto, Paola Giuliano, and Nathan Nunn. 2013. "On the Origins of Gender Roles: Women and the Plough." *Quarterly Journal of Economics*, Vol. 128, No. 2, pp. 469–530.

Alexander, Amir. 2014. *Infinitesimal: How a Dangerous Mathematical Theory Shaped the Modern World*. New York: Farrar, Straus and Giroux.

Alford, William P. 1995. *To Steal a Book Is an Elegant Offense: Intellectual Property Law in Chinese Civilization*.Stanford, CA: Stanford University Press.

Allee, Mark A. 1994. "Code, Culture and Custom: Foundations of Civil Case Verdicts in a Nineteenth-Century County Court." In *Civil Law in Qing and Republican China*, edited by Kathryn Bernhardt and Philip C. Huang, 122–41. Stanford, CA: Stanford University Press.

Allen, F., J. Qian, and M. Qian. 2003. "Law, Finance, and Economic Growth in China." *Journal of Financial Economics*, Vol. 77, No. 1, pp. 57–116.

Allen, F., Y. Qian, G. Tu, and F. Yu. 2019c. "Entrusted Loans: A Close Look at China's Shadow Banking System." *Journal of Financial Economics*, Vol. 133, No. 1, pp. 18–41.

Allen, Franklin, Jun "QJ" Qian, and Meijun Qian. 2019a. "A Review of China's Institutions." *Annual Review of Financial Economics*, Vol 11, pp. 39–64.

Allen, Franklin, M. Qian, and J. Xie. 2019b. "Understanding Informal Financing." *Journal of Financial Intermediation*, Vol. 39, pp. 19–33.

Allen, Robert C., Jean-Pascal Bassino, Debin Ma, Christine Moll-Murata, and Jan Luiten Van Zanden. 2011. "Wages, Prices, and Living Standards in China, 1738–1925: In Comparison with Europe, Japan, and India." *Economic History Review*, Vol. 64, No. 1, pp. 8–38.

Amico, Leonard N. 1996. *Bernard Palissy*. New York: Flammarion.

Amsler, Nadine. 2018. *Jesuits and Matriarchs: Domestic Worship in Early Modern China*. Seattle: University of Washington Press.

Andersen, Thomas B., Jeanet Bentzen, Carl-Johan Dalgaard, and Paul Sharp. 2017. "Pre-Reformation Roots of the Protestant Ethic." *Economic Journal*, Vol. 127, No. 604, pp. 1756–93.

Andrade, Tonio. 2016. *The Gunpowder Age—China, Military Innovation, and the Rise of the West in World History*. Princeton, NJ: Princeton University Press.

Ang, James B., and Per G. Fredriksson. 2017. "Wheat Agriculture and Family Ties." *European Economic Review*, No. 100, pp. 236–56.

Ang, Yuen Yuen. 2012. "Counting Cadres: A Comparative View of the Size of China's Public Employment." *China Quarterly*, Vol. 211, pp. 676–96.

Angelucci, C., S. Meraglia, and N. Voigtländer. 2022. "How Merchant Towns Shaped Parliaments: From the Norman Conquest of England to the Great Reform Act." *American Economic Review*, Vol. 112, No. 10, pp. 3441–87.

Annali. 1190. *Annali Genovesi di Caffaro e dei suoi Continuatori, 1099–1240, 1923–1929*. 4 vols. Translated by Ceccardo Roccatagliata Ceccardi and Giovanni Monleone. Genoa, Italy: Municipio di Genova.

Aristotle. 1932. *Politics*. Translated by H. Rackham. Cambridge, MA: Harvard University Press.

Ascough, Richard S. 1997. "Translocal Relationships among Voluntary Associations and Early Christianity." *Journal of Early Christian Studies*, Vol. 5, No. 2, pp. 223–41.

Ashley, William James. 1909. *An Introduction to English Economic History and Theory. Part 1: The Middle Ages*, 4th ed. Internet Archive, McMaster University.https://archive.org/details/introtoenglishecvol1pt1ashliala/page/n3/mode/2up.

Augier, Mie, Jerry Guo, and Harry Rowen. 2016. "The Needham Puzzle Reconsidered: Organizations, Organizing, and Innovation in China." *Management and Organization Review*, Vol. 12, No. 1, pp. 5–24.

Ayyagari, M., A. Demirgüç-Kunt, and V. Maksimovic. 2010. "Formal Versus Informal Finance: Evidence from China." *Review of Financial Studies*, Vol. 23, No. 8, pp. 3048–97.

Bacon, Francis. [1620] 1999. *The Great Instauration*. Reprinted in *Selected Philosophical Works*, edited by Rose-Mary Sargent, 63–206. Indianapolis: Hackett.

Baechler, Jean. 2004. "The Political Pattern of Historical Creativity." In *Political Competition, Innovation and Growth in the History of Asian Civilizations*, edited by Peter Bernholz and Roland Vaubel, 18–38. Cheltenham, UK: Edward Elgar.

Bai, Chong-En, Chang-Tai Hsieh, and Zheng Song. 2020. "Special Deals with Chinese Characteristics." *NBER Macroeconomics Annual*, Vol. 34, No. 1, pp. 341–79.

Bai, Ying, and Ruixue Jia. 2021. "The Economic Consequences of Political Hierarchy: Evidence from Regime Changes in China, AD 1000–2000 CE." *Review of Economics and Statistics,*pp. 1–45.

Bai, Ying, Ruixue Jia, and Jiaojiao Yang. 2023. "Web of Power: How Elite Networks Shaped War and Politics in China." *Quarterly Journal of Economics*, Vol. 138, No. 2, pp. 1067–108.

———. 2024. "Knowledge Suppression and Resilience under Censorship: Three Centuries Book Publication in China." NBER Working Paper 33258. National Bureau of Economic Research, Cambridge, MA.

Bailey, W., W. Huang, and Z. Yang. 2011. "Bank Loans with Chinese Characteristics: Some Evidence on Inside Debt in a State-Controlled Banking System." *Journal of Financial and Quantitative Analysis*, Vol. 46, No. 6, pp. 1795–1830.

Bairoch, P., J. Batou, and P. Chèvre. 1988. *The Population of European Cities. Data Bank and Short Summary of Results: 800–1850*, Geneva, Switzerland: Librarie Droz.

Bairoch, Paul. 1988. *Cities and Economic Development from the Dawn of History to the Present*. Chicago: University of Chicago Press.

———. 1991. "The City and Technological Innovation." In *Favorites of Fortune: Technology, Growth, and Economic Development Since the Industrial Revolution*, edited by Patrice Higonnet, David S. Landes, and Henry Rosovsky, 159–76. Cambridge, MA: Harvard University Press.

Baker, Hugh D.R. 1979. *Chinese Family and Kinship*. New York: Columbia University Press.

Balch, Emily Greene. 1893. "Public Assistance of the Poor in France." *Publications of the American Economic Association*, Vol. 8, No. 4/5 (July–September), pp. 9–179.

Ballard, Adolphus. 2010. *British Borough Charters 1042–1216*. Cambridge: Cambridge University Press.

Ballard, Adolphus, and James Tait, eds., 1923.*British Borough Charters, 1216–1307*. Cambridge: Cambridge University Press.

Banfield, Edward C. 1958. *The Moral Basis of a Backward Society*. New York: Free Press.

Barber, Malcolm. 1995. *The New Knighthood: A History of the Order of the Temple*. Cambridge: Cambridge University Press.

Bartlett, R. 1994. *The Making of Europe: Conquest, Colonization and Cultural Change 950–1350*. London: Penguin UK.

Barzel, Yoram. 1997. "Parliament as a Wealth Maximizing Institutions: The Right to the Residual and the Right to Vote." *International Review of Law and Economics*, Vol. 17, pp. 455–74.

Barzel, Yoram, and Edgar Kiser. 1997. "The Development and Decline of Medieval Voting Institutions: A Comparison of England and France." *Economic Inquiry*, Vol. 35, No. 2, pp. 244–60.

Bayle, Pierre. 1734. *The Dictionary Historical and Critical of Mr. Peter Bayle*, 2nd ed., collated by Mr Des Maizeaux. London: Printed for J. J. and P. Knapton.Originally published in 1696–1697.

Bedi, Joshua K. 2020. "Shooting an Elephant: A Public Choice Explanation of Caste." Unpublished paper, George Mason University, Fairfax, VA.

Belfanti, Carlo Marco. 2004. "Guilds, Patents, and the Circulation of Technical Knowledge." *Technology and Culture*, Vol. 45, No. 3, pp. 569–89.

Bellavitis, Anna, Riccardo Cella, and Giovanni Colavizza. 2019. "Apprenticeship in Early Modern Venice." In *Apprenticeship in Early Modern Europe*, edited by Maarten Prak and Patrick Wallis, 20–43. Cambridge: Cambridge University Press.

Bellomo, Manlio. 1995. *The Common Legal Past of Europe 1000–1800*. Washington, DC: Catholic University of America Press.

Ben-Amos, Ilana K. 2000. "Gifts and Favors: Informal Support in Early Modern England." *Journal of Modern History*, Vol. 72, No. 2, pp. 295–338.

Beraja, Martin, David Y. Yang, and Noam Yuchtman. 2023. "Data-Intensive Innovation and the State: Evidence from AI Firms in China." *Review of Economic Studies*, Vol. 90, No. 4, pp. 1701–23.

Beresford, M., and Finberg, H.P.R. 1973. *English Medieval Boroughs: A Handlist*. Newton Abbot, UK: David and Charles.

Berg, Maxine. 2007. "The Genesis of Useful Knowledge." *History of Science*, Vol. 45, Pt. 2, No. 148, pp. 123–34.

Berg, Maxine, and Pat Hudson. 2023. *Slavery, Capitalism and the Industrial Revolution*. Cambridge: Polity Press.

Bergeron, Augustin. 2019. "Religion and the Scope of Morality: Evidence from Exposure to Missions in the DRC." Working paper, Harvard University, Cambridge, MA.

Berglas, Eitan. 1976. "On the Theory of Clubs." *American Economic Review*, Vol. 66, No. 2, pp. 116–21.

Berglas, Eitan, and David Pines. 1981. "Clubs, Local Public Goods, and Transportation Models: A Synthesis." *Journal of Public Economics*, Vol. 15, No. 2, pp. 141–62.

Berkowitz, Daniel, and Karen Clay. 2011. *The Evolution of a Nation: How Geography and Law Shaped the American States*. Princeton, NJ: Princeton University Press.

Berlin, Michael. 2008. "Guilds in Decline? London Livery Companies and the Rise of a Liberal Economy, 1600–1800." In *Guilds, Innovation and the European Economy, 1400–1800*, edited by S. R. Epstein and Maarten Prak, 316–41. Cambridge: Cambridge University Press.

Berman, Harold J. 1977. "The Origins of Western Legal Science." *Harvard Law Review* Vol. 90, No. 5 (March), pp. 894–943.

———. 1983. *Law and Revolution: The Formation of the Western Legal Tradition*. Cambridge, MA: Harvard University Press.

Bernholz, Peter, Manfred Streit, and Roland Vaubel, eds. 1998. *Political Competition, Innovation, and Growth*. Berlin: Springer.

Bertucci, Paola. 2017. *Artisanal Enlightenment: Science and the Mechanical Arts in Old Regime France*. New Haven, CT: Yale University Press.

Besley, Timothy, and Maitreesh Ghatak. 2008. "Status Incentives." *American Economic Review*, Vol. 98, No. 2, pp. 206–11.

Besley, Timothy, and Torsten Persson. 2011. *Pillars of Prosperity*. Princeton, NJ: Princeton University Press.

———. 2019. "The Dynamics of Environmental Politics and Values." *Journal of the European Economic Association*, Vol. 17, pp. 993–1024.

Biagioli, Mario. 1990. "Galileo's System of Patronage." *History of Science*, Vol. 28, No. 1, pp. 1–62.

Bian, Y. 1994. "Guanxi and the Allocation of Urban Jobs in China." *China Quarterly*, Vol. 140, pp. 971–99.

Bisin, Alberto, Jared Rubin, Avner Seror, and Thierry Verdier. 2024. "Culture, Institutions and the Long Divergence." *Journal of Economic Growth*, Vol. 29, No. 1, pp. 1–40.

Bisin, Alberto, and Thierry Verdier. 2001. "The Economics of Cultural Transmission and the Dynamics of Preferences." *Journal of Economic Theory*, Vol. 97, No. 2, pp. 298–319

———. 2017. "On the Joint Evolution of Culture and Institutions." NBER Working Paper 23375. National Bureau of Economic Research, Cambridge, MA.

———. 2023. "Advances in the Economic Theory of Cultural Transmission." *Annual Review of Economics*, Vol. 15 (February), pp. 63–89.

Blackstone, William. 1765–1769. *Commentaries on the Laws of England*. Oxford: Clarendon Press. https://avalon.law.yale.edu/subject_menus/blackstone.asp.

Blanning, Tim. 2007. *The Pursuit of Glory: Europe 1648–1815*.New York: Penguin.

Blaydes, Lisa. 2017. "State Building in the Middle East." *Annual Review of Political Science*, Vol. 20, pp. 487–504.

Bloch, Marc. 1962. *Feudal Society—Volume II: Social Classes and Political Organizations*. London: Routledge and Kegan Paul Ltd.

Bo, Zhiyue. 2002. *Chinese Provincial Leaders: Economic Performance and Political Mobility since 1949*. Armonk, NY: M.E. Sharpe.

Bodde, Derk. 1954. "Authority and Law in Ancient China." In *Essays on Chinese Civilization*, edited by Charles Leblanc,161–70. Princeton, NJ: Princeton University Press.

———. 1991. *Chinese Thought, Society, and Science*. Honolulu: University of Hawaii Press.

Bodde, Derk, and Clarence Morris. 1967. *Law in Imperial China, Exemplified by 190 Ch'ing Dynasty Cases*. Cambridge, MA: Harvard University Press.

———. 1970. "Basic Concepts of Chinese Law." In *Traditional China*, edited by James T. C. Liu and Wei-Ming Tu, 92–108. Englewood Cliffs, NJ: Prentice Hall.

Boerner, Lars, and Daniel Quint. 2016. "Medieval Matching Markets." LSE Economic History Working Papers. London School of Economics.

Bohstedt, John. 1983. *Riots and Community Politics in England and Wales*. Cambridge, MA: Harvard University Press.

Bol, Peter Kees. 2003. "The 'Localist Turn' and 'Local Identity' in Later Imperial China." *Late Imperial China*, Vol. 24, No. 2, pp. 1–50.

———. 2008. *Neo-Confucianism in History*. Cambridge, MA: Harvard University Press.

Boone, Marc. 2012. "Cities in Late Medieval Europe: The Promise and the Curse of Modernity." *Urban History*, Vol. 39, No. 2 (May), pp. 329–49.

Boserup, Ester. 1970. *Woman's Role in Economic Development*. London: George Allen and Unwin Ltd.

———. 1981. *Population and Technological Change*. Chicago: University of Chicago Press.

Bosker, M., E. Buringh, and J. L. Van Zanden. 2013. "From Baghdad to London: Unraveling Urban Development in Europe, the Middle East, and North Africa, 800–1800." *Review of Economics and Statistics*, Vol. 95, No. 4, pp. 1418–37.

Boucoyannis, Deborah. 2021. *Kings as Judges: Power, Justice and the Origin of Parliaments*. Cambridge: Cambridge University Press.

Brandt, Loren, Debin Ma, and Thomas G. Rawski. 2014. "From Divergence to Convergence: Re-evaluating the History behind China's Economic Boom." *Journal of Economic Literature* Vol. 52, No. 1, pp. 45–123.

Brandt, Loren, and Thomas Rawski. 2021. "China's Great Boom as a Historical Process." In *The Cambridge Economic History of China*, edited by Debin Ma and Richard Von Glahn, 775–828. Cambridge: Cambridge University Press.

Bray, Francesca. 1984. *Agriculture*. In *Science and Civilization in China*, Vol. 6, Pt. 2, edited by Joseph Needham. Cambridge: Cambridge University Press.

Brenner, Robert. 1987. "Agrarian Class Structure and Economic Development in Pre-industrial Europe." In *The Brenner Debate—Agrarian Class Structure and Economic Development in Pre Industrial Europe*, edited by T. H. Aston and C. H. E. Philpin, 10–63. Cambridge: Cambridge University Press.

Broadberry, Stephen, Hanhui Guan, and David Daokui Li. 2018. "China, Europe and the Great Divergence: A Study in Historical National Accounting, 980–1850." *Journal of Economic History*, Vol. 78, No. 4, pp. 1–46.

Brokaw, Cynthia J. 2005. "On the History of the Book in China." In *Printing and Book Culture in Late Imperial China*, edited by Cynthia J. Brokaw and Kai-wing Chow, 3–54. Berkeley: University of California Press.

Brook, Timothy. 1989. "Funerary Ritual and the Building of Lineages in Late Imperial China." *Harvard Journal of Asiatic Studies*, Vol. 49, No. 2, pp. 465–99.

———. 1993. *Praying for Power. Buddhism and the Formation of Gentry Society in Late-Ming Society*. Cambridge, MA: Harvard University Press.

———. 2010. *The Troubled Empire: China in the Yuan and Ming Dynasties*. Cambridge, MA: Harvard University Press.

Brown, Alfred L. 1989. *The Governance of Late Medieval England, 1272–1461*. Stanford, CA: Stanford University Press.

Brown, Shannon R. 1979. "The Ewo Filature: A Study in the Transfer of Technology to China." *Technology and Culture*, Vol. 20, pp. 550–68.

Brucker, G. A. 2015. *The Civic World of Early Renaissance Florence*. Princeton, NJ: Princeton University Press.

Buchanan, James M. 1965. "An Economic Theory of Clubs." *Economica*, Vol. 32, No. 125, pp. 1–14.

Burgess, John Stewart. 1928. *The Guilds of Peking*. New York: Columbia University Press.

Buringh, Eltjo, and Jan Luiten Van Zanden. 2009. "Charting the 'Rise of the West': Manuscripts and Printed Books in Europe, a Long-Term Perspective from the Sixth through Eighteenth Centuries." *Journal of Economic History*, Vol. 69, No. 2, pp. 409–45.

Burrell, Thomas H. 2011. "A Story of Privileges and Immunities: From Medieval Concept to the Colonies and United States Constitution." *Campbell Law Review*, Vol. 34, No. 1, pp. 7–120.

Cabello, Matías. 2023. "The Counter-Reformation, Science, and Long-Term Growth: A Black Legend?" Unpublished working paper, Martin Luther University, Halle-Wittenberg.

Cai, Hongbin, Hanming Fang, and Lixin Colin Xu. 2011. "Eat, Drink, Firms, Government: An Investigation of Corruption from the Entertainment and Travel Costs of Chinese Firms." *Journal of Law and Economics*, Vol. 54, No. 1, pp. 55–78.

Cai, Jindong, and Sheila Melvin. 2016. *Beethoven in China*. Harmondsworth, UK: Penguin.

Calkins, P. B. 1968–1969. "A Note on Lawyers in Muslim India." *Law & Society Review*, Vol 3, No. 2–3. Special Issue Devoted to Lawyers in Developing Societies with Particular Reference to India.

Calomiris, C. W., R. Fisman, and Y. Wang. 2010. "Profiting from Government Stakes in a Command Economy: Evidence from Chinese Asset Sales." *Journal of Financial Economics*, Vol. 96, No. 3, pp. 399–412.

Cantoni, Davide, Jeremiah Dittmar, and Noam Yuchtman. 2018. "Religious Competition and Reallocation: The Political Economy of Secularization in the Protestant Reformation." *Quarterly Journal of Economics*, Vol. 133, No. 4, pp. 2037–96.

Cantoni, Davide, and Noam Yuchtman. 2014. "Medieval Universities, Legal Institutions, and the Commercial Revolution." *Quarterly Journal of Economics*, Vol. 129, No. 2, pp. 823–87.

Cao, Jarui, Yiqing Xu, and Chuanchuan Zhang. 2022. "Clans and Calamity: How Social Organizations Saved Lives during China's Great Famine." *Journal of Development Economics*, Vol. 157, 102865.

Cao, Shuji. 2022. "Population Change." In *The Cambridge Economic History of China*, Vol. I. edited by Debin Ma and Richard Von Glahn, 300–339. Cambridge, Cambridge University Press.

Caprettini, Bruno, and Joachim Voth. 2020. "Rage against the Machine: Social Unrest and Labor Saving Technological Change in Industrializing England." *American Economic Review: Insights*, Vol. 2, No. 3, pp. 305–20.

Carpenter, Audrey T. 2011. *John Theophilus Desaguliers*. London: Continuum.

Cavanagh, Edward. 2016. "Corporations and Business Associations from the Commercial Revolution to the Age of Discovery: Trade, Jurisdiction and the State, 1200–1600." *History Compass*, Vol. 14, No. 10, pp. 493–510.

Chakrabarty, Bidyut. 2017. *Localizing Governance in India*. New York: Routledge.

Chaney, Eric. 2022. "Islam and Political Structure in Historical Perspective." In *The Oxford Handbook of Politics in Muslim Societies*, edited by Melani Cammett and Pauline Jones, 33–52. Oxford: Oxford University Press.

———. 2023. "Religion and the Rise and Fall of Islamic Science." Unpublished manuscript, Oxford University.

———. 2025. "Tribal Kingdom: The Origins, Economic Impact and Legacy of the Islamic Polity." Unpublished manuscript, Oxford University.

Chang, Chung-li (Zhang Zhongli). 1955. *The Chinese Gentry: Studies on Their Role in Nineteenth-Century Chinese Society*. Seattle: University of Washington Press.

Chang, Jianhua. 2013. *Song yihou de xingchengji diyu bijiao* [The formation and regional comparison of lineages after the Song Dynasty] [in Chinese]. Beijing: Renmin Chubanshe Press.

Chao, Kang. 1986. *Man and Land in Chinese History*. Stanford, CA: Stanford University Press.

Chen, Fanghao, Ruichi Xiong, and Xiaobo Zhang. 2022. "Familiar Strangers: Lineage Connection and Diaspora Direct Investments in China." SSRN working paper.

Chen, Li. 2012. "Legal Specialists and Judicial Administration in Late Imperial China, 1651–1911." *Late Imperial China*, Vol. 33, No. 1, pp. 1–54.

Chen, Lihua. 2022. "Tax System Reform and Its Impacts in the Middle and Late Tang Dynasty." Unpublished paper, University of Sydney Business School.

Chen, Qiang. 2012. "The Needham Puzzle Reconsidered: The Protection of Industrial and Commercial Property Rights." *Economic History of Developing Regions*, Vol. 27, No. 1, pp. 38–66.

Chen, Shuo, Xinyu Fan, and Zhichen Hua. 2023. "Noble No More: *Keju*, Institutional Commitment, and Political Purges." Unpublished manuscript, Fudan University, Shanghai.

Chen, Shuo, Raymond Fisman, Xiaohuan Lan, Yongxian Wang, and Qing Ye. 2024. "The Cost and Benefits of Clan Culture: Elite Control vs. Cooperation in China." NBER Working Paper 32414. National Bureau of Economic Research, Cambridge, MA.

Chen, Song. 2017. "The State, the Gentry and Local Institutions." *Journal of Chinese History*, Vol. 1, pp. 141–82.

Chen, Ting, and James Kai-sing Kung. 2016. "Do Land Revenue Windfalls Create a Political Resource Curse? Evidence from China." *Journal of Development Economics*, Vol. 123, pp. 86–106.

———. 2019. "Busting the 'Princelings': The Campaign against Corruption in China's Primary Land Market." *Quarterly Journal of Economics*, Vol. 134, No. 1, pp. 185–226.

Chen, Y., M. Liu, and J. Su. 2013. "Greasing the Wheels of Bank Lending: Evidence from Private Firms in China." *Journal of Banking and Finance*, Vol. 37, No. 7, pp. 2533–45.

Chen, Yuyu, and David Yang. 2019. "The Impact of Media Censorship: 1984 or Brave New World?" *American Economic Review*, Vol. 109, No. 6, pp. 2294–2332.

Chen, Zhiwu, Chicheng Ma, and Andrew J. Sinclair. 2022. "Banking on the Confucian Clan: Why China Developed Financial Markets so Late." *Economic Journal*, Vol. 132 (May), pp. 1378–1413.

Chen, Zhiwu, and Li Duan. 2024. "Charting the Needham Puzzle: A Long-Term Perspective on Book Writing in China." Unpublished manuscript, University of Hong Kong.

Chen, Zhiwu, and Kaixang Peng. 2022. "Production, Consumption, and Living Standards." In *The Cambridge Economic History of China, Vol. I*, edited by Debin Ma and Richard Von Glahn, 676–709. Cambridge: Cambridge University Press.

Cheng, Jiameng, Yanke Dai, Shu Lin, and Haichun Ye. 2021. "Clan Culture and Family Ownership Concentration: Evidence from China." *China Economic Review*, 70, 101692.

Chesneaux, Jean. 1973. *Peasant Revolts in China, 1840–1949*. Translated by C.A. Current. London: Thames and Hudson.

Ch'ien Mu. 1982. *Traditional Government in Imperial China*. Hong Kong: Chinese University Press.

Ching, Julia. 1979. "The Practical Learning of Chu Shun-shui, 1600–1682." In *Principle and Practicality: Essays in Neo-Confucianism and Practical Learning*, edited by W. Theodore de Bary and Irene Bloom, 189–229. New York: Columbia University Press.

Ch'ü, T'ung-tsu (Qu Tongzu). 1962. *Local Government in China under the Ch'ing*. Cambridge, MA: Harvard University Press.

Clark, D.S. 1987. "The Medieval Origins of Modern Legal Education: Between Church and State." *American Journal of Comparative Law*, Vol. 35, No. 4, pp. 653–719.

Clark, Peter. 2000. *British Clubs and Societies, 1580–1800: The Origins of an Associational World*. Oxford: Clarendon Press.

Clarke, M. V. 1926. *The Medieval City State: An Essay on Tyranny and Federation in the Later Middle Ages*. New York: Routledge

Coad, Jonathan. 2005. *The Portsmouth Block Mills: Bentham, Brunel and the Start of the Royal Navy's Industrial Revolution*. Swindon, UK: English Heritage.

Cohen, Myron L. 1990. "Lineage Organization in North China." *Journal of Asian Studies*, Vol. 49, No. 3, pp. 509–34.

Coker, Francis William. 1926. *Readings in Political Philosophy*. New York: MacMillan.

Colish, Marcia. 1997. *Medieval Foundations of the Western Intellectual Traditions—400–1400*. New Haven, CT: Yale University Press.

Cong, L. W., H. Gao, J. Ponticelli, and X. Yang. 2019. "Credit Allocation under Economic Stimulus: Evidence from China." *Review of Financial Studies*, Vol. 32, No. 9, pp. 3412–60.

Cookson, Gillian. 2018. *The Age of Machinery: Engineering the Industrial Revolution, 1770–1850*. Woodbridge, UK: Boydell Press.

Cooper, Carolyn. 1984. "The Portsmouth System of Manufacture." *Technology and Culture*, Vol. 25, No. 2, pp. 182–225.

Cordery, Simon. 2003. *British Friendly Societies, 1750–1914*. New York: Palgrave.

Cox, Gary W. 2017. "Political Institutions, Economic Liberty, and the Great Divergence." *Journal of Economic History*, Vol. 77, No. 3, pp. 724–55.

Cox, Gary W., Mark Dincecco, and Massimiliano Gaetano Onorato. 2024. "Window of Opportunity: War and the Origins of Parliament." *British Journal of Political Science*, Vol. 54, No. 2, pp. 405–21.

Cranmer-Byng, J.L., and Trevor Levere. 1981. "A Case Study in Cultural Collision: Scientific Apparatus in the Macartney Embassy to China, 1793." *Annals of Science*, Vol. 38, No. 5, pp. 503–25.

Crissman, Lawrence. 1967. "The Segmentary Structure of Urban Overseas Chinese Communities." *Man*, Vol. 2, No. 2, June, pp. 185–204.

Crosby, Alfred. 1972. *The Columbian Exchange; Biological and Cultural Consequences of 1492*. Westport, CT: Greenwood.

Dai, Ruochen, Dilip Mookherjee, Kaivan Munshi, and Xiaobo Zhang. 2020. "The Community Origin of Private Enterprise in China." Institute of Economic Development Working Paper Series, Boston University.

Dari-Mattiacci, Giuseppe, Oscar Gelderblom, Joost Jonker, and Enrico C. Perotti. 2017. "The Emergence of the Corporate Form." *Journal of Law, Economics, and Organization*, Vol. 33, No. 2, pp. 193–236.

Daston, Lorraine. 2005. "All Curls and Pearls: A Review of Neil Kenny, *The Uses of Curiosity in Early Modern France and Germany*." *London Review of Books*, June 23, pp. 37–38.

Daston, Lorraine, and Katherine Park. 1998. *Wonders and the Order of Nature, 1150–1750*. New York: Zone Books.

David, Paul A. 2008. "The Historical Origins of 'Open Science': An Essay on Patronage, Reputation and Common Agency Contracting in the Scientific Revolution." *Capitalism and Society*, Vol. 3, No. 2, pp. 1–103.

Davids, Karel. 2007. "Apprenticeship and Guild Control in the Netherlands, c. 1450–1800." In *Learning on the Shop Floor: Historical Perspectives on Apprenticeship*, edited by Bert De Munck, Steven L. Kaplan, and Hugo Soly, 65–84. New York: Berghahn Books.

———. 2008. *The Rise and Decline of Dutch Technological Leadership*, 2 vols. Leiden, Netherlands: Brill.

Davis, John P. 1961. *Corporations: A Study of the Origin and Development of Great Business Combinations and of Their Relation to the Authority of the State*. New York: Capricorn Books.

Davis, Lewis S., and Claudia R. Williamson. 2019. "Does Individualism Promote Gender Equality?" *World Development*, Vol. 123 (Nov.), 104627.

D'Cruz, Premilla, and Bharat Shalini. 2001. "Beyond Joint and Nuclear: The Indian Family Revisited." *Journal of Comparative Family Studies*, Vol. 32, No. 2 (Spring), pp. 167–94.

De la Croix, David, Frédéric Docquier, Alice Fabre, and Robert Stelter. 2023. "The Academic Market and the Rise of Universities in Medieval and Early Modern Europe (1000–1800)." *Journal of the European Economic Association*, Vol. 22, No. 4, pp. 1541–89.

De la Croix, David, Matthias Doepke, and Joel Mokyr. 2017. "Clans, Guilds, and Markets: Apprenticeship Institutions and Growth in the Pre-industrial Economy." *Quarterly Journal of Economics*, Vol. 133, No. 1, pp. 1–70.

De Long, J. Bradford, and Andrei Shleifer. 1993. "Princes and Merchants: European City Growth before the Industrial Revolution." *Journal of Law and Economics*, Vol. 36, No. 2, pp. 671–702.

De Moor, Tine. 2008. "The Silent Revolution: A New Perspective on the Emergence of Commons, Guilds, and Other Forms of Corporate Collective Action in Western Europe." *International Review of Social History*, Vol. 53, No. S16, pp. 179–212.

De Moor, Tine, and Van Zanden Jan Luiten. 2010. "Girl Power: The European Marriage Pattern and Labour Markets in the North Sea Region in the Late Medieval and Early Modern Period." *Economic History Review*, Vol. 63, No. 1 (February), pp. 1–33.

De Munck, Bert. 2007. *Technologies of Learning: Apprenticeship in Antwerp Guilds from the 15th Century to the End of the Ancien Régime*. Turnhout, Belgium: Brepols.

De Vries, Jan. 2011. "The Great Divergence after Ten Years: Justly Celebrated Yet Hard to Believe." *Historically Speaking*, Vol. 12, No. 4 (September), pp. 13–15.

Dear, Peter. 1995. *Discipline and Experience: The Mathematical Way in the Scientific Revolution*. Chicago: University of Chicago Press.

Debus, Allen G. 1978. *Man and Nature in the Renaissance*. Cambridge: Cambridge University Press.

Defoe, Daniel. 1738. *The Complete English Tradesman*. 4th ed. 2 vols. London: C. Rivington.

Deming, David. 2005. "Born to Trouble: Bernard Palissy and the Hydrologic Cycle." *Ground Water*, Vol. 43, No. 6, pp. 969–72.

Deng, Jianpeng. 2015. "Classifications of Litigation and Implications for Qing Judicial Practice." In *Chinese Law: Knowledge, Practice, and Transformation, 1530s to 1950s*, edited by Li Chen and Madeleine Zelin, 17–46. Leiden, Netherlands: Brill, 2015.

Deng, Kent. 2004. "Unveiling China's True Population Statistics for the Pre-modern Era with Official Census Data." *Population Review*, Vol. 43, No. 2, pp. 32–69.

———. 2016. *Mapping China's Growth and Development in the Long Run, 221 BC to 2020*. Singapore: World Scientific Publishing.

Dennison T., and S. Ogilvie. 2014. "Does the European Marriage Pattern Explain Economic Growth?" *Journal of Economic History*, Vol. 74, No. 3, pp. 651–93.

Desaguliers, John T. 1734–1744. *A Course of Experimental Philosophy*, 2 vols. London: Printed for John Senex.

Desmet, Klaus, Avner Greif, and Stephen L. Parente. 2020. "Spatial Competition, Innovations, and Institutions: The Industrial Revolution and the Great Divergence." *Journal of Economic Growth*, Vol. 25, No. 1, pp. 1–35.

Dharampal. 1971. "Indian Science and Technology in the Eighteenth Century." In *Essential Writings of Dharampal*, 83–118. New Delhi: Publications Division, Ministry of Information and Broadcasting. https://ia803102.us.archive.org/8/items/essentialwriting00dhar/essentialwriting00dhar.pdf.

Diamond, Jared. 1997. *Guns, Germs and Steel: The Fates of Human Societies*. New York: Norton.

Dincecco, Mark, James Fenske, Anil Menon, and Shivaji Mukherjee. 2019. "Pre-colonial Warfare and Long-Run Development in India." *Economic Journal*, Vol. 132, No. 643, pp. 981–1010.

Dincecco, Mark, James Fenske, and Massimiliano Onorato. 2019. "Is Africa Different? Historical Conflict and State Development." *Economic History of Developing Regions*, Vol. 34, No. 2, pp. 209–50.

Dincecco, Mark, and Massimiliano Onorato. 2018. *From Warfare to Wealth—the Military Origins of Urban Prosperity in Europe*. Cambridge: Cambridge University Press.

Dincecco, Mark, and Yuhua Wang. 2018. "Violent Conflict and Political Development over the Long Run: China vs Europe." *Annual Review of Political Science*, Vol. 21, pp. 341–58.

———. 2020. "Internal Conflict, Geopolitics, and State Development: Evidence from Imperial China." Working Paper, Social Sciences Research Network. https://ssrn.com/abstract =3209556.

Dittmar Jeremiah E., and Ralf Meisenzahl. 2020. "Public Goods Institutions, Human Capital, and Growth: Evidence from Early Germany." *Review of Economic Studies*, Vol. 87, No. 2, pp. 959–96.

Dollinger, Philippe. 1970. *The German Hansa*. Stanford, CA: Stanford University Press

Donahue, Charles Jr. 2004–2005. "Medieval and Early Modern Lex Mercatoria: An Attempt at the Probatio Diabolica." *Chicago Journal of International Law*, Vol. 5, pp. 21–38.

Drew, Katherine Fischer. 1991. *The Laws of the Salian Franks*. Philadelphia: University of Pennsylvania Press.

Du, Zhengzhen. 2007. *Cunshe chuantong yu Ming Qing shishen: Shanxi Zezhou xiangtu shehui de zhidu bianqian* [Village Worship Associations and the gentry in Ming and Qing times: Institutional transformations in the local society of Zezhou, Shanxi]. Shanghai: Shanghai cishu chubanshe.

Duan, Li. 2024. "The Development Economics of Meritocracy and Talent Allocation: Evidence from the Keju Exam in Historical China." Unpublished doctoral thesis, Faculty of Business and Economics, University of Hong Kong.

Duby, George. 1974. *The Early Growth of the European Economy*. London: Weidenfeld & Nicolson.

Dupuy, Richard Ernest, and Trevor Nevitt Dupuy. 1986. *The Encyclopedia of Military History from 3500 B.C. to the Present*. New York: Harper & Row.

Dyer, Christopher. 1994. "The English Medieval Village Community and Its Decline." *Journal of British Studies*, Vol. 33, No. 4, pp. 407–29.

Eamon, William. 1994. *Science and the Secrets of Nature*. Princeton, NJ: Princeton University Press.

Eberhard, Wolfram. 1956. "Data on the Structure of the Chinese City in the Pre-industrial Period." *Economic Development and Cultural Change*, Vol. 4, pp. 253–68.

Ebrey, Patricia B. 1986. "The Early Stages in the Development of Descent Group Organization." In *Kinship Organization in Late Imperial China 1000-1940*, edited by Patricia B. Ebrey and James L. Watson, 16–61. Taipei: SMC Publishing.

———. 1990. "Women, Marriage and the Family in Chinese History." In *Heritage of China: Contemporary Perspectives on Chinese Civilization*, edited by Paul S. Ropp, 197–223. Berkeley: University of California Press.

Ebrey, Patricia B., and James L. Watson, eds. 2018. *Kinship Organization in Late Imperial China, 1000–1940*. Los Angeles: University of California Press.

Economy, Elisabeth. 2018. *The Third Revolution—Xi Jinping and the New Chinese State*. Oxford: Oxford University Press.

Ekelund, Robert B., Jr., Robert F. Hébert, Robert D. Tollison, Gary M. Anderson, and Audrey B. Davidson. 1996. *Sacred Trust: The Medieval Church as an Economic Firm*. New York: Oxford University Press.

Ellickson, Robert C. 1991. *Order without Law: How Neighbors Settle Disputes*. Cambridge, MA: Harvard University Press.

Elliott, Mark C. 2001. *The Manchu Way*. Stanford, CA: Stanford University Press.

Elman, Benjamin A. 2000. *A Cultural History of Civil Examinations in Late Imperial China*. Berkeley: University of California Press.

———. 2002. "Jesuit *Scientia* and Natural Studies in Late Imperial China, 1600–1800." *Journal of Early Modern History*, Vol. 6, No. 3, pp. 209–32.

———. 2005. *On Their Own Terms: Science in China, 1550–1900*. Cambridge, MA: Harvard University Press.

———. 2006. *A Cultural History of Modern Science in China*. Cambridge, MA: Harvard University

———. 2013. *Civil Examinations and Meritocracy in Late Imperial China*. Cambridge, MA: Harvard University Press.

Elvin, Mark. 1973. *The Pattern of the Chinese Past*. Stanford, CA: Stanford University Press.

———. 1977. "Market Towns and Waterways: The County of Shanghai from 1480 to 1910." In *The City in Late Imperial China*, edited by G. William Skinner, 442–73. Stanford, CA: Stanford University Press.

Engelfriet, Peter M. 1998. *Euclid in China: The Genesis of the First Chinese Translation of Euclid's Elements*. Leiden, Netherlands: Brill.

Enke, Benjamin. 2019. "Kinship, Cooperation and the Evolution of Moral Systems." *Quarterly Journal of Economics*, Vol. 134, No. 2 (May), pp. 953–1019.

———. 2024. "Moral Boundaries." *Annual Review of Economics*, Vol. 16, pp. 133–57.

Epstein, Stephan R. 2008. "Craft Guilds, the Theory of the Firm, and the European Economy, 1400–1800." In *Guilds, Innovation and the European Economy, 1400–1800*, edited by Stephan R. Epstein and Maarten Prak, 52–80. Cambridge: Cambridge University Press.

———. 2013. "Transferring Technical Knowledge and Innovating in Europe, c. 1200–c. 1800." In *Technology, Skills and the Pre-modern Economy*, edited by Maarten Prak and Jan Luiten van Zanden, 25–67. Leiden, Netherlands: Brill.

Epstein, Steven A. 1991. *Wage Labor and Guilds in Medieval Europe*. Chapel Hill: University of North Carolina Press.

———. 1996. *Genoa and the Genoese, 958–1528*. Chapel Hill: University of North Carolina Press.

———. 2009. *An Economic and Social History of Later Medieval Europe, 1000–1500*. Cambridge: Cambridge University Press.

Eruchimovitch, Israel, Moti Michaeli, and Assaf Sarid. 2024. "On the Coevolution of Individualism and Institutions." *Journal of Economic Growth*, Vol. 29, pp. 391–432.

Esherick, Joseph W. 2011. *Ancestral Leaves: A Family Journey through Chinese History*. Berkeley: University of California Press.

Esherick, Joseph W., and Mary Backus Rankin, eds. 1990. *Chinese Local Elites and Patterns of Dominance*. Berkeley: University of California Press.

Fairbank, John K., and Merle Goldman. 2006. *China—A New History*, 2nd enlarged ed. Cambridge: Belknap Press of Harvard University Press.

Fan, Haichao, Chang Li, Chang Xue, and Miaojie Yu. 2021. "Clan Culture and Patterns of Industrial Specialization in China." Working Paper. China Center for Economic Research, Peking University.

Fan, Jingting, and Ben Zou. 2021. "Industrialization from Scratch: The 'Construction of Third Front' and Local Economic Development in China's Hinterland." *Journal of Development Economics*, Vol. 152, pp. 102698.

Fang, Hanming, Quanlin Gu, and Li-An Zhou. 2019. "The Gradients of Power: Evidence from the Chinese Housing Market." *Journal of Public Economics*, Vol. 176, pp. 32–52.

Faure, David. 2006. *China and Capitalism: A History of Business Enterprise in Modern China*. Hong Kong: Hong Kong University Press.

———. 2007. *Emperor and Ancestor: State and Lineage in South China*. Stanford, CA: Stanford University Press.

———. 2020. "Review of Taisu Zhang (2017)." *Journal of Chinese History*, Vol. 4, pp. 202–10.

Fei, Xiaotong. 1992. *From the Soil—the Foundations of Chinese Society*. Translated by Xiangtu Zhongguo, with an introduction and epilogue by Gary Hamilton and Wang Zheng. Berkeley: University of California Press.

Fernández-Villaverde, Jesús. 2016. "Magna Carta, the Rule of Law, and the Limits on Government." *International Review of Law and Economics*, Vol. 47, pp. 22–28.

Fernández-Villaverde, Jesús, Mark Koyama, Youhong Lin, and Tuan-Hwee Sng. 2023. "Fractured-Land and Political Fragmentation." *Quarterly Journal of Economics*, Vol. 138, No. 2, pp. 1173–231

Fernihough, Alan, and Kevin H. O'Rourke. 2021. "Coal and the European Industrial Revolution." *Economic Journal*, Vol. 131, No. 635, pp. 1135–49.

Findikli, Burhan. 2022. "Rethinking Ancient Centers of Higher Learning: Madrasa in a Comparative Historical Perspective." *British Journal of Educational Studies* Vol. 70, No. 2, pp. 129–44.

Findlen, Paula, ed. 2004. *Athanasius Kircher: The Last Man Who Knew Everything*. New York: Routledge.

Findlen, Paula. 2006. "Natural History." In *The Cambridge History of Science, Vol. 3: Early Modern Science*, edited by Katherine Park and Lorraine Daston, 435–68. Cambridge: Cambridge University Press.

Finer, S. E. 1997. *The History of Government*, Vols. 1–3. Oxford: Oxford University Press.

Fitzsimmons, Michael P. 2010. *From Artisan to Worker: Guilds, the French State, and the Organization of Labor, 1776–1821.*Cambridge: Cambridge University Press.

Folena, Gianfranco. 1971. "Gli antichi nomi di persona e la storia civile di Venezia." *Atti dell'Istituto Veneto di Scienze, Lettere ed Arti*, Vol. 129, pp. 445–84.

Frank, Andre Gunder. 1998. *ReORIENT: Global Economy in the Asian Age*. Berkeley: University of California Press.

Freedman, Maurice. 1958. *Lineage Organization in Southeastern China*. London: Athlone Press.

———. 1966. *Chinese Lineage and Society: Fukien and Kwangtung*. London: Athlone Press.

Friedel, Robert. 2007. *A Culture of Improvement: Technology and the Western Millennium*. Cambridge, MA: MIT Press,

Friedmann, J. 2007. "Reflections on Place and Place-Making in the Cities of China." *International Journal of Urban and Regional Research*, Vol. 31, No. 2, pp. 257–79.

Fu, Feng, Martin A. Nowak, Nicholas A. Christakis, and James H. Fowler. 2012. "The Evolution of Homophily." *Scientific Reports*, Vol. 2, No. 845.

Fu, Zhengyuan. 1993. *Autocratic Tradition and Chinese Politics*. Cambridge: Cambridge University Press.

Fukuyama, Francis. 2011. *The Origins of Political Order*. London: Profile Books.

Gascoigne, John. 2000. "Universities." In *Encyclopedia of the Scientific Revolution*, edited by Wilbur Applebaum, 656–59. New York: Routledge.

Gelderblom, Oscar. 2013. *Cities of Commerce: The Institutional Foundations of International Trade in the Low Countries, 1250–1650*. Princeton, NJ: Princeton University Press.

Gelderblom, Oscar, and Regina Grafe. 2010. "The Rise and Fall of the Merchant Guilds: Rethinking the Comparative Study of Commercial Institutions in Premodern Europe." *Journal of Interdisciplinary History*, Vol. 40, No. 4, pp. 477–511.

Gellhorn, Walter. 1987. "China's Quest for Legal Modernity." *Journal of Chinese Law*, Vol. 1, No. 1, pp. 1–22.

Gennaioli, Nicola, and Joachim Voth. 2015. "State Capacity and Military Conflict." *Review of Economic Studies*, Vol. 82, pp. 1409–48.

Gernet, Jacques. 1982. *A History of Chinese Civilization*. Cambridge: Cambridge University Press.

———. 1995. *Buddhism in Chinese Society: An Economic History from the Fifth to the Tenth Centuries*. Translated by Franciscus Verellen. New York: Columbia University Press.

Gibbon, Edward. 1789. *The History of the Decline and Fall of the Roman Empire*. 3 vols. London: Printed for A. Strahan and T. Cadell.

Giuliano, Paola, and Nathan Nunn. 2013. "The Transmission of Democracy: From the Village to the Nation State." *American Economic Review: Papers and Proceedings*, Vol. 103, No. 3, pp. 86–92.

Glaser, Bonnie, and Jeremy Mark. 2021. "Taiwan and China Are Locked in Economic Co-dependence." *Foreign Policy*. https://foreignpolicy.com/2021/04/14/taiwan-china-econonomic-codependence/.

Golas, Peter. 1977. "Early Ching Guilds." In *The City in Late Imperial China*, edited by G. William Skinner, 555–80. Stanford, CA: Stanford University Press.

Gold, Thomas B. 1985. "After Comradeship: Personal Relations in China since the Cultural Revolution." *China Quarterly*, Vol. 104, pp. 657–75.

Goldstone, Jack A. 2009. *Why Europe? The Rise of the West in World History, 1500–1850*. Boston: McGraw Hill.

Golley, Jane, Rod Tyers, and Yixiao Zhou. 2016. "Contradiction in Chinese Fertility and Savings: Long-Run Domestic and Global Implications." In *Structural Change in China: Implications for Australia and the World*, edited by Iris Day and John Simon, 243–80. Sydney: Reserve Bank of Australia.

Gong, Ting. 2002. "Dangerous Collusion: Corruption as a Collective Venture in Contemporary China." *Communist and Post-Communist Studies*, Vol. 35, No. 1, pp. 85–103.

González de Lara, Yadira. 2008. "The Secret of Venetian Success: A Public-Order, Reputation-Based Institution." *European Review of Economic History*, Vol. 3, pp. 247–85.

Goodman, Bryna. 1995. *Native Place, City and Nation—Regional Networks and Identities in Shanghai, 1853–1937*. Los Angeles: University of California Press.

Goodrich, Luther Carrington. 1935. *The Literary Inquisition of Ch'ien Lung (Qianlong)*.Baltimore: Waverly Press.

Goody, Esther. 1989. "Learning, Apprenticeship, and the Division of Labor." In *Apprenticeship: from Theory to Method and Back Again*, edited by Michael W. Coy, 233–56, Albany: SUNY Press.

Goody, J. 1983. *The Development of the Family and Marriage in Europe*. Cambridge: Cambridge University Press.

———. 1996a. "Comparing Family Systems in Europe and Asia: Are There Different Sets of Rules?" *Population and Development Review*, Vol. 22, No. 1, pp. 1–20.

———. 1996b. *The East in the West*. Cambridge: Cambridge University Press.

Gorodnichenko, Yuriy, and Gerard Roland. 2017. "Culture, Institutions and the Wealth of Nations." *Review of Economics and Statistics*, Vol. 99, No. 3 (July), pp. 402–16.

Gosh, Suresh Chandra. 1978. "The Utilitarianism of Dalhousie and the Material Improvement of India." *Modern Asian Studies*, Vol. 12, No. 1, pp. 97–110.

Gottlieb, Beatrice. 1993. *The Family in the Western World*. Oxford: Oxford University Press.

Gowlland, Geoffrey. 2012. "Learning Craft Skills in China: Apprenticeship and Social Capital in an Artisan Community of Practice." *Anthropology & Education Quarterly*, Vol. 43, pp. 358–71.

Goyal, Sanjeev. 2022. *Networks—an Economic Approach*. Cambridge: Cambridge University Press.

Grafe, Regina, and Maarten Prak. 2020. "Families, Firms and Polities: Premodern Economic Growth and the Great Divergence." In *Global Economic History*, edited by Giorgio Riello and Tirthankar Roy, 83–101. London: Bloomsbury Academic Press.

Grafton, Anthony. 2009. "A Sketch Map of a Lost Continent: The Republic of Letters." In *Worlds Made by Words: Scholarship and Community in the Modern West*(Collected essays), pp. 9–34. Cambridge, MA: Harvard University Press.

Granovetter, Mark S. 1973. "The Strength of Weak Ties." *American Journal of Sociology*, Vol. 78, No. 6, pp. 1360–80.

———. 1983. "The Strength of Weak Ties: A Network Theory Revisited." *Sociological Theory*, Vol. 1, pp. 201–33.

Grant, Edward. 1996. *The Foundations of Modern Science in the Middle Ages*. Cambridge: Cambridge University Press.

Great Britain. 1806. "Select Committee on the State of the Woollen Manufacture of England." *British Parliamentary Papers*, Vol. 3, No. 268. Edgware, UK: Vallentine Mitchell.

Great Britain. 1824. "First Report from Select Committee on Artizans and Machinery." In *British Parliamentary Papers*, Vol. 5, No 51. Edgware, UK: Vallentine Mitchell.

Greif, Avner. 1994. "Cultural Beliefs and the Organization of Society: A Historical and Theoretical Reflection on Collectivist and Individualist Societies." *Journal of Political Economy*, Vol. 102, No. 5, pp. 912–50.

———. 1998. "Self-Enforcing Political Systems and Economic Growth: Late Medieval Genoa." In *Analytic Narratives*, edited by Robert H. Bates, Avner Greif, Margaret Levi, Jean-Laurent Rosenthal, and Barry R. Weingast, 23–63. Princeton, NJ: Princeton University Press.

———. 2005. "Commitment, Coercion, and Markets: The Nature and Dynamics of Institutions Supporting Exchange." In *Handbook for the New Institutional Economics*, edited by Claude Menard and Mary M. Shirley, 727–88. Norwell, MA: Kluwer Academic Publishers.

———. 2006a. "The Birth of Impersonal Exchange: The Community Responsibility System and Impartial Justice." *Journal of Economic Perspectives*, Vol. 20, No. 2 (Spring), pp. 221–36.

———. 2006b. "Family Structure, Institutions, and Growth: The Origins and Implications of Western Corporations." *American Economic Review*, Vol. 96, No. 2, pp. 308–12.

———. 2006c. *Institutions and the Path to Economic Modernity: Lessons from Medieval Trade.* Cambridge: Cambridge University Press.

Greif, Avner, and Murat Iyigun. 2013. "What Did the Old Poor Law Really Accomplish? A Redux." IZA Institute of Labor Economics Working Paper No. 7398.IZA Institute of Labor Economics, Bonn, Germany.

Greif, Avner, Murat Iyigun, and Diego Sasson. 2012. "Social Organizations, Risk-Sharing Institutions, and Economic Development." In *Institutions and Comparative Economic Development*, edited by Masahiko Aoki, Timur Kuran, and Gérard Roland, 48–63.London: Palgrave Macmillan.

———. 2013. "Social Institutions and Economic Growth: Why England Rather than China Became the First Modern Economy." Stanford University Center for International Development Working Paper No. 465.

Greif, Avner, Paul Milgrom, and Barry R. Weingast. 1994. "Coordination, Commitment, and Enforcement: The Case of the Merchant Guild." *Journal of Political Economy*, Vol. 102, No. 4, pp. 745–76.

Greif, Avner, and Jared Rubin. 2023. "Political Legitimacy in Historical Political Economy." In *The Oxford Handbook of Historical Political Economy*, edited by Jeffery A. Jenkins and Jared Rubin, 293–310. New York: Oxford University Press.

Greif, Avner, and Guido Tabellini. 2010. "Cultural and Institutional Bifurcation: China and Europe Compared." *American Economic Review*, Vol. 100, pp. 135–40.

———. 2017. "The Clan and the Corporation Sustaining Cooperation in China and Europe." *Journal of Comparative Economics*, Vol. 45, pp. 1–35.

Grzymała-Busse, Anna. 2023. *Sacred Foundations: The Religious and Medieval Roots of the European State*, Princeton, NJ: Princeton University Press.

———. 2024. "Tilly Goes to Church: The Religious and Medieval Roots of European State Fragmentation." *American Political Science Review*, Vol. 118, No. 1, pp. 88–107.

Guerriero, Carmine. 2016. "Endogenous Legal Traditions and Economic Outcomes." *Journal of Comparative Economics*, Vol. 44, pp. 416–33.

Guiso, Luigi, Paola Sapienza, and Luigi Zingales. 2016. "Long-Term Persistence." *Journal of the European Economic Association*, Vol. 14, No. 6, pp. 1401–36.

Gune, Vithal Trimbak. 1953. *The Judicial System of the Marathas*. Poona (Pune), India: Deccan College, Post Graduate and Research Institute.

Guo, Qiang. 2020. *Essays in Political Economy of State Institutions and Fiscal Capacity in Historical China*. Unpublished doctoral dissertation, New York University.

Hadenius, Axel. 2001. *Institutions and Democratic Citizenship*. Oxford: Oxford University Press.

Hajnal, John. 1965. "European Marriage Patterns in Perspective." In *Demography*, edited by David V. Glass, 101–43. London: Edward Arnold.

———. 1982. "Two Kinds of Preindustrial Household Formation System." *Population and Development Review*, Vol. 8, No. 3, pp. 449–94.

Hall, A. Rupert. 1967. "Early Modern Technology to 1600." In *Technology in Western Civilization*, Vol. 1, edited by Melvin Kranzberg and Carroll W. Pursell Jr., 79–106.New York: Oxford University Press.

Hamilton, Gary G. 1996. "Overseas Chinese Capitalism." In *Confucian Traditions in East Asian Modernity: Moral Education and Economic Culture in Japan and the Four Mini-Dragons*, edited by Tu Weiming, 328–43.Cambridge, MA: Harvard University Press.

———. 2006. *Commerce and Capitalism in Chinese Societies*. Abington, UK: Routledge.

Hannam, James. 2011. *The Genesis of Science: How the Christian Middle Ages Launched the Scientific Revolution*. Washington, DC: Regnery Publishing.

Hao, Yu, Kevin Zhengcheng Liu, Xi Weng, and Li-An Zhou. 2022. "The Making of Bad Gentry: The Abolition of Keju, Local Governance and Anti-Elite Protests, 1902–1911." *Journal of Economic History*, Vol. 82, No. 3, pp. 625–61.

Harkness, Deborah. 2007. *The Jewel House: Elizabethan London and the Scientific Revolution*. New Haven, CT: Yale University Press.

Harper, Kyle. 2021. *Plagues upon the Earth*. Princeton, NJ: Princeton University Press.

Harris, John R. 1988. *The British Iron Industry, 1700–1850*. Houndsmill, UK: MacMillan Education Ltd.

———. 1992a. *Essays in Industry in the Eighteenth Century: England and France*. London: Variorum.

———. 1992b. "Skills, Coal and British Industry in the Eighteenth Century." In *Essays in Industry and Technology in the Eighteenth Century*, edited by John R. Harris, 67–82.Aldershot, UK: Ashgate Variorum.

———. 1998. *Industrial Espionage and Technology Transfer: Britain and France in the Eighteenth Century*. Aldershot, UK: Ashgate.

———. 2006. "Isaac Wilkinson." *Oxford Dictionary of National Biography*.

Harris, Ron. 2020. *Going the Distance: Eurasian Trade and the Rise of the Business Corporation*. Princeton, NJ: Princeton University Press.

Hart, Oliver. 2017. "Incomplete Contracts and Control." *American Economic Review*, Vol. 107, No. 7, pp. 1731–52.

Hartwell, Robert M. 1982. "Demographic, Political, and Social Transformations of China, 750–1550." *Harvard Journal of Asiatic Studies*, Vol. 42, No. 2, pp. 365–442.

Haskins, Charles Homer. 1923. *The Rise of Universities*. New York: Henry Holt.

Hawk, Barry E. 2024. *Family, Partnerships and Companies: From Assur to Amsterdam*. Huntington, NY: Juris Publishing.

Hawkins, Cameron. 2016. *Roman Artisans and the Urban Economy*. Cambridge: Cambridge University Press.

Hayek, Friedrich. 1973. *Law, Legislation and Liberty, Vol. I, Rules and Order*. London: Routledge & Kegan Paul.

He, Alex. 2021. "What do China's High Patent Numbers Really Mean?" Working paper. Center for International Governance Innovation, Waterloo, Canada.

Headrick, Daniel R. 2010. *Power over Peoples: Technology, Environments, and Western Imperialism, 1400 to the Present*. Princeton, NJ: Princeton University Press.

Heblich, Stephan, Stephen Redding, and Hans-Joachim Voth. 2023. "Slavery and the Industrial Revolution." NBER, working paper 30451.

Heijdra, Martin. 1998. "The Socio-economic Development of Rural China during the Ming." In *The Cambridge History of China*, Vol. 8, Part 2, edited by Denis Twitchett and John K. Fairbank, 417–581. Cambridge: Cambridge University Press.

Heilmann, Sebastian. 2008. "From Local Experiments to National Policy: The Origins of China's Distinctive Policy Process." *China Journal*, No. 59 (January), pp 1–30.

Henrich, Joseph. 2020. *The WEIRDest People in the World: How the West Became Psychologically Peculiar and Particularly Prosperous*. New York: Farrar, Straus and Giroux.

Herb, Michael. 2003. "Taxation and Representation." *Studies in Comparative International Development*, Vol. 38, No. 3, pp. 3–31.

Herlihy, David. 1985. *Medieval Households*. Cambridge, MA: Harvard University Press.

Hersh, Jonathan, and Hans-Joachim Voth. 2022. "Sweet Diversity: Colonial Goods and the Welfare Gains from Global Trade after 1492." *Explorations in Economic History*, Vol. 86, p. 101468.

Herzog, Tamar. 2018. *A Short History of European Law*. Cambridge, MA: Harvard University Press.

Hicks, J.R. 1969. *A Theory of Economic History*. New York: Oxford University Press.

Hintze, Otto. 1975. "The Preconditions of Representative Government in the Context of World History." In *The Historical Essays of Otto Hintze*, edited by Felix Gilbert, 302–56. Oxford: Oxford University Press.

Hirschman, Albert O. 1977. *The Passions and the Interests: Political Arguments for Capitalism before Its Triumph*. Princeton, NJ: Princeton University Press.

Ho, Ping-ti. 1964. *The Ladder of Success in Imperial China: Aspects of Social Mobility, 1368–1911*. New York: John Wiley and Sons.

Hoffman, Philip T. 2015. *Why Did Europe Conquer the World?* Princeton, NJ: Princeton University Press.

Hoffman, Philip, and Katherine Norberg, eds. 1994. *Fiscal Crises and Representative Government*. Stanford, CA: Stanford University Press.

Holcombe, Charles. 1994. *In the Shadow of the Han: Literati Thought and Society at the Beginning of the Southern Dynasties*. Honolulu: University of Hawaii Press.

Hsiao, Kung-Chuan. (Gongquan Xiao). 1967. *Rural China: Imperial Control in the Nineteenth Century*. Seattle: University of Washington Press.

Hu, Anning, and Felicia F. Tian. 2018. "Still under the Ancestors' Shadow? Ancestor Worship and Family Formation in Contemporary China." *Demographic Research*, Vol. 38, pp. 1–36.

Hu, Hsien Chin. 1948. *The Common Descent Group in China and Its Functions*. New York: Viking Fund.

Hu, Krystal. 2019. "Inside Huawei's $1.5 Billion 'European Town' Campus in China." Yahoo Finance.https://finance.yahoo.com/news/inside-huawei-european-town-campus-045907581.html.

Huang, Philip C. 1985. *The Peasant Economy and Social Change in North China*. Stanford, CA: Stanford University Press.

———. 1990. *The Peasant Family and Rural Development in the Yangzi Delta, 1350–1988*. Stanford: Stanford University Press.

———. 2010. *Chinese Civil Justice, Past and Present*. Lanham, MD: Rowman & Littlefield Publishers.

———. 2016. "The Past and Present of the Chinese Civil and Criminal Justice Systems: The Sinitic Legal Tradition from a Global Perspective." *Modern China*, Vol. 42, No. 3, pp. 227–72.

———. 2019. "The Sinitic Justice System Past and Present in a Global Perspective." In *The Uses of Justice in Global Perspective, 1600–1900*, edited by Griet Vermeersch, Manon van der Heijden, and Jaco Zuijderduijn, 23–41. Abington, UK: Routledge.

Huang, Ray. 1974. *Taxation and Governmental Finance in Sixteenth-Century Ming China*. Cambridge: Cambridge University Press.

———. 1981. *1587: A Year of No Significance*. New Haven, CT: Yale University Press.

———. 1998. "The Ming Fiscal Administration." In *The Cambridge History of China*, edited by D. Twitchett and F. Mote, 106–71. Cambridge: Cambridge University Press.

Huang, Yasheng. 2012. "How Did China Take Off?" *Journal of Economic Perspectives*, Vol. 26, No. 4, pp. 147–170.

———. 2023. *The Rise and Fall of the East*. New Haven, CT: Yale University Press.

Huang, Yasheng, and Clair Yang. 2022. "A Longevity Mechanism of Chinese Absolutism." *Journal of Politics*, Vol. 84, No. 2, pp. 1165–75.

Huang, Yasheng, Enying Zheng, Wei Hong, Danzi Liao, and Meicen Sun. 2024. "The Needham Question: The Rise and Fall of Chinese Technology in History." Unpublished manuscript, Massachusetts Institute of Technology, Cambridge, MA.

Hucker, C. 1975. *China's Imperial Past*. Stanford, CA: Stanford University Press.

———. 1998. "Ming Government." In *The Cambridge History of China*, Vol. 8, Part 2, edited by Denis Twitchett and John K. Fairbank, 9–105. Cambridge: Cambridge University Press.

Huff, Toby. 2011. *Intellectual Curiosity and the Scientific Revolution*. Cambridge: Cambridge University Press.

Hughes, Diane Owen. 1978. "Urban Growth and Family Structure in Medieval Genoa." In *Towns in Societies*, edited by Philip Abrams and E. A. Wrigley, 105–30. Cambridge: Cambridge University Press. Previously published in *Past and Present* (1975), Vol. 66, No. 1, pp. 3–28.

Hume, David. [1742] 1985. "Of the Rise and Progress of the Arts and Sciences." In *Essays: Moral, Political and Literary*, edited by Eugene F. Miller, 111–37. Indianapolis: Liberty Fund.

Humphries, Jane. 2003. "English Apprenticeships: A Neglected Factor in the First Industrial Revolution." In *The Economic Future in Historical Perspective*, edited by Paul A. David and Mark Thomas, 73–102. Oxford: Oxford University Press.

———. 2010. *Childhood and Child Labour in the British Industrial Revolution*. Cambridge: Cambridge University Press.

Hung, Ho-fung. 2009. "Cultural Strategies and the Political Economy of Protest in Mid-Qing China, 1740–1839." *Social Science History*, Vol. 33, No. 1 (Spring), pp. 75–115.

———. 2011. *Protest with Chinese Characteristics: Demonstrations, Riots and Petitions in the Mid Qing Dynasty*. New York: Columbia University Press.

———. 2016. *The China Boom*. New York: Columbia University Press.

Hunter, Michael. 2009. *Boyle: Between God and Science*. New Haven, CT: Yale University Press.

Hutton, Eric. 2003. "Review of Lloyd, G.E.R., *The Ambitions of Curiosity: Understanding the World in Ancient Greece and China*," *Notre Dame Philosophical Reviews*.https://ndpr.nd.edu /reviews/the-ambitions-of-curiosity-understanding-the-world-in-ancient-greece-and -china/.

Ikegami, Eiko. 2005. *Bonds of Civility: Aesthetic Networks and the Political Origins of Japanese Culture*. Cambridge: Cambridge University Press.

Inikori, Joseph. 2002. *Africans and the Industrial Revolution in England: A Study in International Trade and Economic Development*. Cambridge: Cambridge University Press.

International Monetary Fund (IMF). 2021.*World Economic Outlook*, October. Washington, DC.

Islam, Md. Nazrul. 2016. "Integrating Chinese Medicine in Public Health: Contemporary Trend and Challenges." In *Public Health Challenges in Contemporary China: An Interdisciplinary Perspective*, edited by Md. Nazrul Islam, 55–72. Berlin: Springer.

Iyer, Lakshmi. 2010. "Direct Versus Indirect Colonial Rule in India: Long-Term Consequences." *Review of Economics and Statistics*, Vol. 92, No. 4, pp. 693–713.

Jackson, Matthew. 2008. *Social and Economic Networks*. Princeton, NJ: Princeton University Press.

Jacob, Margaret C. 1988. *The Cultural Meaning of the Scientific Revolution*. New York: Alfred A. Knopf.

Jacob, Margaret C., and Larry Stewart. 2004. *Practical Matter: Newton's Science in the Service of Industry and Empire, 1687–1851*.Cambridge, MA: Harvard University Press.

Jami, Catherine. 2012. *The Emperor's New Mathematics: Western Learning and Imperial Authority during the Kangxi Reign (1662–1722)*. Oxford: Oxford University Press.

Jardine, Lisa. 2008. *Going Dutch: How England Plundered Holland's Glory*. New York: HarperCollins.

Jha, Saumitra. 2015. "Financial Asset Holdings and Political Attitudes: Evidence from Revolutionary England." *Quarterly Journal of Economics*, Vol. 130, No. 3, pp. 1485–545.

Jia, Ruixue. 2014, "Weather Shocks, Sweet Potatoes and Peasant Revolts in Historical China." *The Economic Journal*, Vol. 124, pp. 92–118.

Jia, Ruixue, Masayuki Kudamatsu, and David Seim. 2015. "Political Selection in China: Complementary Roles of Connections and Performance." *Journal of the European Economic Association*, Vol. 13, No. 4, pp. 631–68.

Jia, Ruixue, Xiaohuan Lan, and Gerard Padró i Miquel. 2021. "Doing Business in China: Parental Background and Government Intervention Determine Who Owns Business." *Journal of Development Economics*, Vol. 151, p. 102670.

Jia, Ruixue, Gerard Roland, and Yang Xie. 2020. "A Theory of Power Structure and Political Stability: China vs Europe Revisited." Working Paper, University of California, Berkeley.

Jin, Dengjian. 2016. *The Great Knowledge Transcendence: The Rise of Western Science and Technology Reframed*. Houndmills, UK: Palgrave Macmillan.

Jing, Junjian. 1994. "Legislation Related to the Civil Economy in the Qing Dynasty." In *Civil Law in Qing and Republican China*, edited by Kathryn Bernhardt and Philip C. C. Huang, 42–84. Stanford, CA: Stanford University Press.

Johnson, David G. 1977. *The Medieval Chinese Oligarchy*. Boulder, CO: Westview Press.

Johnson, Noel D., and Mark Koyama. 2014. "Tax Farming and the Origins of State Capacity in England and France." *Explorations in Economic History*, Vol. 51, pp. 1–20.

Johnson, Wallace. 1995. "Status and Liability for Punishment in the T'ang Code." *Chicago-Kent Law Review*, Vol. 71, pp. 217–29.

Johnston, R. Fleming. 1913. *Buddhist China*. New York: E. P. Dutton.

Jones, Eric L. 1981. *The European Miracle*. Cambridge: Cambridge University Press.

————. 2003. *The European Miracle: Environments, Economies and Geopolitics in the History of Europe and Asia*. Cambridge: Cambridge University Press.

————. 2018. *Landed Estates and Rural Inequality in English History*. Cham, Switzerland: Palgrave Macmillan.

Jones, Philip. 1997. *The Italian City-State: From Commune to Signoria*. Oxford: Clarendon Press.

Kadens, Emily. 2015. "The Medieval Law Merchant: The Tyranny of a Construct." *Journal of Legal Analysis*, Vol. 7, No. 2, pp. 251–89.

Kander, Astrid, Paolo Malanima, and Paul Warde. 2013. *Power to the People: Energy in Europe over the Last Five Centuries*. Princeton, NJ: Princeton University Press.

Kaplan, Steven L. 1996. *The Bakers of Paris and the Bread Question*. Durham, NC: Duke University Press.

Karaka, Dosabhai Framji. 1884. *History of the Parsis: Including Their Manners, Customs, Religion and Current Position*. London: Macmillan.

Karayalçin, Cem. 2008. "Divided We Stand, United We Fall: The Hume-North-Jones Mechanism for the Rise of Europe." *International Economic Review*, Vol. 49, No. 3, pp. 973–99.

Keightley, David N. 1990. "Early Civilization in China: Reflections on How It Became Chinese." In *Heritage of China: Contemporary Perspectives on Chinese Civilization*, edited by Paul S. Ropp, 15–54. Berkeley: University of California Press.

Kelliher, Daniel. 1997. "The Chinese Debate over Village Self-Government." *China Journal*, Vol. 37, pp. 63–86.

Kelly, John M. 1992. *A Short History of the Western Legal Theory*. Oxford: Clarendon Press.

Kelly, Morgan, Joel Mokyr, and Cormac Ó Gráda. 2014. "Precocious Albion: A New Interpretation of the British Industrial Revolution." *Annual Review of Economics*, Vol. 6, pp. 363–91.

————. 2023. "The Mechanics of the Industrial Revolution." *Journal of Political Economy*, Vol. 133, No. 1, pp. 59–94.

Kelly, Morgan, and Cormac Ó Gráda. 2016. "Adam Smith, Watch Prices, and the Industrial Revolution." *Quarterly Journal of Economics*, Vol. 131, No. 4, pp. 1727–52.

————. 2018. "From Scientific Revolution to Industrial Revolution: The Role of Mathematical Practitioners." Unpublished manuscript, University College of Dublin.

————. 2022. "Connecting the Scientific and Industrial Revolutions: The Role of Practical Mathematics." *Journal of Economic History*, Vol. 82, No. 3, pp. 841–73.

Kern, Fritz. 1939. *Kingship and Law in the Middle Ages*. London: S. B. Chrimes.

Kessler, A. 2007. *A Revolution in Commerce: The Parisian Merchant Court and the Rise of Commercial Society in Eighteenth-Century France*. New Haven, CT: Yale University Press.

King, Steven. 2000. *Poverty and Welfare in England 1700–1850: A Regional Perspective*. Manchester, UK: Manchester University Press.

Kiser, Edgar, and Xiaoxi Tong. 1992. "Determinants of the Amount and Type of Corruption in State Fiscal Bureaucracies: An Analysis of late Imperial China." *Comparative Political Studies*, Vol. 25, No. 3, pp. 300–331.

Kloppenborg, John D., and Stephen G. Wilson. 1996. *Voluntary Associations in the Graeco-Roman World*. London: Routledge.

Ko, Chiu Yu, Mark Koyama, and Tuan-Hwee Sng. 2018. "Unified China and Divided Europe," *International Economic Review*, Vol. 59, No. 1 (February), pp. 285–327.

Koenig, Michael, Zheng Michael Song, Kjetil Storesletten, and Fabrizio Zilibotti. 2022. "From Imitation to Innovation: Where Is All that Chinese R&D Going?" *Econometrica*, Vol. 90, No. 4, pp. 1615–54.

Korotayev, Andrey V. 2003. "Unilineal Descent Organization and Deep Christianization: A Cross-Cultural Analysis." *Cross-Cultural Research*, Vol. 37, No. 1, pp. 133–57.

Koss, Daniel. 2018. *Where the Party Rules—the Rank and File of China's Communist State*. Cambridge: Cambridge University Press.

Kreps, David M. 1997. "Intrinsic Motivation and Extrinsic Incentives." *American Economic Review*, Vol. 87, No. 2, pp. 359–64.

Ku, Hok Bun. 2003. *Moral Politics in a South Chinese Village: Responsibility, Reciprocity, and Resistance*. Lanham, MD: Rowman & Littlefield.

Kuhn, Dieter. 2009. *The Age of Confucian Rule. The Song Transformation of China*. Cambridge, MA: Harvard University Press.

Kulp, Daniel Harrison. 1925. *Country Life in South China: The Sociology of Familism, Vol. 1*. New York: Bureau of Publications, Teachers College, Columbia University.

Kumar, Deepak. 2003. "India." In *The Cambridge History of Science: Vol. 4: Eighteenth Century Science*, edited by Roy Porter, 669–87. Cambridge: Cambridge University Press.

Kumar, Joginder. 1974. "Family Structure in the Hindu Society of Rural India." In *The Family in India: A Regional View*, edited by George Kurian, 43–74. The Hague: Mouton.

Kumar, Krishna B., and John G. Matsusaka. 2009. "From Families to Formal Contracts: An Approach to Development." *Journal of Development Economics*, Vol. 90, pp. 106–19.

Kung, James, Yongshun Cai, and Xiulin Sun. 2009. "Rural Cadres and Governance in China: Incentive, Institution and Accountability." *China Journal*, Vol. 62, pp. 61–77.

Kung, James Kai-Sing. 2022. "The Economic Impact of the West." In Debin Ma and Richard Von Glahn, eds., *The Cambridge Economic History of China, Vol. II*, edited by Debin Ma and Richard Von Glahn, 354–413. Cambridge, Cambridge University Press.

Kung, James Kai-Sing, and Wenbing Wu. 2025. "The Rise of the Chinese Clan." Working paper, University of Hong Kong. https://ssrn.com/abstract=5100471 or http://dx.doi.org/10.2139/ssrn.5100471.

Kuran, Timur. 1988. "The Tenacious Past: Theories of Personal and Collective Conservatism." *Journal of Economic Behavior and Organization*, Vol. 10, pp. 143–71.

———. 2005. "The Absence of the Corporation in Islamic Law: Origins and Persistence." *American Journal of Comparative Law*, Vol. 53, pp. 785–834.

Kuroda, Akinobu. 2013. "Anonymous Currencies or Named Debts? Comparison of Currencies, Local Credits and Units of Account between China, Japan and England in the Pre-Industrial Era." *Socio-Economic Review*, Vol. 11, No. 1 (January), pp. 57–80.

Lakos, William. 2010. *Chinese Ancestor Worship: A Practice and Ritual Oriented Approach to Understanding Chinese Culture*. Newcastle upon Tyne, UK: Cambridge Scholars Publishing.

Landa, Janet T. 1995. *Trust, Ethnicity, and Identity: Beyond the New Institutional Economics of Ethnic Trading Networks, Contract Law, and Gift-exchange*. Ann Arbor: University of Michigan Press.

———. 2016. *Economic Success of Chinese Merchants in Southeast Asia: Identity, Ethnic Cooperation and Conflict*. Heidelberg, Germany: Springer.

Landes, David S. 1983. *Revolution in Time: Clocks and the Making of the Modern World*. Cambridge, MA: Harvard University Press.

————. 1998. *The Wealth and Poverty of Nations*. New York: W. W. Norton.

Lang, Olga. 1946. *Chinese Family and Society*. New Haven, CT: Yale University Press.

Langford, Paul. 1989. *A Polite and Commercial People: England 1727–1783*.Oxford: Oxford University Press.

————. 2002. "The Uses of Eighteenth-Century Politeness." *Transactions of the Royal Historical Society*, Vol. 12, pp. 311–31.

Lapidus, Ira M. 2002. *A History of Islamic Societies*, 2nd ed. Cambridge: Cambridge University Press.

La Porta, R., F. Lopez-de Silanes, and Andrei Shleifer, 2008. "The Economic Consequences of Legal Origins." *Journal of Economic Literature*, Vol. 46, pp. 285–332.

Lardy, Nicholas R. 2014. *Markets over Mao—The Rise of Private Business in China*. Washington, DC: Peterson Institute of International Economics.

————. 2019. *The State Strikes Back—The End of Economic Reform in China?* Washington, DC: Peterson Institute of International Economics.

Lary, Diana. 2012. *Chinese Migrations: The Movement of People, Goods, and Ideas over Four Millennia*. London: Rowman & Littlefield.

Laslett, Peter. 1969. "Size and Structure of the Household in England over Three Centuries." *Population Studies*, Vol. 23, No. 2, pp. 199–223.

————. 1977. "Characteristics of the Western Family Considered over Time." In *Family Life and Illicit Love in Earlier Generations: Essays in Historical Sociology*, edited by Peter Laslett, 12–49. Cambridge: Cambridge University Press.

Lau, Nap-yin. 2017. "Civil Law and Jurisprudence in Imperial China." In*Oxford Research Encyclopedia of Asian History*. New York: Oxford University Press. https://doi.org/10.1093/acrefore/9780190277727.013.203.

Lavely, W., J. Lee, and W. Feng. 1990. "Chinese Demography: The State of the Field." *Journal of Asian Studies*, Vol. 49, No. 4, pp. 807–34.

Lavely, William, and R. Bin Wong. 1992. "Family Division and Mobility in North China." *Comparative Studies in Society and History*, Vol. 34, No. 3, pp. 439–63.

————. 1998. "Revising the Malthusian Narrative: The Comparative Study of Population Dynamics in Late Imperial China." *Journal of Asian Studies*, Vol. 57, No. 3, pp. 714–48.

Law, Robin. 1986. "Dahomey and the Slave Trade: Reflections on the Historiography of the Rise of Dahomey." *Journal of African History*, Vol. 27, No. 2, pp. 237–67.

Lecoq, Anne-Marie, ed. 2001.*La Querelle des Anciens et des Modernes*. Paris: Éditions Gallimard.

Lee, James Z. 1999. *One Quarter of Humanity: Malthusian Mythology and Chinese Realities, 1700–2000*.Cambridge, MA: Harvard University Press.

Lee, James Z., and Cameron D. Campbell. 2014. *China Multi-generational Panel Dataset, Liaoning (CMGPD-LN), 1749–1909*. ICPSR27063-v10. Ann Arbor, MI: Inter-university Consortium for Political and Social Research, October 7. http://doi.org/10.3886/ICPSR27063.v10.

Lee, James Z., Cameron D. Campbell, and Wang Feng. 2002. "Positive Check or Chinese Checks?" *Journal of Asian Studies*, Vol. 61, No. 2, pp. 591–607.

Lesaffer, Randall. 2009. *European Legal History: A Cultural and Political Perspective*. Cambridge: Cambridge University Press.

Leunig, Tim, Chris Minns, and Patrick Wallis. 2011. "Networks in the Premodern Economy: The Market for London Apprenticeships, 1600–1749." *Journal of Economic History*, Vol. 71, No. 2 (June), pp. 413–41.

Levere, Trevor, and Gerald L'E Turner. 2002. *Discussing Chemistry and Steam: The Minutes of a Coffee House Philosophical Society 1780–1787*. Oxford: Oxford University Press.

Levi, Margaret. 1988. *Of Rule and Revenue*. Berkeley: University of California Press.

Levin, Ari Daniel. 2009. "The Reigns of Hui-tsung (1100–1126) and Ch'in-tsung (1126–1127) and the Fall of the Northern Song." In *The Cambridge History of China, Vol. 5, Part One: The Sung Dynasty and Its Precursors, 907–1279*, edited by Denis Twitchett and Paul Jakob Smith, 596–600. Cambridge: Cambridge University Press.

Levin, Daniel Z., and Rob Cross. 2004. "The Strength of Weak Ties You Can Trust: The Mediating Role of Trust in Effective Knowledge Transfer." *Management Science*, Vol. 50, No. 1, pp. 1477–90.

Levinson, Joseph R. 1968. *Confucian China and Its Modern Fate*. Berkeley: University of California Press.

Lewis, Bernard. 1993. *Islam and the West*. New York: Oxford University Press.

Lewis, Mark Edward. 2000. "The City-State in Spring-and-Autumn China." In *A Comparative Study of the Thirty City-State Cultures*, edited by Mogens Herman Hansen, 359–73. Copenhagen: Royal Danish Academy of Sciences and Letters.

———. 2007. *The Early Chinese Empires*. Cambridge, MA: Harvard University Press.

———. 2009. *China's Cosmopolitan Empire: The Tang Dynasty*. Cambridge, MA: Harvard University Press.

Li, G. 2009. "The PRC Contract Law and Its Unique Notion of Subrogation." *Journal of International Commercial Law and Technology*, Vol. 4, No. 1, pp. 12–21.

Li, Hongbin, and Li-An Zhou. 2005. "Political Turnover and Economic Performance: The Incentive Role of Personnel Control in China." *Journal of Public Economics*, Vol. 89, No. 9–10, pp. 1743–62.

Li Chi. 1967."Book of Rites." In *An Encyclopedia of Ancient Ceremonial Usages, Religious Creeds, and Social Institutions*, edited by Ch'u Chai and Winberg Chai. New York: University Books.

Liang, Linxia. 2007. *Delivering Justice in Qing China: Civil Trials in the Magistrate's Court*. Oxford: Oxford University Press.

Liang, Zhiping. 1989. "Explicating Law: A Comparative Perspective of Chinese and Western Legal Culture." *Journal of Chinese Law*, Vol. 3, No. 1, p. 55–92.

Liangqun, L., and R. Murphy. 2006. "Lineage Networks, Land Conflicts and Rural Migration in Late Socialist China." *Journal of Peasant Studies*, Vol. 33, No. 4, pp. 612–45.

Lin, Justin Yifu. 1995. "The Needham Puzzle: Why the Industrial Revolution Did Not Originate in China." *Economic Development and Cultural Change*, Vol. 43, No. 2, pp. 269–92.

———. 2008. "The Needham Puzzle, the Weber Question, and China's Miracle: Long-Term Performance since the Sung Dynasty." *China Economic Journal*, Vol. 1, No. 1, pp. 63–95.

Lincoln, Toby. 2021. *An Urban History of China*. Cambridge: Cambridge University Press.

Liu, Cong, and Se Yan. 2020. "The Art of Governing: Nomads, Elites, and the Provision of Public Goods in China, 1738–1820." SSRN Working Paper No. 3696307.

Liu, Hiu-Chen Wang. 1959. *The Traditional Chinese Clan Rules*. New York: J.J. Augustin.

Liu, James T. C. 1973. "How Did a Neo-Confucian School Become the State Orthodoxy?" *Philosophy East and West*, Vol. 23, No. 4, pp. 483–505.

Liu, Kwang-Ching. 1988. "Chinese Merchant Guilds: An Historical Inquiry." *The Pacific Historical Review*, Vol. 57, No. 1, pp. 1–23.

Liu, William G. 2005. "Wrestling for Power: The State and Economy in Late Imperial China (1000–1770)." Unpublished PhD dissertation, Harvard University.

Liu, William Guanglin. 2015. *The Chinese Market Economy, 1000–1500*. New York: SUNY Press.

Locke, John. [1690] 1975. "An Essay Concerning Human Understanding." In *The Clarendon Edition of the Works of John Locke*, edited by Peter H. Nidditch. Oxford: Oxford University Press.

Lopez, Robert. 1971. *The Commercial Revolution of the Middle Ages, 950–1350*. Englewood Cliffs, NJ: Prentice Hall.

Lu, Yi, Mengna Luan, and Tuan-Hwee Sng. 2020. "Did the Communists Contribute to China's Rural Growth?" *Explorations in Economic History*, Vol. 75, p. 101315.

Luo, Zhaotian, and Shuyi Yu. 2024. "Great Divergence and Great Convergence: A Theory of Power Dynamics and Social Evolution." Unpublished manuscript, University of Chicago.

Ma, Chicheng. 2021. "Knowledge Diffusion and Intellectual Change: When Chinese Literati Met European Jesuits." *Journal of Economic History*, Vol. 81, No. 4, pp. 1052–97.

———. 2024. "Classicism and Modern Growth: The Shadow of the Sages." *Journal of Economic History*, Vol. 84, No. 2, pp. 395–431.

Ma, Debin. 2004. "Growth, Institutions and Knowledge: A Review and Reflection on the Historiography of 18th–20th Century China." *Australian Economic History Review*, Vol. 44, No. 3, pp. 259–77.

———. 2011. "Rock, Scissors, Paper: The Problem of Incentives and Information in Traditional Chinese State and the Origin of Great Divergence." Working Paper. London School of Economics and Political Science.

———. 2013. "State Capacity and Great Divergence: The Case of Qing China (1644–1911)." *Eurasian Geography and Economics*, Vol. 54, No. 5–6, pp. 484–99.

Ma, Debin, and Jared Rubin. 2017. "The Paradox of Power: Principal-Agent Problem and Fiscal Capacity in Absolutist Regimes." SSRN Working Paper No. 2931096.

Macauley, Melissa. 1994. "Civil and Uncivil Disputes in Southeast Coastal China, 1723–1820." In *Civil Law in Qing and Republican China*, edited by Kathryn Bernhardt and Philip C.C. Huang, 85–120. Stanford, CA: Stanford University Press.

———. 1995. "Review of *Nourish the People: The State Civilian Granary System in China, 1650–1850* by Pierre-Etienne Will and R. Bin Wong, with James Lee." *Journal of Economic History*, Vol. 55, No. 1 (March), pp. 182–83.

———. 1998. *Social Power and Legal Culture: Litigation Masters in Late Imperial China*. Stanford, CA: Stanford University Press.

———. 2021. *Distant Shores: Colonial Encounters on China's Maritime Frontier*. Princeton, NJ: Princeton University Press.

MacFarlane, Alan. 1978. *The Origins of English Individualism*. New York: Cambridge University Press.

Macgowan, Daniel J. 1888–1889. "Chinese Guilds or Chambers of Commerce and Trades Unions." *Journal of North-China Branch of the Royal Asiatic Society*, Vol. 21, pp. 133–92.

MacMullan, Ramsay. 1980. "How Big Was the Roman Imperial Army?" *KLIO*, Vol. 62, pp. 451–60.

Maddicott, John Robert. 2004. *The Origins of the Early English Parliament 924–1327*. Oxford: Oxford University Press

Maddison, Angus. 2007. *The Contours of the World Economy, 1–2030 AD*. Oxford: Oxford University Press.

Makdisi, George. 1970. "Madrasa and University in the Middle Ages." *Studia Islamica* No. 32, pp. 254–64.

———. 1973. "The Sunni Revival." In *Islamic Civilization 950–1150*, edited by D. H. Richards, 155–68. Oxford: Bruno Cassirer.

———. 1981. *The Rise of Colleges: Institutions of Learning in Islam and the West*. Edinburgh: Edinburgh University Press.

Mallik, S.N. 1929. "Local Self-Government in India." *Annals of the American Academy of Political and Social Science*, Vol. 145, Part 2: India (September), pp. 36–44.

Marsh, Robert M. 1960. "Bureaucratic Constraints on Nepotism in the Ch'ing Period." *Journal of Asian Studies*, Vol. 19, No. 2 (February), pp. 117–33.

Marshall, J., 1833. *A Digest of All the Accounts: Relating to the Population, Productions, Revenues, Financial Operations, Manufactures, Shipping, Colonies, Commerce, &c. &c., of the United Kingdom of Great Britain and Ireland, Diffused through More than 600 Volumes of Journals, Reports, and Papers, Presented to Parliament during the Last Thirty-Five Years*. London: Printed by J. Haddon.

Martinez, Luis. 2022. "How Much Should We Trust the Dictator's GDP Growth Estimates?" *Journal of Political Economy*, Vol. 130, No. 10, pp. 2731–69.

Martzloff, Jean-Claude. 1997. *A History of Chinese Mathematics*. Berlin: Springer Verlag.

Maskin, Eric, Yingyi Qian, and Chenggang Xu. 2000. "Incentives, Information, and Organizational Form." *Review of Economic Studies*, Vol. 67, pp. 359–78.

Mather, Richard B. 1981. "The Bronze's Begging Bowl: Eating Practices in Buddhist Monasteries of Medieval India and China." *Journal of the American Oriental Society*, Vol. 101, No. 4 (October–December), pp. 417–24.

Mathias, Peter. 1979. *The Transformation of England*. New York: Columbia University Press.

McClellan, James E. III. 1981. "The Academie Royale des Sciences, 1699–1793: A Statistical Portrait." *Isis*, Vol. 72, No. 4, pp. 541–67.

McCloskey, Deirdre N. 2010. *Bourgeois Dignity: Why Economics Can't Explain the Modern World*. Chicago: University of Chicago Press.

McCloskey, Deirdre Nansen. 2016. "The Great Enrichment: A Humanistic and Social Scientific Account." *Social Science History*, Vol. 40, No. 4, pp. 583–98.

McCulloch, John Ramsay. 1851. *A Dictionary, Geographical, Statistical, and Historical, of the Various Countries, Places, and Principal Natural Objects in the World*. 2 vols. London: Longman, Brown, Green and Longmans.

McDermott, Joseph P. 2011. "Book Collecting in Jiangxi during the Song Dynasty." In *Knowledge and Text Production in an Age of Print: China, 900–1400*, edited by Lucille Chia and Hilde De Weerdt, 63–104. Leiden, Netherlands: Brill.

———. 2013. *The Making of a New Rural Order in South China: Vol. 1, Village, Land, and Lineage in Huizhou, 900–1600*. Cambridge: Cambridge University Press.

———. 2020. *The Making of a New Rural Order in South China: Vol. 2, Merchants, Markets, and Lineages. 1500–1700*.Cambridge: Cambridge University Press.

———. 2022. "Merchants and Commercial Networks." In *The Cambridge Economic History of China*, Vol. 1, edited by Debin Ma and Richard Von Glahn, 597–636. Cambridge: Cambridge University Press.

McLean, Ian, Haidee Lorrey, and Josep Colomer. 2007. "Voting in the Medieval Papacy and Religious Orders." In *Modeling Decisions for Artificial Intelligence,* edited by Vicenç Torra, Yasuo Narukawa, and Yuji Yoshida, 30–44, 4th International Conference, MDAI 2007, Kitakyushu, Japan, August 16–18, 2007. Berlin: Springer.

Mei, Ju-Ao. 1932. "China and the Rule of Law." *Pacific Affairs,* Vol. 5, No. 10 (October), pp. 863–72.

Meisenzahl, Ralf R., and Joel Mokyr. 2012. "The Rate and Direction of Invention in the British Industrial Revolution: Incentives and Institutions." In *The Rate and Direction of Innovation,* edited by Scott Stern and Joshua Lerner, 443–79. Chicago: University of Chicago Press.

Mencius (Meng Ke). 1861. *The Works of Mencius.* In *The Chinese Classics,* Vol. 2, edited by James Legge. London: Trübner & Co.

Meskill, John. 1982. *Academies in Ming China: A Historical Essay.* Tucson: University of Arizona Press.

Milgrom, Paul R., Douglass C. North, and Barry R. Weingast. 1990. "The Role of Institutions in the Revival of Trade: The Law Merchant, Private Judges, and the Champagne Fairs." *Economics and Politics,* Vol. 2, pp. 1–23.

Mitterauer, Michael. 2010. *Why Europe? The Medieval Origins of Its Special Path.* Chicago: University of Chicago Press.

Mitterauer, Michael, and Reinhard Sieder. 1982. *The European Family: Patriarchy to Partnership from the Middle Ages to the Present.* Oxford: Basil Blackwell.

Mok, Kin-wai Patrick. 1995. "Lineage and Elite Dominance in Late Imperial Chinese Society: A Case Study of Shunde Country, Guangdong." Unpublished PhD dissertation, University of Hong Kong.

Mokyr, Joel. 1994. "Cardwell's Law and the Political Economy of Technological Progress." *Research Policy,* Vol. 23, No. 5, pp. 561–74.

———. 2005. "The Intellectual Origins of Modern Economic Growth." [Presidential address.] *Journal of Economic History,* Vol. 65, No. 2, pp. 285–351.

———. 2008. "The Institutional Origins of the Industrial Revolution." In *Institutions and Economic Performance,* edited by Elhanan Helpman, 64–119. Cambridge, MA: Harvard University Press.

———. 2009. *The Enlightened Economy: An Economic History of Britain 1700–1850.* New Haven, CT: Yale University Press.

———. 2016. *A Culture of Growth.* Princeton, NJ: Princeton University Press.

———. 2017. "Culture, Elites and the Great Enrichment." *Annual Proceedings of the Wealth and Well-Being of Nations,* Vol. 9, pp. 39–55.

———. 2018. "Bottom Up or Top-Down? The Origins of the Industrial Revolution." *Journal of Institutional Economics,* Vol. 14, No. 6, pp. 1003–24.

———. 2019. "The Economics of Apprenticeship." In *Learning for Work / Learning the Craft: Apprenticeship in Early Modern Europe,* edited by Maarten Prak and Patrick Wallis, 20–43. Cambridge: Cambridge University Press.

———. 2021a, "Attitudes, Aptitudes, and the Roots of the Great Enrichment." In *Handbook of Historical Economics,* edited by Alberto Bisin and Giovanni Federico, 773–94. New York: Elsevier.

———. 2021b. "'The Holy Land of Industrialism': Rethinking the Industrial Revolution." *Journal of the British Academy,* Vol. 9, pp. 223–47.

———. 2024a. "The Benefits and Costs of Diversity: Lessons from Economic History." In *The Wealth and Well-Being of Nations* (in press).

———. 2024b. "Culture vs Institutions in the Great Enrichment." In *Handbook of New Institutional Economics*, 2nd ed., edited by Mary Shirley and Claude Menard (in press).

Moll-Murata, Christine. 2008. "Chinese Guilds from the Seventeenth to the Twentieth Centuries: An Overview." *International Review of Social History*, Vol. 53, No. 16, pp. 213–47.

———. 2013. "Guilds and Apprenticeship in China and Europe: The Jingdezhen and European Ceramics Industries." In *Technology, Skills and the Pre-modern Economy in the East and the West*, edited by Jan Luiten van Zanden and Maarten Prak, 225–57. Boston: Brill.

Møller, Jørgen, and Jonathan Stavnskaer Doucette. 2022. *The Catholic Church and European State Formation, AD 1000–1500*. Oxford: Oxford University Press.

Møller, Jørgen, and Svend-Erik Skaaning. 2013. *Democracy and Democratization in Comparative Perspective—Conceptions, Conjunctures, Causes, and Consequences*. New York: Routledge.

Mordechai, Lee, Merle Eisenberg, Timothy P. Newfield, Adam Izdebski, Janet E. Kay, and Hendrik Poinar. 2019. "The Justinianic Plague: An Inconsequential Pandemic?" *PNAS*, Vol. 116, No. 51 (December 17), pp. 25546–54.

Moring, Beatrice, and Richard Wall. 2017. *Widows in European Economy and Society, 1600–1920*. Woodbridge, UK: Boydell Press.

Morris, Colin. 1989. *The Papal Monarchy: The Western Church from 1050 to 1250*. Oxford: Clarendon Press.

Morris, Ian. 2010. *Why the West Rules—for Now*. New York: Farrar, Strauss and Giroux.

Morrison, Karl F. 1969. *Tradition and Authority in the Western Church, 300–1140*. Princeton, NJ: Princeton University Press.

Moscona, Jacob, Nathan Nunn, and Jim Robinson. 2020. "Segmentary Lineage Organization and Conflict in Sub-Saharan Africa." *Econometrica*, Vol. 88, No. 5, pp. 1999–2036.

Mote, Frederick W. 1961. "The Growth of Chinese Despotism: A Critique of Wittfogel's Theory of Oriental Despotism as Applied to China." *Oriens Extremus*, Vol. 8, No. 1, pp. 1–41.

———. 1977. "The Transformation of Nanking, 1350–1400." In *The City in Late Imperial China*, edited by William Skinner, 101–53. Stanford, CA: Stanford University Press.

———. 1999. *Imperial China: 900–1800*.Cambridge, MA: Harvard University Press.

Motono, Eiichi. 2000. *Conflict and Cooperation in Sino–British Business, 1860–1911: The Impact of the Pro-British Commercial Network in Shanghai*. New York: St. Martin's Press, Palgrave Macmillan.

Muir, Edward. 2007. *The Culture Wars of the Late Renaissance*. Cambridge, MA: Harvard University Press.

Murray, Alexander C. 1946. *Germanic Kinship Structure*. Toronto: Pontifical Institute of Medieval Studies.

Musson, A. E., and Eric Robinson. 1969. *Science and Technology in the Industrial Revolution*. Manchester, UK: Manchester University Press.

Musson, A. J. 2002. "Sub-keepers and Constables: The Role of Local Officials in Keeping the Peace in Fourteenth-Century England." *English Historical Review*, Vol. 117, No. 470, pp. 1–24.

Nader, Helen. 1990. *Liberty in Absolutist Spain: The Habsburg Sale of Towns, 1516–1700*.Baltimore: John Hopkins University Press.

Nair, Malavika. 2011. "Enforcement of Nineteenth Century Banking Contracts Using a Marriage Rule." *Quarterly Review of Economics and Finance*, Vol. 51, pp. 360–67.

Naquin, Susan, and Evelyn Rawski. 1987. *Chinese Society in the Eighteenth Century*. New Haven, CT: Yale University Press.

Nardi, Paolo. 1992. "Relations with Authority." In *A History of the University in Europe—Vol. I: Universities in the Middle Ages*, edited by Hilde de Ridder-Symoens, 77–107. Cambridge: Cambridge University Press.

Nee, Victor, and Sonja Opper. 2011. *Capitalism from Below—Markets and Institutional Change in China*. Cambridge: Harvard University Press.

Needham, Joseph. 1969. *The Grand Titration*. Toronto: University of Toronto Press.

Nicholas, David. 1992. *Medieval Flanders*. New York: Longman Publishing Group.

———. 1997. *The Growth of the Medieval City: From Late Antiquity to the Early Fourteenth Century*. New York: Addison Wesley Longman.

Nimick, Thomas G. 2008. *Local Administration in Ming China: The Changing Roles of Magistrates, Prefects, and Provincial Officials*. Society for Ming Studies, University of British Columbia.

Noblit, Graham. 2023. "The Origin and Evolution of Chinese Lineages." Unpublished manuscript. Center for Open Science, Charlottesville, VA.

North, Douglass C. 1981. *Structure and Change in Economic History*. New York: W. W. Norton.

North, Douglass C., John Wallis, and Barry Weingast. 2009. *Violence and Social Orders: A Conceptual Framework for Interpreting Recorded Human History*. Cambridge: Cambridge University Press.

Nunn, Nathan, and Nancy Qian. 2010. "The Columbian Exchange: A History of Disease, Food, and Ideas." *Journal of Economic Perspectives*, Vol. 24, No. 2 (Spring), pp. 163–88.

Ober, Josiah. 2015. *The Rise and Fall of Classical Greece*. Princeton, NJ: Princeton University Press.

O'Brien, Kevin J., and Rongbin Han. 2009. "Path to Democracy? Assessing Village Elections in China." *Journal of Contemporary China*, Vol. 18, No. 60, pp. 359–78.

O'Callaghan, Joseph F. 1969. "The Beginnings of the Cortes in León-Castile." *American Historical Review*, Vol. 74, pp. 1503–37.

———. 1989. *The Cortes of Castile-León, 1188–1350*. Philadelphia: University of Pennsylvania Press.

Ogilvie, Sheilagh. 2011. *Institutions and European Trade Merchant Guilds, 1000–1800*. Cambridge: Cambridge University Press.

———. 2019. *The European Guilds: An Economic Analysis*. Princeton, NJ: Princeton University Press.

Ó Gráda, Cormac. 2016. "Did Science Cause the Industrial Revolution?" *Journal of Economic Literature*, Vol. 5, No. 1, pp. 224–39.

Özbek, Nadir. 2018. "Tax Farming in the Nineteenth-Century Ottoman Empire: Institutional Backwardness or the Emergence of Modern Public Finance?" *Journal of Interdisciplinary History*, Vol. 49, No. 2, pp. 219–45.

Pan, Jennifer, and Yiqing Xu. 2018. "China's Ideological Spectrum." *Journal of Politics*, Vol. 80, No. 1, pp. 254–73.

Pang, Yong-Pil. 1981. "Peng Pai and the Origins of Rural Revolution under Warlordism in the 1920s: Haifeng County, Guangdong Province." Unpublished PhD dissertation, University of California, Los Angeles.

Park, Nancy E. 1997. "Corruption in Eighteenth-Century China." *Journal of Asian Studies*, Vol. 56, No. 4 (November), pp. 967–1005.

Parker, G. 2004. *Sovereign City: The City-State Through History*. London: Reaktion Books.

Parthasarathi, Prasannan. 2011. *Why Europe Grew Rich and Asia Did Not: Global Economic Divergence, 1600–1850*. Cambridge: Cambridge University Press.

Pasternak, Burton. 1969. "The Role of the Frontier in Chinese Lineage Development." *Journal of Asian Studies*, Vol. 28, pp. 551–61.

Pei, Minxin. 2016. *China's Crony Capitalism—the Dynamics of Regime Decay*. Cambridge, MA: Harvard University Press.

Peng, Yusheng. 2004. "Kinship Networks and Entrepreneurs in China's Transition Economy." *American Journal of Sociology*, Vol. 109, No. 5, pp. 1045–74.

Peng, Zeyi, ed. 1995. *Zhongguo gongshang hanghui shiliao ji* [Collection of historical materials on Chinese craft and commercial guilds], 2 vols. Beijing: Zhonghua shuju.

Pennington, Kenneth. 1998. "Due Process, Community and the Prince in the Evolution of the *Ordo Iudiciarius*." *Rivista Internazionale di Diritto Commune*, Vol. 9, pp. 9–47.

Perdue, Peter. 2004. "Constructing Chinese Property Rights: East and West." In *Constituting Modernity: Private Property in East and West*, edited by Huri Islamuglo, 35–68. London: I.B. Taurus.

———. 2005. *China Marches West: The Qing Conquest of Central Eurasia*. Cambridge, MA: Belknap Press of Harvard University Press.

Peters, Michael A. "Ancient Centers of Higher Learning: A Bias in the Comparative History of the University." *Educational Philosophy and Theory*, Vol. 51, No. 1, pp. 1063–72.

Pines, Yuri. 2008. "To Rebel Is Justified? The Image of Zhouxin and the Legitimacy of Rebellion in the Chinese Political Tradition." *Oriens Extremus*, Vol. 47, pp. 1–24.

———. 2012. *The Everlasting Empire: The Political Culture of Ancient China and Its Imperial Legacy*. Princeton, NJ: Princeton University Press.

———. 2016. "Review of Zhao Dingxi, *The Confucian-Legalist State*." *Early China*, Vol. 39, pp. 311–20.

———. 2018. "Legalism in Chinese Philosophy." *Stanford Encyclopedia of Philosophy*. https://plato.stanford.edu/entries/chinese-legalism/.

Pirenne, Henri. 1925 [2014]. *Medieval Cities: Their Origins and the Revival of Trade*. Princeton, NJ: Princeton University Press, Princeton, NJ: Princeton University Press.

Piskorski, Jan M. 2008. "Medieval Colonization in East Central Europe." In *The Germans and the East*, edited by Charles Ingrao and Franz A. J. Szabo, 27–36. West Lafayette, IN: Purdue University Press.

Platteau, J.P. 2000. *Institutions, Social Norms, and Economic Development*. London: Academic Publishers and Routledge.

Poggi, Gianfranco. 1978. *The Development of the Modern State—A Sociological Introduction*. Stanford, CA: Stanford University Press.

Pomeranz, Kenneth. 2000. *The Great Divergence: China, Europe, and the Making of the Modern World Economy*. Princeton, NJ: Princeton University Press.

———. 2011. "Ten Years After: Responses and Reconsiderations." *Historically Speaking*, Vol. 12 (September), pp. 20–25.

———. 2022. "The Rural Economy." In *The Cambridge Economic History of China, Vol. I*, edited by Debin Ma and Richard Von Glahn, 484–521. Cambridge: Cambridge University Press.

Porterfield, Amanda. 2018. *Corporate Spirit—Religion and the Rise of the Modern Corporation*. Oxford: Oxford University Press.

Posner, Eric A. 2000. *Law and Social Norms*. Cambridge, MA: Harvard University Press.

Post, Gaines. 1943. "Plena Potestas and Consent in Medieval Assemblies: A Study in Romano-Canonical Procedure and the Rise of Representation, 1150–1325." *Traditio*, Vol. 1, pp. 355–408.

Potter, Pitman B. 2002. "Guanxi and the PRC Legal System: From Contradiction to Complementarity." In *Social Connections in China: Institutions, Culture, and the Changing Nature of Guanxi*, edited by Thomas Gold et al., 179–96. Cambridge: Cambridge University Press.

Pounds, Norman J. G. 1973. *An Historical Geography of Europe, 450 B.C.–A.D. 1330.* Cambridge: Cambridge University Press.

Powell, John. 1827. *Statistical Illustrations of the Territorial Extent and Population, Rental, Taxation, Finances, Commerce, Consumption, Insolvency, Pauperism, and Crime of the British Empire*. Compiled for and published by order of the London Statistical Society. London: Effingham Wilson.

Prak, Maarten. 2018. *Citizens without Nations: Urban Citizenship in Europe and the World, c. 1000–1789*. Cambridge: Cambridge University Press.

Prak, Maarten, and Jan Luiten van Zanden. 2013. "Technology and Human Capital Formation in the East and West before the Industrial Revolution." In *Technology, Skills and the Premodern Economy in the East and the West*, edited by Marten Prak and Jan Luiten van Zanden, 1–22. Boston: Brill.

———. 2022. *Pioneers of Capitalism: The Netherlands, 1000–1800*. Princeton, NJ: Princeton University Press.

Prak, Maarten, and Patrick Wallis. 2019. "Introduction: Apprenticeship in Early Modern Europe." In *Apprenticeship in Early Modern Europe*, edited by Maarten Prak and Patrick Wallis, 1–19. Cambridge: Cambridge University Press.

Price, Derek J. de Solla. 1957. "Precision Instruments to 1500." In *A History of Technology*. Vol. 3, *From the Renaissance to the Industrial Revolution, 1500–1750*, edited by Charles Singer et al., 582–619. New York: Oxford University Press.

Puga, Diego, and Daniel Trefler. 2014. "International Trade and Institutional Change: Medieval Venice's Response to Globalization" *Quarterly Journal of Economics*, Vol. 129, No. 2, pp. 753–821.

Pyatt, T. Roger, and S. Gordon Redding. 2000. "Trust and Forbearance in Ethnic Chinese Business Relationships in Hong Kong and Thailand." *Journal of Asian Business*, Vol. 16, No. 1, pp. 41–63.

Qian, Jiwei, and Tuan-Hwee Sng. 2021. "The State in Chinese Economic History." *Australian Economic History Review*, Vol. 61, No. 3, pp. 359–95.

Qian, Yingyi. 2000a. "The Institutional Foundations of Market Transition in the People's Republic of China." Asian Development Bank Institute Working Paper 9.

———. 2000b. "The Process of China's Market Transition (1978–1998): The Evolutionary, Historical, and Comparative Perspectives." *Journal of Institutional and Theoretical Economics*, March, Vol. 156, No. 1, pp. 151–71.

———. 2017. *How Reform Worked in China: The Transition from Plan to Market*. Cambridge, MA: MIT Press.

Rankin, Mary B. 1990. "The Origins of a Chinese Public Sphere. Local Elites and Community Affairs in the Late Imperial Period." *Études chinoises*, Vol. 9, No. 2, pp. 13–60.

Razi, Z. 1993. "The Myth of the Immutable English Family." *Past & Present*, Vol. 140 (August), pp. 3–44.

Redding, Gordon, and Michael Witt. 2007. *The Future of Chinese Capitalism: Choices and Chances*. Oxford: Oxford University Press.

Reed, Bradly W. 2000. *Talons and Teeth: County Clerks and Runners in the Qing Dynasty*. Stanford, CA: Stanford University Press.

Reed, Frank. 2016. *The Centennial Historical Atlas: Academic Research Edition*. Jamestown, RI: Clockwork Mapping.

Reith, R. 2007. "Apprentices in the German and Austrian Crafts in Early Modern Times: Apprentices as Wage Earners?" In *Learning on the Shop Floor: Historical Perspectives on Apprenticeship*, edited by Steven L. Kaplan, Bert De Munck, and Hugo Soly, 179–99.New York: Berghahn Books.

Reyerson, Kathryn L. 1992. "The Adolescent Apprentice/Worker in Medieval Montpellier." *Journal of Family History*, Vol. 17, No. 4, pp. 355–70.

Reynolds, George W. M. 1869. "The Chinese and Their Peculiarities." *Reynold's Miscellany of Romance, General Literature, Science and Art*, Vol. 42, No. 1080 (February 20), p. 157.

Reynolds, Susan. 1997. *Kingdoms and Communities in Western Europe*. Oxford: Clarendon Press.

Ricci, Matteo. 1953. *China in the Sixteenth Century: The Journals of Matthew Ricci, 1583–1610*. Translated by Louis J. Gallagher. New York: Random House.

Richardson, Gary. 2004. "Guilds, Laws, and Markets for Manufactured Merchandise in Late-Medieval England." *Explorations in Economic History*, Vol. 41, No. 1, pp. 1–25.

Rickett, W. Allyn, ed. 1985. *Guanxi: Political, Economic, and Philosophical Essays from Early China*. Princeton, NJ: Princeton University Press.

Roberts, Lissa, and Simon Schaffer. 2007. "Preface." In *The Mindful Hand: Inquiry and Invention from the Late Renaissance to Early Industrialization*, edited by Lissa Roberts, Simon Schaffer, and Peter Dear, xiii–xxvii. Amsterdam: Royal Netherlands Academy of Arts and Sciences.

Roberts, Lissa, Simon Schaffer, and Peter Dear, eds. *The Mindful Hand: Inquiry and Invention from the Late Renaissance to Early Industrialization*. Amsterdam: Royal Netherlands Academy of Arts and Sciences.

Robertson, Justin. 2015. *Localizing Global Finance: The Rise of Western-Style Private Equity in China*. New York: Palgrave MacMillan.

Robertson, Ritchie. 2021. *The Enlightenment: the Pursuit of Happiness*. New York: HarperCollins.

Rogoff, Kenneth, and Yuanchen Yang. 2021. "Has China's Production Peaked?" *China & World Economy*, Vol. 29, No. 1, pp. 1–31.

Roland, Gerard. 2020a "Culture, Institutions and Development." In *Handbook of Development Economics and Institutions*, edited by J. M. Baland, F. Bourguignon, J. Ph. Platteau, and T. Verdier, 414–48. Princeton, NJ: Princeton University Press.

———. 2020b. "The Deep Historical Roots of Modern Culture: A Comparative Perspective." *Journal of Comparative Economics*, Vol. 48, pp. 483–508.

———. 2024. "Comparative Economic History." Unpublished paper, University of California, Berkeley.

Rolt, L.T.C. 1970. *Victorian Engineering*. Stroud, UK: Sutton Publishing.

Ronan, Colin A., and Joseph Needham. 1981. *The Shorter Science and Civilisation in China*, Vol. 2. Cambridge: Cambridge University Press.

Root, L. Hilton. 1994. *The Fountain of Privilege*. Berkeley: University of California Press.

———. 2020. *Network Origins of the Global Economy*. Cambridge: Cambridge University Press.

Rosenberg, Nathan, and L.E. Birdzell. 1986. *How the West Grew Rich: The Economic Transformation of the Industrial World*. New York: Basic Books.

Rosenthal, Jean-Laurent, and R. Bin Wong. 2011. *Before and Beyond Divergence: The Politics of Economic Change in China and Europe*. Cambridge, MA: Harvard University Press.

Ross, Jack C. 1983. "Differentiation between Gilds and Fraternities in Medieval Europe." *Journal of Voluntary Action Research*, Vol. 12, No. 1 (January),pp. 7–19.

Rosser, Gervase. 2015. *The Art of Solidarity in the Middle Ages—Guilds in England 1250–1550*. Oxford:Oxford University Press.

Rossignoli, Domenico, and Federico Trombetta. 2024."Ora et Guberna: The Economic Impact of the Rule of St Benedict in Medieval England." *Journal of Economic History*, Vol. 84, No. 3, pp. 838–73.

Rowe, William T. 1984. *Conflict and Community in a Chinese City, 1796–1899*. Stanford, CA: Stanford University Press.

———. 1990. "Review Article: *The Public Sphere in Modern China*." *Modern China*, Vol. 16, No. 3, pp. 309–29.

———. 1992. *Hankow: Commerce and Society in a Chinese City, 1796–1889*. Stanford, CA: Stanford University Press.

———. 1993. "The Problem of 'Civil Society' in Late Imperial China." *Modern China*, Vol. 19, No. 2, pp. 139–57.

———. 1998. "Ancestral Rites and Political Authority in Late Imperial China—Chen Hongmou in Jiangxi." *Modern China*, Vol. 24, No. 4, pp. 378–407.

———. 2001. *Saving the World: Chen Hongmou and Elite Consciousness in Eighteenth Century China*. Stanford, CA: Stanford University Press.

———. 2002. "Social Stability and Social Change." In *The Cambridge History of China*, Vol. 9, edited by D. Twitchett and J. K. Fairbank, 473–562. Cambridge: Cambridge University Press.

———. 2009. *China's Last Empire: The Great Qing*. Cambridge, MA: Harvard University Press.

Roy, Tirthankar. 2008 "The Guild in Modern South Asia." *International Review of Social History*, Vol. 53, Supplement 16, pp. 95–120.

———. 2019. *How British Rule Changed India's Economy: The Paradox of the Raj*. London: Palgrave Macmillan.

Rubenstein, Richard E. 1999. *When Jesus Became God*. New York: Harcourt.

Rubin, Jared. 2017. *Rulers, Religion, and Riches: Why the West Got Rich and the Middle East Did Not*. New York: Cambridge University Press.

Rudner, David. 1989. "Banker's Trust and the Culture of Banking among the Nattukottai Chettiars of Colonial South India." *Modern Asian Studies*, Vol. 23, No. 3, pp. 417–58.

Rüegg, Walter. 1992. "Themes." In *A History of the University in Europe—Vol. I: Universities in the Middle Ages*, edited by Hilde de Ridder-Symoens, 3–34. Cambridge: Cambridge University Press.

Ruffini, Edoardo. 1976. *Il Principio Maggioritario. Profilo Storico*. Milan: Adelphi.

Rushton, Peter. 1991. "The Matter in Variance: Adolescents and Domestic Conflict in the Pre-industrial Economy of Northeast England, 1600–1800." *Journal of Social History*, Vol. 25, No. 1 (Autumn), pp. 89–107.

Ruskola, Teemu. 2000. "Conceptualizing Corporations and Kinship: Comparative Law and Development Theory in a Chinese Perspective." *Stanford Law Review*, Vol. 52, No. 6, pp. 1599–1729.

———. 2013. *Legal Orientalism: China, the United States and Modern Law*. Cambridge, MA: Harvard University Press.

Sabine, George Holland. 1960. *A History of Political Theory*. 3rd ed. Calcutta: Oxford and IBH Publishing.

Sakaki, Michiko, Ayano Yagi, and Kou Murayama. 2018. "Curiosity in Old Age: A Possible Key to Achieving Adaptive Aging." *Neuroscience & Biobehavioral Reviews*, Vol. 88, pp. 106–16.

Saleh, Mohamed. 2018. "On the Road to Heaven: Taxation, Conversions, and the Coptic-Muslim Socioeconomic Gap in Medieval Egypt." *Journal of Economic History*, Vol. 78, No. 2, pp. 394–434.

Sarma, K.V. 2001. "Aryabhata: His Name, Time and Provenance." *Indian Journal of the History of Science*, Vol. 36, Nos. 3–5, pp. 105–115.

Say, Jean-Baptiste. [1803] 1821. *A Treatise on Political Economy*. 4th ed. Boston: Wells and Lilly.

Schäfer, Hans-Bernd, and Alexander J. Wulf. 2014. "Jurists, Clerics, and Merchants: The Rise of Learned Law in Medieval Europe and its Impact on Economic Growth." *Journal of Empirical Legal Studies*, Vol. 11, No. 2 (June), pp. 266–300.

Schalk, Ruben. 2019. "Craft Apprenticeships in the Northern Netherlands, 1600–1900." In *Apprenticeship in Early Modern Europe*, edited by Maarten Prak and Patrick Wallis, 187–216. Cambridge University Press, Cambridge.

Scheidel, Walter. 2019. *Escape from Rome: The Failure of Empire and the Road to Prosperity*. Princeton, NJ: Princeton University Press.

Schilling, Heinz. 2008. *Early Modern European Civilization and its Political and Cultural Dynamism*. Hanover, NH: University Press of New England.

———. 2022. *Das Christentum und die Enstehung des Modernen Europa*. Freiburg, Germany: Herder.

Schönholzer, David, and Eric Weese. 2019. "Creative Destruction in the European State System." Working Paper, Yale University.

Schulz, Jonathan F. 2022. "Kin Networks and Institutional Development." *Economic Journal*, Vol. 132, No. 647, pp. 2578–2613.

Schulz, Jonathan, Duman Bahrami-Rad, Jonathan Beauchamp, and Joseph Henrich. 2018. "The Origins of WEIRD Psychology." SSRN Working Paper No. 3201031.

———. 2019. "The Church, Intensive Kinship, and Global Psychological Variation." *Science*, Vol. 366, No. 6466 (November 8), p. 707.

Schwarzschild, Maimon. 2010. "Constitutional Law and Equality." In *A Companion to Philosophy of Law and Legal Theory*, 2nd ed., edited by Dennis Patterson, 160–76. Chichester, UK: Wiley Blackwell.

Scogin, H. 1978. "Poor Relief in Northern Sung China." *Oriens Extremus*, Vol. 25, No. 1, pp. 30–46.

Scogin, Hugh T. Jr. 1994. "Civil 'Law' in Traditional China: History and Theory." In *Civil Law in Qing and Republican China*, edited by Kathryn Bernhardt and Philip C. Huang, 13–41. Stanford, CA: Stanford University Press.

Seabright, Paul. 2010. *The Company of Strangers: A Natural History of Economic Life*. Princeton, NJ: Princeton University Press.

Segal, Richa. 2023. "Institutional Attitudes and the Political Economy of Famine: A Case Study of Colonial India." Unpublished thesis, Northwestern University.

Sella, Pietro. 1904. "The Statutes of the Commune of Bugelle (Biella) and the Documents Which Have Been Added to the Statutes." https://web.archive.org/web/20050208035823 /http://vialardi.org/VdSF/Statuti.Biella-1.html.

Serafinelli, Michel, and Guido Tabellini. 2022. "Creativity over Time and Space—An Historical Analysis of European Cities." *Journal of Economic Growth*, Vol. 27, No. 1, pp. 1–43.

Schelling, Thomas. 1960. *The Strategy of Conflict*. Cambridge, MA: Harvard University Press.

Shapin, Steven. 1994. *A Social History of Truth*. Chicago: University of Chicago Press.

Shapin, Steven, and Simon Schaffer. 1985. *Leviathan and the Air Pump: Hobbes, Boyle, and the Experimental Life*. Princeton, NJ: Princeton University Press.

Sheehan, Brett. 2015. *Industrial Eden: A Chinese Capitalist Vision*. Cambridge, MA: Harvard University Press.

Shiue, Carol H. 2004. "Local Granaries and Central Government Disaster Relief: Moral Hazard and Intergovernmental Finance in Eighteenth- and Nineteenth-Century China." *Journal of Economic History*, Vol. 64, No. 1, pp. 100–124.

Shiue, Carol H, and Wolfgang Keller. 2007. "Markets in China and Europe on the Eve of the Industrial Revolution." *American Economic Review*, Vol. 97, No. 4, pp. 1189–1216.

———. 2023. "Human Capital Strategies for Big Shocks: The Case of the Fall of the Ming." Unpublished working paper, Harvard University.

Siedentop, Larry. 2014. *Inventing the Individual: The Origins of Western Liberalism*. Cambridge, MA: Harvard University Press.

Sivin, Nathan. [1982] 2005. "Why the Scientific Revolution Did Not Take Place in China—or Didn't It?" *Chinese Science*, Vol. 5, pp. 45–66.

———. 1995. *Science in Ancient China*. Aldershot, UK: Variorum.

Skinner, G. W. 1977. "Introduction: Urban Social Structure in Ch'ing China." In *The City in Late Imperial China*, edited by G. William Skinner, 521–55. Stanford, CA: Stanford University Press.

Slack, Paul. 2015. *The Invention of Improvement: Information and Material Progress in Seventeenth-Century England*. Oxford: Oxford University Press.

Smail, John. 1994. *The Origins of Middle-Class Culture: Halifax, Yorkshire, 1660–1780.*Ithaca, NY: Cornell University Press.

Smiles, Samuel. 1883. *Ironworkers and Toolmakers*. Chicago, Belford Clarke & Co.

Smith, Adam. [1762–1763] 1978. *Lectures on Jurisprudence*, edited by R. L. Meek. Oxford: Oxford University Press.

Smith, Adam. [1776], 1976. *The Wealth of Nations*, edited by Edwin Cannan. Chicago: University of Chicago Press.

Smith, Joanna F. Handlin. 1987. "Benevolent Societies: The Reshaping of Charity during the Late Ming and Early Ch'ing." *Journal of Asian Studies*, Vol. 46, No. 2, pp. 309–37.

Smith, Pamela H., and Benjamin Schmidt. 2007a. "Knowledge and Its Making in Early Europe." In *Making Knowledge in Early Modern Europe*, edited by Pamela H. Smith and Benjamin Schmidt, 1–16. Chicago: University of Chicago Press.

———, eds. 2007b. *Making Knowledge in Early Modern Europe*. Chicago: University of Chicago Press.

Smith, Richard. 2008. "Social Security as a Developmental Institution? Extending the Solar Case for the Relative Efficacy of Poor Relief Provisions under the English Old Poor Law." Brooks World Poverty Institute Working Paper No. 56. Brooks World Poverty Institute, University of Manchester.

Smits, Wendy, and Thorsten Stromback. 2001. *The Economics of the Apprenticeship System*. Cheltenham, UK: Edward Elgar.

Sng, Tuan Hwee. 2014. "Size and Dynastic Decline: The Principal-Agent Problem in Late Imperial China 1700–1850." *Explorations in Economic History*, Vol. 54, pp. 107–27.

So, Billy K.L., and Sufumi So. 2022. "Law and the Market Economy." In *The Cambridge Economic History of China, Vol. I*, edited by Debin Ma and Richard Von Glahn, 419–47.Cambridge: Cambridge University Press.

Solar, Peter M. 1995. "Poor Relief and English Economic Development before the Industrial Revolution." *The Economic History Review*, Vol. 48, No. 1, pp. 1–22.

———. 2021. "China, Europe, and the Great Divergence: Further Concerns about the Historical GDP Estimates for China." Working Paper 0217, European Historical Economics Society (EHES) Unpublished working paper.

Sommerville, C. John. 1993. *The Secularization of Early Modern England: From Religious Culture to Religious Faith*. New York: Oxford University Press.

Spagnolo, Giancarlo. 1999. "Social Relations and Cooperations in Organizations." *Journal of Economic Behavior and Organizations*, Vol. 38, No. 1 (January), pp. 1–25.

Spence, Jonathan. 1990. *The Search of Modern China*. New York: W.W. Norton.

Srinivas, M.N., and A. M. Shah. 1960. "The Myth of Self-sufficiency of the Indian Village." *Economic Weekly* (India), September 10, pp. 1375–78.

Stasavage, David. 2011. *States of Credit: Size, Power, and the Development of European Polities*. Princeton, NJ: Princeton University Press.

———. 2016. "Representation and Consent: Why They Arose in Europe and Not Elsewhere." *Annual Review of Political Science*, Vol. 18, pp. 145–62.

———. 2020.*The Decline and Rise of Democracy*. Princeton, NJ: Princeton University Press.

Stewart, Larry. 1992. *The Rise of Public Science*. Cambridge: Cambridge University Press.

Stone, Daniel. 2001. *The Polish-Lithuanian State, 1386–1795*.Seattle and London: University of Washington Press.

Storesletten, Kjetil, and Fabrizio Zilibotti. 2014. "China's Great Convergence and Beyond." *Annual Review of Economics*, Vol. 6, No. 1, pp. 333–62.

Strayer, Joseph. 1970. *On the Medieval Origins of the Modern State*. Princeton, NJ: Princeton University Press.

Strum, Daniel. 2013. *The Sugar Trade Brazil, Portugal, and the Netherlands, 1595–1630*. Stanford, CA: Stanford University Press.

Stubbs, W., ed. 1913. *Selected Charters and Other Illustrations of English Institutional History from the Earliest Times to the Reign of Edward the First*, 9th ed. Oxford: Clarendon Press.

Sun, Xin, Travis J. Warner, Dali L. Yang, and Mingxing Liu. 2013. "Patterns of Authority and Governance in Rural China: Who's in Charge? Why?" *Journal of Contemporary China*, Vol. 22, No. 83, pp. 733–54.

Svolik, Milan W. 2012. *The Politics of Authoritarian Rule*. Cambridge: Cambridge University Press.

Swamy, Subramanian. 1979. "The Response to Economic Challenge: A Comparative Economic History of China and India, 1870–1952." *Quarterly Journal of Economics* Vol. 93, No. 1, pp. 25–46.

Szonyi, Michael. 2002. *Practicing Kinship. Lineage and Descent in Late Imperial China.* Stanford, CA: Stanford University Press.

Tabellini, Guido. 2008a. "Institutions and Culture Presidential Address." *Journal of the European Economic Association,* Vol. 6, No. 2–3, pp. 255–94.

———. 2008b. "The Scope of Cooperation: Values and Incentives." *Quarterly Journal of Economics,* Vol. 123, No. 3, pp. 905–50.

———. 2010. "Culture and Institutions: Economic Development in the Regions of Europe." *Journal of the European Economic Association,* Vol. 8, No. 4 (June), pp. 677–716.

Tackett, Nicolas. 2014. *The Destruction of the Medieval Chinese Aristocracy.* Cambridge, MA: Harvard University Asia Center.

Tait, James. 1936. *The Medieval English Borough. Studies on its Origins and Constitutional History.* Manchester: Manchester University Press.

Talhelm, Thomas, and S. Oishi. 2018. "How Rice Farming Shaped Culture in Southern China." In *Socioeconomic Environment and Human Psychology,* edited by A. Uskul and S. Oishi, 53–76. New York: Oxford University Press.

Talhelm, Thomas, X. Zhang, S. Oishi, C. Shimin, D. Duan, X. Lan, and S. Kitayama. 2014. "Large-Scale Psychological Differences within China Explained by Rice Versus Wheat Agriculture." *Science,* Vol. 344, No. 6184, pp. 603–8.

Tamanaha, Brian Z. 2004. *On the Rule of Law: History, Politics, Theory.* Cambridge: Cambridge University Press.

Tanzi, Vito, and Ludger Schuknecht. 2000. *Public Spending in the 20th Century—a Global Perspective.* Cambridge: Cambridge University Press.

Teiser, Stephen F. 2020. "Terms of Friendship: Bylaws for Associations of Buddhist Laywomen in Medieval China." In *At the Shores of the Sky,* edited by P. W. Kroll and J. A. Silk, 154–72. Leiden, Netherlands: Brill.

Telford, T.A. 1986. "Survey of Social Demographic Data in Chinese Genealogies." *Late Imperial China,* Vol. 7, No. 2, pp. 118–46.

———. 1992. "Covariates of Men's Age at First Marriage. The Historical Demography of Chinese Lineages." *Population Studies,* Vol. 46, pp. 19–35.

Teng, S. Y. 1977. "The Role of the Family in the Chinese Legal System." *Journal of Asian History,* Vol. 11, No. 2, pp. 121–55.

Terpstra, Taco. 2013. *Trading Communities in the Roman World: A Micro-economic and Institutional Perspective.* Leiden, Netherlands: Brill.

———. 2020. "Roman Technological Progress in Comparative Context: The Roman Empire, Medieval Europe and Imperial China." *Explorations in Economic History* Vol. 75, (Winter), p. 101300.

———. 2025. *Rome and the Rise of the West.* Unpublished book manuscript, Northwestern University, Evanston, IL.

Thaplyal, Kiran Kumar. 1996. *Guilds in Ancient India: A Study of Local Guild Organization in Northern India and Western Deccan from c. 600 BC to c. 600 AD.* Delhi: New Age International.

Thøgersen, Stig. 2002. "Village Economy and Culture in Contemporary China." *Modern China*, Vol. 28, pp. 253–74.

Thomas, Emily. 2023. "The Invention of Time." *History Today*, Vol. 73, No. 8 (August 8).

Tierney, Brian. 1982. *Religion, Law, and the Growth of Constitutional Thought, 1150–1650*. Cambridge: Cambridge University Press.

———. 1999. *The Middle Ages. Volume 1: Sources of Medieval History*, 6th ed. New York: McGraw Hill.

Tilly, Charles. 1992. *Coercion, Capital, and European States, AD 990–1992*.Oxford: Blackwell.

Tsai, L.L. 2007. *Accountability without Democracy*. Cambridge: Cambridge University Press.

Turchin, Peter. 2007. *War and Peace and War: The Rise and Fall of Empires*. New York: Penguin.

———. 2012. "Why Europe and Not China?" *Cliodynamica: A Blog about the Evolution of Civilizations*.

Turner, John D. 2017. "The Development of English Company Law before 1900." *QUCEH Working Paper Series* No. 2017–01, Queen's University Centre for Economic History (QUCEH), Belfast.

Twitchett, D.C. 1957. "Monasteries and China's Economy in Medieval Times." *Bulletin of the School of Oriental and African Studies, University of London*, Vol. 19, No. 3, pp. 526–49.

Twitchett, Denis. 1959. "The Fan Clan's Charitable Estate, 1050–1760." In *Confucianism in Action*, edited by David Nivison and Arthur Wright, 97–133. Stanford, CA: Stanford University Press.

———. 1983. *Printing and Publishing in Medieval China*. New York: Frederic C. Bell.

Twitchett, Denis, and John K. Fairbank. eds. 2009. *The Cambridge History of China*: *The Sung Dynasty and its Precursors, 907–1279*. Cambridge: Cambridge University Press.

Van Bavel, Bas. 2016. *The Invisible Hand? How Markets Economies Have Emerged and Declined since AD 500*. Oxford: Oxford University Press.

Van Berkel, Klaas. 2013. *Isaac Beeckman on Matter and Motion: Mechanical Philosophy in the Making*. Baltimore: Johns Hopkins University Press.

Van Doosselaere, Quentin. 2009. *Commercial Agreements and Social Dynamics in Medieval Genoa*. Cambridge: Cambridge University Press.

Van Leeuwen, Marco H.D. 2012. "Guilds and Middle-Class Welfare, 1550–1800: Provisions for Burial, Sickness, Old Age, and Widowhood." *Economic History Review*, Vol. 65, No. 1, pp. 61–90.

Van Zanden, Jan Luiten. 2008. "The Road to the Industrial Revolution: Hypotheses and Conjectures about the Medieval Origins of the 'European Miracle.'" *Journal of Global History*, Vol. 3, pp. 337–59.

———. 2009. *The Long Road to the Industrial Revolution: The European Economy in a Global Perspective, 1000–1800*.Boston: Brill.

Van Zanden, Jan Luiten, Eltjo Buringh, and Maarten Bosker. 2012. "The Rise and Decline of European Parliaments, 1188–1789." *European Review of Economic History*, Vol. 10, pp. 111–45.

Van Zanden, Jan Luiten, and Maarten Prak. 2006. "Towards an Economic Interpretation of Citizenship—The Dutch Republic between Medieval Communes and Modern Nation States." *Economic History Review*, Vol. 65, No. 3, pp. 835–61.

Verboven, Koenraad. 2011. "Introduction: Professional *Collegia*: Guilds or Social Clubs?" *Ancient Society*, Vol. 41, pp. 187–95.

Verbruggen, J. F. 1997. *The Art of Warfare in Western Europe during the Middle Ages*. Woodbridge, UK: Boydell Press.

Verger, Jacques. 2003. "Patterns." In *A History of the University in Europe—Vol. I, Universities in the Middle Ages*, edited by Hilde de Ridder-Simoens, 35–66. Cambridge: Cambridge University Press.

Vogel, Ezra. 2011. *Deng Xiaoping and the Transformation of China*. Cambridge, MA: Harvard University Press.

Vogelsang, Kai. 2020. "The Chinese Concept of 'Progress.'" In *Chinese Visions of Progress, 1895 to 1949*, edited by Thomas Fröhlich and Axel Schneider, 43–74. Leiden, Netherlands: Brill.

Voigtländer, Nico, and Hans-Joachim Voth. 2006. "Why England? Demographic Factors, Structural Change and Physical Capital Accumulation During the Industrial Revolution." *Journal of Economic Growth*, Vol. 11, No. 4, pp. 319–61.

———. 2013. "How the West Invented Fertility Restriction." *American Economic Review*, Vol. 103, No. 6, pp. 2227–64.

Volz, Carl A. 1997. *The Medieval Church*. Nashville: Abingdon Press.

Von Glahn, Richard. 2004. *The Sinister Way: The Divine and the Demonic in Chinese Religious Culture*. Berkeley: University of California Press.

———. 2016. *The Economic History of China: From Antiquity to the Nineteenth Century*. Cambridge: Cambridge University Press.

———. 2022. "The Tang-Song Transition in Chinese Economic History." In *The Cambridge Economic History of China, Vol. I*, edited by Debin Ma and Richard Von Glahn, 243–55. Cambridge: Cambridge University Press.

Vries, Peer. 2001. "Are Coal and Colonies Really Crucial? Kenneth Pomeranz and the Great Divergence." *Journal of World History*, Vol. 12, No. 2 (Fall), pp. 407–46.

———. 2012. "Un Monde de Ressemblances Surprenantes?" In *L'histoire Économique en Mouvement: Entre Héritage et Renouvellement*, edited by Jean Claude Daumas, 311–39. Lille, France: Presses Universitaires Septentrion.

———. 2013. *The Escape from Poverty*. Vienna: Vienna University Press.

Wahl, Fabian. 2016. "Participative Political Institutions in Pre-modern Central Europe. Introducing a New Database." *Historical Methods: A Journal of Quantitative and Interdisciplinary History*, Vol. 49, pp. 67–79.

———. 2018. "Political Participation and Economic Development. Evidence from the Rise of Participative Political Institutions in the Late Medieval German Lands." *European Review of Economic History*, Vol. 23, pp. 193–213.

Wakeman, Frederic. 1975. "The Evolution of Local Control in Late Imperial China." In *Conflict and Control in late Imperial China*, edited by Frederic Wakeman and Carolyn Grant, 1–25. Berkeley: University of California Press.

———. 1993. "The Civil Society and Public Sphere Debate." *Modern China*, Vol. 19, No. 2, pp. 108–38.

Wallis, Patrick. 2025. *The Market for Skill: Apprenticeship and Economic Growth in Early Modern England*. Princeton, NJ: Princeton University Press.

Walsh, Michael J. 2010. *Sacred Economies: Buddhist Monasticism and Territoriality in Medieval China*. New York: Columbia University Press.

Wan, Zheng. 2015. "China's Scientific Progress Hinges on Access to Data." *Nature*, Vol. 520, No. 587.

Wang, H. 2008. *Zhongguo jia pu zong mu* [The comprehensive catalog of Chinese genealogies]. Shanghai: Shanghai gu ji chu ban she.

Wang, Jin, and Keebohm Nahm. 2019. "From Confucianism to Communism and Back: Understanding the Cultural Roots of Chinese Politics." *Journal of Asian Sociology*, Vol. 48, No. 1, pp. 91–114.

Wang, Tongling. 1922. *Zhongguo li dai dang zheng shi* (Chinese Ed.), Vol. 2. Reprints from the collection of the University of Michigan Library, Ann Arbor.

Wang, Yuhua. 2020. "Comprehensive Catalogue of Chinese Genealogies." Harvard Dataverse. https://doi.org/10.7910/DVN/PO0VF6.

Wang, Yuhua. 2022. *The Rise and Fall of Imperial China: The Social Origins of State Development.* Princeton, NJ: Princeton University Press.

Watson, James. 1982. "Chinese Kinship Reconsidered: Anthropological Perspectives on Historical Research." *The China Quarterly*, Vol. 92 (Dec.), pp. 589–622.

Watson, Rubie S. 1985 [2011]. *Inequality among Brothers: Clans and Kinship in South China.* Cambridge: Cambridge University Press. Reprinted in 2011, Cambridge: Cambridge University Press.

Weber, Max. 1927. *General Economic History.* Translated by Frank H. Knight. Reprinted ed. 2009. New York: Cosimo Reprints.

———. 1958. *The City.* Glencoe, IL: Free Press.

Wei, Shang-Jin, Zhuan Xie, and Xiaobo Zhang. 2017. "From 'Made in China' to 'Innovated in China': Necessity, Prospect, and Challenges." *Journal of Economic Perspectives*, Vol. 31, No. 1, pp. 49–70.

Weidenbaum, Murray, and Samuel Hughes. 1996. *The Bamboo Network—How Expatriate Chinese Entrepreneurs Are Creating a New Economic Superpower in Asia.* New York: Martin Kessler Books, Free Press.

Westfall, Richard S. 1985. "Science and Patronage: Galileo and the Telescope." *Isis*, Vol. 76, No. 1 (March), pp. 11–30.

White, Eugene N. 2004. "From Privatized to Government-Administered Tax Collection: Tax Farming in Eighteenth-Century France." *Economic History Review*, Vol. 57, No. 4 (November), pp. 636–63.

White, Lynn. 1978. *Medieval Religion and Technology.* Berkeley: University of California Press.

Whiting, Susan H. 2017. "The Cadre Evaluation System at the Grass Roots: The Paradox of Party Rule." In *Critical Readings on the Communist Party of China* (4 Vols.), edited by Kjeld Erik Brodsgaard, 461–78. Leiden, Netherlands: Brill.

Will, Pierre-Étienne, R. Bin Wong, James Lee, Jean Oi, and Peter Perdue, eds. 1991. *Nourish the People: The State Civilian Granary System in China, 1650–1850.* Ann Arbor: University of Michigan Press.

Williams, Eric. 1944. *Capitalism and Slavery.* Chapel Hill: University of North Carolina Press.

Winchester, Simon. 2008. *The Man Who Loved China.* New York: HarperCollins.

Wolf, Arthur. 2001. "Is There Evidence of Birth Control in Late Imperial China?" *Population and Development Review*, Vol. 27, No. 1, pp. 133–54.

Wong, R. Bin. 1991. "Chinese Traditions of Grain Storage." In *Nourish the People: The State Civilian Granary System in China, 1650–1850*, edited by Pierre-Étienne Will, R. Bin Wong, James Lee, Jean Oi, and Peter Perdue, 1–16. Ann Arbor: Michigan University Press.

———. 1997. *China Transformed—Historical Change and the Limits of European Experience.* Ithaca, NY: Cornell University Press.

Wood. Alan T. 1995. *Limits to Autocracy: From Sung Neo-Confucianism to a Doctrine of Political Rights.* Honolulu: University of Hawaii Press.

Woodside, Alexander, and Benjamin Elman. 1994. "Afterword." In *Education and Society in late Imperial China*, edited by Benjamin Elman and Alexander Woodside, pp. 525–60. Berkeley: University of California Press.

Wootton, David. 2015. *The Invention of Science: A New History of the Scientific Revolution.* London: Allen Lane.

World Bank. 2017. "The World Bank in China: Overview." Accessed March 24, 2025. https://www.worldbank.org/en/country/china/overview.

Wright, Arthur F. 1990. *Studies in Chinese Buddhism.* New Haven, CT: Yale University Press.

Wright, Arthur F., and D. C. Twitchett, eds. 1973. *Perspectives on the Tang.* New Haven, CT: Yale University Press.

Wrigley, E. A. 2004. "The Quest for the Industrial Revolution." In *Poverty, Progress, and Population*, edited by E. A. Wrigley,17–43. Cambridge: Cambridge University Press.

———. 2010. *Energy and the English Industrial Revolution.* New York: Cambridge University Press.

Wrigley, E. A., R. S. Davies, J. E. Oeppen, and R. S. Schofield. 1997. *English Population History from Family Reconstitution, 1580–1837.* Cambridge: Cambridge University Press.

Wuthnow, Robert. 1989. *Communities of Discourse.* Cambridge, MA: Harvard University Press.

Xiao, Yongming 2018. *Ruxue, Shuyuan, shehui: Shehui wenhuashi shiye zhong de shuyuan* [Confucianism, academies, and society: The role of academies in social and culturalhistory]. Rev. ed. Beijing: Shangwu yinshu [Commercial Press].

Xin, Katherine K., and Jone L. Pearce. 1996. "Guanxi: Connections as Substitutes for Formal Institutional Support." *Academy of Management Journal*, Vol. 39, No. 6, pp. 1641–58.

Xu, C. 2011. "The Fundamental Institutions of China's Reforms and Development." *Journal of Economic Literature*, Vol. 49, No. 4, pp. 1076–151.

Xu, Yi, Bas van Leeuwen, and Jan Luiten van Zanden. 2018. "Urbanization in China, ca. 1100–1900." *Frontiers of Economics in China*, Vol. 13, No. 3, pp. 322–68.

Xue, Melanie Meng. 2021. "Autocratic Rule and Social Capital: Evidence from Imperial China." SSRN Working Paper No. 2856803.

Zelin, Madeleine. 1984. *The Magistrate's Tael: Rationalizing Fiscal Reform in Eighteenth-Century Ch'ing China.* Berkeley and Los Angeles: University of California Press.

———. 2004. "A Critique of Rights of Property in Prewar China." In *Contract and Property in Early Modern China*, edited by M. Zelin, J. Ocko, and R. Gardella, 17–36. Stanford, CA: Stanford University Press.

———. 2007. "Informal Law and the Firm in Early Modern China." Unpublished manuscript., Columbia University. https://citeseerx.ist.psu.edu/document?repid=rep1&type=pdf&doi=083e4b7a695da0d137758845fb6cb1d1ed148676

———. 2022. "Chinese Business Organization." In *The Cambridge Economic History of China, Vol. II*, edited by Debin Ma and Richard Von Glahn, 324–53. Cambridge: Cambridge University Press.

Zelin, Madeleine, Jonathan K Ocko, and Robert Gardella. 2004. *Contract and Property in Early Modern China.* Stanford, CA: Stanford University Press.

Zhang, C., and Y. Xie. 2013. "Place of Origin and Labour Market Outcomes among Migrant Workers in Urban China." *Urban Studies*, Vol. 50, No. 14, pp. 3011–26.

Zhang, Chuanchuan. 2017. "Culture and the Economy: Clan, Entrepreneurship, and Development of the Private Sector in China." SSRN Working Paper.

Zhang, Chunlin. 2019. "How Much Do State-Owned Enterprises Contribute to China's GDP and Employment?" Unpublished World Bank report, https://documents1.worldbank.org /curated/en/449701565248091726/pdf/How-Much-Do-State-Owned-Enterprises -Contribute-to-China-s-GDP-and-Employment.pdf.

Zhang, Lawrence. 2022. *Power for a Price: The Purchase of Official Appointments in Qing China*. Cambridge, MA: Harvard University Asia Center.

Zhang, M. 2008. "From Public to Private: The Newly Enacted Chinese Property Law and the Protection of Property Rights in China." *Berkeley Business Law Journal*, Vol. 5, No. 2, pp. 317–63.

Zhang, Taisu. 2017. *The Laws and Economics of Confucianism: Kinship and Property in Pre- industrial China and England*. Cambridge: Cambridge University Press.

———. 2020. "Fiscal Policy and Institutions in Imperial China." *Oxford Research Encyclopedia of Asian History*. New York: Oxford University Press.

———. 2022. *The Ideological Foundations of Qing Taxation: Belief Systems, Politics, and Institu- tions*. Cambridge: Cambridge University Press.

Zhang, Taisu, and Xiaoxue Zhao. 2014. "Do Kinship Networks Strengthen Private Property? Evidence from Rural China." *Journal of Empirical Legal Studies*, Vol. 11, No. 3, pp. 505–40.

Zhao, Dingxin. 2015. *The Confucian-Legalist State: A New Theory of Chinese History*. Oxford: Oxford University Press.

Zhao, Zhongwei. 1997. "Long-Term Mortality Patterns in Chinese History: Evidence from a Recorded Clan Population." *Population Studies*, Vol. 51, No. 2, pp. 117–27.

Zheng, Zhenman. 2001. *Family Lineage Organization and Social Change in Ming and Qing Fujian*. Translated by Michael Szonyi. Honolulu: University of Hawaii Press.

Zhu, Huasheng, Kelly Wanjing Chen, and Juncheng Dai. 2016. "Beyond Apprenticeship: Knowledge Brokers and Sustainability of Apprentice-Based Clusters." *Sustainability*, Vol. 8, No. 12, pp. 1–17.

Zhuo, Xinping. 2012. "Spiritual Accomplishment in Confucianism and Spiritual Transcendence in Christianity." In *Confucianism and Spiritual Traditions in Modern China and Beyond*, edited by Fenggang Yang and Joseph B. Tamney, 277–92. Leiden, the Netherlands: Brill.

Zilibotti, Fabrizio. 2017. "Growing and Slowing Down like China." *Journal of the European Eco- nomic Association*, Vol. 15, No. 5, pp. 943–88.

Zilsel, Edgar. 1942. "The Sociological Roots of Science." *American Journal of Sociology*, Vol. 47, No. 4, pp. 544–60.

Zupko, Jack. 2018. "John Buridan." *Stanford Encyclopedia of Philosophy*. https://plato.stanford .edu /entries/buridan/.

Zurndorfer, Harriet. 2022. "Cities and the Urban Economy." In *The Cambridge Economic history of China*, Vol. 1, edited by Debin Ma and Richard Von Glahn, 522–59. Cambridge: Cam- bridge University Press.

INDEX

Page numbers in *italics* refer to figures and tables

elites, 222, 238; sovereign relations of, 16, 259, 260, 267; the state, Chinese elites cooperating with, 2, 359; in Tang China, 261; tax enforcement, in charge of, 240, 308; as upper-tail human capital, 46; urban elites, 154, 204, 214, 302, 318n17

Elman, Benjamin A., 197, 200, 201, 237, 256, 422

emergent property, 309–10, 469

emperors: central authority of, 231–33, 304; Charlemagne, 58, 270, 288; Chengzu of Ming 256; Hongwu, 167, 234–35, 244, 245, 256, 340; Huizong, 139; Jiajing, 142; Kangxi, 65, 116, 245n22; Mandate from Heaven, deriving legitimacy from, 226, 231; Ming emperors, power of, 232, 234–35; Qing emperors, power of, 232, 252; Renzong of Song, 198; Renzong of Yuan, 198; Rudolph, 62; Tai-Tsung, 232; Taizong, 236; Wu, 347; of Yongle, 64, 167n52, 256, 413n53; of Yongzheng, 65, 245–46, 247n27, 248, 251n34

enforcement, 73, 87, 174, 273, 283, 311, 335, 336, 348, 411, 465; bailiffs and local law enforcement, 166, 360–62; by central government of China, 22, 319, 325, 362; of the Church, 101, 302n89; in clan and corporation model, 88–92; clans, enforcement power of, 24, 164, 239, 240–41, 326, 352, 363; contract enforcement, 155, 195, 311, 342, 344, 368, 407, 455, 467; cooperation, enforcement of, 164–67; corporations, enforcement in, 14, 70, 76, 86, 311; criminal law enforcement, 339, 340, 342, 343–44, 349, 355–57; by English merchant guilds, 180, 183; in kin-based networks, 70, 86; in modern China, 429, 452; self-governing cities, legal enforcement in, 158, 166, 174; social organizations and the enforcement of cooperation, 6–9; tax enforcement, 240, 247, 467; third-party enforcement, 408, 455n

Enke, Benjamin, 6, 12, 13n, 73, 74, 87–88, 96, 141n22

Enlightenment, 5n, 60, 259, 306, 355n, 379, 391, 398, 422; democratic ideas of, 295, 471; Industrial Enlightenment, 32, 50, 393–94, 396, 399, 412, 418, 420–21, 463; intellectualism of the era, 57, 59, 297, 419, 470–71

Epstein, Stephan R., 181

equality before the law, 15, 16, 254, 284nn69–70, 285, 337, 352, 356

Erasmus, 374, 388

European law, 14, 43; bailiffs and local law enforcement, 166, 360–62; civil law, 311, 327, 329n34, 332, 334, 338, 339, 341; constitutional law, 226, 291, 292, 295, 311; criminal law, 310n2, 355–57; *ius commune* law, 330, 331, 334, 336n44, 343; legal institutions of Europe, 285–87, 334–38; legal personality of European corporations, 170–71; legal professions in Europe, 331–33; *lex mercatoria* system, 328, 334–36; private law, 15, 291, 292, 293, 295; Roman *collegia* as legal entities, 153–54; Salic Law, 284, 327, 356; state law, 305, 344, 452; Western Church and, 287–91

European Marriage Pattern (EMP), 11, 40–42, 43, 55, 66, 99–100, 101–4

evolutionary game theory, 81–82

family: Buddhism, family values of, 112, 115; Church policies as influencing family structure, 10, 102, 104; in the clan system, 123–25, 132, 162, 165, 197, 340, 431; in the Confucian tradition, 111, 112, 113, 140, 170–71, 198, 254, 255, 341, 345; cooperation and family structures, 66–68; divergent family structures, 26–27, 40–42, 55, 67; European Marriage Pattern as restructuring, 11, 101; family and lineage in the clan system, 123–25; joint families, 40, 98, 466, 468; in modern China, 430, 434; in neo-Confucianism, 112, 125; nuclear families, 10–11, 40, 67, 68, 96, 97–101, 103, 157, 219, 272, 466; Tang dynasty, communal family units of, 123–24. *See also* ancestor worship